MEDIA ETHICS

Media Ethics: Cases and Moral Reasoning challenges readers to think analytically about ethical situations in mass communication through original case studies and commentaries about real-life media experiences. This text provides a comprehensive introduction to the theoretical principles of ethical philosophies, facilitating ethical awareness. It introduces the Potter Box, with its four dimensions of moral analysis, to provide a framework for exploring the steps in moral reasoning and analyzing the cases. Focusing on a wide spectrum of ethical issues faced by media practitioners, the cases in this Tenth Edition include the most recent issues in journalism, broadcasting, advertising, public relations, and entertainment.

Clifford G. Christians is Research Professor of Communications, Professor of Journalism, and Professor of Media Studies Emeritus at the University of Illinois, Urbana-Champaign.

Mark Fackler is Professor of Communications Emeritus at Calvin College, Grand Rapids, Michigan.

Kathy Brittain Richardson is President of Westminster College in New Wilmington, Pennsylvania. She is the former Provost and a Professor of Communication at Berry College, Rome, Georgia.

Peggy J. Kreshel is Associate Professor of Advertising at the Grady College of Journalism and Mass Communication and an affiliate faculty member of the Institute for Women's Studies at the University of Georgia.

Robert H. Woods, Jr. is Professor of Communication and Media at Spring Arbor University, Spring Arbor, Michigan. He is executive director of the Christianity and Communications Studies Network (www.theccsn.com).

MEDIA ETHICS

CASES AND MORAL REASONING

TENTH EDITION

Clifford G. Christians

Mark Fackler

Kathy Brittain Richardson

Peggy J. Kreshel

Robert H. Woods, Jr.

Routledge
Taylor & Francis Group

NEW YORK AND LONDON

Tenth edition published 2017
by Routledge
711 Third Avenue, New York, NY 10017

and by Routledge
2 Park Square, Milton Park, Abingdon, Oxon, OX14 4RN

Routledge is an imprint of the Taylor & Francis Group, an informa business

Third edition published by Longman Publishing Group 1991
Ninth edition published by Routledge 2016

British Library Cataloguing in Publication Data
A catalogue record for this book is available from the British Library

Library of Congress Cataloging in Publication Data
Names: Christians, Clifford G. author.
Title: Media ethics : cases and moral reasoning / Clifford G. Christians, Mark
Fackler, Kathy Brittain Richardson, Peggy J. Kreshel, Robert H. Woods, Jr.
Description: 10th edition. | New York, NY ; Milton Park, Abingdon, Oxon :
Routledge, 2016. | Includes bibliographical references and index.
Identifiers: LCCN 2016017617 (print) | LCCN 2016024158 (ebook) |
ISBN 9781138672383 (hardback) | ISBN 9780205897742 (pbk.) |
ISBN 9781315544199 (ebook)
Subjects: LCSH: Mass media–Moral and ethical aspects.
Classification: LCC P94 .C45 2016 (print) | LCC P94 (ebook) | DDC 175–dc23

ISBN: 978–1–138–67238–3 (hbk)
ISBN: 978–0–205–89774–2 (pbk)
ISBN: 978–1–315–54419–9 (ebk)

Typeset in Berthold Akzidenz Grotesk
by Keystroke, Neville Lodge, Tettenhall, Wolverhampton

CONTENTS

ACKNOWLEDGMENTS

We incurred many debts while preparing this volume. The McCormick Foundation generously supported our original research into ethical dilemmas among media professionals; many of the cases and the questions surrounding them emerged from this research. Ralph Potter encouraged our adaptation of his social ethics model. Paul Christians wrote Cases 3, 8, 9, 15, and 19, and updated others; his research was invaluable. Conversations with Professor Sun Youzhong while he was translating the ninth edition into Chinese were helpful in preparing this edition. Taran Gilreath gathered information for many of the advertising cases. In Part 4, Kevin Schut contributed Case 61, Sam Smartt wrote case 67, Peggy Goetz did Case 70, John Carpenter wrote Case 71, and Ted Fackler Case 75. Additional thanks to Joel Worsham for designing and developing the companion website for instructors and students that supports this volume (www.mediaethicsbook.com). Joe Rinehart, Department Chair, Director of Broadcasting and Assistant Professor of Communication, Mount Vernon Nazarene University, was instrumental in helping to prepare instructional content for the companion website. Divine Agodzo (Spring Arbor University) and Jessica Wells (Mount Vernon Nazarene University) provided much-needed support in creating and editing companion website content.

Each contributor shares in everything positive this book may contribute to media ethics scholarship. The authors are grateful. We absolve these friends of all responsibility for the weaknesses that remain.

ABOUT THE AUTHORS

Clifford G. Christians is Research Professor of Communications, Professor of Journalism, and Professor of Media Studies Emeritus at the University of Illinois, Urbana-Champaign.

Mark Fackler is Professor of Communications Emeritus at Calvin College, Grand Rapids, Michigan.

Kathy Brittain Richardson is President of Westminster College in New Wilmington, Pennsylvania. She is the former Provost and a Professor of Communication at Berry College, Rome, Georgia.

Peggy J. Kreshel is Associate Professor of Advertising at the Grady College of Journalism and Mass Communication and an affiliate faculty member of the Institute for Women's Studies at the University of Georgia.

Robert H. Woods, Jr. is Professor of Communication and Media at Spring Arbor University, Spring Arbor, Michigan. He is executive director of the Christianity and Communications Studies Network (www.theccsn.com).

PREFACE

Worldwide, people think about doing the right thing. From soccer players to political strategists, doing the right thing weighs against other human motivations: winning at all costs, getting what we want, reducing stress, sometimes plain survival.

We take it as common sense that editors, advertising professionals, public relations pros, and folks with the varied skills of movie making and screen-game playing also think about doing the right thing. In making media, the right thing sometimes collides with concerns about market share, profit, audience, and just getting along in the odd subcultures of Hollywood and Fifth Avenue. Still, doing the right thing is never far from a professional's line of sight.

Few media professionals receive accolades from peers for something so mundane as "doing the right thing," but that impulse still survives all the non-rewards our complex industries can withhold, and all the pettiness and piety that can paint a person who's known for right-thing doing.

Sometimes, we strongly suspect, people who err (that's all of us) wish they would have done the right thing. If only their moral compass had been fixed on North, their careers would not have gone South. Doing wrong is so instantly publicized that there's little chance of escaping public humiliation for moral slippage. The "fallen" among us are reminders that the race to the top, or fame and fortune, or the homage of the Academy, are faint moments of fading grandeur when you're caught doing moral nonsense. So we wonder, given all the many claims to rightness, what right really is. This book is written to address that question.

But wait. Not everyone assigned to read and use this book intends to throw his or her life into media production. All the students, however, in your class and in every single other class are heavy media users and buyers, with emphasis on *heavy*. You say no? Don't even think about it. You could not go cold-turkey from media if free tuition were dangled before you. This book on media ethics—doing the right thing in news, advertising, public relations, and entertainment programming—is for everyone, minus some very few souls who still imagine "mouse" means varmint.

Doing the right thing, as *Media Ethics* presents it, is a discipline to be learned and practiced. We get better at it as we learn to spot the red lights, then, understanding the stakes and stakeholders, apply moral principles toward justifiable solutions. By "justifiable" we mean solutions that can be presented in public as viable, reasonable, fair, honorable, and just. The best descriptor is "good." We want to find the communicative good and do it. We want media industries to understand their *telos* and fulfill it. We want the public to grow more capable of living with a sense of communicative progress and communal support. We celebrate the language of friendship and trust. We want unnecessary violence contained, and necessary violence to be measured and publically accountable. Peace and trust being preferable to deception and warfare, we want media to contribute to public *shalom*, community *salaam*, the *phileo* that inspired the naming of America's first capital city. If that description is too obtuse or linguistically puzzling, just get this: media should contribute to human flourishing, and they can when they are done right, when their practitioners and users do the right thing.

THIS BOOK HAS A PLAN

Case studies help users and professionals achieve focus. You get a set of facts, often built on a historical case, and then you have to solve it, that is, come up with a morally justifiable decision on how to do the right thing. Cases in this book follow the four "functions" of media: news, advertising, public relations, and entertainment. Following each case is moral commentary applying the Potter Box analysis, explained in the Introduction subtitled Ethical Foundations and Perspectives (p. 1).

It should go without mention that not everyone in the room will arrive at an identical solution to any given case. This should not discourage anyone. It is not hopeless moral relativism (everything is just each person's opinion, or bias) to arrive at varying conclusions. We do not aim for uniformity, as you might in a class on algebra. Applying different moral principles, for example, may lead to differing yet fully justifiable moral solutions. Loyalty to different constituencies could produce differing moral action plans. The Potter Box analysis helps parse each approach, and provides a framework for reconsideration based on renewed understanding of the issues at stake.

Why did we authors limit the moral principles applied to media in this book to only five? Surely that must seem like serving asparagus every day in your dining commons when the farms nearby produce a hundred different veggies. First, our choice of five was a workable array, we thought. This book is not intended for a course in philosophical ethics or survey of Western thought. It is a book on applied media ethics, and for that reason alone we do not offer variants on every philosopher's intriguing moral notions (applause, applause).

Second, our choice was a range of time-tested, traditional (in the sense of worldwide and well-used), and diverse moral principles that we could recommend to media professions in all fields. Notice we did not select egoism for commentary in this book. Not that egoism lacks a popular following, only that we believe it has little to offer for the flourishing of community. You may disagree. Fine. We neither spoon-feed what we recommend nor banish by barbed-wire what we don't recommend. The solutions to the dilemmas presented in these cases are yours to decide. If your preferred moral compass is the better option, get it out there. Make it public.

At the end of the day, this book hopes to improve your analytical skills and your ethical awareness. Both require practice. If you enter a media profession, your practice will have already begun. When you ponder your next purchase of mediated stuff, you'll know the why-to-buy better, we hope, than you do now. If not, tear into shreds your tattered old copy of *Media Ethics* and FedEx the mess back to us. OK, we're kidding, sorry for the ethically questionable suggestion.

You will find considerable help in both analysis and ethical awareness at the book's outstanding website, which you may access at www.mediaethicsbook.com.

INTRODUCTION

Ethical Foundations and Perspectives

Anders Behring Breivik terrorized Norway on July 22, 2011. He bombed government buildings in Oslo killing 8, and then killed 69 people, mostly teenagers, at an educational camp of the Workers Youth League on the island of Utoya (together wounding 242). With links to the militant, far-right English Defence League, Breivik protested the government's immigration policy and promoted the deportation of all Muslims from Europe. On August 24, 2012 he was declared sane, found guilty of mass murder, fatal explosion, and terrorism. At thirty-three years of age, Breivik was sentenced to twenty-one years in prison (under the "preventive detention" verdict that extends the sentence as long as he is considered a threat to society).

From November 26 to 29, 2011, ten attackers from Pakistan entered Mumbai, India and over four days of violence killed 164 people and wounded 308. The perpetrators were all members of the Pakistan-based terrorist organization Lashkar-e Taiba. They were trained and armed by this group near Karachi, and aimed to kill 5000 people by bombs and gunfire. Mumbai is India's business capital, and given its November 26 beginning, and parallels with the 9/11 U.S. World Trade Center attack, the Mumbai attacks are often called 26/11.

On March 11, 2004, the biggest attack on European soil at the Atocha Station, Madrid, left 191 dead and 1858 injured. Ten bombs in sports bags exploded on four commuter trains. The governing Popular Party insisted that the Basque guerrilla separatist group ETA (Euskadi Ta Askatasuna), and not Islamist terrorists, was to blame. At national elections three days after the attacks, the Socialist party of José Luis Rodriguez Zapatero won the election in an upset. Three and a half years after the attacks, Spain's National Court found twenty-one people guilty for participating in or abetting the attacks. Two Moroccans were each sentenced to more than 40,000 years in prison for the bombings, although under Spanish law they can only serve a maximum of 40 (Reuters, 10/31/2007).

Timothy McVeigh used a truck bomb to destroy the Alfred P. Murrah Federal Building in Oklahoma City on April 19, 1995. The bomb killed 168 people and injured 800. An army veteran, he became a transient—living with dissidents around the United States, involving himself with the guns and training of different militia groups, protesting the government's siege of Waco, and distributing anti-government propaganda. He was executed by lethal injection on June 11, 2001.

Terrorism is a fact of life in countries around the world. Governments work day and night to prevent it. Psychologists, political scientists, and international relations specialists are challenged to understand it and offer solutions. Ethics is involved too. What can media ethics contribute? Terrorist acts in one country are headline news everywhere. Terrorists typically seek a public stage to communicate their hostility. Breivik, for instance, on the day of his attacks sent an electronic manifesto of 1500 pages calling for the deportation of all Muslims from Europe and condemning what he called "Cultural Marxism." Later he testified that his main motive for the day of slaughter was to call attention to his *2083: European Declaration of Independence*.

Breivik and McVeigh were home grown, attacking their countries' policies from within. The massive attacks on Mumbai and Madrid were from outside India and Spain respectively. The sources inside or outside, the many reasons given for the violence, their surprise and unpredictability—terrorism is complicated and thinking ethically about this global phenomenon cannot be superficial. Moral decision-making is systematic, and these frightening attacks on the common good require careful analysis and orderly reasoning to reach a justified conclusion.

When these cases are presented to a media ethics class for discussion, students usually argue passionately without making much headway. Judgments are made on what Henry Aiken calls the evocative, expressive level—that is, with no justifying reasons.[1] Too often communications ethics follow such a pattern, retreating finally to the law as the only reliable guide. Students and professionals argue about individual sensational incidents, make case by case decisions, and do not stop to examine their method of moral reasoning.

On the contrary, a pattern of ethical deliberation should be explicitly outlined in which the relevant considerations can be isolated and given appropriate weight. Those who care about ethics in the media can analyze the stages of ethical decision-making, focus on the real levels of conflict, and make defensible ethical decisions. These difficult terrorism cases can illustrate how moral justification takes place. Moral thinking is a methodical process: a judgment is made and action taken. Norwegian television must decide how to cover the dead bodies. With ten bombs exploding at the Atocha train station, when do Spain's national newspapers, *El Mundo* and *El Pais*, conclude they have accurate and sufficient information to publish? Newspapers chose the headlines and length of stories about Breivik and his angry text. During the four-day ordeal in Mumbai, internet users sent some shocking photos but not others. What steps are used to reach these decisions? How do media professionals and social media users decide that an action should be taken because it is right and should be avoided because it is wrong?

Any single decision involves a host of values that must be sorted out. These values reflect assumptions about social life and human nature. To value something means to consider it desirable. Expressions such as "her value system" and "Pakistani values" refer to what a woman and a majority of Pakistani citizens, respectively, estimate or evaluate as worthwhile. We may judge something according to aesthetic values (such as harmonious, pleasing), professional values (innovative, prompt), logical values (consistent, competent), sociocultural values (thrifty, hardworking), and moral values (honest, nonviolent). Often we find both positive and negative values underlying our choices, pervading all areas of our behavior and motivating us to act in certain directions.[2] Newspeople hold several values regarding professional reporting: for example, they prize immediacy, skepticism, and their own independence. In the case of the Oklahoma bombing, television viewers, family members, and reporters valued the law and therefore McVeigh's punishment, though they undoubtedly differed on his execution.

Professional values when combined with ethical principles yield a guideline for the television news desk: protect the well-being of the victims and their families at all costs. The good end, in this instance, is compassion for the suffering. The means for accomplishing this is detailed coverage without sensationalism. In the four democratic countries where this terrorism occurred, the public has a right to know public news. But the responsible media do not provide personal information of victims unless it has been officially verified. Overall, professionals value distributing information without hesitation, but recognize the ethical principle of human dignity in these tragedies. The reporters' personal anger—sometimes hostility to the terrorists—confronts the political value, "the right to a fair trial." Ethical principles often must be invoked to determine which values are preferable and how values are to be implemented.

If we do this kind of analysis, we begin to see how moral reasoning works. We understand better why there can be disagreement over exactly how best to cover terrorism. Is it more important to tell the truth, we ask ourselves, or to preserve privacy? Is there some universal principle that applies to these four cases in different countries? As our analysis proceeds, an interconnected model emerges: we size up the circumstances, we ask what values motivated the decision, we appeal to principles, and we choose loyalty to one group instead of to another. Through this examination, we can engage in conflicts over the crucial junctures of the moral reasoning process rather than argue personal differences over the merits of actual decisions. Careful attention to the decision-making process helps us specify where additional discussion and analysis are needed.

THE POTTER BOX MODEL OF REASONING

Creative ethical analysis involves several explicit steps. Ralph B. Potter of the Harvard Divinity School formulated the model of moral reasoning introduced in our review of the terrorist murders. By using a diagram adapted from Professor Potter (the "Potter Box"), we

Figure I.1

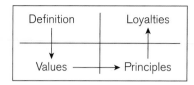

can dissect these cases further (see Figure I.1). The Potter Box introduces four dimensions of moral analysis to aid us in locating those places where most misunderstandings occur.[3] Along these lines we can construct action guides.

Note how the Potter Box has been used in our analysis: (1) We gave a *definition* of the situation, citing details of the attacks, information on the terrorists, and results of the trials. In all four cases, there were convictions and sentencing in court, with punishment ranging from the death penalty for McVeigh to twenty-one years of a rolling containment for Breivik. (2) We looked beneath the facts to values, citing values that might have been the most important. Reporters in all four cases valued timely release of the information. The terrorists valued violence and hatred. The police and government officials valued law and order. The news media valued their reputation, and defended themselves to the public whenever their integrity or professionalism was criticized. Each value was seen as influencing discourse and reasoning. (3) We named at least two ethical *principles* and we could have listed more. Most television stations concluded that the principle of other-regarding care meant protecting the victims' right to privacy. Many of the media outlets invoked truth-telling as an ethical imperative. But other principles could have been summoned: do the greatest good for the greatest number, even if innocent people such as the murderers' families might be harmed. (4) Throughout the reporting, from initial attack to court decision, *loyalties* are evident. Some reporters were loyal first of all to their own career; they saw these sensational events as an opportunity to win awards. Some media firms were loyal to themselves, wanting above all to win competition over their rivals in circulation and audience numbers. In general, the media were loyal to their country, seeing no validity in Breivik's diatribes against Norway's immigration policy, and supportive of the government's attempt to stop the viciousness in Mumbai. The public media overall attempted to express their loyalties only on the editorial pages and in background stories, seeking balance and fairness in their news accounts.

Moving from one quadrant to the next, we finally construct our action guides. But moral decision-making can be examined in more depth (see Figure I.2). For working through the Potter Box in greater detail, the Norway case will be featured.[4] The most recent of the four, it continues to produce headlines and public discussion over the nation's trauma. The latest controversy is about the location and character of a memorial to the seventy-seven victims. Mumbai, Atocha, and Oklahoma will be included as they clarify the four steps needed for a justified conclusion. The purpose of the Potter Box is to tell us what we ought to do. What should the media have done in the Norway terrorism case to be ethical? The two quadrants on the left side describe "what is," what the media did. But they are only the

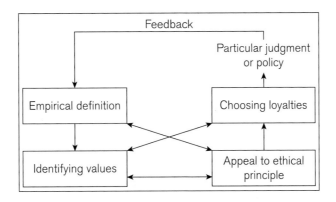

beginning steps toward the right-side quadrants 3 and 4 where we determine the right action to take.

Quadrant 1 (facts) should include all the relevant details. The more specifics, the better, is the rule. All four cases have hundreds of pertinent facts, so what to include is debatable. Choices of what is relevant and where to end need to be made, and a rationale for both is necessary.

We know what Breivik did. The content of his bulky manifesto is important but only needs to be summarized for quadrant 1. Breivik's day of murder was planned over nine years, while he lived with his mother in her apartment. His video game obsession, his relationship to the Knights Templar, his building a truck bomb on the family farm, his religious training in the Lutheran Church of Norway (confirmed at age fifteen)—all such particulars are pertinent. But how much is necessary without giving him the public platform he wanted? His parents divorced when he was one, and after skirmishes with the law between the ages of thirteen and sixteen, his father severed all contact with him. His mother was under psychiatric care, and Breivik rejected her feminism and the Norwegian values of her generation. The trial hinged on whether the first court diagnosis (he was a paranoid schizophrenic and could not be convicted) or the second evaluation (where he could stand trial—sane but with a narcissistic personality disorder) was correct. Must all of this personalia be told for the public to assess whether its institutions were failing or Breivik was a lone wolf? The police responded erratically. Not equipped for terrorism of this magnitude, they were delayed in their ferrying to the island. How much of this incompetence to include in quadrant 1 is an issue.

After working out the empirical definition of the situation, the values of quadrant 2 need special attention. Knowing values helps us understand people's behavior. Values motivate our actions, and where values can be identified the more accurate is the Potter Box process. At least five values are prominent in this case: (1) legal value, obey and enforce the law; (2) compassion for victims; (3) social value, expecting the public to stay peaceful and not retaliate in mob fury; (4) white-supremacy values of Breivik; and (5) professional value, the public's right to know. At the trial, a 12-minute video produced by Breivik was shown. Many media professionals declined to show it or report on it, choosing compassion for the victims and the social value of peace rather than airing Breivik's white-supremacy madness.

Often we value certain things without thinking about them. Debating values with those who are not easily convinced will make us more critical of ourselves in the positive sense. Our professional values are often honestly held, but having them challenged periodically leads to maturity. In the process of clarification and redefinition, deeper insight is gained in how to connect to the other quadrants.

Often in real-life practice, media professionals act on the values of step 2 in deciding what to do. Step 3 on ethical principles and step 4 about choosing loyalties are ignored, resulting in a decision that is not justified morally. But the values of quadrant 2 are typically a long list and contradictory to one another. They need to be put in context and choices made among them by using quadrant 3. Particular judgments of policy (step 5), to be ethical, must follow the guidelines of steps 3 and 4. Breivik's white-supremacy values are so strong and offensive that he calls the seventy-seven "criminals" for supporting Norway. Breivik's ideology distorts and challenges the press's responsibility to report fairly. (Is CNN justified in calling him "the Norway monster"?) And value 5 sometimes conflicts with values 2 and 3. Breivik was the self-proclaimed murderer, but his right to a fair trial was sometimes ignored in valuing the public's right to know. Quadrant 2 has good and bad values competing with one another, and, in complex situations, values are often too narrow to serve as the basis for a justified action. The "ought" or normative side of the Potter Box is the crucial next phase toward ethical judgment.

Two ethical principles are the most credible at this stage of the process. Telling the truth is a moral imperative for Kant and applicable for first news reports, through the trial, and until the aftermath now as Breivik serves his prison sentence (asking by mail or of visitors whether his thinking is taking hold in Norway). The ethical principle of other-regarding care is pertinent too, given the enormous tragedy the terrorism was for the victims and for the country.

After identifying principles, the matter of choosing loyalties needs close scrutiny. The Potter Box is a model for social ethics and consequently forces us to articulate precisely where our loyalties lie as we make a final judgment or adopt a particular policy. And in this domain, we tend to beguile ourselves very quickly.

Examine the decisions made once again: withhold names until families have been officially notified; reject the showing of Breivik's video or his tears in court, but photos of his clenched fist ought to appear. Should *El Mundo* and *El Pais* report on the Breivik trial in detail, given Spain's horrific struggle with Nazism, which the clenched fist represents to its readers? Details of Breivik's nine years of planning, disclose them or not? Who were the news staffs thinking about when they made their decisions? Perhaps they were considering themselves first of all and their competitive advantage. They may claim that they were restrained in their coverage, not wanting to stir up the public to violent hatred toward Breivik or to protests against inept police. But on additional reflection, their loyalties actually may be different. Are they protecting the victims or themselves?

The various media enterprises appear to be interested in a gain for society. What is more important: the welfare of the readers or the welfare of those involved in the crime? On the face of it, the former's welfare, but should this be to the total sacrifice of the latter? Can the people directly involved in the event—including government personnel acting in an extreme emergency—become more than objects of curiosity? Will the truth of this event outweigh idle speculation about Breivik, and cool the gossip about a broken marriage and often clueless mother? Important issues such as these are encountered and clarified when the loyalty quadrant is considered thoroughly.

The crucial question must be faced once more. For whom did the press do all this? If we do not return to the top right-hand quadrant of the diagram and inquire more deeply where the media's allegiances lie—for whom they did what—we have not used the Potter Box adequately.

Choosing loyalties is an extremely significant step in the process of making moral decisions. As the preceding paragraphs indicate, taking this quadrant seriously does not in itself eliminate disagreements. Honest disputes may occur over who should benefit from a decision. Media personnel who are sincere about serving society must choose among the various segments of that society: subscribers and viewers, sources of information, politicians, ethnic minorities, children, law-enforcement personnel, judges, and lawyers. Their calculations need to consider that flesh-and-blood people, known by name, ought not to be sacrificed for euphemisms and abstractions such as the public, clients, audience, or market. The Potter Box is an exercise in social ethics. Ethical principles are crucial, of course, in the overall process of reaching a justified conclusion. However, in the pursuit of socially responsible media, clarity regarding ultimate loyalties is of paramount importance.

In addition to considering each step of the Potter Box carefully, we must see the box as an organic whole. It is not merely a random set of isolated questions, but a linked system. The Potter Box gives us a mechanism to link together facts, values, principles, and loyalties, and doing so yields a justified decision. But the Potter Box can also be used to adopt policy guidelines that will govern future behavior in similar circumstances. On the basis of this case, the broadcast station or newspaper might decide to alter its policy regarding interviews with those still in traumatic shock. Through the five steps of the Potter Box, media institutions can establish or strengthen their policy regarding anonymous sources, police work, confidentiality, and trial coverage.

But we are still left with the important question: which of the two ethical principles is the most appropriate in terrorism coverage? Which one directs us best to a justified conclusion? And this leads to a central inquiry raised by this exercise: is there a transnational ground for making ethical decisions, an overarching theory that directs the news coverage of terrorism worldwide?[5] Or is ethical decision-making a process of adjusting to the mores and commitments of a given community?

Potter's cyclical model, with its potential for continual expansion and feedback through the cycles, takes both aspects seriously. Community mores are accounted for when we elaborate on the values people hold and when we identify our loyalties before we make a final choice. But these sociological matters are tempered in the Potter Box by an appeal to an explicit ethical principle. Without such an appeal, a conclusion is not considered morally justified.

In the terrorism case, both truthtelling and other-regarding care are defensible. But put newsroom values into perspective. Both aim toward media decisions that are widely accepted in democratic societies. Both prevent a media company from justifying immoral behavior—breaking promises, cheating, and deception. Resolution of competing values usually occurs in step 3 while working on ethical theory. But, in this case, two different ethical

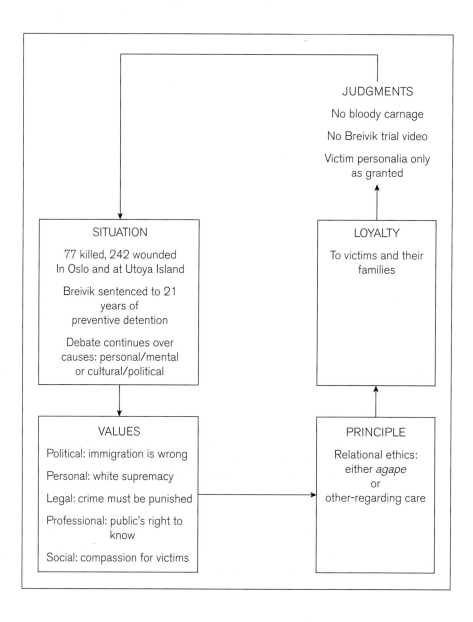

SITUATION

77 killed, 242 wounded
In Oslo and at Utoya Island

Breivik sentenced to 21 years of
preventive detention

Debate continues over causes: personal/mental or cultural/political

VALUES

Political: immigration is wrong

Personal: white supremacy

Legal: crime must be punished

Professional: public's right to know

Social: compassion for victims

JUDGMENTS

No bloody carnage

No Breivik trial video

Victim personalia only as granted

LOYALTY

To victims and their families

PRINCIPLE

Relational ethics:
either *agape*
or
other-regarding care

Figure I.3

theories remain relevant. The *agape* principle of other-regarding care gives victims priority. Telling the truth as a categorical imperative directs the news media to make every effort to verify the facts.

When two different ethical theories appear to be relevant as in this situation, the appropriate ethical choice does not appear until quadrant 4. Although most cases come to a head over ethical principles in quadrant 3, the loyalty issue is the deciding factor here (see Figure I.3). Loyalty to the innocent victims of tragedy is paramount in dealing with the outrage of terrorism, rather than using the tragic circumstances for the media's own gain and busily publishing all the gory details. The ethical principle of other-regarding care is more explicit about sufferers being able to control private information rather than surrendering this prerogative to others who are promoting their own agendas. Truthtelling is the recommended norm under ordinary circumstances. The life and death drama of terrorism in all four countries is best guided by the ethical principle of other-regarding care.

The process by which moral decisions are made is of the greatest importance. Media professions are demanding, filled with ambiguous situations and conflicting loyalties. The practitioner must make decisions quickly and without much time for reflection. Knowing the elements in moral analysis sharpens our vocabulary, thereby enhancing our debates in media ethics. By understanding the logic of a four-quadrant social ethics, we improve the quality of our conceptual work and thereby the validity of the choices actually made in media practice over the long term. The four dimensions introduced with the Potter Box instruct media practitioners and students in developing normative ethics instead of leaving situations trapped in a crisis or in confusion.

USING ETHICAL PRINCIPLES

The Potter Box can help guide us through the various cases presented in this book. In the Norway terrorism case, the relevant empirical matters are complicated but not impossible to sort out. The Potter Box insists that we treat the specifics carefully and research the events thoroughly.

Our disagreements often result from our seeing the actual events differently. For example, when a newspaper purchases a building secretly, sets up a bar, and records city officials on camera, a host of details must be clear before a conclusion can be reached, before we can decide whether the paper is guilty of entrapment, invasion of privacy, or deception. Or, when debating a television station's responsibility to children, much of the disagreement involves the station's profits and how much free programming of high quality it can contribute without going broke. Discussions of controlling advertising are usually divided over the question of the actual effect advertising has on buyer behavior. Often we debate whether we must overthrow the present media system or work within it. These quarrels are usually not genuine moral disagreements. Both sides may appeal to a utilitarian principle that institutions must promote the greatest amount of good possible. The debate might simply be over facts and details, over conflicting assessments of which strategy is more effective, and so forth.[6]

Also, our values need to be isolated and accounted for. Several values usually enter and shape the decision-making process. Development of an exhaustive list of the values held by participants is never possible. Nevertheless, paying attention to values helps to prevent us from basing our decisions on personal biases or unexamined prejudices.

Our values constitute the frame of reference in which theories, decisions, and situations make sense to us. Sometimes our moral values correspond favorably to carefully articulated ethical theories. We may value gentleness and compassion so highly, for example, that our attitudes and language mesh with a stringently systematic ethics of pacifism. It is more likely, however, that stepping into quadrant 3 to examine principles will critique the values that may cloud our judgment. For example, journalists sometimes defend the "smoking out" process—making public an accusation about a politician under the assumption that guilt or innocence will emerge once the story gets played out fully in public. This professional value is usually contradicted by ethical principles regarding truth and protecting privacy.

Patrick Plaisance is helpful in connecting values to the media professions. He sees the code of ethics adopted by the Public Relations Society of America (PRSA) as more practical than most because it includes a statement of professional values. The PRSA defines values this way: "Fundamental beliefs that guide our behaviors and decision-making process." These are the key professional values that the PRSA code considers vital for public relations practice: advocacy, honesty, expertise, independence, loyalty, and fairness.[7]

Values motivate human action. Values are a distinctive mark of the human species. But our values are never pure. We tend to become defensive about them and typically rationalize our behavior when we violate them. Professional values are inscribed in power.[8] Professions such as journalism, law, or engineering are very influential; generally, they operate in their own interests. Often our professional values are high-minded. Film producers may be strongly committed to aesthetic values and advertisers to hard work, for example. But no values are innocent. In institutions, values are a complicated mixture of ideas that often need to be checked, questioned, or corrected. Steps 3 and 4 in the Potter Box (naming the principles and loyalties) help us to think critically about the conflicting or inappropriate signals we receive from quadrant 2 (identifying the values).

The format in this book of first describing cases and then giving commentaries attempts to clarify the first two quadrants in the Potter Box. Case studies, by design, give the relevant details and suggest the alternatives that were considered in each situation. The cases themselves, and the commentaries particularly, explicate the values held by the principal figures in the decision-making process. Usually in conversations, speeches, memos, and animated defenses of one's behavior, a person's important values become clear. Ethicists examine rhetoric very carefully in order to determine what material is relevant for quadrant 2. The manager of a public relations agency, for example, may value innovation so highly that other dimensions of the creative process are ignored; efficiency may be so prized in a film company that only subordinate values survive; and a reporter's commitment to the adversary relationship may distort his or her interpretation of a politician's behavior.

Occasionally, the commentaries extend even further and offer ethical principles by which the decision can be defended—yet, on the whole, these norms, or principles, must be introduced by readers themselves. To aid this process, the following pages (Five Ethical Guidelines) summarize five major options. As the Potter Box demonstrates, appealing to ethical principles that illuminate the issues is a significant phase of the moral reasoning process. Often one observes newspapers and broadcasters short-circuiting the Potter Box procedures. They typically act on the basis of professional values, in effect deciding in quadrant 2 what their action will be. For example, in the Pentagon Papers dispute, the *New York Times* decided to publish the story because it valued First Amendment privileges so strongly that no other considerations seemed important. In this classic case, the Pentagon's review of Vietnam policy in secret documents were stolen by Daniel Ellsberg in early 1971 and leaked to the *New York Times.* Though the documents were under National Security protection, the newspaper saw duplicity and abuse of the Constitution by the U.S. government, and concluded the American people had a right to know. However, on the basis of the Potter Box, we insist that no conclusion can be morally justified without a clear demonstration that an ethical principle shaped the final decision. The two quadrants on the left side, including values, explicate what actually happens. The two on the right side, including ethical principles, concern what ought to happen. The left half of the box is descriptive and the right half normative.

We will follow the standard definitions that locate the act of valuing deep within the human will and emotions, whereas ethics involves critical reasoning about moral questions. As Sigmund Freud argued in *Totem and Taboo*, all societies, as far as we know, raise up certain ideals to emulate—but they also separate themselves from other cultures by establishing boundaries or taboos. A totem pole may indicate that a tribe supremely values the strength of a lion or the craftiness of a weasel. Similarly, rituals are maintained to pronounce a curse on behaviors considered totally unacceptable. In other words, valuing occurs as an aspect of our human condition as moral beings; it automatically comes to expression in everyday circumstances.[9] Values pervade all dimensions of human experience; even scientific experiments are saturated with value components. However, ethics involves an understanding of theology and philosophy as well as debates in the history of ideas over justice, virtue, the good, and so forth. Ethics also emphasizes reasoning ability and adequate justification.

Sometimes a working journalist will ask: "Why worry about principles? We know what we should do!" Such a comment often reflects a professional impatience with the idea of a moral dilemma, but it sounds a note that many moral philosophers are also asking: "Why principles? What principles? Whose principles?" The philosophical mind and social critics today tend to challenge the practice of searching for moral norms.[10] Yet norms rightly understood are foundational for moral commitment. Along those lines, Charles Taylor writes: "A framework is that in which we make sense of our lives spiritually. Not to have a framework is to fall into a life which is spiritually senseless."[11]

However, while morally appropriate options can be outlined, the imposition of ethical principles by teachers and authors is normally counterproductive in that it undercuts the analytical process. The purpose of sound ethical reasoning is to draw responsible conclusions that yield justifiable actions. For this purpose, several ethical norms are introduced below. In analyzing the cases in this book, these principles can be incorporated wherever appropriate and beneficial to given situations. Theories arise in specific historical circumstances and address specific issues. Therefore, no one theory can satisfactorily resolve all the questions and dilemmas in media ethics. One of the important tasks for instructors and students is learning which theory is the most powerful under what conditions. While other texts may focus on one approach across the board—utilitarianism or virtue ethics, for instance—identifying the right theory is a significant step in the decision-making process with the Potter Box. In coming to grips with privacy, for example, *agape* and caring are more penetrating than utility.

Historically, ethicists have established many ethical principles.[12] However, ethicist Louis Hodges is correct in organizing all the various options into five categories—ethical theories based on virtue, duty, utility, rights, and love. For four of them, we provide the most influential time-tested representative of each of these traditions. For example, within the contractarian tradition of John Locke emphasizing rights, Rawls has been selected as the dominant contemporary theorist in that category. Judeo-Christian *agape* is included as the historic and pervasive ethical theory based on love; the "ethics of care" (Nel Noddings) is included as a contemporary example of this approach. By working with these theories, students learn how they apply in situations close to their own experience. Readers acquainted with other theories from across the globe and with moral issues in other cultures are encouraged to substitute them instead. Confucius and Islamic ethics are included in the following discussion to stimulate work in other traditions and to illustrate how such theories enrich the Potter Box model for teaching ethics.

These master theories are not canonical, that is, they are not a body of self-evident truths without contradiction. Such a celebration is too glib and ignores the cultural power that dominant theories represent. The Greek *kanon* means measuring stick, a taxation table, or a blueprint. Canons do grant privilege to certain texts on the grounds that without boundaries, there is only chaos, dissipated energies, "a babble of . . . complaints rather than a settled critique." Diversity arises out of unity; without a buffer zone, struggle is impossible. The canon "depends on who is teaching it and how; . . . living in the same place does not mean living with the same history." The French philosopher Maurice Merleau-Ponty once wrote: "What is original about Machiavelli is that having laid down the source of struggle, he goes beyond it without ever forgetting it." Socrates makes the same point in the *Crito*—recognizing that the fact he criticizes, what he criticizes, and how he criticizes is made possible by the very city he is criticizing. Throughout this text, theorists provide a common language not as abstract authority, but in order that we can think on our own rebelliously or amiably, as circumstances demand it.[13]

FIVE ETHICAL GUIDELINES

1A. Aristotle's Mean: "Moral virtue is a middle state determined by practical wisdom."[14]

From Aristotle's predecessor, Plato, the Greeks inherited the four cardinal virtues: temperance, justice, courage, and wisdom. Of these virtues, temperance was the capstone, the virtue through which the others flowed. When doing his ethics, Aristotle emphasized moderation, or temperance, and sharpened it. Just as intellectual life is reasoning well, moderation is living well. In Aristotle's philosophy, justice is a mean lying between indifference and the selfish indulgence of insisting on personal interests. Courage is a mean between cowardice and temerity. Wisdom is a middle state between stultifying caution and unreflective spontaneity.

Propriety is stressed rather than sheer duty or love. As a biologist, Aristotle notes that both too much food and too little spoil health. Whereas many ethical theories focus on behavior, Aristotle emphasizes character rather than conduct per se. Outer behavior, in his view, reflects our inner disposition. Virtuous persons have developed habits in terms of temperance; in order for them to flourish as human beings, the path they walk is that of equilibrium and harmony.[15]

In Aristotle's own words, the principle is this: "Moral virtue is a fixed quality of the will, consisting essentially in a middle state, as determined by the standard that a person of practical wisdom would apply."[16] Practical wisdom (*phronesis*) is moral discernment, a knowledge of the proper ends of conduct and the means of attaining them. Practical wisdom is distinguished in Aristotle's teaching from both theoretical knowledge and technical skill. Humans who are not fanatics or eccentrics, but of harmonious character, develop their proportion and balance through everyday habit, guided by reason:

> Over a career of moral growth . . . [we develop] acuity in our perceptions and a disposition to reason wisely. . . . [We acquire] states of emotional maturity and character traits that dispose us toward the virtuous mark in our choices. . . . The wise person within whom there are well-integrated traits of character is the ultimate arbiter of right and wrong.[17]

Aristotle challenges those of practical wisdom to apply this discernment "to individual facts" by locating "the mean between two vices, that which depends on excess and that which depends on defect."[18] And the basic principle of the middle state applies to several diverse areas. In journalism, the sensational is derided, and the virtues of balance, fairness, and equal time are recognized. When faced with a decision of whether to prohibit all raising of tobacco or to allow unregulated promotion, the Federal Trade Commission operated in a middle state—they banned cigarette ads from television and placed warning labels on cigarette packages. Recommendations about liquor advertising fall between the extremes of not advertising at all and no restrictions on it whatsoever. The legitimate claims of two legally appropriate entities must be negotiated, Aristotle would contend. Regarding violence in cinema, sensationalist violence on the one hand, and bloodless romanticism on the other, are both rejected. Aesthetic realism is the pathway in between. The middle-state mean is the fairest and most reasonable option for honorably resolving disputes between labor and management, between school board and striking teachers, and between Palestinian and Israeli politicians. Generally speaking, in extremely complicated situations with layers of ambiguity and uncertainty, Aristotle's principle has the most intelligent appeal. This is the path recommended, for example, in the *Philadelphia Inquirer* bankruptcy case (Case 3).

However, some issues are not amenable to a center. A balanced diet positioned between famine and gluttony is undoubtedly wise, but occasionally our bodies require drastic surgery also. There were slaves in Greece; Aristotle opted for treating them well and fairly but not for the radical change of releasing them altogether. In considering action regarding a hostile editor, a reporter cannot say: "If one extreme is to murder him, I will merely pummel him senseless in a back alley." In the same way, bank robbers cannot justify themselves by operating at night so that customers will not be hurt and by taking only $10,000 instead of $100,000.

As the *Nicomachean Ethics* makes clear, not every action or every emotion admits of a middle state. The very names of some of them suggest wickedness. For instance, spite, shamelessness, envy, and, among actions, adultery, theft, and murder; all these and similar emotions and actions are blamed as being intrinsically wicked and not merely when practiced to excess or insufficiently. Consequently, it is not possible ever to feel or commit them rightly; they are always wrong.[19]

Extreme oppression demands extreme resistance. Fascism needs opposition. Suicide bombing requires protest.

It bears repeating that Aristotle was not advocating a bland, weak-minded consensus or the proverbial middle-of-the-road compromise. The mean is not isolated action reduced to political wheeling-and-dealing or bureaucratic fixing. We say of an artistic masterpiece, "Nothing can be added or subtracted without spoiling it." This is Aristotle's intent with the middle state as well. Although the word *mean* has a mathematical flavor and a sense of average, a precise equal distance from two extremes is not intended. Aristotle speaks of the "mean relative to us," that is, to the individual's status, particular situation, and strong and weak points.[20] Thus, if we are generally prone to one extreme, we ought to lean toward another this time. Affirmative-action programs can be justified as appropriate in that they help correct a prior imbalance in hiring. The mean is not only the right quantity, but also, as Aristotle puts it, "the middle course occurs at the right time, toward the right people, for the right motives, and in the right manner."[21] This is the best course and is the mark of goodness. The distance depends on the nature of the agents as determined by the weight of the moral case before them. Consider the Greek love of aesthetic proportion in sculpture. The mean in throwing a javelin is four-fifths of the distance to the end, and in hammering a nail, nine-tenths from the end.

1B. Confucius's golden mean: "Moral virtue is the appropriate location between two extremes."

Virtue ethics rooted in temperance emerged at the earliest beginnings of Western philosophy in fourth-century B.C. Greece. But the theory of the mean—more exactly rendered as "Equilibrium and Harmony"—was developed before Aristotle by the grandson of Confucius in fifth-century B.C. China.[22]

Confucius (551–479 B.C.) worked as a professional teacher in the states of Qi and Chou. In his fifties, he became a magistrate, then minister of justice in Chou. At age fifty-six, however, he fell out of favor and spent the next thirteen years traveling and teaching. Finding the rulers of other states uninterested in his ideas, he returned to Lu (the small state where he was born) at sixty-eight and taught there until his death eight years later. He is reported to have had over 3000 students.[23]

A century and a half before Aristotle, Confucius rooted his ethical theory in virtue. Confucius turned on its head the traditional idea of a superior person as born into an aristocratic family. Human excellence is seen as depending on character rather than on social position. "The virtuous person, according to Confucius . . . is benevolent, kind, generous, and above all balanced, observing the mean in all things. . . . Confucius thinks of virtue as a mean between extremes."[24]

From one of his four major books, *The Doctrine of the Mean*, representative sayings describe his teaching on virtue:

Equilibrium (*chung*) is the great root from which grow all human actings in the world. And . . . harmony (*yung*) is the universal path all should pursue. Let the states of equilibrium and harmony exist in perfection, and happy order will prevail throughout heaven and earth, and all things will be nourished and flourish [*Four Books*, vol. I, I.4, I.5].

The superior man embodies the course of the mean; the mean man acts contrary to the course of the mean. . . . The superior man's embodying the course of the mean is because he is a superior man, and so always maintains the mean [*Four Books*, vol. I, II.1, II.2].

The master said, "Perfect is the virtue which is according to the mean" [*Four Books*, vol. I, III].

The superior man cultivates friendly harmony without being weak. . . . He stands erect in the middle, without inclining to either side. How firm is he in his energy [*Four Books*, vol. I, X.5].

One begins operating with this principle by identifying extremes—doing nothing versus exposing everything, for example, in a question of how to report some event. In cases where there are two competing obligations, they often can be resolved through the golden mean. Should newspaper staffs be actively involved in community affairs, for example? The journalist's role as practitioner may at times contradict the journalist's role as citizen. In terms of Confucius's mean, the newspaper rejects both extremes: the defect of excluding all outside involvements and the excess of paying no attention to external affiliations. In this situation, the application of Confucius's principle would recommend that the newspaper publish a financial disclosure of the publisher's holdings, withdraw from potential conflicts of interest such as local industry boards, report all staff connections, and so forth but allow other civic involvements.[25]

On another level, the idea of *jen/ren* in Confucius enriches international media ethics. Confucius uses *ren* (humanity) as the term for virtue in general. Humaneness (*ren*) is the key virtue in the *Analects*. It has had a variety of translations, such as perfect virtue, goodness, and human-heartedness. However, it does not mean individual attainment—such as generosity or compassion—but refers to the manifestations of being humane. It derives from a person's essential humanity. Before Confucius, the idea of humaneness did not have ethical importance, and its centrality is certainly one of the great innovations of the *Analects.*

2A. Kant's categorical imperative: "Act on that maxim which you will to become a universal law."

Immanuel Kant, born in 1724 in Königsberg, Germany, influenced eighteenth-century philosophy more than any other Western thinker. His writings established a permanent contribution to epistemology and ethics. Kant's *Groundwork of the Metaphysic of Morals* (1785) and *Critique of Practical Reason* (1788) are important books for every serious student of ethics.[26]

Kant gave intellectual substance to the golden rule by his categorical imperative, which implies that what is right for one is right for all. As a guide for measuring the morality of our action, Kant declared: "Act only on that maxim whereby you can at the same time will that it should become a universal law."[27] In other words, check the underlying principle of your decision, and see whether you want it applied universally. The test of a genuine moral obligation is that it can be universalized. The decision to perform an act must be based on a moral law no less binding than such laws of nature as gravity. *Categorical* here means unconditional, without any question of extenuating circumstances, without any exceptions. Right is right and must be done even under the most extreme conditions. What is morally right we ought to do even if the sky should fall, that is, despite whatever consequences may follow.

Kant believed there were higher truths (which he called *noumena*) superior to our limited reason and transcending the physical universe. Conscience is inborn in every person, and it must be obeyed. The categorical imperatives, inherent in human beings, are apprehended not by reason but through conscience. By the conscience one comes under moral obligation; it informs us when we ought to choose right and shun evil. To violate one's conscience—no matter how feeble and uninformed—brings about feelings of guilt. Through the conscience, moral law is embedded in the texture of human nature.

The moral law is unconditionally binding on all rational beings. Someone breaks a promise, for example, because it seems to be in his or her own interest; but if all people broke their promises when it suited them, promises would cease to have meaning, and societies would deteriorate into terror. Certain actions, therefore, are always wrong: cheating, stealing, and dishonesty, for example. Benevolence and truthtelling are always and universally right.[28] These moral duties are neither abrogated by the passage of time nor superseded by such achievements as the Bill of Rights. Even if one could save another's life by telling a lie, it would still be wrong. Deception by the press to get a good story or by advertisers to sell products cannot be excused or overlooked in the Kantian view. Dishonesty in public relations is unacceptable. Violent pornography in entertainment is not just one variable among many; it is too fundamental an issue to be explained away by an appeal to the First Amendment.

Kant's contribution is called *deontological ethics* (*deon* from the Greek word for duty). The good will "shines like a jewel," he wrote, and the obligation of the good conscience is to do its duty for the sake of duty.[29] Ethics for Kant was largely reducible to reverence for duty, visible in his work as a hymn on its behalf. With exercising the good will an end in itself, the will–duty relationship can be elaborated this way. We have a duty

> to interact with others in ways that maximize their ability to exercise free will, or reason. To fail to do so is to fail to recognize our existence as rational beings who, by the presence of our will to reason, are obligated to act morally toward others.[30]

For Kant, categorical imperatives must be obeyed even to the sacrifice of all natural inclinations and socially accepted standards. Kant's ethics have an austere quality, but they are generally regarded as having greater motivating power than subjective approaches that are easily rationalized on the basis of temporary moods. His categorical imperative encourages obedience and faithful practice.

Sir David Ross, a twentieth-century Oxford philosopher, developed a different version of duty ethics in his books *The Right and the Good* (1930) and *The Foundation of Ethics* (1939). Moral duties such as keeping your promises were compelling to him as they were for Kant. But rather than constructing such principles rationally, he argued that "objective moral truths are intuitively known, self-evident facts about the world."[31] Obligations not to lie and duties of justice, gratitude, and noninjury have inherent value, and Ross called them "prima-facie duties"—prima facie meaning upon first view or self-evident. Since it is immediately obvious to human beings that they should not kill, Kant's universalizability construction was unnecessary, and accepting a universe of formal laws was not required. Telling the truth is a self-evident obligation to media professionals, and attempting to justify it further in Ross's view only divides and deters potential adherents. While *Media Ethics: Cases and Moral Reasoning* emphasizes the classic deontological ethics of Kant, Ross's prima-facie duties will be helpful at various points as an alternative.

2B.   Islam's divine commands: "Justice, human dignity and truth are unconditional duties."

Islamic morality is known through the original sources of Islam, that is, the Qur'an and the revelations to successive prophets and messengers, the last of whom was Muhammad of Arabia (A.D. 572–632).

In Islamic ethics, justice, human dignity, and truth are divine commands. This is a duty ethics based on unconditional imperatives. Rather than a system of formal laws as in Kant, ethical principles are commanded by Allah. Islam is based on the oneness (*Tawhid*) of God. Whatever denies a belief in God is unacceptable: "Do not make another an object of worship" (Qur'an 51:51).[32] No God exists but Allah. All Islamic virtues specifically and human responsibility generally are grounded in monotheism (the belief in one God).

From *Tawhid* is the overarching duty to command the right and prohibit the wrong. All Muslims have the responsibility to follow Islamic principles and to encourage others to adopt them. "Let there arise out of you a band of people inviting all that is good, and forbidding what is wrong" (Qur'an 3:104). "Commanding to the right and prohibiting from the wrong" is one of Islam's best-known precepts.

This system of ethics, commanded by Allah and revealed in the holy Qur'an, is comprehensive for all of life. The teachings of Islam cover all fields of human existence. As Muhammad Ayish and Haydar Badawi Sadig observe: "This ethical system is broad enough to tackle general issues confronting the Islamic community and specific enough to take care of the slightest manifestations of human behavior."[33] Muhammad the prophet is described in the Qur'an as "a perfect model" (33:21) and "the exemplar of virtues" (68:4). Patience, moderation, trust, and love are all included in Islamic morality, and prudence is a core virtue among all the others. It is well known that moral decadence portrayed in the media is unacceptable, regardless of political guarantees of free expression. But three principles are basic and of special importance to communication: justice, human dignity, and truth.[34]

Islam emphasizes justice ('adl), considering justice, in fact, the essence of Islam itself. The goal of the Prophet Muhammad and the purpose of the Qur'an was "to establish justice among the people" (Qur'an 57:25). "Justice is God's supreme attribute; its denial constitutes a denial of God Himself."[35] The injunctions are clear: "O believers. Stand firmly for justice as witnesses of God, even if it be against yourself, your parents and relatives, and whether it be against the rich or poor" (Qur'an 4:135). "When you judge among people, judge with justice" (Qur'an 4:58). As Ali Mohamed observes, this umbrella concept "balances between rights and obligations without discrimination, without an emphasis on one at the expense of the other." Islam gives priority to justice as "the supreme value that underpins other values such as freedom and equality."[36]

Respecting human dignity is the second major principle revealed in the Qur'an as commanded by Allah. God honors humans above all His creatures, and therefore, the human species is to honor its members to the maximum. Allah "created man in the best of molds" (Qur'an 95:4). In secular ethics, the concept of dignity is individualistic and horizontal, but in Islamic ethics it is rooted in the sacredness of human nature: "Humans are not just one element in the vast expense of God's creation but are the *raison d'être* for all that exists."[37]

To safeguard the individual's dignity, the Qur'an warns against defamation, backbiting, and derision. Respecting others as human beings is a wide-ranging theme, including the smallest details:

> Let not some men among you laugh at others. It may be that the latter are better than the former. Nor let some women laugh at others. It may be that the latter are better than the former. Nor defame nor be sarcastic to each other, nor call each other by offensive nicknames.
>
> (Qur'an 49:11)

Many of the virtues on Islam's extensive list are rooted in the honor owed to the human species. As Malaysian scholar Zulkiple Abdullah Ghani puts it: "Islam provides universal values and ethics in designating communication functions and verifying its end products, with the main objective of enhancing the dignity of mankind."[38] Kant uses different language but, for him, human dignity is an unconditional imperative also. In his language: "Act so that you use humanity, as much in your own person as in the person of every other, always at the same time as an end and never merely as means."[39]

And truth is a pillar of Islamic ethics also. The Prophet speaks the truth, and Allah's word in the Qur'an is true. Therefore, truthfulness is likewise at the center of human affairs and fundamental to Islamic communication. "Telling lies is as evil as worshipping idols, which is the worst offence Muslims can commit."[40] As it says in the Qur'an, "[s]hun the abomination of idols, and shun the word that is false" (22:30). There is no other pathway to Paradise than telling the truth, as the Prophet said: "Truthfulness leads to righteousness and righteousness leads to Paradise."[41] Muslims are able to uphold the truth when they follow the Islamic way of life: "They are steadfast, truthful, obedient, charitable, and they pray for forgiveness at dawn" (Qur'an 3:17).

> Muhammad emphasized the propagation of truth and the common good for the people as a whole. He insisted on verification of information before spreading it among people. As such, he disliked rumors, and slanderous characterization of individuals or groups. His most famous saying is "Actions are based on intentions." He asked people to have open and sincere dialogue.[42]

In Islam, the principles provided by the Qur'an and the Prophetic examples are the framework for believers. The First International Conference of Muslim Journalists held in Jakarta in 1981 recommended that all Muslims in the media should follow the Islamic rules of conduct, and the Association of Muslim Journalists has lived this way ever since. But Islamic ethics also testifies to the human race as a whole that following these principles brings fulfillment and well-being to societies everywhere. These three principles are directly relevant to media ethics. In those situations where unconditional imperatives are the most appropriate, justice, human dignity, and truth recommend themselves as enduring standards.

Sadig and Guta call on Islamic media ethicists to follow these principles and not the reactionary strands of Islamic thought. They remind Muslim media professionals that Islam is a religion of peace. The essence of Islam is in the word itself, "*Salam*," which in Arabic means peace. Sadig and Guta also remind us that over the thirteen years the Qur'an was revealed to the prophet in Mecca, he was instructed to spread the word of Allah with grace, wisdom, and gentle admonition, and to preach the equality of men and women in all walks of life.[43]

3.   Mill's principle of utility: "Seek the greatest happiness for the aggregate whole."[44]

Utilitarianism is an ethical view widespread in North American society and a notion well developed in philosophy. There are many different varieties, but they all hold in one way or another that we are to determine what is right or wrong by considering what will yield the best consequences for the welfare of human beings. The morally right alternative produces the greatest balance of good over evil. All that matters ultimately in determining the right and wrong choice is the amount of good promoted and evil restrained.

Modern utilitarianism originated with the British philosophers Jeremy Bentham (1748–1832) and John Stuart Mill (1806–1873). Their traditional version was hedonistic, holding that the good end is happiness or pleasure. The quantity of pleasure depends on each situation; it can be equal, Bentham would say, for a child's game of kickball as for writing poetry.[45] Mill contended that happiness was the sole end of human action and the test by which all conduct ought to be judged.[46] Preventing pain and promoting pleasure were for Bentham and Mill the only desirable ends.

Later utilitarians, however, have expanded on the notion of happiness. They have noted that if pleasure is upheld as the one object of desire (in the sense of "wine, women, and song"), then all people do not desire it (Puritans did not), and, therefore, it cannot be the only desired goal. Thus these utilitarians argue that other values besides pure happiness possess intrinsic worth—values such as friendship, knowledge, health, and symmetry. For these pluralistic utilitarians, rightness or wrongness is to be assessed in terms of the total amount of value ultimately produced. For example, after burglars broke into the Democratic Party's National Committee offices in the Watergate Hotel in 1972, the press's aggressive coverage did not yield a high amount of pleasure for anyone except enemies of Richard Nixon. Yet, as described in Case 13, for utilitarians, the overall consequences were valuable enough so that most people considered the actions of the press proper, even though pain was inflicted on a few.

Worked out along these lines, utilitarianism provides a definite guideline for aiding our ethical choices. It suggests that we first calculate in the most conscientious manner the possible consequences of the various options open to us. We would ask how much benefit and how much harm would result in the lives of everyone affected, including ourselves.

Once we have completed these computations for all relevant courses of action, we are morally obligated to choose the alternative that maximizes value or minimizes loss. The norm of utility instructs us to produce the greatest possible balance of good over evil. Actors should focus on "the greatest amount of happiness altogether."[47] To perform any other action knowingly would result in our taking an unethical course.

Two kinds of utility are typically distinguished: act and rule utilitarianism. For act utilitarians, the basic question always involves the greatest good in a specific case. One must ask whether a particular action in a particular situation will result in a balance of good over evil. Rule utilitarians, also attributing their view to Mill, construct moral rules on the basis of promoting the greatest general welfare. The question is not which action yields the greatest utility, but which general rule does. The principle of utility is still the standard, but at the level of rules rather than specific judgments. The act utilitarian may conclude that in one specific situation civil disobedience obtains a balance of good over evil, whereas rule utility would seek to generate a broadly applicable moral rule such as "civil disobedience is permitted except when physically violent."[48]

Although happiness is an end few would wish to contradict, utilitarianism does present difficulties. It depends on our making accurate measurements of the consequences, when in everyday affairs the result of our choices is often blurred vision, at least in the long term. For instance, who can possibly calculate the social changes that we will face in future decades in the wake of converging media technologies? Moreover, the principle of the greatest public benefit applies only to societies in which certain nonutilitarian standards of decency prevail. In addition, utilitarians view society as a collection of individuals, each with his or her own desires and goals; the public good is erroneously considered the sum total of private goods.[49]

These ambiguities, although troublesome and objectionable, do not by themselves destroy the utilitarian perspective, at least for those who are intellectually sophisticated. For our purposes in examining media ethics, no moral norms can be considered free of all uncertainties. However, the obvious difficulties with utilitarianism usually can be addressed in round two or three when circulating through the Potter Box for specificity and clarification.[50] Occasionally, in resolving the cases considered in the following pages, utility is the most productive principle to include in the lower right-hand quadrant. In the classic case of Robin Hood accosting the rich in order to provide for the poor, act utilitarianism appropriately condones his behavior as morally justified.

4.   Rawls's veil of ignorance: "Justice emerges when negotiating without social differentiations."

John Rawls's book, *A Theory of Justice* (1971), has been widely quoted in contemporary work on ethics. From Rawls's perspective, fairness is the fundamental idea in the concept of justice.[51] He represents a return to an older tradition of substantive moral philosophy and thereby establishes an alternative to utilitarianism. He articulates an egalitarian perspective that carries the familiar social contract theory of Hobbes, Locke, and Rousseau to a more fundamental level.

In easy cases, fairness means quantity: everyone in the same union doing similar work would all fairly receive a 10 percent raise; teachers should give the same letter grade to everyone who had three wrong on a particular test; and at a birthday party, each child should get two cookies. Eliminating arbitrary distinctions expresses fairness in its basic sense. However, Rawls struggles more with inherent inequalities. For example, players in a baseball game do not protest the fact that pitchers handle the ball more times than outfielders do. We sense that graduated income taxes are just, though teachers pay only 22 percent and editors, advertisers, public relations staff, and film producers perhaps find themselves in the 50 percent bracket.

When situations necessitating social contracts are inherently unequal, blind averages are unfair and intuitional judgments are too prone to error. Therefore, Rawls recommends his now classic "veil of ignorance," asking that all parties step back from real circumstances into an "original position" behind a barrier where roles and social differentiations are eliminated.[52] Participants are abstracted from individual features such as race, class, gender, group interests, and other real conditions and are considered equal members of society as a whole. They are men and women with ordinary tastes and ambitions, but each suspends these personality features and regains them only after a contract is in place. Behind the veil, no one knows how he or she will fare when stepping out into real life. The participants may be male or female, ten years old or ninety, Russian or Polish, rookie or veteran, black or white, advertising vice president or sales representative for a weekly magazine. As we negotiate social agreements in the situation of imagined equality behind the veil of ignorance, Rawls argues, we inevitably seek to protect the weaker party and to minimize risks. In the event that I emerge from the veil as a beginning reporter rather than a big-time publisher, I will opt for fair treatment for the former. The most vulnerable party receives priority in these cases. Therefore, the result, Rawls would contend, is a just resolution.

Because negotiation and discussion occur, the veil of ignorance does not rely merely on intuition. Such individual decisions too easily become self-serving and morally blind. Nor is the veil another name for utility, with decisions based on what is best for the majority. Again, the issue is morally appropriate action, not simply action that benefits the most people. In fact, Rawls's strategy stands against the tendency in democratic societies to rally around the interests of the majority and give only lip service to the minority.

Two principles emerge from the hypothetical social contract formulated behind the veil. These, Rawls declares, will be the inevitable and prudent choices of rational women and men acting in their own self-interest. The first principle calls for a maximal system of equal basic liberty. Every person must have the largest political liberty compatible with a like liberty for all. Liberty has priority in that it can never be traded away for economic and social advantages. Thus the first principle permanently conditions the second. The second principle involves all social goods other than liberty and allows inequalities in the distribution of these goods only if they act to benefit the least advantaged party. The inequalities in power, wealth, and income on which we agree must benefit the members of society who are worse off.[53]

Consider the press coverage in the well-known case of William Kennedy Smith for the alleged rape of a woman at the Kennedy Palm Beach compound in 1991. The case continues to be used as a learning tool, though Senator Kennedy is now deceased. The extensive media coverage at that time was justified on the basis of Senator Edward Kennedy's role at the bar earlier in the evening and public interest in the Kennedy family. Given conventional news values, the public's right to know supersedes the Kennedy family's right to privacy. But what if we go beyond values to ethical theory? Put Ted Kennedy and a newsperson behind the veil of ignorance, not knowing who will be who when they emerge. Undoubtedly they would agree that reporting on the public acts of public officials is permissible but that publicizing the alleged rape incident itself, now several years later, would be undue harassment in the absence of any new material. Rawls's principle precludes reporters from using their power to pester without end those who are caught in a news story.

On a broader level, place politicians and journalists behind the veil and attempt to establish a working relationship agreeable to all after the veil is parted and space/time resumes. All stark adversary notions would disappear. There would be no agreement that elected officials as a class should be called the enemy or liars because those who emerge as politicians would resent such labels. Independence, some toughness, and persistence seem reasonable for media professionals, but a basic respect for all humans would replace an unmitigated and cynical abrasiveness among those wielding instruments of power.

5A.   Judeo-Christian persons as ends: "Love your neighbor as yourself."[54]

Ethical norms of nearly all kinds emerge from various religious traditions. The highest good in the *Bhagavad Gita*, for example, is enlightenment. Of all the options, however, the Judeo-Christian tradition has dominated American culture to the greatest extent, and its theological ethics have been the most influential. By studying a prominent religious perspective in terms of the issues and cases in this textbook, students should be inspired to take other religious ethics seriously as well. The intention here is pedagogical—to learn a system of ethical reasoning and ethical concepts within a familiar context. On that foundation, other frameworks can be added, and dilemmas in different cultural contexts can be addressed responsibly. As summarized above, Islam and Confucianism have developed sophisticated ethical traditions.[55]

The ethics of love is not exclusively a Judeo-Christian notion. Already in the fourth century B.C., the Chinese thinker Mo Tzu spoke in similar terms: "What is the Will of Heaven like? The answer is—To love all men everywhere alike."[56] Nor are all Judeo-Christian ethics a pure morality of love; some ethicists in that tradition make obedience, justice, or peace supreme.[57] But the classic contribution of this religious perspective, in its mainline form, contends that ultimately humans stand under only one moral command or virtue: to love God and humankind. All other obligations, though connected to this central one, are considered derivative.

"Love your neighbor" is normative, and uniquely so in this tradition, because love characterizes the very heart of the universe. Augustine is typical in declaring that divine love is the supreme good.[58] The inexhaustible, self-generating nature of God Himself is love. Therefore, human love has its inspiration, motive, and ground in the highest reaches of eternity. Humans are made in the image of God; the more loving they are, the more like God they are. At this very point the Judeo-Christian norm differs from other ethical formulations. Love is not only a raw principle, stern and unconditional, as in Kant's categorical imperative. Regard for others is not simply based on just a contract motivated by self-interest, as in John Rawls's theory. It remains personal at its very roots and, although rigorously dutiful, it is never purely legalistic.[59] As Heinrich Emil Brunner noted in summarizing the biblical exhortations:

> "Live in love." Or, still more plainly: "Remain in love." . . . It is the summons to remain in the giving of God, to return to Him again and again as the origin of all power to be good and to do good. There are not "other virtues" alongside the life of love. . . . Each virtue, one might say, is a particular way in which the person who lives in love takes the other into account, and "realizes" him as "Thou."[60]

The Old Testament already spoke of loving kindness, but the Christian tradition introduced the more dramatic term *agape*—unselfishness; other-regarding care and other-directed love, distinct from friendship, charity, benevolence, and other weaker notions. In the tradition of *agape*, to love a human being is to accept that person's existence as it is given; to love him or her as is.[61] Thus human beings have unconditional value apart from shifting circumstances. The commitment is unalterable; loyalty to others is permanent, indefectible, in sickness and in health. It is unloving, in this view, to give others only instrumental value and to use them merely as a means to our own ends. Especially in those areas that do not coincide with a person's own desires, love is not contradicted. In this perspective, we ought to love our neighbors with the same zeal and consistency with which we love ourselves.

Agape as the center of meaning in Judeo-Christian ethics raises significant issues that ethicists in this tradition continue to examine: the regular failure of its adherents to practice this principle; the relationship of love and justice, of the personal and institutional; the role of reason as distinguished from discernment; and whether *agape* is a universal claim or, if not, what its continuity is with other alternatives.[62]

However, all agree that loving one's neighbor in this tradition is far from sentimental utopianism. In fact, *agape* is strong enough to serve as the most appropriate norm in Chapters 4, 5, and 14. Moreover, it is thoroughly practical, issuing specific help to those who need it. (*Neighbor* was a term for the weak, poor, orphans, widows, aliens, and disenfranchised in the Old Testament.) Even enemies are included. This love is not discriminatory: no black or white, no learned or simple, no friend or foe. Although *agape* does not deny the distinctions that characterize creaturely existence, it stays uniquely blind to them. Love does not first estimate rights or claims and then determine whether the person merits attention. The norm here is giving and forgiving with uncalculating spontaneity and spending oneself to fulfill a neighbor's well-being. Because of its long attention to understanding the character of humanness, the *agape* principle has been especially powerful in its treatment of social injustice, invasion of privacy, violence, and pornography.

5B.   Noddings' relational ethics: "The 'one-caring' attends to the 'cared-for' in thought and deeds."

Feminist scholarship in the past decade has given more precise development and higher status to the central terms in love-based ethics: nurturing, caring, affection, empathy, and inclusiveness.[63] For Carol Gilligan, the female moral voice roots ethics in the primacy of relationships. Rather than the basic standard of avoiding harm to others, she insists on compassion and nurturance for resolving conflicts among people.[64] Nel Noddings' *Caring* rejects outright the "ethics of principle as ambiguous and unstable," insisting that human care should play the central role in moral decision-making.[65] "Relationships themselves, and more generally real, lived experiences rather than intellectual and theoretical constructs, are considered the genesis of philosophical feminist ethics."[66] For Julia Wood, "an interdependent sense of self" undergirds the ethic of care, wherein we are comfortable acting independently while "acting cooperatively . . . in relationship with others."[67] In Linda Steiner's work, feminists' ethical self-consciousness also identifies subtle forms of oppression and imbalance and teaches us to "address questions about whose interests are regarded as worthy of debate."[68]

For Noddings, ethics begins with particular relations, and there are two parties in any relation. The first member she calls the "one-caring," and the second, the "cared-for." The one-caring is "motivationally engrossed in the cared-for," attending to the cared-for in deeds as well as thoughts. "Caring is not simply a matter of feeling favorably disposed toward humankind in general. . . . Real care requires actual encounters with specific individuals; it cannot be accomplished through good intentions alone." And, "when all goes well, the cared-for actively receives the caring deeds of the one-caring."[69]

Noddings does not explicitly define a care ethics, but she emphasizes three central dimensions: engrossment, motivational displacement, and reciprocity. The one-caring is engrossed in the needs of the other. "The one-caring is fully disposed and attentive toward the cared-for, has regard for the other, desires the other's well-being, and is responsive and receptive to the other." Through motivational displacement, those caring retain but move beyond their "own interests to an empathy for or 'feeling with' the experiences and views of the cared-for." The cared-for must reciprocate in order to complete the caring relationship. "Reciprocity may be a direct response or it simply may be the delight or the personal growth of the cared-for witnessed by the one caring."[70]

Through an ethics of care, we rethink the purpose of public communication. Instead of objectivity, neutrality, and detachment, an ethics of care is compassionate journalism.

Beyond the limited mission of transmitting information, feminist ethics wants to see public life go well. The vitality of the communities reported on is considered essential to a healthy news profession. Readers and viewers are connected to one another, not just to the press. The public is considered active and responsible. Citizens themselves arrive at their own solutions to public problems. The watchdog role of journalism is not emphasized as much as its responsibility to facilitate civil society. Public life outside government and business needs special attention. For education, science, communities, nongovernmental organizations, and culture to flourish, the involvement and leadership of women in the media needs serious attention.

TO WHOM IS MORAL DUTY OWED?

The Potter Box forces us to get the empirical data straight, investigate our values, and articulate an appropriate principle. Once these steps are accomplished, we face the question of our ultimate loyalties. Many times, in the consideration of ethics, direct conflicts arise between the rights of one person or group and those of others. Policies and actions inevitably must favor some to the exclusion of others. Often our most agonizing dilemmas revolve around our primary obligation to a person or social group. Or we ask ourselves: is my first loyalty to my company or to a particular client?

To reach a responsible decision, we must clarify which parties will be influenced by our decision and which ones we feel especially obligated to support. When analyzing the cases in this book, we will usually investigate five categories of obligation:

1. *Duty to ourselves.* Maintaining our integrity and following our conscience may be the best alternative in many situations. However, careerism is a serious professional problem and often tempts us to act out of our own self-interest while we claim to be following our conscience.

2. *Duty to clients/subscribers/supporters.* If they pay the bills, and if we sign contracts to work for them, do we not carry a special obligation to them? Even in the matter of a viewing audience that pays no service fee for a broadcast signal, our duty to them must be addressed when we are deciding which course of action is the most appropriate. Patrick Plaisance is correct that the principle of transparency is essential for trust to develop between media practitioners and these stakeholders.[71]

3. *Duty to our organization or firm.* Often company policy is followed much too blindly, yet loyalty to an employer can be a moral good. Whistle blowing, that is, exposing procedures or persons who are harming the company's reputation, is also morally relevant here. Reporters might even defy court orders and refuse to relinquish records in whistle-blowing cases, under the thesis that ultimately the sources on which media companies depend will dry up. Thus duty to one's firm might conceivably take priority over duty to an individual or to a court.

4. *Duty to professional colleagues.* A practitioner's strongest obligation is often to colleagues doing similar work. Understandably, reporters tend to prize, most of all, their commitments to fellow reporters and their mutual standards of good reporting. Some even maintain an adversarial posture against editors and publishers, just short of violating the standards of accepted etiquette. Film artists presume a primary obligation to their professional counterparts, and account executives to theirs. However, these professional loyalties, almost intuitively held, also must be examined when we are determining what action is most appropriate.

5. *Duty to society.* This is an increasingly important dimension of applied ethics and has been highlighted for the media under the term *social responsibility*. Questions of privacy and confidentiality, for example, nearly always encounter claims about society's welfare over that of a particular person. The "public's right to know" has become a journalistic slogan. Advertising agencies cannot resolve questions of tobacco ads, political commercials, and nutritionless products without taking the public good fully into the equation. When some Tylenol bottles were laced with cyanide, the public relations staff of Johnson and Johnson had its foremost obligation to the public. Violence and pornography in media entertainment are clearly social issues. In such cases, to benefit the company or oneself primarily is not morally defensible. In these situations, our loyalty to society warrants preeminence.

Our duty to society requires a world vision. International trade and global communication have fundamentally altered the boundaries in which we live. Many social issues are worldwide in scope—global warming, food supply and distribution, risks of nuclear and chemical warfare, health and infectious diseases, world travel networks. Regardless of our home country, we are citizens of the world. Stephen Ward has developed a global journalism ethics based on cosmopolitan values such as human rights, freedom, and justice. "We live simultaneously in two communities: the local community of birth and a community of common human aspirations. . . . We should not allow local attachments to override fundamental human rights and duties."[72] Instead of the fragmented "act locally and think globally," world citizens think and act locally and globally at the same time.[73]

Throughout this volume, the media practitioner's moral obligation to society is stressed as critically important. Admittedly, the meaning of that responsibility is often ill-defined and subject to debate. For example, when justifying one's decision, particular social segments must be specified: the welfare of children, the rights of a minority, or the needs of senior citizens. We have emphasized that, in spite of the difficulties, precisely such debate must be at the forefront when we are considering the loyalty quadrant in the Potter Box. No longer do the media operate with a crass "public be damned" philosophy. Increasingly, the customer is king, whereas belligerent appeals to owner privilege have been lessened. However, these gains are only the beginning. They need to be propelled forward so that a sincere sense of social responsibility and a genuine concern for the citizenry become characteristic marks of all contemporary media operations in news, advertising, public relations, and entertainment.

The version of the Potter Box described in this chapter furthers this textbook's overall preoccupation with social responsibility. Consider the upper tier of the Potter Box (empirical definition and ultimate loyalties), which stresses the social context. As was noted earlier, the Potter Box as a schematic design is not just an eclectic, random gathering of several elements for justifying a decision or policy. Although the lower half (values and ethical principles) deals more with analytical matters than it does with sociological ones in everyday experience, it also feeds into the higher half. Additionally, the two levels are integrated at crucial junctures so that social situations initiate the process and the choice of cultural loyalties forces one toward the final decision. Thus the loyalty component especially provides a pivotal juncture in moral discourse and indicates that conceptual analysis can hardly be appraised until one sees the implications for institutional arrangements and the relevant social groups. Along those lines, Nel Noddings strongly urges that caring—a notion of relatedness between people—should take a central role in decision-making. From her perspective, mere subscription to principle without concentrating on the people involved has caused much needless wrong.[74]

The line of decision-making that we follow, then, has its final meaning in the social order. Certainly, precision is necessary when we are dealing with ethical principles, just as their relation must always be drawn to the values held and empirical definition described. But the meaning becomes clear when the choice is made for a particular social context or a specific set of institutional arrangements. Considered judgments, in this view, do not derive directly from normative principles but are woven into a set of obligations one assumes toward certain segments of society. In this scheme, debate over institutional questions is fundamental, and ethical thinking is not completed until social applications and implications have been designated. In social ethics of this kind, the task is not just one of definition but also an elaboration of the perplexities regarding social justice, power, bureaucracies, and cultural forms. Social theory is central to the task, not peripheral.[75]

WHO OUGHT TO DECIDE?

During each phase of ethical reasoning, some actor or group of actors is directly involved in deciding, determining values, selecting moral norms, and choosing loyalties. The cases in this book cannot be read or discussed fruitfully without constant attention to the question of who is making the decision. At every step, applied ethics always considers seriously the issue of who should be held accountable.

Usually numerous decision-makers are involved. In simple cases, it is an organizational matter where an editor or executive decides rather than a reporter or sales representative. In more complicated areas, can producers of entertainment dismiss their responsibility for quality programming by arguing that they merely give the public what it wants? Are parents to be held solely accountable for the television programs that children watch, or do advertisers and networks carry responsibility also? If advertisers and networks have responsibility, in what proportions? Does the person with the greatest technical expertise have the greatest moral obligation? We must be wary of paternalism, in which consumers and informal social networks are removed from the decision-making process. When is the state, through the courts, the final decision-maker? Giving absolute authority or responsibility to any person or group can be morally disastrous. Requiring accountability across the board helps to curb the human penchant for evading one's own liability.

For all the emphasis in this textbook on social ethics, individual practitioners ought not become lost. The individual is the authentic moral agent. A firm or institution, when infused and animated by a single spirit and organized into a single institution, is more than a mere sum of discrete entities—it has a personality of its own. It is also true that such institutions can, in a sense, be held accountable for their deeds and become the object of moral approval or disapproval but only in a limited sense. Such institutions are real enough, but they lack concreteness. It is the individual who reasons morally that we consider the responsible agent. These individuals alone can be praised or blamed.[76] Such accountability is especially relevant in this new era of user-based social media.

Certainly, corporate obligation is a meaningful notion. The British company, Guardian News and Media, is a prime example of how corporate responsibility can be taken seriously. Over fifty years ago, its *Manchester Guardian* adopted specific corporate values that continue to this day, a charter that employees practice and the public knows.[77] When individuals join an organization, and for as long as they remain members, they are coresponsible for the actions taken by that organization. What is most important, however, is that ultimate responsibility finally rests on individuals. It should be obvious that this is not a plea for a heavy-handed individualism; that would stand directly at odds with the social ethics of the Potter Box model. The point is that responsibility, to be meaningfully assigned and focused, must be distributed among the individuals constituting the corporation. Individuals are not wholly discrete, unrelated, atomistic entities; they always stand in a social context with which they are morally involved. But individuals they nevertheless remain. And it is with each person that ethics is fundamentally concerned. Gross attacks and broad generalizations about entire media systems usually obscure more than they enlighten. On most occasions, such assessments are not normative ethics but hot-tempered moralism. The cases and commentaries that follow, filtered through the Potter Box model, steer media practitioners toward socially responsible decisions that are justified ethically.

NOTES

1. Henry D. Aiken, *Reason and Conduct* (New York: Knopf, 1962), 65–87.
2. For helpful background, see Richard L. Morrill, "Values as Standards of Action," in his *Teaching Values in College* (San Francisco: Josey-Bass, 1980), 56–73; David Boeyink, "What Do We Mean by Newspaper Values?" unpublished paper, February 8, 1988, Southern Newspaper Publishers Association, St. Petersburg, FL; Everette E. Dennis, "Values and Value-Added for the New Electronic Journalism," The Freedom Forum Media Studies Center, March 15, 1995; and the pamphlet (n.d.) *Journalism Values Handbook* (Boston: The Harwood Group, American Society of Newspaper Editors). For values among

artists, see Horace Newcomb and Robert Alley, *The Producer's Medium: Conversations with Creators of American TV* (New York: Oxford University Press, 1983). Here are examples of the values that are often important in media practice:

> *Professional values:* proximity, firstness, impact, recency, conflict, human interest, entertainment, novelty, toughness, thoroughness, immediacy, independence, watchdog, public's right to know, no prior restraint, independence.
>
> *Moral values:* truthtelling, humanness, fairness, honesty, stewardship, nonviolence, commitment, self-control.
>
> *Sociocultural values*: thrift, hard work, energy, restraint, heterosexuality.
>
> *Logical values:* consistency, competence, knowledge.
>
> *Aesthetic values:* harmonious, pleasing, imaginative.

3. Karen Lebacqz of the Pacific School of Religion named the model the "Potter Box" after the original version described in Ralph B. Potter, "The Structure of Certain American Christian Responses to the Nuclear Dilemma, 1958–63." Ph.D. Diss., Harvard University, 1965. See also Ralph B. Potter, "The Logic of Moral Argument," in *Toward a Discipline of Social Ethics*, ed. Paul Deats (Boston: Boston University Press, 1972), 93–114.

4. Details regarding Anders Breivik and references to the Atocha Station terrorism are solicited from "Cases and Commentaries," edited by Ginny Whitehouse with commentaries by Kirsten Mogensen and Mónica Codina, *Journal of Mass Media Ethics* 28:1 (2013): 57–69.

5. Potter himself labeled it the "ground of meaning" level. As he describes it: "Even when ethical categories have been explicated with philosophical exactitude it is possible for one to ask, 'Why ought I to be moral?' or 'Why ought I to consider your expressions of ethical judgment and your pattern of ethical reasoning to be convincing?'" Further inquiry "drives men ultimately to reflect on their more fundamental ideas concerning God, man, history, and whatever is behind and beyond history," Potter, "The Structure of Certain American Christian Responses," 404–405.

6. Taking the empirical dimension seriously does not imply a commitment to neutral facts and what is called "abstracted empiricism" in C. Wright Mills, *The Sociological Imagination* (New York: Oxford University Press, 1959), 50–75. W. I. Thomas's "definition of the situation" is actually a more sophisticated way of explicating the empirical dimension of moral questions; see W. I. Thomas, *Primitive Behavior: An Introduction to the Social Sciences* (New York: McGraw-Hill, 1937), 8. For a comprehensive introduction to this strategy, see Norman K. Denzin and Yvonna S. Lincoln, eds., *Handbook of Qualitative Research*, 5th ed. (Los Angeles, CA: Sage Publications, 2016).

7. Patrick Plaisance, *Media Ethics: Key Principles for Responsible Practice*, 2nd ed. (Thousand Oaks, CA: Sage Publications, 2013), 30–31.

8. See Karen Lebacqz, *Professional Ethics: Power and Paradox* (Nashville: Abingdon Press, 1985).

9. Obviously, the anatomy of values and their relation to beliefs and attitudes are complex issues both in psychology and in axiology. In terms of the Potter Box model, our concern is to identify the values invoked in various cases and to ensure that they are understood as only one phase of the decision-making process. In that sense, instead of the values-clarification approach of Louis Rath, Sydney Simon, and Merrill Harmin, we insist on the critical normative reflection represented in quadrant 3.

10. Richard Rorty, *Contingency, Irony, Solidarity* (New York: Cambridge University Press, 1989).

11. Charles Taylor, *Sources of the Self* (Cambridge, MA: Harvard University Press, 1989), 18; see also his *Ethics of Authenticity* (Cambridge, MA: Harvard University Press, 1991), and his *Multiculturalism and the Politics of Recognition* (Princeton, NJ: Princeton University Press, 1992).

12. Ethical egoism has not been included in the list despite its immense popularity. The authors stand with those who doubt its adequacy and coherence as an ethical theory. Furthermore, the view that everyone ought to promote his or her own self-interest does not agree with the emphasis on social responsibility in the Potter Box model. There are several formulations of ethical egoism, however. Students interested in pursuing this option should see Edward Regis's significant attempt to present a conception that

overcomes the standard objections. Edward Regis, "What is Ethical Egoism?" *Ethics* 91 (October 1980): 50–62. For a history of the debates in this area, see Tibor R. Machan, "Recent Work in Ethical Egoism," *American Philosophical Quarterly* 16 (1979): 1–15.

13. Peter Euben, "The Debate over the Canon," *The Civic Acts Review* 7:1 (Winter 1994): 4–15. Euben gives a comprehensive overview of the canonicity issue in this article. The ideas in this paragraph and the cited material are taken from Euben's essay. See also Clifford Christians, "Media Ethics in Education," *Journalism & Communication Monographs* 9:4 (Winter 2008): 186–187.

14. For a summary of Aristotle's work and its application to media ethics, see Lee Anne Peck, "Aristotle: Self-Development," in C. Christians and J. Merrill, eds., *Ethical Communication: Moral Stances in Human Dialogue* (Columbia: University of Missouri Press, 2009), 55–60.

15. For example, see *Nicomachean Ethics*, in Richard McKeon, ed., *Introduction to Aristotle* (New York: Modern Library, 1947); (1104a), 333; (1106a), 340; (1107a), 341; (1138b), 423.

16. *Nicomachean Ethics*, Bk. II, ch. 6. This is H. Rackham's translation in William Alston and R. B. Brandt, *The Problems of Philosophy* (New York: Allyn and Bacon, 1978), 187. In J. A. Stewart's version: "Moral Virtue may then be defined, as a habit involving choice, lying in a relative mean fixed by reason, that is, as the prudent man would fix it." For up-to-date research and theory in virtue ethics, see Patrick Lee Plaisance, *Virtue in Media: The Moral Psychology of Excellence in News and Public Relations* (New York: Routledge, 2015).

17. Stanley B. Cunningham, "Getting It Right: Aristotle's 'Golden Mean' as theory Deterioration," *Journal of Mass Media Ethics* 14:1: 10. Cunningham correctly insists that "congruent behavior within a career of character and emotional development, rather than isolated answers to textbook-style conflicts, defines the Aristotelian moral enterprise" (11).

18. *Nicomachean Ethics*, ed. McKeon (1107A), 340. For practical wisdom in Aristotle, see Christopher L. Johnstone, "Aristotle's Ethical Theory in the Contemporary World: Logos, Phronesis, and the Moral Life," in S. Bracci and C. Christians, eds., *Moral Engagement in Public Life: Theorists for Contemporary Ethics* (New York: Peter Lang, 2002), 16–34.

19. *Nicomachean Ethics*, ed. McKeon (1107A), 340–341.

20. Ibid. (1107a), 340.

21. Ibid. (1106b), 340.

22. For "The Doctrine of the Mean" by Confucius, selected from *The Four Books*, see Daniel Bonevac, William Boon, and Stephen Phillips, eds., *Beyond the Western Tradition: Readings in Moral and Political Philosophy* (Mountain View, CA: Mayfield Publishing Co., 1992), 264–269. See also James Legge, ed., *Four Books of the Chinese Classics: Confucian Analects, the Great Learning, Doctrine of the Mean, Works of Mencius*, 4 vols. (Corona, CA: Oriental Book Store, 1991). For background and application to communication ethics, see Virginia Whitehouse, "Confucius: Ethics of Character," in Christians and Merrill, *Ethical Communication*, 167–172.

23. Bonevac et al., *Beyond the Western Tradition*, 252.

24. Ibid., 252–253.

25. For an application of Confucius to business, see Stefan Rudnicki, ed., *Confucius in the Boardroom: Ancient Wisdom, Modern Lessons for Business* (Vancouver, BC: Newstar Press, 1998). See also Tom R. Reid, *Confucius Lives Next Door: What Living in the East Teaches Us about Living in the West* (New York: Random, 1999). For Confucius as the basis of human rights, see Dong-Hyun Byung and Keehyeung Lee, "Confucian Values, Ethics and Legacies in History," in Bracci and Christians, eds., *Moral Engagement in Public Life*, 73–96. For a discussion of Confucian values for press theory, see Jiafei Yin, "Beyond Four Theories of the Press: A New Model for the Asian and World Press," *Journalism & Communication Monographs* 10:1 (2008): 5–62. Daniel Bell reviews the status of Confucianism in modern China, *China's New Confucianism: Politics and Everyday Life in a Changing Society* (Princeton, NJ: Princeton University Press, 2008); see also William T. deBary, *Asian Values and Human Rights: A Confucian Communitarian Perspective* (Cambridge, MA: Harvard University Press, 1998).

26. For general background and an application of Kant's thinking to media ethics, see Lee Anne Peck, "Immanuel Kant: Importance of Duty," in Christians and Merrill, *Ethical Communication*, 145–150.

27. Immanuel Kant, *Groundwork of the Metaphysic of Morals*, trans. H. J. Paton (New York: Harper Torchbooks, 1964), 69–71, 82–89.

28. Patrick Plaisance elaborates on the truthtelling imperative in Kant based not only on Kant's *Groundwork* but also his *Metaphysic of Morals* published twelve years later in 1797. He demonstrates that Kant's deontological system should not be grounded first of all in the universalist maxim but in the philosophical basis for his categorical imperatives—human dignity. Kant's claim regarding the distinctive rational agency and free will of the human species expands our understanding of truthtelling as an imperative so that transparency in communication may be considered Kant's "greatest gift to media ethics today" (191). Patrick Plaisance, "Transparency: An Assessment of the Kantian Roots of a Key Element in Media Ethics Practice," *Journal of Mass Media Ethics* 22:2–3 (2007): 187–207. For elaboration, see Plaisance, *Media Ethics*, ch. 3.

29. Kant, *Groundwork of the Metaphysic of Morals*, 62.

30. Plaisance, *Media Ethics*, 54.

31. Christopher Meyers, "Appreciating W. D. Ross: On Duties and Consequences," *Journal of Mass Media Ethics* 18:2 (2003): 81–97.

32. The translation is from A. Yusuf Ali, *The Holy Qur'an*, 10th ed. (Beltsville, MD: Amana Corp., 2001). The description of Islamic ethics in this section relies principally on Ali Mohamed, "Journalistic Ethics and Responsibility in Relation to Freedom of Expression: An Islamic Perspective," in S. J. A. Ward and H. Wasserman, eds., *Media Ethics beyond Borders: A Global Perspective* (Johannesburg, S.A.: Heinemann Publishers, 2008), 142–156. See also Muhammad A. Siddiqi, "New Media of the Information Age and Islamic Ethics," *Islam and the Modern Age* 31:4 (2000): 1–5. For a Jewish version of monotheistic ethics, see William Babcock, "Moses: Deontological Norms," in Christians and Merrill, *Ethical Communication*, 151–157.

33. Muhammad Ayish and Haydar Badawi Sadig, "The Arab-Islamic Heritage in Communication Ethics," in C. Christians and M. Traber, eds., *Communication Ethics and Universal Values* (Thousand Oaks, CA: Sage Publications, 1997), 108. For background, see Abderrahmane Azzi, "The Morality of Journalism Ethics: Readings of Al Nursi's Theory of God's Attributes," *Journalism Studies* 12:6 (2011): 757–767.

34. Hamid Mowlana explains some of the different emphases in Islamic ethics over history, among varied schools of thought, and in different geographic regions (137–141). For applications to media issues and practices, see Hamid Mowlana, "Communication Ethics and the Islamic Tradition," in Thomas Cooper, ed., *Communication Ethics and Global Change* (New York: Longman, 1989), 137–146.

35. Ayish and Sadig, "Arab-Islamic Heritage in Communication Ethics," 115.

36. Mohamed, "Journalistic Ethics and Responsibility in Relation to Freedom of Expression," 8–9. For a comprehensive review of justice in Islamic ethics, see Muhammad I. Ayish, "Justice as an Islamic Journalistic Value and Goal," in Shakuntala Rao and Herman Wasserman, eds., *Media Ethics and Justice in the Age of Globalization* (Basingstoke, UK: Palgrave Macmillan, 2015), 139–154.

37. Ayish and Sadig, "Arab-Islamic Heritage in Communication Ethics," 109.

38. Zulkiple Abdullah Ghani, "Islamic Ethics and Values in the Life of a Communication Scholar," *Journal of Communication and Religion* 27 (March 2004): 58.

39. Kant, *Groundwork of the Metaphysic of Morals*, 429.

40. Ayish and Sadig, "The Arab-Islamic Heritage in Communication Ethics," 113.

41. From *The Translation of the Meanings of Sahih al-Bukhari* (Chicago: Kazi Publication, 1979), 75.

42. Mohammad A. Siddiqi, "Muhammad: Honor-Centered Morality," in Christians and Merrill, *Ethical Communication*, 143.

43. B. H. Sadig and H. A. Guta, "Peace Communication in Sudan: Toward Infusing a New Islamic Perspective," in R. Fortner and M. Fackler, eds., *The Handbook of Global Communication and Media Ethics*, vol. 2 (Walden, MA: Wiley-Blackwell, 2011), 602–625.

44. When utilitarianism is linked to both Jeremy Bentham and John Stuart Mill, the principle of utility is ordinarily stated as "seek the greatest happiness for the greatest number." Deni Elliott argues that when speaking of Mill's theory, "the greatest good for the greatest number" is misleading. Mill's principles of justice come before the utility calculus, and throughout his work Mill seeks to protect individuals who may be sacrificed for the good of the whole. "The greatest number" is an arithmetic statement, implying that the majority wins. Elliott suggests that "the aggregate good" is more accurate to Mill—those actions are right that produce the most overall good for the community as a whole or "for all the people who can be identified as being affected by a particular action" (Deni Elliott, "Getting Mill Right," *Journal of Mass Media Ethics* 22:2–3 [2007]: 100). In order to indicate the importance in Mill of valuing all people involved, the term *aggregate whole* is used here.

45. Bentham suggested a scheme for measuring the quantity of pleasure in human acts in Jeremy Bentham, *An Introduction to the Principles of Morals and Legislation* (New York: Hafner, 1948), chs. 3–7.

46. John Stuart Mill reached this conclusion in the last chapter of *A System of Logic* (London: J. W. Parker, 1843). He attempted eighteen years later to expand and defend this conviction. See John Stuart Mill, *Utilitarianism* (London: J. M. Dent & Sons, 1861), esp. ch. 2.

47. Mill, *Utilitarianism* (1863), in *Utilitarianism: Text and Critical Essays*, ed. Samuel Gorovitz (Indianapolis: Bobbs Merrill, 1971), 59–401.

48. The Potter Box can function without this distinction, but a working knowledge of act and rule utility increases the Potter Box's sophistication. Students are therefore encouraged to read additional descriptions of these two forms of utilitarianism, such as William Frankena, *Ethics* (Englewood Cliffs, NJ: Prentice-Hall, 1962), 29–35; C. E. Harris, Jr., *Applying Moral Theories*, 2nd ed. (Belmont, CA: Wadsworth, 1992), 123–154; and Robert L. Holmes, *Basic Moral Philosophy* (Belmont, CA: Wadsworth, 1993), 154–174. A twentieth-century act utility is presented in George E. Moore, *Principia Ethica* (Cambridge, UK: Cambridge University Press, 1954), ch. 5. Richard Brandt and J. O. Urmson are prominent rule utilitarians. See Richard Brandt, "Toward a Credible Form of Utilitarianism," in H. N. Castaneda and G. Nakhnikian, eds., *Morality and the Language of Conduct* (Detroit: Wayne State University Press, 1963), 107–143; and J. O. Urmson, "The Interpretation of the Moral Philosophy of J. S. Mill," *The Philosophical Quarterly* 3 (1953): 33–39.

49. For a detailed critique of utilitarian ethics, see Clifford G. Christians, "Utilitarianism in Media Ethics and Its Discontents," *Journal of Mass Media Ethics* 22:2–3 (2007): 113–131.

50. For an exceptional analysis of utilitarianism for beginners, see Arthur J. Dyck, *On Human Care: An Introduction to Ethics* (Nashville: Abingdon Press, 1977), 57–71.

51. John Rawls, *A Theory of Justice* (Cambridge, MA: Harvard University Belknap Press, 1971), 3–53. For an assessment of Rawls, see Martha Nussbaum, *Frontiers of Justice: Disability, Nationality, Species Membership* (Cambridge, MA: Harvard University Press, 2006).

52. Ibid., 118–192.

53. For a critique and elaboration of the two principles, see *Reading Rawls: Critical Studies of a Theory of Justice*, ed. Norman Daniels (New York: Basic Books, 1976), 169–281. For an effective classroom strategy to teach Rawls's theory, see Ronald M. Green, "The Rawls' Game: An Introduction to Ethical Theory," *Teaching Philosophy* 9:1 (March 1986): 51–60. For elaboration and application, see Plaisance, *Media Ethics*, 85–104.

54. A secularized account of this principle was developed by Kant, who contended that we ought to treat all rational beings as ends in themselves and never as means only. The Judeo-Christian version is included here because of its vast influence on the popular level. William Frankena judged Judeo-Christian ethics to be even more important to Western society than utilitarianism.

55. For an introduction to the central concepts and relevant literature, see Part IV, "East Asia," in Bonevac et al., *Beyond the Western Tradition*; and Mowlana, "Communication Ethics and the Islamic Tradition," 137–146. The best historical background for Confucianism is Kai-wing Chow, *Ethics, Classics, and Lineage Discourse: The Rise of Confucian Ritualism in Late Imperial China, 1600–1830* (Stanford, CA: Stanford University Press, 1993). A comprehensive list of the relevant material is included in

Bibliography of Comparative Religious Ethics, eds. John Carmen and Mark Jürgensmeyer (New York: Cambridge University Press, 1991). For a theoretical attempt to integrate diversity and universality, see Christians and Traber, *Communication Ethics and Universal Values*. Important essays on intercultural studies and moral norms are included in Ellen F. Paul et al., eds., *Cultural Pluralism and Moral Knowledge* (Cambridge, UK: Cambridge University Press, 1994), and in Bo Shan and Clifford Christians, eds., *The Ethics of Intercultural Communication* (New York: Peter Lang, 2015).

56. See E. R. Hughes, *Chinese Philosophy in Classical Times* (London: J. M. Dent and Sons, 1942), 48.

57. Pedro Gilberto Gomes, *Direto de ser: A ética da Comunicáção na Americana Latina* (*The Right to Be: An Ethics of Communication in Latin America*) (São Paulo, Brazil: Ediciones Paulinas, 1989).

58. Augustine, *The Confessions*, trans. J. G. Pilkington (New York: Liveright Publishing Corp., 1943); (2.2), 40; (4.10–4.13), 71–75; (7.12), 150; (9.1), 188; (10.1), 218; (10.29), 249; (13.1–13.4), 340–343. God's love is a basic theme throughout Augustine's writings. For a summary, see Frederick Copleston, "St. Augustine: Moral Theory," in his *A History of Philosophy*, vol. 2 (Westminster, MD: Newman Press, 1960), 81–86. Augustine's impact on the larger philosophical tradition is outlined in *Augustine for the Philosophers: The Rhetor of Hippo, the Confessions, and the Continentals*, ed. Calvin L. Troup (Waco, TX: Baylor University Press, 2014).

59. For elaboration, see Mary Hulst, "Jesus: Loving Neighbors," in Christians and Merrill, *Ethical Communication*, 18–24.

60. Heinrich Emil Brunner, *The Divine Imperative*, trans. Olive Wyon (Philadelphia: Westminster Press, 1947), 165, 167.

61. For a comprehensive review of this concept, see Gene Outka, *Agape: An Ethical Analysis* (New Haven: Yale University Press, 1972); pages 7–16 are particularly helpful in understanding the meaning of *agape*.

62. For the best available introduction to the historical and contemporary issues in Christian ethics, see Edward LeRoy Long, Jr., *A Survey of Christian Ethics* (New York: Oxford University Press, 1967); and his *A Survey of Recent Christian Ethics* (New York: Oxford University Press, 1982). See also E. Clinton Gardner, *Justice and Christian Ethics* (Cambridge, UK: Cambridge University Press, 1995). James M. Gustafson develops a systematic approach to theological ethics in his *Ethics from a Theocentric Perspective* (Chicago: University of Chicago Press, 1981 and 1984). As an alternative to both rationalist and narrative ethics, see Oliver O'Donovan, *Resurrection and the Moral Order*, 2nd ed. (Grand Rapids, MI: William B. Eerdmans, 1994), and his *Self, World, and Time: Ethics as Theology*, vol. 1 (Grand Rapids, MI: William B. Eerdmans, 2013).

63. For an evaluation of the role of gender in contemporary theoretical ethics, see Seyla Benhabib, *Situating the Self: Gender, Community and Postmodernism in Contemporary Ethics* (Cambridge, UK: Polity Press, 1992). Of particular interest to students of communication is Charlene Siegfried's *Pragmatism and Feminism: Reweaving the Social Fabric* (Chicago: University of Chicago Press, 1996); Virginia Held's *Feminist Morality: Transforming Culture, Society, and Politics* (Chicago: University of Chicago Press, 1993); Lea P. Stewart's "Facilitating Connections: Issues of Gender, Culture, and Diversity," in Josina M. Makau and Ronald C. Arnett, eds., *Communication Ethics in an Age of Diversity* (Urbana: University of Illinois Press, 1997), 110–125; Julia T. Wood, "Gender and Moral Voice: Moving from Woman's Nature to Standpoint Epistemology," *Women's Studies in Communication* 15 (1992): 1–24; Virginia Held, *The Ethics of Care: Personal, Political, and Global* (New York: Oxford University Press, 2006); and Linda Steiner, "Feminist Media Ethics," in L. Wilkins and C. Christians, eds., *The Handbook of Mass Media Ethics* (New York: Routledge, 2009), 366–381. For a general overview of the current theorists and issues, see Rosemarie Tong, *Feminine and Feminist Ethics* (Belmont, CA: Wadsworth, 1993); C. Card, ed., *Feminist Ethics* (Lawrence: University of Kansas Press, 1991); Maurice Hamington and Dorothy C. Mille, eds., *Socializing Care: Feminist Ethics and Public Issues* (Oxford, UK: Rowan and Littlefield, 2000). Paul Martin Lester and Susan Dente Ross's *Images That Injure*, 3rd ed. (Santa Barbara, CA: Praeger, 2011) includes a section of eight chapters on "Gender Stereotypes."

64. Cf. Carol Gilligan, *In a Different Voice: Psychological Theory and Women's Development* (Cambridge,

MA: Harvard University Press, 1982); Carol Gilligan et al., *Mapping the Moral Domain* (Cambridge, MA: Harvard University Graduate School of Education, 1988). For background and application to media ethics, see Lee Wilkins, "Carol Gilligan: Ethics of Care," in Christians and Merrill, *Ethical Communication*, 33–39.

65. Nel Noddings, *Caring: A Feminine Approach to Ethics and Moral Education* (Berkeley: University of California Press, 1984), 5. Cf. Nel Noddings, *Starting at Home: Caring and Social Policy* (Berkeley: University of California Press, 2002).

66. Wilkins, "Carol Gilligan: Ethics of Care," 36.

67. Julia T. Wood, *Who Cares? Women, Care and Culture* (Carbondale: Southern Illinois University Press, 1994), 108–110. Cf. also her *Relational Communication*, 2nd ed. (Belmont, CA: Wadsworth, 2000).

68. Linda Steiner, "Feminist Theorizing and Communication Ethics," *Communication* 12:3 (1991): 158; cf. Linda Steiner, "A Feminist Schema for Analysis of Ethical Dilemmas," in Fred L. Casmir, ed., *Ethics in Intercultural and International Communication* (Mahwah, NJ: Lawrence Erlbaum, 1997), 59–88; Linda Steiner and C. M. Okrusch, "Care as a Virtue for Journalists," *Journal of Mass Media Ethics* 21:2–3 (2006): 102–122; and Steiner, "Feminist Media Ethics," 366–381. Daryl Koehn, *Rethinking Feminist Ethics: Care, Trust, and Empathy* (New York: Routledge, 1998) supports the turn away from an abstract rationalistic ethics and likewise emphasizes a relational rather than individualistic understanding of persons. She insists on an empathic rather than legalistic approach to community life. However, in her view, the Gilligan–Noddings tradition tends to favor caregivers over those on the receiving end. She calls for a dialogic ethics that is shaped by feminist ethics but is broader in scope.

69. Tong, "Nel Noddings' Relational Ethics," in her *Feminine and Feminist Ethics*, 109.

70. Quotations from Richard Johannesen's summary of Noddings' *Caring* (12–19, 69–75, 176–177, 182–197), "Ned Noddings' Uses of Martin Buber's Philosophy of Dialogue," unpublished paper, 4.

71. Plaisance, *Media Ethics*, 33–72.

72. Stephen J. A. Ward, "Philosophical Foundations for Global Journalism Ethics," *Journal of Mass Media Ethics* 24:1: 15. See Stephen J. A. Ward, *Global Journalism Ethics* (Montreal: McGill-Queen's University Press, 2010) and his *Radical Media Ethics: A Global Approach* (Malden, MA: Wiley-Blackwell, 2015). Also see Stephen J. A. Ward, *Global Media Ethics: Problems and Perspectives* (Malden, MA: Wiley-Blackwell, 2013).

73. M. S. Ronald Comers, "Global Ethics and World Citizenship," in M. S. Comers, Wim Vanderckhove, and An Verlinden, eds., *Ethics in an Era of Globalization* (Aldershot, UK: Ashgate, 2008), 75–94.

74. Noddings goes further than urging that human loyalty mitigates stern application of principles; she rejects outright the "ethics of principle as ambiguous and unstable," *Caring*, 5. As further background to Noddings' work, refer to Nel Noddings, "Ethics from the Standpoint of Women," in D. L. Rhode, ed., *Theoretical Perspectives on Sexual Difference* (New Haven: Yale University Press, 1990), 160–173; also helpful is Nel Noddings, *Women and Evil* (Berkeley: University of California Press, 1989), and Noddings et al., eds., *Justice and Caring: The Search for Common Ground in Education* (New York: Teachers College Press, 1999).

75. The precise role of philosophical analysis and social theory has been debated even among those who generally follow this decision-making paradigm. Potter himself emphasized philosophical analysis as the primary element in moral deliberation, highlighting, in effect, the third quadrant as the key to a tough-minded social ethics. James Childress follows the spirit of Potter's apparent focus on philosophical ethics in the analytical tradition. See James Childress, "The Identification of Ethical Principles," *Journal of Religious Ethics* 5 (Spring 1977): 39–66.

     The desire for precision threatens the power of a comprehensive method. But the issue is not over the desirability of philosophical rigor versus the benefit of social theory. Both are indispensable forms of knowledge for ethical reflection. The question is which domain galvanizes the total process of reaching a justifiable moral decision. Which particular emphasis achieves a superior disciplinary coherence for applied ethics? Stassen argues for a "focus upon social theory which includes philosophical analysis but extends beyond it" (Glen H. Stassen, "A Social Theory Model for Religious Social Ethics,"

The Journal of Religious Ethics 5 [Spring 1977]: 9). In this volume, we provide a streamlined version of Stassen's adaptation of Potter, a schematic model that seeks to be both useful and rigorous.

76. Henry Stob, *Ethical Reflections: Essays on Moral Themes* (Grand Rapids, MI: Eerdmans, 1978), 3–6. For a distinction between task and collective responsibility, see Clifford G. Christians, "Can the Public Be Held Accountable?" *Journal of Mass Media Ethics* 3:1 (1988): 50–58.

77. Walter Jaehnig and Uche Onyebadi, "Social Audits as Media Watchdogging," Southern Illinois University manuscript, April 2010, 1–35.

1

NEWS

Democratic theory gives the press a crucial role. In traditional democracies, education and information are the pillars on which a free society rests. Informed public opinion is typically believed to be a weapon of enormous power—indeed, the cornerstone of legislative government. Therefore, a free press is also central to Thomas Jefferson's understanding of politics, for example; Jefferson characteristically referred to an independent information system as "that liberty which guards our other liberties."[1]

Because of the press's privileged position (commonly termed the *enlightenment function*), outside critics and inside leaders have persistently urged it toward responsible behavior. Thomas Jefferson himself lamented how such a noble enterprise could degrade itself by publishing slander and error. Joseph Pulitzer worried that without high ethical ideals, newspapers would fail to serve the public and could even become dangerous. Early in the seventeenth century, the French moralist La Bruyère chided newswriters for reporting trivia and demeaning their high obligation: "They lie down at night in great tranquility upon a piece of news . . . which they are obliged to throw away when they awake." A few years earlier, John Cleveland cautioned against respecting diurnal makers, "for that would be knighting a Mandrake . . . and giving an engineer's reputation to the maker of mousetraps."[2]

Modern criticisms of journalism seem merely to echo complaints that are centuries old. However, the number of today's cavilers and the bitterness of their attacks set the present decade apart. A free press remains an urgent ideal in a complicated world where expectations of journalistic performance are higher than ever before. Actually, the intense and widespread criticism may have yielded a modest dividend: never before have the media been so aware of the need for responsible behavior.

A self-conscious quality hangs heavily over newsrooms and professional conventions. Aside from the bandits and the pompous who remain untouched by any attacks, some movement is evident. How can journalists fulfill their mission credibly? Should Pulitzer Prizes be given to reporters who use deception to get a story? Why not form an ethics committee?

Are codes of ethics helpful? Do the new-media technologies require a new ethics? Should journalism schools teach ethics courses? Such well-intentioned questions crop up more and more. The cases in Part 1 present the primary issues and problems that are currently being debated among those with a heightened awareness of journalism's ethical responsibility.

The fresh interest in ethics and the profit to be gained from working through these cases may be threatened by the Western press's commitment to independence. There is a rhetoric from as far back as Jefferson, who called for a nation "where the press is *free*." Others have argued: "you cannot chain the watchdog"; "allowing controls over the news media by anyone makes it a mockery." And in countries where freedom is valued, accountability is not often understood clearly. Accountability, properly requested and unreservedly given, is alien territory. Although the belief in a free press is sincere and of critical importance, it often plays tricks on the press's thinking about ethics. Ethical principles concerning obligation and reckoning do not find a natural home within a journalism hewn from the rock of negative freedom. Part 1 advocates freedom of the press, but it promotes an accountable news system and attempts to provide content for that notion.

Ethical questions concerning conflict of interest, truthfulness, privacy, social justice, confidentiality, and the other issues we address here must be considered in an environment of stress. The latest Gallup polls reveal press credibility at 16 percent in the United States, the lowest figure in decades and an alarming one by anyone's measure. For some, it represents kicking the chair on which you stubbed your toe. The anxieties experienced in a nation uncertain of its world leadership role often provoke outbursts against the messenger. Nonetheless, we must continue working on media ethics, even in these hard times. Restrictions tend to make newspeople feel stifled, yet the contemporary cultural climate demands that journalism employ restraint and sobriety.[3] Although all the problems cannot be solved in the five chapters in this part, the analysis and resolution of the moral dilemmas presented here address matters of high priority on the journalist's agenda.

LEARNING OBJECTIVES

The learning objectives for Part 1, Chapters 1–5, are straightforward but tremendously important:

◼ Know the pressures from businesses and the new technologies that influence ethical reporting.

◼ Understand the nature of truth and its centrality in news.

◼ Understand the importance of ethics for source–reporter relationships.

■   Distinguish reporting that recognizes issues of social justice from journalism that is insensitive to these issues.

■   Explain how the public's right to know must be balanced against the public's right to privacy.

NOTES

1. Thomas Jefferson, "Address to Philadelphia Delegates," May 25, 1808, in Andrew J. Lipscomb, ed., *The Writings of Thomas Jefferson* (Washington, DC: The Thomas Jefferson Memorial Association, 1903), vol. 16, 304. For similar highly quoted passages, see his "Letter to Marquis de Lafayette," November 4, 1823, and his "Letter to Dr. James Currie," January 18, 1786, in *The Writings of Thomas Jefferson*, ed. Paul L. Ford (New York: G. P. Putnam's Sons, 1894), vol. 4, 132.

2. La Bruyère and Cleveland are quoted in William Rivers, Wilbur Schramm, and Clifford Christians, *Responsibility in Mass Communication*, 3rd ed. (New York: Harper and Row, 1980), 2.

3. An important line of scholarship accounts for some of these shifts and stresses by understanding news as social narrative. See Gertrude J. Robinson, "Making and Manufacturing Consent: The Journalistic Narrative and Its Audience," in Theodore L. Glasser and Charles T. Salmon, eds., *Public Opinion and the Communication of Consent* (New York: Guilford Press, 1995), ch. 14, 348–369; James A. Ettema and Theodore L. Glasser, *Custodians of Conscience: Investigative Journalism and Public Virtue* (New York: Columbia University Press, 1998); Stuart Allan, *News Culture* (Buckingham, UK: Open University Press, 1999); Michael Schudson, *The Sociology of News* (New York: W. W. Norton, 2003); Brian Goss, *Rebooting the Herman & Chomsky Propaganda Model for the Twenty First Century* (New York: Peter Lang, 2013); and Einar Thorsen and Stuart Allan, eds., *Citizen Journalism: Global Perspectives*, 2 vols, 2nd ed. (Bern, Switzerland: Peter Lang, 2014).

1

INSTITUTIONAL PRESSURES

William Peter Hamilton of *The Wall Street Journal* once argued that "[a] newspaper is private enterprise owing nothing whatever to the public, which grants it no franchise. It is emphatically the property of the owner, who is selling a manufactured product at his own risk."[1] This is an extreme statement, yet over the past two centuries many shared this attitude. Based on the principles of classical democracy and traditional capitalism, the individual's right to publish has been a strongly held convention in countries such as the United States. But this mood may be shifting somewhat, at least in theory. Increasingly, enlightened newspaper owners and executives realize their special obligation precisely because news—and not widgets—is their business.

Nothing is more difficult in the mass-media enterprise than promoting the public good, even though the rewards—professionally and financially—are not commensurate with such altruism. In actual practice, it becomes extraordinarily difficult to separate the media's financial interests from the public's legitimate news interests. The law may protect the media from government constraint, but the news is under the perpetual risk of corporate control. Granted, a conflict between the public's need for unpolluted information and the stockholders' need for profit is not inevitable. Needing to earn a respectable income and deciding to stop a dead-ended investigation could both be appropriate; moral questions emerge when the two are connected as cause and effect. Without a press pool to help pay expenses for a charter, a minor party candidate could not conduct a modern political campaign. One person serving in two potentially conflicting capacities—for example, as executive for Columbia Broadcasting and board member for Columbia University—may indeed be working ethically.[2] Not every owner or executive is automatically suspect.

Nonetheless, ever since much of the mass communications took on the character of big business at the turn of the twentieth century, there have been built-in commercial pressures. The angry critic Upton Sinclair said accusingly in 1920:

The Brass Check is found in your pay envelope each week . . . the price of your shame—you who take the fair body of truth and sell it in the market-place, who betray the virgin hopes of mankind into the loathsome brothel of Big Business.[3]

As the ominous trend continues toward concentrated ownership of media properties, cost-conscious publishers threaten to overwhelm the press's noble mission.[4] The four cases that follow demonstrate how media practitioners are often caught in conflicting duties to their employers, to their readers or viewers, and to their own professional conscience. They illustrate some of the conundrums that occur regularly in today's news business. It is no wonder the public remains enormously concerned whether media enterprises spend money honorably.

The first case, "Fox News," describes the rise of niche news using internet technology. With digital technology making interaction between senders and receivers possible, specialized audiences live in an echo chamber polarized from others.

The second case, "Access to the Internet," raises the problem of distribution. Justice requires equal access to all and the National Broadband Plan promotes it, but market economics limits accessibility.

The third case, "Bankruptcy at the *Philadelphia Inquirer*," traces the history of this quality newspaper from its golden era to receivership in the U.S. Bankruptcy Court. The question is whether ethics can be maintained as the news industry downsizes.

The fourth case, "Paid Journalism Worldwide," deals with payola, freebies, gifts, and hush money that create conflicts of interest for journalists and threaten the news media's credibility with the public.

Since biblical times, sages have warned against serving two masters. Nearly all professions—politics most notably—confront the same problem. Yet the issues cut especially deep in reporting. The highly publicized conviction of former *Wall Street Journal* reporter R. Foster Winans has become a classic reminder that easy cash is always a temptation—for individuals as well as for companies. Leaking advance information from his "Heard on the Street" column to stockbroker Peter Bryant yielded a $30,000 under-the-table payment. Apparently even small amounts of money are occasionally worth more than our integrity as journalists. As some observers have noted, the issues of handling profit responsibly and spurning fattened pockets are not just a chapter in a book, they are the cornerstone of media ethics.

CASE 1. FOX NEWS

The Fox News Channel was launched on October 7, 1996 by Australian Rupert Murdoch. In 1989 Murdoch started Sky News in the United Kingdom, Europe's first 24-hour news channel. He used that experience to establish what he called a "worldwide platform" of cable and satellite systems with its headquarters in New York. Murdoch hired Roger Ailes from America's Talking (now MSNBC) to begin Fox News and Ailes continues as CEO at the time of writing.[5]

The Fox News Channel maintains a website featuring both video and audio clips from its newsgathering operations, columns from its radio, television, and online personalities, and discussion programs such as the *The Five*, *Business Hour*, *News with a View*, and the *Stossel Show*. Its live streaming segment, *The Strategy Room*, includes informal discussion and running commentary. Fox News Mobile formats the website for video-enabled mobile phones. Fox News Radio was introduced in 2003 and includes both short newscasts and talk radio.

Shephard Smith is Fox's news anchor, and correspondents and news staff contribute to his twice-daily news show in mid-afternoon and early evening. Fox's visibility and notoriety as a network centers on its big-name personalities, who all host programs that are in the top ten most-watched nightly news programs: Margo Kelly, Neil Cavuto, Sean Hannity, Bill O'Reilly, and Greta Van Susteren. Its ratings began climbing dramatically during the Iraq invasion and occupation (300 percent in 2003). During the Republican National Convention in 2004, Fox became a larger news source than the three broadcast networks (ABC, CBS, NBC). In 2006, during the North Korean Missile Crisis and Lebanon War, Fox became the number one cable news channel. By 2009 Fox News had its highest ratings ever, beating all cable news competitors in daytime programming; it has continued that dominance every year since. Since April 2010, Fox News has led in the primetime ratings also—the first time in history that a news network beat entertainment programs in evening primetime, both over-the-air networks and cable. In April 2014, Fox led the Cable News Daily Ratings in all age categories.

In 2004, Robert Greenwald produced the documentary film *Outfoxed: Rupert Murdoch's War on Journalism*, which argues that Fox News has a conservative bias, including as evidence internal memos that demonstrate Fox's attempt to alter news content. In the Pew Research Center report on public attitudes toward various national news organizations, 72 percent of Republican viewers rated Fox as "favorable", while 43 percent of Democrat viewers share this opinion. However, Fox had the highest unfavorable rating of all national outlets studied at 25 percent of all viewers. The report concludes that "partisan differences in views of Fox News have increased substantially since 2007." A Pew Research poll released in October 2009 found that Fox News is viewed as the most ideological network in America. Murdoch reacts against these charges of bias toward the political right by claiming that Fox "has given room to both sides, whereas only one side had it before."[6]

The Fox News Channel as a whole is typically considered ideological but the most severe criticisms are directed to its big-name personalities. Bill O'Reilly has topped the cable news show rankings for eleven years in a row and is a lightning rod for controversy. House Minority leader Nancy Pelosi and Senate Majority leader Harry Reid are always under attack, at one point O'Reilly wishing Reid would be kidnapped and Pelosi waterboarded. He wished Hurricane Katrina would have flooded the United Nations Building and its occupants, instead of New Orleans. Karl Rove, a political contributor to the Fox News Channel, often makes himself the headlines with sensational claims such as Hillary Clinton suffering brain damage since a fall in 2012. *Huckabee* is rated the number one weekend cable news show, with viewers apparently attracted to his controversial claims and political humor. A harsh critic of Islam, in reference to what he considered its propensity for violence during their holidays, Mike Huckabee compared Muslims to "uncorked animals" encouraged by their religion to "murderous mayhem." Intolerant of the LGBT community, he compares homosexual relationships to illegal drug abuse. A committed Christian, Huckabee claimed that the Newtown shooting was because America has removed God from the schools. His recent comments about the Affordable Health Care Act are his most outrageous:

> If the Democrats want to insult the women of America by making them believe that they are helpless without Uncle Sugar providing for them a prescription each month for birth control because they cannot control their libido or their reproductive system without the help of government then so be it.[7]

The White House spars frequently with Fox also. In September 2009 President Obama appeared on all major news programs except Fox News. Commentator Sean Hannity was berating Obama's health care proposal and falsifying the facts, so the President snubbed them. Fox News Sunday host Chris Wallace called White House administration officials "crybabies" in response. Two weeks later, Anita Dunn, then the administration's Director of Communications, complained on Howard Kurtz's CNN program, *Reliable Sources*:

> The reality of it is that Fox News often operates almost as either the research arm or the communications arm of the Republican Party. They take Republican talking points and put them on the air, take their opposition research and put it on the air. And that's fine. But let's not pretend they're a news organization like CNN is.

President Obama agreed: "If the media is operating basically as a talk radio format, that's one thing, and if it's operating as a news outlet, then that's another."[8]

The Fox News Channel, its success and controversy, reflects today's fracturing of news. Fragmentation of the audience, the "news niche" phenomenon, polarization of the public—the terms and labels refer to a distinctive feature of media technology at present. When only three major over-the-air channels existed—ABC, CBS, and NBC—the audience for broadcast news gathered around these national platforms. With the proliferation of delivery systems, from cable TV first to the iPad and DirecTV now, technological fragmentation inevitably means the disruption of a common news audience:

> The neutral media environment changed dramatically with the diffusion of cable television and the Internet. The new, more diversified information environment makes it not

only possible for consumers to seek out news they might find agreeable, but also provides a strong economic incentive for news organizations to cater to their viewers' political preferences.[9]

As Terry McDermott puts it in his analysis ("Dumb Like a Fox"), "Fox News has simply (and shamelessly) mastered the confines of cable."[10] Roger Ailes self-consciously adopted the Republican Party as Fox's audience from the beginning, identifying the "silent majority" that his former boss Richard Nixon served. But Ailes chose this market for reasons of technology as much as for politics. The Republicans had no explicit television home in 1996, one that connected them to the news flow, and the narrowcasting of cable technology could serve them primarily. Ailes is a brilliant tactician, a mastermind of the way the technological infrastructure works. "He turned a fledgling news operation that barely existed a decade ago into the runaway market leader in cable news and a profit engine that turns out more than $500 million annually for Rupert Murdoch's global News Corporation."[11] MSNBC interconnects with a specific cable audience too. The business channel CNBC with a viewership of only 200,000 is in "its fourth year of double digit record-breaking profits."[12] Taking the new media's infrastructure into account, Fox's so-called bias doesn't cover the issues fully. "Fragmentation, or the ability to get news from hundreds of different sources, is the main culprit of declining viewership, declining revenue and struggling news channels."[13]

Interactive technologies that link sender and receiver create the "echo chamber" effect. We select stories from the media that interest us. We participate in blogs that confirm our prejudices. The social glue that societies need to make responsible decisions together is replaced by information ghettos and insularity. Digital media enable us to link into sympathetic perspectives and avoid discordant ones. Those who live in an "information cocoon" are typically ignorant about the views of those who live outside it. When major issues such as health care reform are on the national agenda, the plethora of media technologies does not promote understanding and consensus, but an echo effect. Rumors, myths, conspiracy theories, and self-indulgence all generate their own audiences who talk among themselves and reinforce the status quo.

Harvard University professor, Cass R. Sunstein, has put this concern in compelling terms in his book *Republic.com 2.0*.[14] He argues that "The Daily Me," as he calls life on the internet, is unhealthy for democracy. Rather than enhancing public discourse, limitless news and information, in his view, are "a nightmare" for it. Living within those news programs, blogs, podcasts, and social media that reinforce their own views, citizens tend to filter out alternatives and exist in an ideologically exclusive "Daily Me." The members of a democratic society are prone to equate this personal empowerment with freedom and individual rights. The ideals of unity and the common good—crucial to the survival of democratic government—are replaced by accelerating polarization. In our "cybercascade," as Sunstein calls it, diverse publics do not hear multiple voices; abundant technology does not cultivate a culture where people want to hear what others have to say, where we actually believe that learning from one another is important.

In a similar vein, the German thinker, Jürgen Habermas, famous for his concept of the public sphere, worries about computer-mediated communication becoming dominant: "The rise of millions of fragmented chat rooms across the world tends to lead to the fragmentation of large but politically focused mass audiences into a huge number of isolated issue publics."[15] The overall question is still unresolved: does the internet "gather the public together, not as spectators, followers or atomized egos, but as *demos* capable of self-articulation."[16]

The research of Matthew Gentzkow and Jesse M. Shapiro of the University of Chicago tends toward a negative answer to that question.[17] Apparently most internet users roam widely. While a majority may start with giant sites such as Google and Yahoo News, typically they cruise about checking Sara Palin's website, MSN Money, celebrity gossip, real estate, or wherever the content and links may lead them. As David Brooks puts it: "If this study is correct, the Internet will produce . . . a free-wheeling, multilayered public square."[18]

Today's polarization may only be partially explained by technology. Digital technology and citizenship is an issue we all face together. But what is the specific responsibility of those creating and profiting from information cocoons? The Fox channel is a news niche. How do ethical principles apply? Fox's newscast twice per day with anchorman Shephard Smith is basically straight news. "Their bevy of more notorious personalities—Bill O'Reilly, Neil Cavuto, Sean Hannity, and Greta Van Susteren," by Fox's own accounting, is not made up of "news people; they are editorialists and ought to be analyzed as such. They are analogous to the editorial and op-ed opinion pages of newspapers, which ought not to be confused with straight news coverage."[19] While CNN and Fox are "each seeking its own distinct niche in the modern television ecology," and each distinguishes news and commentary, Fox is distinct from CNN. Opinion and analysis are adjuncts to CNN's news programming, but

> Fox is the opposite. It includes the news operations as an adjunct to opinion and analysis. It is much more of a talk-show network than a news-network. . . . [Fox's] news portion is very small and the opinion portion very large. . . . Fox has a reporting and editing staff about one-third the size of CNN's. . . . Fox has many fewer bureaus, both domestic and international (again, about one-third CNN's total).[20]

For Fox Channel News as narrowcast, oriented to opinion, the ethical principles of truth and other-regarding care are not pre-eminent. There is frequent error of facts, misrepresentation, and rumor in the talk-show format. And for the flamboyant personalities who specialize in ridicule, judgment of people as a class, profiling, and hostility, the Judeo-Christian principle of persons as ends and Noddings's relational ethics are obvious moral guidelines.

CASE 2. ACCESS TO THE INTERNET

A global information order has come into its own. Massive multimedia conglomerates are at war for the $3.5 trillion annually at stake—Pearson plc in England, Bertelsmann in Germany, Alibaba in China, Microsoft and Google in the United States, Rupert Murdoch's empire, and Sony of Japan. An interactive industry of giant companies is emerging from television, telecommunications, electronics, mobile phones, financial services, texting, computers, and book-publishing firms. Today's business tycoons do not specialize in steel but in images, data, software, and ideas.

Clusters of high-tech electronic firms are remapping what they call the virtual planet. Silicon Valley, California and Silicon Alley, New York are home to more than 5,000 companies. Israel's Silicon Wadi is coming on strong as a cyber superpower. Bangalore, India is a magnet for multinational information technology firms. Singapore is transforming itself into an internet island in which every office, home, and school will be linked to an ultrafast multimedia network. South Korea has the world's largest broadband capacity. Zhongguancun is Beijing's international home for computer merchandizing and high-tech startups. Previous geographic alignments organized by political power are being reordered in terms of electronic megasystems.

Networking is the critical concept: the storage capacity of digital data banks integrated with the unlimited transmission capabilities of fiber optics and satellites; video imaging and the switching capabilities of smart phones. Thanks to services such as iTunes, TiVo, and Netflix, we no longer need to settle for whatever happens to be on at a particular time. We can select any item from an encyclopedic menu of offerings and have it routed directly to our television or computer screen. Tomorrow's newspaper or yesterday's episode of *The Office*? The latest gag on YouTube? Type in what you want and it appears just when you need it. Welcome to the information superhighway.[21]

Electronics are rapidly engulfing our family life, schools, professions, and religious institutions. Twitter, WeChat, iPads, Amazon.com, video games, the World Wide Web, and virtual reality—the electronic world is increasing our native habitat. This megaindustry is by all odds the most important and lucrative marketplace of the twenty-first century.

The pressures on media institutions from this new delivery system are multiple and complex. As global media empires take shape, the public is more concerned than ever about surveillance, commercialism, privacy, and offensive speech. Will government agencies misuse the abundance of confidential data? Will nonprofit uses and information services be central or marginalized? How can users protect themselves from the intrusion of unnecessary and unwarranted messages? Will hate speech and violence have free reign in cyberspace?[22]

Although these problems are important, the overriding issue is distribution. Will the participation of citizens be more inclusive than before? Can we ensure that the institutional need to survive financially will not limit accessibility? This challenge from the media's technological transformation needs to be understood in both legal and ethical terms.

The U.S. Federal Communications Commission (FCC) has developed the National Broadband Plan designed to keep the right to the internet open to everyone, including those in rural areas. The plan makes clear that only an accessible and secure internet serving communities without exception can sustain a vibrant democracy. The key idea is *net neutrality* in which all internet content is to be treated equally by network providers. One of the legal struggles has revolved around Comcast's prerogatives online; the latest decision of a Federal Appeals Court has ruled in Comcast's favor. The ruling allows internet service companies to "block specific sites, charge video sites like YouTube to deliver their content faster to users, and slow its cable customers' access to a file-sharing service called BitTorrent."[23] Along with Comcast, broadband providers such as AT&T and Verizon argue that after spending billions of dollars they should be able to manage their systems to prevent some services from hogging internet capacity. The Free Press organization has been coordinating the protests here, fearing that the Federal Appeals Court ruling effectively places the internet in the hands of big phone and cable companies (www.freepress.net).

You hear the rallying cry from the Save the Internet Coalition: "It's our Internet, not theirs. Let's take it back."[24] In addition to promoting FCC regulations to protect equal access for all consumers, another argument for regulation stresses innovation and investment in technology: "You can't have innovation if all the big companies get the fast lane," said Gigi B. Sohn, president of Public Knowledge, which advocates for consumer rights on digital issues. "Look at Google, eBay, Yahoo—none of those companies would have survived if 15 years ago we had a fast lane and a slow lane on the Internet."[25]

While the legal struggle over online accessibility centers on the FCC's regulatory authority, ethics speaks to the access issue in broader public terms. The question is justice. Will there be universal, affordable access to digital technology? With the global media almost exclusively in the private sector, there is little incentive to include the information-poor. Business firms do not consider themselves charitable organizations. From the perspective of private ownership, we can best admit from the beginning that some people will be left behind. Universal diffusion driven by profits alone is unlikely. The history of the communications media indicates that the media follow existing political and economic patterns; inequalities in society lead to inequalities in technology. Therefore, the important question is whether one can justify allocation of electronic resources to all parties without discrimination. On what basis can one argue that it is morally desirable to ensure comprehensive information for every person regardless of income or geographic location?

The pressures of marketplace economics, to be sure, do not accede to this concern. Private enterprise represents a view of social justice based on merit. There are several variants of this approach, but all of them judge on the basis of conduct or achievement, not solely on the inherent value of human beings. Thus, the argument goes, those who have expended the most energy or taken the greatest risk or suffered the most pain deserve the highest reward. Even though not all differences in people result from varying amounts of their own effort or accomplishment, in this view, ability to pay is considered a reasonable basis for determining who obtains the service. The information structure would be unjust only to the degree that supply and demand or honest dealings are ended.

However, another notion of justice, "to each according to one's essential needs," does validate a concern for universal, affordable access. This concept of justice is rooted in the principle of other-regarding care. The contention here is not that all felt needs or frivolous wants ought to be met, but that basic human requirements must be satisfied equally. The basis for judging is not activity or achievement but being human. Although there is a legitimate argument over which needs qualify, agreement is rather uniform on most fundamental issues such as food, housing, safety, and medical care. People as persons share their generic endowments that define them as human. Thus we are entitled—without regard for individual success—to those things in life that permit our existence to continue in a humane fashion. Whenever a society allocates the necessities of life, the distribution ought to be impartial. Free competition among goods and services has been the historically influential rationale for media practice, but in the case of an all-encompassing national structure performing a vital function, the need-based criterion appears to be the more fitting ethical standard. Meanwhile, the British magazine *Prospect* speaks to the FCC–Comcast dispute. It would take only a small contribution from internet users "to finance the expansion of bandwidth the Web desperately needs,"[26] and a system should be found to implement it.

VIRTUE: Justice

The technology gap between rich and poor nations is growing. The United Nations Development Programme "endorses a tax of one cent on lengthy emails to raise $70 billion a year to connect the world's Internetless."[27] Does justice require us to consider this possibility?

Through the principle of justice we ought to be concerned not just with physical access but also with the deeper divide over social practices. What is most important about internet technology long term is not so much the availability of the computing device or the internet connection, but rather people's ability to make use of the device as a conduit for meaningful social practices. People who cannot read, who have never learned to use a computer, and who do not know the major languages of software and internet content will have difficulty even getting online, much less using the internet productively.[28]

CASE 3. BANKRUPTCY AT THE *PHILADELPHIA INQUIRER*

On February 22, 2009, the parent company of the third oldest newspaper in the United States declared bankruptcy in federal courts, no longer able to service debts of around

$400 million. Philadelphia Media Holdings, a consortium of Philadelphia investors led by publisher Brian Tierney, had purchased the *Philadelphia Inquirer* along with the tabloid *Philadelphia Daily News* and their share website, Philly.com, for more than $500 million only three years before. What happened?

The *Philadelphia Inquirer* has had a long and varied history. Founded in 1829 as the *Pennsylvania Inquirer* and tracing its lineage via mergers all the way back to 1771, the paper grew rapidly during the Civil War due to its strong reputation for accurate reporting.[29] By the end of the nineteenth century, however, the paper waned as competition increased— with more than half a dozen other local newspapers in Philadelphia. Sold to James Elverson in 1889, the paper remained in Elverson family hands until 1930. In 1925, Elverson's son, James, Jr., constructed the paper's eighteen-story building.

Offloaded to Curtis-Martin Newspapers in 1930, the *Inquirer* was again sold six years later to Moses L. Annenberg. A mere two years later, Annenberg had increased daily circulation from 280,000 to 345,000. The new publisher also sought to eliminate explicit political perspective from the paper for the first time.[30] However, in 1939, Annenberg was indicted, pled guilty, and was sent to prison for income tax invasion. Upon his death in 1942, son Walter took over. Though the paper continued to grow, the younger Annenberg's tenure was marked by several significant problems, including a major strike in 1958 and the 1968 conviction of star reporter Harry Karafin for extorting Philadelphia individuals and institutions. Many authors, of the period and later, also noted Walter Annenberg's penchant to blacklist from the paper those he disagreed with.[31]

Annenberg's 1969 sale of the *Inquirer* and *Daily News* (purchased in 1957) to John S. Knight was the precursor to what has subsequently been dubbed the paper's golden age. New executive editor Eugene Roberts, Jr., hired from the *New York Times* in 1972, embarked on a radical transformation from a paper with little to distinguish it to one of the nation's best news outlets. Told by one *Inquirer* editor on the first day that "you're making the dumbest mistake of your life," in the coming years, Roberts nevertheless created a new philosophy at the paper. Michael Shapiro has chronicled the *Inquirer*'s golden age in detail, and writes:

> The men and women who worked for Roberts talk, wistfully, of the possibilities that awaited them each day when they came to work. They were not guided, they say, by a journalistic sense of "should." Their responsibility was not to be comprehensive but to be different, to be bold and, they admit without hesitation, to please the boss.[32]

Injected with dozens of new hires and a pugnacious sense of doing what other papers would not or could not, the *Philadelphia Inquirer* soon gained ground on its competitors. By the end of the 1970s, the *Philadelphia Bulletin*, the city's once dominant paper, was hemorrhaging subscribers and cash. Roberts responded with the Alpha Plan, designed to ensure that the *Inquirer* would become the local paper of record as the *Bulletin* collapsed. It worked. By 1982 the *Bulletin* folded. Roberts boldly hired many of the paper's reporters and doubled the *Inquirer*'s bureaus.

The combination of aggressive investment in reporters and a creative, alternative outlook paid huge dividends. By the mid-1980s, Roberts's *Inquirer* produced annual profits in excess of $100 million. From 1975 to 1990, the *Inquirer*'s staff received no less than seventeen Pulitzer Prizes—matched only by the *New York Times*.[33] *Time* magazine called the *Philadelphia Inquirer* one of the nation's ten best newspapers. Staff turnover was almost nonexistent; reporters and editors wanted to work at the *Inquirer*, and they came to stay.

In 1986, however, Tony Ridder took over as head of newspapers for what had become Knight Ridder in 1974. Whereas John Knight had focused largely on journalism itself, Ridder took a more business-oriented outlook. Roberts, by now a legend in the news world, increasingly clashed with corporate executives over budgets. By 1990, clearly out of favor and tired of struggling, Roberts retired from the *Inquirer*.

Preoccupied with profitability (though in most years the paper maintained annual profits between 10 and 20 percent), the 1990s and early 2000s saw a steady decline in staff and slowly decreasing circulation. By the end of the century, almost all of the senior editors under Roberts had moved on, along with many reporters. Several rounds of cuts left the newsroom significantly smaller. The party seemed to be over.

Yet much of the paper's troubles were caused by very real issues and changes faced by news outlets across the United States. News was always a highly competitive national industry. Philadelphia as a city grew slowly while its surrounding suburbs expanded rapidly. Difficulty covering all of the suburbs adequately meant readership continued to decline. Labor negotiations were difficult for the *Inquirer* and its sister the *Daily News*: contracts had to be negotiated with over a dozen unions making up the paper's employees. Especially with the rise of the internet, ad revenues began to decline sharply. Even though there was plenty of discussion about harnessing the explosion of new information technology to provide novel revenue streams, no one could quite figure out how, exactly, to make it work.[34] In Alicia Shepard's memorable words, the *Philadelphia Inquirer* had hit a midlife crisis.[35]

March 2006 brought a new low; as revenue declined precipitously and costs continued to increase, the rival McClatchy news conglomerate announced it was buying out Knight Ridder. While doing so, McClatchy stated that Knight Ridder's twelve least profitable papers would be put up for sale again, effective immediately. That included the *Inquirer* and the *Daily News*.

In late June of the same year, however, a small hope emerged when it was announced that Philadelphia Media Holdings, a group of area business people led by public relations magnate Brian Tierney, would pay $515 million for the two papers and the Philly.com website. Nevertheless, inevitable steep cuts were made. The new labor contracts cut sick pay, health benefits, the wage structure, and the pension fund. The *Inquirer*'s newsroom, already slashed to 412 staff from its peak of 721 in 1989, lost 71 more people in layoffs at the beginning of 2007.[36] Many criticized Tierney, who had never run a newspaper before. Others considered it positive news that Philadelphia Media Holdings brought in William

Marimow, a Pulitzer-winning former reporter for the *Inquirer* as editor-in-chief.[37] Despite the struggle, Marimow and staff continued to aim for high-quality work wherever possible.

Although the *Philadelphia Inquirer* tried many new revenue models and kept cutting costs, it was unable to replace the revenue lost as advertising continued to crater. After declaring bankruptcy in 2009, Philadelphia Media Holdings entered a long, contentious process of revamping the *Inquirer* and *Daily News* to reenter the marketplace. Much of the investment lost was unsecured, leaving creditors out to dry for hundreds of millions. In 2010 a court ruled that Philadelphia Media Holdings's major creditors could not use the balance owed them in a bid to buy the papers, paving the way for an auction. On April 29, 2010, after an intense twenty-nine hours in the auction room, Brian Tierney and a Keep It Local campaign of Philadelphia businesses narrowly lost buying back the company. The purchaser? A consortium of the newspapers' major lenders led by Angelo, Gordon & Co., a New York-based distressed-assets specialists with stakes in other major, struggling media groups such as the Tribune Company.[38]

Although the $139 million final price was well over the $80 million or so expected before the auction, both the *Inquirer* and *Daily News* faced further cuts, though the investment group has stated it will not close the *Daily News* entirely. At the time of writing, the layoffs continue for both the *Inquirer* and *Daily News*.[39] The *Digital Edition* has helped strengthen the Philadelphia Media Network, and the *Inquirer* has become the first newspaper in the country to create an online fantasy sports betting system that produces income.[40] The story continues, as does the struggle to create a more sustainable news industry in the U.S.

The *Philadelphia Inquirer*'s golden era is one of the legends of journalism history: seventeen Pulitzer Prizes in eighteen years, across an astonishing variety of award categories. The *Inquirer* was a destination for the best reporters and editors in the business. With its ownership changing hands multiple times since its glory days (1972–1990), the same *Inquirer* finally went bankrupt in February 2009, unable to make payments on $400 million in loans. And at its lowest point conceivable, only a whisker short of closing its doors for good, it was put up for public auction in 2010. "Philadelphia news outlets, like those across the country, have been battered by the recession and the historic shift of readers and advertisers to the Internet."[41] Whether the Angelo, Gordon & Co. auction winner of April 29, 2010, is good or bad for the papers remains debatable. At the time of the auction, newspaper analyst John Morton argued: "Their hearts are not in the newspaper business. . . .You'll see a lot of cost-cutting."[42] To date it is still unknown whether award-winning journalism can survive foreclosure.

This fall of a noble institution is only the tip of the iceberg. Bankruptcies are the visible form of turmoil underneath the news industry as a whole. As the history of the *Inquirer* makes clear, the economic, legal, and professional issues are complex, and bankruptcies need to be analyzed from several perspectives to understand them adequately. In the process, media ethics contributes; the relevant ethical principles can prevent decision-makers from being consumed by finances, profit margins, legal contracts, and markets. As we know from ethics scholarship and practice, Aristotle's golden mean is typically the most appropriate principle when the issues are complex and there are obvious conflicts of interest. Applying that principle to the *Inquirer*'s bankruptcy provides an orientation and assessment that is valuable for examining the massive restructuring of the news business currently underway.

Here are some suggestions for putting to work Aristotle's mean: "Moral virtue is a middle state determined by practical wisdom." The middle state can only be known when the extremes are identified. With temperance the capstone virtue, both extremes—of excess and of defect—are unethical. The ownership was frequently the most intemperate. In 1986, when Tony Ridder became head of the newspaper division, the *Inquirer* had just won three Pulitzers. Ridder visited the newsroom and told the editors and managers

> that while he wanted to congratulate them on the prizes, he wanted to speak with them about "something more important." "Next year," he said, "I would like you to win a Pulitzer for cost cutting." He preached this ethic ever since, adhering to a business strategy that focused on the moment. . . . His one solution to all financial difficulties was to cut the payroll.[43]

Also as evidence of the extreme of excess: after the paper became a publicly held corporation, the shareholders demanded relentless cutting across the board, including newsrooms. To stave off a stockholder revolt, management often had to violate their deepest beliefs and act as though "you can cut your way to quality."[44]

At the other extreme, of deficit, are those who made little effort to find new ways to do journalism. They refused to innovate or saw no need for changing to new technologies. For the *Philadelphia Bulletin*, the standard market-oriented model was assumed to be sufficient, and by 1982, it disappeared.

The middle state between these two extremes makes public affairs reporting nonnegotiable. The amount and quality of public affairs reporting must be adequate for holding public officials and government institutions accountable. When lost readership and decline in advertising revenue no longer made robust reporting of public affairs possible, some editors and dedicated reporters still found a way to produce high-quality work. During the *Inquirer*'s darkest days, editorial-page editor, Chris Satullo, acted on Aristotle's mean. He built his downsizing and reordering around the paper's core values: investigative reporting, setting the region's agenda, accuracy, fairness, and ethics.[45] On occasion, extra measures were taken so the cost-cutting and restructuring were handled fairly and with transparency.

While these and other approximations of Aristotle are glimmers of hope, the golden mean requires bolder thinking and action. In its ideal form, the middle state balances profit with public purpose. The Hutchins Commission already in 1947, in its report "A Free and Responsible Press," insisted on the media's duty to serve society even as a business. C. P. Scott of the *Manchester Guardian* put Aristotle's golden mean in classic terms:

"A newspaper has a moral as well as a material existence, and its character and influence are in the main determined by the balance of these forces."[46] The principle of stewardship summarizes the middle state also: being entrusted with the management of estates or affairs not one's own. A mind for sustainability helps define stewardship, too, in the literature on corporate responsibility. "Economic development that meets the needs of the present generation without compromising the ability of future generations to meet their own needs."[47]

To accomplish the middle state in its fullest sense, Robert McChesney and John Nichols propose government subsidies in their book, *The Death and Life of American Journalism.*[48] They conclude that because the commercial model is unable to meet the challenges of the technological revolution, news journalism cannot survive without some kind of government support. Despite resistance to government aid from the media in the United States, consider these facts: the United States had postal subsidies in the 1700s, and the U.S. government supports public broadcasting now. The BBC in Britain, CBC in Canada, and many Scandinavian media are examples of government support without censorship. Philanthropy for nonprofit news organizations, and worker and community cooperative ownership on the local level, are solutions worth considering too, consistent with the practical wisdom by which the middle state is determined.

CASE 4. PAID JOURNALISM WORLDWIDE

"Paid news" is a common term for the practice of bribing journalists for favorable media coverage. Sometimes called red- or brown-envelope journalism, it refers to the envelopes for cash bribes given in secret or at public news conferences for news stories that the donor appreciates. China prefers "red envelope" terminology for its reference to their tradition of gift-giving. Nigeria uses "brown envelope" journalism for what is understood in that country as corruption.[49] "Payola" is typical in the United States, a term for the radio industry scandal of the 1950s when money from record companies guaranteed that their music would be played by disc jockeys. Ethicists in the Philippines usually refer to the straightforward terms "payments" and "gifts," which are prohibited in the code of ethics for Filipino journalists. While accepting money and gifts is an ethical issue for journalism worldwide, South Africa, China, and the United States are among the nations and regions giving it special attention at present.

Paid journalism drew national attention in South Africa with the scandal at the *Cape Argus* newspaper. Two of its journalists were accused of being paid for writing stories favorable to then Western Cape Premier Ebrahim Rasool and opposing his political opponent Mcebisi Skwatsha.[50] Not long afterward, a journalist was accused of accepting 100,000 rand for a positive story on a police officer suspected of murder, and 50,000 rand for not publishing a story on a senior police officer. Also *Mpumalanga News* admitted to accepting "beer, a promised municipal job and a BMW" for writing negative stories about a political challenger to Premier David Mabuza.[51]

There is no scientific evidence for widespread abuse of this type in South Africa. Witnesses are reluctant to come forward and surveys are inconclusive. Oryx Media, the company that first reported the *Cape Argus* scandal, maintains that brown-envelope journalism is a normal feature of the news in South Africa. Most newspaper editors believe that "such instances of outright bribery are too few to constitute a crisis and are promptly nipped in the bud whenever they are proven."[52] Michael Coetzee, news editor of *The Citizen* argues that payola cannot be widespread; whenever it is, the press's credibility plummets. But there is no such crisis in South Africa: "South Africans trust the media more than any other democratic institution in the country, including Parliament and the police."[53]

Though there are different assessments of the seriousness of the problem, both academics and professionals in South Africa concur on the credibility issue. They agree that there is a serious negative impact, whether the corruption of paid journalism is large or small. "South Africa is in an interesting but dangerous phase of development," says Moegsien Williams of Independent Newspapers. In his view, corruption in politics and business are a detriment to the country's moving forward, and so is any and all corruption in the news media. "We as editors need to set an example. Under no circumstances do I take freebies."[54] Tim DuPlessis, editor-in-chief of Media24 also believes South Africa cannot blur the line between acceptance and rejection. The public trust depends on the press's integrity in all phases of the reporting process.

In China, gift-giving is a custom. Gifts of appreciation and as awards are commonplace, including money-gifts.[55] But in a business networking context, the line between gift-giving and bribery is not always clear. According to the *Global Times*, government departments, public relations companies, and business owners "all routinely hand out *hong bao* (red envelopes) to journalists seeking favors. So-called 'transport fees' can range from a 50-yuan note for a local newspaper reporter to thousands of yuan for a top TV reporter."[56] The system is reciprocal: "Government officials give out red envelopes for media coverage to their advantage and journalists take cash to boost their income."[57]

China has stringent regulations against bribery. The "Professional Ethical Principles for Chinese Journalists" prohibits all forms of paid news, including hush money to kill or ignore important stories. "Unrighteous profits at the convenience of the profession" is the terminology of the Chinese Journalists Association. And there are legal regulations prohibiting red envelopes. Government officials have been imprisoned for paying money to silence media coverage. But the regulations within journalism are not enforceable and, according to critics, the red envelopes are too vast to be policed effectively. However, Weizhi Yin in her research on red envelopes, concludes that media organizations can play an important role in controlling this phenomenon.[58]

In the 1990s, as economic reforms expanded, government financial support was withdrawn from smaller media outlets and concentrated on the Xinhua News Agency, China Central Television, and the *People's Daily*. "Most newspapers in China are now struggling," says Professor Zhan Jiang, "and to cut costs and maximize profits, intentionally offer reporters extremely low salaries. This pushes journalists to take red envelopes."[59] For many in the profession, the issue is social not ethical. Red envelopes, in this view, are not corruption, but necessary working conditions. Many journalists have a precarious livelihood and payola is essential for survival. Agnés Gaudu of the *Courier International* puts it this way: "China's journalists do not have independent working conditions; they are paid to represent either state or business interests. This is the reason there is no respect for the ethics of journalism."[60]

Whether they see red envelopes as ethical or as social, professionals are united in making hush money a separate category. Hush money typically involves 10,000 yuan or more, and is considered bribery. Reporters who are willing to accept a red envelope for "soft news," themselves reject "hush fees" as ethically and legally wrong. The former may be excused for journalists who depend on them for their primary income source. The latter is considered a violation of journalistic integrity. However, while acknowledging the importance of this distinction, ethicists such as Zhan Jiang judge that taking either kind of red envelopes is unacceptable. He argues that red envelopes are understood by the public as corruption and thus they damage society's support for journalism. Accusations against one individual or media company hurt the profession as a whole.[61]

The issue of paid news not only revolves around individuals in China. Companies are often able to buy from media outlets the coverage they want. According to David Barboza of the *New York Times*, for a chief executive to appear in the Chinese version of *Esquire*, it costs $20,000 per page. For the head of a company that has a new product, to appear on a news program of China Central Television costs about $4000 per minute. A five-page feature about a European audio company costs $50,000, with no indication that it was actually a paid advertisement. "Though Chinese laws and regulations ban paid promotional material that is not labeled as such, the practice is so widespread that many publications and broadcasters even have rate cards listing news-for-sale prices."[62] So much "money is sloshing around, analysts say, that enforcement is rare. Instead the government issues general warnings which go widely ignored."[63]

Paid journalism or "pay-to-play" is on the agenda in the United States because of blogging and upheavals in the news business. "Marketers have rushed to build relationships with bloggers, many of whom have developed a substantial following. And in building these relationships, the bloggers sometimes get—or demand—free products and even cash payments."[64] Clothing companies hold "blogger previews" for its fall collections or new designs, offering gift cards to bloggers who write about their products. Construction companies solicit interest from bloggers who specialize in home construction. Some bloggers, to attract attention to their site, give prizes that are supplied by companies wanting to promote their products. Bloggers whose purpose is to keep their networks up to date on health and electronics are especially vulnerable. "News releases" prepared by manufacturers that promote their new medication or revolutionary device blur the distinction between journalism and advertising. The prepared content and free samples make endorsements of this kind tempting. The Federal Trade Commission now requires "disclosure by bloggers who receive money or freebies in return for reviewing or endorsing products."[65] But many bloggers retort that they have built their own audience and why shouldn't they make a profit from it?

Ethicist Edward Wasserman focuses on the dramatic changes in the news business. Traditional full-time employment is becoming increasingly rare. He quotes Doug Bandow writing in the *Los Angeles Times*, whose career became a patchwork of jobs: "I ghostwrote op-ed articles, drafted political speeches, prepared internal corporate briefings and strategized business media campaigns. All the while, I also wrote commentary and opinion pieces. Virtually everyone I worked with or wrote for had an ax to grind."[66] While ethics codes can forbid full-time employees from accepting outside money, "it is no longer feasible to apply such a prohibition universally to the journalism profession, which for many practitioners is morphing into one long series of moonlightings."[67] Wasserman worries about payola becoming uncontrollable "if mainstream journalism and commentary become the work of professional wordsmiths who are perpetually on the hustle."[68]

While the problem of paid journalism online dominates the agenda in the U.S., many critics insist on a broader agenda. Travel and tourism journalists routinely accept in-kind support—travel, lodging, food, weekend getaways, exclusive clubs, free passes, memorabilia. "Glossy, high-end magazines catering to fashion and entertainment" traditionally have looser restrictions on freebies.[69] Embedded reporting as in the U.S. invasion of Iraq is criticized by many as paid news. With automation dominating radio, safeguards against company-generated material are nearly impossible to engineer and monitor. "About.com," in its list of media ethics for today's media professionals, recognizes the severity of the payola issue. Its first guideline is this: "Avoid Accepting Payola."[70]

Wherever paid journalism is seen as a social issue, the answer is often said to be socioeconomic, that is, pay journalists well. For journalists to be truthful at all costs, their salaries should be competitive. Journalists who have good salaries won't solicit gratuities. When journalism is poorly remunerated, insisting on purity is only moralism from an upper class.

You Think?

"Pay journalists well and hidden payments will disappear." Agree or disagree? Is the solution to payola economic or moral?

Within the journalism profession, accepting rewards under the table is understood as a conflict of interest. Franz Kruger summarizes the standard view: "Journalists need to avoid not just actual conflicts of interest, but also perception of such conflicts."[71] Those who understand the profession of journalism and its significance in society recognize that it depends for its very existence on the public trust. Bribery is everything journalism is not.

In the Potter Box, conflict of interest is called "conflicting loyalties." Quadrant 4 requires our being completely transparent about our loyalties, and when they conflict, a choice must be made consistent with the ethical principle of quadrant 3. Pretending to be loyal to readers, for example, when journalists in fact are loyal to a paying source, prevents us from reaching a justified conclusion. When the public doubts the authenticity of a story before believing it, journalism is no longer viable.

For the Potter Box step 3, two principles are directly applicable. In utilitarian ethics, decisions are justified if they benefit the largest number and do minimal harm. Whether bloggers receive sample gifts can be seen as minimal harm. In some areas of journalism, support from manufacturers is essential for providing up-to-date information to readers and audiences. In certain countries of the world, without payola, journalism could not even exist except through big and profitable organizations. Society would be ill-served in those regions. Utilitarian ethics, however, may not always be helpful. "Minimal harm" and "serving the majority" are subject to debate and open to different interpretations. Often in deciding what is "minimal harm," reporters may be thinking only of themselves and not hearing the voice of the public.

Whereas utilitarian ethics is helpful but not decisive, the duty ethics of Kant is explicit. Payola is deception. The categorical imperative is stated in both positive and negative terms: "Tell the truth" and "do not deceive." In Kant there is a short list of moral laws that ought not to be violated. Telling the truth is one of those, along with such commands as "don't kill," "keep your promises," and "don't steal." We have a duty to obey these imperatives, regardless of our moods or rationalizations. To deceive is wrong and therefore the deception of paid news is unethical. Independent bloggers and online journalists who deceive by presenting company-written material as though it is news are wrong. The source of the news story must be clear for the truth of the event to be known. To tell an audience that something is information when it is actually advertising is deception. Kant does not allow us to call payola "perks of the job." The categorical imperative rejects the language of innocence: "just a little appreciation," "a token for your transport [fuel]," or "they aren't asking for anything." Kant's idea of truthtelling includes both commission and omission; that is, to deceive deliberately is wrong, and to omit important facts is wrong. For Kant, the audience, readers, network users are rational beings and they need full information to exercise their reason correctly.

NOTES

All website addresses throughout this book were accessed in April 2016.

1. Fred S. Siebert, Theodore Peterson, and Wilbur Schramm, *Four Theories of the Press* (Urbana: University of Illinois Press, 1956), 72.
2. The question is whether one's dual obligation in this instance prevents the fulfilling of both contracts. See Joseph Margolis, "Conflict of Interest and Conflicting Interests," in Tom L. Beauchamp and Norman E. Bowie, eds., *Ethical Theory and Business* (Upper Saddle River, NJ: Prentice Hall, 1979), 361–372.
3. Upton Sinclair, *The Brass Check: A Study of American Journalism* (Pasadena, CA: Published by author, 1920), 436. New edition with introduction (9–33) by Robert McChesney and Ben Scott (Urbana: University of Illinois Press, 2003).

4. For a comprehensive account of concentration in various media, see Robert McChesney, *Rich Media, Poor Democracy: Communication Politics in Dubious Times* (New York: New Press, 2000); cf. also Robert McChesney, *The Problem of the Media: U.S. Communication Politics in the 21ˢᵗ Century* (New York: Monthly Review Press, 2004).

5. For the details of how Murdoch built his media empire, News Corporation, see Michael Wolff, *The Man Who Owns the News: Inside the Secret World of Rupert Murdoch* (Louisville, KY: Broadway Press, 2010).

6. http://pewresearch.org/pubs/1341; www.people-press.org/2009/10/29/Fox-news-viewed-as-most-ideological-network/; "News Corp Denies Fox News Bias," Australian Associated Press, October 24, 2004.

7. Alexandra Petri, "Mike Huckabee and Women's Uncontrolled Libido, or, Uncle Sugar," *The Washington Post*, January 23, 2014, www.washingtonpost.com/blogs/compost/wp/2014/01/12/23/mike-huckabee.

8. "Fox's Volley with Obama Intensifying," *New York Times*, October 12, 2099, www.nytimes.com/2009/10/12/business/media/12fox.html; "The Fox News War: What's the Upside for Obama?" *Christian Science Monitor*, October 23, 2009, www.csmonitor.com/USA/Politics/2009/1023/the-fox-news-war-whats-the-upside-for-obama.

9. Shanto Iyengar and Kyu S. Hahn, "Red Media, Blue Media: Evidence of Ideological Selectivity in Media Use," *Journal of Communication* 59 (2009): 19–39.

10. Terry McDermott, "Dumb Like a Fox," *Columbia Journalism Review* (March/April 2010): 26.

11. Ibid., 32.

12. "CNBC in Fourth Year of Profit Growth," *The Hollywood Reporter*, December 9, 2009, www.hollywoodreporter.com/news/cnbc-fourth-year-profit-growth-92178.

13. Rafael Guerro, "Kaplan Speaks on Fracture, Future," *Daily Illini*, April 20, 2010, 1A, 3A.

14. Cass R. Sunstein, *Republic.com 2.0* (Princeton, NJ: Princeton University Press, 2012).

15. Jürgen Habermas, "Does Democracy Enjoy an Epistemic Dimension?" *Communication Theory* 16 (2009): 423.

16. S. Coleman and Jay G. Blumer, *The Media and Democratic Censorship: Theory, Practice and Policy* (Cambridge, UK: Cambridge University Press, 2009), 197.

17. Matthew Gentzkow and Jesse M. Shapiro, "Ideological Segregation Online and Offline," Online Appendix, University of Chicago, April 12, 2010, www.nber.org/papers/w15916.

18. David Brooks, "Riders on the Storm," *New York Times*, April 20, 2010, A19.

19. McDermott, "Dumb Like a Fox," 26.

20. Ibid., 30.

21. The authoritative and comprehensive book on convergence and ethics is Michael Bugeja's *Living Ethics: Across Media Platforms* (New York: Oxford University Press, 2007). See also Charles Ess, *Digital Media Ethics*, 2nd ed. (Cambridge, UK: Polity, 2014).

22. For a comprehensive review of the legal and ethical dimensions of these issues internationally, see Raphael Cohen-Almagor, *Confronting the Internet's Dark Side: Moral and Social Responsibility on the Free Highway* (Cambridge, UK: Cambridge University Press, 2015).

23. "U.S. Court Curbs F. C. C. Authority on Web Traffic," *New York Times*, April 7, 2010, 1A.

24. The Save the Internet Coalition (www.savetheinternet.com) includes hundreds of nonprofit organizations, bloggers, and businesses across the United States (totaling over one million people) concerned about maintaining a free and open internet. The coalition is coordinated by Free Press, a national, nonpartisan organization supporting media freedom, including that of the internet.

25. *New York Times*, April 7, 2010, B7.

26. "The Case for Taxing E-Mail," in *Idea of the Day* (blog), *New York Times*, May 26, 2009, www.ideas.blogs.nytimes.com/2009/05/26/the-case-for-taxing-e-mail/?_r=0.

27. Judith Miller, "Globalization Widens Rich-Poor Gap, U.N. Report Says," *New York Times*, July 13, 1999, A8.

28. Mark Werschaver, "Reconceptualizing the Digital Divide," *First Monday*, July 26, 2002, 1–17.

29. Gerry Wilkinson, "History of the *Philadelphia Inquirer*," The Philadelphia Press Association, April 30, 2010, 1–7, www.phillyppa.com/inquirer.html.

30. Ibid.

31. Michael Sokolove, "What's a Big City without a Newspaper?" *New York Times*, August 9, 2009, www.nytimes.com/2009/08/09/magazine/09Newspaper-t.html?_r=0.

32. Michael Shapiro, "Looking for Light: *The Philadelphia Inquirer* and the Fate of American Newspapers," *Columbia Journalism Review* (March/April 2006): 31.

33. Sokolove, "What's a Big City," 1–13.

34. Shapiro, "Looking for Light," 26.

35. Alicia C. Shepard," The *Inquirer*'s Midlife Crisis," *American Journalism Review* (April 29, 2010): 1–11, www.ajrarchive.org/article.asp?id=1600.

36. Julia M. Klein, "Dark Days: Labor Loses More Ground in the Newsroom," *Columbia Journalism Review* (March/April 2007): 16–17.

37. Devin Leonard, "A PR Magnate Struggles to Revive a Newspaper," CNNMoney.com, November 13, 2006, 1–3, http://archive.fortune.com/magazines/fortune/fortune_archive/2006/11/27/8394325/index.htm.

38. Christopher K. Hepp and Harold Brubaker, "Creditors Buy Paper at Auction," Philly.com, April 29, 2010, 2–4, http://articles.philly.com/2010-04-29/news/25213075_1_new-owners-bidding-defeat-ends.

39. "Owner: Over 40 Layoffs at *Philadelphia Inquirer, Daily News*," Associated Press, *The Seattle Times*, November 3, 2015. www.seattletimes.com/business/owner-over-40-layoffs-at-philadelphia-inquirer-daily-news.

40. "*Philadelphia Inquirer* Web Site Launches 'Fantasy' Sports Betting That Pays Real Money," *Editor and Publisher*, April 9, 2010, 1–2, www.editorandpublisher.com/news/philadelphia-inquirer-web-site-launches-fantasy-sports-betting-that-pays-real-money/. Foundation support to fund local journalism projects such as this are also a possible source of revenue; see Abby Brownback, "New News for Philly?" *American Journalism Review* (April 29, 2010): 1, www.ajrarchive.org/article.asp?id=4865.

41. Ibid., 1.

42. Ibid., 2.

43. Shapiro, "Looking for Light," 33.

44. Ibid., 35.

45. Ibid., 30.

46. Quoted in Walter Jaehnig and Uche Onyebadi, "Social Audits as Media Watchdogging," Southern Illinois University, unpublished paper, 2010, p. 3.

47. Quoted in Jaehnig and Onyebadi, p. 6, from Marc J. Epstein, *Making Sustainability Work*, 2008, p. 20.

48. Robert W. McChesney and John Nichols, *The Death and Life of American Journalism: The Media Revolution that Will Begin the World Again* (New York: Nation Books, 2010).

49. Shola Oshunkeye, "Journalism vs. Brown Envelopes," *The Media Project*, August 4, 2011. Vipul Mudgal, "News for Sale: 'Paid News', Media Ethics, and India's Democratic Public Sphere," in Shakuntala Rao and Herman Wasserman, eds., *Media Ethics and Justice in the Age of Globalization* (Basingstoke, UK: Palgrave Macmillan, 2015), 100–120.

50. Thabo Leshilo, "Is South African Journalism Plagued by Payola?" *The Media Online*, June 11, 2012, http://themediaonline.co.za/2012/06/is-south-african-journalism-plagued-by-payola/.

51. Ibid.

52. Ibid.

53. Ibid.

54. Ibid.

55. For a review of red-envelope practices, see Shixin Ivy Zhang, *Impact of Globalization on the Local Press in China: A Case Study of the Beijing Youth Daily* (Lanham, MD: Lexington Press, 2014, ch. 6).

56. Donghuan Xu, "The Rotten Red Envelope," *Global Times* 22:19 (January 5, 2010).

57. Ibid.

58. Weizhi Yin, "Research Report of Journalists Taking 'Traffic Allowance' in Mainland China," Fourth Roundtable, Beijing, April 2014.
59. Xu, "The Rotten Red Envelope."
60. Ibid.
61. Jiang Zhan, "Red Envelope for Journalists and Soft Information in Media," Chapter 3 of his *Journalistic Morals and Ethics: Case-Based Teaching* (Beijing: Communication University of China Press, 2014).
62. David Barboza, "In China Press, Best Coverage Cash Can Buy," *New York Times*, April 3, 2012.
63. Ibid.
64. John Reinan, "Journalism and Marketing Debate: Blogging for Payola," *MinnPost*, March 22, 2010, www.minnpost.com/business/2010/03/journalism-and-marketing-debate-blogging-payola.
65. Ibid.
66. Edward Wasserman, "Payola Journalism: A Breach of Ethics," Philly.com, January 11, 2006, http://articles.philly.com/2006-01-11/news/25410750_1_abramoff-affair-institute-for-policy-innovation-doug-bandow.
67. Ibid.
68. Ibid.
69. Reinan, "Journalism and Marketing Debate."
70. Glenn Halbrooks, "The Dangers of Accepting Payola in Media," *About.com*, Media Newsletter, May 5, 2014, http://media.about.com/od/mediaethics/a/Media-Ethics-For-Todays-Media-Professionals.htm.
71. Franz Kruger, "Seal the Brown Envelope for Good," January 12, 2010, www.mg.co.za/article/2010-01-11-seal-the-brown-envelope-for-good.

2

TRUTHTELLING

The press's obligation to print the truth is a standard part of its rhetoric. Virtually every code of ethics begins with the newsperson's duty to tell the truth under all conditions. High-minded editors typically etch the word on cornerstones and on their tombstones. Credible language is pivotal to the communication enterprise.

When Pontius Pilate asked, "What is truth?" he posed the question people of every kind have struggled to answer. And as ideas and worldviews shift, so does the definition of truthfulness. Newspeople must live within the larger ambiguities about truth in Western and Eastern scholarship and culture today. Their situation is further complicated by budget constraints, deadlines, reader expectations, editorial conventions, and self-serving sources. Journalism is often referred to as "history in a hurry"; providing a precise, representative account can rarely occur under such conditions. At the same time, sophisticated technology generates unceasing news copy so that the journalistic gatekeeper must choose from a mountain of options, often without the time to sift through the moral intricacies.

The cases that follow introduce several dimensions of the truthtelling issue. Although not every conceivable aspect is offered, truth is enlarged beyond a simple facts-only definition.[1] One way to broaden our scope, for example, is to consider the antonym of truthfulness and to account for newsgathering as well as newswriting. The opposite of truthtelling is deception, that is, a deliberate intention to mislead. Outright deceit occurs infrequently in the newswriting phase; only rarely, if ever, does a reporter or editor specifically and consciously give the wrong story. But deception in newsgathering is a persistent temptation because it often facilitates the process of securing information.

The first case in this chapter, on the obesity epidemic in the United States and elsewhere, centers on the Institute of Medicine's report of 2004 authorized by the U.S. Congress. The issue is the press's ability to communicate scientific findings to the many parties involved.

The second case introduces Al Jazeera, the independent news organization based in Qatar, which is in a region where state-owned media dominate the airwaves. As an Arab news network, it reflects Arab culture. Is Al Jazeera a truthful news source, or does it slant its broadcasts against the West?

The third case, "The Unabomber's Manifesto," struggles with the ethical issues of violence and technology. Does someone advocating and engaged in violent attacks against an evil technological order deserve a hearing?

The fourth case introduces the worldwide controversy over the publication of the Muhammad cartoons, a complicated story involving religion, politics, and press freedom. The challenge for the news media is to present a truthful account of highly emotional issues in a multicultural context.

CASE 5. OBESITY EPIDEMIC

Over the past two decades, the diet and health of millions of people across the world have changed. For most developing nations, obesity has become a more serious health threat than hunger. In Mexico, Egypt, and South Africa, more than half the adults are either over-weight or obese. In virtually all of Latin America and much of the Middle East and North Africa, one of four adults is overweight. Malnutrition and hunger are significant problems in sub-Saharan Africa and South Asia, but even poor countries such as Nigeria and Uganda face the dilemma of obesity.

You Think?

Worldwide, more than 1.3 billion people, are overweight; about 800 million are underweight. This difference continues to grow.[2] How are these statistics relevant, if at all, to the issue of obesity?

The problem of obesity is especially acute in the larger cities, where the population has a more sedentary lifestyle and greater access to soft drinks, caloric sweeteners, vegetable oils, and animal foods.[3] In Mexico, in 1989 fewer than 10 percent were overweight. In 2013, seven out of ten Mexicans were overweight, with one-third clinically obese. Mexico is now ranked as the most obese country in the world.[4]

Over the past several decades, the number of overweight Americans has grown dra-matically. In 1996, the National Center for Health Statistics reported that obese or overweight people outnumbered other Americans for the first time. In 2014, about 66 percent of adults over the age of twenty were overweight, and the rates of obesity (body mass index of 30 or higher) have doubled from 15 percent in 1980 to over 30 percent today. The prevalence of type 2 diabetes among children and youth (adult-onset diabetes) has more than doubled in the past decade. Diets that are high in calories and saturated fats and low in certain nutrients are putting American children and youth at risk later in life for heart disease, stroke, circulatory problems, diabetes, some cancers, and osteoporosis. The surgeon general now reports that obesity will overtake cigarette smoking as the leading cause of preventable death.

In 2004, Congress through its Health, Labor, and Education Committee directed the Centers for Disease Control and Prevention (CDC) to undertake a study of the role that the marketing of food and beverages may play in determining the nutritional status of children and youth and what marketing approaches might be used as a remedy. The CDC turned to the Institute of Medicine (IOM) of the National Academies to conduct this study, and its report is the most comprehensive review to date of the scientific studies available.[5] Among IOM'S findings are these:

- The preponderance of television food and beverage advertising promotes high-calorie and low-nutrient products and influences children and youth to prefer and request high-calorie and low-nutrient foods and beverages.
- Exposure to television advertising is associated with adiposity (body fatness) in children two to eleven years of age and teens twelve to eighteen years of age.
- Food and beverage companies, restaurants, and marketers have underutilized resources for supporting healthy diets for children and youth.
- Achieving healthy diets for children and youth will require sustained and integrated efforts across society, including industry leadership.

The IOM's ten recommendations for dealing with obesity in America cover a broad spectrum of society—education, homes, government, industry, and the media. These are illustrative of the ways obesity can become a public health priority of the highest order. Six of these are listed below:

Recommendation 1: Food and beverage companies should use their creativity, resources, and full range of marketing practices to promote and support healthful diets for children and youth.

Recommendation 3: Food, beverage, restaurant, retail, and marketing industry trade associations should assume transforming leadership roles in harnessing industry creativity, resources, and marketing on behalf of healthful diets for children and youth.

Recommendation 6: Government, in partnership with the private sector, should create a long-term, multifaceted, and financially sustained social-marketing program supporting parents, caregivers, and families in promoting healthful diets for children and youth.

Recommendation 7: State and local educational authorities, with support from parents, health authorities, and other stakeholders, should educate about and promote healthful diets for children and youth in all aspects of the school environment (e.g., commercial sponsorships, meals and snacks, curriculum).

Recommendation 8: Government at all levels should marshal the full range of public policy levers to foster the development and promotion of healthful diets for children and youth.

Recommendation 10: The secretary of the U.S. Department of Health and Human Services should designate a responsible agency, with adequate and appropriate resources, to formally monitor and report regularly on the progress of the various entities and activities related to the recommendations included in this report.

When the source of news is a scientific report on a complicated social issue, how should the press handle it? What is necessary to tell the truth? On a basic level, statistical data will be presented accurately and in readable fashion. But describing the problem and the conclusions involves interpretation. Winners and losers are identified. The importance of the issue itself and whether it can be solved at all are central to reporting this kind of material, and the choices made influence the quality of the public discussion about it. And is the tone correct, that is, no more pessimistic or optimistic than the report itself? The report genre is inherently boring, bringing the tendency to sensationalize the content or even initiate a moral panic when reporting on it as news. One study of news coverage of obesity concluded that "journalists tended to exaggerate the risks of obesity by reporting disproportionately on the most alarmist scientific studies."[6]

A ten-year study of newspaper articles and television news centered on the question of news framing—who is considered responsible for causing the obesity problem and who must fix it. The research presumed that the media tell the audience which crises to think about and also how to think about them. Therefore, the way responsibility is framed is an important moral issue in news.

A content analysis showed these results: an *unhealthy diet* is cited most often as the cause of obesity (23 percent of the news stories). Following next was a *sedentary lifestyle*, principally a lack of exercise (18.2 percent). *Food industry practices*, including heavy advertising of its junk food products, was the chief institutional cause, mentioned 12.4 percent of the time. *Genetic conditions* and body chemistry appeared less often (11.8 percent); reports did include medical research identifying genes that contribute to obesity. *Schools* (i.e., unhealthy cafeteria food and lack of physical education) only appeared in 4.2 percent of the news as a major cause. And *socioeconomic factors* (i.e., eating patterns and education among low-income families) was cited least at 3.4 percent of the time.[7]

Consistent with the same results, personal-level solutions were mentioned most often: healthy diet, physical activity, and medical treatment (i.e., surgeries and weight-loss medications). Together, personal solutions were included as the best alternative in 90 percent of the news stories. Regulation of the food industry and changes in schools and education together accounted for 18.2 percent of the articles and transcripts. Socioeconomic changes were mentioned in only three newspaper articles as an important solution and never appeared in television news.[8] None advocated drastic societal solutions, such as regulation of the food industry and its aggressive marketing. On the policy level, taxing junk food or sugar-rich drinks (the so-called Twinkie tax) was noted but not seriously developed. Lawsuits filed against fast-food restaurants appeared intermittently, but without the presumption that fast-food restaurants are responsible for making Americans obese and sick.[9]

Meanwhile, the sobering fact is that despite surging news coverage over the past decade, large-scale changes in the public's eating habits, and growth in exercise gym membership and diet programs, obesity continues to increase at a faster rate than before.[10]

An ethics of other-regarding care is sympathetic in its outlook. News that follows this principle does not condemn unfairly. It is cautious about generalizations, recognizing that medical conditions explain obesity for some. However, it is also important to report the truth that people are accountable for their decisions, although how to do so without being judgmental and alienating is difficult. Truthtelling in the context of other-regarding care is one of the greatest challenges an ethical journalist can face.

CASE 6. AL JAZEERA

Mention Al Jazeera to the average American, and the response is likely to be less than positive. Al Jazeera is the Qatar-based Arab network that has become a household name in the United States primarily because it chose to air audio and videotapes received from the elusive Osama bin Laden, as it did from Saddam Hussein when he was in power. Due to what he considered this unseemly connection, then Vice President Dick Cheney accused Al Jazeera of providing "a platform for terrorists." But what North Americans may find interesting is that Al Jazeera isn't uniformly embraced by Arab leaders either.

After he seized ruling power from his father, Sheikh Hamad bin Khalifa Al Thani of Qatar established Al Jazeera (which means "The Peninsula") to promote modernization and democracy. Al Thani set aside $137 million for Al Jazeera, hoping that it would be self-sustaining within five years of its November 1, 1996 debut.

Before Al Jazeera went on the air, state-owned media dominated the airways in most Arab countries, and government leaders were accustomed to controlling the message. Citizens of Arab countries expected the media to serve as a voice for the government.

The creation of Al Jazeera changed that. Suddenly there was an Arabic news channel unconcerned with the promotion of any government's agenda. Al Jazeera sought to present the news in an unbiased and objective way, which often meant unflattering portrayals of existing Arab leaders.

Because of Al Jazeera's insistence on independent reporting, the agency has been the recipient of various punishments doled out by Arab leaders. The government in Algiers once cut its signal. Egypt's state media ran a campaign against Al Jazeera, stating that they aired a "sinister salad of sex, religion, and politics" topped with "sensationalist seasoning."[11] The station's repeated interviews of Hamas's spiritual leader Sheikh Ahmed Yassin angered Yasir Arafat. The religiously conservative government of Saudi Arabia bars Al Jazeera from its territory. And on it goes.

If it were not for the events of September 11, 2001 and the conflicts that followed in Afghanistan and Iraq, Al Jazeera would have remained a Middle Eastern station known primarily to Arabs. Its focus would have remained on the leadership of the Arab states and on the ongoing conflict between Israel and Palestine, and Al Jazeera would be relatively unknown and uncontroversial to citizens of the West. However, as the world's attention turned to Afghanistan, and then to Iraq, the world's journalists had to rely on this relatively small media outlet based in Qatar.[12]

Following September 11, the Taliban evicted Western journalists from Kabul. Al Jazeera, which had a history of covering Afghanistan, was allowed to stay. When the air strikes against Iraq began on October 7, Al Jazeera had exclusive access to the sights and sounds of the bombing campaign. It then sold the images to the other news agencies. It became the hit station of the war. Al Jazeera was transformed in the way that CNN was by the Gulf War a decade earlier.

This access has been financially profitable for Al Jazeera. Exclusive footage from places no one else can get to but that everyone wants to see has allowed it to rise in international prominence as a news leader. While Western journalists struggle to understand the language and culture of the Middle East, Al Jazeera's reporters are on the ground and among the people, speaking the language and knowing the customs.

In 2003, Imad Musa, a news producer at the Washington bureau of Al Jazeera, wondered how "this tiny station"—with a worldwide staff of fewer than 650 and short lifespan of seven years—has become a household name in the United States, where many people cannot name any media outlet in France, Germany, Mexico, or even Canada. The news outlet has continually expanded its reach, launching an English-language website in 2003 and an English-language satellite channel in 2006. Al Jazeera English has its headquarters in Doha, with studios in Kuala Lumpur, London, and Washington, D.C. It reaches some 80 million households worldwide[13] and it recently has begun to offer segments of its broadcast on YouTube in order to overcome its limited availability in the United States.[14] However, nineteen years after its founding by a country that is a U.S. ally, Al Jazeera is still commonly called "the terrorist network."

Many Western governments remain unconvinced of Al Jazeera's neutrality. Its special status in Afghanistan made it suspect to the forces trying to root out the Taliban. Because of Al Jazeera's airing of his tapes, its link to Osama bin Laden was questioned. Two months after 9/11 and six weeks after Colin Powell expressed his concerns about Al Jazeera to the Qatari emir, its agency in Kabul was bombed.

American officials claim it was accidental. But Al Jazeera's leadership knows that the location of its building was common knowledge among other news agencies and among the military forces invading Afghanistan. When asked about the loss, Al Jazeera's Managing Director Mohamed Jasem al Ali said, "Whether it was targeted or not, I can't answer. But I can say for 100 percent that the United States knew about the office. Everyone knew we had an office in Kabul. It was very easy to find."[15] The site in Kabul was not the only one hit. Al Jazeera's Iraq station also was leveled in the bombing run that hit Baghdad on April 8, 2003, and speculation about the intentional nature of the bombings was further fueled when the *Daily Mirror* obtained a leaked memo from a 2004 meeting between then Prime Minister Tony Blair and President Bush in which the U.S. president allegedly revealed a plan to bomb the Qatar headquarters of Al Jazeera.[16] Two British government employees were jailed in 2006 for leaking the memo, but Al Jazeera's efforts to obtain its contents did not yield any results.[17]

Some wonder if the hits were intended to send a message to Al Jazeera to cease airing the tapes of bin Laden and Hussein. Some said that when Al Jazeera aired such speeches in their entirety, it was serving as a mouthpiece for terrorists. The leaders of Al Jazeera object. They point out that they air the complete speeches of all world leaders, lest the station be accused of editing out words they didn't think people should hear. "Are we a mouthpiece for bin Laden?" asks Dana Suyyagh, an Al Jazeera news producer who was educated in Canada. "Maybe, but that would make us Bush's mouthpiece as well. He gets more airtime, actually."[18]

While talking heads make up a significant part of their coverage, what really sets Al Jazeera apart from other media outlets is its use of images. Unlike agencies that seek moderation in the airing of objectionable scenes, Al Jazeera is unapologetic in showing images that disturb.

The images that Al Jazeera beamed from inside Iraq displayed the horrors of war. Unlike on CNN, no anchor prepares viewers for what is to come. Without warning, gory images of dead bodies or wounded children fill the screen. On Al Jazeera, the blood is part of the story:

> It's pretty hard to adequately describe the level of bloodiness during an average Al Jazeera newscast. It's mesmerizing bloodiness. It's not just red but gooey. There's no cutaway. They hold the shot for the full vicious effect. It's vastly grislier than anything that's ever been shown on television before. It's snuff-film caliber.[19]

While Western journalists may focus on the humanitarian aid extended to the citizens of Afghanistan or Iraq, Al Jazeera's inside look at bombed-out houses and wounded people communicates a different message to the world. As Samir Kahder, a senior producer, says: "We don't show the faces of the dead. We don't show the faces of the wounded, especially in this time of satellite television. We don't want to be in a position where we on television are notifying the next of kin."[20]

The message Al Jazeera communicated in airing pictures of American and British war dead and POWs was not warmly welcomed. Then U.S. Secretary of Defense Donald Rumsfeld claimed that the footage was a violation of the Geneva Convention rulings on the rights of prisoners of war. Following this, Al Jazeera economic correspondents on Wall Street, Ramsey Shibar and Ammar al Sankari, had their press credentials revoked by the

New York Stock Exchange—the first time NYSE had ever withdrawn them. The next day, Nasdaq followed suit. "[T]he corpses, the sea of blood, the POWs' faces . . . 'Since when is a television network governed by the Geneva Conventions?' [The Al Jazeera staff] were confidently turning the free-press argument on the free press itself."[21]

The turmoil reveals the crux of the issue: is Al Jazeera a neutral news source, or does it slant its broadcasts against the West and for the Arab world? In November of 2001, the *New York Times Magazine* ran a cover story by Fouad Ajami, a professor of Middle East studies at Johns Hopkins, who accused Al Jazeera of exactly that:

> One clip juxtaposes a scowling George Bush with a poised, almost dreamy bin Laden. Between them is an image of the World Trade Center engulfed in flames. . . . [I]n its rough outlines, the message of Al Jazeera is similar to that of the Taliban: there is a huge technological imbalance between the antagonists, but the foreign power will nonetheless come to grief.[22]

Ajami went on to accuse the station of "mimicking Western norms of journalistic fairness while pandering to pan-Arabic sentiments." The Canadian Jewish Congress and B'nai Brith Canada have labeled Al Jazeera "virulently anti-Semitic." The Canadian Arab Federation counters with the assertion that "the views of the people who make the news should not be confused as the views of the station that airs it."[23]

Imad Musa points out that Al Jazeera is an Arab news medium and therefore reflects Arab culture. In referring to their choice to air images of POWs, Musa states:

> To Al Jazeera, war is ugly, and these were the images of war. . . . [W]e realize that the right time to air bad news will never come, so it is preferable not to play politics with the news and air whatever is timely, relevant, accurate, and of interest to our viewers. . . . Al Jazeera's preference is to give its viewers unfiltered information as soon as possible before political pressures begin to flood in from all over the globe and despite accusations of hurting morale.[24]

Josh Rushing was a U.S. Marines information officer during the Iraq invasion. Based at the U.S. media center in Doha, Qatar, he spoke for the military at Central Command. Becoming an inadvertent star in the documentary *Mission Control*, he was ordered not to comment on the film or U.S. engagement in Iraq. Josh Rushing resigned from the Marines after sixteen years of duty and signed on as a reporter for Al Jazeera English. Believing that the public knows the truth after hearing the various sides of a story, Rushing opposes the U.S. government's policy of refusing to cooperate with Al Jazeera Arabic and Al Jazeera English:

> The U.S. government would be wise to recognize the value of Al Jazeera's reach in the Middle East, as its viewers regard the network as "the most trusted name in news." If

the United States would accept using the network as an emissary, their messages to the Arab world would be tempered with a much greater credibility than could be gained through domestic networks. . . . Engaging all sides needs to be standard operating procedure for our government on this new media battleground, otherwise they are simply ceding the turf to the other side. Even if the Arab audience might not like what the U.S. government has to say, it should see the benefit of arguing its case intelligently, thus possibly deflating some of America's demonization that otherwise might go unchecked.[25]

In Rushing's view, the Iraqi government banishing Al Jazeera in 2004 and the United States establishing its own Arabic language satellite network, Al Hurra (The Free One), are counterproductive. For the latter,

Viewers stayed away, and small wonder. People in the Arab world are all too familiar with state-controlled media, press organs that run only good news about the king or government, and bad news about any dissidents or insurgents. . . . Propaganda machines are prone to breaking down, no matter how pure the intentions.[26]

CASE 7. THE UNABOMBER'S MANIFESTO

On September 19, 1995, the *Washington Post* and the *New York Times* jointly published a 35,000-word manifesto from an unknown person identified as the Unabomber.[27] The Justice Department had been trailing him for more than seventeen years, during which time he mailed bombs that injured twenty-three people and killed three. In late June, the document arrived with a cover letter that gave the newspapers three months to publish it, upon which time he promised to "desist from terrorism." He warned that if they refused, he would "start building [his] next bomb" when the deadline expired on September 29. The Unabomber also demanded that he be allowed to publish 3000-word rebuttals for the next three years directed to any critics who attacked his manifesto.

New York Times publisher Arthur O. Sulzberger, Jr., and *Washington Post* publisher Donald E. Graham issued this joint statement:

For three months the *Washington Post* and the *New York Times* have jointly faced the demand of a person known as the Unabomber that we publish a manuscript of about 35,000 words. If we failed to do so, the author of this document threatened to send a bomb to an unspecified destination "with intent to kill."

From the beginning, the two newspapers have consulted closely on the issue of whether to publish under the threat of violence. We have also consulted law enforcement officials. Both the Attorney General and the director of the Federal Bureau of

Investigation have now recommended that we print this document for public safety reasons, and we have agreed to do so.

In a statement to his staff, Sulzberger insisted that the case was unique and not likely to become a journalistic precedent. "Newsrooms regularly receive messages from people threatening dire action unless their demands are met. Our traditional response will continue to serve us well—we notify law enforcement officials, when appropriate, and print nothing." Sulzberger explained: "You print and he doesn't kill anybody else, that's a pretty good deal. You print it and he continues to kill people, what have you lost? The cost of newsprint?"

The Unabomber's central point in the manifesto is that the industrial-technological system in which we live is a disaster for the human race. Therefore, he seeks to "propagate anti-industrial ideas" and to encourage "those who hate the industrial system." The task of those who oppose the industrial system is to advance its breakdown by promoting "social stress and instability," which presumably includes bombing. For lasting change, "reform is insufficient" and "revolution is necessary." Revolution, in the Unabomber's terms, involves destroying and wrecking "the system" and seeing "its remnants . . . smashed beyond repair."[28]

When he saw the text, the Unabomber's brother informed the Federal Bureau of Investigation (FBI) that his sibling was the likely author of the manifesto. On April 1, FBI agents surrounded the cabin of Theodore Kaczynski in the mountains of Montana and arrested him. In June, Kaczynski was indicted in Sacramento, California, on federal charges that he mailed two fatal bombs from that city, as well as two other bombs that injured their targets. On October 1, 1996, a federal grand jury in Newark, New Jersey, indicted him on charges that one of his mail bomb attacks killed a North Caldwell, New Jersey, advertising executive, Thomas J. Mosser. The Newark indictment charged Kaczynski with mailing a bomb that arrived at Mosser's home on December 9, 1994. Mosser was killed when he opened the package the next day.

In a letter published in the *New York Times* in April 1995, the Unabomber said that Mosser had been killed because his company, Burson-Marsteller, had "helped Exxon clean up its public image after the *Exxon Valdez* incident" in Alaska in 1989. Burson-Marsteller has denied working with Exxon in connection with the oil spill.

The Justice Department ruled that Theodore Kaczynski would be tried first in California. A prison psychiatrist, Sally Johnson, declared him competent to stand trial, and after often dramatic proceedings, Kaczynski was sentenced to four consecutive life terms in return for a guilty plea. He is now detained in solitary confinement in a federal prison in Colorado.

In October 1993, federal authorities had announced a $1 million award for helping them find the elusive terrorist. On August 21, 1998, the government paid the award to David Kaczynski. Some of the money has been used to pay off the family's legal bills. For months prior to Theodore Kaczynski's guilty plea, the family had lobbied the government not to seek the death penalty. The rest of the award is set up in a trust fund for the victims' families.[29] In February 1999, Theodore Kaczynski signed a book deal to tell his story, with the proceeds also designated for the victims' families.[30]

For two reasons, several journalists objected strongly to the *Times* and *Post's* decision to publish the manifesto. First, that "these two champions of a free press" would publish on "recommendation of federal law enforcement authorities" was reprehensible to Jane Kirtley of the Reporters Committee for Freedom of the Press: "It signaled a dangerous erosion of the line between the media and government, a line that should be fixed and immutable."[31] Second, objections also centered on conceding to the demands of an anonymous terrorist. As Rem Rieder, editor of the *American Journalism Review*, put it:

> Ours is a society filled with rage: against women, against minorities, against government. And many of those angry people possess the anger of righteousness. Their cause is so right, their opponents so wickedly misguided, that violence to advance the former and hurt the latter is justified in their minds.
>
> Publishing the Unabomber's manifesto says to the true believer: Do enough damage, wreak enough havoc, take enough innocent lives, injure enough people, and the printing press is yours.[32]

Paul McMasters, First Amendment ombudsman of the Freedom Forum in Arlington, Virginia, wondered whether publication in the name of public safety would expose "other newspapers and television and radio stations to a higher risk of being hijacked for similar purposes."[33]

Thus the issues can be understood in terms of quadrant 2 of the Potter Box. Important professional values are at stake here—the independence of newspapers from government and their independence from hostile groups who make threats. From this perspective, the *Times* and *Post* violated two basic journalistic values that will hurt the press's integrity and effectiveness over the long term.

However, there are ambiguities in quadrant 2. Richard Harwood of the *Post* called the criticism a "species of poppycock" saying: "The government had no . . . power to dictate the papers' decision. . . . Newspapers on many occasions have consulted with government officials on matters of national security that might put lives at risk."[34] And appearing to cave into the Unabomber's remarks is at least understandable if the decision to publish could save lives and help generate leads to the Unabomber's identity.

Regarding the debate over professional values, the issue of newsworthiness is also involved. Sulzberger and Graham did not use newsworthiness as a rationale for publication. However, they could have justified publishing the manuscript by using the public interest argument: journalists don't withhold important information from their readers and viewers. Different aspects of the Unabomber story had been developing for months, the newspapers had published excerpts already, and executives from the papers had met with public officials. Some of the Unabomber's concerns about technology were relevant. Defending publication as a journalistic decision connected to an ongoing story is at least plausible and keeps editors and reporters in control rather than following the dictates of outside interests.

An analysis of professional values in quadrant 2 leaves ambiguity over appropriate action. What about quadrant 3? Are ethical theories helpful? Aristotle's mean is not applicable because the two parties are not both legitimate. A position of ideal balance is not possible when one party is engaged in criminal activity. *Agape* specializes in justice and privacy, but not as explicitly regarding sources and truthtelling. Because the Unabomber's response is unpredictable, utilitarianism is unhelpful; refusal to publish may create intolerable risk and harm. The categorical imperative typically is most decisive when a short list of moral questions is at stake—promise keeping, deception, theft, and so forth.

But, clearly, the first principle in Rawls's theory of justice is relevant—the largest amount of political liberty for all. The Unabomber's practice of violence and threat of violence does not pass this first principle. Violence against technological growth is not a credible alternative. It need not demand the journalist's attention. Several broadcasters and newspapers refuse to publish or air blatantly racist material. Similarly, terrorist propaganda advocating violence ought not be published either. According to Rawls's first principle, actions or messages that deprive equal liberty for everyone are immoral.

CASE 8. MUHAMMAD CARTOON CONTROVERSY

On September 30, 2005, the *Jyllands-Posten*, Denmark's largest newspaper, published a series of twelve cartoons depicting the Prophet Muhammad. Flemming Rose, *Jyllands-Posten*'s culture editor, commissioned the cartoons in response to the incidents of self-censorship and intimidation within Islam that he observed in Denmark and across Europe. He wanted moderate Muslims to speak out in favor of healthy criticism. He insisted that the paper had a tradition of satire with the royal family and public figures and that the cartoonists were treating Islam in the same way they treat Christianity, Hinduism, Buddhism, and other religions.

Although there have been irreverent portrayals of the Prophet by Europeans since the Middle Ages, the right-of-center *Jyllands-Posten* was known for its anti-immigrationist stance, and publication of the cartoons appeared to many Muslims as racial hatred toward a besieged community. The act of even creating an image of Muhammad is blasphemous according to a tradition in Islam so, not surprisingly, many Muslims were outraged for that reason alone. To a neutral observer, some of the cartoons were mild and innocuous. A few were aimed at the editor's call for cartoons, not at Muhammad directly. One showed Muhammad as a Bedouin flanked by two women in burqas. But others were more explosive. One depicted Muhammad wielding a cutlass, and another had him saying that paradise was running short of virgins for suicide bombers. In the most offensive cartoon, the Prophet is wearing a bomb-shaped turban, complete with burning fuse—a reference to the Aladdin story where an orange falling into his turban brought him great fortune. Those who took offense at the cartoons viewed their publication as yet another instance of Western religious intolerance and prejudice.[35]

In mid-November 2005, some Danish fundamentalist imams set off on a journey through the Middle East. They took with them the twelve cartoons, ten others from a November publication of the Danish *Weekend Avisen*, and three more of unknown origin (one showing Muhammad with a pig's nose). The violence that occurred in the beginning of 2006 as a result of this dossier of cartoons outweighed the attention the *Jyllands-Posten* set received immediately after their publication. As such, some view the imams's visit and inclusion of additional incendiary cartoons as the major cause of the worldwide turmoil that ensued. A baseless rumor that Danes planned to burn copies of the Qur'an in Copenhagen's City Square fanned the protests even more. In late January, the imam of the Grand Mosque of Mecca issued an ultimatum, "He who vilifies the Prophet should be killed."[36]

On January 30, 2006, gunmen raided the European Union's offices in Gaza, demanding an apology for allowing the paper to publish the cartoons. While the Danish paper apologized, Danish Prime Minister Anders Fogh Rasmussen defended freedom of speech as essential to democracy. In a show of support for freedom of the press, papers in Spain, Germany, Italy, and France reprinted the cartoons the following day.

A battle of wills ensued in a cycle of publication and subsequent protests. On February 4, 2006, Syrians retaliated by attacking the Norwegian and Danish embassies in Damascus. Protesters also stormed Danish embassies in Beirut and Tehran. Protests in Afghanistan and Somalia turned deadly, and in Libya, ten people were killed in riots. Pakistan's Jamaat-e-Islamic party placed a bounty of 50,000 Danish kroner on the cartoonists.[37] Editors in Jordan who dared to reprint the cartoons were arrested. The prime minister of Malaysia called for calm but described the cartoons as an act of provocation, and editors in Malaysia considering publication were threatened with injunctions.[38] The newspaper *France Soir* published the cartoons, along with Buddhist, Jewish, and Christian caricatures, and declared defiantly: "No religious dogma can impose its view on a democratic and secular society. We have a right to caricature God." Its managing editor was sacked.[39] Several days later, the French magazine *Charlie Hebdo* also published the cartoons. Muslim groups filed charges of racism against Philippe Val, the magazine's editor, but lost their case in 2007.

Western newspapers continued to champion freedom of the press by printing the cartoons, whereas many Muslims likewise have defended their freedom of religion by protesting the publications. Some have referred to this situation as the most contentious one since the events surrounding the 1988 publication of the novel *The Satanic Verses*, when Iran's then leader, Ayatollah Ruhollah Khomeini, declared a *fatwa* death sentence on the book's author, Salman Rushdie:

> The broader issues raised by the furor are certain to persist. To some, the dispute over the cartoons is a bellweather of a deepening divide between Western societies and Islam, a civilizational clash on issues as basic as the role of religion in society, and the limits of liberty.[40]

Publication of the twelve cartoons brought to the surface a number of competing values. The debate and actions around the world were driven by contending political, religious, and social values. These deeply rooted beliefs produced both moderate and extreme reactions, depending typically on the group's leadership.[41]

Those who valued free expression in democratic societies wanted the cartoons published. For many in Europe, defending the cartoons was a defense of the superior core values of Western democracy. One dimension of this social value is the public's right to know, prompting several papers to publish in order to inform their constituencies of the source of the furor. The Danish prime minister refused to meet with ambassadors of eleven Muslim countries on the grounds that governments in democracies do not control the press, although it appeared to be inflexibility and political ineptitude.

For Muslims, an assault on the Prophet cuts across all political issues and unites Muslims everywhere. In fact, all religions in various ways respect their leaders and forbid blasphemy of the sacred. Religion is the core of Islamic identity and needs to be taken seriously, beyond a right to worship freely. Given the religious values, as might be expected, at a meeting in the Muslim Holy City of Mecca in early 2006, leaders of the world's fifty-seven Islamic countries issued a joint statement that condemned "the desecration of the image of Muhammad."

Economic values surfaced also. Some newspapers declined publication out of fear of the consequences. They decided not to risk offending their readership on this issue. The *Daily Illini* at the University of Illinois was the only student newspaper to publish all twelve cartoons (on February 9, 2006). As the editor saw it:

> All across this nation, editors are gripped in fear of printing. As a journalist, this flies in the face of everything I hold dear. If anything, journalists all over this country should be letting the public decide for themselves what to think of these cartoons.[42]

In addition, aesthetic values complicated the debates. Cartoons are an important genre in newspaper publishing. By character, they are provocative and often unflattering, but not necessarily inspired by hatred. Their purpose is to stimulate further reading and thinking, not preclude them. For a large segment of Islam, with any drawings of the Prophet forbidden, this genre cannot be appreciated on its own terms. Satirical depictions of leadership figures are taken for granted in Western democratic nations, but in this instance these assumptions clash with those who regard the sanctity of a religious icon to be untouchable.

Following the Potter Box strategy, quadrant 3 is crucial after the values are clarified in quadrant 2. When values conflict, as they often do, an ethical principle is needed to move forward toward resolution. If action is taken already after step 2 based on one's values, those actions typically lead to inadequate decisions and continuing disputes. While the two major values in this case are social—freedom of the press and freedom of religion—economic and aesthetic values complicate mutual understanding and motivations. Step 3 is necessary for justified conclusions and unified action.

When cultures clash and religious beliefs are in dispute, the ethics of other-regarding care is ordinarily the strongest ethical principle for quadrant 3. The imperative to love our neighbors as ourselves means that we begin with the other. The other's needs, desires, and aspirations establish our attitudes and actions. Others are treated with dignity and respect because they are human beings, regardless of their status or achievements. Granting others their right to the freedom of religion also means religious toleration.

Editors and publishers following the ethical principle of other-regarding care would decline publication. The democratic political value of free expression is suspended in this case by editors who want to act ethically, believing that in the long run ethics produces the best journalism. The right to take action does not mandate the action.

For Muslims adhering to Islamic ethics, the Qur'an's principle of human dignity leads to the same conclusion against publication. It also supports the moderates in Islam who reject violence to others based on the same principle. Muslims honoring human dignity is typical and extremists the exception.

VIRTUE: Fairness

Of the more than 1.6 billion Muslims in the world, fewer than 0.001 percent were involved in protests or violence over the cartoons.[43] Shouldn't reporters use statistics like these, instead of photographs and news clips of embassies being burned?

The Qur'an's principle of human dignity agrees with other-regarding care that condemnation of entire groups (Danes, Muslims, Europeans, Western democracies) is unacceptable rhetoric.[44]

NOTES

1. For a classic statement of truthfulness in context, see Dietrich Bonhoeffer, *Ethics* (New York: Macmillan, 1955), 363–372.
2. On worldwide poverty, see Per Pinstrup-Anderson and Cheng Fuzhi, "Still Hungry," *Scientific American*, September 2007, 88–95.
3. Much of the data in this paragraph are from Barry M. Popkin, *The World is Fat: The Fads, Trends, Policies and Products that Are Fattening the Human Race* (New York: Avery Books, 2008).
4. For world statistics on obesity, see Harvard School of Public Health, www.hsph.harvard.edu/obesity-program.
5. *Food Marketing to Children and Youth: Threat or Opportunity?* (Washington, D.C.: National Academics Press, 2006).
6. T. Boyce, "The Media and Obesity," *Obesity Reviews* 8:suppl. 1 (November 2006): 201–205. For an overview, see "*Supersize Me* and Marketing Fat," in Clifford Christians, Mark Fackler, and John Ferré, *Ethics for Public Communication* (New York: Oxford University Press, 2012), 95–112.
7. Sei-Hill Kim and L. Anne Willis, "Talking About Obesity: News Framing of Who Is Responsible for Causing and Fixing the Problem," *Journal of Health Communication* 12:4 (June 2007): 359–376.

8. Ibid., 367.

9. Ibid., 374.

10. Ibid., 374.

11. Quoted in Rick Zednik, "Inside Al Jazeera," *Columbia Journalism Review* (March/April 2002): 47.

12. Imad Musa, "Al Jazeera TV: When the Medium Becomes the Story," *IPI Global Journalist*, second quarter 2003, p. 20. For more details on the history and sociology of Al Jazeera, see Mohammed el-Nawawy and Adel Iskandar, *Al Jazeera: The Story of the Network that Is Rattling Governments and Redefining Modern Journalism* (Cambridge, MA: Westview Books, 2003).

13. Jonathon Curiel, "Al-Jazeera Speaks English," *The San Francisco Chronicle*, November 16, 2006. For an overview of Al Jazeera English, see *Ethics for Public Communication*, ch. 2.

14. Sara Ivry, "Now on YouTube: The Latest News from Al Jazeera in English," *New York Times*, April 16, 2007.

15. Neil Hickey, "Perspectives on War: Different Cultures, Different Coverage," *Columbia Journalism Review* (March/April 2002): 45.

16. Kevin Maguire and Andy Lines, "Bush Plan to Bomb His Arab Ally," *Daily Mirror*, November 22, 2005.

17. "Al Jazeera Pursues Bush Bomb Claim as Civil Servant Jailed," *Brand Republic News*, May 11, 2007, www.brandrepublic.com/News/656892.

18. Rick Zednik, "Inside Al Jazeera," April 16, 2013, www.masspersuasion.blogspot.com/2013/04/inside-al-jazeera.html.

19. "Al Jazeera's Edge," August 21, 2003, http://nymag.com/nymetro/news/media/columns/medialife/n_8648/.

20. Ted Koppel, "Deciding What Images to Show," *Nieman Reports*, Summer 2003, 95.

21. "Al Jazeera's Edge."

22. Fouad Ajami, "What the Muslim World Is Watching," *New York Times Magazine*, November 18, 2001, 48.

23. Norman Spector, *Globe and Mail*, August 21, 2003. File copy, Institute of Communications Research, University of Illinois, cchrstns@illinois.edu.

24. Musa, "Al-Jazeera TV," 21.

25. Josh Rushing, *Mission Al Jazeera* (New York: Palgrave Macmillan, 2007), 156, 160. Mohammed el-Nawaw and Shawn Powers put these issues into a global perspective, *Mediating Conflict: Al-Jazeera English and the Possibility of a Conciliatory Media* (Los Angeles: Figueron Press, 2008).

26. Rushing, *Mission Al Jazeera*, 178. For more details, see Philip Seib, *The Al Jazeera Effect: How the New Global Media Are Shaping World Politics* (Dulles, VA: Potomac Books, 2008).

27. For elaboration of this case and four responses from journalists, see Louis Hodges, "Cases and Commentaries," *Journal of Mass Media Ethics* 10:4 (1995): 248–256. For a book-length treatment, see Alston Chase, *Harvard and the Unabomber: The Education of an American Terrorist* (New York: Norton, 2003).

28. Cf. Kirkpatrick Sale, "Unabomber's Secret Treatise: Is There Method in His Madness?" *The Nation*, September 25, 1995, 305–311.

29. Karen Brandon, "$1 Million Paid to Unabomber Kin," *Chicago Tribune*, August 26, 1998, sec. 1, p. 3.

30. "Unabomber Gets Book Deal to Tell His Story," *Los Angeles Times*, February 12, 1999, A 1; Theodore J. Kaczynski and David Skrbnia, *Technological Slavery: The Collected Writings of Theodore J. Kaczynski, a.k.a. The Unabomber* (Port Townsend, WA: Feral House, 2010).

31. Hodges, "Cases and Commentaries," 249.

32. Ibid., 253. A *Presstime* online survey on September 21 showed ninety-nine answering "yes" and ninety-six checking "no" to the question whether these editors would have published or not.

33. Hodges, "Cases and Commentaries," 256.

34. Richard Harwood, *Washington Post*, September 23, 1995.

35. The culture editor, Flemming Rose, objects to this interpretation. "When I commissioned the cartoons, it was not 'Draw cartoons making fun of the prophet,' but 'Draw Mohammad as you see him,' which is very neutral. . . . I just don't accept the point that the cartoons are demonizing or stereotyping or racist.

Many people said, 'When you printed this one [bomb in the turban], you're saying that every Muslim is a terrorist.' That's a kind of illiteracy to see the cartoon that way. It makes the point that some people in the name of the Prophet are committing terrorist acts and that is a fact of life." Ali Malek, "Beyond the Cartoon Controversy," *Columbia Journalism Review* (March/April 2007): 19.

36. Romesh Ratnesar, "Fanning the Flames," *Time*, vol. 167, February 20, 2006.

37. Paul Marshall, "The Mohammed Cartoons," *The Weekly Standard*, February 13, 2006, 14–15.

38. For these and other details on reactions around the world, see Maha Azzam, "Cartoons, Confrontation and a Cry for Respect," *The World Today* 62:4 (April 2006): 7–8.

39. Marshall, "The Mohammed Cartoons," 14.

40. Ratnesar, "Fanning the Flames."

41. For a different perspective centered on competing ideologies, see Risto Kunelis, "Lessons of Being Drawn In: Global Free Speech, Communication Theory and the Mohammed Cartoons," in A. Kierule and H. Rønning, eds., *Freedom of Speech Abridged? Cultural, Legal and Philosophical Challenges* (Gøteborg, Sweden: University of Gothenburg Nordicom, 2009), 139–151.

42. Acton H. Gordon, "Editor's Note," *The Daily Illini*, February 9, 2006, 5a.

43. Before the international story broke, but when it was big in Denmark, the *Jyllands-Posten* ran "three full pages with short interviews with forty-seven Muslims in Denmark with photos, and the headline was: 'We say no to the imams'" (Malek, "Beyond the Cartoon Controversy," 18).

44. Clifford Christians, "The Ethics of Human Dignity in a Multicultural World," in Bo Shan and Clifford Christians, eds., *The Ethics of Intercultural Communication* (New York: Peter Lang, 2015), 337–356. For a thoughtful application of Islamic ethics to this controversy, see Ali Mohamed, "Journalistic Ethics and Responsibility in Relation to Freedom of Expression: an Islamic Perspective," in S. J. A. Ward and H. Wasserman, eds., *Media Ethics Beyond Borders: A Global Perspective* (New York: Routledge, 2010), 142–156.

3

REPORTERS AND SOURCES

Well-informed sources are a reporter's bread and butter, and dependence on them creates some genuine complexities. A news medium's pledge to divulge its sources of information is welcomed by the public; however, publishing names usually results in the sources thereafter speaking guardedly or even drying up. Several tactics are used in confronting this dilemma so that audiences are served and sources remain content. As Hugh Culbertson wrote: "The unnamed news source has been called a safety valve for democracy and a refuge for conscience, but also a crutch for lazy, careless reporters."[1] A classic *Washington Post* editorial captured some of the struggle in its description of "Source's" family tree:

> Walter and Ann Source (nee Rumor) had four daughters (Highly Placed, Authoritative, Unimpeachable, and Well-Informed). The first married a diplomat named Reliable Informant. (The Informant brothers are widely known and quoted here; among the best known are White House, State Department, and Congressional.) Walter Speculation's brother-in-law, Ian Rumor, married Alexandre Conjecture, from which there were two sons, It Was Understood and It Was Learned. It Was Learned just went to work in the Justice Department, where he will be gainfully employed for four long years.[2]

The complications here are not easily resolved. Walter Lippmann noted this journalistic bind nearly a century ago in *Public Opinion*, where he distinguished news from truth. News he saw as fragments of information that come to a reporter's attention; the pursuit of truth, according to him, followed explicit and established standards.[3] In this sense, the judicial process, for example, adheres to rigorous procedures for gathering evidence. Academics footnote and attribute sources so that knowledgeable people can verify or dispute the conclusions. Medical doctors rely on technical precision and expertise. Reporters, however, cannot compete with these other professions. They have found no authoritative way of examining, testing, and evaluating their information, at least not in a public arena and not under risky, often hostile conditions. The abundance of data available now with the new digital technologies has complicated journalism's task even more.

The difficulties result primarily from the multitude of practical considerations that need to be jockeyed under deadline pressures. On occasion, reporters must be adversarial, at least skeptical; at other times, friendliness and cooperation work better. If newspeople become too intimate with important men and women, they lose their professional distance or develop unhealthy biases protecting them. However, to the degree that powerful sources are not cultivated and reporters establish no personal connections, the inside nuance and perspective may be lost. At times, written documents supplemented by public briefings are superior to information painfully dug out by a conscientious reporter. On most other occasions, the official source is blinded by self-interest. But who can predict? Regarding sources, the American Society of Newspaper Editors' Statement of Principles correctly warns: "Journalists must be vigilant against all who would exploit the press for selfish purposes."[4] Little wonder that as information came to light about the burglary of the headquarters of the Democratic National Committee at the Watergate hotel, several "scoops" proved to be stories leaked originally by Mr. Nixon's staff.

Most news operations have developed specific procedures to help prevent chaos and abuse. Certain conventions also hold together journalistic practice. It is typically assumed that all information must be verified by two or three sources before it can be printed. Most codes of ethics and company policies insist on attribution and specific identification whenever possible. A few news operations allow reporters to keep sources totally secret, but a majority of them openly involve editors as judges of the data's validity. The rules also require accurate quotation marks, correction of errors, and an account of the context. However, even with these safeguards, a responsible press must continually agonize over its treatment of sources in order to prevent lapses.

This chapter chooses five entangled aspects of the reporter–source relationship, all of them actual occurrences of some notoriety. The first case, on the WikiLeaks website, illustrates the enormous difficulties in getting reliable information from the emerging technologies. In the second case, the debate revolves around the use of stolen materials. The *Cincinnati Enquirer's* investigation of Chiquita Brands provides an opportunity to examine Kant's restrictions against theft and lying. The third case, on the Israeli–Palestinian conflict, concerns the question of reliable and balanced sources amid ongoing conflict. The fourth case involves the increasingly complex issue of knowledgeable sources when covering social protests. The fifth case is the classic Watergate scandal, which continues to instruct reporters and sources and ethics. Cheap answers are not forthcoming, but at every point the ethical issues ought to form a prominent part of the resolution.

CASE 9. THE WIKILEAKS WEBSITE

On April 3, 2010, two previously unreleased videos, titled "Collateral Murder," surfaced online at websites WikiLeaks[5] and YouTube.[6] The videos, one full-length at thirty-eight minutes, the other an edited version at seventeen minutes, claimed to show the actual deaths of two reporters for Reuters news network, along with ten other Iraqis, by gunfire from a U.S. Army Apache helicopter on July 12, 2007. The footage contained an onboard gun-sight view of the events, accompanied by corresponding audio of the radio exchanges between the helicopter's crew, mission control, and on-the-ground soldiers.

In the graphic video, the helicopter crew spots a group of Iraqis walking through New Baghdad, a suburb of Baghdad and, at the time, a center of conflict. Seeing what could be weapons—but in reality were most likely the reporter's camera equipment—the crew asks for and receives permission to engage. Rounds of cannon fire from the Apache leave the air grey with dust, and the street below littered with bodies. A dry chuckle comes over the radio:

"All right, I hit 'em."
"Oh, yeah, look at those dead bastards," a crew member states.
"Nice . . . good shootin'," comes the reply.
"Thanks."

As the air clears the helicopter sight zooms in on one person wounded but still alive. As the individual crawls out of the street (in fact one of the Reuters employees), the helicopter's gunner responds with "Come on buddy—all you gotta do is just pick up a weapon," presumably so that he can engage the target again.

A few minutes later, an unmarked van pulls up; two unarmed men jump out and run to the aid of the wounded. The crew notes this event, and asks ground command for new permission to engage. Receiving the go-ahead, a second round of fire pours into the van and the men, killing all three. The Apache crew then radios navigation instructions to ground forces, for follow up. Upon learning from the foot soldiers that two small children were in the van, one of the crew comments: "Well, it's their fault for bringing kids into a battle." The other responds: "That's right." Ground soldiers rush the wounded kids to a local hospital.

Was it just another day at war? Murder? Reuters had tried for three years to obtain the video, through the Freedom of Information Act. Less than a month after its leak, the shorter video had been viewed over 6.5 million times on YouTube alone, in addition to being posted on WikiLeaks itself and linked to many other websites. Searches of Google Insights, the company's analytical tool, reveal that on April 5, "wikileaks" was the engine's number one search term. In the aftermath, Julian Assange, a founder and spokesperson for WikiLeaks, was interviewed by a number of media outlets. The U.S. military's Central Command (CENTCOM), meanwhile, told the Associated Press that it was unable to locate its original copy of the footage.[7]

Launched in 2007, WikiLeaks.org is an online clearinghouse that uses wiki collaborative software to publish the submissions of anonymous whistleblowers from around the world. In its own words, WikiLeaks aims to be "the first intelligence agency of the people."[8] Anyone can upload documents or other materials via a secure connection, which are then reviewed by a staff panel and made available on the site; the policy is to leak everything of significance. WikiLeaks has now gathered over three million leaked items on every topic imaginable—from classified American government documents to political membership lists and financial records. Assange states that WikiLeaks has survived over 100 legal challenges from governments and private entities, and has yet to give up a single source. In 2008 the website was briefly shut down, by American court order, after being sued by the Swiss bank, Julius Baer Holding. It had published confidential records from the bank that detailed more than 1,600 accounts located in the Cayman Islands, often used by investors as a tax shelter. However, a mere two weeks later WikiLeaks was up and running again: after hearing arguments from more than ten organizations on WikiLeaks's behalf, the case judge reversed his original ruling on grounds it might violate free speech and the First Amendment.[9]

The site reports that it uses military-grade encryption to protect anonymity. It does not keep logs of its data, which are spread around the world in countries perceived to have strong privacy laws. (In fact, its main services are hosted by the same Swedish internet service provider that provided infamous file-sharing network "The Pirate Bay" with bandwidth.) Its founders consistently maintain that the site does not take money from governments or other institutions, relying on donations for its operations and pro bono legal aid from newspapers, free-speech organizations, media foundations, and so forth. WikiLeaks associates have worked closely with the government of Iceland on the Icelandic Modern Media Initiative, a proposed resolution that aims to radically decrease censorship by providing sweeping changes to strengthen privacy laws and protect whistleblowers.[10]

Organized as a nonprofit with a small core staff and hundreds of volunteers, WikiLeaks aims not only to leverage internet technologies for investigative journalism but also to help whistleblowers advocate against unethical or illegal acts by institutions and governments.[11] In the aftermath of the "Collateral Murder" video's release, Assange commented to the *New York Times* that a main goal is "to get maximum political impact—to do justice to our material."[12] Indeed, it was actually TV satirist and comedian Stephen Colbert who asked Assange, in an interview on *The Colbert Report*, whether titling the video of the killing of the Iraq Reuters journalists "Collateral Murder" meant WikiLeaks had moved from objectivity to "pure editorial."[13]

Responses to WikiLeaks and its founders have varied widely. Perhaps ironically and probably in self-interest, WikiLeaks itself published a Central Intelligence Agency (CIA) report highly critical of the site. Then U.S. Defense Secretary Robert Gates strenuously defended the actions of U.S. troops appearing in the "Collateral Murder" video, arguing that WikiLeaks did not provide the proper context for the events depicted. WikiLeaks disputed Gates's claim about "proper context"; it has contended there was no active firefight between

U.S. forces and those killed. Moreover, Gates argues that WikiLeaks has no legitimacy: "These people can put out anything they want, and they're never held accountable for it."[14] On the other hand, because of the video's release, the Committee for the Protection of Journalists called for the Army to reopen the closed investigation into the Reuters reporters' deaths. The Army had found no wrongdoing among any party and continued to claim that the affair occurred in the course of combat. More broadly, secrecy expert Steven Aftergood of the Federation of American Sciences has questioned whether or not WikiLeaks's undiscriminating editorial policy is in the long-term best interests of all concerned.[15] Yet Kelly McBride, veteran reporter and ethics group leader at the Poynter Institute for Media Studies, also suggested at the time of its launch in 2007 that WikiLeaks could become a highly important tool for journalists to help document their work.[16]

In situations filled with controversy and ambiguity, such as with WikiLeaks, Aristotle's mean is typically the most appropriate theory. This is especially true when two extremes emerge, the one an evil of excess and the other an evil of defect. The response of the extreme of defect is total rejection, a refusal to consider this new technology for any reason or use:

> It [WikiLeaks] is currently banned in China and can only be accessed via proxy names; over the past two years it has been issued with legal challenges by the Scientologists, the Mormons, and several banks; and it is blocked in the offices of the British Ministry of Defense.[17]

And a Pentagon report elaborates: in addition to China as noted, "the governments of Israel, North Korea, Russia, Vietnam and Zimbabwe have all sought to block access to or otherwise impede the operations of WikiLeaks."[18] The extreme of excess is represented by WikiLeaks itself upon its debut, audaciously claiming it will "crack the world open" by becoming a global watchdog more reliable than conventional media.[19] Assange adds: "Of course, there's a personal psychology to it, that I enjoy crushing bastards. I like a good challenge; so do a lot of the other people involved in WikiLeaks."[20]

In order to find Aristotle's middle state between the extremes, WikiLeaks's role in journalism needs examination:

> The international scope of WikiLeaks (documents relevant to over 100 countries are already included on the site) allows for the circulation of politically sensitive material from countries without a free media, and also provides a central repository for documents of international interest to compensate for the lack of on-the-ground reporters overseas.[21]

Three different kinds of relationships between investigative reporters and this huge resource have become evident.

For many journalists, WikiLeaks is a jumping-off tool, an occasional source for fresh leads in old stories and for new possibilities also. In one study of the relationship of journalists and this website, a first core group of reporters from the mainstream media was identified who found the information in WikiLeaks newsworthy on occasion. "For these reporters, WikiLeaks was not something that changed their methods, but rather a source that was useful," more by happenstance and periodic checking than from systematic pursuit.[22]

A second group of reporters knows WikiLeaks and recognizes its potential value but is ambivalent about it. Though WikiLeaks is an outlet for political information that might otherwise remain secret, these journalists criticize the ethics of its very structure and policies. As one reporter puts it: "Society does set limits on information disclosure in many ways; even in the journalism community there are rules. WikiLeaks is radical in that it recognizes very few such rules." Though this journalist uses WikiLeaks, it raises serious questions for him about "the ethics of quoting anonymous people you can't meet or verify."[23]

While these two responses to WikiLeaks avoid the two extremes and are therefore in the middle state, Aristotle's practical wisdom searches for the maximum alternative. A third option is closer to what is sometimes called the golden mean: journalists trained in the best practices of investigative reporting use WikiLeaks in that context and not in isolation. Advocates of this position describe the site "as important a journalistic tool as the U.S. Freedom of Information Act."[24] As with the *New York Times* story described here, WikiLeaks has proved to be invaluable in the investigation of high-profile stories. The earliest example is from 2005, when the *New York Times* and Reuters used the *Standard Operating Manual for Guantanamo* in their investigation of prisoner abuse at that location. Since that time, several important investigations have been done by major newspapers that included WikiLeaks documents in establishing the overall picture:

> A U.S. Army Intel brief on Afghani insurgent groups; the membership list of the British National Party; over 6000 US Congressional Research Service reports; briefs on UN activity around the world; and leaks suggesting improprieties at banks including Northern Rock, Barclays, Julius Baer, and Iceland's Kaupthing.[25]

Professor Lisa Lynch of Concordia University considers the site "one of the best existing examples of a phenomenon described by Yochai Benkler in *The Wealth of Networks*–the emergence of a critical information media that is indebted neither to states nor markets."[26]

WikiLeaks poses a major challenge to traditional investigative journalism.[27] Its rigorous anonymity provides a new way of dealing with sources. It forces journalists to examine the press's long-accepted role as the arbiters of fact:

> WikiLeaks has emerged as something of a strange bedfellow to a beleaguered industry, one that holds itself up as a champion of principles many journalists hold dear–freedom of information and the sanctity of the source–yet embeds these principles in a

framework of cyberlibertarianism that is frequently at odds with the institutional ethics of journalists and editors.[28]

Several other online entities have been created recently to aid reporting, investigative journalism in particular, such as

> the *Huffington Post Investigative Fund*, *Propublica*, *Spot.us*, and a Knight-funded multimedia project at the Center for Investigative Reporting. . . . How WikiLeaks fits in along this spectrum of new online ventures—and whether investigative journalism and the industry as a whole will be reshaped or revolutionized in the process—is yet to be determined.[29]

CASE 10. STOLEN VOICE MAIL

On May 3,1998, the *Cincinnati Enquirer* published an eighteen-page special section of ten stories on Chiquita Brands International, Inc. The *Enquirer* had spent hundreds of thousands of dollars investigating one of Cincinnati's most prominent businesses, controlled since the 1970s by the city's most powerful corporate executive, Carl Lindner. "Chiquita Secrets Revealed: Power, Money and Control" charged the company with environmental recklessness, bribery, and constructing secret trusts to evade land and labor regulations. *Enquirer* reporters had been working on the story since May 1997 and had traveled from the Caribbean, Honduras, and Panama to Brussels and Antwerp in Belgium, plus Vancouver, New York, and Washington.

Mike Gallagher, a decorated and highly respected reporter, led the investigation, and the editor, Lawrence Beaupre, praised its "thorough reporting." Beaupre had upgraded the *Enquirer* substantially since becoming editor in 1995, with the Gannett Company honoring him as one of its top ten editors in 1996. The *Enquirer* expected the Chiquita stories "to complete the paper's metamorphosis from middling corporate protector to purveyor of a journalism worthy of the ultimate accolade, the Pulitzer Prize."[30]

Less than two months later, on June 28, the *Enquirer* withdrew its story, with "An Apology to Chiquita" spread across the entire front page. The apology was reprinted on two later occasions, admitting that the report created "a false and misleading impression of Chiquita's business practices." While the May 3 story had promoted some 3000 internal Chiquita voice mail messages as documentation, apparently the paper now believed Gallagher had illegally taped some of them. As the apology stated: "Despite [Gallagher's] assurances to his editors prior to publication that he had obtained his information in an ethical and lawful manner, we can no longer trust his word." The apology was part of a $10 million settlement from Gannett in which Chiquita removed the threat of litigation against the paper and its corporate sponsor. Instead of repudiating Gallagher's conduct but defending the contents of the report, the *Enquirer* guaranteed that the allegations would be lost to history.

Mike Gallagher was fired, and on July 2, Chiquita filed suit against him in federal district court for "defamation, trespass, conversion, violations of state and federal wiretapping
laws and other intentional misconduct." Editor Lawrence Beaupre was removed and given
a responsibility in Gannett's corporate headquarters for conducting ethics seminars.
Gallagher's assistant in the investigation, Cameron McWhirter, was reassigned to the
Detroit News. In September, Michael Gallagher pleaded guilty to two felony counts. But he
likely kept himself from jail by signing a cooperation agreement with law authorities to provide "a full, truthful and complete disclosure as to all sources and their activities." Former
Chiquita lawyer George Ventura was indicted—after Gallagher turned over to authorities
"his notes, thirty-nine computer disks, a series of e-mails, his hard drive, and at least seven
taped telephone conversations between Ventura and reporters."[31] Ventura's lawyer, Marc
D. Mezibov, believed it was

> the first time a source has been prosecuted criminally as a result of a reporter refusing
> to live up to his promises of anonymity. . . . He's Judas. He committed the ultimate sin
> in journalism. He's Benedict Arnold or any other scoundrel you can think of.[32]

In January 1999, Gannett brought in Ward H. Bushee III from its Reno *Gazette-Journal*
as the *Enquirer's* new executive editor, with the task of repairing its damaged reputation and
rescuing a shambolic news operation.

From a Kantian perspective, lying, theft, and breaking promises are always wrong. The full
details of the case are constrained within the judicial process—the editor's agreement not to
discuss it publicly, for example. But the *Enquirer* declared in its apology that the staff believe
Mike Gallagher lied to them. Precisely how Gallagher obtained the voice mail information is
unclear, but Gannett's willingness to settle meant that its lawyers concluded Gallagher stole
at least some of them by recording the voice mail himself and finding others in locked files.

The categorical imperative suggests that we do not permit for ourselves what we do
not wish to make a universal law. From this viewpoint, societies cannot exist—and the institutions within them have no integrity—if stealing, lying, and breaking one's promises are allowed.
When these basic moral duties are violated, the tragic circumstances are understandable.

The investigation followed the standards of traditional reporting—interviews, extensive
travel for onsite observation, examining court records and company documents obtained
legally, financial resources for veteran reporters, and the courage to examine a powerful
local company.[33] But from Kant's perspective, unless we tell the truth, keep our promises,
and honor property that's not ours, the entire well-intentioned enterprise will fail. Instead of
fulfilling its purpose of informing the public on matters of vital importance to it, the *Enquirer*
seriously jeopardized its public role for the foreseeable future.

This case has a number of complications, and other analyses of the debacle are possible. The cause of the breakdown could center on Gallagher's alleged criminal behavior: "He almost certainly violated federal wiretapping law, according to several experts . . . we can do these stories without breaking laws."[34] Gallagher's zealous and self-righteous style could explain the excesses also; thus he could be said to have made an error in judgment but is not a devil. The *Enquirer*'s management, reporting, and editing policy and procedures may need to be corrected or strengthened. But Kant's deontological ethics appears to provide the most persuasive framework for analysis and for reorganizing this newspaper's policies and culture.

VIRTUE: Nobility

Colleen Gallagher gave this explanation of her brother's role in the Chiquita story: "With his trip to South America, when he saw firsthand the suffering of the people he perceived to be victims of Chiquita, he became emotionally involved, incensed, and believed that he needed to do what he could to right what he saw as a grievous wrong. . . . I do not believe he made his choices for personal gain or with criminal intent.[35] Are "good intentions" important in journalism? If so, to what extent? In law, we distinguish between robbing a bank and stealing a loaf of bread to feed starving children. Shouldn't "good intentions" play a major role in reporting?

CASE 11. COVERING THE MIDDLE EAST

In 1947, the United Nations established the State of Israel and the Palestinian settlements from the former British mandate of Palestine. Three regional wars have followed, that is, two Palestinian intifadas, and Israeli incursions into Arab-populated territories. During each war, Israel expanded its boundaries. In 1948, it extended the Jewish areas in the original partition plan to its current internationally recognized borders. In 1967, it took the West Bank from Jordan and the Gaza strip from Egypt—what remained of British-administered Palestine:

> Significantly these were areas that large numbers of Palestinian refugees were forced to flee to when the Jewish state was created in 1948. So while the 1967 war had defended Israel against combined Arab armies massed on its borders, it had also put a significant Arab population under Israeli rule. It was in the following years that Israel began an illegal programme of settlement building in the now occupied territories, which it successfully defended in the 1973 Yom Kippur war.[36]

The 1980s intifada took place in a decade when Israel made peace with Egypt and pursued Yasser Arafat's Palestinian Liberation Organization (PLO) into Lebanon. The intifada demonstrated the rage the Palestinians felt toward the Israeli occupation, which resurfaced again in September 2000 with the beginning of the al-Aqsa intifada.

A major peace initiative—the Oslo process—began in 1992 with secret negotiations between Yasser Arafat, the exiled head of the PLO, and the then Israeli prime minister, Yitzhak Rabin, who was later assassinated by a Jewish fanatic. The Oslo process continued through the 1990s and into January 2001, despite suicide bombings in Jerusalem and Tel Aviv, the continued building of Israeli settlements in the occupied territories, and the beginning of the al-Aqsa intifada:

> Ehud Barak, then the Israeli prime minister, made a series of offers to Yasser Arafat on what Israel would concede to a Palestinian state, but none of them was accepted. The final offer, made in January 2001 at Taba in Egypt, was the best of the lot but whether it was the best Mr. Arafat could reasonably expect remains controversial. [37]

Early in 2003, President George W. Bush unveiled a new "road map to peace." It was drawn up by the United States, the United Nations, the European Union, and Russia, with Israeli and Palestinian consultation. It sought an independent Palestinian state in the West Bank and the Gaza strip alongside Israel. The plan proposed a three-stage plan to achieve this by 2005. The first stage demanded an immediate cessation of Palestinian violence, reform of Palestinian political institutions, the dismantling of Israeli settlement outposts built since March 2001, and a progressive Israeli withdrawal from the occupied territories. In the second phase, an independent Palestinian state would be created. The third stage sought a permanent end to the conflict by agreeing on the final borders, the status of Jerusalem, the fate of Palestinian refugees, and peace deals between Arab states and Israel.

Like the Oslo peace process, the plan left the difficult issues until last: borders, the status of Jerusalem, Israeli settlements, and four million Palestinian refugees. Its early advocates pointed to the backing of the United Nations, the European Union, and Russia and hoped that after three years of fighting and civilian deaths, the militant group Hamas and the Israeli army might consider a truce. However, the road map's status among the principal parties was controversial from the outset. Skeptics suggested that then Prime Minister Sharon might have accepted it only to ride out U.S. pressure or in the expectation that it had no chance to succeed. Internal Palestinian politics, Mr. Arafat's objections to governmental restructuring, and his longstanding animosity with Sharon were likely to sidetrack the process as well. In fact, six months after its introduction, with the resignation of Palestinian Prime Minister Abu Mazen, Israel's building of a security fence in the West Bank, and unrelenting violence, pundits from around the world had already declared the Bush initiative dead.

By the summer of 2004, President Bush conceded that the 2005 goal was unrealistic.[38] That winter, Arafat died, and the following year, Abu Mazen was elected president of the Palestinian Authority. Shortly thereafter, Sharon and Abu Mazen convened a summit with the Egyptian and Jordanian presidents at which the leaders restated their support for the road map.[39] When Sharon suffered an incapacitating stroke in 2006, his successor, Ehud Olmert, continued discussions with Abu Mazen. The victory of Hamas in the 2006 Palestinian elections raised alarm among Israeli and U.S. officials and caused conflicts within the Palestinian government itself. Throughout 2006, Israel engaged in violent conflicts with Hamas in the Gaza strip and with Hezbollah in Lebanon. These conflicts once again caused pundits to declare the road map dead. While President Bush tried, in the last year of his administration, to revive negotiations for peace, no tangible results were evident.

The Obama administration has not offered a fundamentally different strategy. In the nuances of its policy, it has appeared to be more sympathetic to Palestine than to President George W. Bush. It has also engaged in high-profile disputes with Prime Minister Binyamin Netanyahu over Israel's settlements in the West Bank and in East Jerusalem. When General David Petraeus declared in April 2010 that Israel had become a threat to U.S. security, some pundits saw a significant shift in U.S. thinking. But whatever the changes in posture and detail, the Secretary of State Hillary Clinton, former Senator of a state with a large Jewish population, insisted during her term on America's total support for Israel. Israel knows that it has the majority of votes in the U.S. Congress. Meanwhile, peace talks between Israel and Palestine—a White House and John Kerry priority—have been intermittent and not tangibly productive.

In terms of Palestinian initiatives in the West Bank, the "Fatah-dominated Palestinian Authority, joined by the business community, is trying to forge" another way. "The public feels trapped between failed democracy and failed armed struggle."[40] Fatah is attempting to be a governing party. Prime Minister Salam Fayyad says the goal is

> to build the makings of a state. . . . It's about putting facts on the ground. If we create services, it gives people a sense of possibility. I feel we are on a path that is very appealing both domestically and internationally.[41]

The world's newsrooms feel constant heat from their coverage of the Middle East conflict. Attacks come from both sides. The Committee for Accuracy in Middle East Reporting condemns National Public Radio's (NPR) coverage as "false" and "skewed" against Israel. At the same time, Fairness and Accuracy in Reporting attacks what it sees as NPR's pro-Israeli bias. As the *Columbia Journalism Review* observes, "No news subject generates more complaints about media objectivity than the Middle East in general and the Israeli–Palestinian conflict in particular."[42] "As a hard news subject, [Middle East coverage] is probably the no. 1 issue that consistently comes up across the country," says Mike Clark, reader advocate of the Florida *Times-Union* and web editor for the Organization of News Ombudsmen.[43] Allegations of pro-Israeli bias include more prominent attention to Israeli deaths than Palestinian casualties and the use of words such as *retaliation* for Israeli attacks and *terrorists* or *gunmen* for Palestinians. Pro-Palestinian bias is indicated by more attention to Palestinian children and by violence being softened to *protests*.

But complaints that come from both sides are no indication that the press is doing its job correctly:

> The media do indeed love to point out that they are getting it from both sides. The fact that both sides attack them and accuse them of bias comes in quite handy for them during heated meetings with media activists. . . . But that is almost always used as an end-all argument and a way to avoid dealing with specific concerns that are raised.[44]

Charges of unfair coverage are not new; they have persisted since 1948. But criticism has intensified since Israeli military incursions into Gaza and Palestinian suicide bombings. David Demers of the Center for Global Media Studies accounts for the dual response in this way: "The two sides in a conflict will always see the mainstream media as biased on the other side. When the conflict flares up, and especially when violence increases, both sides become more vociferous in their criticism."[45]

Temperance in Classical Greece and in Aristotle is the most appropriate virtue in complicated, multilayered cases where two legitimate entities are at odds with each other. The Israeli–Palestinian conflict fits that guideline explicitly, and news reporters typically seek the appropriate location between two extremes. The ethical challenge is implementing Aristotle's middle state effectively.

Executing the right balance is complicated by several factors, such as a "lack of understanding of the underlying historical and political background."[46] Ira Stoll identifies a "structural imbalance" as the greatest impediment to fairness, one that comes "from journalists being able to work mostly free and uninhibited in Israel but being subject to severe restrictions in countries like Syria or Iran."[47] David Demers draws a slightly different conclusion:

> Content analyses by scholars generally conclude that media coverage tends to favor Israel over Palestine. It's not a conspiracy by any means, but what it boils down to is they depend on government officials. And these government officials represent the administration, which tends to be pro-Israel.[48]

Ahmed Bouzid adds another perspective:

> The media have very easy access to Israeli spokespersons, who are always on the ready with a statement, a TV appearance, who actively promote their point of view. Access to the Palestinians, meanwhile, is made extremely difficult by the realities of the occupation, the curfews, the town closures, the checkpoints, and, of course, by deliberate harassment from the Israeli army against journalists.[49]

But using one highly publicized episode as an example, easier access to Israeli sources may result in inferior (lazy?) reporting. When Israel barred reporters from entering

Gaza during its recent invasion, CNN's cameras watched from outside the border. "The BBC, by contrast, hired Palestinian camera crews and covered the devastation live. Only midway through the twenty-two day war, since the evidence of massive destruction was inescapable, did CNN start airing extensive footage from Palestinian crews."[50] In this case, being virtuous in Aristotle's sense requires a keenly developed moral discernment and an especially sophisticated professional practice.

Physical violence to solve the issues is contrary to Aristotle's temperance. An aggressive Israeli military and Palestinian mortar and rocket attacks have both sidetracked negotiations and as Aristotelian extremes cannot be justified morally. The Palestinian online hacker group "Anonymous" is trying a nonviolent alternative.[51]

Anonymous has launched a series of cyber attacks against websites in Israel, with data bombardments knocking their sites offline. An "OpIsrael Campaign" was organized in retaliation for Israel's military operation against Hamas in Gaza and the threats by the Israeli government to cut all Gaza's telecommunication links. Anonymous has posted a list of eighty-seven sites it claims had been defaced or attacked as part of OpIsrael. Many of the sites had their homepages replaced with messages in support of Hamas and the Palestinians. This attempt to follow Aristotle's mean may not be fully productive. But it illustrates thinking that is not trapped in either the extreme of defect or the extreme of excess.[52]

CASE 12. KOREA BANS U.S. BEEF: CANDLELIGHT VIGIL

On April 17, 2008 President Lee Myung-bak of South Korea, on the eve of his summit with then President George W. Bush, decided to open the market to American beef. The Korean government had banned imports of American beef since 2003 when a case of "mad cow disease" was found in the United States. President Lee hoped that his decision would encourage the United States Congress to ratify a free-trade agreement between the two countries. However, he did not sound out public opinion or seek the understanding of South Korea's citizens. The deal that the government proposed, moreover, had less rigorous safeguards against the dangers of "mad cow disease" than the U.S. government had reached with other countries.[53]

Lifting the ban mobilized the majority of South Korea's people. Tens of thousands began to hold candlelight vigils in Seoul. These vigils spread to other cities and the number of participants expanded to hundreds of thousands of people. The government used police force to stop the protestors, but the candlelight vigils continued to take place on a nearly daily basis for more than four months. President Lee and his administration were bewildered by these unexpected mass demonstrations. The entire cabinet, the prime minister, and all the top aides to the president submitted their resignations. The ban was re-imposed.

One of the most conspicuous features of this candlelight demonstration was the diversity and heterogeneity of its participants—high-school students in their uniforms, mothers carrying babies in prams, businessmen wearing suits and ties, parents holding hands with their children, young couples, Buddhist monks, Catholic nuns, Protestant clergy, college students, retirees, blue-collar workers and small-business owners.

They had a wide range of different grievances against President Lee's decision. Some demonstrators feared "mad cow disease." Others disliked President Lee's authoritarian style of leadership. Others had national sentiment, criticizing Lee for making too many concessions to the United States. Lee's decision triggered the people's widespread unhappiness with his leadership, and in the tradition of South Korea's protests, they chose nonviolence and took to the streets.

The peaceful demonstrations were not planned by organizations with a policy agenda. The vigils were not arranged by Korea's legal experts, market strategists, or professional protest leaders. The people were articulating their own values, creating solidarity, and advancing their own sphere outside commerce and the state.

On July 3, 2008, Amnesty International dispatched its investigator, Norma Kang Muico, to South Korea to investigate whether the police had violated the protestors' human rights. She said in an interview with the Korean newspaper *Hankyoreh*:

> It's a wonderful expression of people power at the most organic level. It just grows on its own. It doesn't have leadership. It doesn't have specific political groups leading it: for example, trade unions, university students, or normal and traditional leaders of any protests. It's a very peaceful demonstration. It's remarkable to see so many different types of people.[54]

A South Korean political scientist said that "most demonstrators are just ordinary people networking through the Internet and spontaneously and voluntarily joining the rally."[55]

Peace vigils have a long history in South Korea. When the country was under the rule of the authoritarian military regime, political struggles took place in the street. These street demonstrations contributed, to a great extent, to the democratization of the country in 1987. And, once again, peaceful mobilization, nonviolent civic action, totally transformed the government's beef decision. Nonviolence is not a weakness, but effective for social change.

When there are social protests, the media are attracted by violence. Throughout the Middle East upheavals in spring 2013, violent protests drew the media's attention. Dramatic social conflict makes interesting news television and peaceful vigils do not. The Potter Box helps us locate the issues, and in this case, quadrants 1 and 2 need to be examined in depth. Before working on ethical principles and choosing loyalties, the definition of what is newsworthy ought to be critiqued.

The French thinker Jacques Ellul introduces the distinction between ends and means. Because of the overwhelming amount of means at our disposal, ends have lost their meaning. In the technological society, we have become experts on instruments, but neglect ends.

"In this terrible dance of means that has been unleashed, no one knows where we are going; the aim of life has been forgotten."[56] When we are satisfied we are enamored of tools, we tend to be satisfied with means rather than ends. Obviously public communication still invokes lofty ends such as happiness or justice. However, Ellul contends, these goals are obsolete illusions; they no longer inspire and their formative power has dissipated. As means triumph, the goals of technological societies disappear in the busyness of perfecting methods.

The prevailing worldview in industrial societies is instrumentalism—the idea that technology is neutral and does not condition our humanness. The overwhelming power of instrumentalism tends to trap electronic technologies such as the new digital media within its efficiency. Society has sacralized the genius behind machines and uncritically allowed *la technique* to infect not just industry, engineering, and business but also politics, education, the church, labor unions, and international relations. *La technique* is for Ellul the mystique of machineness behind machines, an omnivorous administrative force in which efficient ordering saturates human values, culture, and institutions. Technical efficiency becomes a force so powerful that it makes other imperatives of secondary importance.

In Ellul's framework, the media represent the meaning-edge of the technological system. Communication technologies incarnate the properties of technology while serving as agents for interpreting the meaning of the very phenomenon they embody. As the media organize our conversations, influence our decisions, and impact our self-identity, they do so with a technological cadence, massaging in our souls a technological rhythm and disposition—enabling us to adapt efficiently to the technological world. Moral and social values are disrupted as communication technologies grow.

The media, themselves co-opted by instrumentalism, do not transmit neutral messages but subtly weave audiences and users into the fabric of an efficiency-dominated culture. The media's data "codify social, political and moral standards."[57] In the process, information and communication technologies have become so powerful, Ellul contends, that congruity with the social system is considered normal, even desirable. Our own voice and identity are replaced by a technicized worldview. Particular deviations from the prevailing cyber patterns are of secondary importance and actually divert attention from the human and social values of the dominant culture. The Web 2.0 is not an exchange system of neutral messages, but through it humans are subtly stitched into the warp and woof of an efficiency-dominated culture.

In the Potter Box model, a professional value that tends to dominate in technological societies is the mastery of technology. The technological imperative is the typical term, where the capabilities of media technologies set the agenda and define the issues. Human values are replaced by the machine-like value of efficiency. When the technological imperative is supreme, whether we cover the peace vigil and how we do so are driven by what is best technologically. We go wherever the technology tells us gives the most technically precise visuals. The technological imperative demands impact, rather than what is newsworthy in historical and sociological terms.

■ Give "the technological imperative" a hard critique. What does it mean for broadcast news? Can you think of examples?

OR

■ Jacques Ellul was a Professor at the University of Bordeaux (France) and author of *The Technological Society* and 40 other books. Is "the technological imperative" an ivory-tower idea irrelevant for journalism?

When the news media give peace vigils priority, peaceful means to peaceful ends, then the problem of the technological imperative will be overcome. In order to achieve this turn in direction from violent news to newsworthy nonviolence, for step 3 the ethical principle that is appropriate is the one most radically opposite of instrumentalism and efficiency.

CASE 13. WATERGATE AND GRAND JURY INFORMATION

At 2:31 a.m. on June 17, 1972, five men were arrested by police in the Watergate Hotel building. They were inside the offices of the Democratic National Committee. Frank Wills, a security guard, had noticed that a door leading into the room had been taped open, alerted the police and the men were caught rifling desks and files. The five burglars had lock-picks and door jimmys, a radio walkie-talkie and scanner for listening to police frequencies, cameras and film, tear-gas guns, and recording devices presumably to be planted in the offices for listening to conversations there. One of the men, James McCord, was a former CIA employee and at the time of this arrest was a member of President Nixon's Committee to Re-elect the President (CRP).

After leading the pack in the early going on this break-in, *Washington Post* reporters Carl Bernstein and Bob Woodward ran into rough waters.[58] On October 25, 1972, a major coup had turned into a major disaster. They had written that H. L. (Bob) Haldeman, President Nixon's chief of staff, had been personally involved in espionage and sabotage. The charge moved the Watergate break-in to the door of President Nixon. But then, through his attorney, their source for the report denied before a grand jury that he had given such a testimony. The White House used the opportunity to respond with a vigorous counterattack on the *Washington Post*.

In an effort to discover how they had gone wrong, Woodward and Bernstein revealed their primary source (an agent of the FBI) to his superior. Back at the office, the two reporters and *Post* executives discussed revealing all five sources of their erroneous information, but they decided against it.

After that debacle, Woodward and Bernstein ran into more trouble; now the problem was not erroneous stories but no stories at all. They had hit a lull. The timing was bad. The *Post*'s executive editor, Benjamin Bradlee, became frustrated. The Nixon forces were shooting at him. Charles Colson, speaking to a group of New England editors, said, "If Bradlee ever left the Georgetown cocktail circuit where he and his pals dine on third-hand information and gossip and rumor, he might discover out here the real America." Bradlee told an interviewer that he was "ready to hold both Woodward and Bernstein's heads in a pail of water until they came up with another story." That dry spell was anguish.

Such was the pressurized atmosphere in the *Post* newsroom at the time that Woodward and Bernstein and their editors decided to seek information from members of the Watergate grand jury. They came to the idea by happenstance. One night late in November, a *Post* editor told Woodward that his neighbor's aunt was on a grand jury, that, judging from remarks she had made, it was the grand jury on Watergate, and that, in the words of the editor, "My neighbor thinks she wants to talk."

The two reporters checked the Federal Rules of Criminal Procedure—grand jurors take an oath of secrecy. But it appeared that the burden of secrecy was on the jurors; nothing in the law directly forbade questioning them. The *Post*'s lawyers agreed with that interpretation but urged "extreme caution" in approaching the jurors. Bradlee, nervous, echoed that warning: "No beating anyone over the head, no pressure, none of that cajoling."

All the consultation and advice were for nothing. The woman, Woodward and Bernstein were to learn, was not on the Watergate grand jury after all. But the episode "whetted their interest." The day after the abortive interview, Woodward went to the courthouse, found the list of Watergate grand jurors, and memorized the names; he had been forbidden to take notes.

After typing up the list of jurors, Woodward and Bernstein had a session with Bradlee, *Post* Metropolitan Editor Harry M. Rosenfeld, Managing Editor Howard Simons, and City Editor Barry Sussman. They went over the list looking for members "least likely to inform the prosecutors of a visit," eliminating civil servants and military officers. By considering the occupations of the jurors, they sought individuals "bright enough to suspect that the grand jury system had broken down in the Watergate case" and "in command of the nuances of the evidence." "Ideally," Woodward and Bernstein wrote, "the juror would be capable of outrage at the White House or prosecutors or both; a person who was accustomed to bending rules, the type of person who valued practicality more than procedure." *All the President's Men* describes the mental state of those in the room:

> Everyone had private doubts about such a seedy venture. Bradlee, desperate for a story, and reassured by the lawyers, overcame his own. Simons doubted out loud the rightness of the exercise and worried about the paper. Rosenfeld was concerned most about the mechanics of the reporters not getting caught. Sussman was afraid that one of them, probably Bernstein, would push too hard and find a way to violate the law. Woodward wondered whether there was ever justification for a reporter to

entice someone across the line of legality while standing safely on the right side himself. Bernstein, who vaguely approved of selective civil disobedience, was not concerned about breaking the law in the abstract. It was a question of *which* law, and he believed that grand jury proceedings should be inviolate. The misgivings, however, were unstated, for the most part.[59]

The procedure for interviewing the jurors was agreed on. The reporters were to iden-tify themselves and say that through a mutual but anonymous friend, they understood he or she knew something about the Watergate case. They would then ask if he or she was will-ing to discuss it. If the answer was no, the reporters were to leave immediately.

Visits to about half a dozen grand jurors yielded nothing but trouble. One of the jurors reported the visit to a prosecutor, who informed Judge John Sirica. *Post* attorney Edward Bennett Williams met with Sirica. After the meeting, he told Woodward and Bernstein he thought they would get off with a reprimand. He was right. The chiding came in open court, in a room packed with reporters. But Sirica did not identify them or the *Post.* The reporters present were out for the story, questioning each other, seeking the identity of the reporters mentioned by the judge. Woodward and Bernstein agreed they would make an outright denial "only as a last resort." A colleague caught up with them as they headed for the elevator. *All the President's Men* describes the scene and thinking of the two reporters:

> He (the reporter) caught up with Woodward near the elevator and asked point-blank if the judge had been referring to him or Bernstein.
>
> "Come off it, what do you think?" Woodward answered angrily. The man persisted. "Well, was it one of the news media representatives there or wasn't it? Yes or no?"
>
> "Listen," Woodward snapped. "Do you want a quote? Are we talking for the record? I mean, are you serious? Because if you are, I'll give you something, all right." The reporter seemed stunned. "Sorry, Bob, I didn't think you'd take me seriously," he told Woodward.
>
> The danger passed. The nightmare vision that had haunted them all day—Ron Ziegler at the podium demanding that they be the object of a full federal investigation, or some such thing—disappeared. They tried to imagine what choice phrases he might use ("jury tampering"?), and they realized that they didn't have much stomach for it. They felt lousy. They had not broken the law when they visited the grand jurors, that much seemed certain. But they had sailed around it and exposed others to danger. They had chosen expediency over principle, and, caught in the act, their role had been covered up. They had dodged, evaded, misrepresented, suggested, and intimidated, even if they had not lied outright.[60]

This case involves a long sequence of ethical choices. It reveals many of the pressures on the *Post*'s staff. Bradlee's desire, for example, for a story, "any story," to take the heat off the *Post* could be examined as a nonethics of self-interest, principles be damned. In this way, the case is realistic in its reflection of conditions under which journalistic decisions are frequently made. Under most conditions, these pressures are much less strong than they were for the *Post* in this instance. However, knowledge of these circumstances does not help resolve the ethics of the case. Surely, the existence of pressures, even intense ones, cannot itself justify a reporter's conduct. At best, the reality of pressure may help one sympathize with a reporter who, feeling it strongly, made bad moral judgments. But that is not ethics in the sense of reaching justified conclusions.

Perhaps the best way to begin examining this multisided situation is to identify some of the moral choices made along the way:

1. They decided to reveal the identity of a source to his superior "in an effort to find out how they had done wrong." But they also decided not to reveal all five sources. The decision to reveal their source likely involved the violation of promises, though the case itself does not tell us.
2. They decided to seek information from the grand jury. Clearly, they were aware of potential legal problems, as evidenced by their check into the Federal Rules of Criminal Procedure and by their conversation in the planning session.
3. They decided to get the list of grand jurors by memorization rather than by taking notes. This is already a step in the direction of misusing the grand jury system and violating the important ethical principles on which it stands.
4. They decided to do everything possible to avoid being caught in interviews with grand jurors. This was not a case of deliberately violating the law toward the end of changing an unjust law; it was a case of violating the law in order to serve the interests of the newspaper at the moment.
5. They decided to deceive, beginning with their approach to the grand jurors, and said that they got the juror's name "through a mutual friend." This lie was told in order to open the possibility of getting jurors to talk, to use jurors toward the *Post*'s own ends.
6. They decided to lie if they were identified by fellow reporters as those reprimanded by Sirica. Admittedly, they would stoop to that only "as a last resort."

Certainly the nation can be grateful to Woodward and Bernstein for the final results of their investigation (Nixon's resignation), but the morality of their investigation was seriously flawed. If they had known at the time that issues of overriding national importance were involved, their improprieties could be seen as outweighed by the enormous public benefits. Their lying and their serious tampering with the grand jury resulted in uncovering one of the biggest threats to American democracy in its history. But it's not obvious that this vital end can be used to justify immoral means. The ethical problem is that they employed these immoral means toward immoral ends, namely, the self-interest of protecting themselves and the *Post*.

At the time that they chose to lie and violate the grand jury system, they could not have known, and did not claim to know, the final dimensions of the story they would uncover. In this case, then, democracy benefited, but not by their conscious intent to aid society. The benefit was an unforeseen, and unforeseeable, consequence of decisions to violate not only the law but also basic moral principles. Their decisions cannot, therefore, be justified *ex post facto* in light of the fortunate results. Bad choices do sometimes unwittingly evoke good ends. But such results do no more than place us in the awkward position of being glad that immoral people were at work on the case.[61] Journalists cannot morally follow in the *Post*'s footsteps as a general rule. Lying must always be justified in terms of some higher value; truthtelling need never be justified.

In 2003, the Harry Ransom Center at the University of Texas at Austin purchased the Woodward and Bernstein Watergate files for $5 million. In 2006, Robert Woodward published *The Secret Man: The Story of Watergate's Deep Throat* about their legendary source, Mark Felt. Felt, as an FBI executive and protégé of Herbert Hoover, resented the choice of L. Patrick Gray, rather than himself, to succeed Hoover as FBI Director.[62] But this wealth of material has not resolved questions that

> matter far more than Deep Throat's identity: How important was the *Washington Post*'s reporting to the exposure of the full Watergate scandal? . . . Critics such as Edward Jay Epstein have argued that the journalists simply published information that would have doomed Nixon anyway once the prosecutors brought it to light.[63]

Although it is likely that Woodward and Bernstein helped prevent the burglary from being seen as an isolated incident separate from the White House, the massive Woodward and Bernstein documents have not been conclusive. Their decisions to circumvent the law out of self-interest undoubtedly contribute to the debate that remains today about their precise role in the termination of Richard Nixon's presidency.

NOTES

1. Hugh M. Culbertson, "Leaks a Dilemma for Editors as Well as Officials," *Journalism Quarterly* 57 (Autumn 1980): 402–408.
2. Editorial in the *Washington Post*, February 12, 1969. Quoted in John L. Hulteng, *The Messenger's Motives*, 2nd ed. (Englewood Cliffs, NJ: Prentice-Hall, 1985), 79.
3. Walter Lippmann, *Public Opinion* (New York: The Free Press, [1922] 1949), Part 7, 201–230.
4. John L. Hulteng, *Playing It Straight* (Chester, CT: Globe Pequot Press, 1981), 15.
5. www.wikileaks.org. For details on the release of this and 92,000 classified military documents by Private First Class Bradley Manning, see Denver Nicks, *Private: Bradley Manning, Wikileaks, and the Biggest Exposure of Official Secrets in American History* (Chicago: Chicago Review Press, 2012). Chelsea Elizabeth Manning is now serving a thirty-five-year prison sentence (known as Bradley Edward Manning until August 22, 2013; see www.chelseamanning.org/learn-more/bradley-manning.
6. www.youtube.com/watch?v=5rXPrfnU3G0&feature=player_embedded#!.

7. Anne Flaherty and Pauline Jelinek, "CENTCOM Unable to Find Copy of Shooting Video," *Army Times*, April 8, 2010, www.armytimes.com/news/2010/04/ap_iraq_shooting_video_040610.

8. Noam Cohen, "Calling on Leakers to Help Document Local Misdeeds," *New York Times*, December 20, 2009.

9. Phillip Gollner, "Judge Reverses Ruling in Julius Baer Leak Case," Reuters (San Francisco), February 29, 2008, http://Uk.reuters.com/article/oukin-uk-baer-idUKN2927431720080301.

10. Alexander Hotz, "What WikiLeaks Means for Journalism and Whistle-Blowers," *Poynter Online*, February 25, 2010, www.poynter.org/2010/what-wikileaks-means-for-journalism-and-whistle-blowers/101060/. Iceland has been working on the strongest protection for whistleblowers that exists in the world. Last year when it suffered economic collapse, it was discovered "that numerous nefarious causes (corrupt loans, off-shore transactions, concealed warning signs) were hidden completely from the public and even from policy-makers, preventing detection and avoidance." The media and legislative bodies were not able "to penetrate this wall of secrecy, allowing this corruption to fester until it brought about full-scale financial ruin" ("The War on WikiLeaks and Why It Matters," *Salon.com*, March 27, 2010, 4).

11. Noam Cohen and Brian Stelter, "Airstrike Video Brings Notice to a Website," *New York Times*, April 7, 2010, A1, A9.

12. Noam Cohen, "What Would Daniel Ellsberg Do with the Pentagon Papers Today?" *New York Times Reprints*, April 18, 2010, www.nytimes.com/2010/04/19/business/media/19link.html?_r=0.

13. "Julian Assange," interview by Stephen Colbert, *The Daily Show*, April 12, 2010, www.cc.com/video-clips/5mdm7i/the-colbert-report-exclusive---julian-assange-extended-interview.

14. "Gates Assails Internet Group over Attack Video," Reuters, April 13, 2010, www.reuters.com/article/us-iraq-usa-journalists-idUSTRE63C53M20100413.

15. Steven Aftergood, "WikiLeaks and Untraceable Document Disclosure," *Secrecy News*, January 3, 2007, 1, www.fas.org/blogs/secrecy/2007/01/wikileaks_and_untraceable_docu/.

16. Tracy Samantha Schmidt, "A Wiki for Whistle-Blowers," *Time* magazine, Washington, April 28, 2010, www.time.com/time/nation/article/0,8599,1581189,00.html#ixzz1ExtfiKg4.

17. Lisa Lynch, "'We're Going to Crack the World Open': WikiLeaks and the Future of Investigative Reporting," *Journalism Practice*, iFirst, 1751-2794, March 24, 2010, 2.

18. Glenn Greenwald, "The War on WikiLeaks and Why It Matters," *Salon.com*, May 27, 2010, 3; see WikiLeaks website, https://wikileaks.org/.

19. Lynch, "We're Going to Crack the World Open," 3.

20. Greenwald, "The War on WikiLeaks," 5.

21. Lynch, "We're Going to Crack the World Open," 2.

22. Ibid., 7.

23. Ibid., 6.

24. Schmidt, "A Wiki for Whistle-Blowers," quoted in Lynch, "We're Going to Crack the World Open," 2.

25. Ibid., 2.

26. Ibid., 2.

27. For a book-length review of the issues for journalism, see Charlie Beckett and James Bull, *Wikileaks: News in the Networked Era* (Cambridge, UK: Polity, 2012).

28. Lynch, "We're Going to Crack the World Open," 9.

29. Ibid., 9.

30. For quotations and details, see Nicholas Stein, "Banana Peel," *Columbia Journalism Review* (September/October 1998): 46–51. For the case and three commentaries, see "The *Enquirer* and Chiquita," *Journal of Mass Media Ethics* 16:4 (2001): 313–321.

31. Alicia C. Shepard, "The Chiquita Aftermath," *American Journalism Review* (May 1999): 48.

32. Stein, "Banana Peel," 46.

33. For a thoughtful analysis, see Mike Hoyt, "Essay: Just How Far Is Too Far?" *Columbia Journalism Review* (September/October 1998): 48–49. Bruce Shapiro expands: "A 'false and misleading' picture? The

Enquirer's lawyers have found it necessary to bend over fast and far. But in fact the 'Chiquita Secrets Revealed' series presents a damning, carefully documented array of charges, most of them 'untainted' by those stolen executive voice mails. Gallagher's and McWhirter's allegations are largely based on old-fashioned reportorial legwork: land records in Central America, interviews with environmental scientists and trade unions, lawsuit records, leaked corporate memoranda and the reporter's own visits to workers' villages and campuses" (Bruce Shapiro, "Rotten Banana," Salon.com, July 8, 1998, www.salon1999.com/archives/1998/media.html).

34. Hoyt, "Essay" 49.

35. Shephard, "The Chiquita Aftermath," 48. For a detailed account of the aftermath, see Donald Challenger and Cecilia Friend, "Fruit of the Poisonous Tree: Journalistic Ethics and Voice-Mail Surveillance," *Journal of Mass Media Ethics* 16:4 (2001): 255–272.

36. Simon Jeffrey, "The Road Map to Peace," *The Guardian Review*, June 4, 2003, 2, www.theguardian.com/world/2003/jun/04/israel.qanda.

37. Jeffrey, "The Road Map to Peace," 3.

38. "Newspaper Interview with George W. Bush," Federal News Service, May 9, 2004.

39. Steven Erlangen, "Urging New Path, Sharon and Abbas Declare Truce," *New York Times*, February 9, 2005.

40. Ethan Bronner, "Palestinians Try Less Violent Path to Resistance," *New York Times*, April 7, 2010, A1, A10.

41. Ibid, A10.

42. "Questions of Balance in the Middle East," *Columbia Journalism Review* (May/June 2003): 54.

43. Charles Burress, "U.S. Newspapers Catch Flak for Mideast Coverage," *The News-Gazette*, 21 April 2002, B4.

44. Ahmed Bouzid, "The Other War: A Debate," *Columbia Journalism Review* (May/June 2003): 55.

45. Quoted in Burress, "U.S. Newspapers Catch Flak for Mideast Coverage," B4.

46. Ira Stoll, "The Other War: A Debate," *Columbia Journalism Review* (May/June 2003): 54.

47. Ibid.

48. Quoted in Burress, "U.S. Newspapers Catch Flak for Mideast Coverage," B4.

49. Bouzid, "The Other War: A Debate," 54–55.

50. J. J. Goldberg, "A Matter of Trust," *Columbia Journalism Review* (May/June 2009): 43.

51. See the website of the Palestinian hacker group "Anonymous," www.anonrelations.net and also forum.caergybi.com/index.php?topic=6627.5;wap2.

52. "Anonymous Hacker Group Attacks Israeli Websites," BBC News, November 16, 2012, www.bbc.com/news/technology-20356757.

53. This summary of events is based primarily on research by Dr. Jeong-ho Kim, Seoul, Korea.

54. See "Amnesty International to Investigate Police Violence in South Korea," *The Hankyoreh*, July 3, 2008.

55. Choe Sang-Hun, "Shaken Korean Leader Promises New Beginning," *New York Times*, June 12, 2008.

56. Jacques Ellul, *Presence of the Kingdom*, trans. O. Wyon. (Philadelphia: Westminister, 1951), 69.

57. Jacques Ellul, *Propaganda: The Formation of Men's Attitudes*, trans. K. Kellen and J. Lerner (New York: Alfred A. Knopf, 1965).

58. Quotations for this case are taken from Robert Woodward and Carl Bernstein, *All the President's Men* (New York: Simon and Schuster, 1974), 205–224.

59. Ibid., 210.

60. Ibid., 224.

61. This commentary focuses on the contributions of journalists in uncovering Watergate, with an emphasis on their relationship to sources. Measuring the size of the reporters' contribution is debatable. Judge Sirica attempted to document that the judiciary (including special prosecutors) was primarily responsible for developing the case and securing its resolution. See John Sirica, *To Set the Record Straight* (New York: W. W. Norton, 1979).

62. Robert Woodward, *The Secret Man: The Story of Watergate's Deep Throat* (New York: Simon and Schuster, 2006).

63. David Goldberg, "Beyond Deep Throat," *Columbia Journalism Review* (September/October 2005): 51–52. For a recent review of the issues, see Roger Stone, *Nixon's Secrets: The Truth about Watergate and the Pardon* (New York: Skyhorse Publishing, 2014).

4

SOCIAL JUSTICE

Historian Charles Beard once wrote that freedom of the press means "the right to be just or unjust, partisan or nonpartisan, true or false, in news columns and editorial columns."[1] Very few people still have confidence in such belligerent libertarianism. There is now substantial doubt whether the truth will emerge from a marketplace filled with falsehood. The contemporary mood among media practitioners and communication scholars is for a more reflective press, one conscious of its significant social obligations. But servicing the public competently is an elusive goal, and no aspect of this mission is more complicated than the issue of social justice. The Hutchins Commission mandated the press to articulate "a representative picture of the constituent groups of society." The commission insisted that minorities deserved the most conscientious treatment possible and chided the media of their day for tragic weaknesses in this area.[2]

Often a conflict is perceived between minority interest on the one hand and unfettered freedom of expression on the other. The liberty of the press is established in the First Amendment. Thus this freedom continues to be essential to a free society. Practitioners thereby tend to favor an independent posture on all levels. Whenever one obligates the press—in this case, to various social causes—one restrains its independence in some manner. Obviously, the primary concern is government intervention, but all clamoring for special attention from the press ought to be suspect.

In spite of debate over the precise extent of the media's obligation to social justice, there have been notable achievements. Abolitionist editors of the nineteenth century crusaded for justice even though the personal risks were so high that printing presses were thrown into rivers and printing shops burned down by irate readers. A symbiosis between television and the black movement aided the struggle for civil rights in the 1960s.

This chapter introduces five problems of social justice on a different scale but involving typical issues of justice nonetheless. In all cases, a responsive press is seen to play a critical role. All five situations assume that genuine social concerns are at stake, and not just high-powered special-interest groups and authoritarian governments seeking their own ends. Each of the five examples pertains to the disenfranchised: the victims of genocide in the first case, the poor in the second, women in the third, Native Americans who had run out of options in the fourth, and the victims of war in the fifth example. In all cases, the reporters felt some measure of obligation. Although press response is sometimes extremely weak, no cause is dismissed out of hand by journalists in these situations.

Social ethicists typically show a strong commitment to justice. We assume this principle here and try to apply it in complicated situations.[3] The heaviest battles in this chapter usually occur over questions in the middle range, issues that media personnel confront along with the larger society. For example, do the media carry a particular mandate from subscribers and audiences, in the same way politicians may sense a special obligation to represent the people who voted for them—or who at least live in their district? And further, does the press have a legitimate advocacy function, or does it best serve democratic life as an intermediary, a conduit of information and varying opinions? In a similar vein, should the press just mirror events or provide a map that leads its audience to a destination? The kind of responsibility for justice that a particular medium is seen to possess often depends on how we answer these intermediate questions about the press's proper role and function.

CASE 14. CRISIS IN DARFUR

After the Rwandan genocide that occurred during the 1990s, many people vowed never to allow such atrocities to go unnoticed again. Yet ethnic cleansing has ravaged the Darfur region of Sudan, and, once again, the international community has been slow to act. In the larger context, the Second Sudanese Civil War from 1983–2005, more than two million people died. In one of the largest civil wars in history, millions have been displaced, with many fleeing to neighboring Chad and the Central African Republic.

Darfur for several hundred years was an independent Islamic sultanate with a population of both Arabs and black African tribes—both of them Muslim. Darfur was annexed to Sudan by the British in 1916, but it was neglected by the colonial power. When Sudan became independent in 1956, the new government continued to overlook Darfur. The core area around Khartoum and inhabited by riverine Arabs has largely ignored all the rural territory in the country, although it covers the largest geography and has the largest population.[4]

Sudan is no stranger to conflict. In 1962, just six years after achieving its independence, a decade-long civil war broke out between the Arabs residing in the north and the Africans living in the south. After eleven years of peace, another civil war erupted, this time raging on for two decades. Things appeared to be calming down when, in February 2003, a rebellion occurred in the Darfur region of Sudan—an area plagued not only by drought and desertification but also by continued tensions between the farmers and nomads who inhabit the area. The rebels began attacking government targets, claiming that the Sudanese government was discriminating against them because of their black African identity. The

Sudanese government retaliated by employing local Arab militias to quash the uprising—nicknamed the *Janjaweed* (translated as "the evil horsemen"). Because the insurgents were mostly black, choosing the Darfuri Arab tribes was a brilliant strategy for terrorizing them.

While the Sudanese government is reluctant to admit its complicity in this tragedy, the events that have transpired in Darfur are nothing less than genocide. (The December 1948 International Convention on the Prevention and Punishment of Crimes of Genocide defines *genocide* as "deliberately inflicting on the group, conditions of life calculated to bring about its physical destruction in whole or in part.") After the government conducted air strikes on targeted villages, the *Janjaweed* descended on the area, murdering, and raping anyone left alive. To ensure that no one returned, the militias burnt any remaining structures and poisoned the water supply. By backing the militias, the Sudanese government was able to engage in ethnic cleansing and at the same time deny responsibility for the human rights violations, claiming the violence was due to "tribal conflicts."[5]

Attempts by the international community to bring an end to this crisis were slow and ineffective. The United States and the European Union have contributed to humanitarian efforts but showed no resolve to do anything meaningful in terms of policy. Furthermore, Sudan has been reluctant to keep its word when negotiations have led to ceasefire or peace agreements. In July 2007, the United Nations Security Council passed a resolution authorizing a peacekeeping force made up entirely of African troops, but without authorization to act. The Western countries were let off the hook easily, and Khartoum got an impotent and probably mute presence with no clear mandate to intervene.[6]

The International Criminal Court issued ten charges of war crimes and genocide against Sudan's president Omar Hassan al-Bashir in July 2008. He was re-elected as president on April 26, 2010, in a blatantly manipulated election. As Sudan continues to hemorrhage citizens to neighboring countries, the region has become increasingly unstable. This instability has had a negative impact on humanitarian efforts in the area and has caused many to scale back or abandon their efforts entirely.

A referendum in 2011 resulted in the Christian and animist south becoming an independent state from the Arab Muslim north, the Republic of South Sudan. Unfortunately, civil war, rampant ethnic strife, and tribal conflict continue as before.[7]

What is known as the "greatest humanitarian crisis of the twenty-first century" requires the best possible international reporting. The ethical principle is justice. The world deserves to see Darfur in terms of justice rather than the sensationalism of bloody violence. The news media as the only global form of communication have a major responsibility to provide this perspective.

Standard definitions of news are not adequate. Fairness and balance are important but not sufficient. Accuracy is required on the details, but the complications are enormous, and being accurate is not strong enough either. Hard news coverage that is spectacular and crisis-oriented is obviously inadequate.

To meet the ethical principle of social justice in this case means comprehensiveness. The term *interpretive sufficiency* is one way to define it. A sufficient interpretation opens up public life in all its dynamic dimensions. A newsworthy account that makes justice explicit represents complex cultures and religions adequately. The people involved at all levels are portrayed authentically without stereotype or simplistic judgments.[8]

In this deeper understanding of reporting in international news, news means authentic disclosure. Journalists disclose the essence of the events or, in other words, get to the heart of the matter. And on this level, the truth about Darfur is still debated, even though this crisis has been unfolding since early 2003. According to Gerard Prunier, director of the French Center for Ethiopian Studies and author of *Darfur: The Ambiguous Genocide*, four different explanations are being disputed yet today: (1) the Khartoum government claims that it is an explosion of tribal conflicts exacerbated by drought; (2) some leading specialists and governments see it as a counterinsurgency gone wrong with the *Janjaweed* militias brutal and out of control; (3) a few call it "ethnic cleansing," with the African tribes being replaced by Arabs who are more supportive of Arab rule in Khartoum; and (4) a stronger version of number 3 is genocide, with genocide meaning the violent annihilation of one race by another.[9]

Meeting the standard of reporting as authentic disclosure is complicated by unending difficulties with sources. Visas to Sudan and South Sudan are difficult to get for journalists and typically involves months of waiting. Reporting in Darfur itself is expensive and dangerous. The news networks presume a lack of interest in Africa on the part of their audiences, and several have exhausted their budgets and personnel covering Iraq and Afghanistan. The government assigns "minders" to accompany correspondents, and local sources who speak honestly to the media have to be protected for their own safety.

VIRTUE: Compassion

Research has identified "compassion fatigue" as a reality. Journalists and the public become weary of ongoing crises that are difficult to sort out with no end in sight. What is the moral status of this phenomenon? Or, another way to ask the same question: "Is it fair to criticize a decline in news coverage and in audience interest over unending conflict?"

In addition to knowing events on the ground—gang rape, bombings, murder, burned-out villages, children slaughtered in daylight—reporters need to interview government administrators and rebel commanders. Aid workers and United Nations workers are accessible, but leaders of both countries are typically evasive or deceptive. Professor and diplomat Haydar Badawi Sadig describes a speech by President Omar Hassan al-Bashir given in Qatar as an example of rhetorical spin that's difficult to report in terms of social justice:

The President of Sudan enumerated his grievances with the West in general, and the United States in particular. He condemned the U.S. for Native Indian genocide. He talked about U.S. atrocities committed in Iraq, "based on a lie," he said. Then he went on to say that the Sudan government ordered the Ambassador of Great Britain out of the country. . . . Al Bashir was passionately, feverously, and very loudly, speaking while the crowd cheered "Alahu Akbar" (God is Great) between statements. He himself used the cheer "Alahu Akbar" as he always does to conclude his emotionally charged address.[10]

Meanwhile, al-Bashir's National Conference Party has almost total control of electronic broadcasting in Khartoum and heavy censorship of the print media.[11]

Some serious reporting does overcome the hurdles and meets the justice principle. Nicholas Kristof of the *New York Times* and Emily Wax of the *Washington Post* are distinguished in the United States, and the BBC covers Darfur at length and regularly. According to the Tyndall Report, however, the failures of U.S. television are inexcusable. In 2004, for the entire year, ABC News had eighteen minutes on Darfur, NBC five minutes, and CBS three minutes. In contrast, Martha Stewart received 130 minutes of coverage by the three networks. CNN, Fox News, NBC, MSNBC, ABC, and CBS together ran fifty-five times as many stories about Michael Jackson as they did about Darfur.[12]

Haydar Badawi Sadig and Hala Asmina Guta call for peace communication in and about Sudan built on a new Islamic perspective. No political solutions are sustainable, in their view, without "good-faith and goodwill communication." Reflecting C. F. Alger, they see peace communication as not promoting an absence of violence, but in social justice terms "[a]ddressing structural inequalities, cultural and global threats to [Sudan's] world fabric and natural environment." They see the relationship between the mass media and peace articulated in the UNESCO (United Nations Educational, Scientific and Cultural Organization) constitution: "Since wars begin in the minds of men [sic], it is in the minds of men [sic] that the defenses of peace must be constructed." Following Johan Galtung, Sadig and Guta conclude that violence from the oppressor and counter violence from the oppressed will continue to intensify, unless the dehumanization that drives them can be overcome. Communication is crucial to this cultural shift in which different ethnicities and religions are respected rather than polarized. A change in language and attitudes is required for changes in policy and institutions. They quote S. Keen approvingly: "We first kill people with our minds, before we kill them with weapons." Along with the schools, the news media are crucial for rising above stereotypes, fanaticism, us/them binaries, and seeing the other as an evil enemy.[13]

In this case on the Darfur region, there is general agreement about which ethical principle is most relevant. And this principle, justice through news as the authentic disclosure of truth, is readily understandable. The challenge is overcoming the failure to act on this principle. There are examples of overcoming the problems by reporting comprehensively. How can they be disseminated and used effectively by journalism educators and professionals?

CASE 15. "A HIDDEN AMERICA: CHILDREN OF THE MOUNTAINS"

More than 10.9 million viewers tuned in for *20/20*'s "A Hidden America: Children of the Mountains," broadcast on ABC during a Friday night in February 2009—the audience that night the show's largest in five years.[14] It begins with a montage of scenes—most troubling—from Appalachia. Host Diane Sawyer's voice comes in on the audio, describing the region's people and history, then setting the stage with a question:

> So how is it so many of these people have been left behind? We take you tonight to one of the poorest regions in the nation. Where men and women die younger than other Americans, where there is a documented epidemic of drug addition, cancer, toothlessness, alcoholism, depression. And yet everywhere in these hills there are so many people filled with courage and hope.

More images, clips from across time and place. A different voice saying: "We need to reinvest in those people. It's a lot easier to blame people for their poverty than to figure out what's next." The title screen arrives, then Sawyer superimposed over a regional map. Over the following hour, she sketches a portrait of central Appalachia via the stories of young people.

Shawn, a high-school football star with the "will of a lion," sleeps in his truck, showers at a friend's, and dreams of a sports scholarship to "get out" while saving his anger for Friday nights on the field. He mostly stays away from home, which is in the hills outside town. At one point, his family is rocked by allegations of incest and abuse.

Courtney, twelve, lives in a small home with eleven extended-family members; the family struggles to make food stamps last all month. Her mother, thirty, a recovering addict, walks eight miles each way to her General Educational Development (GED) classes. Grandma, forty-nine, prays for both. Viewers see Courtney's uncle pour Pepsi into her two-year-old sister's sippy cup.

An aside, back to the big picture: Sawyer is visibly shocked to learn that Oxycontin goes for $120 per pill in parts of eastern Kentucky, the drug of choice in a region struggling with addiction to methamphetamines and prescription painkillers. One dealer remarks, as she's led away in handcuffs, that it's about "survival," not hurting people.

Erica, now eleven, was first profiled by local news five years ago. Her mother, too, battles addiction to painkillers. In a moment of lucidity, Mom comments: "I'm sorry you had to go through this." Erica replies: "It's okay, Mommy," but in that second looks as if she's lived many lifetimes. Her mother returns from court-mandated treatment, lapses again, and Diane Sawyer catches up with Erica wandering local streets to get some space. Why does Mom do it? "The pain," Erica responds.

Next, on to more uplifting . . . material. Sawyer heads to the Mud Creek Clinic, run by Eula Hall and serving 19,000 people a year. People pay only what they can; she keeps a gun to protect the pharmacy. Another "hero," Dr. Edwin Smith, is a dentist who travels the region with a mobile clinic financed by himself. "The stereotype rooted in fact," much of his work aims to reverse what's known as "Mountain Dew mouth."

Jeremy, nineteen, is an apprentice miner. With a baby on the way, he has a family to support and gives up thoughts of becoming an Army engineer. While only one in ten men in the region earns a college degree, coal miners start at $60,000 a year. It's dangerous, but almost half of the energy used in the U.S. comes from coal—and West Virginia provides 16 percent of it. Sawyer heads into a mine and interviews workers; glancing at the mine management standing nearby, they respond warily.

Meanwhile Shawn is off to college, accepted on a football scholarship. But two months in it's clear he doesn't have the money to make it work. He's isolated and decides to return home. Jeremy, on a steady salary, gets a loan and buys a home for his new family. Courtney's mother finishes her GED, and the family moves out of the grandparents' home. Quickly, "A Hidden America" concludes with a few thoughts on education and the possibility of federal stimulus money for the region. Sawyer closes by referring viewers to ABC's website, for watchers to find organizations that help Appalachian kids and to provide feedback on the documentary.

Audience reactions pour in: by the following Monday, ABC's website has received over 1,600 comments from around the country. A week later, *20/20* has a brief update. It focuses mostly on recapping the documentary's stories, but gives some insight into people's responses. Shawn gets another chance, offered a full financial package to another school that provides more support. Concerned citizens send clothes, food, and a carriage for Jeremy's new baby. Erica receives an educational trust fund. The governor comments that Kentucky will get $3 billion in the federal Economic Recovery Act. More computers may help Appalachian kids be more competitive with their international peers. And after initially declaring "this is old, irresponsible news" in the film, Pepsi decides to donate a mobile dentist clinic to Dr. Smith and vows to help mobilize volunteers, technicians, and dentists.

Debate broke out just as quickly. In an interview with Diane Sawyer appearing on Fox News's *The O'Reilly Factor* the same night as "A Hidden America," host Bill O'Reilly remained pessimistic: "There's really nothing we can do about it," he said; "their parents are drunks."[15] Newspapers, television stations, radio broadcasts, and other media outlets around the country picked up the issue—from a variety of perspectives. A local uploaded a newscast to YouTube from WSAZ News in Paintsville, Kentucky, that profiles Johnson Central High School, Shawn's alma mater—as a "cool school" of the week.[16] It detailed Johnson's multi-million dollar development efforts, new computer labs, and world champion problem-solver team. In a thoughtful response, award-winning journalist and WYMT TV (Hazard, Kentucky) news director Neil Middleton weighed both sides:

> Yes, I wish ABC would have balanced the segment and focused on some of our
> successes. . . . But if we are honest, we must admit the facts of the documentary are

true and sometimes the truth hurts. . . . Are we really mad at Diane Sawyer for reporting on a serious problem, or are we upset that someone is reminding us of images we would rather ignore? Remember, our mandate as journalists is to "give voice to the voiceless," or as newsman Harry Golden once described his job: "To comfort the afflicted and afflict the comfortable." The images we saw the other night should make us all uncomfortable.[17]

Just over a year later, in March 2010, ABC News reported that the network won a Peabody Award for "A Hidden America," which is considered the most prestigious prize in electronic media broadcasting.

■ ■ ■ ■

In the aftermath of the *20/20* special, Neil Middleton—among many others in the media and outside it—implied that something more was at stake in "A Hidden America" than questions of accuracy and stereotypes alone. Following Harry Golden, Middleton included a claim for justice in his reflection: in this particular case the reporter's obligations move beyond simply reporting the facts (though as he notes, getting that right is still crucial) toward moral ground. While questions of stereotyping the residents of Appalachia is certainly an issue of merit, deeper critiques of Diane Sawyer's approach suggest that, despite its Peabody, "A Hidden America" failed to live up to this standard.

In her defense, Sawyer did endeavor to make it clear in her introduction that she spoke of the 500,000 living in poverty among central Appalachia's 2.2 million residents. Her tone and approach was mostly seen as compassionate. After all, as she noted upfront, "we want to take you to a part of America I love: my home state of Kentucky." The project was a two-year endeavor that logged over 1400 miles through the region; yet the overall feel was not one of rootedness, of layered connection to and understanding of the communities in question. As Appalachian author and West Virginia native Betty Dotson-Lewis asked:

> When Sawyer's documentary was over, I thought maybe an hour wasn't long enough to explore such a complex issue. Maybe that's why the show lacked much real information. But I wondered why Sawyer didn't explore the causes of the poverty and the cycle that kept these places poor.[18]

Why, Dotson-Lewis asked, were people who want to help not given instructions? Why was the coal scene not covered better—mountaintop removal, for example, and why were the coal operators contributing so little to their communities?

Despite briefly mentioning historical precedents such as President Lyndon Johnson's declaration of "war on poverty" from eastern Kentucky over forty years ago, and Bobby Kennedy's activism after that, it seems that "A Hidden America" failed to answer its own premise question: how did Appalachians get left behind? Al Cross, director of the Center for Rural Journalism and Community Issues, referenced Neil Middleton in a column that clarified the challenge: "When journalism illuminates problems that raise questions of public policy, it's obliged to offer suggestions for solutions. That was the main flaw many journalists saw in the documentary, which was long on emotion and short on context."[19]

Jeff Biggers, a cultural historian with deep knowledge and lived experience of Appalachia, put it even more starkly: "Sawyer left a lot of key issues hidden in 'A Hidden America.'"[20] For Biggers, those issues are deeply embedded in the region's history, culture, people, social fabric, traditions and religious beliefs, and economy. Chief among that context is coal: "While touching on the extreme conditions of poverty in eastern Kentucky, replete with toothless enthusiasm, Sawyer failed to notice the 800-pound gorilla in the room: Mountaintop removal strip mining that has devastated eastern Kentucky's communities and economy."[21] While "A Hidden America" mentioned coal's importance and related that its staff was unable to get statistics on corresponding health issues such as black lung disease, Sawyer's only onsite interactions with miners seemed to occur while company bosses were present. How could they be expected to speak openly and in detail about the struggles, problems, and dangers they faced? A social justice approach thirsts for deeper analysis.

Another event may shed further light in gaining a critical, justice-based perspective. A mere five days after ABC News announced that "A Hidden America" won a Peabody, on April 5, 2010, a gigantic explosion ripped through the Upper Big Branch coal mine in southern West Virginia. In the aftermath, twenty-five miners were found dead, and the entire United States watched for days as rescuers led a desperate effort to find the remaining four miners trapped in the mine. In the end it was too late, the result was the worst American mining tragedy in forty years. In a crass sense, it was also a bona fide story—the kind of scoop that increases circulation and makes reputations. Heroic rescuers, an unapologetic mine boss (widely perceived in public opinion as a heartless villain), a pattern of safety violations, lives and millions of dollars on the line in an industry that continues to fill almost half of the United States' energy needs.

Many national outlets moved on quite quickly to other news after asking similar, basic questions, but some coverage strove to get a multifaceted, layered approach to the "Montcalm disaster." In the flurry of events and reporting after the tragedy, official statements whizzing back and forth between government officials, politicians, industry spokespeople, miners, bosses, and investors, the *Charleston Gazette* found a unique voice as a result of dogged investigative reporting, tenacious commitment to the facts, and a rich understanding of the coal industry and Appalachian life. In the month after the disaster, Ken Ward Jr., the *Gazette*'s decorated and veteran reporter on environment issues and the coal industry,[22] and other staff filed dozens of stories that approached Upper Big Branch from every possible angle.[23] While many journalists looked to the previous decade for historical context, *Gazette* stories went fifty or even a hundred years back in time. They used legal depositions, government records, interviews, and a variety of sources all while respecting families grieving over the loss of twenty-nine loved ones. Perhaps keys to this perspective may be found in two statements by Ward during a 2007 interview:

With a few exceptions, journalists are forgetting about the value of being an expert on the issue and having a reporter who specializes in things. The fact that I'd spent a lot of time trying to do a lot of these issues, I knew the backdrop of it, the people to call and where the documents were, and we were able to do more stories and better stories than anyone else had.

And later: "It's a difference between the national media folks who parachute in to West Virginia. It doesn't matter if people trust them, because they're doing one story and moving on. But we live here and work here."[24]

Notably, in the wake of "A Hidden America: Children of the Mountains," a number of journalists and thinkers began to answer Middleton's rhetorical call to think more deeply and creatively about the issues Diane Sawyer and her team raised, if incompletely. In the special's conclusion, Dee Davis asked why we tend to see bank failures and other broad social issues as systemic problems, while we tend to see the Appalachian poor as needing to "pull themselves up by their bootstraps." Davis runs the Center for Rural Strategies, a Kentucky-based nonprofit that looks to create economic advancement and better national discussion about rural life and culture. Other editorials responding to *20/20* referenced comments by Ed Roller, a professor and Appalachian expert at the University of Kentucky quoted at the end of the follow-up segment on *20/20*, who reminded viewers "there are ways to think about the future in the mountains, in different kinds of ways than we've thought about it in the past. We just need to be willing to dream." Roller himself is doing just that. Based on his extensive research and recent book examining the roots of inequality between Appalachia and elsewhere in the United States, he advocates beginning to address Appalachia's long-term issues by decentralizing education and health care, among other suggestions. For Roller, "if we stop at charity, we never get to the point where we address the underlying issues that generated the problems that exist. We never get to the 'justice' side of the social equation."[25]

CASE 16. GLOBAL MEDIA MONITORING PROJECT

The Global Media Monitoring Project (GMMP) is the largest research study of gender in the world's media. Every five years since 1995, GMMP research has examined women's presence in the media compared to men, gender bias, and stereotyping in news media content. The fourth study in 2010 was done in 108 countries and involved hundreds of research volunteers. The project includes participants ranging from local community organizations to university students and researchers, to media practitioners. The 2010 data contains 16,734 news items, 20,769 news personnel (announcers, presenters and reporters), and 35,543 total news subjects. The GMMP has become the largest advocacy initiative in history on changing the representation of women in the media (http://whomakesthenews.org/gmmp).

The idea for a one-day study of the portrayal of women in the world's media was first discussed in Bangkok in 1994. From the beginning, a grassroots research instrument was considered essential. To create media awareness and develop media monitoring skills on an international level, using local talent was chosen over professional research teams. The methodology and results of the first study were published as *Global Media Monitoring: Women's Participation in the News*. This report was presented to the United Nations Fourth World Conference on Women in Beijing in September 1995 and confirmed there as an effective implementation of the Beijing Declaration and Platform for Action, Strategic Objective J2: "Promote a balanced and non-stereotypical portrayal of women in the media."

Bringing media accountability into the struggle for gender equality was the original impetus for the GMMP. Given its global perspective, the project also has been committed to ensure "comparable and accurate results from data collected by researchers in different contexts."[26] The news media are the most influential source of ideas and information for most people around the world. "Who and what appears in the news and how people and events are portrayed matters. . . . In many countries, the cultural underpinnings of gender inequality and discrimination against women are reinforced through the media."[27] The GMMP seeks to have this statement adopted and implemented by media organizations everywhere: "Fair gender portrayal is a professional and ethical aspiration, similar to respect for accuracy, fairness and honesty."[28]

The methodology has been refined in each study, but the structure for 2015 has been fundamentally the same as 1995 in order to chart progress and make comparisons. On the same day (November 10, 2009 for the 2010 research) news coverage in three media—radio, TV, newspaper—was analyzed. In the U.S., the research included seven newspapers, eleven television stations (including PBS and cable), and four radio stations. Internet news was monitored on a pilot basis in sixteen countries. International news included such websites as CNN International, Al Jazeera, Euronews, Africa 24, Deutsche Welle World, Telesur, and BBC World. The online sources yielded 1061 news items containing 2710 news subjects and reported by 1044 news personnel.[29]

GMMP 2010 showed that women are dramatically under-represented in the news. A comparison of the 2010 results with the previous GMMP studies in 1995, 2000, and 2005 revealed that change in the gender dimensions of news media has been small and slow across the two decades. Only 24 percent of news subjects—the people who are interviewed, or whom the news is about in print, radio and television—are female. Women's points of view are rarely heard in the topics that dominate the news agenda. Even in stories that affect women profoundly, such as gender-based violence, it is the male voice (64 percent of news subjects) that prevails. Stories about economic development (59 percent) reinforce gender stereotypes. When women do make the news it is primarily as "stars" or "ordinary people," not as persons of authority. As newsmakers, women are under-represented in professional categories. As authorities and experts, women barely feature in news stories. While the study found a few excellent examples of exemplary gender-balanced and gender-sensitive journalism, it demonstrated an overall glaring deficit in the news media globally, with the female half of the world's population barely present.[30]

You Think?

- Are research reports such as this GMMP study effective?
- Could you take this report to local newspapers or broadcast stations and ask them to evaluate their gender practices in light of this research?
- Rather than protesting gender inequality through oral communication, would these written documents give a rational basis for assessment and change?

The results of GMMP have been used in multiple ways by gender and communication groups worldwide, in teaching research, training for media practitioners, media literacy education for media audiences, advocacy with local stations and newspapers, lobbying work for nongovernmental organizations. In Malta, the Gender Advisory Committee of the Broadcasting Authority uses the results of the GMMP in their research and training programs. In Jamaica, upon receiving the 2010 report, the Broadcasting Commission noted its value in communication policy development. In Senegal, the Inter-African Network for Women, Media, Gender and Development uses the GMMP methodology for research and training in francophone West and Central Africa. In Argentina, the GMMP reports have inspired the formation of a network of journalists for gender-responsive media. The Arab Human Development Report published by the United Nations uses the GMMP reports as a resource, and the studies' results are included in the work of the United Nations International Research and Training Institute for the Advancement of Women.

Women have been stereotyped regularly by the press. The problem has long, historical roots. During the women's suffrage movement, for example, news accounts often distorted the issues. Editorials regularly denounced women's "petty whims," spoke of "appalling consequences," and even used labels such as "insurrection." Sample twentieth-century writing of any kind (including journalism) and the failures become obvious: overemphasis on clothes and physical appearance, the glorification of domesticity, the portrayal of women as empty-headed or at least nonintellectual.

Evidence abounds that such problems persist. Pay scales are still not equitable across genders. Joann Byrd and Geneva Overholser have been ombudspersons for the *Washington Post*, and some women are high-ranking executives now, but women are still under-represented in influential positions. Jane O'Reilly assails the "pale male" pundits (in skin color and perspective) who dominate editorials and commentary.[31] In fact, the existence of sexism in the media has been proven so repeatedly, and with so little change over time, that one scholar has concluded we should quit doing studies that prove what we already know about media sexism and start teaching "readers to talk back to their newspapers in ways that make clear their dissatisfaction with how women are represented and portrayed."[32]

Why does sexist language continually creep into reporting? How could women be included as sources? How can we bring more women onto the staff and into management positions so that their points of view are more likely to be represented? In order to help promote change in the news, readers and viewers should be researched with precision and comprehensiveness. The GMMP covers roughly 57 percent of the world's surface. The data are scientifically rigorous and broad enough in scope that station managers cannot ignore the results, and they provide instructive materials for training journalists (www.whomakes-thenews.org/gmmp). The GMMP makes it obvious that old ideas of authority with diminished voices for women get in the way of new ideas of community and leadership.[33]

Sexual harassment is another entangled issue that demands accurate, knowledge-able, non-sensational reporting. Educational institutions, government agencies, health organizations, and religious bodies over the last decade all have adopted some form of harassment policies based on gender and sexual orientation. They vary in detail, but all such policies advocate non-tolerance and insist on mandatory action against offenders. Elaborate procedures for implementation are required so that violators are prosecuted, the innocent protected, and retaliation does not result later. Overall the aim is preventative rather than focusing on violations themselves. The news media play a crucial role in ensuring that policies are implemented actively and fairly, but to do so without creating a public trial or spectacle is nearly impossible. Basing news reports on scientific studies rather than on informal opinion helps give journalism credibility.

Sexism is embedded in our culture and social order. It will take the persistent, thoughtful attention of editors everywhere to identify and expunge it. We could fairly conclude that the best professionals are not sexist, but instead, they are aggressive reporters or sometimes uncertain in their judgment as social mores shift. However, the broader agenda remains. Even if press behavior is improving rapidly in particular cases, there is an urgent need for institutional and structural reform. Otherwise, a long and entrenched history will not be permanently changed.[34]

CASE 17. TEN WEEKS AT WOUNDED KNEE

One of this century's leading civil libertarians, Zechariah Chafee, Jr., once wrote:

> Much of our [national] expansion has been accomplished without attacking our neigh-bors. . . . There were regrettable phases of our history, such as breaches of faith with the Indians, but these are so far in the past that they have left no running sores to bother us now. . . . We have not acted the bully."[35]

If a distinguished Harvard law professor, a man considered a champion of oppressed minor-ities, could write so casually about the plight of American Indians, little wonder a tight circle of American Indian Movement (AIM) leaders thought they needed a major event to publicize their concerns. And what better event than an old-fashioned "uprising" complete with teepees, horses, rifles, war paint, and television cameras?

On February 27, 1973, some 200 Indians seized the hamlet of Wounded Knee on the Pine Ridge Sioux Indian Reservation in southwest South Dakota.[36] Tension had been growing steadily for three weeks, ever since a group of Indians clashed with police in Custer, South Dakota, protesting the light charge (second-degree manslaughter) returned against a white man accused of stabbing and killing an Indian there. Thirty-six Native Americans were arrested in that melee, eight policemen were injured, and a Chamber of Commerce building was burned.

But the problem at Wounded Knee was of a different magnitude. Indians were thought to have taken hostages (eleven townspeople who later declared they were not being held against their will and who refused to be released to federal authorities) and were prepared to hold their ground by violence if necessary. They gathered considerable public support, trading on sympathy for Chief Big Foot's band slaughtered there in 1890 by the U.S. Seventh Cavalry— the last open hostility between American Indians and the U.S. government until February 1973.

As the siege began, news crews rushed to cover the developing story. On February 28, Indians demanded that the Senate Foreign Relations Committee hold hearings on treaties made with Indians and that the Senate begin a full investigation of the government's treatment of Native Americans. George McGovern, a liberal Democrat and South Dakota senator at the time, flew home to negotiate, but to no avail. Meanwhile, FBI agents, federal marshals, and Bureau of Indian Affairs (BIA) police surrounded Wounded Knee, hoping to seal off supplies and force a peaceful surrender.

But the siege turned violent. On March 11, an FBI agent was shot and an Indian injured as gunfire erupted at a roadblock outside town. On the same day, AIM leader Russell Means announced that Wounded Knee had seceded from the United States and that federal officials would be treated as agents of a warring foreign power. A marshal was seriously wounded on March 26, and two Indians were killed in gunfire as the siege wore on into April. Finally, on May 6, with supplies and morale nearly expended, AIM leaders negotiated an armistice and ended the war.

An incredible 93 percent of the population claimed to follow the story through television, but Indian attorney Roman Roubideaux did not think they were seeing the real story:

> The TV correspondents who were on the scene filmed many serious interviews and tried to get at the essence of the story, but that stuff never got on the air. Only the sensational stuff got on the air. The facts never really emerged that this was an uprising against the Bureau of Indian Affairs and its puppet tribal government.[37]

Television critic Neil Hickey summarized the feelings of many:

> In all the contentiousness surrounding the seizure of Wounded Knee last winter, a thread of agreement unites the disputants: namely, the press, especially television,

performed its task over a quality spectrum ranging from "barely adequate" to "misguided" to "atrocious." For varying reasons, no party to the fray felt that his [sic] views were getting a decent airing.[38]

The lack of compelling evidence foiled prosecutors at the subsequent trial of AIM leaders Russell Means and Dennis Banks. Defense attorneys Mark Lane and William Kunstler argued that the Indians were not guilty because they were merely reclaiming land taken from them by treaty violations. But the real defense was an inept offense. In September 1974, U.S. District Judge Fred Nichol accused the FBI of arrogance and misconduct and the chief U.S. prosecutor of deceiving the court. After an hour's lecture to the government, he dismissed the case.

The occupation at Wounded Knee was deliberately staged for television. AIM leaders knew that the legends of Chief Big Foot and the recent popularity of Dee Brown's *Bury My Heart at Wounded Knee* would virtually guarantee a good amount of press coverage. And it was a newsworthy event. The Indians at Pine Ridge had just witnessed what they perceived to be a breakdown in the judicial system at Custer. The AIM had tried other forums for airing their argument: that 371 treaties had been violated by the U.S. government, including failed grievance procedures through the BIA.

The moral issue concerns the degree to which the conflicting voices were fairly represented. In fact, the ten-week siege produced so many aggrieved parties that fairness to all became impossible. How accurately did reporters cover the law officials ordered to the scene, for example? After the event, FBI agents and marshals were hissed by hostile crowds near Wounded Knee and ordered to leave lest another outbreak occur. And how could the press treat the BIA fairly? Its policies became the lightning rod of attack, catching all the fury born from 200 years of alleged broken promises. An inept Justice Department, abuses from ranchers and storekeepers, racism from area whites, and inadequate congressional leadership also contributed to the situation but received only a minor part of the blame. How does one evaluate where accusations are appropriate and yet recognize legitimate achievements in a volatile setting? The BIA contended, for example, that it was not responsible for every abuse and that it had sponsored nearly all the vocational training and employment on the reservation.

But the hardest questions concern treatment of the Sioux grievances. According to the ethical principle that human beings should be respected as ends in themselves, the moral ideal entails an account that clearly reflects the viewpoint of these aggrieved. And even minimum fairness requires avoidance of stereotypes. A young Ogalala Sioux bitterly criticized the press for stories that cast the standoff as a "Wild West gunfight between the marshals and Indians." On December 30, 1890, the *New York Times* warped its account of the original Pine Ridge battle with biased phrases about "hostiles" and "reds." The story concluded:

It is doubted if by night either a buck or squaw out of all Big Foot's band is left to tell the tale of this day's treachery. The members of the Seventh Cavalry have once more shown themselves to be heroes of deeds of daring.[39]

After eighty-three years, many newspapers and broadcasters had still not eliminated clichés, prejudices, and insensitive language.[40]

Russell Means complicated the press's task with his quotable but stinging discourse. Years later, in fact, Means was working to erect a monument at the site of the 1876 Battle of the Little Big Horn. In the process, he called for razing the statue of the "mass murderer" George Custer. "Can you imagine a monument to Hitler in Israel?" he asked in a news conference. "This country has monuments to the Hitlers of America in Indian country everywhere you go."[41] Means called for a fitting memorial to a battle that "continues to epitomize the indigenous will to resist oppression, suppression, and repression at the hands of European parasites."[42]

Fairness, at a minimum, requires that news coverage reflect the degree of complexity inherent in the events themselves. Admittedly, when events are refracted through the mirrors of history, separating fact from fiction becomes impossible. Moreover, the Pine Ridge Indians themselves disagreed fundamentally about the problems and the cure. Richard Wilson, president of the tribal council, despised the upstarts of AIM: "They're just bums trying to get their braids and mugs in the press." He feared a declaration of martial law on the reservation and considered Means and Banks to be city-bred leaders acting like a "street gang," who could destroy the tribe in the name of saving it.

"No more red tape. No more promises," said Means in response. "The federal government hasn't changed from Wounded Knee to My Lai and back to Wounded Knee." Raymond Yellow Thunder, after all, had been beaten to death earlier by whites and the charges limited to manslaughter by an all-white jury in Custer. The average annual wage at Pine Ridge was $1800, with alcoholism and suicide at epidemic rates. Why were the AIM occupiers, speaking for thousands of Indians, unable to get a hearing for them? Where is the truth in all the highly charged rhetoric?

Some reporters did break through the fog with substantive accounts. NBC's Fred Briggs used charts and photos to describe the trail of broken treaties that reduced the vast Indian territory to a few small tracts. CBS's Richard Threlkeld understood that AIM really sought a revolution in Indian attitudes. ABC's Ron Miller laid vivid hold of life on the Pine Ridge Reservation itself by "getting inside the Indians and looking at what was happening through their eyes." But, on balance, journalists on the scene did not fully comprehend the subtleties or historical nuances of tribal government. Reporters covering Wounded Knee complained that their more precise accounts often were reduced and distorted by heavy editing. After seventy-one days, the siege ended from weariness—not because the story was fully aired or understood. The press could have unveiled a political complaint to be discussed sensibly and thoroughly; instead, it was caught up in the daily drama of quoting accessible sources and finding attractive visuals.

Maybe the principle of fairness can operate only before and after a spectacle of this kind, when the aggrieved knock on doors more gently. If that is true, owners of news businesses in the Wounded Knee region carry an obligation to develop substantial and balanced coverage of the oppression of Native Americans over the long term, even though such coverage may threaten some of their established interests. Often reporters sensitive to injustice receive little support and thus have no choice but to break stories of injustice when they fit into traditional canons of newsworthiness.[43]

This regrettable weakness in Native American coverage did not end with Wounded Knee. A decade later, 100 miles east of the Grand Canyon, the federal government began the largest program of forced relocation since the internment of Japanese Americans during World War II. Thousands of Navajos were taken from a million acres awarded to the neighboring Hopi tribe. The Navajo–Hopi turmoil is the biggest story in Indian affairs for a century and an "issue of national significance." But, Jerry Kammer complained, major newspapers have hurried past "the way some tourists hurry across the reservations en route to the Grand Canyon. They have regarded the dispute and its people as little more than material for colorful features."[44] Violence is a likely possibility even for years after the resettlement is completed—given the sacred burial grounds involved, disputes over oil and minerals, Navajo defiance, and so forth. Periodically, banners emblazoned with "WK 73" (Wounded Knee 1973) appear to remind everyone that a battle to the death may be at hand with authorities.

If federal marshals sent to evict Navajos do battle with an unlikely guerrilla force of AIM members, Navajo veterans of Vietnam, and grandmothers in calico skirts, the press will descend like Tom Wolfe's fruit flies, just as they did at Wounded Knee. They would feast on the violence of a tragedy that was spawned by competing tribes, compounded by the federal government, and neglected by the national press.[45]

Mainstream journalism seems unable to grasp Native American culture. In May 1993, journalists from around the world descended on Littlewater, New Mexico, a small Navajo town on a 25,000-square-mile reservation, the largest in the United States. An unknown disease had killed six Navajos initially and then spread to thirty-nine people in eleven states and left twenty-six dead (including Hispanics, Hopi Indians, African-Americans, and Anglos). "A front-page headline in *USA Today* called the illness 'Navajo flu,' the *Arizona Republic* labeled it the 'Navajo epidemic,' and *NBC News* referred to it as the 'Navajo disease.'"[46] That headline stuck, said one man burying his wife, because "people think we live in tepees and our homes are dirty." Navajos chased journalists away from funerals of victims, with the president of the Navajo nation complaining that they

> violated many of our customs and taboos. . . . In Navajo tradition, the four days after a burial are especially sacred. That was blasted apart by journalists aggressively pursuing a story. They were disrespectful, disruptive, and upsetting to the whole idea of harmony.

The mystery illness was later identified as a noncontagious strain of hantavirus, a deadly disease carried by the deer mouse.[47] Some journalists had used offensive labels such as "witchcraft," and photographers had taken pictures of sacred objects. A tribal resolution criticized sensational news coverage for inspiring "discriminatory attitudes and activities against Navajo people."

And the beat goes on. Because of this historic pattern of failure, observers predict that the confrontations now will move to the state and county levels. For example, seventy-two Wisconsin counties have formed an association to resolve the costly and complex jurisdictional disputes between the Oneida Indians and local governments over fishing rights, timber, minerals and water, property taxes, welfare, and education.[48] Jumbled federal policies, many of them as old as the U.S. Constitution, fan the disputes rather than clarify them. Increasingly, local journalists face the same contentious issues of social justice brought to a head on the national level at Wounded Knee. Native American journalists themselves are leading the way. More than 400 belong to a thriving Native American Journalists Association, and their news stories meet all the tests of excellent journalism.[49]

Perhaps other media can redeem press failure here. In 1993, HBO produced an excellent documentary entitled *Paha Sapa: The Struggle for the Black Hills*, which described vividly Native American beliefs and legends, the "Sacred Hogs" of the Black Hills, and the meaning of the tribal name *Lakota* ("people together"). On May 11, 2009, "Wounded Knee" was shown on PBS as a documentary in its film series of five episodes on Native Americans: *American Experience–We Shall Remain*. It includes archival footage from 1973, along with present-day interviews with Banks and Means. Dennis Banks has had roles in the movies *War Party*, *The Last of the Mohicans*, and *Thunderbolt*. He released a music video in 1995, *Still Strong*, featuring his original work as well as traditional Native American songs. Banks's video autobiography, *The Longest Walk*, was released in 1997. Russell Means has recorded two musical albums, *The Radical* and the *Electric Warrior*, on his own label, the American Indian Music Company. His autobiography, *Where White Men Fear to Tread*, introduces Wounded Knee to young people and children. In 2001, Means founded TREATY, a total-immersion school for Ogalala Sioux children (K–third grade) based on the Sioux language, culture, and modes of learning. In addition, Means uses the internet to reach audiences not available to him through the traditional news outlets. In trying to press the contractual claims of the Ft. Laramie Treaty of 1868, Russell Means said recently: "I feel a sadness for the white man. He has no roots. No foundations." That challenge must extend to the journalist on assignment: why am I covering this story? For whose agenda? To what purpose? All of Means's projects have slowed since he died of cancer on October 12, 2012 but he leaves behind a legacy of ideas for understanding and action on the ethics of social justice.

CASE 18. PEACE JOURNALISM

Peace journalism is a new way of thinking about reporting on violent conflicts worldwide. The Norwegian scholar Johan Galtung has developed and applied the principle systematically through peace studies, concerned not simply with war reporting, but with what he calls "positive peace." He promotes a creative, nonviolent approach to all cultural, social, and political conflicts.[50] Following Galtung, Jake Lynch recognizes that military coverage feeds the very violence it reports, and therefore he has developed an on-the-ground theory and practice of peace initiatives and conflict resolution.[51] As Cai Yiping puts it:

> In contrast to War Journalism which is journalism about conflict that has a value bias towards violence and violent groups that usually leads audiences to overestimate violent responses to conflict by ignoring non-violent alternatives, peace journalism, by identifying and avoiding these reporting conventions, aims to correct this bias. And, by doing so, allow opportunities for society at large to consider and value non-violent responses to conflict.[52]

Conflict has significant news value. Dramatic violence appeals to journalists and their audiences alike. Standard journalistic norms favor conflict, directly or indirectly. Peace journalism is a self-conscious, working concept that denies this premise. Galtung wants to reroute journalism on the "high road to peace," instead of the "low road" often taken by the news media. The "low road" for Galtung is when the media fixate "on a win–lose outcome, and simplify the parties to two combatants slugging it out in a sports arena."[53]

In her literature review of war and peace journalism, Seow Ting Lee sees three contrasting features of each.[54] The three characteristics of mainstream war journalism are: (1) Focus on the here and now, on military action, equipment, tangible casualties, and material damage. Embedding journalists during the U.S. invasion of Iraq illustrates an effective strategy for meeting this objective. (2) An elite orientation: use official sources, follow military strategy, quote political leaders, and be accurate with the military command perspective. (3) A dichotomy of good and bad. Simplify the parties to two combatants, them versus us. Make the war a zero-sum game of binaries, such as Arab intransigence and Israeli militarism.

There are three salient features of peace journalism: (1) Present context, background, and historical perspective. Use linguistic accuracy—not Muslim rebels but rebels identified as dissidents of a particular political group. (2) An advocacy stance editorially for peace, and focusing in news on common values rather than on vengeance, retaliation, and differences. The people's perspective is emphasized in news. Reporting should not be limited to the organized violence between nations, but include stories of cooperation and integration among people. (3) A multiplicity orientation: All sides, all parties are represented. Create opportunities for society at large to consider and value nonviolent responses to conflict. Include the ways in which the conflict can be resolved without violence. Consensus-building efforts are considered newsworthy.

Seow Ting Lee is from Singapore and Jake Lynch is based in Australia. Johan Galtung, from the land of the Nobel Peace Prize, Norway, started using the term, "peace journalism" in the 1970s.[55] The peace journalism model was further developed by Conflict and Peace Forums, a think tank based in England in a series of international conferences in the late

1990s. Isis International is a communication organization in the Philippines that conducts workshops for media professionals and community leaders on peace and conflict. Search for Common Ground in Brussels trains journalists and students in media and conflict resolution, in Europe, the Middle East, Sri Lanka, and Turkey.[56] Jolyon Mitchell of Scotland sees potential in the documentary genre for peacemaking.[57] He recommends three examples: *War Photographer* (Swiss filmmaker Christian Frei), *Long Night's Journey Into Day* (South Africa), and the British documentary *The Imam and the Pastor*. While peace journalism is routinely criticized as "unprofessional activism" by the conventional media, its rationale and practice are taking hold around the world.

Peace journalism faces a heavy agenda.[58] In order to advance it, journalism needs to give up its neutrality and detachment, and adopt the Judeo-Christian ethical principle: "Love your neighbor as yourself." This principle can inspire journalists to give peace priority even while reporting on a violent world. The standard professional values of immediacy, objectivity, and relevance do not put reporters on "the high road to peace." Utilitarian ethics, the typical principle for journalism in democratic societies, does not lead to the three features of peace journalism as summarized by Seow Ting Lee. However, the Judeo-Christian ethics of love provides a way of thinking that makes peace the moral ideal and conflict a social practice that needs transformation.

You Think?

Gandhi believed that nonviolence was a powerful force. What about you? "Turning the other cheek" is weakness, isn't it? Insisting on peace seems to be naive when there's violence. Assume that Gandhi is right and try to answer these objections.

The issues in peace journalism are especially complicated, and the ethical principle of loving one's neighbor needs to be elaborated if it is to serve as the foundation for this kind of reporting. The golden rule is one such way of showing how the ethics of love is a guide for morally appropriate action.[59] To think and act nonviolently "do unto others as you would have them do unto you." This is a norm that is not just hypothetical and conditional, but is also apodictic and unconditional. Hans Küng is correct in saying that it is fully practicable in the face of the extremely difficult situations in which individuals or groups ought to act when there are crises and conflicts.[60] Its secret is avoiding a list of prohibited acts and providing a way to think about behaving toward others.

Küng assumes that the golden rule is so clear and intuitive that we feel no need to ask what it really means. Acting toward others as we wish them to act toward us is not an abstract theory, but readily understandable. The rule of reciprocity between others and myself seems unarguable, intuitive, the natural way to live harmoniously in the human world.

As Tod Lindberg observes, its brevity and simplicity obscure its radical implications. In his words, it proceeds from the assumption of human dignity—we regard others as basically like ourselves. Thus when followed it produces a community of goodwill.[61] Instead of categories such as enemies and criminals dominating news reports on war and conflict, human relationships are understood in more sophisticated terms with reciprocal relations primary.

As Young Ahn Kang concludes, the golden rule can function effectively as a moral procedure because, as he believes, it expresses the common moral wisdom of almost all humanity.[62] Judeo-Christian ethics systematizes it, but it is also a social value that enables the human race to survive. There is no reason not to make use of golden-rule thinking among peoples, nations, and for multinational cooperation in order to build a world in which cultural diversities are respected and shared. Media organizations as social institutions can resonate with it also as their ethical standard for public affairs reporting. As Jolyon Mitchell concludes regarding the golden rule, it "provides a different description of reality which challenges the claim that violence has either the first or the last word"; it discredits the myth "that by using violence lasting peace can be achieved—sustained."[63]

A semiotics of news reporting from around the world of conflict and war needs to continue unabated.[64] Hard work on epistemology is required of media scholars and professionals. As Seow Ting Lee puts it: "If peace journalism is to succeed, journalists must assess their notions of hard news, objectivity, and traditional news values."[65] Peace journalism is typically understood as an innovation in mainstream newsgathering—along with developmental and public journalism.

In addition to this demanding agenda—and one could argue, our first order of business—peace journalism must transform its philosophy of the human. When we start intellectually with humans-in-relation, the golden rule becomes a credible normative standard for both the general morality and professional journalism ethics in this contentious age.

NOTES

1. Charles Beard, "*St. Louis Post-Dispatch* Symposium on Freedom of the Press," 1938. Quoted in William L. Rivers, Wilbur Schramm, and Clifford Christians, *Responsibility in Mass Communication*, 3rd ed. (New York: Harper and Row, 1980), 47.

2. Commission on the Freedom of the Press, *A Free and Responsible Press* (Chicago: University of Chicago Press, 1947), 26–27.

3. For a description of the concepts of justice as background to the social justice of this chapter, see Patrick Plaisance, *Media Ethics: Key Principles for Responsible Practice* (Los Angeles: Sage, 2009), 77–83.

4. Gerard Prunier, "The Politics of Death in Darfur," *Current History* (May 2006): 195–196. For further details, see his book, *Darfur: The Ambiguous Genocide* (Ithaca, NY: Cornell University Press, 2005).

5. Matthew Lippman, "Darfur: The Politics of Genocide Denial Syndrome," *Journal of Genocide Research* 9:2 (2007): 192–213.

6. Prunier, "The Politics of Death in Darfur," 199.

7. See Faith Karimi and Mohammed Osman, "Sudanese Woman Sentenced to Death for her Christianity Gives Birth in Prison," *CNN World*, May 27, 2014, http://religion.blogs.cnn.com/2014/05/27/Sudanese-woman-sentenced-to-death-for-her-Christianity-gives-birth-in-prison/.

8. For an authoritative study of eight daily newspapers from around the world on the question of interpretive sufficiency, see Bella Mody, "Uncovering Darfur Sudan 2003–2005: Which News Organization Offered the Most Comprehensive Coverage?" unpublished paper, University of Colorado–Boulder, July 7, 2006). For a full review and analysis of the media's role and responsibility in Darfur, see Bella Mody, *The Geopolitics of Representation in Foreign News: Explaining Darfur* (Lanham, MD: Rowman & Littlefield, 2010.

9. Prunier, "The Politics of Death in Darfur," 200.

10. Haydar Badawi Sadig and Hala Asmina Guta, "Peace Communication in Sudan: Toward a New Islamic Perspective," in R. Fortner and M. Fackler, eds., *Blackwell Handbook of Global Communication and Ethics*, vol. 2 (Oxford, UK: Blackwell, 2011), 602–625.

11. Ibid., 606.

12. Sherry Ricchiardi, "Déjà Vu," *American Journalism Review* (February/March 2005).

13. This summary and quotations from Sadig and Guta, "Peace Communication in Sudan," 602–625. For a political and economic perspective on what is needed for peace to be possible, see Hamid Eltgani Ali, ed., *Darfur's Political Economy: A Quest for Development* (New York: Routledge, 2014).

14. ABC News, "ABC News Honored with Peabody Award for Diane Sawyer's Report "A Hidden America: Children of the Mountains," March 31, 2010, http://blogs.abcnews.com/pressroom/2010/03/abc-news-honored-with-peabody-award-for-diane-sawyers-report-a-hidden-america-children-of-the-mounta. html.

15. Bill O'Reilly, *The O'Reilly Factor*, February 13, 2009. For additional commentary on the interview, see *The Mountain Eagle*, "Fox News commentator says Appalachia is 'hopeless,'" February 18, 2009, www.themountaineagle.com/news/2009-02-18/front_page/005.html.

16. "A Hidden America: Children of the Mountains? A Rebuttal from Johnson Central," www.youtube.com/watch?v=9bkyGBAY-MY.

17. Neil Middleton, "Diane Sawyer's Hidden America: Children of the Mountains Made Me Mad as Hell," February 16, 2009, http://appalachianforums.com/forum/dcdb/arch.pl/md/read/id/186229.

18. Betty Dotson-Lewis, "Speak Your Piece: Diane Sawyer in Eastern Kentucky," *Daily Yonder*, February 15, 2009, www.dailyyonder.com/speak-your-piece-diane-sawyer-eastern-kentucky/2009/02/15/1933. The *Daily Yonder* is a publication of the Center for Rural Strategies, a nonprofit organization dedicated to Appalachian issues whose founder, Dee Davis, was featured in "A Hidden America."

19. Al Cross, "Will Sawyer's Report Lead to Local Action?" *Mountain Eagle*, February 25, 2009.

20. Jeff Biggers, "Dear Diane Sawyer: The Other Children of the Mountains," *Huffington Post*, February 17, 2009.

21. Jeff Biggers, "Diane Sawyer: Talk to Ashley Judd, Don't Overlook the 800-LB Gorilla on 20/20," *Huffington Post*, February 19, 2009. For the role of women in protesting mountaintop removal, see Joyce M. Barry, *Standing our Ground: Women, Environmental Justice, and the Fight to End Mountaintop Removal* (Athens: Ohio University Press, 2012).

22. Ken Ward won a 2007 Investigative Reporters and Editors medal for his *Charleston Gazette* series on the 2006 Sago mine disaster, in which a dozen miners died. He also received a 2006 Annual Medal from the Investigative Reporters and Editors' Association.

23. The *Charleston Gazette* keeps a complete list of articles related to the Montcalm disaster on its website, see http://wvgazette.com/News/montcoal/201004100542.

24. Leann Frola, "How a Small Newspaper Won a Big Award," *Poynter Online*, April 9, 2007, www.poynter.org/2007/how-a-small-newspaper-won-a-big-award/81636.

25. Jeff Worley, "A Walk across Uneven Ground: A Conversation With Appalachian Historian Ron Eller," *Odyssey* (Summer 2009): 12–15.

26. Lavina Mohr, "Preface," *Global Media Monitoring Project 2010*, September, iv, www.whomakesthe-news.org/gmmp.

27. Ibid.

28. Aidan White, *Getting the Balance Right: Gender Equality in Journalism*, International Federation of Journalists report, 2009, www.unesco.org/new/en/communication-and-information/resources/publications-and-communication-materials/publications/full-list/getting-the-balance-right-gender-equality-in-journalism/.

29. The data in this paragraph are largely from "Who Makes the News?" *Global Media Monitoring Project 2010.*

30. For data and conclusions in this paragraph, see ibid., 4.

31. Jane O'Reilly, "The Pale Males of Punditry," *Media Studies Journal* (Winter/Spring 1993): 125–133.

32. Barbara Luebke, "No More Content Analyses," *Newspaper Research Journal* 13 (Winter/Spring 1992): 1–2.

33. For other monitoring projects, see "Media Report to Women," published by Communication Research Associates since 1972 (www.mediareporttowomen.com). FAIR, another national media watchdog, keeps a continually updated online directory of media stories dealing with sexism (www.fair.org/index.php?page=7&issue_area_id=13).

34. For a comprehensive review of the issues and challenges, see Linda Steiner, "Feminist Media Ethics," in Lee Wilkins and Clifford G. Christians, eds., *The Handbook of Mass Media Ethics* (New York: Routledge, 2009), 366–381.

35. Zechariah Chafee, Jr., "Why I Like America," commencement address at Colby College, Waterville, Maine, May 21, 1944.

36. For a detailed review of this case, see C. Christians, M. Fackler, J. Ferré, *Ethics for Public Communication* (New York: Oxford University Press, 2012), ch. 12.

37. Neil Hickey, "Only the Sensational Stuff Got on the Air," *TV Guide*, December 8, 1973, 38. For details on which this case and commentary are based, see the other three articles in Hickey's series: "Was the Truth Buried at Wounded Knee?" December 1, 7–12; "Cameras Over Here!" December 15, 43–49; "Our Media Blitz Is Here to Stay," December 22, 21–23.

38. Hickey, "Only the Sensational Stuff Got on the Air," 34.

39. Arnold Marquis, "Those 'Brave Boys in Blue' at Wounded Knee," *Columbia Journalism Review* 13 (May/June 1974): 26–27; and Joel D. Weisman, "About That 'Ambush' at Wounded Knee," *Columbia Journalism Review* 14 (September/October 1975): 28–31. For background, see Mario Gonzalez and Elizabeth Cook-Lynn, *The Politics of Hallowed Ground: Wounded Knee and the Struggle for Indian Sovereignty* (Urbana: University of Illinois Press, 1998).

40. For a historical overview of photography, see Joanna C. Scherer, "You Can't Believe Your Eyes: Inaccuracies in Photographs of North American Indians," *Studies in the Anthropology of Visual Communication* 2:2 (Fall 1975): 67–79. For an analysis of Native Americans in the twentieth-century press, see Mary Ann Weston, *Native Americans in the News* (Westport, CT: Greenwood, 1996).

41. Daniel Wiseman, "Indians Will Erect Own Monument Over Defeat of 'Murderer' Custer," *Casper* (Wyoming) *Star-Tribune*, June 23, 1988, A1.

42. "Statement of Russell Means, Lakota Nation," *Akwesasne Notes* (Summer 1989): 12.

43. For a description of the ongoing struggle of the press with Indian tribal governments over First Amendment freedoms and reporting positive news from the reservation, see Karen Lincoln Michel, "Repression of the Reservation," *Columbia Journalism Review* (November/December 1998): 48–52.

44. For details on this story and the quotations, see Jerry Kammer, "The Navajos, the Hopis, and the U.S. Press," *Columbia Journalism Review* 24 (July/August 1986): 41–44.

45. Ibid.

46. For details and quotations, see Bob M. Gassaway, "Press Virus Strikes Navajos: Journalists Invade another Culture, Stumble over Traditions," *Quill* 81:9 (November/December 1993): 24–25.

47. Leslie Linthicum, "Of Mice and Mistrust," *Albuquerque Journal*, December 19, 1993, 1E–2E.

48. For a review of the challenges of state-level reporting, see Ron Seely, "Native Americans Have Been Stewards of Wisconsin Land for Centuries," *Wisconsin State Journal* (October 5, 2003); for background, see Ron Seely, "Tribal Culture is Still Vibrant," October 5, 2003, www.highbeam.com/doc/1G1-108575812.html.

49. For a study of four tribal newspapers between 1995 and 1999, see Patty Leow and Kelly Mella, "Black Ink and the New Red Power: Native American Newspapers and Tribal Sovereignty," *Journalism and Communication Monographs* 7:3 (Autumn 2005): 111–133.

50. Johan Galtung, *Conflict Transformation by Peaceful Means: A Participants' and Trainers' Manual* (Geneva, Switzerland: UNDP, 2000); and Johan Galtung, *Transcend and Transform: An Introduction to Conflict Work (Peace by Peaceful Means)* (London: Pluto Press, 2004).

51. Jake Lynch, *Debates in Peace Journalism* (Sydney, Australia: University of Sydney Press, 2008). J. Lynch and A. McGoldrick, *Peace Journalism* (Glasgow, Scotland: Hawthorn Press, 2005).

52. Cai Yiping, "Revisiting Peace Journalism with a Gender Lens," *Media Development* 2 (2011): 16–20.

53. Johan Galtung, "High Road, Low Road: Charting the Course for Peace Journalism," *Track Two* 7:4 (December 1998): 7–10.

54. Seow Ting Lee, "Peace Journalism," in Lee Wilkins and Clifford Christians, eds., *The Handbook of Mass Media Ethics* (New York: Routledge, 2009), 258–275.

55. See Jake Lynch and Johan Galtung's co-authored, *Reporting Conflict: New Directions in Peace Journalism* (Brisbane, Australia: University of Queensland Press, 2010). See also Johan Galtung and Dietrich Fischer, *Johan Galtung: Pioneer of Peace Research* (London: Springer Heidelberg, 2013).

56. Georgios Terzis, "Mediatizing Peace," *Media Development* 4 (2007): 40–46.

57. Jolyon Mitchell, "Peacemaking in the World of Film," *Media Development* 4 (2007): 13–16.

58. Bruce W. Dayton and Louis Kriesberg, *Conflict Transformation and Peace Building: Moving from Violence to Sustainable Peace* (London: Routledge, 2009).

59. Clifford Christians, "Non-violence in Philosophical and Media Ethics," in Richard Keeble, John Tulloch, and Florian Zollmann, eds., *Peace Journalism, War and Conflict Resolution* (New York: Peter Lang, 2010), 15–30.

60. Hans Küng, *Global Responsibility: In Search of a New World Ethics* (New York: Continuum, 1993); and Hans Küng, *A Global Ethics for a Global Politics and Economics* (New York: Oxford University Press, 1997).

61. Tod Lindberg, *The Political Teachings of Jesus* (New York: HarperCollins, 2007).

62. Young Ahn Kang, "Global Ethics and a Common Morality," *Philosophia Reformata* 71 (2006): 79–95. For another intellectually informed discussion of the golden rule, see Jeffrey Battles, *The Golden Rule* (New York: Oxford University Press, 1996).

63. Jolyon Mitchell, *Media Violence and Christian Ethics* (Cambridge, UK: Cambridge University Press, 2008). See also his *Promoting Peace, Inciting Violence: The Role of Religion and Media* (New York: Routledge, 2012).

64. As an illustration of the work accomplished to date and still needed, detailed case studies of violent conflict across the globe are included in Dayton and Kriesberg, *Conflict Transformation and Peace Building*; cf. peace journalism website (www.peacejournalism.org).

65. Lee, "Peace Journalism," 207.

5

PRIVACY

The right of individuals to protect their privacy has long been cherished in Western culture. Samuel Warren and Louis D. Brandeis gave this concept legal formulation in their famous essay "The Right to Privacy" in the December 1890 *Harvard Law Review*. Thirty-eight years later, Brandeis still maintained his concern:

> The makers of the U.S. Constitution undertook to secure conditions favorable to the pursuit of happiness. . . . They conferred, as against the Government, the right to be let alone–the most comprehensive of rights and the right most valued by civilized man.[1]

Since that time, the protection of personal privacy has received increasing legal attention and has grown in legal complexity. Although the word *privacy* does not appear in the U.S. Constitution, its defenders base its credence on the first eight amendments and the Fourteenth Amendment, which guarantee due process of law and protection against unreasonable intrusion.

The many laws safeguarding privacy now vary considerably among states and jurisdictions. Yet the general parameters can be defined as proscriptions "against deep intrusions on human dignity by those in possession of economic or governmental power."[2] Privacy cases within this broad framework generally are classified into four separate, though not mutually exclusive, categories: (1) intrusion on seclusion or solitude; (2) public disclosure of embarrassing private affairs; (3) publicity that places individuals in a false light; and (4) appropriation of an individual's name or likeness for commercial advantage.

However, for all of privacy's technical gains in case law and tort law, legal definitions are an inadequate foundation for the news business. Merely following the letter of the law certainly is not sufficient–presuming that the law can even be determined reasonably. There are several reasons why establishing an ethics of privacy that goes beyond the law is important in the gathering and distribution of news.

First, the law that conscientiously seeks to protect individual privacy excludes public officials. Brandeis himself believed strongly in keeping the national business open. Sunlight for him was the great disinfectant. And while he condemned intrusion in personal matters, he insisted on the exposure of all secrets bearing on public concern. In the United States, the courts have upheld that political personalities cease to be purely private persons, as well as that First Amendment values take precedence over privacy considerations. Court decisions have given the media extraordinary latitude in reporting on public persons. The U.S. Supreme Court in a 1964 opinion (*New York Times v. Sullivan*) concluded that even vilifying falsehoods relating to official conduct are protected unless made with actual malice or reckless disregard of the facts. The Court was profoundly concerned in its judgment not to impair what they considered the press's indispensable service to democratic life. In 1971, the Court applied its 1964 opinion to an individual caught up in a public issue—a Mr. Rosenbloom, who was arrested for distributing obscene books. Subsequent opinions have created some uncertainties, although continually reaffirming broad media protection against defamation suits. Thus, even while adhering to the law, the press has a nearly boundless freedom to treat elected officials unethically.

Second, the press has been given great latitude in defining newsworthiness. People who are catapulted into the public eye by events generally are classified with elected officials under privacy law. In broadly construing the Warren and Brandeis public interest exemption to privacy, the courts have ruled material as newsworthy because a newspaper or station carries the story. In nearly all important cases, the U.S. courts have accepted the media's definition. But is not the meaning of newsworthiness susceptible to shifting trends in news values and very dependent on presumed tastes and needs? Clearly, additional determinants are needed to distinguish gossip and voyeurism from information necessary to the democratic decision-making process.

Third, legal efforts beg many questions about the relationship between self and society. Democratic political theory since the sixteenth century has debated that connection and shifted over time from a libertarian emphasis on the individual to a twenty-first century version that is much more collectivistic in tone. Within these broad patterns, several narrower arguments have prevailed. Thomas Jefferson acquiesced to the will of the majority, whereas John Stuart Mill insisted that individuals must be free to pursue their own good in their own way. Two of the greatest minds ever to focus on American democracy, Alexis de Tocqueville and John Dewey, both centered their analysis of this matter on a viable public life. Likewise, Walter Lippmann worried about national prosperity in his *Public Opinion* and *The Public Philosophy*. Together these authors and others have identified an enduring intellectual problem that typically must be reduced and narrowed in order for legal conclusions to be drawn. Professor Thomas Emerson's summary is commonly accepted:

> The concept of a right to privacy attempts to draw a line between the individual and the collective, between self and society. It seeks to assure the individual a zone in which to be an individual, not a member of the community. In that zone he can think

his own thoughts, have his own secrets, live his own life, reveal only what he wants to the outside world. The right of privacy, in short, establishes an area excluded from the collective life, not governed by the rules of collective living.[3]

Shortcuts and easy answers arise from boxing off these two dimensions. Glib appeals to "the public's right to know" are a common way to cheapen the richness of the private–public relationship. Therefore, sensitive journalists who personally struggle with these issues in terms of real people put more demands on themselves than on considering what is technically legal. Such reporters recognize that privacy is not only a legal right but also a moral good. And they realize that ethically sound conclusions can emerge only when various privacy situations are faced in all their complexities. The cases that follow illustrate some of those intricacies and suggest ways of dealing with them responsibly. The first case introduces the challenges from the new online social networks to our traditional understanding of privacy. The second case deals with the press's responsibility to report effectively on the major post-September 11 attack on privacy, the USA PATRIOT Act. In this case, the massive amounts of data available through blogs complicate the protection of privacy to an unprecedented degree. The privacy situations in the third and fourth cases, involving small-town gossip and a tragic drowning accident, represent typical dilemmas involving both elected officials and persons who became newsworthy by events beyond their control.

Woven through the commentary are three moral principles that undergird an ethics of privacy for newspeople. The first principle promotes decency and basic fairness as nonnegotiable. Even though the law does not explicitly rule out falsehood, innuendo, recklessness, and exaggeration, human decency and basic fairness obviously do. The second moral principle proposes "redeeming social value" as a criterion for selecting which private information is worthy of disclosure. This guideline eliminates all appeals to prurient interests as devoid of newsworthiness. Third, the dignity of persons ought not be maligned in the name of press privilege. Whatever serves ordinary people best must take priority over some cause or slogan.[4]

At a minimum, this chapter suggests, private information in news accounts must pass the test of these three principles to be ethically justified, although the commentaries introduce the subtleties involved. In most surveys of public opinion and the media, privacy is a premiere issue if the press wishes to maintain its credibility. But privacy matters cannot be treated sanctimoniously by ethicists. They are among the most painful that humane reporters encounter. Often they surface among those journalists with a heart in a recounting of battles lost.

CASE 19. FACEBOOK AND SOCIAL MEDIA NETWORKS

The creation and rise of Facebook is already the stuff of Silicon Valley and social media legend. Developed by Harvard computer science student Mark Zuckerberg at age nineteen from his dorm room in early 2004, what started as a simple way for college students to interact with each other online exploded into an online phenomenon. Two weeks in, more than 4,300 people at Harvard had joined.[5] Soon after that, Facebook added a number of other elite schools, then more colleges and universities. By summer of the same year Zuckerberg had dropped out of school and headed west to Palo Alto to find his fortune and—as so many young Web 2.0 entrepreneurs put it—"change the world." One story goes that he spent his college money on servers to host all the new user data pouring in.

These were heady times once again for the tech industry and internet startups. The devastating dot-com crash of the late 1990s was becoming for many insiders just a receding memory as new "social" websites sought to move beyond the direct commerce of Web 1.0 by developing possibilities for human interactions on the net. Venture capitalists and investors embraced Zuckerberg and his rapidly expanding startup's vision to create a social utility that people all over the world could use to connect with each other. Still, Zuckerberg and other twenty-something entrepreneurs such as Firefox coder Blake Ross and YouTube founders Chad Hurley and Steven Chen—dubbed "baby billionaires" by *Rolling Stone*—understood that focus and smart business plans were required to scale up their ideas to millions of users.[6]

In 2005 Facebook opened up to high schools ("the horror!" cried many college users). By January 2006, the site received 250 million hits per day, and ranked ninth among all websites in overall traffic.[7] It opened to corporate networks, then to anyone by that September. Now at the helm of a juggernaut, in the wake of Google's $1.65 billion acquisition of YouTube, twenty-two-year-old CEO Zuckerberg and Facebook's board turned down Yahoo, which made a billion-plus offer to buy out the company. Growth accelerated: by mid-2007, more than one million new people signed up for Facebook weekly. Clearly, users continued to respond. Millions logged in daily to update their statuses, share photos of their experiences, and chat with friends and family. The voyeurism of being able to view all that delicious data about your friends probably didn't hurt.

Facebook's success invariably meant competition. After a bidding war with Google, in 2007 Microsoft purchased a 1.6 percent stake in the company for a whopping $240 million. Microsoft valued the startup at $15 billion. Industry tea-leaf readers suggested that fantastical sum was designed to price out any possible takeover efforts by other companies. Meanwhile, taking one step closer to becoming the go-to platform for the entire planet's social web needs, Facebook opened its code to developers, allowing anyone to create applications directly within Facebook's interface.

With the stakes now so high, Facebook came under increasing pressure to create revenue. Despite its $15 billion valuation, the company generated only $150 million annually in actual cash. Just as Google didn't generate significant income until it managed to pair advertising with search, Facebook too relied on advertising and the market research data created by its users who constantly shared their preferences, habits, and demographic data online. And it's here that things started to get tricky. In 2007 Facebook released a new advertising system called Beacon, which was designed to share with its users Facebook purchases and other data. It didn't give users a clear way to opt out, and Facebook adjusted the program in the wake of significant public outcry. Over the following years, this cycle of unilateral change, public outcry, and organizational adjustment recurred several times.

User backlash reached critical mass in late 2009 and the first half of 2010, fueled both by shifts in policy at Facebook, new additions to the website's expanding ad and net-working arsenal such as the Facebook Connect system, and one or two inadvertent but high-profile leaks of personal data by the company. At first, complaints over privacy issues largely originated from tech luminaries. With the brio typical of online debate, several pub-licly deleted their accounts in protest. Well-known internet entrepreneur Jason Calacanis declared the general sentiment via a rather vitriolic post on his own website that

> over the past month, Mark Zuckerberg, the hottest new card player in town, has over-played his hand. Facebook is officially "out," as in uncool, amongst partners, parents and pundits all coming to the realization that Zuckerberg and his company are—simply put—not trustworthy.

Others took a more measured, but nonetheless concerned, approach. Several members of Congress led by Senator Charles Schumer of New York wrote an open letter to Facebook expressing their reservations about its recent changes to privacy policies and the publication of its user data. Government agencies from other nations also began investigations into Facebook, for various reasons. The Norwegian, Canadian, and German governments all largely focused on privacy issues and possible violations of their respective national codes. The Electronic Frontier Foundation, the United States' leading legal defense group for online civil liberties and law, filed against court claims by Facebook that sought to criminalize the use of third-party services to aggregate Facebook data by Facebook's own users.[8]

By late spring in 2010, the debate also reached fever pitch among media outlets and the public at large. While Facebook changed default privacy options to opt-in during December 2009, in April it started making Facebook user data available to third-party sites. Ryan Singel, who covered Facebook's privacy issues at influential tech magazine *Wired*, captured the moment in "Facebook's Gone Rogue; It's Time for an Open Alternative." Several user groups sprung up that vowed to commit digital mass suicide of their Facebook accounts on given days; admittedly, the largest coalitions had only low five-figure member-ships. *Time* magazine put Facebook on the cover of all four of its May 31 editions, worldwide, with the lead story "How Facebook is Redefining Privacy." This saturation coverage, the majority critical, is likely what led Mark Zuckerberg to reveal, via a *Washington Post* op-ed, that Facebook would soon implement a revised privacy control system. Absent from the editorial, as many news outlets immediately noted, were any specifics or reversals of existing privacy policy at Facebook.

Despite ongoing concerns over privacy, Facebook continues to head for the stratosphere. By early 2010 the website surpassed Google as the internet's number one most-visited destination. It reached 1.3 billion users around the world in early 2014, with 48 percent logging on every day. On its public "Statistics" page, Facebook reported that over 70 percent of its use occurs outside the United States, and the site is translated into more than seventy languages. Moreover, over 1 million people develop applications for Facebook, and more than 700 million users access it via mobile devices.[9]

Yet many technologists have started to wonder if Facebook's stance on privacy is sowing the seeds of its own long-term destruction. On the one hand, it's highly unlikely that the world's largest website is going down anytime soon—especially as it continues to develop its advertising businesses based on ever-evolving ways of gleaning consumers' preferences from their digital selves. On the other hand, Facebook quickly superseded its competitor MySpace largely on the perceived strength of its user experience, features, and general elegance. Microsoft and Google, too, were once each considered invincible. The growing number of alternative social networking sites, many of which are direct responses to Facebook's privacy policies, may suggest that a new generation of young entrepreneurs see an opportunity, or at least a niche.

Even as Facebook's privacy crisis peaked in the spring of 2010, but is not fully resolved, four computer science undergrads from New York University made international headlines with their idea for a new social networking project, called Diaspora: "Facebook Challenged by Ambitious Upstarts" screamed one BBC News headline. Inspired during a lecture about online privacy by Eben Moglen, a renowned Columbia University law professor and founder of the Software Freedom Law Center, the four students set up a project fund on Kickstarter.com, aiming to raise $10,000. The worldwide response was overwhelming: in a couple of weeks Diaspora received over $180,000 in funding to develop a free, open-source social network system that would allow users to retain full control over their data. Diaspora's developers knew better than to challenge Facebook directly, commenting in the same BBC article that

> Facebook is not what we are going after. We are going after the idea there are all these centralized services where people are giving up their personal information. We want to put users back in control of what they share.[10]

In a *New York Times* article that began with the memorable question "How angry is the world at Facebook for devouring every morsel of personal information we are willing to feed it?" a Diaspora coder reflected on the intense response: "We were shocked. For some strange reason, everyone just agreed with the whole privacy thing."[11] Though Diaspora has died, for programmers of projects like it such as OneSocialWeb, maybe it isn't so far-fetched to believe that consumer concerns can drive a privacy revolution on the web.

Finally, on May 26, 2010, Facebook responded to the escalating pressure from users and privacy groups, and announced a simplified version of its privacy controls. Mark Zuckerberg said the revised settings would make it easy for users to know how much of their personal information was publicly accessible. The new settings help users to control whether the information is visible only to friends, friends of friends, or to everyone on the internet. "The settings have gotten complex, and it has become hard for people to use them effectively to control their settings," said Mr. Zuckerberg. These new settings "dramatically reduce access" to personal information. Those who want access "to anything specifically" will "have to ask permission."[12] Kevin Bankston, senior staff attorney for the Electronic Frontier Foundation (EFF) said the "changes are pretty good, though more is needed." But along with other critics, EFF still is concerned about third-party access to individual profile information. Amichai Schulman of the net security firm Imperva put the challenge this way: "Privacy does not coincide with the interests of Facebook creators."[13]

Social media were the heart and soul of the mid-2000 "Web 2.0" revolution: YouTube, Facebook, Twitter, Friendster, and so forth. But for all its human-focused promise, Web 2.0 was grafted onto the existing internet, which since the late 1990s was largely characterized by commercial enterprise. (Remember eBay was a web Cinderella in the 1990s.) Therefore, any consideration of Facebook and privacy issues has to start with an understanding of how Facebook actually works. Users tend to think of Facebook as a free, benevolent service. You sign up, agree to some terms—it only takes a few seconds, these days—and you're well on your way to creating a digital self to share with others.

Yet, at its core, Facebook is a for-profit company that must generate revenue to survive. As such, it offers a different product than might be suggested on the surface. At its most fundamental level, it is an advertising and marketing provider, not just a social network. In a 2009 interview with *BusinessWeek*, Facebook's Chief Operating Officer, Sheryl Sandberg, was unabashedly clear about the site's business model:

> Our business is advertising. There is a real imbalance right now: Between 28% and 29% of people's [free] time is spent online, but only 8% [to] 10% of the ad dollars are spent online. So there is this migration of ad dollars from other places going online. The question is how do advertisers make that useful? What we do is enable connections. We enable people to connect with users and provide advertising in a way that is not obtrusive. And so we're doing really well financially.[14]

It's worth adding that Sandberg arrived from Google, where she is credited with creating AdSense and AdWords, the company's main advertising applications, which generate the majority of its income.

Technology columnist Farhad Manjoo wisely noted that Mark Zuckerberg has consistently pushed users to share more information, more often. Rather than increasing privacy as Facebook grows, "indeed, the numbers tell the opposite story—Facebook's gradual erosion of privacy correlates precisely with growing activity on the site."[15] The more people using Facebook, and the more data they provide, the more useful the service is to Facebook's business partners. How concerned should users be that Facebook's business model seems to inversely correlate profits to privacy and user preferences? Is it disingenuous for Facebook to continue emphasizing publicly that it seeks only to construct the one-stop hub for our digital selves, in Zuckerberg's terms the "open graph" that connects people to each other through a benevolent network, when there are actually billions of dollars at stake? Is there a conflict of interest?

Given this additional understanding of Facebook, there are real concerns for privacy and civil liberties here. Facebook's public relations officers often note, fairly, that the website is voluntary. But does the site make it adequately clear what it does with material that users choose to post? Much of the criticism leveled at the company suggests that the public does not believe that it does. When members of Congress and advertisers alike mention their concerns, a key factor is that Facebook's current baseline stance is "opt-out," that is, a user by default would share everything, rather than have to opt-in to make the data public. In addition, the *New York Times* examined the increasing complexity of Facebook's privacy statement and settings. Its reporters found a bewildering maze of 50 settings, with over 170 total options.[16] While Facebook's 2005 privacy statement was 1,004 words long, it has grown to a bloated 6,910 words. These figures engender an obvious question: if Facebook really cares about users, why does it make it so hard to control what they share? The predicament of Facebook is that its repeated pledges to return to simplicity have not in themselves engendered confidence on the part of its users who have become skeptical of management's intentions.[17] In an interview with tech magazine *Wired*, Will Moffat, one of Openbook's creators, summarized his perspective: "They are trying to change society to make it less private. But given they have such a monopoly on social networking, I think they have a moral responsibility to respect social norms."[18]

Facebook's internal attitudes may not coordinate with the website's own ideology as a globe-spanning service that enables new ways of relating to others. Senior employees strike many as acerbic in their attitudes toward privacy. Zuckerberg himself is on record as taking a negative stance on whether privacy is still a social norm. Predictably, word flew around the internet at warp speed when Nick Bilton, a *New York Times* reporter, sent a message over Twitter that an unnamed Facebook employee had laughed when Bilton asked what Zuckerberg thought of privacy, responding simply "He doesn't believe in it." Others note that, fairly or not, Facebook has been quick to capitalize on many of the features of Twitter and other sites, adapting their innovations into the site. A final, much earlier series of events also may shed light on the company's underlying position on privacy. In 2008, after a long and bloody lawsuit, Facebook settled with ConnectU for $65 million. ConnectU's founders, three fellow Harvard alumni, alleged that in 2004 Mark Zuckerberg improperly stole their idea to create a social networking hub after they hired him to code their version of an interactive website for Harvard students.

VIRTUE: Empathy

The University of Michigan's Institute for Social Research finds a steep 47 percent drop in the "empathy index" (much of it in the last decade) among today's college students, increased bonding through the social media but sharp decline in emotional concern for others.

▪ What might be the causes?
▪ Is the decline in empathy an important social issue or not?

In a piece called "Your Facebook Profile Makes Marketers' Dreams Come True," tech journalist Eliot Van Buskirk got it right when he wrote that

> social networking feels free, but we pay for it in ways that may not be readily apparent. The rich personal data many of us enter into these networks is a treasure trove for marketers whose job it is to target us with ever-increasing precision.[19]

While that's not inherently wrong, it does create a new reason for reflection among many online social media users, young and old alike. How should we respond in an age when the Library of Congress is now cataloguing every tweet, or message, sent on Twitter?[20] According to two studies by University of California-Berkeley and the Pew Research Center's Internet and American Life Project, a shift is occurring. More than half of young adults are more concerned about privacy than they were in 2005, and twenty-somethings now exert noticeably more control over social networking privacy than older adults.[21] The Pew Internet Project's Mary Madden also suggests we should keep in mind

> what seems to rarely get mentioned—perhaps because we haven't yet found great ways to articulate the user experience—is that the choices people make to share personal information on social networking sites and other places online are highly contextual ones.[22]

And we can all always remember the perspective of media analysts such as Michael Bugeja, author of *Interpersonal Divide: The Search for Community in a Technological Age*, who gently remind us of the value of face-to-face communication.[23]

CASE 20. THE CONTROVERSIAL USA PATRIOT ACT

Six weeks after September 11, 2001, President George W. Bush signed the USA PATRIOT (Uniting and Strengthening America by Providing Appropriate Tools Required to Intercept and Obstruct Terrorism) Act into law. Written quickly and pushed through Congress in record time, the bill "shifted the Department of Justice's goal from prosecuting terrorists to preventing terrorism."[24] Then Attorney General John Ashcroft declared that the Act provides cautionary measures that preserve freedom by providing the means to stop terrorist activity even before it begins. "It's a fundamental and unprecedented shift," says Viet Dinh of the Georgetown University Law Center, "We are fighting guerrilla warfare on steroids, an attempt [by terrorists] to destabilize and defeat the Western order."[25]

Among its controversial provisions dealing with privacy are the following:

- It grants the FBI access to records maintained by businesses—ranging from medical, financial, library, and purchase records—if law-enforcement agents certify that the request is connected to a foreign intelligence investigation or is intended to protect against clandestine intelligence activities or international terrorism.
- It permits law enforcement to conduct unannounced "sneak and peek" searches that the target is notified of only at a later date.
- It activates SEVIS (Student Exchange Visitor Information System), which was first legislated in 1996. The records of international students must be kept up to date and made available because such students are considered a potential source of espionage and terrorism.

Supporters insist that the USA PATRIOT Act is an essential tool for investigating terrorists who have targeted the country. For its advocates, the Act only amends existing federal laws, that is, the federal criminal code and the Foreign Intelligence Surveillance Act. Rather than introduce new laws, its purpose is said to be threefold: (1) apply existing federal law and law enforcement to terrorism investigations; (2) allow intelligence-gathering and law-enforcement agencies to share information; and (3) enable the use of modern techniques and business practices to gather information. As U.S. Attorney Jan Paul Miller puts it:

> Before September 11, 2001, a federal law enforcement officer could apply for a wiretap for a drug dealer's telephone, but he couldn't for a terrorist. Our office could be investigating someone who was planning to blow up a building. I could talk to his co-conspirators or to Al-Qaida, if we knew where they were and could get a hold of them. But I could not walk down the hall and talk to the FBI if they were investigating the same person.[26]

From this perspective, the provisions of the USA PATRIOT Act are measured responses that enable law enforcement to keep up with post-September 11 threats while still preserving our civil rights.

To its critics, the USA PATRIOT Act is a vague, overbroad law of questionable constitutional validity enacted in a climate of fear. While the information-sharing provisions are valuable, it establishes a secret information-gathering process that does not require a showing of probable cause to obtain confidential records—only that the records are relevant to an investigation. As lawyer Steven Beckett argues: "That's a drastic change in the privacy rights in our country."[27] In addition, critics say the law opens the door to broader uses of information. It expands the definition of domestic terrorism so significantly that it could be used against anti-abortion protesters, environmentalists, AIDS activists, or other movements with a history of robust activism. In fact, according to Section 501 of a proposed revision of the USA PATRIOT Act, any persons can be taken off the street and brought to a secret military tribunal if their activity has suspicious intent.[28] Using the bill inappropriately to prosecute standard criminal suits "guts the Fourth Amendment."[29]

One year after 9/11, the federal government held 762 immigrants, many for months, without charges or counsel. Not one of them was prosecuted for terrorism. Attorney General John Ashcroft refused to disclose information on how the government used library, business, computer, and other records of individuals. In one example that made the news, Jose Padilla, a U.S. citizen, was arrested after returning from a trip to Pakistan. He was held in a military jail and refused an attorney until a judge ordered the government to allow him counsel.

Major provisions of the USA PATRIOT Act were set to expire in December 2005. The House passed a bill that would have made most of the provisions permanent, but the Senate was wary. Democratic Senator Russ Feingold, who had issued the lone vote against the Act in 2001, rallied forty other Democrats and four Republicans to filibuster its renewal.[30] The legislators wanted to extend debate to address the protection of civil liberties. By March 2006, the House and Senate reached a compromise that made most of the Act's provisions permanent while adding some safeguards. A vocal minority voted against the bill, convinced that the legislation was still seriously flawed.[31] Opposition has continued, on the grounds that the Act allows the government to secretly obtain a range of personal records, in violation of the First Amendment and the separation of powers doctrine. But after overwhelming majority votes in the House and Senate for a four-year USA PATRIOT Act extension, President Obama signed the legislation on May 27, 2011.

Surveillance in a democratic society is a crucial issue. Clearly, the news media should be vitally involved in promoting awareness of it. But, rather than playing a substantial role in educating the public about the legislation's pros and cons, the media's record has been mixed.

In a study of the news media's role in the passage of the legislation, researchers at the University of Washington have concluded that the media largely mimicked the Bush administration.[32] They have documented that then President Bush and the Attorney General engaged in a pattern of strategic public communications with the goal of pressuring Congress to adopt the proposed legislation. Their overall purpose was to engender confidence among citizens that the administration had an effective strategy for countering terrorism. The researchers' findings indicate that communications from the Bush administration "were echoed by the press, and created an environment in which Congress had little choice but to pass the USA PATRIOT Act with remarkable speed."[33]

Project Censored, an annual Sonoma State University study run by several hundred faculty and students, named "Homeland Security" as one of the most important, yet little reported, stories of the year during its passage and then during its renewal in 2005–2006. During the legislative renewal cycle of 2011, "Homeland Security" no longer qualified as a "Most Important Story." In fact, many of the Act's dangers have been largely ignored by the mainstream press—except on its op-ed pages. The *New York Times* is the exception and sets the standard for all news media to follow. It pays close attention to the ways the Act is implemented. It editorializes against the government's power to search financial records, conduct roving wiretaps, and track terrorism suspects.[34]

Even though the press has not aggressively investigated the issues itself, it has been responsive to specific agencies and to individual voices. The American Civil Liberties Union and the American Library Association adamantly oppose the loss of civil liberties and are frequently cited. The Center for Public Integrity leaked Justice Department proposals for tightening the USA PATRIOT Act and continues to update the press on its status. The National Association of Foreign Student Advisors has concluded that the United States will no longer be the destination of choice for international students, and higher education will lose 15 to 30 percent of its future graduate students to Australia, Canada, and the United Kingdom. Some of these unintended consequences make it into the news. A former *New York Times* reporter has started the Transactional Records Access Clearinghouse, a gigantic database that obtains information through the Freedom of Information Act; the organization sued John Ashcroft to release terrorism data.[35] The *Herald News* of Paterson, New Jersey, became very active in the fight to gain information about the hundreds of Arab immigrants detained in their city. Although "the government's obsessive secrecy made it hard to report this story," the paper was able to expose the plight of detainees in a community with large Palestinian and Muslim populations.[36]

In addition to news about the Act's implementation and consequences, and beyond legal analyses of it, the press ought to be reporting on this legislation in ethical terms. Understanding the moral dimensions of privacy provides the public with a foundation for coming to grips with the law and politics of the Act. Privacy is a moral good because privacy is a precondition for developing a unique sense of self. Violating it therefore violates human dignity. Privacy is a moral good in a political sense also, in that respecting privacy distinguishes democratic from totalitarian societies. As persons, we need privacy, both for our own dignity and for our social relationships with others. Healthy human existence is impossible without it.[37] Educating the public on the ethics of privacy accomplishes the long-term goal of taking the USA PATRIOT Act out of political disputes and legal wrangling and focusing on the central substantive issues instead.[38]

CASE 21. BLOGGERS' CODE OF ETHICS

The weblog has arrived, with the great virtual space in which millions of blogs exist called the "blogosphere."[39] The mainstream media have been integrating blogs into their channel mix, and now this computer-mediated technology is a recognized source of news, political commentary, religion, entertainment, and advertising.

Is a code of blogging ethics necessary or even possible? Rebecca Flood proposed one in 2002 in *The Weblog Handbook*, and Jonathon Dube, founder of CyberJournalist, maintains a code for online journalism patterned after the Society of Professional Journalists Code of Ethics (www.cyberjournalist.net). Norway's Morten Rad-Hendriksen of the "Pink and Yellow" digital media company, proposes a code of ethics for "Online Content Creators" that parallels the Norwegian Press Association Code and includes such standards as separating fact from opinion and giving opponents full opportunity to respond (www.mor10.com/code-of-ethics-for-bloggers). These three are explicitly tied to online journalism, and Martin Kuhn argues for a broader code that is helpful to political blogs but is also credible to bloggers more generally. He surveyed the field of computer-mediated communication (http://blogethics2004.blogspot.com) and created a system of moral imperatives:[40]

PROPOSED CODE OF BLOGGING ETHICS

Promote Interactivity

- Post to your blog on a regular basis.
- Visit and post on other blogs.
- Respect blog etiquette.
- Attempt to be entertaining, interesting, and/or relevant.

Promote Openness

- Do not restrict access to your blog.
- Do not self-censor by removing posts or comments once they are published.
- Allow and encourage comments on your blog.

Strive for Factual Truth

- Never intentionally deceive others.
- Be accountable for what you post.

Be as Transparent as Possible

- Reveal your identity as much as possible.
- Reveal your personal affiliations and conflicts of interest.
- Cite and link to all sources referenced in each post.

Promote the "Human" Element in Blogging

- ■ Minimize harm to others when posting information.
- ■ Promote community by linking to other blogs and keeping a blogroll.
- ■ Build relationships by responding to e-mails and comments regularly.

When the ethical principles of blogging are debated, some stories from blogging and politics are typically used as examples for and against. Matthew Drudge is a talk-radio host and internet journalist. His *Drudge Report* on the web is financed by advertising. The *Drudge Report* was the first to break the news in 1998 of the Clinton–Lewinsky scandal. By 2002, his website had reached the one-billion-page view mark.

On U.S. Election Day (November 2, 2004), several blogs ran exit-poll numbers throughout the day that erroneously predicted an easy victory for John Kerry. "Many of the sites posting exit poll information stressed the provisional nature of incomplete polls. For example, the poll numbers on Wonkette.com came with the disclaimer: 'All with grains of salt. Huge tablespoons of salt.'"[41] But most simply reported the data, trusting website users to interpret them accurately:

> Many sites displaying poll numbers experienced surges in visitors: Slate.com traffic increased from 153,000 visitors on November 1 to 412,000 on election day. Wonkette.com increased to 200,000 from 6000, and the *Drudge Report* drew nearly 700,000 visitors according to Nielsen/NetRatings.[42]

During the 2012 campaign, stories often moved from blogs to the mainstream media. As Alex Jones of Harvard's Shorenstein Center on the Press put it: "Things start on the fringes of the blogosphere, become the buzz, and then move to cable."[43] Blogging proved to be valuable on the whole, but running the early exit polls distinguished this medium sharply from the traditional news outlets, where verification of data is considered essential to their credibility.

Based on this background of thinking and experience, the Radio Television Digital News Association (RTDNA) adopted a set of "Social Media and Blogging Guidelines." These ethical standards are introduced in this way: "Social media and blogs are important elements of journalism. They narrow the distance between journalists and the public. They encourage lively, immediate and spirited discussion. They can be vital news-gathering and news-delivery tools."[44] As an association of media professionals, the Ethics Committee of RTDNA, in preparing the guidelines, focused them on online journalism. Therefore, this summary of the major principles: "As a journalist you should uphold the same professional and ethical standards of fairness, accuracy, truthfulness, transparency and independence when using social media as you do on-air and on all digital news platforms."[45]

Using this material and other cases of blogging and politics, what ethical principles ought to be included in a weblog code of ethics? Assume for the sake of discussion that the proponents of such a code are right, and codes are both credible and possible. Is Kuhn correct that the two primary principles are truth and human dignity? Truthtelling means for him "factual truth." Never intentionally deceive. Cite all relevant links to your sources. Do not erase posts, and encourage comments and reaction that help to keep your information valid. Promoting human dignity is especially important for him in a technology that tends to be anonymous and lacking in accountability. Adapting human dignity to blogging, he recommends two major principles ("Be as transparent as possible," and "Promote the human element"), each with three guidelines for implementation.[46]

Jane Singer also makes truth a primary principle in blogging ethics.[47] She observes that the codes of journalism ethics around the world include truth as a central norm. Therefore, for bloggers who concentrate on the same areas as journalists (i.e., politics, policy, and civic information), a similar standard is reasonable. She notes that people who use blogs see them as quite credible, but think of truth differently than those in mainstream news. Blogs are considered a source of open information without spin and censorship. Blogs are understood to be independent and designed for people who prefer to trust their own judgment rather than accept the narrow agenda and constraints of the usual sources:

> Bloggers do not see truth as resting on the decisions of one autonomous individual or groups of individuals within a news organization or anywhere else. Instead, bloggers see truth as emerging from shared, collective knowledge, from an electronically enabled marketplace of ideas. . . . The bloggers' truth is created collectively rather than hierarchically. Truth, in this view, is the result of discourse rather than a prerequisite to it.[48]

The RTDNA guidelines also put "Truth and Fairness" first. RTDNA elaborates for reporters using weblogs:

> Information gleaned online should be confirmed just as you must confirm scanner traffic or phone tips before reporting them. If you cannot independently confirm critical information, reveal your sources; tell the public how you know what you know and what you cannot confirm. Don't stop there. Keep seeking confirmation. You should not leave the public "hanging." Lead the public to completeness and understanding.[49]

Transparency is an important standard also: "You should not write anonymously or use an avatar or username that cloaks your real identity on newsroom or personal websites. You are responsible for everything you say. Commenting or blogging anonymously compromises this core principle,"[50] that is, the principle of Accountability and Transparency.

Bloggers generally resist rules established by others. Jeff Jarvis, former columnist and editor and now blogger, is typical:

What I have a problem with is the idea that one person presumes to come up with an ethical code for an entire culture. This is complex and can't be handled in a single code. It's as complex as human character.[51]

For bloggers who are not professionals connected through associations and business networks, Kuhn believes that the code he proposes can be adopted personally and made transparent in one's weblog practices. Also, A-list bloggers are key resources for both citizens and journalists, and if they actively use and promote codes, it will enhance influence and credibility. The RTDNA code integrates online journalism into the newsroom. It demonstrates how weblog technology can be used with the same integrity in news as are print and broadcast technologies now.[52]

CASE 22. DEAD BODY PHOTO

John Harte was the only photographer working on Sunday, July 28, at the *Bakersfield Californian*. After some routine assignments, he heard on the police scanner about a drowning at a lake twenty-five miles northeast of Bakersfield. When he arrived on the scene, divers were still searching for the body of five-year-old Edward Romero, who had drowned while swimming with his brothers.

The divers finally brought up the dead boy, and the sheriff kept onlookers at bay while the family and officials gathered around the open body bag. The television crew did not film that moment, but Harte ducked under the sheriff's arms and shot eight quick frames with his motor-driven camera.[53]

The *Californian* had a policy of not running pictures of dead bodies. So Managing Editor Robert Bentley was called into the office on Sunday evening for a decision. Concluding that the picture would remind readers to be careful when kids are swimming, Bentley gave his approval. On Monday, Harte transmitted the picture over the Associated Press wire "after a 20-minute argument with an editor who was furious we ran the picture . . . and accused [Harte] of seeking glory and an AP award."[54]

Readers bombarded the 80,000 circulation daily with 400 phone calls, 500 letters, and 80 cancellations. The *Californian* even received a bomb threat, forcing evacuation of the building for ninety minutes.

Distraught by the intensity of the reaction, Bentley sent around a newsroom memo admitting that "a serious error of editorial judgment was made. . . . We make mistakes—and this clearly was a big one." He concluded that their most important lesson was "the stark validation of what readers—and former readers—are saying not just locally but across the country: that the news media are seriously out of touch with their audiences."

For photographer John Harte, Bentley's contrition was "disappointing to me and many of my coworkers." And editorial page editor Ed Clendaniel of the *Walla Walla* (Washington) *Union Bulletin* was not apologetic either about running it in his paper, even though it was out of context. "First, the foremost duty of any paper is to report the news," he argued, adding:

> One of the hard facts of life is that the world is filled with tragic moments as well as happy moments. . . . Second, we believe the photograph does more to promote water safety than 10,000 words could ever hope to accomplish.

Later Bentley entered Harte's photo in the Pulitzer Prize competition. "I really don't see any contradiction," he explained. "I think the photograph should never have been published. . . . But the Pulitzer Prize is given for journalistic and technical excellence. It is not given for reader approval."

Michael J. Ogden, executive director of the *Providence Journal-Bulletin*, condemns photographs that capitalize on human grief:

> I can understand the printing of an auto accident picture as an object lesson. What I can't understand is the printing of sobbing wives, mothers, children. . . . What is the value of showing a mother who has just lost her child in a fire? Is this supposed to have a restraining effect on arsonists? I am sure that those who don't hesitate to print such pictures will use the pious pretense of quoting Charles A. Dana's famous dictum that "whatever the Divine Providence permitted to occur I was not too proud to print." Which is as peachy a shibboleth to permit pandering as I can imagine.[55]

But Ogden is a rare editor. Every day in newspapers and on television, photographs and film footage emphasize grief and tragedy. Though Harte's photo did not win the Pulitzer, in fact, professional awards are regularly given to grisly pictures regardless of whether they pander to morbid tastes.

Defending photos of this type usually centers on newsworthiness. The broken-hearted father whose child was just run over, a shocked eight-year-old boy watching his teenage brother gunned down by police, the would-be suicide on a bridge—all pitiful scenes that communicate something of human tragedy and are therefore to be considered news. Photojournalists sum up a news event in a manner the mind can hold, capturing that portrayal "rich in meaning because it is a trigger image of all the emotions aroused by the subject."[56] Harte, in this case, acted as an undaunted professional, fulfilling his role as reporter on everyday affairs—including the unpleasantries. From the photographer's perspective, to capture the newsworthy moment is an important self-discipline. Photographers are trained not to panic but to bring forth the truth as events dictate. They are schooled to be visual historians and not freelance medics or family counselors.

On what grounds, however, can the photographer's behavior be condoned in the Bakersfield drowning? The principals at the scene tried to prevent him from intruding, though, it should be granted, the authorities' judgment is not always correct. The warning-bell thesis was generally used by the picture's proponents, asserting that the photo could make other parents more safety conscious. However, this utilitarian appeal to possible consequences has no factual basis.[57] Perhaps in the name of reporting news, the photojournalist in this case was actually caught in those opportunistic professional values that build circulation by playing on the human penchant for morbidity.

No overarching purpose emerges that can ameliorate the direct invasion of privacy and insensitivity for these innocent victims of tragedy. In all jurisdictions, the reporting of events of public concern involves no legal issue of privacy invasion. But it is here that the photographer should consider the moral guideline that suffering individuals are entitled to dignity and respect, despite the fact that events may have made them part of the news.

Photojournalism is an extremely significant window on our humanity and inhumanity. In pursuing its mission, the ethical conflict typically revolves around the need for honest visual information and for respecting a person's privacy. Bob Greene of the *Chicago Tribune* is exaggerating only slightly in calling the Harte picture "pornography." "Because of journalistic factors they could not control," he wrote, "at the most terrible moment of their lives," the Romeros were exposed to the entire country.[58] The older brother's hysteria for not watching his little brother closely enough is presented without compassion before an audience who had no right to become a participant in this traumatizing event for a suffering family. And even those who find the photo acceptable are upset by the context: the *Californian* printing the photo right next to a headline about teen killings by a satanic cult.[59]

Figure 5.1

Source: The *Bakersfield Californian*, July 29, 1985, p. 1. Photo by John Harte. Reprinted by permission.

NOTES

1. *Olmstead v. United States*, 277 U.S. 438, 478 (1928). Brandeis dissenting.
2. *Briscoe v. Reader's Digest Association*, 4 Cal. 3d 529, 93 Cal. Reptr. 866, 869 (1971).
3. Thomas I. Emerson, *The System of Free Expression* (New York: Vintage Books, 1970), 545.
4. Candace Gauthier presents two principles as guidelines for the press and privacy: respect for persons and avoid causing unjustified harm in her "Understanding and Respecting Privacy," in Christopher Meyers, ed., *Journalism Ethics: A Philosophical Approach* (Princeton, NJ: Princeton University Press, 2010), ch. 15, 215–230.
5. Steven Levy, "Facebook Grows Up," *Newsweek* 150: 8/9 (2007): 40–46.
6. David Kushner, "The Baby Billionaires of Silicon Valley," *Rolling Stone*, November 16, 2006, www.davidkushner.com/article/413/.
7. Michael Bugeja, "Facing the Facebook," *The Chronicle of Higher Education*, January 23, 2006, http://chronicle.com/article/Facing-the-Facebook/46904/.
8. See Adi Kamdar, "How to Protect Your Privacy from Facebook's Graph," *Electronic Frontier Foundation*, January 18, 2013, www.eff.org/deeplinks/2013/01/how-protect-your-privacy-facebooks-graph-search.
9. See Facebook's latest statistics at www.statista.com/statistics/264810/number-of-monthly-active-facebook-users-worldwide/. For an overview of this growth, see "Facebook: 10 Years of Social Networking in Numbers," *The Guardian DataBlog*, February 4, 2014, www.theguardian.com/news/datablog/2014/feb/04/facebook-in-numbers-statistics.
10. Jonathan Frewin, "Facebook Challenged by Ambitious Upstarts," *BBC News*, May 23, 2010. Also see Jenna Wortham, "Founders of Diaspora, Intended as the Anti-Facebook, Move On," *New York Times*, August 27, 2012, and *Stop Facebook from Spying on You and Other Ways to Protect Your Online Privacy* (Bottom Line Publications: Kindle eBook, 2015).
11. Kristen Burnham, "Facebook Privacy Changes Explained," *Information Week*, May 24, 2014. See Vindu Goel, "Some Privacy Please? Facebook, Under Pressure, Gets the Message," *New York Times*, May 22, 2004, www.nytimes.com/2014/05/23/technology/facebook-offers-privacy-checkup-to-all-1-28-billion-users.html.
12. Quotations and details from Jenna Wortham, "Facebook Unveils Simplified Approach to Privacy," *New York Times*, May 26, 2010.
13. Quoted in "Facebook Changes are 'Not Enough,' Say Groups," *BBC News*, May 27, 2010, www.bbc.co.uk/news/10171575.
14. "Facebook Gets Down to Business," *BusinessWeek*, April 2, 2009, p. 30. For the overall framework, see Bala A. Masa, "Social Media and the Invasion of Privacy by Corporations," in Jim Willis and Bala A. Masa, eds., *From Twitter to the Tahrir Square: Ethics in Social and New Media Communications*, 2 vols. (Santa Barbara, CA: Praeger ABC-CLIO, 2014), 203–210.
15. Farhad Manjoo, "Can We Get Some Privacy?" *Slate.com*, May 13, 2010, www.slate.com/id/2253827.
16. Christian Fuchs, "What Is Facebook's New Privacy Policy All About? More Complexity," September 17, 2011, http://fuchs.uti.at/699/.
17. "Facebook Privacy: A Bewildering Tangle of Options," *New York Times*, May 12, 2010. See also Martin Kaste, "Facebook's Dilemma: When Privacy Hits the Fan," *All Things Considered*, May 25, 2010, www.npr.org/templates/story/story.php?storyId=127118179.
18. Ryan Singel, "Openbook Creator Offers Privacy Design Solution for Facebook," *Wired*, May 24, 2010, www.wired.com/2010/05/openbook-facebook-design/.
19. Jessi Hempel and Beth Kowitt, "How Facebook is Taking Over Our Lives," *Fortune* 159:4: 48–56.
20. Eliot Van Buskirk, "Your Facebook Profile Makes Marketers' Dreams Come True," *Wired*, April 28, 2009, www.wired.com/epicenter/2009/04/your-facebook-profile-makes-marketers-dreams-come-true/.
21. "Twitter Donates Entire Tweet Archive to Library of Congress," Library of Congress News Release PR 10-081, April 14, 2010, www.loc.gov/today/pr/2010/10-081.html.
22. Laura Holson, "Tell-All Generation Learns to Keep Things Offline," *New York Times*, May 8, 2010, www.nytimes.com/2010/05/09/fashion/09privacy.html.

23. Mary Madden, "Facebook's Latest About-Face," Pew Internet, Pew Research Center, November 30, 2007, www.pewinternet.org/2007/11/30/facebooks-latest-about-face/.

24. Associated Press, "Some Tech Gen Youth Go Offline," *Wired News*, October 6, 2009, http://archive.wired.com/techbiz/media/news/2006/10/71918?currentpage=all.

25. Tony Carnes, "Curbing Big Brother: Christians Urge Ashcroft to Respect Freedom in Surveillance Law," *Christianity Today*, September 2003, 27.

26. Ibid.

27. Jodi Heckel, "Patriot Act Debated at UI College of Law," *News Gazette*, September 16, 2003, B1.

28. Ibid., B2.

29. Eric Lichtblau, "In a Reversal, Ashcroft Lifts Secrecy of Data," *New York Times*, September 17, 2003, www.nytimes.com/2003/09/18/politics/18PATR.html.

30. Ryan Singel, "A Chilly Response to Patriot II," *Wired*, February 12, 2003, http://archive.wired.com/politics/law/news/2003/02/57636.

31. Sheryl Gay Stolberg, "Once-Lone Foe of Patriot Act Has Company," *New York Times*, December 19, 2005, www.nytimes.com/2005/12/19/politics/oncelone-foe-of-patriot-act-has-company.html.

32. Sheryl Gay Stolberg, "Senate Passes Legislation to Renew Patriot Act," *New York Times*, March 3, 2006, www.nytimes.com/2006/03/03/politics/03patriot.html.

33. Erica S. Graham et al., "Follow the Leader: The Bush Administration, News Media, and Passage of the U.S.A. Patriot Act," paper presented at the Association for Education in Journalism and Mass Communication conference, Kansas City, Missouri, July 2003. The research included a content analysis of fifteen leading newspapers from around the country and the nightly evening newscasts of ABC, NBC, and CBS for a total of 230 texts (pp. 12–13).

34. Ibid., 2.

35. For example, "Editorial: Patriot Act Excesses," *New York Times*, October 8, 2009, A28, www.nytimes.com/2009/10/08/opinion/08thu1.html.

36. Michael Scherer, "Keeping TRAC: A Tool for Mining Federal Data," *Columbia Journalism Review* (March/April 2003): 10.

37. Hilary Burke, "A Question of Security: Blanket Security Is Not the Answer," *Columbia Journalism Review* (November/December 2002): 80.

38. For elaboration, see Clifford Christians, "The Ethics of Privacy," in Christopher Meyers, ed., *Journalism Ethics: A Philosophical Approach* (Princeton, NJ: Princeton University Press), ch. 14, 213–214.

39. For details on this case and theoretical background, see Martin Kuhn, "Interactivity and Prioritizing the Human: A Code of Blogging Ethics," *Journal of Mass Media Ethics* 22:1 (2007): 18–36. Also see David D. Perlmutter and Mary Schoen, "'If I Break a Rule, What Do I Do, Fire Myself?' Ethics Codes of Independent Blogs," *Journal of Mass Media Ethics* 22:1 (2007): 37–48.

40. Kuhn, "Interactivity and Prioritizing the Human," 27–30.

41. Matt Carlson, "Blogs and Journalistic Authority," *Journalism Studies* 8:2 (April 2007): 264–279.

42. Ibid., 269.

43. David Usborne, "Bloggers Rewrite Political Opinion," *Seattle Post-Intelligencer*, November 2, 2004, B9.

44. RTNDA, "Social Media and Blogging Guidelines," *Media Ethics*, 21:2 (Spring 2010): 12, www.rtdna.org/article/social_media_blogging_guidelines. For RTNDA/RTDNA Code of Ethics and Professional Conduct, see www.rtdna.org and www.rtdna.org/content/rtdna_code_of_ethics. The Online News Association encourages individual bloggers and non-traditional news organizations to construct their own code of ethics; see Online News Association, "Build Your Own Ethics Codes," http://journalists.org/resources/build-your-own-ethics-code/.

45. RTNDA, "Social Media and Blogging Guidelines," 12.

46. Kuhn, "Interactivity and Prioritizing the Human," 33–34.

47. Jane B. Singer, "Contested Autonomy," *Journalism Studies* 8:1 (February 2007): 79–95; Cecilia Friend and Jane B. Singer, *Online Journalism Ethics* (Armonk, NY: M. E. Sharpe, 2007); also see Jane

B. Singer et al., *Participatory Journalism: Guarding Open Gates at Online Newspapers* (Malden, MA: Wiley-Blackwell, 2011), ch. 7.

48. Singer, "Contested Autonomy," 85.

49. RTNDA, "Social Media and Blogging Guidelines," 12.

50. Ibid.

51. Quoted in Kuhn, "Interactivity and Prioritizing the Human," 25.

52. Many new books and manuals are appearing that describe how blogging can be used effectively in business. But they typically do not include the establishing of ethical standards as an important step in the process. See, for example, Alex Newson et al., *Blogging and Other Social Media: Exploiting the Technology and Protecting the Enterprise* (Farnham, UK: Gower Publishing Limited, 2009). For a review of the issues that both online journalism and business face, see Kord Davis, *Ethics of Big Data: Balancing Risk and Innovation* (Sebastopol, CA: O'Reilly Media, Inc., 2012).

53. "Graphic Excess," *Washington Journalism Review* 8:1 (January 1986): 10–11. In 1994, a court case alleging that John Harte interfered with a rescue operation of a drowned boy in a local canal (*California v. John Harte*) was dismissed by a judge (see *News Photographer* [January 1995]: 16).

54. For the quotations and details in this case, unless otherwise noted, see "Grief Photo Reaction Stuns Paper," *News Photographer* (March 1986): 16–22. For John Harte's reflections, see "The Hart Park Drowning Photo," December 10, 2014, https://johnhartephoto.wordpress.com/2014/12/10/the-hart-park-drowning-photo/.

55. John Hohenberg, *The News Media: A Journalist Looks at His Profession* (New York: Holt, Rinehart and Winston, 1968), 212.

56. Harold Evans, *Pictures on a Page: Journalism, Graphics and Picture Editing,* rev. ed. (London: Pimlico, 1997), 5.

57. Obviously beneficent results sometimes follow. As in Stanley Foreman's *Boston Herald-American* photos of a baby and woman falling from a broken fire escape, better safety standards and tighter inspection can be initiated after tragedies.

58. Bob Greene, "News Business and Right to Privacy Can Be at Odds," 1985–1986, report of the SPJ-SDX Ethics Committee, 15.

59. This case study also appears in Paul Martin Lester's *Photojournalism: An Ethical Approach* (Mahwah, NJ: Lawrence Erlbaum, 1991), ch. 14. He takes, primarily, the approach that Harte's photo fell under a categorical imperative to report what happened in as powerful a manner as possible.

THE HEART OF THE MATTER IN NEWS ETHICS

You remember the ancient wisdom: "Give someone a fish and save the day; teach someone how to fish and secure a lifetime." *Media Ethics* follows that good thinking. We've gone through cases and theory and five major issues in the news, with the purpose of teaching you to do ethics yourself. Mini-ethicists know how to fish, and not just eat when hungry from the textbook's cafeteria.

Doing ethics means reaching justified conclusions. It means going carefully through all the steps of the process and making the best decision each time. Ethicists of credibility don't just follow their intuitions or make snap judgments or condemn the scruffy and disagreeable people. They gather the facts, clarify the important values involved, choose the most appropriate principle, decide who deserves support, and then make a decision that can stand the light of day. Whether or not you experience any of the twenty-two cases or their equivalents in the future, you should have an understanding of what counts as moral questions and how to deal with them. When truth or social justice or conflict of interest or privacy is debated in the newsroom and in public, a mini-ethicist is able to contribute an intelligent perspective.

What really matters, then, if you want to do media ethics for a lifetime? Whether as a news professional or a citizen, what quality is indispensable? Keeping up with the news is crucial, that is, being informed rather than living with clichés and gossip. Knowing theory is important. Yes, no question. But the heart of the matter is moral discernment. Insight. Wisdom. Seeing through to the nub of the issue. In the standard definition, moral discernment means discovering which actions promote human fulfillment. Not just intelligence that organizes facts, but assessment, evaluation, making distinctions. We're told not to just work harder, but smarter. The same idea here with doing ethics: those with moral discernment identify a problem, put it in the right proportions, and find a solution that is appropriate. To do ethics over a lifetime requires the quality of moral discernment.

Moral discernment does not mean you see immorality everywhere and are outraged by it, filled with condemnation. That's a hot-tempered moralist. Moral discernment doesn't mean you ignore the political and economic dimensions of news, and speak only of moral turpitude in government and business. Discernment is a scalpel rather than a sledgehammer. It's keen and sharp rather than a bludgeon. It calls for appropriate punishment, but not the dissolution of a profession or rejection of an entire social order.

If moral discernment is *sine qua non* for being an ethicist, where is it found and how can it be sustained over a career or lifetime? Aristotle speaks in his own way to the question: it's grounded in habit. By playing the drums we become an accomplished drummer. Virtue is practiced day by day. The analogue is physical fitness: exercise and the right diet year after year—not just a one-time decision—means a healthy body. For Confucius, when we walk the pathway of equilibrium and harmony, our character is nurtured into wholeness. As we learn the general morality, and observe moral insight in others, moral discernment is being cultivated. The ethical theorists of this book agree that we are moral beings, that the human species has a moral dimension. When this native human capacity is exercised, the result is moral discernment.

This book is academic; it teaches theoretical moral reasoning. It describes intellectual procedures and gives facts on the ground. But this is only introductory to the heart of the matter. *Media Ethics* intends to launch a thicker understanding of cases and dilemmas in the news. Moral discernment is the ultimate aim, and those stirrings in your conscience are signs that it's coming to life.

2

PERSUASION IN ADVERTISING

Each year, on a Sunday early in February, millions gather to watch the Super Bowl, an advertising extravaganza. Oh, and there's a football game too. In 2016, an estimated 111.9 million viewers watched the average minute of the game between the Denver Broncos and the Carolina Panthers, making it the third-most watched broadcast in television history. And, those numbers didn't include internet streaming. CBS set a new streaming record with an average 1.4 million viewers per minute, and reported that, with the addition of those viewers, 167 million viewers watched all or part (at least six minutes) of the game. That made Super Bowl 50 the most-watched broadcast in television history.[1] Peak viewing occurred not during the game, but during the half-time show, which featured Coldplay, Beyoncé, and Bruno Mars.

At a moment in time when we are purportedly in the "post-television age," some fifty-three brands, including seventeen Super Bowl "rookies," made the decision that paying $5 million for a thirty-second spot was a sound strategy.[2] Brands purchased sixty-two ads for a total of thirty-nine minutes and fifteen seconds of advertising, 22 percent of the total broadcast.[3] According to the executive vice president and director of strategic planning at McCann Erickson, the Super Bowl is "less about the relevance of a message but more about the entertainment quotient. [Marketers] aren't selling a product; they are creating brand buzz."[4] A writer in *Fortune* noted that "companies spend so much on Super Bowl ads chasing the . . . hope that after the game, people will be talking about them."[5] Another advertiser agreed: "It's never about the Super Bowl ad itself. It's the best online buzz for the buck."[6]

Live polling to determine the "most popular" or "most buzzed about" commercials took place on a number of sites; winners varied. However, according to the *USA Today* Ad Meter, one of the most-watched sites, Hyundai was at the top, the first time in twenty-eight years an automobile topped big advertisers such as Anheuser Busch and PepsiCo.[7]

What about the effectiveness of those Super Bowl spots? Ad agency chief Linda Kaplan Thayer noted that in the absence of real water coolers around which to gather information about "how they'd done," advertisers would go to their "digital water coolers."[8] A writer in *USA Today* wrote:

> [E]veryone measures everything to see if they got their money's worth. Advertisers will count tweets. They'll count the number of folks who visit their Facebook pages. They'll count visits to the brand. . . . They'll measure the "buzz" factor online—seeking a running tab on how often their company or their Super Bowl ad gets mentioned.[9]

Granted, the Super Bowl is not typical network fare; it is both a football *and* an advertising showcase. Thinking about this "event," what can we learn about advertising? First, we recognize that advertising is an economic power in the United States, and globally. Advertising is a major player in the global economy. It is estimated that global advertising expenditures in 2016 will reach approximately $525 billion;[10] $200 billion will be spent in the United States.[11] These expenditures alone stand as testimonial to the value of advertising as a strategic marketing tool.

Amid trade press conversations about return on investment, metrics, tracking studies, and so on, it is easy to lose track of advertising as anything *other* than a marketing tool. Yet, in a discussion of the development of modern American advertising, historian Daniel Pope reminds us that "[f]or advertising to play a large part in market strategy, consumers had to be willing to accept this kind of self-interested persuasion as a tolerable substitute or complement to more objective product information."[12] That is, in order for advertising to *work* as a business tool, it has to "fit" into the culture. It has to *work* as a vehicle of social communication. One look at the Super Bowl—live polling of commercial popularity, pre- and post-game buzz about advertising, podcasts, consumer-generated advertising, and of course, Super Bowl parties where people gather to watch the game *and* the advertising—and there can be no question. Advertising is indeed a part of our culture, a part of our everyday lives, a part of what we have come to recognize as a media culture.

Some contemporary scholars, while in no way suggesting that advertising fails to provide information or has no influence on consumer choices, invite us to examine what they view to be advertising's more critical role, that of social communication. Rick Pollay speaks of what he calls the unintended social consequences of advertising, the "social by-products of exhortations to 'buy products.'"[13] Canadian scholars Leiss, Kline, Jhally, and Botterill too suggest:

> Advertising is not just a business expenditure undertaken in the hope of moving some merchandise off the store shelves, but it is rather an integral part of modern cultures. The least important aspect of advertising's significance for modern society is its role in influencing specific consumer choices—whether wise or unwise—about purchasing products. . . . [A]dvertising's transmittal of details about product characteristics is a trivial sidelight.[14]

Building on these scholars' observations, we glimpse fertile ground for ethical debate. It is from this perspective of advertising as a vehicle of social communication that most critical questioning occurs.

Historically, the dialogue underlying advertising controversies has been stated overly simplistically in terms of the mirror/shaper debate. Advertisers and their advocates view advertising as a mirror, passively reflecting society. By contrast, critics are likely to view advertising somewhat less benignly, as a shaper, a powerful, *selective* reinforcer of social values. "So," you might ask, "which is it?" After an intensive study of the social content of advertising in the 1920s and 1930s seeking the answer to that question, historian Roland Marchand concluded:

> I regret to say that I have not resolved these dilemmas. I cannot prove conclusively that the American people absorbed the values and ideas of the ads, nor that consumers wielded the power to ensure that the ads would mirror their lives. In fact, as advertisers quickly perceived, people did not usually want ads to reflect themselves, their immediate social relationships, or their broader society exactly. The wanted not a true mirror but a *Zerrspiegel*, a distorting mirror that would enhance certain images. Even the term *Zerrspiegel*, denoting a fun-house mirror, fails to suggest fully the scope of advertising distortions of reality. Such a mirror distorts the shapes of the objects it reflects, but it nevertheless provides some image of everything within its field of vision. Advertising's mirror not only distorted, it also selected. Some social realities hardly appeared at all.[15]

Perhaps then it is best said that advertising both *defines* and *is defined by* culture.

As we approach the topic of ethical decision-making, it is valuable to pause and reflect upon the ideological web in which the institution of advertising, its processes, practices, practitioners, creations, and audiences are grounded.

Chief among these are:

■ **We live in a democratic political system.** Citizens participating in public life elect their government officials. Citizens possess basic human rights and freedoms, among them, those provided in the First Amendment to the U.S. Constitution. Media scholar James W. Carey articulated those rights this way:

> [The First Amendment] says that the government can't tell you how to worship. It says that if you have something to say you can say it. If you want to, you can write it down and publish it. If you want to talk about it with others, you can assemble. And if you have a grievance, you can let your government know about it, and nobody can stop you.[16]

As citizens, we must exercise those rights peaceably and with respect to the law. Democracy, then, is frequently described in terms of freedom, fairness, individualism, and choice.

■ **We live in a capitalist economic system** in which individuals and firms decide what to do based on their own best interests. Profit is the difference between what a product costs to provide, and what the producer gets back in return—and it is this return that drives the system forward. Thus, when we say, "that corporation is only in it for the money," we do well to recognize the principles of our economic system.

■ **We live in a media culture.** It is becoming increasingly difficult and perhaps impossible to separate media and culture in any meaningful way. A blogger recently gave a succinct description of media culture when he wrote:

> Mass media has done such a good job at embedding their copyright into culture that it has become culture itself. The watercooler effect is what happens when media becomes the bits of communication—it's what lets us share our values and interests, determine common ground, etc. Conversations swirl around TV characters, brands, and movie quotes. I remember two kids in college deciding to only express themselves through Monty Python quotes in conversation. They felt that every question or comment necessary was already present in the movie.[17]

■ **We have a commercial media system**, largely profit-motivated, advertising-supported, and highly consolidated.

■ **We live in a consumer culture**, a culture preoccupied with things and with the act of acquiring those things. Consumption is both a concrete institution (we have an infinite number of tools—you can use your smartphone as your wallet—to make it easier for us to buy and reward us for buying) and a guiding myth.[18] In an article entitled, "Why the U.S. Will Always Be Rich," columnist David Brooks described consumer culture this way:

> The most obvious feature of the land of abundance is that people work feverishly hard and cram their lives insane fully. That's because there are candies all around, looking up and pleading to you "taste me, taste me, taste me." People in this realm live in a perpetual aspirational state.[19]

■ **Our media culture is image-based.** Individuals actively, perhaps sometimes unconsciously, work to construct identities that are both fluid and multiple and frequently grounded in consumption. Images are powerful and ideological because they speak in a different grammar. Media scholar Neil Postman noted that when we deal in images, we move "out of the realm of logic and into the realm of aesthetics."[20] That is, we either like an image or we don't; truth and falsity no longer apply. Take, for instance, an image of a young man spraying a particular cologne, then smiling with self-satisfaction as scantily clad women—seemingly hundreds of scantily clad women— run to get close to him. If the image were to be articulated in words (as I have just done)—you'll put on this body spray and the young women literally will stampede to get near you—we would find the premise unbelievable, and yet, when we see an image suggesting exactly that, we often accept it uncritically.

■ **Technology strengthens and amplifies these ideological threads.** The techno-logical/digital revolution has rocked the industry. Advertising's long-established rela-tionships with media industries have blurred, increased in complexity, and often have become maddeningly opaque. The advertising industry is now a major player in the seemingly indistinguishable "ad-tech" and "big data" industries. What this has meant for advertising is an accelerated expansion of media platforms, cluttered media, and indeed, a media culture cluttered with commercial messages. As Ruskin and Schor note, "commercial culture has oozed into nearly every nook and cranny of life."[21] It means fragmented and multitasking audiences, increasingly said to be taking control of their media exposure, making it increasingly difficult for advertisers to get attention for their messages. Yet, those very audiences that now more than ever before indicate their desire to escape from advertising, and turn to technology for the ability to do so (the current explosion of ad blocking stands as testimonial) are at the same time inter-acting with a wonder world of interactive activities on corporate websites, creating ads independently or at the invitation of marketers, "friending" brands on social networking sites, and tweeting their approval or disapproval with lightning-like speed from wherever they might be to others, wherever *they* might be, literally in a matter of seconds.

Finally, adding to this already complex mixture, marketers, recognizing that their "tar-gets" view sources of communication as indistinguishable, have adopted a strategy of integration in an attempt to *guarantee* that advertising messages in fact *are* indistinguish-able from other messages. Coupled with social media—blogs, social networks, buzz—the result is 360-degree marketing, where consumers talk about a brand outside as well as inside the brand's boundaries. In this context, the definition of advertising is fluid.

The chapters in this part ask you to confront a number of ethical dimensions that you may not have considered. Some invite you to look at institutional values and practices; others take a more practical focus. We look at two related dynamics inherent in our work and in our culture: the increasing infringement of advertising/promotional speech into public and private spaces; and the commodification of aspects of culture never intended to be marketed as commodities. We ask: what complexities arise when advertising talks not in words, but in images? We examine the implications of a media system that is supported by advertising, motivated by profit, and increasingly concentrated in the hands of a few large corporations. Finally, we invite you to look at the values and principles that guide our profession. The ethical dilemmas are complex, intriguing, dynamic, and well worth reflection.

LEARNING OBJECTIVES

Upon completing Part 2, you should:

1. recognize and reflect upon the increasing interjection of advertising/promotional speech into public and private spaces;

2. recognize and reflect upon the insertion of a commercial logic into aspects of culture never intended to be traded as marketable commodities;

3. understand the implications and impact of an advertising and media culture increasingly dominated by images rather than words, and the ethical issues arising in that image-based context;

4. identify the implications of a media system that is supported by advertising, motivated by profit, and becoming ever more consolidated in a few corporations, as well as the ethical decisions that arise within that system in a democratic society;

5. critically examine the values and principles that guide the advertising profession and consider avenues of intervention when/if necessary.

NOTES

1. http://money.cnn.com/2016/02/08/media/super-bowl-50-ratings/.
2. www.businessinsider.com/super-bowl-50-ad-rates-reach-a-record-5-million-on-cbs-2015-8.
3. http://variety.com/2016/tv/news/super-bowl-commercials-tv-advertising-stuffed-1201700950/.
4. www.oneupweb.com/blog/super_bowl_bust/.
5. http://fortune.com/2016/02/07/super-bowl-ads-spend-millions/.
6. www.usatoday.com/money/advertising/2010-02-04-super-bowl-hype_N.htm.
7. www.usatoday.com/story/money/business/2016/02/07/.
   super-bowl-ad-meter-picks-winner/79886286/.
8. www.usatoday.com/money/advertising/2010-02-04-super-bowl-hype_N.htm.
9. Ibid.
10. Nathalie Tadena, "Firms Trim Ad Spending Growth Forecasts for 2016," *Wall Street Journal*, December 7, 2015, www.wsj.com/articles/firms-trim-ad-spending-growth-forecasts-for-2016-1449464401.
11. "Total Media Advertising Spending in the United States from 2011 to 2018 (in Billion US Dollars), Statistica, www.statista.com/statistics/272314/advertising-spending-in-the-us/.
12. Daniel Pope, *The Making of Modern Advertising* (New York: Basic Books, 1983).
13. Richard W. Pollay, "The Distorted Mirror: Reflections on the Unintended Consequences of Advertising," *Journal of Marketing* 50 (April 1986): 19.
14. William Leiss, Stephen Kline, Sut Jhally, and Jacqueline Botterill, *Social Communication in Advertising: Consumption in the Mediated Marketplace* (New York: Routledge, 2005), 5, 18.

15. Roland Marchand, *Advertising the American Dream: Making Way for Modernity, 1920–1940* (Berkeley: University of California Press, 1985), xvii.
16. Personal conversation.
17. www.zephoria.org/thoughts/archives/2005/09/29/when_media_beco.html.
18. Lawrence B. Glickman, "Born to Shop? Consumer History and American History," in *Consumer Society in American History: A Reader* (Ithaca, NY: Cornell University Press, 1999), 1–14.
19. www.nytimes.com/2002/06/09/magazine/why-the-us-will-always-be-rich.html.
20. *The Public Mind: Consuming Images*, PBS documentary with Bill Moyers, 1989.
21. Gary Ruskin and Juliet Schor, "Every Nook and Cranny: The Dangerous Spread of Commercialized Culture," in Joseph Turow and Matthew P. McAllister, eds., *The Advertising and Consumer Culture Reader* (New York: Routledge, 2009), 410.

6

THE COMMERCIALIZATION OF EVERYDAY LIFE

Promotional communication permeates and blends with our cultural environment, punctuating our television watching, saturating our magazines and newspapers, and popping up in our Internet surfing, movies, and video games. In short, advertising has become an accepted part of everyday life. . . . [A]t the individual level the discourse through and about objects sidles up to us everywhere, beckoning, teasing, haranguing, instructing, cajoling, and informing our daily interactions with each other in most settings. . . . The symbolic attributes of goods, as well as the characters, situations, imagery, and jokes of advertising discourse, are now fully integrated into our cultural repertoire.[1]

Advertising is a major player in the global economy. It is estimated that global advertising expenditures in 2016 will reach approximately $525 billion;[2] $200 billion will be spent in the United States.[3] Advertising helps consumers make $7 trillion of spending decisions annually.[4] An indispensable business tool, advertising, at the same time, is an integral part of our media culture. It is the commercial foundation that supports most media, and a considerable portion of media content *is* advertising.

To say that the character of advertising and advertising work has changed dramatically is a gross understatement of the intensity of the "revolution" rocking the industry. Technological innovation is bolstered by a seemingly limitless exuberance for all things digital, optimistic and imaginative visions of the future, and ambitious entrepreneurship. This has accelerated the development of "new" media platforms: digital, interactive, and mobile; social networks such as the constantly shape-shifting Facebook, Twitter, Snapchat, Pinterest, Instagram, and their global counterparts; and the transformation of "legacy" media. At this moment, one might legitimately ask how long "new" is an appropriate descriptor for any innovation—a year?

Six months? What's "new" at the time of writing may very well have become routinized in advertising practice and unexceptional in everyday life by the time you're reading this. Alternatively, that which was so recently "new" may have disappeared. That's the way technological innovation "lives" today.

Technological capabilities are fundamentally altering the very "rules of engagement" in our "participatory culture."[5] Boundaries of all kinds seem to blur or disappear with amazing rapidity. Individuals once relegated to the role of "audiences" have become not only content producers, but also media channels themselves, taking content from one channel and sending it along another digital pathway, often remixing, shaping, and reframing it without much, if any, intervention from the content provider.[6] Brands and individuals alike engage and interact on social media to gather likes, tweets, retweets, and followers: the social currencies of internet culture.

Much to the delight of marketers (as well as others), technology not only makes it possible to reach consumers through an ever-growing array of channels, but it also makes it possible to track, analyze, and store our online activity. Each interaction shapes our "digital footprint." Customer concerns regarding the extent and "stealth" of this tracking has kept concerns of privacy at the forefront, so much so that "surveillance" frequently replaces the more benign term in everyday vernacular. Media scholar Mark Andrejevic notes:

> On some intuitive level, I do think that we're reaching a point where more and more Internet users understand that they are participating in a monitored environment about which they have little knowledge and over which they have very little control. . . . I don't think they've got a well-developed understanding of what the potential implications of that are down the road.[7]

The advertising industry is now a major player in "big data" and "analytics," morphing, it seems, into "ad-tech." Data obtained through tracking are joined through analytic processes with other "big data," contributing to technological achievements in the world of health, science, and education; and providing and shaping information and capabilities essential for monetization of internet platforms. Today, advertisers are able to target "a customer of one" with pinpoint accuracy.[8] Theoretically, advertisers powered by algorithms can provide highly relevant (and hence, welcomed?) advertisements based upon particular consumer interests in a matter of milliseconds. Indeed, "programmatic buying," basically using machines to buy advertising, has become part of everyday advertising practice. The cover of the June 1, 2015 issue of *Advertising Age* declared: "This year, $15 billion in digital advertising will be bought without speaking to a single person. Love it or hate it . . . the programmatic revolution is here."[9]

In this increasingly "cluttered" media environment, media themselves are increasingly "cluttered" with commercial messages. Nielsen found that the average non-program time during a typical hour on network television is fourteen minutes; on cable, the average is fifteen and a half minutes, with some networks including as many as twenty-five minutes of commercial time.[10] Not only is more time being allotted to advertising, but also more spots are being jammed into commercial breaks as advertisers move from thirty-second to fifteen-second spots. The *Wall Street Journal* reported that cable networks are speeding up programming in order to create more commercial time.[11] As advertising dollars have shifted to digital, pages oversaturated with advertising have become an increasing concern, for advertisers and for consumers who are increasingly turning to ad-blocking technology.

Nielsen, a global information and research company, reported that adult Americans spend more than eleven hours a day watching television, listening to radio, and using smart-phones and other electronic devices.[12] Noting that most people are awake sixteen to eighteen hours a day, one media analyst wrote somewhat sarcastically: "It's a good thing people were given the ability to multitask; otherwise we wouldn't get a whole lot done these days."[13] How many commercial messages do we see each day? A Media Dynamics study suggested that despite a steady growth in time spent with media, consumers were not being exposed to proportionally greater numbers of commercials due to the availability of avoidance technology and the greater number of channels from which to choose.[14] In this media milieu, depending on who you talk to and how they define advertising, each of us is exposed to anywhere from 362 to 20,000 messages a day.[15] Simply getting consumers' attention is both difficult and urgent. Yet, a writer in *Advertising Age*, commenting on the "clutter problem," noted somewhat ironically:

> Like a fly repeatedly bouncing off a closed window, the ad industry is trying to fix the problem by doing more of the same. That is, by creating more ads. What that absurdly clichéd mission statement of "cutting through the clutter" has really yielded is an industry that shotgun blasts commercial messages into sexy new places as quick as it can identify them, whether it's emerging digital platforms or nooks and crannies in an increasingly buyable physical world—dry-cleaning bags, coffee cups, door hangers and even houses. Yes, clutter is leading to more clutter.[16]

Advertisers use buzz and word-of-mouth marketing, seeking "trendsetters . . . and subtly pushing them into talking about their brand to their friends and admirers."[17] Online, marketers are looking for "influencers," individuals with the ability to affect other people's thinking in social online communities.[18] Guerrilla marketing techniques use "unusual and unpredictable tactics"—flashmobs, street art, viral videos—to get maximum attention using minimal resources. We receive "recommendations" from online retailers ("as someone who bought . . ., we thought you might like . . .") perhaps never giving a thought as to how that recommendation came to be. Critics point to Tropicana Field (home of the Tampa Bay Devil Rays), *The M&M's Brand Counting Book* ("Pour out the candies. Get Ready. Get Set. This counting book is the tastiest yet."),[19] and corporate sponsorships of charity events as evidence of a creeping infringement of commercial logic into public and private arenas.

The blurring of editorial, entertainment, and advertising content—product placements, celebrity endorsers, native advertising/branded content—further contributes to an increasingly commercialized landscape. One certainly can argue that in the context of integrated marketing communication, advertising, public relations, and promotional messages are *by design* virtually indistinguishable in their persuasive intent, if not in form.

All this occurs at the same time that consumers express discomfort, dismay, and occasionally something bordering on outrage with hyper-commercialization. It is something of a paradox that even as audiences are turning to ad-blocking technology, challenging "the implicit agreement that in return for free content we will tolerate a constant barrage of ads,"[20] marketers are finding increasing success in engaging consumers through websites that provide interactive opportunities and promotions in which consumers are asked to create ads for brands.[21] What has come to be called consumer-generated advertising (CGA) first garnered attention in the 2007 Super Bowl when the National Football League, Frito Lay, and General Motors conducted promotions inviting consumers to create ads that were run during the Bowl telecast. Today, CGA is viewed not as a promotion but as a widely used strategy to create brand engagement and interaction even as it gathers data from those who participate. Such is our media culture.

Another dimension of the commercialized landscape, more subtle perhaps, and for that very reason, some critics argue, more insidious, is the commodification of everyday life. In a PBS documentary, *Consuming Images*, Bill Moyers argued that "advertising" has become the primary mode of public address.[22] That is to say, a commercial logic is increasingly finding its way into institutions, ideas, and processes never intended to be traded as marketable commodities. Quite simply, Moyers noted, we think about more and more things as if they were products.

Some twenty-five years later, Harvard professor Michael Sandel echoed Moyers's observation. In his book *What Money Can't Buy: The Moral Limits of Markets*, Sandel noted: "Today, the logic of buying and selling no longer applies to material goods alone but increasingly governs the whole of life. It is time to ask whether we want to live this way."[23]

It is possible to buy prison-cell upgrades and the right to shoot an endangered black rhino, to earn money by renting space on your forehead or holding a place in line for a lobbyist who wants to attend a congressional hearing.[24] It is not unusual for infertile couples to "advertise" in college newspapers for egg donors, sometimes offering to pay top price for a donor with the desired qualities. In a *New York Times* ad, a company advertised that its "diverse donor pool includes doctoral donors with advanced degrees and numerous other donors with special accomplishments and talents."[25] Educational institutions routinely "package" their courses into specialized curricula—for example, advanced-degree executive programs on a satellite campus—deliverable commodities that can be exchanged for a profit on the market.[26] Political candidates—not unlike toothpaste, cereal, and automobiles—market themselves as brands.[27] Books, webinars, and consultants are available to help you perfect your own personal brand. Reality programming, now seemingly a staple of television and cable, breaks down the distinction between what is public and viewable and what is private and closed to outside viewing. Privacy, and indeed an individual's "reality," is turned into a commodity by and for money.[28] Some have argued that even anti-corporate activism and resistance to commodification have become commodities, something you can "buy into" to distinguish yourself from others.[29]

The interjection of a decidedly corporate ethos into our everyday lives has not come about by deliberate choice, but has come about casually, yet consistently, overwhelming the public sphere in sometimes obvious and sometimes not so readily obvious ways. A commercial imperative has come to seem natural and even expected. As a result, it has remained largely unexamined and unquestioned.

The four cases in this chapter focus on various dimensions of commercialization in our modern media culture. The first case, "All Is Not What it Seems: Pondering Guerrilla Marketing," explores the ethical dimensions of how marketing messages are presented and where they are presented. The increasingly complex relationship between pharmaceutical companies, the health care profession, patients, and advertising is the focus of the second case, "DTC Advertising: Prescription Drugs as Consumer Products?" In the third case, "Cause-Related Marketing: Are You Buying It?," we probe the complex ethical dimensions that arise when corporate logic enters the arena of social welfare in the guise of corporate social responsibility (CSR). The final case, "'Like' as Social Currency: Empowerment or Exploitation?" asks us to reflect on the consequence of the commercial models that underline our online environments.

CASE 23. ALL IS NOT WHAT IT SEEMS: PONDERING GUERRILLA MARKETING

Guerrilla Marketing: getting consumers "seeing things that they aren't used to seeing, creating something that lives in the context of what they do but that is out of context with what they are used to."[30]

There was a time when we recognized advertising when we saw it—on billboards lining our highways, in the pages of our magazines and newspapers, a familiar presence as we watched television or listened to our favorite radio station, and as we've moved into the digital world, on many of the various screens that surround us. Today, the cluttered advertising landscape is "tougher to crack than ever."[31] In response, marketers are creating ever-more-inventive ways to get our attention, frequently taking marketing performances into the "real world."

The term guerrilla marketing was first coined in 1984 in *Guerrilla Advertising* by business writer Jay Conrad Levinson, who identifies the "soul and essence" of guerrilla marketing as "achieving conventional goals, such as profits and joy, with unconventional methods."[32] Levinson suggests that guerrilla advertising "gives small businesses a delightfully unfair advantage: certainty in an uncertain world, economy in a high-priced world, simplicity in a complicated world, marketing awareness in a clueless world."[33]

In the thirty-plus years since it was introduced, guerrilla marketing has become a recognized part of the marketing mix for businesses and nonprofit organizations both small and large. Even the U.S. government has used guerrilla marketing tactics.[34] Today, guerrilla marketing has come a long way from Levinson's early suggestions: sponsoring a Little League team, joining a civic group, or offering to be a public speaker. Strategies and tactics for guerrilla marketing are bounded only by marketing imagination (Red Bull asks, skydiving anyone?[35]). Then too, in our digital world, guerrilla marketing is no longer confined to local efforts: video of a guerrilla event (frequently called pranking) often goes straight to YouTube and around the globe in a matter of minutes, for better or worse.

Connor, an intern at a mid-sized advertising agency, had been doing a lot of thinking about guerrilla marketing. His boss had heard about a local guerrilla campaign, and become intrigued by the possibility of bringing in new clients by expanding the agency services to include guerrilla marketing. She asked Connor to do some research; today he was to "report back." The problem was that he still wasn't sure how he really felt about guerrilla marketing. Campaigns he'd read about were usually good-natured fun; some bordered on hilarious. But Connor knew guerrilla efforts by their very nature were designed to be deceptive, to disguise the fact that marketing was occurring altogether. He looked over his notes one last time.

One of the best-known guerrilla campaigns (it turned up in almost every web search) was Sony Ericsson's 2002 "Fake Tourist" effort for its new camera phone. Sixty actors wandered the streets of Seattle and New York City asking others to take pictures of them using their phone. Voilà, an instant product demonstration by actors who didn't identify themselves as working on behalf of Sony Ericsson. It all seemed very innocent to Connor, but it had created quite a stir. Gary Ruskin of Commercial Alert, an advertising monitoring organization, said: "It's absolutely unethical to deceive people like this. . . . [I]t's taking advantage of the kindness of strangers and that's pretty low."[36] A marketing executive called it "reprehensible and desperate."[37] Connor thought these criticisms were a bit over the top, but one remark by Rob Walker in the *New York Times Magazine* made him pause. After describing the incident, Walker said very simply, if somewhat cynically, "and thus, an act of civility was converted into a branding event."[38]

The abundance of sites celebrating guerrilla marketing's successes stand as testimonial to the popularity of the tactic. Some guerrilla efforts have gone far beyond the use of "unconventional messages in unconventional places." Connor often found himself awestruck by the creativity involved. The so-called "2007 Bombscare," was a classic case of guerrilla marketing gone wrong. Interference, a guerrilla marketing company, placed magnetic signs promoting Turner Broadcasting System's Cartoon Network's *Aqua Teen Hunger Force* in ten cities. Boston citizens mistook the electronic gadgets hanging under bridges for terrorist devices. Repeated bomb scares around the city prompted closure of bridges and a portion of the Charles River. Ultimately, Turner Broadcasting paid Boston-area authorities $2 million to compensate for the marketing stunt.[39] A cautionary tale, certainly. Turner and Interference had simply shown poor judgment in a post-9/11 world.

Connor had *experienced* a guerrilla effort when he'd gone to the South By Southwest (SXSW) film festival in Austin, Texas. Companies had to pull some wild ideas to get noticed amid the throngs of people, speakers, brands, bands, and everything that was "the latest." The movie *Ex Machina* was premiering at the festival, and the marketing team created an automated Tinder profile for Ava, the seductive robot starring in the movie. Tinder, a dating app boasting a user base of 50 million, 1.4 billion daily swipes, and 26 million daily matches,[40] seemed the ideal platform on which to market a technology-based movie. Connor had been taken in, one of hundreds of "suitors" who had chatted with Ava, only to find himself on Ava's Instagram profile, a promotion for the film. A writer on *Stuff.tv* wrote: "Using the hashtag #ExMachina, Twitter users were overwhelmingly impressed by the marketing campaign, calling it 'genius', 'wild' and 'wicked smart.'"[41] The effort seemed to have been a success; Connor had to admit that the whole thing was harmless and "impressively deceptive." Still, he considered himself to have been duped.

Connor knew Tinder didn't accept advertising, yet a month or so after SXSW, he heard that Amnesty International had won a Webby Award in the "Guerrilla and Innovation Category." The category description noted that, "by nature, guerrilla marketing is subtle, often deceptive."[42] Amnesty International, an international human rights organization, presented women browsing Tinder with the message, "THE CHOICE. You have the power to choose how you live your life. Many women don't." If the browser chose to "stand up for women's rights," they were directed to a microsite to show support of Amnesty International's campaign to promote women's rights.[43] Though the effort was called Tinder Takeover, the group had collaborated with rather than hijacked Tinder. Amnesty International wasn't trying to sell anything, but it *was* trying to get the browsers "on board" with their cause. Is a guerrilla strategy deceptive even if it isn't commercial?

Connor became even more conflicted when he read about a guerrilla effort in Belgium. Reborn-to-be-Alive, an organ donor association, wanted to inform people that they must register to become organ donors. The organization describes the effort this way:

> Raising awareness for issues like this one isn't always an easy task. We considered the opening of the Apple store in Brussels the perfect opportunity to make people aware of the fact that, for some, waiting could be a matter of life or death.
>
> Three people who are currently waiting for an organ donation made some of the people standing in the queue a very special offer. They would take their place in the queue, because they themselves are used to waiting for something. The only thing the customers had to do in return: Register themselves as organ donors.[44]

The "activists" who took over standing in the queue held signs that read, "We're waiting for you." Watching the video on YouTube, Connor was touched by people's reactions. He wondered: was this guerrilla marketing? Was this deceptive?

Connor walked into the boss' office. She motioned him to a seat across from the desk, smiled, took out a notepad, and asked: "Well Connor, what are your thoughts on guerrilla marketing? A good idea?"

Is guerrilla marketing a good idea?

Guerrilla marketing tactics are an intriguing ethical area. At one end, we see private enterprise at its most inventive, working, sometimes ingeniously, to reach potential customers and sell them something. At the other end, we have practices that some have labeled deceptive, intrusive, and offensive. At times, relatively small firms attempt to joust with the "gorilla" marketers (i.e., large firms) in the great spirit of commercial self-interest, yet Turner Broadcasting and Sony—certainly "gorillas" by any standards—are guerrilla marketers as well. And in today's digital world, video of any guerrilla event can go straight to YouTube and go global in a short time.

Are guerrilla efforts ethical? A virtue ethics framework, which emphasizes character as the basis of action, challenges people to act with honesty, integrity, compassion, and respect in all situations. The central question is not "What should I do?" but rather, "What sort of person should I become?"[45] Given that, by definition, guerrilla marketing is deceptive, attempting to catch people when their defensive shields are down, the practice clearly would be unethical within the framework of virtue ethics.

Using a consequentialist framework, the ethicality of an action is judged by its ends rather than its means. Within this framework, it isn't the manner in which the action is presented but the effect that determines ethicality. How do the efforts by *Ex Machina*, Amnesty International, and Reborn-to-be-Alive fare under this framework?

One can contend that if guerrilla practices truly offended individuals, the marketers would be failing to achieve their goals. But guerrilla marketing webpages and newsletters celebrate seemingly unending success stories. Even if Sony's ploys made some uncomfortable, sales of the telephone/camera in the promotional cities were 54 percent higher than anywhere else. *Ex Machina*'s effort was heralded as a success by those who'd heard of it, and even by those who had "swiped right" on Ava. Amnesty International earned a Webby Award. The signals that sellers are receiving from the feedback mechanism of the market (sales) are that they must be doing something right, resting on familiar—and comforting—utilitarian soil.

Sometimes the number of "votes in the economic marketplace" doesn't tell the whole story. The *Aqua Teen Hunger Force* effort was clearly unethical, the negative consequences for the greater number of people far outweighing what might be viewed as the positive consequences for Turner. Indeed, there *were* some benefits for Turner. A columnist in the *Boston Globe* pointed out the irony of that situation when he wrote:

> The bottom line, as the corporate types like to measure these things, is that Turner Broadcasting's guerrilla marketing assault on Boston was a fabulous success. Suddenly a no name cartoon about a talking box of French fries is the talk of the town from coast to coast. . . . Bottom line, in a world where you get famous by being infamous . . . the ratings get a big bump at the Cartoon Network.[46]

Other ethical questions about guerrilla marketing might be raised. Is the "greatest good for the greatest number" achieved when people have virtually no choice but to participate in a promotion—be it commercial or cause-related—that may or may not have been of interest to them even as it adds yet another degree of commercialism to an already highly commercialized culture? Should consumers be allowed to control when, where, and how they are marketed to?

At least on the surface, many efforts seem harmless, even socially responsible; who would argue with sponsoring a Little League team? But even there, at the most benign level, we encounter the classic question of means and ends; it might be contended that the only reason to (say) join a civic club, give public speeches, or sponsor a Little League team is ultimately to reap marketing outcomes. This, of course, resonates with one of the essential themes of the market system—private gains ultimately will result in public good. A consequentialist approach judges ethicality by the outcomes achieved, not by the motivations that led to those outcomes.

One thing remains certain. In our increasingly cluttered media culture, we will see more and more efforts to sell us—on products and causes—not only through traditional advertising but also through more creative, unexpected tactics as well. In light of this, one might pause to consider again Walker's remark: "and thus, an act of civility was converted into a branding event."[47] Communication scholar Stuart Ewen warns:

> The main thing these [guerrilla tactics] "add" to our lives is an intensified sense of distrust of and alienation from others. This grows out of the suspicion that any human interaction, any product used or opinion expressed may be a commercially staged event designed to get us to buy, think, or behave in certain ways.[48]

CASE 24. DTC ADVERTISING: PRESCRIPTION DRUGS AS CONSUMER PRODUCTS?

AMA Calls for Ban on Direct to Consumer Advertising of Prescription Drugs and Medical Devices. Today's vote in support of an advertising ban reflects concerns among physicians about the negative impact of commercially-driven promotions, and the role that marketing costs play in fueling escalating drug prices. Direct-to-consumer advertising also inflates demand for new and more expensive drugs, even when these drugs may not be appropriate.[49]

Here's a switcheroo: HIV activists target Gilead for holding back on Truvada marketing. At a time when the pharma industry is drawing fire for marketing its drugs to doctors, Gilead is drawing fire for not marketing enough.[50]

These comments—the first drawn from a press release from the American Medical Association (AMA) dated November 17, 2015, the second from *FiercePharma*, a pharmaceutical industry newsletter—illustrate the complex relationships between the medical profession, patients, and the pharmaceutical industry, and highlight the wide range of opinions on direct-to-consumer (DTC) pharmaceutical advertising. Total DTC drug advertising spending in the United States peaked in 2006 at $5.4 billion, dropped to $3.47 billion in 2012, and today appears to be roaring back from that "pharmageddon." Spending in 2014 rose to $4.5 billion, up 18 percent from the previous year.[51] New Zealand is the only other country in the world to allow drug advertising to consumers.

The volume of spending on DTC advertising is, perhaps, surprising given the strength of the time-honored doctor–patient relationship and the fact that public perceptions of the pharmaceutical industry are low. In the most recent Gallup poll measuring American views on twenty-five business and industry sectors (2015), the pharmaceutical industry ranked twenty-third. Only the oil and gas industry and the government ranked lower.[52] In fact, since Gallup began the poll in 2001, the pharmaceutical industry was viewed positively only three times, in 2001, 2003, and 2014.[53] Then too, DTC advertising has been beset by controversy since the Food and Drug Administration (FDA) lifted the ban on DTC broadcast advertising in 1997. The intensity of public discourse on the topic has escalated recently, in part due to concern over rising drug and health care costs as suggested in the AMA call to ban DTC advertising.

The positions taken in the controversy have remained largely unchanged.[54] Advocates suggest that DTC advertising is "the successful marriage of the drug companies' profit motive and their patients' interests":

- DTC advertising educates consumers about common yet serious conditions such as hypertension, elevated cholesterol levels, and depression that often go undiagnosed and untreated. Increased awareness brings patients into doctors' offices seeking help.
- It helps to avert underuse of medicines among individuals requiring them for the ongoing treatment of chronic conditions.
- Patients become more involved in their health care; advertising encourages them to seek more information from their physicians, websites, or medical sites.

Detractors suggest that DTC advertising turns patients into "unwitting tools" of the drug manufacturers' marketing departments. They argue that:

- Advertising is overtly persuasive in intent, so it is ill-suited to educate. Studies have found that DTC ads tend to include more emotional than informational content, frequently rely on images, and rarely mention lifestyle changes as an alternative to medication.[55]
- Consumers do not understand the technicalities, are confused into believing that inconsequential changes are major breakthroughs, and develop unrealistic expectations about drug performance.[56]

■   Advertising contributes to consumers' increased anxiety, self-diagnosis, and requests to doctors for particular drugs.

The controversy persists, now with the added dimension of escalating prices. Americans spent approximately $329.2 billion on prescription drugs in 2013. And, while DTC advertising expenditures are rising, pharmaceutical companies spent far more (approximately $24 billion) advertising directly to health care professionals in 2014. Critics call attention to the fact that pharmaceutical companies spend more on marketing than on research and development.[57] The dynamics of the promotion of pharmaceuticals are fraught with charges and counter charges. In a recent (2015) episode of "Last Week Tonight with John Oliver," Oliver examined marketing to doctors, ending the episode with a spoof of drug advertising that suggested the tension underlying the phenomenon:

"Ask your doctor today if he's taking pharmaceutical company money. Then ask your doctor what the money is for," the narrator says. "Ask your doctor if he's taken any money from the companies who make the drugs he just prescribed for you. Then ask yourself if you're satisfied with that answer."[58]

Truvada, manufactured by Gilead Sciences, has become a part of the discussion. Truvada is an HIV PrEP drug. That is, it is a drug taken to reduce the risk of HIV transmission in uninfected individuals. It is the drug "drawing fire for not marketing enough," even as the AMA calls for a ban on DTC advertising. Let's begin by learning a bit more about Truvada:

■   **2004.** Truvada was approved by the FDA to be used in combination with other medications to treat HIV.

■   **2012.** The FDA approved Truvada for pre-exposure prophylaxis. Truvada became the first approved PrEP medication.

■   **2014.** The Centers for Disease Control and Prevention (CDC) recommended Truvada be taken daily by anyone using injectable drugs or having unprotected sex with partners of HIV status. If *taken properly* the CDC said PrEP reduces the risk of men having unprotected sex getting HIV by 90 percent, and provides more than 70 percent protection to drug injectors.[59]

■   **2014.** The World Health Organization (WHO) "strongly recommended men who have sex with other men consider taking antiretroviral medicines [Truvada] as an additional method of preventing HIV transmission alongside the use of condoms." WHO estimated that approximately one million new HIV cases among this group could be averted over a ten-year period.[60]

■   **2015.** CDC reported that one-third of primary care doctors and nurses had never heard of Truvada. "Despite the fact that an estimated half million Americans could be good candidates for PrEP treatment, relatively few actually take Truvada."[61]

Why the low numbers? Let's dig a bit deeper. At the outset, Truvada had an image problem. Many, even some within the gay community, denigrated those individuals who took the drug as "Truvada Whores." Grindr, a gay hookup app, surveyed Truvada users (2015) and found that the stigma appears to be subsiding.[62] Still, a blogger in the *Huffington Post* wrote: "instead of educating and promoting safe sex practices, the FDA is encouraging the continuation of unsafe sex and most likely contributing to the spread of other sexually transmitted infections."[63] Doctors, even pioneer AIDS advocates were hesitant, fearful that long years of education and safe-sex behavior would be undone. Calling Truvada a "party drug," Michel Weinstein President of the AIDS Healthcare Foundation warned of an increase in irresponsible sexual practices.[64]

Cost was also a factor. Though covered by most insurers, co-payments made Truvada unaffordable, particularly compared to condoms. However, Gilead Sciences initiated an assistance program that can lower out-of-pocket expenses to under $25 per month depending on the plan.

Many patients don't know where to get the drug, and sometimes struggle to get the prescription. Jim Pickett of the AIDS Foundation of Chicago spoke of "a circle of pointing fingers. . . . 'HIV specialists are like, I don't see HIV-negative people,' and you see a primary care physician, and they say, 'you need to see a specialist.'"[65] Another patient wrote: "The [doctors'] assumption is if you're using Truvada to prevent HIV, you're engaging in fabulous orgies while high on meth."[66] As a result, thousands of people who could significantly lower their HIV risk are not taking the drug.

Truvada has been a financial success due to its use in HIV treatment, bringing Gilead $1.79 billion in the U.S. in 2014, but, according to a Gilead spokesperson, the company "does not view PrEP as a commercial opportunity and is not conducting marketing activities around Truvada as PrEP."[67] The company supports communication organizations' education efforts around the U.S.; however the Truvada sales force focuses on HIV specialists not primary care physicians who see healthy people.

There are an estimated 50,000 new cases of HIV in the United States each year.

Much of the controversy swirling around the issues of DTC pharmaceutical advertising seemingly arises from a discomfort with the fit of profit motive, the inviolability of the doctor–patient relationship, and differences in the perceived rationality of consumers. *If* we assume that individuals will not be prone to developing symptoms to match those described in the advertising, *if* we assume that individuals will not be "taken in" by the uplifting images that populate many DTC ads, and *if* we assume that consumers will be diligent in discerning and assessing all the possible side effects of the promoted drug, then the relationship between profit-seeking pharmaceutical companies and health-seeking consumers may well be a sound one. This is particularly true if we view consumers not only as "information processors," carefully reflecting on information in the ads, but also as "information seekers," encouraged by the ads to go to websites, medical sites, or their physician. Thus, when patients and physicians *support* DTC advertising, they do so largely in utilitarian terms, judging ethicality based on consequences. The assumption is that both the patient and the doctor are being well served—the patient via the empowerment that comes with awareness and knowledge and the doctor by a patient more informed about treatment options.

When patients and physicians *object* to DTC advertising, they seem to do so from two ethical positions. The utilitarian argument suggests that, on balance, the greatest good for the greatest number is *not* being served by attempts at self-medication in these complex areas, which have been made to seem simpler largely to satisfy the demands of the techniques of modern advertising. Others adopt the absolutist Kantian position: it's just wrong in any way to apply pressure on the presumed expertise of the physician in the time-honored doctor–patient relationship. As patients, we are used to having drug companies attempt to persuade us about over-the-counter, that is, nonprescription, drugs. With prescription drugs, however, we pass through the gatekeeper of the physician, who, we expect, knows far more about the condition and the treatment than we do. It is noteworthy that part of the argument advanced by those opposed to DTC advertising is that the doctors will succumb to patient pressure to prescribe advertised medications. There is a certain irony in the dueling images of doctor as knowledgeable professional and doctor as willing to prescribe based on little more than patient suggestion.

And what of the rationality of the patients? While we cannot judge individual motivations for seeking the medication, the patient in this case, once aware of Truvada, seems primarily to be an information seeker, active and persistent in attempting to get a prescription.

Physicians' reluctance to prescribe the medication may be due in part to lack of awareness in light of Gilead's very limited marketing. That reluctance but may also be based on professional values and boundaries, that is, on the limitations of physicians' specialty areas. Physicians are bound by a Hippocratic Oath, which in its modern version says both: "I will not be ashamed to say 'I know not,' nor will I fail to call in my colleagues when the skills of another are needed for a patient's recovery" and "I will prevent disease whenever I can, for prevention is preferable to cure."

And what of Gilead Sciences? On the surface, it would be easy to suggest the pharmaceutical company has been negligent in its refusal to market the drug, particularly on the grounds of it not being a commercial opportunity. From Gilead's perspective, we might ask to whom is duty owed? The situation is a complicated one. Gilead offers financial assistance to lower co-payments and engages in educational efforts with community groups. "Where is the line between what a corporation can be expected to do in serving public health and what it actually needs to do in advertising products in the most efficient and profitable manner possible?"[68]

CASE 25. CAUSE-RELATED MARKETING: ARE YOU BUYING IT?

It is difficult to avoid the ubiquitous messages at the grocery store, pharmacy or shopping mall that conscientious consumption choices can change the world. Consider that by purchasing a certain brand of bottled water one can "help to alleviate the global water crisis." A chocolate bar purchase can help children in developing countries "be who they want to be." Buying laundry detergent helps to "change lives," and designer clothing allows the consumer to "empower women globally."[69]

Shopping to save the world is easier [than joining together to make a difference], promising consumers that they can improve someone else's life without having to change their own.[70]

Social responsibility has not always fit easily into a business culture where, to quote a well-known economist and Harvard business professor, Theodore Levitt, "the business of business is profits; . . . virtue lies in the vigorous, undiluted assertion of the corporation's profit-making function."[71] Once, corporations were hesitant to link themselves to a cause, fearing that their involvement would appear to be exploitation of the cause for commercial gain. Today, however, that fear appears to be unfounded. According to the 2015 Cone Communication/Ebiquity Global CSR Study, nearly all global consumers expect companies to act responsibly: "most global customers believe CSR is simply part of doing everyday business."[72] The Cone Communication 2015 Millennial CSR Study identified that group as "far and away, America's most ardent CSR supporters."[73]

What is CSR? CSR is generally understood to include any business practice that signals that a company is taking responsibility for its environmental and social impact beyond what may be required by regulators.[74] Corporations engage in CSR activities for a variety of reasons, including, among others: engaging with customers and employees; benefiting themselves while benefiting society; and differentiating brands. The nature of CSR initiatives are equally wide ranging, among them: corporate philanthropy; sustainability and environmental programs; ethical labor practices and sourcing of raw materials; diversity initiatives; and cause-related marketing.

Cause-related marketing, expected to reach $2 billion in 2016,[75] refers to CSR initiatives that depend on consumer participation. These initiatives too are diverse; the degree and nature of consumer involvement vary. Consumers simply may be asked to purchase a product they might buy regularly; a percentage of sales will go to the cause. Some companies create items particularly sold to raise money for a cause; again, a percentage of the profits will go to the cause. In still other instances, consumers are asked to buy a symbol of their support of a cause—breast cancer's looped pink ribbon, a red-dress pin for heart disease, a FEED Project tote bag for the United Nations World Food Programme, the "Live Strong" bracelet for cancer research—"wearable proof . . . a visible declaration of concern."[76]

Global connectivity made possible by technology has increased consumer awareness of global social inequities, and created opportunities for corporations to engage in cause-related marketing activities that enable consumers to take part in solving the social problems of "distant others" through the act of consumption.[77] For example, Danone's "1L = 10L for Africa" campaign linked the purchase of one liter of Volvic bottled water with the promise to provide 10 liters of drinking water in Africa. In this way, the campaign successfully transformed a bottle of water into a tool of consumer activism and regular consumers into consumer activists, while strengthening consumer ties with their brand.[78] A similar campaign, Pampers' One Pack = One Vaccine partnership with UNICEF (the United Nations Children's Emergency Fund), is credited with saving 500,000 newborns in seventeen countries. "How many times in your life can you say, 'I'm helping to eliminate a disease?'" asked a Procter and Gamble executive in *Advertising Age*. "We liked that there was something that you could measure, and the results would be really rewarding."[79]

Amidst these recurring celebratory success stories, international development scholars are more cautious in their assessments of the success of global cause-related marketing efforts. For example, in an analysis of the Pampers campaign, Samantha Beattie noted that

> while helpful, [the effort] only pays for the vaccine itself. The entire (and considerably more expensive) vaccination process, including hiring the professionals, buying the equipment and maintaining the health care facilities, is left uncovered. . . . The projects themselves may not be addressing the full extent of the problem.[80]

Similarly, Brei and Böhm suggested that, despite short-term contributions, cause-related marketing efforts can be risky in that "when certain social issues no longer fit into the marketing strategy of corporations, then these private actors can simply walk away."[81] Their analysis highlights what they identify as the pitfalls of "the neoliberal shift from government to governance."[82] Such differences in definitions of "success" are characteristic of the cause-related model and symptomatic of the varied goals of participants.

Corporate cause-related marketing fits comfortably, almost seamlessly, in our consumer culture. Individuals routinely construct their identities and announce their allegiances and generosity: buying, charging, cooking for a cause; accessorizing with yellow bracelets, pink ribbons, red Converse sneakers, FEED tote bags. Indeed, cause-related marketing initiatives are so much a part of our business and cultural landscape that we participate almost unconsciously. Ten years ago, Martin Glenn, a British businessman, wrote that "one day soon marketers will drop the prefix 'cause-related' and see campaigns that stir the consumer's conscience as plain, simple marketing—unremarkable and barely worthy of comment."[83] Perhaps we have reached that day. Still, if we look beyond the seeming normality of consuming for a cause, *are* these cause-related marketing campaigns truly "unremarkable and barely worthy of comment"?

Cause-related marketing as a business strategy raises questions about the nature of social responsibility, corporate philanthropy, and social participation. How might the ethical dimensions of cause-related marketing be assessed? Certainly, corporations should be commended for using their assets in positive ways to make a difference, be it locally, nationally, or globally. Without such corporate involvement, organizations addressing issues ranging from education and arts to environment, health, and social welfare, from providing drinkable water to eliminating disease, would be hard-pressed to operate. Indeed, the long-term relationships created through corporate–nonprofit alliances often provide the nonprofits with a far greater ability to engage in long-term planning than more traditional, grant-based funding.

Adopting a consequentialist approach whereby the ethicality of an action is based on the outcome of that action, cause-related marketing is often touted as a win–win–win scenario. The nonprofit organization raises money to sustain its good work and creates awareness of the cause using the expertise of the corporate partner. Corporations are able to sell their products, improve their image and create a connection with consumers who are able to do good while shopping. The greater good of social welfare and civic action is served. Certainly this is true in the short term; however, given our inability to discern long-term political and social ramifications of interventions, any assessment of consequences beyond the short term may elude us.

Brei and Böhm suggest that CSR might be categorized in two streams. Corporations taking a "societal approach" go beyond the companies' immediate stakeholders, demonstrating "a continuing commitment by businesses to contribute to economic development and, simultaneously, improve the quality of life for the workforce, their families, the community and society at large as well as 'distant others.'" The second stream, a "stakeholder approach," focuses primarily on the CSR implications for the corporation and less on the social impact of those efforts.[84] We might ask: does a corporation's motive for undertaking a cause-marketing social initiative need to be totally without an expectation of reward for it to be ethically virtuous? A gift genuinely altruistic in nature, that is, to demonstrate other-centered love, must have benefit to the recipient as its primary motive and purpose but not necessarily its *only* motivation or purpose. Perhaps the concept of "strategic giving" strikes a balance, Aristotle's golden mean between pure altruism and economic return? Then too, adopting a consequentialist approach denies motivation in assessing ethicality, focusing instead on the outcome, the greater good.

Let's return to Theodore Levitt's logic mentioned at the outset. Certainly, the stark position that he and others, most notably economist Milton Friedman, advocated decades ago is no longer defensible. Yet, in the article from which Levitt's observation is drawn, "The Dangers of Social Responsibility," he continues:

[A]t bottom [a corporation's] outlook will always remain narrowly materialistic. What we have, then, is the frightening spectacle of a powerful economic functional group whose future and perception are shaped in a tight materialistic context of money and things but which imposes narrow ideas about a broad spectrum of unrelated noneco-nomic subjects on the mass of man and society. Even if its outlook were the purest kind of good will, that would not recommend the corporation as an arbiter of our lives.[85]

Levitt encourages us to reflect on the values and principles on which decisions regarding public welfare should be made. Are we comfortable with the insertion of a commercial imperative into this social realm? Are we comfortable with corporate decision-makers, who by professional necessity are motivated primarily by the needs and objectives of the *corpo-ration* rather than by social welfare, making decisions about the relative importance of social needs in achieving/maintaining public welfare? Certainly the realization that the decision to support one cause (let's say breast cancer) over another (AIDS) may be the result of no greater urgency than to create an image among a particular target market gives one pause.

Other dimensions might enter into our assessment making the situation even more complex. Corporate decision-makers rarely have expertise in the relevant areas of public welfare. This may particularly be the case when corporations partner with causes serving the needs of "distant others." A decision to form an alliance with a particular group related to a cause is simultaneously a decision to advocate a particular solution to the problem, that is, to say, "This is the way that the problem should be solved." Here, in the absence of a firm knowledge base and familiarity with the actual situation in distant arenas, the application of a utilitarian perspective of "greatest good for the greatest number" becomes a bit more fragile.

Critics have noted that cause-related marketing legitimizes and reinforces consump-tion not only as a route to social benevolence but also as an act of activism. To appeal to consumption amid concerns about exploitation and depletion of resources, environmental degradation, social inequities, escalating energy consumption, and so on might seem inde-fensible to many. Writing about the Red campaign for the Global Fund to Fight AIDS, Tuberculosis and Malaria launched by rock star and activist Bono, a columnist in the *Chicago Tribune* asked plaintively, "Do you have to suffer and sacrifice to make the world a better place? Or can you just buy more cool stuff?"[86] Indeed, has "buying more cool stuff" replaced political activity?

Finally, consider the nonprofit organizations whose causes do not align easily with corporate or business objectives. Is the greater good being served when nonprofits are forced to simplify complex development problems as well as solutions to those problems in order to provide "catchy" slogans and sound bites required by marketing efforts? More troubling is that in an era of "cause clutter," nonprofits may find themselves tempted to reposition their groups or reconstruct their cause into a more marketable commodity. Hawkins noted that "competition for corporate partners leads to the practice of NPOs [non-profit organizations] framing themselves as 'the best' at certain development tasks."[87] The temptation to dramatize and over-emotionalize need in order to attract donors may only be exacerbated in this new giving environment. A utilitarian focus may emphasize the urgency of fund-raising, and the acquisition of a corporate partner as the route to generating the greatest benefit. Yet consequences of challenges, transformation, and perhaps even the violation of values and principles supporting the cause require careful consideration at both the individual and organizational levels. A balance of emotional and logical argumentation in fund-raising appeals may be needed to avoid the extremes that would justify using any means to raise funds for worthwhile ends.

CASE 26. "LIKE" AS SOCIAL CURRENCY: EMPOWERMENT OR EXPLOITATION?

> I like to imagine a hypothetical scenario in which somebody came to a town and said, "Hey, look, we can build an amazing new type of high-tech road system for your community that will improve commerce and give people new ways to communicate with each other and see each other and interact, but you have to understand that we are going to track you and monitor everything you do, and we are going to use that information to try and influence you according to our priorities."
>
> If somebody came and said that to you as a proposition, you'd probably say, "No, that sounds a little creepy."[88]

Sophie had worked in advertising a long time, more than twenty years. She was used to the hustle, client demands, and creative disagreements that characterized the profession; she was no stranger to controversy. On this particular day, Sophie was, as she liked to say, pausing, taking a deep breath, and reflecting on advertising work. More particularly, she was thinking about the internet culture, technology, big data, advertising, and the media ecosystem. She had watched a PBS documentary, *Generation Like*, which focused on teens interacting with culture through social media.[89] Since then, she'd been troubled. She kept returning to the question of manipulation. Were adolescents being empowered or exploited?

Her thoughts began with the longstanding controversies surrounding advertising to children. Few issues generated as much controversy as marketing's pursuit of children. Parents, critics, and regulators asked key questions about understanding. Did children understand the difference between reality and advertising? Did they understand that advertising tried to sell them something? Did they recognize the difference between advertising and programming? The industry had gone to great lengths in its efforts to respond to those concerns and protect the vulnerable and impressionable child audience, though there was no doubt that children were a very profitable market today. Then, her thoughts turned to adolescents. Certainly they were "digital natives," navigating the internet to search, play games, interact with friends and celebrities, and announce to the world, "this is who I am." Indeed, they were masters of the internet.

Theoretically, teens were empowered, validated, and enriched by social media relationships. Interaction provided a sense of belonging. The internet was a place to be creative, to "be yourself." Likes. Tweets. Retweets. Shares. Followers. These were the currencies of the internet. Brands sought them as eagerly as adolescents. Still, Sophie thought about those adolescents who shared so easily; befriended celebrities; crafted and recrafted their profile pictures then waited anxiously to see how many "likes" they'd get and how quickly; became fans of their favorite program, or movie, or YouTube superstar, tweeting and post-ing in order to express their affinity and be rewarded with badges, stars, or a better position on a leader board.

Sophie didn't for a minute diminish the value of the experiences, yet she couldn't help but wonder: did adolescents understand what happens to the data they share? Did they realize that the benefits of the internet were only possible through the collection and use of personal data, data mining, and sharing in ways they cannot control? Did they understand the "work" they were doing each time they clicked share, retweet, or like? Research suggests that adoles-cents have only a low level of knowledge about the type of information tracking that takes place, and they know even less about the sophisticated forms of data mining emerging.[90]

The internet, so pervasive, so commonplace, it almost seems like a utility. What was it Alexander Furnass had said? "We are handing out the largest most powerful trove of infor-mation to advertisers ever in human history, and in exchange, we get free email."[91] Sophie could almost hear the teens she'd seen in the documentary: "Look at the cool things I can do. And YIPPEE! It's free." Except it isn't.

Douglas Rushkoff noted:

When you're socializing and self-expressing and your sense of personal worth is also based in how many "likes" you have, it's kind of important, I think, for people to under-stand not that this is bad, but for people to understand that they're living their social lives in a marketplace, and what does that do to the way you think about yourself?

In this world, getting "likes" is the way to get ahead, the way to "leverage your network to make money. . . . If you're doing it transparently and openly and authenti-cally, this is not evil. This is life.[92]

It's an important question. If adolescents don't understand the virtually invisible com-mercial rules of the internet game—heck, if anyone doesn't understand that game—then even as they're being empowered through social media interactions or just using the internet in daily life, they're being exploited. Manipulated.

Sophie sighed. Clearly, the technology genie is out of the bottle, and she won't be going back in. What now?

As often happens with technological innovations, exuberance over newly discovered capabilities coupled with optimistic and perhaps idealistic visions of never-before-possibilities finds us doing things because we *can* before we've given sufficient thought to unintended consequences or varied perspectives. Sophie's reflection raises many ethical considerations.

Let's think now about the longstanding issue of privacy and Sophie's concern about manipulation.

Lou Hodges wrote that "as our *ability* to invade privacy has increased, so too has our *willingness* to invade."[93] Though he was talking about the press, the statement is no less true here. At the core, the most obvious ethical dilemmas in behavioral targeting are those of privacy and the accompanying values of trust and respect. And, what *is* privacy? The definiton offered by Alan Westin is a useful one: "the claim of individuals, groups, or institutions to determine for themselves when, how, and to what extent information about them is communicated to others."[94]

At the outset, the discussion is complicated by differences in our understanding of privacy and the value we place on it. Mark Zuckerberg, Facebook CEO, has advocated for years that users should be more open to sharing information. Others argue that private information is a property, that it belongs to the individual. In short, they argue that privacy is a commodity. In what seems to be a mood of online openness, however, many provide "seemingly innocuous bits of self-revelation" without a second thought.[95] One writer noted: "This new world owes its origin to the rampant sharing of photos, resumes and personal news bites on services like Facebook, LinkedIn and Twitter, which have acclimated people to broadcasting even the most mundane aspects of their lives."[96]

Insofar as we give consent for our personal information to be collected and to be handled in particular ways, that is, that we consent to its being shared with third parties, it might be argued that collecting data for behavioral targeting is ethical and, indeed, perhaps beneficial. Still, to what degree are individuals aware that their "digital footprint" is defining and redefining who they are to parties unknown for purposes perhaps not yet known? Jon Kleinberg, a professor of computer science at Cornell University, has told us that when online we should behave as if we were in public. We might know that intellectually, nod our heads in agreement, and even mumble "of course." But do we actively incorporate that information the next time we order a book, chat with a friend, retweet a news story, or like a YouTube superstar? Or do we come to the "relationship" with a foundation based in trust and a reasonable expectation of privacy?

And what of transparency? Consider the hypothetical scenario opening this case. Monitoring online behavior is one thing; inclusion in a detailed database that is shared with others is quite another. Selling that information for profit, too, is something quite different:

> Would you find it acceptable for someone to stand behind you while you surf the Internet, write down everything you look at and them keep those notes for themselves? Would you trust that person to safeguard those notes? To not turn them over to anyone else, particularly someone who you didn't know? How would you feel if that individual sold the notes for profit?

The very technologies that threaten our privacy have resulted in many benefits. It is the means to those ends that are in question. How much are we willing to "pay" for information that is customized to our interests? Are we aware of long-term consequences—consequences beyond those of possible harm when the information is misused? Andrejevic writes:

> Rumors of the death of privacy in the 21st century have been greatly exaggerated. The increasingly important role of on-line surveillance in the digital economy should be constructed not as the disappearance of privacy per se, but as a shift in control over personal information from individuals to *private* corporations. The information in question—behavioral habits, consumption preferences, and so on—is emphatically not being publicized. It is, rather, being aggregated into proprietary commodities, whose economic value is dependent, at least in part, upon the fact that they are privately owned. Such commodities are integral to the exploitation of customized markets.[97]

Are we not, in these instances, in Kantian terms, diminished as human beings when we are so objectified?

The technology genie *is* out of the bottle and she's *not* going back. As we encounter new technologies, we'll encounter problems never faced before. These problems are not inherent in the technology, but in how human beings develop, exploit, and utilize it. Henry Jenkins has noted that "what people collectively and individually decide to do with those technologies as professionals and as audiences, and what kinds of culture people produce and spread in and around these tools, are still to be determined."[98]

At their core, questions raised here are not merely technical questions. They are questions of trust, respect, and responsibility. It is imperative that we consider our choices, our decisions, and take responsibility for our actions. It is important that taking action doesn't become more important than the consideration of consequences of that action. As Socrates noted in Plato's *Republic*, "we are discussing no small matter, but how we ought to live."

NOTES

1. William Leiss, Stephen Kline, Sut Jhally, and Jacqueline Botterill, *Social Communication in Advertising: Consumption in the Mediated Marketplace*, 3rd ed. (New York: Routledge, 2005), 3, 6.
2. Nathalie Tadena, "Firms Trim Ad Spending Growth Forecasts for 2016," *Wall Street Journal*, December 7, 2015, www.wsj.com/articles/firms-trim-ad-spending-growth-forecasts-for-2016-1449464401.
3. "Total Media Advertising Spending in the United States from 2011 to 2018 (in billion US dollars), Statistica, July 2014, www.statista.com/statistics/272314/advertising-spending-in-the-us/.
4. Randall Rothenberg, "Ad-blocking Unnecessary Internet Apocalypse," *Advertising Age*, September 22, 2015, http://adage.com/article/digitalnext/ad-blocking-unnecessary-internet-apocalypse/300470/.
5. Henry Jenkins, Sam Ford, and Joshua Green, *Spreadable Media: Creating Value and Meaning in a Networked Culture* (New York: New York University Press, 2013).
6. These ideas are drawn from Jenkins, Ford, and Green, *Spreadable Media*.
7. Mark Andrejevic, "We Are All 'Lab Rats' Online," interview with Sara Childress, *Frontline*, February 18, 2014, www.pbs.org/wgbh/frontline/article/mark-andrejevic-we-are-all-lab-rats-online/.
8. This phrase is used by many in the advertising industry in discussions of the importance of personalization and individualization of the advertising experience.

9. Cover, *Advertising Age*, June 1, 2015.

10. www.tvweek.com/tvbizwire/2014/05/how-many-minutes-of-commercial/.

11. www.wsj.com/articles/cable-tv-shows-are-sped-up-to-squeeze-in-more-ads-1424301320.

12. *Nielsen Total Audience Report 2014*, cited in www.statista.com/chart/1971/electronic-media-use/.

13. Felix Richter, "Americans Use Electronic Media 11+ Hours a Day," March 13, 2015, www.statista.com/chart/1971/electronic-media-use/.

14. http://sjinsights.net/2014/09/29/new-research-sheds-light-on-daily-ad-exposures/.

15. Ibid.

16. Matthew Creamer, "Caught in the Clutter Crossfire: Your Brand," *Advertising Age*, April 2, 2007, p. 1.

17. www.bloomberg.com/news/articles/2001-07-29/buzz-marketing.

18. http://searchcrm.techtarget.com/definition/Social-media-influence.

19. Barbara Barbieri McGrath and Roger Glass, *The M&M's Brand Counting Book* (Watertown, MA: Charlesbridge Publishers, 2002).

20. Farhad Manjoo, "Ad Blockers and the Nuisance at the Heart of the Modern Web," August 19, 2015, www.nytimes.com/2015/08/20/technology/personaltech/ad-blockers-and-the-nuisance-at-the-heart-of-the-modern-web.html?_r=0.

21. Laura Petrecca, "Amateur Advertisers Get a Chance; Companies Pick Up Ads Made by Novices and Regular Old Customers," *USA Today*, March 28, 2006, p. 2B.

22. *The Public Mind: Consuming Images*, PBS documentary with Bill Moyers, 1989.

23. Michael J. Sandel, *What Money Can't Buy* (New York: Farrar, Straus and Giroux, 2012), 5.

24. Ibid.

25. Genetics & IVF Institute, advertisement, "Over 40 and Thinking of Having a Baby?" *New York Times*, September 30, 2007, p. 18S.

26. David F. Noble, "Technology and the Commodification of Higher Education," *Monthly Review*, March 2002.

27. Ibid.

28. Jane Deery, "Reality Television as Advertainment," *Popular Communication* 2:1 (2004): 1–20.

29. Nate Thompson, "The Flip Side to the Commodification of Revolution: a Critique of the Activist Scene," *Journal of Aesthetics and Protest*, www.joaap.org/4/nato.html. See also, Thomas Frank, "Why Johnny Can't Dissent," in *Commodify Your Dissent: Salvos from the Baffler* (New York: W. W. Norton, 1997) and Joseph Heath and Andrew Potter, *Nation of Rebels: Why Counterculture Became Consumer Culture* (New York: HarperCollins, 2004).

30. Brooke Capps, "The Reserved Ruler of In-Your-Face Marketing," *Advertising Age*, March 5, 2007, p. 12.

31. www.foxnews.com/opinion/2011/08/23/why-afs-silly-jersey-shore-stunt-hurts-us-all.html.

32. http://gmarketing.com/.

33. Ibid.

34. www.wemarket4u.net/fatfoe.

35. www.redbullstratos.com/the-mission/world-record-jump/.

36. http://abcnews.go.com/Business/IndustryInfo/story?id=130164&page=1.

37. www.wsj.com/articles/SB1028069195715597440.

38. Rob Walker, "The Hidden (in Plain Sight) Persuaders, *New York Times Magazine*, December 5, 2004, p. 68.

39. Michael Learmonth, "Turner Pays in Boston," *Daily Variety*, February 6, 2007, p. 4.

40. http://expandedramblings.com/index.php/tinder-statistics/.

41. https://watsondg.com/work/ex-machina-sxsw-tinder-stunt.

42. http://webbyawards.com/winners/2015/advertising-media/individual/online-guerilla-innovation/tinder-takeover/.

43. Ibid.

44. http://creativecriminals.com/reborn-to-be-alive/waiting-queue.

45. Sherry Baker, "The Model of the Principled Advocate and the Pathological Partisan: a Virtue Ethics Construct of Opposing Archetypes of Public Relations and Advertising Practitioners," *Journal of Mass Media Ethics* 23 (2008): 237.

46. Steve Bailey, "Laughing to the Bank," *The Boston Globe*, February 2, 2007, p. C-1.

47. Walker, "The Hidden (in Plain Sight) Persuaders," *New York Times Magazine*, December 5, 2004, p. 68.

48. www.metropolismag.com/March-2007/Going-Overground/.

49. AMA Press Release, November 17, 2015, www.ama-assn.org/ama/pub/news/news/2015/2015-11-17-ban-consumer-prescription-drug-advertising.page.

50. www.fiercepharma.com/story/heres-switcheroo-hiv-activists-target-gilead-holding-back-truvada-marketing/2015-02-18.

51. www.fiercepharma.com/dtc-advertising/some-ad-types-are-calling-it-pharmageddon-over-dtc-back.

52. Ibid.

53. www.gallup.com/poll/185432/americans-views-pharmaceutical-industry-tumble.aspx.

54. The stances taken on the DTC controversy are frequently and widely discussed in the trade and popular press. See, e.g., www.pharmaceutical-technology.com/features/feature-big-pharma-ethics-of-tv-advertising/.

55. Rita Rubin, "Analysis: Prescription Drug Ads Leave Out Risks, Alternatives; Consumers Urged to Be Skeptical," *USA Today*, January 30, 2007, p. 7D; Ira Teinowitz, "Stage Set for Senate to Shackle DTC Advertisers; Bill Would Allow Ban of Up to 2 Years and Require FDA to Pre-Clear Drug Ads," *Advertising Age*, February 26, 2007, p. 43.

56. http://yourbusiness.azcentral.com/pros-cons-directtoconsumer-advertising-14119.html.

57. www.washingtonpost.com/news/wonk/wp/2015/02/11/big-pharmaceutical-companies-are-spending-far-more-on-marketing-than-research/.

58. http://time.com/3700497/john-oliver-last-week-tonight-big-pharma/.

59. Donald G. McNeil Jr., "Many Doctors Unaware of Truvada, Drug for Preventing H.I.V.," *New York Times*, November 25, 2015, http://nyti.ms/1T4jVaH.

60. www.who.int/mediacentre/news/releases/2014/key-populations-to-hiv/en/.

61. www.pbs.org/newshour/rundown/8-things-didnt-know-truvadaprep/.

62. Ernesto Londoño, "Grindr Polls Users on H.I.V. Prevention Pill," *New York Times*, December 2, 2015.

63. www.huffingtonpost.com/david-duran/truvada-whores_b_2113588.html.

64. www.pbs.org/newshour/rundown/8-things-didnt-know-truvadaprep/.

65. www.bloomberg.com/news/articles/2015-02-18/gilead-s-pill-can-stop-hiv-so-why-does-almost-nobody-take-it-.

66. Ibid.

67. Ibid.

68. Michael Mackert and Marie Guadagno, "DTC Prescription Drug Advertising: Focusing on Ethics," in Minette E. Drumwright, ed., *Ethical Issues in Communication Professions: New Agendas in Communication* (New York: Routledge, 2014), 231.

69. Roberta Hawkins, "A New Frontier in Development? The Use of Cause-related Marketing by International Development Organisations," *Third World Quarterly*, 33:10 (2012): 1783.

70. Samantha Beattie, "Selling Consumer Goods by Linking to Good Causes Questions at the U of G [University of Guelph]. Cause-related Marketing May Obscure Deeper International Development Issues, Study Says," *Guelph Mercury* (ON), September 5, 2012. Accessed through Newspaper Source Plus, #Q4K050954221312.

71. Theodore Levitt, "The Dangers of Social Responsibility," *Harvard Business Review* (September/October 1958): 42.

72. Cone Communications/Ebiquity Global CSR Study, www.conecomm.com.

73. www.conecomm.com/2015-cone-communications-millennial-csr-study/.

74. www.investopedia.com/terms/c/corp-social-responsibility.asp.
75. "2016 IEG Sponsorship Report," www.causemarketingforum.com/site/c.bkLUKcOTLkK4E/b.6412299/apps/s/content.asp?ct=8965443.
76. Rob Walker, "Live Strong Bracelet," *New York Times Magazine*, August 29, 2004.
77. Vinicus Brei and Steffen Böhm, "'1L = 10L for Africa': Corporate Social Responsibility and the Transformation of Bottled Water into a 'Consumer Activist' Commodity," *Discourse & Society* 25:1 (2014): 3.
78. Ibid., 5.
79. http://adage.com/article/cmo-strategy/p-g-s-pampers-unicef-effort-succeeds-17-countries/300609/.
80. Beattie, "Selling Consumer Goods by Linking to Good Causes Questions at the U of G."
81. Brei and Böhm, "'1L = 10L for Africa'," 24.
82. Ibid.
83. Martin Glenn, "There's a Simple Rationale behind Ties with Causes," *Marketing* (UK), March 20, 2003, p. 18.
84. Brei and Böhm, "'1L = 10L for Africa'," 6–7.
85. Levitt, "The Dangers of Social Responsibility."
86. Nara Schoenberg, "BUY(LESS) Targets Cause-Related Marketing," *Chicago Tribune*, March 23, 2007.
87. Hawkins, "A New Frontier in Development?," 1798.
88. Andrejevic, "We Are All 'Lab Rats' Online"; Manjoo, "Ad Blockers and the Nuisance at the Heart of the Modern Web."
89. http://www.pbs.org/video/2365181302/.
90. www.nola.com/tv/index.ssf/2014/02/frontline_generation_like_expl.html.
91. Ibid.
92. www.nola.com/tv/index.ssf/2014/02/frontline_generation_like_expl.html.
93. Lou Hodges, "Privacy and the Press," in Lee Wilkins and Clifford Christians, eds., *The Handbook of Mass Media Ethics* (New York: Routledge, 2009), 276.
94. Alan Westin, *Privacy and Freedom* (New York: Atheneum, 1967), 7, quoted in Wilkins and Christians, *The Handbook of Mass Media Ethics*, 277.
95. Steve Lohr, "How Privacy Vanishes On-line," *New York Times*, March 16, 2010, www.nytimes.com/2010/03/17/technology/17privacy.html?emc=eta1.
96. Brad Stone, "For Web's New Wave, Sharing Details Is the Point," *New York Times*, April 22, 2010.
97. Mark Andrejevic, "The Work of Being Watched: Interactive Media and the Exploration of Self-Disclosure," *Critical Studies in Mass Communication* 19:2 (2002): 243–244.
98. Jenkins, Ford, and Green, *Spreadable Media*.

7

ADVERTISING IN AN IMAGE-BASED MEDIA CULTURE

> Life on Earth in the twenty-first century is characterized by the near inability to avoid being constantly bombarded by images, day in and day out. . . . It does not matter whether you are in a public space or in the comfort of your own home; the endless barrage of imagery is almost inescapable.[1]

Today, in the context of what might rightly be called be called an "explosion" of technological innovations, it is becoming increasingly difficult, and perhaps impossible, to separate the media in their varied platforms in any meaningful way from thoughts, behavior, relationships, values, and ideas that *are* culture. We no longer talk of media *and* culture, but instead, of *media culture*. In this context, the question of whether advertising is a mirror, passively reflecting society and its values, or a shaper, actively constructing those social values, is rendered moot. Advertising both *defines* and *is defined by* culture, and is perhaps best characterized as a *Zerrspiegel*, a fun-house mirror, reflective but rich with distortion. Consider Michael Schudson's observation in his book, *Advertising*, *The Uneasy Persuasion*:

> The pictures of life that ads parade before consumers are familiar, scenes of life as in some sense we know it or would like to know it. Advertisements pick up and represent values already in the culture. But these values, however deep or widespread, are not the only ones people have or aspire to, and the pervasiveness of advertising makes us forget this. Advertising picks up some of the things that people hold dear and re-presents them to people as *all* of what we value.[2]

Yet the analogy of the mirror, even a fun-house mirror, isn't quite right. As historian Roland Marchand noted: "Advertising's mirror not only distorted, it also selected. Some social realities hardly appeared at all."[3]

Advertising was once primarily informational in both its purpose and content. Advertising told consumers about product features and uses. As our culture gradually evolved from a production-based to a consumption-based culture, advertising became what historian Rick Pollay has identified as transformational. We've come not to sell the steak, but to sell the sizzle. That is, advertising focuses on consumer benefits rather than product characteristics, often trying to influence "attitudes . . . toward brands, expenditure patterns, lifestyles, techniques for achieving personal and social success, and so forth."[4] Today, our media culture increasingly is image-based. The implications are nothing short of phenomenal, for images challenge our traditional ways of deciding whether an argument is true or false. Christine Rosen tells us: "Images appeal to emotion. . . . They claim our attention without uttering a word. . . . They seem to speak for themselves."[5] Perhaps no one better explained the emotional power of the advertising image than fictional ad man Don Draper in a now-classic "Carousel" clip from the television series *Mad Men*.[6]

A short discussion by Neil Postman, drawn from the PBS documentary *Consuming Images* serves to illustrate:

> We have recognized, reputable ways of judging the truth or falsity of statements. We have means, to use a phrase from Bertrand Russell, defenses against the seduction of eloquence. But, we know more or less how to do that, how to analyze what people say, how to measure the truth or falsity of something.
>
> Now let's take a McDonald's commercial. We see a young father taking his six-year-old daughter into McDonald's, and they're eating a cheeseburger, and they're ecstatic.
>
> Is that true or false?
>
> Is the image true or false?
>
> Well, the words don't seem to apply to that sort of thing. There is just no way to assess that in the way we assess statements, linguistic utterances.
>
> So we now build up a whole world of imagery where basically we are out of the realm of logic and perhaps, into the realm of esthetics. . . . You either like McDonald's or you don't. But you can't talk about their truth or falsity. So we now need a different kind of defense against the seduction of eloquence.[7]

In an image-based media culture, the commodity has relinquished its importance to the brand. And, what of the advertising images that surround us in an image-based media culture? They, indeed, are the commodities in which we traffick.[8]

The cases in this chapter ask you to consider some of the ethical dilemmas encountered and questions raised with regard to our marketplace of images. "Altering Images: Attaining the Unattainable?" examines the digital manipulation of advertising imagery that persists in celebrating an ideal feminine beauty that is unattainable to the majority of women. "Stereotyping Disability" explores advertising's use of images and language related to disability. The last two cases look at the use of shocking images in very different contexts. "Spectacle for Social Change: Celebration or Co-optation?" raises several issues simultaneously through the examination of a single advertising campaign: creating spectacle to draw attention to social injustice, exploitation, and the co-optation of a cause to sell merchandise. The final case, "Anti-Obesity: A Question of Images" considers the complexity of using images of obese individuals in advertising campaigns challenging the obesity epidemic, looking at a recent effort that drew national controversy.

CASE 27. ALTERING IMAGES: ATTAINING THE UNATTAINABLE?

It's like the frog in the water: If you slowly turn up the heat, it doesn't know it's being boiled to death. After a while, a size 0 starts to seem normal, not cadaverous.[9]

That's the key: We've begun to make a habit of questioning how women are depicted and what tools are being used to change or edit their appearance for public consumption. Yes, the visual landscape is still awash with altered images, surgically altered models, and the pressure to be thinner, younger, and closer to the narrow beauty ideal that so much marketing pushes on us.

Marketers aren't going to stop selling us and the insecurity that comes with it. So we can't stop asking questions and developing the tools to deconstruct these carefully crafted images.[10]

As advertisers, we are responsible for the creation of the estimated thousands of ads to which the average American is exposed daily. Yet, for all our pride in "pushing the envelope" and "cutting-edge" creativity and innovation, the images we produce and distribute are strikingly and alarmingly similar. This is especially obvious in portrayals of women and girls. The world of advertising is populated by women who no longer resemble even their iconic predecessors, much less the average American women to whom they represent an ideal. They are an entire society, narrowly constructed to represent our notions of perfection—in silence—on the runway and in our advertisements. In repeatedly casting women (and in many cases, girls) who meet an ever-shrinking standard of beauty, we reinforce practices and mindsets that are damaging to those who look to the ideal for a suggestion of what it is to "be beautiful." In a culture of Botox, plastic surgery, and digital retouching, this ideal not only may be lofty, but also is likely to be distinctly unattainable for most women. One graphic director states the problem this way: "When you look at a magazine, 98% of what you see in the fashion industry is unreal. . . . We have taken the human beauty to an extreme that beauty itself cannot compete with."[11]

The relationship between women and girls, cultural norms, advertising, and the fashion industry, with its star-studded fashion extravaganzas, is fraught with tension. The actors involved seek to satisfy their separate goals—some economic, others cultural, still others creative—against a backdrop of persistent critique that seems to remain almost singularly focused on the celebration of the unattainable image. Let's consider the complex "cultural conversation":

■ **2006.** Dove introduces the "Evolution" video to "understand how easy it is for our perception of beauty to be manipulated and distorted."[12]

■ **August 2006.** Luisel Ramos, a young Uruguayan model, collapsed on the runway and died of heart failure, assumed to have been the result of anorexia nervosa.[13] Six months later, her sister Eliana, also a model, died of a heart attack associated with malnutrition.[14]

■ **November 2006.** Ana Carolina Reston, a Brazilian model weighing eighty-eight pounds, at five feet, eight inches, died of complications of anorexia.[15] The ensuing "ultra-skinny-model uproar" began an industry-wide conversation.

■ **2007.** Encouraged by the positive feedback to its "Campaign for Real Beauty," Unilever banned size zero models from its advertisements. The company said it wished to take into account "the possible negative health effects that could occur should people pursue unhealthy or excessive slimness."[16]

■ **2012**. *Seventeen* publishes a "Body Peace Treaty" in their August editions vowing to show "real girls and models." The treaty was a response to a Change.org petition began by a 14-year-old girl. "Those 'pretty women' that we see in magazines are fake," the petition said, in requesting "one unaltered—real—photo spread per month." "They're often Photoshopped, air-brushed, edited to look thinner and to appear like they have perfect skin. A girl you see in a magazine probably looks a lot different in real life."[17]

■ **2012.** Global Democracy, an organization that "uses social media to identify popular solutions to global problems" releases a "Body Evolution" video in which a "girl turns into a bombshell with the help of hair and make-up artists and, of course, Photoshop." The video announced that Global Democracy had created a proposal to encourage mandatory disclaimers when manipulated bodies appear in advertising.[18]

■ **2014.** Feminist website Jezebel "calls out" Beyoncé for a Photoshop-created "thigh gap."[19]

■ **2014.** American Eagle's sister lingerie store, Aerie, pledges not to use retouching tools such as Photoshop in the company's advertising.[20]

■ **2016.** *Sports Illustrated* puts the first plus-size model, Ashley Graham (size 16), on one of three covers of the *Sports Illustrated Swimsuit Edition*.[21]

■ **2016.** The back cover of the *Sports Illustrated Swimsuit Edition* is a Snickers ad satirizing retouching, "Photo retouchers get confused when they're hungry." According to *MediaPost* writer Karlene Lukoviz:

> The back-cover features a tanned, bikini-clad model with a perfect shape in a perfect beach setting. Well, not quite perfect. A closer look reveals a disembodied third hand resting on her right shoulder. Then there's her oddly misplaced belly button. (And those are just two of nearly a dozen mistakes.)[22]

Suddenly, or perhaps not so suddenly, manipulation of photos (once known to many as air-brushing and now almost universally called Photoshopping, a reflection of the fact that an estimated 90 percent of creative professionals has Photoshop software on their desktop) has been "outed" as the "culprit." It seems Photoshop is behind all those unattainable images of perfection we've been viewing for decades. Perhaps it is good to remember that Photoshop can do nothing without us. Photoshop doesn't create those images, *we do*. Still, it seems swearing off Photoshop is the latest addition to the current climate of "female empowerment" in advertising. After years of being told otherwise, women seemingly have become beautiful and real just the way they are. Have attitudes toward beauty really changed? Or, is this media literacy lesson simply a new marketing strategy? And if it's the latter, how long will it last? Jumping the queue gets you ahead, until everyone jumps the queue.

We've been here before. Dove's Campaign for Real Beauty started the conversation in 2004, and in 2006 produced the "Evolution" video, a "60 second journey from real beauty to retouched glamour."[23] To use a phrase taken from Bob Dylan, "the times they were a changing." Or were they?

On the runway, the women of fashion continue to push their physical limits in order to maintain a standard the public simultaneously spurns and reveres. In 2015, more than a decade after Dove launched its Campaign for Real Beauty, Victoria Beckham was slammed for using models that "needed feeding" during New York Fashion Week[24] and France joined Israel, Spain, and Italy in banning excessively skinny models from working in the ultra-chic country's fashion industry.[25]

The unattainable ideal. She's complicated.

On a collective and an individual level, advertisers have available a number of ways to confront this ethical dilemma. We may opt to:

- "Pass the buck" to the fashion industry, thus maintaining the status quo.
- Blame society for superficial standards, prompting society to shift its values so advertising might reflect them more realistically.
- Maintain the standards but publicize the unnatural and/or unhealthy circumstances surrounding the marketing of these ideal images. This option also allows advertisers to continue down their current path but introduces a disconnect between the coveted images in advertising and the reality of their attainability. This is essentially the media literacy effort some advertisers are undertaking today.
- Accept responsibility for perpetuating unhealthy practices and thought patterns, thereby paving the way for a new set of standards. The danger in this option is, of course, that any individual actor in an industry comprised of individual actors renders himself or herself vulnerable to professional criticism, public opposition, and societal resistance.

Let's examine some of these options. Advertisers might dismiss, even comfortably dismiss, the unrealistic representations as an offense residing within the fashion industry, essentially shifting the burden of what is right to the client. But can we so easily wash our hands of the matter? Is it not our industry that takes the remote model and repackages her for mass-distribution? Walking down the street, would Gigi Hadid have the same effect on women if advertising had not elevated her to the "Guess Girl"? We have a professional duty to our client to do what we can to advocate for their best interests, and the marketplace seems to be showing its approval at the cash register. Yet, maybe the marketplace isn't telling the whole story. To whom do we owe more loyalty when girls are (literally) dying to be on the runway and in the ads?

Another avenue of retreat from responsibility for unattainable images might be to suggest that the problem lies not in the retouched photo but in the audience "who misguidedly lets themselves believe that the image is true, when clearly it isn't."[26]

> When young women look at fashion magazines in this current society, they should be well aware that the photos are retouched. They should know by now the photos are not 100 percent truthful or realistic. Choosing to consider the photos real is a naïve mistake on the consumers' part, not an unethical mistake by the fashion magazine.[27]

The editor of a leading fashion magazine quipped defiantly: "Our readers are not idiots."[28]

Inherent here, though unspoken, are two interrelated assumptions common in today's digital world. The first is quite simply that the use of manipulation techniques in the media is something of a moot point at a moment when anyone with a smartphone can digitally alter an image. Hidden in this claim is a silent "everybody's doing it" that relieves advertising of responsibility, embracing misrepresentation as a part of the nature of advertising as self-interested communication.

Advertisers, on the one hand, might choose to deny their power noting that advertising messages are merely the reflections of existing cultural beliefs and values. Certainly the images of perfection in advertising are not surprising in a culture that celebrates beauty—albeit a particular kind of beauty—and its frequent companion, youth, almost to the point of obsession. Advertising's role as the "mirror" (as opposed to the "shaper") is, in essence, benign. If, on the other hand, we acknowledge that the efficacy of our work as advertisers relies at least in part on our ability to shape attitudes in a direction favorable to our client (that is, after all why they use our services), then should we not also assume some degree of responsibility for the standards that we transmit and so perpetuate and reinforce? Unlike journalists' news images, advertising photos can be manipulated "for aesthetic effect." Important questions to ask when we manipulate photos are: why are we doing it, what are our purposes and intentions, and where do we draw the line? Certainly intentional efforts to deceive are unethical. Photos are infinitely pliable. Perhaps the solution lies in moderation? There is considerable difference between retouching a few stray hairs or adjusting the reflection of light on an earring and altering the physique.

The appeal of an advertised good lies in the perception that it has the ability to enhance our existence. To convey that potential, advertisers draw from a narrow pool of images that appear exceptional when juxtaposed with an average American's life. Advertisers choose to use thin models, and they sometimes choose to use the "culprit" Photoshop, because they assume those models will be regarded by their target audience as attractive either directly (e.g., choose our diet plan and look like this) or indirectly (e.g., Jennifer Aniston uses this product and *she's* an appealing celebrity). Given the ambiguity of advertising effects, these advertisers would generally receive no clear confirmation that these assumptions are in fact correct, so they are probably choosing to conform to an unwritten group norm—the assumption that slim is better than not slim. In so doing, advertising perpetuates a standard that exists only within the borders of the ads themselves. Advertisers in part are responsible for the creation of that standard. Are they likewise responsible for the consequences associated with promoting an unattainable ideal?

Of course, none of this would be an issue if women demonstrably resisted the "ideal" with which they are presented and expressed their dissatisfaction to advertisers through their behavior in the marketplace.

If we agree that the digital manipulation of images to create a virtually unattainable ideal contributes to what is essentially a health hazard, does advertising have a responsibility to make changes? And will society—one that acknowledges a problem and even expresses outrage at the problem—ultimately be receptive to that change?

CASE 28. STEREOTYPING DISABILITY

A while back, a headline in *Adweek* had caught Meryl's eye: "A Girl With a Disability Appears as Princess Elsa in Target's Halloween Ad. When quiet inclusion speaks volumes." The mother of a disabled little girl, Jen Spickenagel Kroll, had posted the ad on Facebook saying:

> I love you. Thank you for including a child with braces and arm crutches into your advertising campaign! And as Elsa, no less! My daughter (with arm crutches and prosthetic legs) is going to FLIP when she sees this! Including children with special needs into advertising makes them less of a spectacle to the general public when they venture out into the real world. Normalizing disabilities in children is PRICELESS.[29]

The ad and Jen's message went viral. Once again, Target had made a positive social justice move. Earlier, the company had taken the gender labels off the toy section in their stores; they'd also included a little boy with Down's Syndrome in an ad. Meryl thought Target was making all the right moves. They were being socially responsible *and* they were letting people know of their efforts. Research has shown that nearly all consumers expect companies to act responsibly; they only take note of extraordinary actions (good or bad).[30] Well, unfortunately it seems including a disabled child in an advertisement *is* extraordinary.

And just a couple of days ago, Meryl read that LEGO was going to unveil its first young, disabled figure in June 2016. Rebecca Culler, writing in *Adweek* noted: "everyone wants to talk about it. I know what you're thinking. With all the millions of kinds of Legos out there, how could this possibly be a first? Well, it's a qualified first."[31]

Meryl had been into LEGO when she was a child, and she still kept current on what the company was doing. She knew that today LEGO had something of a "cult" following of adults, AFOLs they called themselves–Adult Fans of LEGO. And there were LUGs–LEGO user groups.[32]

She also remembered that LEGO hadn't always been "cutting edge." She was thinking back to the introduction of LEGO Friends for girls. Good idea. The only problem was that the set featured five women living in Heartlake, an area that included a salon, vet, swimming pool, and convertible car all in pastel colors. She chuckled. But LEGO had learned its lesson. In 2014, they introduced three new characters–a paleontologist, an astronomer, and chemist–all women. It seemed LEGO had become a gender battleground.[33] And, with this step toward inclusivity, a disability battleground as well.

ToyLikeMe, an organization celebrating diversity and calling on the industry to do a better job at representing disability, circulated a Change.org petition:

> There are 150 million children with disabilities worldwide. Yet these kids are arriving into a world where, even before they've left their mums' laps, they're excluded or misrepresented by the very industry that exists to create their entertainment, the objects that fuel their development, the starting blocks of life: Toys!
>
> Please, Lego, put some wheelchair vroom vroom into the toy box and help generations of kids, (both with and without disabilities), grow up with a more positive attitude to human difference![34]

Of course Meryl had signed it. It was the least the company could do. According to Rebecca Atkinson, co-founder of ToyLikeMe, the introduction of the wheelchair LEGO boy was "pretty momentous . . . even though it's just a little toy. It's about the message behind it, which is far, far bigger than a little one-inch-tall plastic guy."[35]

Meryl scrolled down to the comments, expecting cheerful expression of gratitude. But she was instantly infuriated. The first comment read: "Let me see if I've got this right. . . . So now little kids get to build people with no arms or legs? Build little buildings with handicapped ramps? Gee, what fun!" That's precisely the attitude that needed to be overcome. Meryl was especially happy to witness the subsequent "take down":

> If the kid is handicapped why shouldn't he or she feel like being handicapped is normal, and a part of the view on society? Hey here's a crazy idea, maybe if kids think of handicapped ramps as an essential part to buildings, later when they get to a position to be able to do something about it, they will, and we'll have a better society for everyone. I'm sick and tired of handicap being swept under the rug by disgusting

mindsets such as yours. This isn't about representation; it's about acknowledging an aspect of life that kids should be aware of.

That's more like it she thought. Later comments were full of "thank-yous," and "'bout times," and people just being thrilled.

By the time she was through, Meryl had become *exasperated with herself*. She realized that she had never really thought much about the disabled before. As a copywriter and artist, she thought she was being particularly careful to be inclusive, and not rely on stereotypes, particularly in the case of race and ethnicity. And she was *very careful* about her representations of women. Still, disability had never been on her radar. She wondered why. Was it because she had never come across a client who needed or wanted to include the disabled in an ad? Or was she hesitant because she didn't know how to "do it right"? She remembered the headline, "quiet inclusion speaks volumes."

Meryl reproached herself; she'd never thought about what it must feel like to never see yourself included in the media. Then she recalled another comment: "I have no problem with LEGO choosing to make such toys but is it really in these children's best interest to glamorize being disabled?" One thing was clear: representation of the disabled was complicated. You certainly don't want to cause more harm than good. The disabled were on Meryl's radar now. She was determined to keep them there and do something about it.

Meryl should be congratulated for taking time amid the demands and time constraints of her copywriting job to pause and reflect on "what she was doing when she was doing her work" (and what she wasn't doing), and for making a commitment to thoughtful, appropriate inclusion of the disabled in the future.

Advertising may pride itself on being insightful, cutting edge, and savvy about popular culture, but it relies heavily on stereotypes. In fact, in advertising, stereotyping is almost an essential part of the business of effective and efficient communication. Is stereotyping unethical? Given that stereotypes are "misrepresentations" of a group, the use of stereotypes is deceptive and morally wrong. And, if stereotypes cause harm, using them is also morally wrong. In short, stereotypes are ethically problematic.

What's the solution? Given the media's power to "teach culture," it is important that printed and visual representations benefit people, individually and collectively, and that they are never degrading. Advertising can contribute to discrimination through the use of inappropriate and dated stereotypes as well as through marginalization through exclusion. The ramifications are far-reaching and long-lasting. In an article on NPR, "On the Image of Disability," Laura Block noted:

[W]hen someone learns today that she will have a disability or a condition understood as disabling, when a parent-to-be learns that his child will have a physical or cognitive impairment, when television reports that a public figure has become disabled, certain specters are likely to arise—emotionally freighted, irrational, even mutually contradictory—of what the life of a person with a disability must be like.[36]

Why does the use of stereotyping persist? What we see, hear, and read in advertisements is often the product of a small group of decision-makers. Each of these individuals brings his/her own "picture in their head" of people with disabilities; those pictures are often stereotypes. In *What Media Classes REALLY Want to Discuss*, Greg Smith suggests that because the decision-makers are focused on what they believe will bring in consumers, on success in the marketplace, they may be reluctant to move outside stereotypes that have "sold well" in the past. In these instances, the risk involved—the possibility of consumer protest or declining sales—trumps the goals of social justice and fairness. Popular culture images can circulate for a long time with little connection to anything real. "As long as there is a market for images, Hollywood will be tempted to perpetuate them, regardless of whether they portray a 'realistic' vision of a group."[37]

This may not be done with any intentionality, and may be largely unconscious. It is possible and indeed, very likely, that the power of stereotypes in culture—to foster or reinforce (or to challenge) prejudices and discrimination—never enters into our thinking. The reliance on stereotypes suggests a lack of reflection, laziness, or possibly, ignorance. In "Spanish Gold: Stereotypes, Ideology, and the Construction of a U.S. Latino Market," Roberta Astroff writes that in constructing the Hispanic market, advertisers retained traditional stereotypes simply re-interpreting them to suggest "market" potential that could be "sold" to advertisers.[38]

To create fair, respectful representations of the disabled, it is vital first to recognize destructive stereotypes haunting popular culture. Numerous lists of the most frequently used stereotypes of the disabled are available. The list here is adapted from *Beyond Affliction: The Disability History Project*:[39]

1. People with disabilities are different from fully "human" people; they are partial or limited people, in an "other" and lesser category.

2. The successful "handicapped" person is superhuman, triumphing over adversity in a way which serves as an example to others; the impairment gives disabled persons a chance to exhibit virtues they didn't know they had, and teach the rest of us patience and courage. (Disabled individuals call this the "supercrip" stereotype.)

3. The burden of disability is unending; life with a disabled person is a life of constant sorrow, and the able-bodied stand under a continual obligation to help them. People with disabilities and their families—the "noble sacrificers"—are the most perfect objects of charity; their function is to inspire benevolence in others, to awaken feelings of kindness and generosity.

4. A disability is a sickness, something to be fixed, an abnormality to be corrected or cured. Tragic disabilities are those with no possibility of cure, or where attempts at cure fail.

5. People with disabilities are a menace to others, to themselves, and to society. This is especially true of people with mental disability. People with disabilities are consumed

by an incessant, inevitable rage and anger at their loss and at those who are not disabled. Those with mental disabilities lack the moral sense that would restrain them from hurting others or themselves.

6. People with disabilities, especially cognitive impairments, are holy innocents endowed with special grace, with the function of inspiring others to value life. The person with a disability will be compensated for his/her lack by greater abilities and strengths in other areas—abilities that are sometimes beyond the ordinary.

People with disabilities should not be misrepresented, ignored, or hidden from the general public. In assessing advertising representations, it may be useful to step behind Rawls's veil of ignorance and, unsure whether you would emerge as able-bodied or disabled, ask: would I find the representation to be fair and just?

To whom is duty owed? Duty-based ethics would require reflection on loyalties. Does loyalty to a client suggesting continued reliance on "tried and true (stereotypical)" representations trump a commitment to fair and equitable representations for the disabled individual and society at large? Or, does a sense of social justice coupled with a professional duty as a client advocate compel efforts to change the client's mind? Does a sense of commitment to the disabled, individually and collectively, supersede you own hesitation?

Because stereotypes are both an essential part of advertising and ethically problematic, advertisers necessarily must take great ethical care in their use. The American Association of People with Disabilities warns of the reliance on stereotypical representations so often found in popular culture:

> Deaf people don't always know how to lipread and blind people don't always identify people by touching their faces. People using wheelchairs don't suddenly stand up at a particularly emotional moment of their lives. People with autism do not have magical powers. People with disabilities don't always want to be "cured" or have our disability magically go away—we simply want to be included in the mainstream and be respected as equals. And we most definitely aren't evil; nor are we absolutely helpless. We are contributing members of the larger society and we want to be independent with full access.[40]

CASE 29. SPECTACLE FOR SOCIAL CHANGE: CELEBRATION OR CO-OPTATION?

FCKH8 describes itself as "a for-profit T-shirt company with an activist heart and a passionate social change mission: arming thousands of people with pro-LGBT equality, anti-racism and gender equality shirts that act as 'mini-billboards' for change." Visitors are invited to "Join the FCKH8 community to shed light on these issues and to educate yourself in order to speak out against inequality."[41]

In October 2014, FCKH8, a for-profit advocacy organization introduced a video, "Potty-Mouthed Princesses Drop F-bombs to Support Feminism." In the video, girls (aged six–thirteen) in princess costumes (the press release calls the girls "adorably articulate little ladies in sparkling tiaras") speak out about sexual assault, race, and gender inequality, and edicts to "be pretty," all the while "dropping the F-bomb" over and over and over again. In fact, the satin-clad princesses "dropped the F-bomb" sixteen times in two and a half minutes all the while emoting with exaggerated gestures and extreme facial expressions:

> What the f*ck? I'm not some pretty f*ckin' helpless princess in distress. I'm pretty f*ckin' powerful and ready for success!
>
> What is more offensive . . . a little girl saying "f*ck" or the f**king unequal and sexist way society treats girls and women?

Entertainment Tonight aired a story on the video and the *ET* online site included the video with a disclaimer: "WARNING: This video does contain explicit language. But for a good cause!"[42] The shock value was enormous. The campaign generated mountains of publicity: in news, blogs, and of course, in social media. Reactions tended toward the negative but focused not on the "feminist message," but primarily on the message delivery, which was said to be: "Shameful," "Absolutely disgusting," "Absolutely nothing cute, funny or redeeming in this video." "Horrible. Horrible. Horrible. This is a disgrace." *Adweek*'s Michelle Castillo identified the clip as an effective use of "shock-vertising," advertising that intentionally startles and offends by violating shared understandings, moral or social codes, or moral sensibilities.[43] According to Castillio, "People are sharing the clip and it's going viral. And that's the best form of advertising. . . . They've definitely made their point."[44]

Luke Montgomery, the director of the spot, appeared on *Entertainment Tonight* with mother and daughter Brooklyne and Caige Coulter the following day. Six-year-old Caige appears as one of the princesses in the clip. Challenged by one of two hosts on the necessity of using an approach that was so obviously going to offend so many, Montgomery defended the idea of using a bad word for a good cause in an effort to get people's attention:

> A lot of people are focusing on that we use the "F" word in this video. . . . The reason we did use the "F" word is because we want people to focus on statistics like one out of five women will be raped or sexually assaulted in their lifetime, or the fact that women and men doing the exact same job, the woman gets paid 23 percent less than men. In 2014, that's what's shocking, not the "F" word.[45]

All five (Caige, Brooklyne, Luke Montgomery, and the two hosts) sat together around a table, talking about sexual assault, a topic which they indicated made them uncomfortable. The host asked Caige if she understood what the words she was saying in her performance meant. Caige replied, "I don't know." When asked, "Do you use these words at home?" Caige shook her head; the host replied, "Good."

When Brooklyne was asked by a seemingly disbelieving host why she allowed her daughter to be in the video, her first response was that she and her daughter were there [Hollywood] from Colorado for Caige's acting. "First of all. It's a job. It's a craft." Then, a tearful Brooklyne said:

People who know us know that we are a good family, and if this didn't mean something to me as a woman who was inappropriately touched at the age of four, I would not have let my daughter do this. . . . Getting a message out like that is so important for me. . . . And, you know what? It's done in a crazy way, but like I was telling [Luke] earlier, we've been sitting here for decades of people talking about women's rights and where is it? . . . I don't see the stats that say women are equally paid . . . or somebody's foundations for getting sexual awareness or sexual help or something like that. Where's [the] charities and people who are doing stuff to educate at an early age? Teen pregnancy! It's out there, these kids know this kind of stuff.[46]

Following these interviews, comments turned to questioning the girls' parents. "What's wrong with parents these days?" "This totally made me sick. Are parents so driven to ruin their kids?" Still others turned on *Entertainment Tonight*:

YOU SHOULD ALL BE SUED FOR CHILD ABUSE!! ET [*Entertainment Tonight*], the parents and director!! ET you should be ashamed for your reckless conduct in broadcasting this with total disregard for the viewer AND look at the time slot you are showing this in?!!! exposing the viewing public's children to this outrageous abuse of innocent children!!! Has any of you thought of the psychological effect this is going to have on these kids that were pushed before the cameras by their irresponsible parents?

I can't believe you would have this little girl ON STAGE and PARTICIPATING in the discussion about sexual assault. You are hypocrites to THEN attack the mother when you are guilty of the EXACT SAME THING.

Interspersed with these critical remarks was an occasional comment from someone who focused on the importance of the message and was frustrated by the fact that all the focus seemed to be on the delivery of that important message. Perhaps not realizing that she echoed the princesses' words nearly verbatim, one writer commented: "What I think is absurd is that almost everybody here is more concerned with swear words than they are about pay inequality, and rape and violence."

Those defending the use of young girls to deliver the message were often as adamant as the detractors:

"I would say that yes although shocking and as uncomfortable as it [talking about sexual assault] may very well be, not armoring our young girls and boys with this serious and very important information is child abuse." Another wrote:

[F]or ET Cohost (female) to say the sexual topic is too early for a six year old. I strongly disagree. When you have pedafiles [sic] make statements that "eight is too late", parents must empower their children at an early age as early as two as to what is good touch and bad touch. Too many cases of unreported incest, rape, molestation, and assault . . . in this country and abroad. So many people have been scarred by this [sic] acts of violence and left disillusioned, life altered, and forever changed.

CNN commentator Sally Kohn somewhat sarcastically remarked: "at least the video has a positive message about girl power and women's rights. But it is also an ad."

Not an ad for a feminist cause, as the title, "Potty-Mouthed Princesses Drop F-bombs to Support Feminism," implied, but an ad for FCKH8, "an on-line, for-profit, advocacy group selling 'anti-sexism' 'anti-racism,' and 'LGBT equality' clothing and gear."[47] The "pitch" arrived in the last thirty seconds of the two-and-a-half minute video. Two women sporting T-shirts that read "Girls just want to have FUN-damental rights," and "This is what a feminist looks like" entered the picture, talking just as loudly and gesturing just as manically as the girls. The "call to action" came at the conclusion of the video when one of the women held up a five-dollar bill and announced that five dollars from every shirt sold would be given to "kick-ass charities."

The video was parodied the very next day;[48] and soon YouTube was rife with parodies and video reactions. Many called the statistics presented in the clip into question, debunking them as "bad science" or selective use of statistics. One of the most ambitious of these challenges came from TL;DR, a site devoted to "exposing human stupidity in all its forms using my glorious super-power or common sense . . . and Google search."[49] The TL;DR host asks "Who's Still Exploiting Children? Feminists." Claiming to be "troubled by things that can't be proven or indeed things that can be disproven with even a five-minute Google search," he goes on to provide information and visual evidence debunking each of the claims.[50]

In November, the princesses returned in a video focused on domestic abuse. That video opened with one of the girls appearing in a stained white T-shirt pretending to be a rough-neck man. After delivering an offensive joke regarding domestic abuse, the princesses appeared. This time, they sported heavy, realistic-looking bruises and arms carried in slings. Perhaps not surprisingly, this video stirred even more controversy; one might say the conversation was "much louder and more intense." In December, FCKH8 released a third video with a sexist Santa; all the princesses wanted for Christmas was equal pay.

The videos have more than ten million hits, and the "delivery technique" has spawned a number of copy-cat "expletive-laden" advocacy efforts.[51]

This "charity T-shirt fundraising campaign," while getting a lot of attention and notoriety, raises a number of ethical questions. At the outset, the information provided in the ad— information that purportedly is the motivation for the campaign—is inaccurate. Though statistics reveal a deplorable degree of inequality, they don't approach the startling numbers presented in the clip. The video is deceptive, and as such is not only unethical but also illegal. Deception is defined as "a statement or omission likely to mislead a reasonable consumer in a material way." False and deceptive advertising have no First Amendment protection.

Even if the statistics provided had been accurate (that is, even if the ad had not been deceptive), adopting Kant's belief that human beings should not be treated merely as a means to an end, but are to be respected as ends in themselves, the FCKH8 effort is clearly unethical. Virtually everyone involved—audiences, young girls performing as princesses, the "equality causes"— is seemingly used to serve FCKH8's utilitarian goal of selling merchandise.

Is this FCKH8 video a campaign for social justice or an ad for T-shirts? The Potty-Mouth Princesses videos lack transparency. They have every appearance of being a social movement effort to draw attention to social injustices, calling attention to the magnitude of the problem (unfortunately using inaccurate statistics) then asking for the donation, which in this case is asking viewers to buy a T-shirt. It isn't until the final thirty seconds that the source (and the purpose?) of the message is revealed except for a small logo in the upper right corner of the screen. CNN's Sally Kohn points to the irony of the effort saying: "The video wants you to channel all your outrage, not into volunteering at a domestic violence shelter or calling for the reintroduction of the Equal Rights Amendment, but into buying a T-shirt."[52] The receivers of the message may be unaware they are being persuaded; the execution of the messages leaves little room for counterargument.

While FCKH8 might defend its effort, identifying the campaign as a cause-marketing campaign in which donations are tied to consumer purchases, evidence of that is sparse. The company's website indicates that FCKH8 has given "over $250,000 to the equality causes through directly funded projects and donations to LGBT charities." Again, the "equality causes" remain unspecified, as do the "LGBT charities." Additionally the amount FCKH8 has donated is less than might be expected over the four-year period of the company's existence. A commenter on the feminist website Jezebel wrote sarcastically: "Hahaha, they are keeping that extra . . . profit for themselves, no way it's $6 to make them [T-shirts]." This led another to reply: "I wonder how much money the seamstresses in Honduras or Vietnam make per shirt."[53]

The cause, always vague, and broadly identified as "causes of equality" (another transparency problem), is co-opted, in service to the brand. Equality becomes nothing more than a sales appeal. Some recognize it as such. For example, TL;DR takes FCKH8 to task saying: "I hope you're not planning on exploiting those little girls as a means of making money now from people's knee-jerk emotional reactions."[54]

It is clear that the many who viewed the clip identified feminists as the source of the message. For example, one writer on the conservative online site *The Federalist* noted:

> You've got to hand it to feminists: Just when you think they can't get any crazier, they go ahead and up the ante. If I've written some version of this line before—and I'm sure I have, because today's feminists are truly the unwanted gift that keeps on giving— please forgive me. My brain tissue is a little scarred by what I've just seen.[55]

In fact, the title of the video, "Potty-Mouthed Princesses Drop F-bombs to Support Feminism," suggests that feminism is indeed the "cause." The exploitation of the cause of equality is especially troubling, not because of the "mistaken identity" of any particular cause, but because the effort in a sense exploits *every* equality cause: a "slap in the face." Viewers, equality causes, individuals supporting and supported by those causes are all diminished by this effort.

FCKH8's blatant effort to deliberately "shock" the audience through the violation of social and moral codes goes beyond questions of taste and decency. Respect for message recipients is at the heart of ethical communication. Sexualized and demeaning images of children are some of the most sensitive issues. Judging from the volume and character of the comments in response to these efforts, it is readily apparent that the majority of the audience was emotionally offended. Children aged six to thirteen remain vulnerable and any use of child actors demands thoughtful reflection. The potential for harm, not only physical but also psychological, should be taken into account. It is hard to believe that "spouting vulgarities" or being "artfully" bruised and battered will have no impact on these girls' psyches. The use of vulnerable children, performing in roles they apparently don't understand, "spouting vulgarities" is exploitation of that vulnerability, offensive, and disturbing to the moral sensibilities of the viewers.

This leaves the question: is "shock-vertising" inherently unethical? Certainly in the absence of resources with which to buy advertising time and space and in light of difficulty getting editorial coverage for marginalized groups or controversial causes, social movement groups often resort to sensationalism, shocking images, and advertising rhetoric.[56] People for the Ethical Treatment of Animals (PETA) president Ingrid Newkirk once noted: "The truth is that extremism and outrage provide the fundamental fuel for many special interest groups."[57] Media ethicist Thomas Bivins suggests that the question to be asked when considering the use of shock advertising is: "whom are we offending and why?" He continues:

> The part of the question that goes to the morality of the act is the "why" part. By applying the criteria of means and ends, we could say that using shock advertising to draw attention to a moral cause is probably ethical—remembering that unethical techniques are still suspect, even in a good cause. However, if we accept that selling a product or simply drawing attention to a brand is an amoral end [that is, neither moral nor immoral] then the morality of using potentially offensive tactics to accomplish that end deserves a much harder scrutiny.[58]

The ethicality of using words, actions, and images deliberately to offend hinges on the morality of the ends sought. Is the end so morally worthy that it mitigates the use of morally questionable means in order to achieve it?

CASE 30. ANTI-OBESITY: A QUESTION OF IMAGES

Georgia has the second highest obesity rate in the country. In 2012, Children's Healthcare of Atlanta, a pediatric hospital, was determined to do something about it. They created the Strong4Life program, a five-year, $50 million wellness movement to reverse the epidemic of childhood obesity in Georgia. The program includes community partnerships, health care provider programs, school programs, policy change efforts, and public awareness.[59]

As a part of the Strong4Life program, Children's Healthcare created an ad campaign modeled after anti-smoking campaigns. That is, the ads were designed to shock families into recognizing that obesity is a problem. The ads have been described as: "in-your-face," "grim," "harsh," "stark," and "scary."

According to Linda Matzigkeit, vice president of Children's Healthcare, the ads were intended to be harsh because nobody would listen if they weren't. Research had shown that 50 percent of the people surveyed didn't know childhood obesity was a problem and 75 percent of Georgia parents with overweight kids didn't recognize the problem. "We wanted to come up with something arresting and hard-hitting to grab people."[60]

> If you don't believe me, visit our hospital and see the kids we are now taking care of—that more and more have Type 2 diabetes, have hypertension, need knee replacements—and its breaking our heart to see these adult-type diseases in the children that we serve.[61]

The billboards, which also appeared on buses and in train stations, used stark black-and-white images of overweight children with warnings of health risks linked to obesity. The messages: "Being fat takes the fun out of being a kid"; "It's hard to be a little girl when you're not"; "Chubby isn't cute if it leads to type two diabetes"; "Big bones didn't make me this way – big meals did."

Children's Healthcare also released two similarly themed videos. In one, a little boy and a mom, both clearly overweight, enter a room with two folding chairs. They sit and look at each other. The boy asks: "Mom, why am I fat?" The mother hangs her head and the tag line appears: "75% of Georgia parents with overweight kids don't recognize the problem." In another video, a sad, overweight girl says: "I don't like going to school, because all the other kids pick on me. It hurts my feelings."

The ads were intended to spark conversation in order to raise awareness and encourage action. The buzz was almost immediate. News sites around the country talked about the "controversy swirling about harsh anti-obesity ads." A petition on forechange.com called for removal of the Strong4Life ads. In part, the petition read:

> These ads put too much shame onto overweight kids, insinuating that they are not happy or cute simply due to their weight. As you know, children do not eat unhealthily on their

own accord, they do so because parents don't have the time, means, or knowledge of how to provide their kids with healthy foods and schools serve them awful options.[62]

The campaign divided and even angered health providers. "We need to fight obesity, not obese children," noted one professional in a special report on ABC news.[63] "The ads can hurt the very market they are targeting . . . stigmatization leads to lower self-esteem, potential depression." Alan Guttmacher, a leading child health expert at the National Institutes of Health, agreed, saying the ads carry "a great risk of increasing stigma" around childhood obesity and as a result pose "risks to the psychological health of obese adults." Children's Healthcare was repeatedly charged with fat-shaming.

The use of children in advertising communications requires careful consideration and reflection on possible consequences. Children's Healthcare took the responsibility for the well-being of the child actors in the ad seriously. Children and their parents who responded to an ad seeking overweight children on Facebook heard about the substance of the ads and also heard about the possible backlash they could face. One actor, Maya Bradley, told CNN she had been hesitant at first, but thought the ads might help others like her. Feedback from peers was generally positive and she then became actively involved in defending the ads in the ensuing melee, even appearing on the *Today Show*.[64]

The campaign has ended but the controversy over Children's Healthcare's approach continues unabated. Regardless of the reaction, Children's Healthcare is unapologetic, saying that as far as it is concerned, the ads achieved their goal: they got people talking.

Children's Healthcare of Atlanta finds itself in a difficult situation. Childhood obesity is a grave problem in the state. Research has shown that in addition to physical health risks, obese children struggle with diminished self-confidence, anxiety, and depression. Equally compelling is evidence that societal prejudice against obesity is widespread. According to the Obesity Action Coalition, peers are frequent critics and school is a common setting where "weight bias" occurs:

> Research shows that negative attitudes toward obese children begin as early as preschool age, from three to five years old. Preschoolers report that their overweight peers are mean and less desirable playmates compared to non-overweight children, and they believe that overweight children are mean, stupid, ugly, unhappy, lazy and have few friends.[65]

Both the decision to run the campaign and the question of whether or not the campaign should continue were no doubt difficult ones. The use of images in any advertising communication requires careful reflection on possible consequences. This is particularly true when images of children are used or when images are used in communication directed to vulnerable child audiences. In this instance, obesity added another dimension of vulnerability. While there is nothing inherently unethical in using the images, or in using images of children, the decision to develop an approach that would undoubtedly shock many—particularly in a culture heavily invested in perfection and beauty as well as protective of children—was a carefully considered one.

By all accounts, conversations with the parents and child actors were forthright and transparent. Health care professionals, parents, and the children considered how a child might react to seeing him or herself in an advertisement about obesity, how the child would react to the likelihood that peers will see the advertising, possible ramifications given the propensity toward bullying and exclusion of obese children, how the parents would react to the fact that the advertising might be seen as calling their parenting skills into question or perhaps acknowledging their own weight problems if that was the case.

Children's Healthcare felt its professional responsibilities as a health care provider and its duty to the state of Georgia trumped any concerns of offensiveness that might arise. Although the campaign wasn't targeted at children but at parents, the ads were placed in the most public of venues, billboards, buses, and train stations, and most certainly would be seen by the children and their peers. The charges of shaming and the possible stigmatization of obese children that might result thus raised concerns far greater than that of offensiveness, and certainly concerns that ran counter to Children's Healthcare's intentions. Still, successful public health campaigns often portray real people with real problems. Ultimately, the ethicality of the decision might best be judged by its consequences. In the short term, the ads appeared to be working;[66] yet, given the inability to foresee long-term consequences, it is impossible to make a decision as to the ethicality of the action on that basis.

In addition to the concerns related to health care and the possibility of stigma associated with the advertising images, public perceptions of the institution, its credibility and compassion, could have lasting impact on its reputation, reducing its effectiveness at serving the health needs in the state. "The trick is figuring out how to be anti-obesity without being anti-obese people—and boiling these issues down to a slogan makes this difficult to do."[67]

NOTES

1. Nick Clyde, "The Society of Spectacle: The Unsettling Consequences of Living in an Image-Based Culture," www.refinethemind.com/society-of-spectacle/.
2. Michael Schudson, *Advertising, The Uneasy Persuasion* (New York: Basic Books, 1987), 233.
3. Roland Marchand, *Advertising the American Dream: Making Way for Modernity, 1920–1940* (Berkeley: University of California Press, 1985), xvii.
4. William Leiss, Stephen Kline, Sut Jhally, and Jacqueline Botterill, *Social Communication in Advertising: Consumption in the Mediated Marketplace* (New York: Routledge, 2005), 75.
5. Christine Rosen, "The Image Culture," *The New Atlantis*, Fall 2005.
6. https://vimeo.com/20736616.

7. Ibid.
8. Naomi Klein, *No Logo* (New York: Picador, 2002).
9. Robin Givhan, fashion editor of the *Washington Post*, in Rebecca Johnson, "Walking a Thin Line," *Vogue*, April 2007, p. 384.
10. www.takepart.com/article/2014/01/30/10-years-after-doves-real-beauty-campaign-brands-are-fighting-female-form.
11. www.artinstitutes.edu/blog/picture-imperfect-digital-image-manipulation-ethics.
12. Ibid.
13. Rebecca Seal, "The Incredible Shrinking Woman," *The Observer*, September 9, 2007.
14. Ibid.
15. Valli Herman, "Is Skinny Going Out of Style?" *Los Angeles Times*, December 16, 2006, p. E-1.
16. Unilever press release.
17. www.change.org/p/seventeen-magazine-give-girls-images-of-real-girls.
18. www.youtube.com/watch?v=17j5QzF3kqE.
19. http://jezebel.com/the-enigmatic-mystery-of-beyonces-golf-thighs-1562154200.
20. www.huffingtonpost.com/2014/01/17/aerie-unretouched-ads-photos_n_4618139.html.
21. www.adweek.com/news/press/which-sports-illustrated-swimsuit-cover-leading-conversation-social-media-169723.
22. www.mediapost.com/publications/article/269209/snickers-satirizes-retouching-in-si-swimsuit-iss.html?utm_source=newsletter&utm_medium=email&utm_content=headline&utm_campaign=90432.
23. http://theinspirationroom.com/daily/2006/dove-evolution/.
24. www.dailymail.co.uk/femail/article-3321748/Victoria-Beckham-defends-use-skinny-models-showcase-designs-New-York-fashion-week.html.
25. http://time.com/3770696/france-banned-ultra-thin-models/.
26. www.harrington.edu/student-life/blog/august-2013/is-photo-retouching-ethical.
27. Ibid.
28. http://nymag.com/thecut/2010/08/photoshop_retouching.html.
29. www.facebook.com/photo.php?fbid=10153816866666004&set=a.10150224898921004.360771.644796003&type=3.
30. Cone Communications/Ebiquity Global CSR Study, www.conecomm.com.
31. www.adweek.com/adfreak/lego-unveils-its-first-disabled-minifigure-good-week-inclusivity-169305.
32. www.usatoday.com/story/news/nation/2014/11/28/lego-builds-adult-fan-base/19637025/.
33. www.bbc.com/news/magazine-28660069.
34. www.change.org/p/lego-please-positively-represent-disability-in-your-toys.
35. www.adweek.com/adfreak/lego-unveils-its-first-disabled-minifigure-good-week-inclusivity-169305.
36. www.npr.org/programs/disability/ba_shows.dir/children.dir/highlights/stereot.html.
37. Smith, Greg M., "Role Models and Stereotypes: an Introduction to the 'Other,'" in *What Media Classes REALLY Want to Discuss* (New York: Routledge, 2011), 88–113.
38. Roberta Astroff, "Spanish Gold: Stereotypes, Ideology, and the Construction of a U.S. Latino Market," *Howard Journal of Communications* 1:4 (Winter 1988–1989): 155–173.
39. www.npr.org/programs/disability/ba_shows.dir/children.dir/highlights/stereot.html.
40. www.aapd.com/resources/power-grid-blog/positive-images-of-people.html.
41. www.FCKH8.com.
42. www.etonline.com/news/152912_princesses_drop_f_bombs_to_support_feminism/.
43. Thomas Bivins, *Mixed Media: Moral Distinctions in Advertising, Public Relations and Journalism* (New York: Routledge, 2009), 220–222.
44. www.etonline.com/news/152977_f_bombs_for_feminism_is_this_viral_video_exploiting_girls_or_empowering_them/.
45. www.etonline.com/news/152991_potty_mouth_princess_director_defends_controversial_campaign/?utm_content=buffer0e489&utm_medium=social&utm_source=facebook.com&utm_campaign=buffer.

46. Ibid.
47. www.FCKH8.com.
48. www.youtube.com/watch?v=SgNV3FbottE.
49. www.youtube.com/watch?v=PHmuPrFymjc.
50. Ibid.
51. www.politico.com/story/2015/11/donald-trump-latino-advocacy-ad-215591.
52. www.cnn.com/2014/10/24/opinion/kohn-potty-mouthed-princesses/.
53. http://jezebel.com/the-potty-mouth-princesses-are-back-and-now-they-have-b-1663329964.
54. www.youtube.com/watch?v=PHmuPrFymjc.
55. http://thefederalist.com/2014/10/23/potty-mouthed-princesses-and-the-feminist-rabbit-hole/.
56. Carrie Packwood Freeman, "A Greater Means to the Greater Good: Ethical Guidelines to Meet Social Movement Organization Advocacy Challenges," *Journal of Mass Media Ethics* 24:4 (2009): 269–288.
57. Ingrid Newkirk, PETA president, quoted in Michael Specter, "The Extremist: The Woman Behind the Most Successful Radical Group in America," *New Yorker*, April 14, 2003, 57, www.newyorker.com/magazine/2003/04/14/the-extremist.
58. Bivins, *Mixed Media*, 222.
59. www.strong4life.com/en/pages/about/ArticleDetails.aspx?articleid=AboutStrong4Life&sectionid=overview.
60. www.cnn.com/2012/02/07/health/atlanta-child-obesity-ads/.
61. www.npr.org/2012/01/09/144799538/controversy-swirls-around-harsh-anti-obesity-ads%20Strong%204Life...GA...NPR.
62. www.change.org/p/childrens-healthcare-of-atlanta-end-the-stop-sugarcoating-obesity-campaign.
63. http://abcnews.go.com/Health/Wellness/stop-sugarcoating-child-obesity-ads-draw-controversy/story?id=15273638.
64. www.cnn.com/2012/02/07/health/atlanta-child-obesity-ads/.
65. www.obesityaction.org/educational-resources/resource-articles-2/childhood-obesity-resource-articles/childhood-obesity-and-stigma.
66. www.prnewswire.com/news-releases/strong4life-addresses-growing-number-of-children-who-likely-will-become-overweight-or-obese-adults-139469903.html.
67. www.theatlantic.com/health/archive/2012/09/obesity-campaigns-the-fine-line-between-educating-and-shaming/262401/.

8

THE MEDIA ARE COMMERCIAL

The United States media are commercial. What exactly does this mean? A casual response might be, "There are ads." And indeed, that's part of the answer; advertising makes up a substantial portion of our media content. Advertising provides the financial support for most media, and for some media is the *only* source of revenue. The ensuing trade-offs are the ongoing stuff of pride—advertising helps make media available free or at lower cost, without possible dependence on government subsidy—and controversy.

The media are also commercial in the sense that in our capitalist economic system, the media are structured so that their primary goal is profit. Audiences become commodities, essentially products, produced and sold to advertisers. Insofar as advertisers are looking for people who are likely to buy what they have to sell, and have both the resources and the willingness and opportunity to spend those resources, not all audiences are equal; some are more desirable than others. Advertisers "shop" for audiences in the media marketplace much the same way consumers shop for products.

As a result, the media shape their content to attract those audiences advertisers want to reach. So, for example, our media landscape has been shaped in large part by the advertising industry's preoccupation with millennials (those born from the early 1980s to around 2000). Individuals in this group are "digital natives" and have embraced online television such as Netflix, Amazon, and Hulu. They have preference for binge viewing (all episodes of a program released at one time). The increased number of original programs released by online streaming services stand as testimonial to that preoccupation.

This arrangement between advertising and the media gives rise to some of advertising's most common ethical charges:

Advertising may exercise control over non-editorial content, or may attempt to do so. Maintaining a barrier between advertising and editorial content is a hallmark of journalistic integrity in a democratic society, a responsibility clearly stated in the Society of Professional Journalists' Code of Ethics.[1] Charges of the media allegedly "selling out" to advertiser interests are a longstanding concern, and that concern has escalated as media struggle in the current economic climate. Nearly twenty-five years ago, Ronald K. L. Collins and Todd Gitlin wrote in the introduction to their book, *Dictating Content*:

> Typically, we associate censorship and related problems with meddling or authoritarian government. [This book] documents that in modern America, censorship is far more likely to be imposed by advertisers and advertising-related pressures, and far more likely to be tolerated by our commercially supported media.[2]

Advertiser attempts to shape non-advertising content are not limited to news, but extend to other media content as well. Advertisers have been known to withdraw their support if certain popular programs don't change "offensive" content. Sometimes, the effort to exert control is explicit: a statement that advertising will be pulled in the event of some "offense" to the advertiser. Consumer threats of advertiser boycott or public outrage over inappropriate media content can also lead advertisers to withdraw advertising support. At still other times, a medium might practice self-censorship, "softening" or choosing not to publish a story simply to avoid the possibility of a disconcerted advertiser. In many women's interest and fashion magazines, a "supportive editorial environment" or "complementary copy" is almost essential to attracting advertisers.[3] In recent years, native advertising and product placement/integration have become popular techniques, blurring the distinction between advertising and non-commercial content.

Advertising influences media choices available, that is, it "creates" the media landscape. As noted, that landscape tends to be designed to attract the "haves," usually defined in terms of consumption potential. This means that entire segments of the population might be ignored if advertisers don't deem them "desirable" as a target market, if advertisers aren't interested in talking to them. In this way, advertisers play a powerful role in shaping the marketplace of ideas.

These concerns are particularly troubling given the normative role of the press in a democracy, and have intensified in the face of persistent media consolidation. The number of corporations that control the majority of the media has been shrinking rapidly, placing enormous political, economic, and indeed cultural power in the hands of a few corporate giants. Corporate owners may view the media primarily as profit centers, treating media essentially as products rather than recognizing the foundational role of supporting media in a democracy. Robert McChesney, media scholar, activist, and co-founder of Free Press, a "national non-partisan organization working to reform the media" articulates this point repeatedly and vehemently, calling attention to the "clash" of democratic and capitalist ideologies in the context of our media system: "the tensions between democracy and capitalism is becoming increasingly evident, and communication—so necessary to both—can hardly serve two masters at once."[4] McChesney elaborates on freepress.net, the activist website he founded: "Media must not be considered just another business: They are special institutions in our society. Information is the lifeblood of democracy—and when viewpoints are cut off and ideas cannot find an outlet, our democracy suffers."[5]

Though advertisers rarely call attention to the role advertising plays in serving democracy, the recent ad-blocking controversy led one *Advertising Age* reporter to do exactly that, asking: "Could Ad Blocking Really Dampen Democracy?" The reporter suggested that candidates in the 2016 presidential campaign "might make plans to reach prospective voters online, . . . only to be automatically stiff-armed by ad blockers," concluding "some think ad blockers could actually be the death knell for democracy."[6]

The digital revolution has transformed the media ecosystem in fundamental ways. New platforms emerge at an accelerating pace, providing an increasing array of opportunities for advertisers to interact with media audiences in a variety of formats on a variety of devices. Because digital content can easily move from platform to platform (you can view "television" programming "live" or time-shift viewing to a more convenient time; you can stream programming on your computer, tablet, or smartphone), media are no longer controlled distribution systems for marketing messages. The ability of any one medium to create an audience has diminished. The "stickiness" of a site, that is, its ability to draw an audience in order to generate advertising revenue, has given way to "spreadability," "the potential—both technical and cultural—for audiences to share content for their own purposes, sometimes with permission of rights holders, sometimes against their wishes."[7]

Advertising continues to be the primary source of revenue for these new platforms. Monetization of the internet is made possible by tracking individuals' online activity. This tracking, itself a point of substantial controversy and concern, enables advertisers to deliver and consumers to receive advertising relevant to their interests. Programmatic buying, machines using algorithms to buy online advertising, has become standard in the industry, enabling advertisers to individualize and personalize advertising messages to a "customer of one" in a matter of milliseconds.[8] In *The Filter Bubble*, Eli Pariser argues that increased personalization made possible by algorithms leads to decreased exposure to unfiltered information. Instead, what we see reinforces what we already believe and hides opinions different from our own.[9]

The cases in this chapter examine several complex ethical dilemmas that arise in our commercial media system. "Media Gatekeepers" reminds us that while media depend on advertisers and the revenue they provide, advertisers also depend on the media to reach audiences effectively and efficiently. This case explores power wielded by media vehicles to accept or reject advertising. The remaining three cases focus on marketers' efforts to counter audiences' apparent diminishing "patience" with advertising and the resultant decrease in advertising effectiveness. "Native Advertising: Advertising and Editorial Content" examines something of a "hybrid" of product placement, variously identified as native advertising, sponsored content, or branded content. It probes ethical dilemmas posed by the blurring of advertising and editorial content. "Welcome to Madison and Vine" examines the ever-increasing presence of product placement in media content. The final case, "Ad Blocking: A Perfect Storm" examines the constellation of activities that led to the current ad-blocking controversy and the industry's reaction to ad-blocking efforts in the context of an individual's decision-making regarding installation of ad-blocking software.

CASE 31. MEDIA GATEKEEPERS

The marketplace of ideas, the belief that "the best way to discover truth is through robust competition of a multitude of voices," is a metaphor deeply entrenched in American culture and democracy.[10] In the introduction to this chapter, we noted that because our media system is advertising-supported, media routinely craft their content to attract audiences that advertisers find desirable. As such, it is possible and indeed quite likely that entire segments of the population may be ignored; they are not participants in the marketplace of ideas.

This case explores the marketplace of ideas from another perspective, examining the power of any medium to reject advertising messages (political broadcast advertising being an exception; media are subject to a complex set of requirements in this regard) for whatever reason it chooses. Identified as "media clearance," this power is viewed to be a vital component of advertising's regulatory mix. Certainly, this has economic implications for particular advertisers, making it difficult, if not impossible, for them to have a voice in the economic marketplace. However, if we recognize advertising as a vehicle of social communication as well as a business tool, it is quite possible that through media rejection of advertising, entire groups of people as well as particular ideas seeking to be heard via advertising messages may be rendered voiceless. The Adbusters Media Foundation, for example, has tried to buy commercial time for a variety of "subvertisements," only to be repeatedly rejected by U.S. and Canadian media.[11]

At the outset, it is should be noted that media clearance of advertising messages or asking advertisers to amend their messages is not uncommon. Usually, this occurs without fanfare; many individuals may not even be aware that the media regularly approve or reject advertising according to the medium's established guidelines. However, in some instances, typically in cases of controversial groups or issues, media rejection becomes news.[12]

The following examples illustrate that media clearance of advertising is not confined to any particular medium. Indeed, clearance issues arise in a number of media, and in varied contexts.

In 2011, the National Association for the Advancement of Colored People (NAACP), and the American Civil Liberties Union (ACLU) filed a lawsuit against the City of Philadelphia and Clear Channel for violation of the group's First Amendment rights (Clear Channel was later dropped from the suit). The suit grew out of the Philadelphia International Airport's rejection of an NAACP ad promoting criminal justice reform. City officials rejected the ad that read: "Welcome to America, home to 5% of the world's people & 25% of the world's prisoners. Let's build a better America together."[13] The ads were part of a public awareness campaign surrounding an NAACP report exploring the relationship between high incarceration rates and poorly performing schools. Although the city claimed they did not accept "issue" or "advocacy" advertisements at the airport, ads for other social and political issues, among them the World Wildlife Foundation, had been accepted in the past. ACLU attorney, Chris Hansen claimed the city's "unwritten and undefined policy" was abitrary.

"The government cannot pick and choose which speech it deems acceptable and which it does not. It is a clear violation of the First Amendment's prohibition against the government favoring some speakers over others."[14]

After the suit was filed, the city agreed to post the billboard for a limited time, but in March 2012 adopted a written policy barring all advertising that did not propose a commercial transaction. The NAACP contended the policy was unconstitutional. In May, the city filed for dismisal of the suit; dismissal was denied.

In August 2014, U.S. District Judge Cynthia Rufe ruled in favor of the NAACP; in rejecting the ad, the city of Philadelphia had violated the NAACP's free-speech rights. Additionally, the airport's written policy allowing only commercial advertising violated the First Amendment. In the opinion she noted:

> The NAACP has pointed to considerable evidence that supports the conclusion that to display non-commercial ads, like the NAACP's, would be perfectly compatible with a multipurpose terminal containing many adult-oriented potentially controversial media. By contrast, the city has failed to demonstrate why allowing non-commercial advertisements would diminish advertising revenue, diminish the airport's efficacy, or make the airport a meaningfully less positive, family oriented place than permitting commercial and city-sponsored advertisements only.[15]

In October 2014, Hulu, the online streaming video service owned by 21st Century Fox, the Walt Disney Company, and NBC Universal rejected an ad from the Vote No 67 Campaign featuring a rape victim opposing Colorado's proposed "personhood" Amendment 67. The amendment would expand the definition of a person to include "unborn human beings" in the Colorado criminal code, and would have far-reaching implications for reproductive rights. Hulu's objection was not with the ad, but with abortion, a controversial issue. Hulu explained the service's decision this way: "According to our advertising bylaws, we are not able to accept 'ads that advocate a controversial political or other public position,' which unfortunately No 67 falls under due to the subject matter of abortion."[16] However, Hulu *had* run ads endorsing a political candidate who co-sponsored the "Life at Conception Act" as well as ads attacking fracking and the Affordable Care Act, certainly controversial issues. These apparently contradictory decisions led *Newsweek* to ask: "Is Hulu silently advocating for Colorado's personhood amendment?"[17] Vote No 67 Campaign ads were accepted on other sites including Facebook, Twitter, Pandora, and Google Adwords. Colorado voters rejected Amendment 67 in November.

In October 2015, CBS rejected a multi-million dollar ad buy for *Truth*, a movie revisiting "an embarrassing episode in the Company's history."[18] The movie, starring Cate Blanchett as producer Mary Mapes and Robert Redford as Dan Rather, details a 2004 *60 Minutes II* report alleging that President George W. Bush had received preferential treatment as a member of the Air National Guard in the late 1960s and early 1970s. The documents used in the report were later discredited. CBS producer Mary Mapes was fired, as were three other CBS executives. Dan Rather, who had anchored the *60 Minutes* story, later apologized for a "mistake in judgement." He was eased out of his role as *CBS Evening News* anchor. CBS told the Associated Press it had rejected the advertising because of "inaccuracies and distortions in its portrayal of the events."[19] Earlier that month, a CBS spokesperson, Gil Schwartz declared that it was "astounding how little truth there is in *Truth*." He continued:

> There are, in fact, too many distortions, evasions and baseless conspiracy theories to enumerate them all. The film tries to turn gross errors of journalism and judgment into acts of heroism and martyrdom. That's a disservice not just to the public but to journalists across the world who go out every day and do everything within their power, sometimes at great risk to themselves, to get the story right.[20]

The film-makers responded that they were "disappointed" in the reaction from CBS, noting that "the events depicted in *Truth* are still vigorously debated, and that's a good thing. It's a fascinating story at the intersection of politics, media and corporate America."[21]

While Rather admits that he and the members of his team had made mistakes in putting the story together, he remains convinced that the substance of the story remains true.[22]

The publicity surrounding the CBS decision was well timed for the studio. Callan Advertising, the agency making the media buys for the movie, had been informed two weeks earlier that CBS would not run the ads, but the first Associated Press news story appeared on the day the film opened in U.S. cinemas.[23]

■ ■ ■ ■

These examples call our attention to an ethical dilemma that many may not view as an ethical issue. Media, after all, have the right to refuse any advertising; the medium need not specify the reason for rejection. Media clearance is viewed as an integral part of the regulatory mix, having the advantage of pre-empting public exposure to ads that might be false or deceptive. Common justifications for rejection provided include a violation of company guidelines, consumer protection from deception, the belief that some products (ideas?) are objectionable to the target audience, and fear of offending audiences.

While we cannot know the motivations for advertising rejection in any of these cases were anything other than those stated, one might speculate the possibility that personal beliefs played some role, particularly given the apparent contradictions in the nature of the ads that had been accepted previously by the City of Philadelphia and Hulu. "Controversial" can be interpreted in a multitude of ways. If the decision-makers had shaped their social contracts from behind the veil of ignorance, they would have been rendered unaware of their own positions on the political and social spectrums involved. Thus, in making their decisions, they would have had to employ the principle of "justice as fairness." As self-serving individuals, they could neither condemn nor elevate any particular group's message for fear of condemning themselves.

A more familiar example of this thought process involves two people sharing one cake. If it is agreed that one person will cut the cake and the other will choose his or her piece, the cutter cannot be aware of which piece he or she will receive in the end. Thus, it follows logically that the individual cutting the cake will divide it as evenly as possible, not to ensure the chooser a fair piece but to protect his or her own share. From this perspective, ethical behavior does not necessarily arise from altruism, but from a human inclination toward self-preservation.

Realistically, we are not expected to engage in an internal, Rawlsian debate on each decision we encounter. We may, however, consider if we would feel ourselves to have been fairly treated if the tables had been turned.

Quite simply, because media *can* reject particular ads doesn't necessarily mean that they *should* reject those ads. Such decisions should be made with an obligation to fairness and justice and a commitment to freedom of expression. Before leaving these examples, we might reflect upon the following questions:

1. Is it ethical to reject an advertisement, or request it be amended for no reason other than that it is inconsistent with our personal beliefs?
2. Do the media have an obligation to subject rejection decisions to strict scrutiny, recognizing the role those advertisements might play in the social marketplace *as well as* the economic marketplace?
3. Is identifying an advertising message as "too controversial" a legitimate reason for rejecting an ad in a culture that celebrates the "marketplace of ideas"? If so, who should determine what constitutes "controversial" subject matter?

BRANDED CONTENT: IT'S COMPLICATED

[C]ontent sometimes seems to have taken over marketing, to the point that it's surprisingly hard to define or distinguish from many other activities. It arguably encompasses not just branded entertainment and native advertising but in various ways social media, search ads, events, product placement, digital video and much more. In fact, you could make the case that all advertising is content, and vice versa.[24]

[Content marketing is] an approach where instead of distracting our audience with advertising that's not relevant to them, we're going to create valuable, compelling and relevant content on a consistent basis and build an audience over that time in order to see some profitable customer action.[25]

The next two cases examine what might be viewed as "two sides of the same coin." Product placement and what we'll call here "native advertising" are not new; both have existed for years, though in formats very different than those of today. Product placement, once little more than "sending out props and hoping for the best," has become product integration, and thanks to technological innovation, placements can even be made in old movies retro-actively, though that is not a common practice. Native advertising had its birth, perhaps, in what used to be called advertorials, advertisements that provided information on a product in the style of the editorial content.

Product placement and native advertising, both of which are mentioned in the recent Federal Trade Commission (FTC) "Enforcement Policy Statement on Deceptively Formatted Advertising," have assumed a new importance for a number of reasons, among them: the ubiquity of commercial messages and the perceived decline in advertising effectiveness in an environment cluttered with media that are themselves cluttered with advertising; adver-tisers seeking new ways to connect with audiences who are seemingly less inclined to view and are actively avoiding advertising content; and media seeking new, innovative ways to generate revenue during challenging economic times.

Ever more effectively blurring the boundaries of editorial, entertainment, and advertis-ing content, product placement and integration raise complex ethical questions.

CASE 32. NATIVE ADVERTISING: ADVERTISING AND EDITORIAL CONTENT

> Broadcast outlets and publishers need to keep their advertisers happy, and if that means creating new avenues and formats for brands to tap into their audiences, so be it. Lines will continue to become blurred and no doubt, it will be interesting to see [what] will happen to the integrity of editorial report as brands exert more and more influence over content.[26]

> Native advertising—articles paid for and/or written by a brand that live on a publisher's site—has emerged as a powerful and popular new advertising tool over the past few years. Media companies like BuzzFeed, *The New York Times*, *The Wall Street Journal*, and *The Atlantic* have all invested heavily in the creation and distribution of native advertisements on behalf of brands.[27]

A barrier between advertising and editorial content has been a hallmark of journalistic integ-rity in a democratic society since the nineteenth century. Maintaining that barrier is a respon-sibility clearly stated in the Society of Professional Journalists' Code of Ethics ("Distinguish news from advertising and shun hybrids that blur the lines between the two") and the guide-lines of the American Society of Magazine Editors ("Media consumers should always be able to distinguish between content produced by journalists and content delivered on behalf of advertisers").

Over the years, persuasive formats such as advertorials, infomercials, video news releases, press releases, and paid endorsements have blurred the line between editorial and advertising content. However, native advertising, which "at its basic level . . . is advertising paid for by outside companies in an online news outlet that takes the appearance of editorial content produced by that outlet"[28] (essentially, an "ad trying not be an ad") in many ways emerged as something of a perfect storm.

Publishers, seeing profits shrinking, are getting more creative in their efforts to identify "'new,' shiny, monetization methods"[29] that will attract advertiser dollars. Marketers are looking for new ways to reach consumers resistant to conventional advertising and believe those consumers are more likely to respond positively to tactics that don't look like ads in today's ever-more-commercialized culture. Then too, audiences are purportedly seeking more content they value, and if that content is advertising, so be it. "People are ignoring advertising, but they're not ignoring content."[30] Native advertising is thus seen to be a win–win–win situation for all parties involved.

The number of native advertisers jumped to 1595 in November 2015. Those advertisers ran across 218 publisher sites. Clearly clutter could become a problem in the future, leading to the native advertising equivalent of "banner blindness." In fact, despite the increases in brand content, interactions with that content (likes, shares, retweets) declined 60 percent in 2014.[31] And what of audience response? A Contently Survey in September 2015 sought to answer the question: do consumers interpret native advertising as an advertisement or a published article? Nearly half of the respondents felt deceived after discovering the content was created by a brand.[32]

The FTC first examined native advertising in a 2013 workshop "Blurred Lines: Advertising or Content?" The ethical dilemmas posed by the new arrangement of the media ecosystem and the discomfort among publishers in that arrangement were palpable, even if often unspoken. Instead of reflection and open dialogue, publishers frequently presented "a fantastic example of collaboration based on our shared values. . . . [W]e brainstormed ideas . . . and built the campaign together."[33] In December 2015, the FTC issued an "Enforcement Policy Statement on Deceptively Formatted Advertising," which provided principles supporting the FTC approach to native advertising, when disclosure of native advertising content was necessary, and how to make that disclosure clear and prominent. In that document, as in industry discussion more generally, "transparency" seemed to be the key ingredient of (ethical?) native advertising. Additionally, the FTC indicated that they would take action against all parties who participate directly or indirectly in creating or presenting native ads the FTC found deceptive (including ad agencies and operators of affiliate advertising networks).

Clearly, "going native" raises practical and ethical issues both on the advertiser/client side and on the publisher side, particularly in the sense of "deception." Somehow often less visible in this discussion is the extension of that concern, the preservation of media ability not only to sustain itself, but also to serve its role in democratic society.

According to the Society of Professional Journalists Code of Ethics, "Journalists believe that public enlightenment is the forerunner of justice and the foundation of democracy.... Professional integrity is the cornerstone of a journalist's credibility."[34] The mandate to maintain a distinct separation between commercial interests, advertising, and editorial content is fundamental to the integrity of the news product. It is essential to a newspaper's ability to fulfill its responsibilities to its readers, the organization, and the profession.

Times are tough for all media; in making concessions in the name of survival, the wall between advertising and editorial content is becoming more and more strained. And yet, maintaining that wall remains a shared responsibility.

Adopting a utilitarian perspective, one would believe the greatest good for the greatest number would be served by maintaining the strictest of barriers between advertising and editorial content. Monetizing content in any manner might provide a short-term solution; however, in the long-term the very foundations of the news and the profession will erode. Given the reduction in perceived credibility of news and news sources that already exists, what might further advertising–editorial collaboration mean for the integrity of the media? For the perceived integrity of media more generally as a viable source of news? How long will it be before the news department will find itself at the mercy of the advertisers, stop reporting news, and start running content that pleases advertisers? Some would say, then, and did say, "It is simply wrong!" For these individuals, monetizing content is not viable in the long run; professional consequences, the sacrifice of journalistic integrity, trump the immediate concern with the economic viability.

Robert Niles, a former journalism professor at the University of Southern California, warned that advertising incursion into editorial content "is pretty dangerous.... It really shows a lack of respect for the audience and a lack of confidence in your editorial product."[35] "This is exactly the wrong way to go about surviving," noted independent journalist and educator Geneva Overholser. Blurring of the line between editorial and advertising "breaks perhaps the most important bond that newspapers have with their readers, which, to me, is a bond of trust."[36]

And yet, it is difficult to argue with the view that the greatest good would be served by the media's continued survival, a perspective not without its merits. Faced with what might rightfully be termed dire economic straits, one can sense resignation in many comments of critics, or industry professionals, and even of readers. Dan Kennedy, media critic for the *Guardian* of London, said:

> Given that we're in pretty desperate times, far better that the *L.A. Times* do this [this is a reference to a native advertising effort on the front page in 2009] than say no to the revenue and end up having to cut back on their actual news coverage.[37]

Then too, one must necessarily pose the ethical question to those on the advertising side of the equation, for advertising too depends upon the integrity of the news product. Advertising in newspapers is deemed useful, in part, because of the halo of credibility cast from the editorial. In this case, efforts appear to have been conceptualized and spear-headed by the *Times*'s marketing department. As professionals employed by the paper, the advertising department certainly has a responsibility to maintain the commercial foundations of the paper. As an advocate for the client, they have some responsibility to act in their best interests as well. Don't they also have a duty to the public? Is the integrity of the news product partially their responsibility?

Are we at an ethical impasse? Is there possibility of compromise for all parties involved—the advertisers, the media, the readers? How do newspapers protect their journalistic integrity at the same time they develop new revenue streams? The stakes are high. The Poynter Institute's Bob Steele notes: "It's unwise and ethically problematic to have advertising morph into news content and style. Each step may seem like a small one. But each time you cut a corner, you create weakness in the overall product."[38]

CASE 33. WELCOME TO MADISON AND VINE

> Never has it been more clear that commercials and content are fast becoming one and the same, wholly indistinguishable from each other. . . . At some point, ads and shows might blur so much that the notion of a "commercial break" becomes a silly, antiquated thing of the past.[39]

Product placement, paying to have a brand embedded in media content, is hardly a new phenomenon. The Lumière brothers are said to have made the first product placement recorded on film for Unilever's Sunlight Soap in 1896.[40] In the 1950s, Gordon's Gin paid to have Katherine Hepburn's character in *The African Queen* toss their product overboard.[41] Currently, there appears to be something of a "frenzied resurgence" of the strategy fueled by a number of factors, among them: technological innovations; digital competition; clients seeking creative ways to reach an ever-harder-to-reach, fragmented audience in relevant ways; high production costs, a decline in television viewing, and advertising clutter.

Buoyed by successful promotions of products in films and television, brand placement has become almost ubiquitous, spreading to novels, recorded songs, music videos, plays, video games, and blogs. Expenditures on product placements, though difficult to measure, reached an estimated $4.75 billion in 2014 and are estimated to rise to $11.4 billion by 2018.[42]

Once, product placement was little more than "sending out props and hoping for the best." Today, advertisers seek ever-deepening integrations coupling placements with other promotions, online activities, and traditional advertising. The term "product placement" has been replaced with "brand integration" in industry conversations and in concept. Product placements are strategic and highly managed, "elaborately woven into the plot, with advertisers calling the shots."[43]

As advertising representatives become more involved and more demanding, writers have become particularly watchful of their creative freedom and the integrity of their work.

The president of the Screen Actors Guild described product integration as "an intrusive process that is getting more and more out of hand."[44] Let's consider Pepsi's recent meta-product placement deal in Fox network's drama *Empire*.

Premiering in 2014, *Empire* drew record-breaking audience numbers, growing its rating week-to-week, a feat rarely accomplished. In its second season, the program, which already had a placement deal with Lincoln, added Pepsi for a meta-product placement. Pepsi was heavily featured in the plotline of three episodes, culminating with a commercial starring the fictional character in the show. An *Advertising Age* writer described the effort this way (spoiler alert):

> Rising star Jamal Lyon, son of Empire Entertainment CEO Lucious Lyon, is approached by Pepsi about an endorsement deal. But he must beat out competing artists to become the new face of the brand. Jamal wins the assignment after creating a song for a Pepsi ad called "Ready to Go."
>
> On the show, the commercial is directed by Lee Daniels, "Empire" co-creator and executive producer, who will make a cameo. Mr. Daniels did in fact direct the commercial in real life.
>
> Then, in the [final] episode, Jamal will introduce the commercial during an awards nomination ceremony. Fox will cut from the show directly into the real 60-second commercial break, where it will debut the spot, and then go directly back into "Empire."[45]

The Pepsi effort has been heralded by a Pepsi spokesperson as a "truly authentic integration of life imitating art, . . . a break thru for [Pepsi] and the industry."[46] And, indeed, many agree. Product integration is celebrated for its creativity, innovation, and "ability to break the fourth wall." The ability to "prove that advertising can be just as creative and exciting as the content viewers tuned in to watch," underlies the advertising industry buzz about the necessity of telling a good story.[47] Morgan Spurlock, creator and producer of *The Greatest Movie Ever Sold*, a documentary film about product placement funded by product placements, now creates branded content himself. In a recent *Adweek* interview Spurlock noted that the biggest mistake marketers make in creating branded content is "trying to turn it into advertising." He continued:

> Nobody wants to watch commercials. People want stories. They want something that is going to be compelling and different. They don't care who brings it to them—Haagen Dazs or Columbia Pictures—so long as it's a great story and not anybody selling something to them.[48]

But isn't "selling something" precisely the intention?

Here, once again, we encounter a dilemma of commercial incursion into non-commercial space. When contemplating the ethical dimensions of product integration, it might be useful to recall that the use of this strategy increased as marketers attempted to counter consumer advertising avoidance efforts. An *Advertising Age* writer recently commented on the "seismic shifts" occurring in product integration due to the fact that "viewers aren't just skipping ads with DVRs [digital video recorders] these days, many are watching shows on ad-free streaming services like Netflix or staring into smartphones during commercial breaks."[49] Despite the fact that brand names may very well add authenticity to program content—one might argue that replacing a plain box labeled "cereal" on the kitchen table with a box of Kashi Go-Lean Crunch (oops! but not a paid placement) adds a sense of reality and seems a relatively benign intrusion—the strategy emerged as a fundamentally adversarial one: consumers don't want to see ads so marketers "create ads that look less like ads and slip them in front of potential customers." Is this a violation of responsibility to the public? Does product placement simply serve the needs of the media while disregarding those of the public? Is product placement/integration unethical, given that viewers are unaware that they are watching a promotional message? Is this deception?

Judgment of the ethicality of the brand integration is primarily based on two key issues: the extent to which media and brands make the placement explicit, and the perceived sophistication of the entertainment audience.[50]

Robert Weissmann, managing director of Commercial Alert, a nonprofit group that aims to limit commercial marketing, believes that advertising involvement in shaping scripts is a "fundamental encroachment on the independence of programming." More importantly, product placement is "dishonest, deceptive, and manipulative":

> TV networks send programs into living rooms that are packed with embedded advertising. . . . TV stations pretend that these are just ordinary programs rather than paid ads. This is an affront to basic honesty. . . . Product placements are inherently deceptive, because many people do not realize that they are, in fact, advertisements.[51]

The FCC, in its examination of the phenomenon, agrees: "[Product placement and other 'stealth advertising' are] particularly insidious because viewers often are unaware that someone is trying to influence, persuade or market to them."[52]

Calls for regulation have revolved around mandatory disclosure and how that disclosure might best be effected. Current rules require that when money or "another consideration" has been received, the station must broadcast full disclosure of that fact at the time of the airing of the material, and must identify who provided or promised to provide consideration. "Viewers should be informed about who is secretly pitching to them in the TV shows they are watching."[53] The requirement is typically met with a disclosure in the end credits ("promotional consideration paid by . . .") that remains on the screen long enough to be read or heard by the average viewer but after viewing has already occurred. Critics have suggested variations: disclosures should be longer, larger, and on the screen at the time placements occur. Insofar as they perceive current disclosures to be inadequate, consumers are being deceived.

The advertising industry and the media disagree. "Our audience is aware that product placement exists and that advertisers are probably paying for some of the more branded mentions that they see in the body of the show . . . the audience gets it."[54] The fact that product placement is frequently spoofed in popular culture suggests that perhaps placement is an acknowledged and understood practice. Ask any college student about product placement and they're likely to mention Spurlock's *The Greatest Movie Ever Sold*, *Wayne's World*, *Josey and the Pussycats*, and, perhaps, *The Truman Show*. They very possibly can also identify the car driven by James Bond in the latest 007 movie.

Then too, some suggest that product placement not only increases the commercialization of entertainment but also may be an unwarranted violation of privacy on essentially "captive" audiences. If one views privacy as "the right to be left alone," the interjection of paid integration into entertainment programming without disclosure may be an invasion of privacy in that the viewer is not being told of the commercial insertion and was not given the right to choose whether to view or not.

In a capitalist economy, brand integration, in its unannounced presence, raises a number of ethical questions, among them:

- Do consumer have the right to know whether they are viewing or hearing paid advertising from the product manufacturer?
- Do advertisers have some moral and perhaps legal obligation to be certain their messages are understood to be promotional?
- Alternatively, do advertisers have freedom in their efforts, relying on consumer sophistication?
- Is product placement socially responsible given its contribution to the escalation of commercial voices and monopolization of cultural space?
- Are there possible points of compromise between critics and advocates on issues of product placement? If so, what actions might be taken to effect such a compromise?

Taking note of the increased sales attributed to the brand integration, which can be interpreted as indicative of consumer satisfaction, lower production costs for the brand, and a greater sense of authenticity for audience enjoyment, a utilitarian perspective might well suggest the ethicality of product integrations. However, concerns raised by the Writers Guild and the Actors Guild related to the integrity of the creative process and product should also be considered. A deontologically based approach necessarily acknowledges the marketers' advocacy role. Kant's categorical imperative that one should "[a]ct only on that maxim whereby thou canst at the same time will that it should become a universal law," might also judge the effort ethical if it is acceptable to live in a world in which product placement plays an ever-increasing role. Product integration would be less likely to meet the second version of Kant's imperative, that one should "act as to treat humanity, whether in thine own person or in that of any other, in every case as an end, never as means only." A common deontological assessment suggests that marketing focuses on getting consumers in their target market to buy what they have to sell rather than on improving consumers' lives. That is, consumers are viewed as means to an end rather than respected as individuals. This view led Baker and Martinson to suggest:

> There is a very real danger that advertisers and public relations practitioners will play an increasingly dysfunctional role in the communication process if means continue to be confused with ends in professional persuasive communications. Means and ends will continue to be confused unless advertisers and public relations practitioners reach some level of agreement as to the moral end toward which their efforts should be directed.[55]

Finally, a virtuous marketing ethics might approve of some aspects of product integration (in terms of the improved audience experience and resultant benefit to the brand and the media), but would recognize that deception might occur in instances in which the integration is not made explicit.

CASE 34. AD BLOCKING: A PERFECT STORM

Tommy, an advertising major looking toward graduation at the end of the year, was perplexed. He was wondering why ad blocking was creating such a stir. The industry had faced "ad avoidance" technologies before—remote control, VCR, and then the DVR—and survived. Certainly technology would come up with something. Still, it seemed like the discussion had been going on for months. At the outset, some had denied the significance of Apple's announcement that it would enable ad-blocking apps through its new mobile operating system. Counter technology would prevail, folks said; it always did. Tommy remembered what he'd read about the dynamics of technology: "In a remarkable process of self-referentiality, technology now creates the problems for which it has to create ever new solutions, which in turn create further side-effects that again have to be dealt with technologically."[56] Others said they weren't worried because ad blockers on browsers don't really matter nearly so much as apps on mobile devices. "That's where the technology is taking us."

For the last two months, the trade press had been teeming with naysayers, apologists, apocalyptic predictions, and people who simply were fighting mad. There was a "war on advertising." Ad blocking was "robbery, plain and simple—an extortionist scheme."[57] It seemed to Tommy that the advertising industry had lost its confidence. There was endless questioning. Who or what is to blame? Plenty of culprits there: advertisers, publishers, technology companies, tracking, consumers who somehow had forgotten they had made an implicit agreement that in exchange for free content they'd watch a seemingly endless barrage of commercials. Who stands to win? Who's going to lose?

It seemed advertising was flummoxed. What should we do? Sue? Put up paywalls? "Rethink digital advertising before more consumers want to annihilate it?"[58] Advertising went on the defensive. An article in *Advertising Age* asked readers to imagine a world without ads. Simon Dumenco estimated the cost of advertising-free media and concluded: it's expensive.[59] Tommy thought it was odd that Dumenco never mentioned all the other things advertising does such as provide product information, entertain, keep the marketplace going. He thought the illustration of a darkened Times Square was just plain eerie.

But what perplexed Tommy most was the difficulty he was having deciding if he should purchase an ad-blocker app. He was an advertising major for heaven's sake. He was all about advertising. But he'd read an article by Joe Mandese, "The Pot Calling the Kettle Blocked."[60] Mandese said that advertising and agency executives indexed higher than the overall consumer marketplace when it came to ad blocking. And the reason industry pros install and use ad blockers is "probably for the same reason average consumers do: because they can."[61]

So, that was the dilemma–to block or not to block? It seemed all his friends had ad-block apps, and they were advertising majors too. And to hear them talk . . . it was "magical. Pages loaded so much faster, and no pop-ups, no pre-rolls when you watch YouTube videos." It was only $3.99. But then, he was an advertising major.

It seems Tommy had arrived at the point at which we may all have arrived at some time when confronting difficult decisions–decisions about our immediate world that somehow seem to extend far beyond our world. Tommy can't determine if and how his decision to block advertising would have any impact on the so-called "grander scheme of things." Of course, many might not think of this as an ethical dilemma, but ethics is not something to which we resort only in times of crisis. It is thoughtful consideration of how we live in and act on the world. Ethics should be at the core of decisions we make every day.

What will Tommy do? He believes advertising plays an important role in sustaining the economy and even "holding society together." It operates for the greater good, at least economically. He didn't think he should block advertising. It didn't seem right. But, ad blockers weren't illegal so it really was just like any other product, wasn't it? You bought it if you wanted it. It would be great not to have pop-up ads interrupting your web search, and pages *would* load faster. Those were pluses. But then, there was loyalty to the profession and all it values, though at least some professionals didn't let loyalty prevent them from the convenience of ad blocking. But was the decision just about him?

> Thing is, you can only use ad blockers to consume ad-free content if there are enough people looking at the ads to make it worthwhile for somebody. Ad blocking is like queue-jumping: if you're the only one doing it, you win, but if everybody does it, the whole thing falls apart.[62]

What would you do?

NOTES

1. www.spj.org/ethicscode.asp.
2. Ronald K. L. Collins and Todd Gitlin, *Dictating Content* (Washington, DC: The Center for the Study of Commercialism, 1992), 41.
3. Gloria Steinem, "Sex, Lies, and Advertising," *Ms.*, July/August 1990.
4. Robert W. McChesney, "The Communication Revolution: The Market and the Prospect for Democracy," in Mashoed Bailie and Dwayne Winseck, eds., *Democratizing Communication? Comparative Perspectives on Information and Power* (Cresskill, NJ: Hampton Press, Inc., 1997), 74.
5. Free Press Beginner's Guide: Why Care about Media, http://subsol.c3.hu/subsol_2/contributors3/freepresstext.html.
6. http://adage.com/article/campaign-trail/ad-blocking-dampen-democracy/301429/.
7. Henry Jenkins, Sam Ford, and Joshua Green, *Spreadable Media: Creating Value and Meaning in a Networked Culture* (New York: New York University Press, 2013).
8. The "customer of one" is a widely used moniker in the advertising industry in discussions highlighting personalization and individualization of the advertising experience.
9. TED talk available at www.ted.com/talks/eli_pariser_beware_online_filter_bubbles?language=en.
10. W. Wat Hopkins, "The Supreme Court Defines the Marketplace of Ideas," *Journalism and Mass Communication Quarterly* 73:1 (Spring 1996): 40.
11. http://inthesetimes.com/article/3581/adbusters_ads_busted.
12. We would be remiss if we failed to note that there are instances in which advertisers are believed to create advertising messages they know will be rejected in order to garner the publicity that will follow and the notoriety that comes with being a "banned commercial" on YouTube. The ethical issues surrounding this "strategy" will be addressed in later chapters.
13. NAACP press release, www.naacp.org/pages/BillboardLawsuit.
14. Ibid.
15. www.law360.com/articles/563611/philly-shouldn-t-have-refused-naacp-airport-ad-judge-says.
16. http://rhrealitycheck.org/article/2014/10/20/hulu-rejects-anti-personhood-ad-labels-controversial/.
17. Lauren Walker, "Is Hulu Silently Advocating for Colorado's Personhood Amendment?" *Newsweek*, October 24, 2014, www.newsweek.com/hulu-silently-advocating-colorados-personhood-amendment-279790.
18. www.theguardian.com/film/2015/oct/19/cate-blanchett-robert-redford-truth-cbs-wont-advertise.
19. http://zap2it.com/2015/10/cbs-refuses-air-ads-truth-dan-rather-movie-cbs-news-scandal/.
20. Widely quoted, here taken from www.theguardian.com/film/2015/oct/19/cate-blanchett-robert-redford-truth-cbs-wont-advertise.
21. Ibid.
22. http://money.cnn.com/2015/10/16/media/dan-rather-movie-truth-cbs/.
23. http://variety.com/2015/film/news/cbs-truth-dan-rather-ads-refuses-1201620016/.
24. Jack Neff, "Is it Content or Is it Advertising? *Advertising Age*, October 12, 2015, http://adage.com/article/ad-age-research/content-advertising/300858/.
25. Ibid. Definition from Joe Pulizzi, purportedly the man who first used the term.
26. Richard L. Tso, "Native Advertising: Coming Soon to a TV Near You," February 25, 2014, www.adotas.com/2014/02/native-advertising-coming-soon-to-a-tv-near-you/.
27. https://contently.com/strategist/2015/09/08/article-or-ad-when-it-comes-to-native-no-one-knows/.
28. Tom Kutsch, "The Blurred Lines of Native Advertising," *Al Jazeera America*, March 8, 2014, http://america.aljazeera.com/articles/2014/3/8/the-blurred-linesofanativeaadvertising.html.
29. Jason Del Ray, "Native Advertising: Media Savior or Just the New Custom Campaign?" *Advertising Age*, October 29, 2012, http://adage.com/article/digital/native-advertising-media-savior-custom-campaign/238010/.
30. Robert X. Cringely, "Here Lies Web Journalism, Dead at the Hand of the Almighty Advertiser," March

20, 2013, www.infoworld.com/article/2614404/cringely/here-lies-web-journalism--dead-at-the-hand-of-the-almighty-advertiser.html.

31. Surveys from MediaRadar and Track Maven reported in Lucia Moses, "Publishers Are about to Hit the Wall with Native Ads," Digiday, January 8, 2016, http://digiday.com/publishers/peak-native-ads/.

32. https://contently.com/strategist/2015/09/08/article-or-ad-when-it-comes-to-native-no-one-knows/.

33. Mark Sweney, "GNM Launches Branded Content Division Guardian Labs," *Guardian* (UK), February 13, 2014, www.theguardian.com/media/2014/feb/13/guardian-labs-branded-content.

34. www.spj.org/ethicscode.asp.

35. www.thewrap.com/ind-column/la-times-sells-disney-entire-front-page-14953.

36. www.nytimes.com/2009/04/10/business/media/10adco.html.

37. Stephanie Clifford, "Front of LA Times has an NBC 'Article,'" *New York Times*, April 9, 2009, www.nytimes.com/2009/04/ 10/business/media/10adco.html.

38. Ibid.

39. Brian Steinberg, "Don't Like Product Placement? Here's Why It's Your Fault," *Advertising Age*, February 11, 2010, http://adage.com/article/madisonvine-news/branded-entertainment-product-placement-fault/142069/.

40. www.facebook.com/video/video.php?v=123667494316611.

41. Rick D. Saucier, *Marketing Ethics* (Lewiston, NY: Edwin Mellen Press, 2008), 25.

42. www.statista.com/statistics/261454/global-product-placement-spending/.

43. Clifford, "Front of LA Times has an NBC 'Article.'"

44. T. L. Stanley, "A Place for Everything," *Adweek*, February 28, 2010.

45. http://adage.com/article/media/pepsi-s-meta-integration-fox-s-empire/301420/.

46. Ibid.

47. http://adage.com/article/media/donny-deutsch-putting-brands-front-center-tv-show/300849/.

48. Tim Baysinger, "How Morgan Spurlock Created a Branded Content Revolution," *Adweek*, October 2, 2015, www.adweek.com/news/television/how-morgan-spurlock-started-branded-content-revolution-167335.

49. http://adage.com/article/media/interrupt-nbc-program-bring-word-sponsor/300785/.

50. Chris Hackley, Rungpaka Amy Tiwsakul, and Lutz Preuss, "An Ethical Evaluation of Product Placement: a Deceptive Practice?" *Business Ethics: A European Review* 17:2 (April 2008): 109–120.

51. www.commercialalert.org/issues/culture/product-placement.

52. Federal Communications Commission, https://apps.fcc.gov/edocs_public/attachmatch/FCC-08-155A1.pdf.

53. Ibid.

54. Brian Steinberg, "Product Ads Gain More Screen Time, *The Boston Globe*, July 28, 2009.

55. Sherry Baker and David L. Martinson, "The TARES Test: Five Principles for Ethical Persuasion," *Journal of Media Ethics* 16:2&3: 148–175.

56. Bernhard Debatin, "The Future of New Media Ethics," in Thomas W. Cooper, Clifford G. Christians, and Anantha S. Babbili, eds., *An Ethics Trajectory: Visions of Media Past, Present and Yet to Come* (Urbana: University of Illinois Institute of Communications Research, 2008), 257.

57. Randall Rothenberg, "One-Two Punch: Go after Ad-Blocking Companies while Treating Consumers Better," *Advertising Age*, September 28, 2015, 52.

58. Maureen Morrison and Tim Peterson, "The War on Advertising," *Advertising Age*, September 14, 2015, 12.

59. Simon Dumenco, "Imagine a World without Ads," *Advertising Age*, September, 28, 2015, 30.

60. Joe Mandese, "The Pot Calling the Kettle Blocked," mediapost.com, October 19, 2015, www.mediapost.com/publications/article/260728/the-pot-calling-the-kettle-blocked.html.

61. Ibid.

62. www.mediapost.com/publications/article/259121/ad-blocking-is-destroying-the-internet-and-that.html?edition=.

ADVERTISING'S PROFESSIONAL CULTURE

Professions occupy a position of great importance in America; they influence the relationships between individuals and their work and between their work and society.[1] The tendency toward professionalization began to emerge in the United States around 1840; occupations as widely varied as baseball, morticians, and private detectives sought to join law, medicine, and the clergy as recognized professions.[2] Beginning in the late nineteenth and early twentieth centuries, advertising too sought the credibility, authority, and "job security" that comes with professional stature. Earliest efforts sought primarily to distance advertising work from the hucksterism so characteristic of its founders: P. T. Barnum and "snake oil" salesmen hawking patent medicines (Dr. Winslow's Soothing Syrup: "Makes 'em lay like the dead 'til morning"[3]). The introduction of the rationality and rhetoric of science to the practice of advertising became the "scientific advertising" movement.[4] Among other early efforts undertaken by practitioners to attain professional stature were:

- The formation of local clubs and national associations, which served to bring the community together, foster a sense of self-identification and recognition, and "announce" the existence of the profession to clients and the broader public.[5]
- The appearance of a number of trade journals in which practitioners negotiated and renegotiated the boundaries of the profession, celebrated its victories both large and small, mourned its defeats, applauded the victors, and dissected the strategies of the losers as cautionary tales.[6]
- The establishment of academic programs in advertising at universities, signaling the special knowledge required to practice.[7]
- The development of internal efforts to gain ethical control of the field; the industry's first code of ethics was the Printers' Ink Statute (1911).

The success of these efforts—that is, the answer to the question, "Is advertising a profession?"—remains a point of continuing debate. In part, this may be a reflection of the fact that, even today, there is only limited consensus on "what makes a profession a profession"; you need only to Google that question to see evidence. Then, too, the term *professional* has entered everyday vernacular, frequently used to indicate little more than that someone has worked at something for an extended period of time. Even so, two characteristics are found in virtually all but the most colloquial definitions. The first, sometimes stated explicitly and at other times implied, is the possession of theoretical knowledge, in some sense, a "magic circle of knowledge," that distinguishes the profession from the laity. Others, be they clients, patrons, or patients, convinced of the need for the professional's knowledge, provide "job security." A second component inherent in our cultural understanding of what it means to be a professional is ethics. That is, the responsibility to look beyond one's own self-interest. Because professional stature is a societally granted privilege, "its proper use becomes a moral duty."[8] "Society's granting of power and privilege is premised on [the profession's] willingness and ability to contribute to social well-being and to conduct their affairs in a manner consistent with broader social values."[9]

The answer to the question of advertising's professional stature, however, is not the subject of this discussion. What is more important for our purposes here is the recognition that much of "what we are" as an industry, what we value, and what we dismiss, are reflections of advertising's early efforts to professionalize, and current acknowledgment of the importance of professional recognition. While advertising practitioners may use the term infrequently today, it is evident that their concerns—providing a rational basis for decision-making, maintaining authority in their relationships with clients—clearly are grounded in issues of professional stature and credibility.[10] Inherent in those efforts is the belief that advertising's primary role is to "be a constructive force in business."[11] This understanding has both structural and moral dimensions, establishing the boundaries of our work and at the same time bracketing areas of obligation and moral responsibility. Have we clung too tenaciously to that singular objective? Have we overlooked our responsibilities as professionals to other constituencies?

The advertising profession is what Bivins identifies as a "consulting" profession. Unlike journalism, with its responsibility to inform and enlighten, advertising is "almost always speaking on behalf of someone else,"[12] contractually obligated to be an advocate for the client, working to advance the client's ends. Yet, as noted in the Introduction to this book "Ethical Foundations and Perspectives," we do well to remember that as media professionals we are variously obligated. Davidson summarizes the complexity of ethical decision-making faced by the advertising profession:

> [T]here is tension—sometimes conflict—between *economic* goals and *ethical* goals. . . . The great challenge . . . is to accomplish these goals simultaneously: to operate economically *and* efficiently to build market share and establish brand names and a

good customer base *and* behave ethically, and to make a satisfactory profit *and* still contribute to the well-being of society overall.[13]

Each advertising agency has its own culture grounded in philosophy/approach, tradition, organization, goals, recognitions, and history. Individual agency cultures vary widely, but exist in the context of a larger *professional culture.* You might think of advertising's professional culture as a shared understanding of what it means to *be* an advertising professional, how we make sense of the profession and its obligations and responsibilities, what we think we are doing when we are "doing advertising work." Professional culture encompasses a number of dimensions, grounded in the values, attitudes, beliefs, and experiences of a profession. It includes both a private ethos and public perceptions. Professional culture, then, is an ever-evolving constellation of:

- *What we value.* Our professional values certainly are apparent in our *output* (i.e., our ads), but also in *awards* we give and to whom we give them (Are they based on creativity? Effectiveness? What are the criteria used to bestow the title "Agency of the Year" or "Marketer of the Year"?); *codes of ethics* and our attention to those codes; client relationships; policies of inclusion and exclusion; pro bono work, etc.
- *How we go about our work.* This includes routines, payment processes, relationships and interactions with constituencies—clients, the public, colleagues, and the media; the persistent debate about the "the pitch" process, the consolidation, organization and ownership patterns; do we discuss ethical concerns freely? etc. The technological/digital revolution is altering a number of our profession's longstanding processes (e.g., programmatic buying, which enables a customer-of-one targeting).
- *How we think about ourselves.* As noted, advertising initially sought to establish an image of rationality and continues to do so given clients' emphasis on accountability and return on investment. At the same time, we work hard to create an image of advertising as glamorous, youthful, willing, and indeed eager, to take a risk, push the envelope, be edgy, and always be innovative and creative. Do we think of our work as a business tool? A vehicle of social communication? Both?
- *How others think about us.* Among our stakeholders are clients, the media, our colleagues and associates, and the public. The public views advertising variously as entertaining, disturbing, innovative, offensive, informative, exploitative, and unbelievably intrusive until they find the "coolest advergame," or create their own commercial either by corporate invitation or out of spite. Those who practice advertising consistently rank low in public opinion polls based on trust and honesty.[14] Our professional response to these perceptions—a shrug of the shoulders or a thoughtful editorial or column in *Advertising Age*?—reveals quite a lot about our industry's values.

Professions and their cultures are constantly evolving in response to the technological, political, economic, social, and cultural milieu. Today, more so perhaps than ever in the past, the industry's linkages to tech companies and big data are apparent, so much so that many advertising agencies have morphed into adtech companies. It is not surprising that with the changes occurring at an ever-accelerating pace in response to technology, innovative entrepreneurship, and a seemingly undeterred exuberance for all things digital, come new controversies, concerns, and ethical dilemmas.

Looking at all the cases in this part of the book, you'll recognize that each has told us something about advertising's professional culture. Each has asked you to reflect on what it means to "do advertising work." This chapter does so explicitly. The first case, "'. . . perhaps the absence of a code of ethics'?" considers the role of ethical codes in defining behavior, providing guidance in day-to-day decision-making, and fostering an environment in which ethical decision-making is the norm. In that case, you are invited to examine the American Association of Advertising Agencies' (AAAA or 4As) *Standards of Practice* and the Institute for Advertising Ethics (IAE) *Principles and Practices for Advertising Ethics* (both available on the *Media Ethics* website) and consider their adequacy, their usefulness, and the profession's attentiveness to them. The next two cases, "Branding: Making the Same Different, Again" and "Niche Markets, Niche Media," invite reflection on the ethical considerations inherent in two activities at the core of advertising work—branding and the construction of target markets. The goal is to encourage thoughtful consideration of activities that seem almost routine and to consider the social as well as the practical consequences of our decisions in these areas. The last two cases, "Ethical Vision: What Does It Mean to Serve Clients Well?" and "The Risky Client: Yes? No?," look at hypothetical decision-making scenarios to probe the ethical dilemmas and constraints that might occur day-to-day in the advertising workplace. They explore the concept of responsibility and the relationships among advertising practitioners, clients, and the public.

CASE 35. "'. . . PERHAPS THE ABSENCE OF A CODE OF ETHICS'?"[15]

> Through these codes [of ethics], professional institutions forge an implicit social contract with other members of society: Trust us to control and exercise jurisdiction over this important occupational category. In return the profession promises, we will ensure that our members are worthy of your trust—that they will not only be competent to perform the task they have been entrusted with, but they will conduct themselves with high standards and integrity.[16]

"Advertising ethics? That's an oxymoron!" You've likely heard it a dozen times: the suggestion that practicing advertising and practicing ethics are mutually exclusive activities. It is no secret that negative public perception of the honesty and trustworthiness of advertising and the professionals working in the industry has persisted for decades. Yet, the industry has recognized the importance of ethical codes for more than a century. The advertising industry's first professional code of ethics emerged in the context of advertising practitioners' earliest drive to be recognized as a profession. That code, the Printers' Ink Statute, was adopted by the Associated Advertising Clubs of America in 1911.[17] What is now often called the *4As Standards of Practice* was adopted by the AAAA in 1924; its Creative Code was incorporated into the document in 1931. The creation of these codes stands as testimonial to the profession's long-held recognition of the importance of ethics in advertising practice. Today, several ethical codes are in place in the advertising industry, among them: *4As Standards of Practice*, the American Advertising Federation's (AAF) *Advertising Ethics and Principles*, and the most recently developed IAE *Principles and Practices for Advertising Ethics.*

And still it seems, the advertising–ethics relationship is a fragile one. Let's begin considering this disconnect by looking at two "incidents" that speak to the importance of a code of ethics, and the role of that code in advertising practice.

Incident #1. In 2005, two former Ogilvy & Mather executives, Shona Seifert and Thomas Early, were found guilty of one count of conspiracy and nine false claims in a case involving overbilling of the White House Office of National Drug Control Policy. In handing down the sentence, Judge Richard M. Berman pointed to what he identified as advertising's "culture of carelessness," indicating that the case was essentially about the "slippage in ethics and perhaps the absence of a code of ethics."

Judge Berman's remarks drew our attention to the industry's existing code, the *4As Standards of Practice*,[18] the code to which all member agencies must adhere. At the time, the advertising industry appeared reluctant to engage in self-reflection. One industry analyst noted, that "it was difficult to find anyone who thinks the industry needs another ethics statement."[19] Similarly, O. Burtch Drake, the president and CEO of the 4As at the time noted: "The 4As has in place strong standards of practice that have served the industry well over the years. I don't see a need for a change or addition to these standards."[20]

Incident #2. In 2004, Drumwright and Murphy conducted a study of advertising practitioners to discover how they think about, approach, and deal with ethical issues.[21] Their findings were disheartening in that a "substantial portion" of the respondents did not see ethical issues or rationalized them away. These practitioners were what the authors called morally myopic, that is, they did not see a problem, or morally mute in that they may have recognized a moral problem but didn't communicate their concerns. They also found that failure to recognize the "unintended consequences" of advertising work existed at the individual, organizational, and societal levels, but was most acute at the societal level. That is, advertising practitioners had little sense of their work having any impact on broader social issues.

Still, there was good news. "There are and can be successful advertising professionals who are ethically aware and respond accordingly." The researchers identified these individuals as "talking, seeing advertising practitioners."

Theoretically, ethical codes institutionalize the collective moral conscience of the profession, reminding us of varied obligations to our stakeholders and to society at large, and creating an environment that fosters ethical conduct—a community in which ethical decision-making can thrive. At the same time, the codes signal external others of our industry's willingness and ability to "contribute to social well-being and to conduct our affairs in a manner consistent with broader social values."[22] What can we learn about the role of ethical codes in advertising practice from these two "incidents"?

Judge Berman's remarks reflect the importance of a code of ethics in guiding an industry's actions, but also in signaling to others the commitment we have made to do so. Judge Berman's perception of the "absence of a code of ethics" served as at least a partial explanation for the illegal activity that had occurred and his sense that advertising operated in a "culture of carelessness." And what to make of the industry reactions? Judge Berman's remarks were viewed rather casually at the time; perhaps in part because he ironically sentenced Seifert, then a convicted felon, to eighteen months' imprisonment, two years' probation, 400 hours of community service, a $125,000 fine, and an assignment—to write a professional code of ethics (see http://adage.com/images/random/seifertethics.pdf). Should we instead have seen those remarks as a challenge to the advertising industry's professional stature, a suggestion that perhaps the industry couldn't after all be trusted to "exercise jurisdiction over this important occupational category"?

It is commonly understood that in order to be relevant, professional codes of ethics should be viewed as a "living document," frequently revisited and revised to reflect changes in the profession and in the arenas in which that profession operates. The advertising industry actively constructs its image and indeed, seemingly "lives" at the forefront of creativity and innovation and yet, those "strong standards of practice" to which Drake referred, had been adopted in 1924 and revised—for the first time—sixty-six years later, in September 1990. Yet Drake saw no need for change or revision of those standards fifteen years later in his response to Judge Berman. Sixteen years passed before the *4As Standards of Practice* were revised again (most recently) in 2011. The fact that the *4As Standards of Practice* were in place at the time both of these incidents occurred might lead one to ask: are the codes of ethics serving the industry well?

It is perhaps not the myopic, mute practitioners that have something to tell us, but instead the "talking, seeing practitioners." Drumwright and Murphy noted that these practitioners appeared to have "developed and articulated ethical norms." It was not clear, they noted, that other agencies had done so "at least not in a purposeful, premeditated manner." These talking, seeing practitioners recognized moral issues readily; "tried to be clear in communicating their ethical values" not only in their day-to-day interactions but also in new business solicitations; and exhibited "moral imagination, envisioning moral alternatives that others do not."[23] The researchers concluded: "The point is not that these agencies had statements or codes, but that the statements or codes appeared to articulate authentic norms of the agency communities and efforts were made to put them into action."[24] Might it be that the conversation about ethics is as important as or more important than the codes?

Let's pause now to consider another dimension of the role of ethics in advertising: the distinction between ethicality and legality, for indeed, there is a distinction. Consider this comment from an advertising practitioner:

I think [advertising] is probably one of the most ethical businesses there is. It is so regulated. Everything that we do has to go through our lawyers to make sure that it's conforming to law, and then our client's lawyers, and then we have to send it through to the networks and their lawyers. . . . It's really hard to be unethical in this business even if you wanted to.[25]

Here, the practitioner has "passed the buck" for ethical decision-making to the legal profession, essentially saying: "They'll take care of it. If it's legal, it's ethical, right?" Cunningham suggests that ethics is "concerned with questions of what ought to be done, not just with what legally must be done."[26] Weinstein, writing in *Bloomberg Business*, concurs, noting that "the ultimate standards for deciding what we ought to do are ethical, not legal, ones."[27] Finally, in an attempt to sharpen the distinction, advertising legal scholar Ivan Preston said somewhat sarcastically:

Now, I *have* heard . . . people . . . say that you're doing an ethical thing simply by choosing to obey the law. I regard that at best as an awfully low form of ethics, and in fact so low that I personally don't regard that as ethics at all. Doing something useful for your fellow human beings doesn't deserve much credit when your purpose includes avoiding the punishment you could get for not doing.[28]

Ethics "kicks in" when there is no law governing the situation. This is particularly important in advertising. Advertising is regulated by the same laws that regulate business as well as by a host of other federal, state, and local bodies, with regard to truthfulness, deception, and fairness. Beyond that, the industry operates primarily under the auspices of guidelines and self-regulation.

If we recognize the roles advertising plays beyond being a tool of business, that is, if we acknowledge advertising as a vehicle of social communication, we discover that a number of the key concerns voiced about advertising are ethical not legal concerns. Consider, for example, the matter of taste. Indeed, tastefulness of advertising content (or the lack thereof) emerges again and again in controversies surrounding advertising and society. Keith Reinhard, Chairman Emeritus of DDB Worldwide, addresses this issue in an article entitled, "The Taste Debate: Making a Case for Decency in Advertising."[29] He acknowledges that taste is neither arguable nor able to be regulated, but continues, quoting Kirk Carr of *The Wall Street Journal*: "The fact that constructive measures are not easily crafted and that universal agreement is not likely to emerge doesn't relieve the leaders of our community from the responsibility of tackling this difficult issue [taste]."[30] Taste, then, is an ethical issue.

The very nature/character/possibilities, players, and process of our profession and our practices have altered dramatically in today's rapidly evolving digital media culture: a culture in which accelerated technological developments provide seemingly endless opportunities to reach anyone (everyone?) anywhere (everywhere?) almost immediately; a culture cluttered with commercial messages; a global culture that knows virtually no boundaries; a technological tsunami in which legal frameworks simply cannot keep pace, and then too, "ethical reflection often begins only after damage has been done."[31]

The times virtually demand that we reflect on our values as individuals, as professionals, and citizens of the world, consider how we want to act in and on the world, view society as our ultimate client, and always be certain that intrinsic values—respect, trust, humaneness, and justice—enter into our understanding of "doing advertising work."

Jay Black, noted media ethicist and co-founder of the *Journal of Mass Media Ethics*, noted the importance of *meaningful* codes of ethics in the communication professions:

> The bottom line: If we want to be taken seriously as ethical communicators, we need codes that mean something to practitioners and the general public. If we want to be ethical, we need to articulate our ideals, remind ourselves and others of our unique contributions to the world's civic health, and then act accordingly. If we want to continue to claim freedoms to communicate and advocate, then we should accept concomitant responsibilities. To some extent codes of ethics can help on all counts.[32]

This case differs from others in this section in that it doesn't ask you to reflect on an ethical dilemma. Instead, it asks you to reflect on ethics. What is the role of ethics in advertising? What is the normative role of ethics in advertising? How does (or how might) a code of ethics enter into the process of ethical advertising decision-making?

As noted in the case, several ethical codes are in place in the advertising industry, among them: *4As Standards of Practice*, the AAF's *Advertising Ethics and Principles*, and the most recently developed IAE *Principles and Practices for Advertising Ethics*. Take time to look at these codes and ask: do these codes serve the industry well?

Key points made in the case are the importance of relevance, timeliness, and the necessity of being attentive to codes, creating a moral community in which ethical decision-making is a routine part of doing our work. Consider the following:

In 1924, the opening statement of the *Standards of Practice* articulated the relatively young industry's perception of its role:

> We hold that a responsibility of advertising agencies is to be a constructive force in business. We hold that, to discharge this responsibility, advertising agencies must recognize an obligation, not only to their clients, but to the public, the media they employ, and to each other. As a business, the advertising agency must operate within the framework of competition. It is recognized that keen and vigorous competition, honestly conducted, is necessary to the growth and the health of American business. However, unethical competitive practices in the advertising agency business lead to financial waste, dilution of service, diversion of manpower, loss of prestige, and

tend to weaken public confidence both in advertisements and in the institution of advertising.[33]

That statement has remained unchanged for nearly a century. Both the AAF *Advertising Ethics and Principles* and the *4As Standards of Practice* have statements regarding taste: "Advertising shall be free of statements, illustrations or implications that are offensive to good taste or public decency" (AAF). "We will not knowingly create advertising that contains statements, suggestions, or pictures offensive to public decency or minority segments of the population" (4As). Think about the industry's attentiveness to existing codes.

It is no exaggeration to say that advertising is in the midst of a revolution: the industry regularly enters into a variety of relationships with adtech and analytic sectors; and programmatic buying demands behavioral targeting, a practice that brings privacy, security, and what many have come to view as "surveillance" to the forefront of consumer concerns. Are the existing codes relevant to this new media ecosystem?

Media ethicist Jay Black notes:

Drafting, reconsidering, and revising codes should encourage further conversation within the field and better dialogue with the public and other stakeholders. And then, after a couple of years, it is probably useful to tear up the code and start over—if only because the process of drafting a code of ethics is intellectually invigorating and pragmatically cathartic.[34]

It just *might* be that the conversation about ethics is as important as or more important than the codes.

CASE 36. BRANDING: MAKING THE SAME DIFFERENT, AGAIN

It got me thinking about the premium bottled-water category, and what a challenge it must be to break through with a new brand. This is the one category in which the product itself is an internationally recognized commodity that is colorless, tasteless, and (hopefully) odorless. It is a brand category that only mad dogs and marketers would venture to enter.[35]

Bottled water has become the indispensable prop in our lives and our culture. It starts the day in lunch boxes; it goes to every meeting, lecture hall, and soccer match; it's in our cubicles at work; in the cup holder of the treadmill at the gym; and it's rattling around half-finished on the floor of every minivan in America.[36]

The bottled-water industry in the U.S. is a $15 billion business and is estimated to grow to $20 billion in 2020. More than half the population drinks bottled water. Americans drink more bottled water than milk, and bottled water is scheduled to overtake carbonated beverage sales in the next few years. Nearly fifty billion twelve-ounce bottles of water were sold in 2014; only 23 percent was recycled.

Why do people drink bottled water? The estimated growth in bottled-water consumption is predicated on the fact that customers are seeking "better-for-you beverages" and turn to bottled water rather than tap water because they believe it to be better for them. The truth of this belief is highly contested. The International Bottled Water Association identifies many of the claims made by tap water–bottled water costs 1,000–3,000 times more than tap water, FDA standards for tap water are higher than for bottled water, bottled water is just water from the tap–as myths. Critics of bottled water remain undaunted, continuing to repeat their claims vehemently.

Many claim that bottled water tastes better, though taste tests have tended to show that tap water fares well against bottled waters; few can tell the difference between premium bottled waters and less-expensive brands.

In what is arguably one of the most pointed examples of social commentary (though now quite dated), an episode of *Penn & Teller: Bullshit* conducted its own experiment. The show, a documentary-style television series on Showtime, which prides itself on identifying and exposing popular sociopolitical misconceptions, aired an episode called "Bottled Water." The episode introduces an actor posing as a "water steward" at a fancy restaurant, offering a menu of fake bottled waters to unsuspecting diners. As each table places their water order, subsequently commenting on the "unique freshness" of one or the "sweetness" of the next, the screen juxtaposes images of the water steward filling each and every bottle with water from the garden hose.

America's best-selling brands, Aquafina and Dasani, Pepsi and Coke's contributions to the bottled-water industry respectively, start with water from public sources (tap water) and "refine" it using the same reverse-osmosis techniques to which the water already has been subjected, as required by the Environmental Protection Agency's standards for safe drinking water.

Still, the question remains unanswered. If evidence suggests that bottled water is neither better for you nor better tasting than tap water, and indeed, may only be one unnecessary process away from tap water, why are we, as consumers, only too happy to spend between $1 and $40 per bottle for a resource that costs us less than 1 cent per gallon from the tap? The answer, as you've likely guessed, has to do with marketing, branding, and the construction of an image. In terms of bottled water a major consideration is the argument that advertising efforts for bottled water distinguish brands from tap water, detracting from its appeal.

We have waters that purportedly come from springs, mountain streams, and volcanoes; that are pure, purified, enriched, and mineralized; that will satisfy, invigorate, help us feel young; and that originate in far-away places–Italy, France, and Fuji. Advertisers call this brand equity.

The challenge faced by advertisers in the bottled-water industry parallels that of any number of industries selling parity products, products that are essentially alike: how do we make the same seem different? In a market of virtually indistinguishable products, our job as advertisers is to create the illusion of a difference where there may or may not be one. What are the ramifications of this branding process?

In February 2016, *Business Insider* announced that Coke and Pepsi, both of which are experiencing a decline in sales of the leading carbonated beverages, will be engaging in "the trick of the century." No longer positioning their brands against other bottled waters, or tap water, they have identified a new "competitor." They will be trying to convince Western consumers that buying water is a healthier choice than sugary soda. John Jewell, a writer for *The Week*, notes that "the comparison is a case of false equivalence. Bottled water isn't simply an alternative to soda—it's an alternative to the much more inexpensive and eco-friendly tap water."

> Our problem is—a client comes into my office and throws two newly minted half-dollars onto my desk and says, "Mine is the one on the left. You prove it's better."[37]

Let's consider more generally the dilemmas characteristic of nearly all parity product advertising. According to marketing scholar David Aaker, the creation of differentiated brands is a distinguishing characteristic of modern marketing. He notes:

> Unique brand associations have been established using product attributes, names, packages, distribution strategies, and advertising. The idea has been to move beyond commodities to branded products—to reduce the primacy of price upon the purchase decision, and accentuate the bases of differentiation.[38]

In the process of constructing a brand and a brand image, then, marketers are responsible for every detail that affects consumers' perceptions, from the font to the graphics in the packaging, from the copy to the placement of ads, and even in the careful distribution of a product. In so doing, we create the perception of a product that is truly superior when we know as well as its manufacturers know that it is, in essence, interchangeable with most other products in its category. The ethical question we must ask ourselves is a fundamental one: regardless of whether it *can* be done, is it wrong to imply differences where, functionally, there are none?

In answering this question, we might start by recalling that ours is an image-based culture; much of our knowledge of the world around us is based on images. In this sense, we are not ill-served by communications that suggest more than they may ultimately deliver. We may in fact feel more "comfortable" with one virtually identical brand over another—such as Dasani over Fuji or over tap water—based on the symbolic content that makes a difference to us. We can contend that this is an ethical issue without a constituency: if customers in fact want to perceive their brand choices as different, for whatever reason, so be it. And, the success of the products in the marketplace suggests consumers are satisfied.

In justifying our efforts, we also might argue that rational, reasonable consumers are well aware of the parity in many of their choices. But can we be sure? Would it make a difference if people knew that certain brands were virtually identical in performance? Perhaps. Yet, if knowledge of the parity nature of some products *would* make a difference in purchasing decisions, then the greatest good for the greatest number is not being served by concealing it. The utilitarian justification is weakened if not eliminated.

Are other justifications for making the same different available to us? Certainly the conviction that moral duty is owed specifically to the client ("It is my job to establish a difference."), or, more generally to advertising as a communication form ("That's the way the game is played.") is an option. And, perhaps, there could be an expanded vision of utilitarianism in this context to contend that–beyond purchase consequences–the greatest good for the greatest number is served through allowing individuals freedom of choice, including the freedom to choose to pay more for a functionally identical product if it suits their particular needs.

Certainly making the same different is legal. Adopting a viewpoint that what is good is what is legal, we choose to continue business as usual. Even recognizing it is *not* necessarily what is good for the public, branding will continue; it is essential to the smooth functioning of the marketplace. Advertising as we know it today originated when manufacturers took their commodities "out of the cracker barrel," packaged them and attached brand names to distinguish one from the other. Even Adbusters, a nonprofit organization "fighting back against hostile takeover" by corporations and consumerism, discovered the importance of branding. In their effort to "unbrand Nike," they created Blackspot Unswoosher Sneakers with a red spot on the toe (to kick Nike's butt), simply another brand.[39]

CASE 37. NICHE MARKETS, NICHE MEDIA

> Every consumer market is a construction of reality. This realization does not mean that the categories used to construct consumer markets have no basis in actuality. It does mean that the categories designed and the questions asked that contribute to the categories are for the benefit of advertisers and their clients, not consumers.[40]

Targeting is an everyday convention of marketing practice; as advertisers, we routinely identify a group, define that group using any number of characteristics, and subsequently direct our marketing efforts toward it. Targeting is an effective and efficient approach to creating and delivering marketing messages. While rarely acknowledged as such, stereotyping is an inherent part of the targeting process. Most anyone, even if they are not in advertising, can tell you what characterizes a baby boomer, a millennial, or a tween; "the coveted eighteen to thirty-four market" conjures up images and ideas that go well beyond age, as does the "55+" demographic. Target marketing is so much a part of what advertisers do that we rarely give it a thought. Perhaps we should.

As the opening quotation suggests, a group's recognition as a market is neither natural nor automatic; it occurs in the context of social relations.[41] That is, a market isn't "out there" waiting to be discovered; advertisers in effect define it into existence for commercial purposes. And yet, the definition of a target market has consequences that extend far beyond the marketplace.

While targeting will always be a necessary part of marketing, it's grounding in stereotyping is ethically problematic. The routine process of constructing market segments should be carefully considered. Let's briefly examine the construction of two of today's recognized markets: the Hispanic market and the gay market.

The Hispanic Market[42]

The Latino market came to the attention of advertisers in the mid-1960s. Conversations in the advertising trade press identified that group as untargeted, ignored, neglected, and invisible. Marketing to Hispanics primarily was local; brokers bought time on English-speaking television stations. Emilio Azcarraga, a Mexican TV entrepreneur with Televisa, had long been looking for a way to get Televisa programs into the United States. Rather than buying time on American stations, he decided instead to buy stations. At the time, FCC rules precluded noncitizens from owning more than 20 percent of a network. Azcarraga began by buying television stations in San Antonio and Los Angeles in 1961 and established the Spanish International Network and Spanish International Communications Corporations (SIN/SICC). Azcarraga circumvented the FCC rule by making the purchases through an association of employees and business partners, though he and Televisa maintained operational control:

▦　By the mid-1970s, SIN owned sixteen stations.
▦　The network became the first U.S. network connected by satellite in 1976.
▦　By 1982, SIN claimed a 90 percent reach of Latino households through its 16 networks, 100 repeater stations, and over 200 cable systems.
▦　SIN was later sold to Hallmark and renamed Univision.

As noted in Chapter 8, in a commercial media system, audiences are commodities, products sold to advertisers. In order to interest advertisers in supporting Spanish-language broadcasting, Latinos were identified, "called into existence" as a lucrative, untapped market. The broadcasters had to convince advertisers that Latinos were desirable consumers, that Latinos were a group large enough and possessing enough spending power to make it a worthwhile target market. In an article titled "Spanish Gold: Stereotypes, Ideology, and the Construction of a U.S. Latino Market," Roberta Astroff analyzes discussion in the advertising trade press and notes:

> [T]he U.S. Latino population was transformed from an "invisible market" into "Spanish gold"; through the redefinition, but not the elimination, of traditional stereotypes:

though basic elements of the stereotypes persist, values useful to advertisers are now assigned to the stereotyped ascriptions and behaviors.[43]

The market also had to be identified as having unique characteristics that required separate media. In short, Latinos had to be packaged as a marketable, commercially valuable identity. In this process, Latinos, be they Cuban, Mexican, or Puerto Rican, came to be identified in the marketing sense as a "nation within a nation," possessing a distinct culture, ethos, and language.[44] They became identified as Spanish-speaking. Arlene Davila notes:

> "Hispanics" remain a protected segment by their mere definition as a homogeneously bounded, "culturally defined" niche. It is this definition that makes all "Latinos" part of the same undifferentiated "market"—whether they live in El Barrio or in an upscale New York high-rise, or whether they watch *Fraser* or only Mexican *novellas*.[45]

She goes on to argue that the implications of this construction go far beyond marketing. Recognition as a vital market and commercial representations have not translated into expansion of the Hispanic role in participatory democracy:

> [C]ommercial representations may shape people's cultural identities as well as affect notions of belonging and cultural citizenship in public life. . . . Latinos are continually recast as authentic and marketable, but ultimately as a foreign rather than intrinsic component of U.S. society, culture, and history. . . . [M]arketing discourse is not without economic and political repercussions.[46]

Carl Kravetz, chairman of the Association of Hispanic Advertising Agencies, made a similar argument with regard to what he clearly viewed as the objectification of Hispanic advertising agencies:

> [W]e allowed the Hispanic advertising industry to be dragged into a Spanish vs. English debate, and . . . in order to get ourselves out of the language corner, there [are] three things we need to do: One. To move beyond defining our market in terms of English or Spanish. Two. To insist on permission to be complex. Three. To adopt a new language . . . the language of agency . . . the language of marketing . . . the language of business-building . . . it is up to *us* to define our consumers or risk having them defined for us.[47]

The Gay Market[48]

When the Gay Liberation Movement began in 1969, gay males and lesbians (at the time, identified as "homosexuals," a term now viewed to be offensive) were one of the most marginalized and stigmatized minority groups in the U.S. Once the movement began, however, it didn't take long for discussions in the trade press raising the possibility of marketing to the gay market to begin. At that time, most gay men remained in the closet, and advertisers were reluctant to have their products associated with a gay market, arguing they could reach gay consumers in mainstream media through advertising aimed at the straight market.

The lack of marketing data on the gay community also contributed to advertisers' hesitation to target the group. The first marketing study of gay men was conducted in 1977 by the *Advocate*, at the time the only gay publication with a national circulation. The study, based on a sample of readers, presented a picture of gay men as white, upscale professionals. These men had no families and so were able to consume high-end items: liquor, clothing, and travel. As national advertisers gradually found their way into the *Advocate* and local gay newspapers, they became aware that in urban areas, "the consumption habits and fashion tastes of gay men were being imitated by straight men, particularly in clothing designs that emphasize a highly eroticized masculinity."[49] Rather than being viewed as an isolated, marginalized niche, "hyper-consumer" and "trend setter" became a part of the constellation of qualities ascribed to the gay male, the gay male stereotype.

Advertisers, who were becoming increasingly interested in reaching the gay market, were hindered by the limited number of ways to do so. The only gay publications that existed in the 1980s lacked the production quality national advertisers sought and tended toward content that was too sexually explicit. Advertisers who sought the gay market's dollars but remained reluctant to have their products associated with the gay market resorted to "gay window dressing"—ads with subtexts recognized by gay males but unnoticed by others—in mainstream media.

Gay publications began to appear in the late 1980s and early 1990s, and for the most part adopted the strategy of using high-quality glossy paper and emphasizing lifestyle. Sexual content was isolated to the back pages. Local and regional gay periodicals followed suit, likewise altering their formats and focus to attract national advertiser dollars. Studies were conducted in an attempt to create a picture of a more "marketable" gay market. Although results of these studies were often contradictory, and sometimes revealed a gay population quite different from that constructed in the advertising mind, the number of publications targeting gay males increased; more media representations of the (stereo)typical gay male filled the pages of those publications. Fred Fejes notes that someone coming out who turned to gay media would discover:

> [T]o be a homosexual in today's society is to be masculine, young white male, with well-muscled body and handsome face, a good education, and a professional job. Moreover . . . all the members of the gay community are alike. There may be a few African Americans or Asians, albeit with very Caucasian features, and a few women, but aside from their race or gender, there is very little difference. They all live in a gay-friendly environment where this is no sexism, racism, homophobia, or poverty.[50]

This image bore little resemblance to the majority of the gay population.

The construction of Hispanics and gays as economic subjects has not been without conse-quence. Rather than signaling progress toward legal and social equality, some argue that commercially motivated representations "created and regulated identities and desires" of these groups and actually *hampered* their political progress. Stereotypical representations, though not representative, became the basis of political discourse. Others have called attention to the apparent consequences in communities. Writing particularly of the gay and lesbian communities, Fejes noted that:

> media images and consumption played a more important role in the construction of a definition of the lesbian and gay community . . . and identity than they do in the process of identity formation of individuals in other groups. . . . [Y]ouths and adults with primarily same-sex desires and orientation have little or no help in understanding or defining themselves as gay or lesbian. . . . Where in the past coming out was chiefly about sex, today it is as much about consumption.[51]

> [A]dvertising may be presenting a very biased and very partial view of society, one that excludes many groups of individuals who do not fall into those selected advertising types. If, as we are often told, advertising is a reflection of society, then it is a very limited, partial, and biased reflection. In fact, it is a reflection that is itself a grand stereotype.[52]

The stereotyping inherent in the targeting process commodifies individuals, placing them in groups on the basis of some composite of "typical" characteristics that has meaning to the advertisers but may or may not be meaningful to the individuals targeted. Nowhere is this more true than in the behavioral tracking that makes monetization of the internet possible. There, algorithms sort individuals into categories based on correlations of data collected, about some of which we know nothing. Mark Andrejevic describes it this way: "The commer-cial model that underlines . . . online environments tends to reinforce what we already know about this person: Find a way to sort them into a particular category and sell them based on that category that we have."[53] Stereotypes simplify complexity, sacrifice individuality, and are always misrepresentations. In that sense, stereotypes are deceptive. The use of stereo-types will continue because marketing segmentation and targeting are essential to the practice of advertising and the smooth functioning of the marketplace. However, the process should not be viewed as routinized, but instead should be considered with great ethical care.

Targeting appears to be a valuable tool in an instrumental sense. It provides the basis of efficient communication with a group of desirable consumers, and it minimizes monetary waste as well as message delivery to individuals to whom the message might not be relevant and so might be particularly annoying. In all fairness, it should also be noted that the Hispanic and gay media created to facilitate targeted marketing efforts have been welcomed by many in the those communities, despite the failure of those media to recognize the communities' diversity. Those media provide not only entertainment but also information on issues important to the group and an opportunity for dialogue. In short, Hispanics and gay males have been given a voice, albeit a commercially driven voice.

To help clarify the construction of any target market, we might ask ourselves:

▪ How do a variety of people come to be identified as belonging to a single group?
▪ What characteristics determine membership in that group?
▪ Who attributes the meanings (and value) given to these characteristics?

In the examples discussed here, Hispanics were defined by Hispanic media entrepreneurs who subsequently assumed roles as "professional consultants" for the purpose of packaging Hispanics as a marketable audience. The market was constructed, one might say "othered," by language and identified as a nation within a nation. In being distinguished in this manner, Hispanics were marginalized as outside the mainstream, "forever needy of culturally special marketing."[54]

The gay market too was a product of commercial initiative, emerging from marketing data that created an unrealistic picture of a complex market. Media created and recreated their publications to appeal to marketers' images of the gay male. And what of lesbians? It appears that even in the gay market, men are more equal than women. Advertisers did not find lesbians to be an attractive market or one easily identified. Efforts to reach lesbians, they said, could be made through ads aimed at women generally.[55] Gay women remain marginalized.

In examining this process, the question to be asked is this: were these markets constructed in response to the market's genuine needs or as a means to achieve a marketer-defined end?

If the latter, Kant would question the morality of the process, for in its strictest sense, to "use" others in pursuit of our goals, or perhaps more clearly, in *mere* pursuit of our own goals, is immoral. To show disrespect for the humanity of another human being is morally wrong.

Another factor to be considered is the *vulnerability* of these markets; to be recognized as economic subjects suggested a level of acceptance that the groups had not enjoyed previously. Brooks reminds us that "it is through the discourses of advertisers and their clients that the categories of consumers get established."[56] The Hispanic community was vulnerable to stereotypical interpretations and misinterpretations by a larger community that knew very little about its many and varied cultures. To the degree that the Hispanic community lacked control of its representations, it was at a decided disadvantage. In fairness, the complicity of Hispanic professionals as brokers of that understanding should be acknowledged. So too were the gay and lesbian communities complicit in their own construction. Fejes writes that:

lesbians and gays often take advertising directed at their community as a sign of validation and legitimation. If they have not yet achieved the status of citizens with full and equal rights, they at least have achieved the status of desirable consumers.[57]

Seeking both validation and the advertising dollars, the gay media recrafted themselves to attract; those advertising then filled their pages with representations that created an unrealistic identity of the gay market, an identity available only to a privileged minority.

Finally, we should call into question the persistence with which the marketing community has addressed these markets rhetorically as well as instrumentally as precisely and solely that: markets, commodities. Advertiser-constructed images and representations play a vital role in how individuals in each of those markets are understood more broadly as social, economic, and political participants. Given that, we should ask: is there not some ethical middle ground where we recognize at one and the same time their value as consumers *and* their value and rights as citizens?

Again, as is true of branding in the previous case, it is unrealistic to harbor any illusions that targeting or the stereotyping implicit in the construction of target markets can or will disappear. Targeting is a fundamental component of advertising work. As advertising professionals we must use the greatest ethical care to consider the consequences of decisions that often seem routine, and we must do so in each new situation, with each new product, and each new "target." While we certainly have a professional obligation to be an advocate for our clients, advancing their interests and the achievement of their goals, we have at the same time a responsibility to do our work with fairness and sensitivity.

ETHICS IN THE EVERYDAY

Eroticism and fast food come together in an unlikely combination to announce the arrival of the Patty Melt Thickburger at the Hardee's restaurant chain.[58]

Carl's Jr., a subsidiary of CKE Restaurants and sister to Hardee's, is a regional chain operating in the western and southwestern states. They're well known for their use of scantily clad, sexy models in advertising targeted to "young, hungry guys" who are "apt to find it appealing."[59]

In 2007, Carl's Jr. and Hardee's aired a spot for their new patty melt sandwich served on a flat bun. The "flat buns" spot featured a young, sexy "teacher" in a pencil skirt gyrating to the front of the classroom (later atop her desk) to a rap song "celebrating flat booty" sung by the teen boys in her class. The response from the Tennessee Education Association was quick and vehement. Hardee's cancelled the ad; the Carl's Jr. ad was modified. Still, the brands knew from experience that the surest way to draw viewers to an ad that has been canceled in response to public criticism or media rejection is to identify it as a "banned commercial" and place it on YouTube. Hardee's and Carl's Jr. did just that. There the ad joined another Hardee's/Carl's Jr. effort: "Patty Melts for You," in which Swedish model Helena Mattson cooingly gyrates, tosses her hair, licks her lips, and then invites the viewer to join her as she bites into a patty melt sandwich. There too was an earlier—one might say infamous—ad for Carl's Jr. in which a very scantily clad Paris Hilton seductively soaps herself and her Bentley before biting into her sandwich. That spot has recently been reprised, this time featuring *Sports Illustrated* model Hannah Ferguson washing a Ford pickup truck, and a cameo appearance by Hilton. In 2013, Carl's Jr. featured Heidi Klum as a kind of Mrs. Robinson from *The Graduate*, to introduce their Jim Beam Bourbon Burger calling it a "fun and irreverent way to introduce the mature taste of bourbon to hungry guys." *Sports Illustrated* cover models continue to populate Carl's Jr. and Hardee's commercials, some of which are banned and never broadcast.

Carl's Jr. is a tough client. In 2011, they fired their agency of less than a year because they had "become concerned about the recent direction of the advertising and determined that we needed to make a change."[60] That was industry speak for the ads not being sexy enough. They hired 72nd and Sunny, which remains their agency today.

Note: The preceding facts are true. The scenario in the following case, "Ethical Vision," is hypothetical and was created to invite you to reflect on some of the decision-making processes that *might have occurred* in the conceptualization, creation, and airing of the new spot. Although there are elements of fact in the scenario, *they did not happen* as presented here.

CASE 38. ETHICAL VISION: WHAT DOES IT MEAN TO SERVE CLIENTS WELL?

Jeff was relatively new in his position as an assistant account planner on the Carl's Jr. account. Maybe that was why he felt so uncomfortable at this meeting with the agency creative team, the Carl's Jr. marketing team and Eric, the account planner, his boss. He was excited to be working on an account that was going to be in the Super Bowl. Okay, so the ad was only going to be shown in the West, but, still, it was the Super Bowl! Then too, Jeff was worried that his dislike for the product would be evident. He didn't like the very *idea* of the product: 1410 calories, 70 percent of the average person's daily caloric intake. The rest of the world is worrying about the obesity epidemic.[61] He even wondered if he should have asked to be removed from the account for that reason alone.

But, there was no use denying it, Jeff knew he was unnerved because he thought the execution the agency was going to suggest was offensive. It objectified women; it was demeaning. Sure, the ad they would be proposing was "on strategy"; very obviously targeted to the "young hungry guys" the restaurant was seeking. But, the execution was . . . what? Well, in a word it was "raunchy." It was just too much! Okay, so sex sells, or so we say in the industry. But again? Hamburgers? He had been hoping that the agency would create something new rather than the clichéd sexy girl in a bikini.

Jeff reflected on what had come before. How *had* they gotten to this point? The Carl's Jr. people had come with a new product, the All Natural Burger. "This is the way I see it," the client's marketing officer had told them. "We're talking to young men–young *hungry* men. You remember when you were that age?" He looked pointedly at Jeff who had just turned 24 and was the youngest in the room. "All you cared about was food and girls." Now Jeff thought he looked accusatory! "So that's what we want in our ad. A really big, delicious, juicy, decadent burger, and a girl. That's it! Oh, and it only costs $4.69."

Jeff had looked at the research. The client was right about the link between boys, food, and girls. "There is a connection, at least in the young man's mind," the director of the Cornell University Food and Brand Lab had noted in a recent *Advertising Age* article, "of having a healthy appetite for food and having an identity that you believe is appealing to the opposite sex."[62] He had to admit, the previous ads seemed to have worked. Sales were up and an expansion plan was being drawn up. With the client mandate in hand, the creative team had set to work.

Jeff's agency was one of the "hot shops" in the industry, noted for its innovation and sometimes "off the wall" creative efforts. That's why this client had come to them in the first place. They wanted an agency that would be willing to push the envelope, be "over the top," edgy. A week ago, Jeff and Eric met with their creative team to see what they'd come up with and the creatives were pumped. Carl's Jr. had hired Charlotte McKinney, "the Guess Jeans girl" for the ad. "WOW!!!!!!" The creative team (all men, Jeff noted) had a spot the client would be wild about.

When Jeff noticed they'd labeled the ad "au naturel" he thought "Oh please, no. Surely not." But, yes. He watched the model walking through a farmers market, looking very "au naturel." "She won't really be naked," the creative team assured Eric and him. But the coy views, suggestively but strategically placed fruits and vegetables, and the gawking vendors made you wonder. Finally, as Charlotte approached the camera with what appears to be a monstrous burger, she cooed in a sultry voice: "I love going all-natural. . . . It just makes me feel better." Even if she didn't make it to the Super Bowl, the team thought she could become sort of an extra treat on the website. And after that? YouTube. "What do you think?" they asked.

"I think you must be kidding," Jeff said somewhat sarcastically. But again, no. The creative folks were serious. He hoped Eric would round them up, but no, Eric praised the executions.

Jeff wasn't going to say anything because he thought he'd be laughed out of the room. He could hear the creative team now: "The client will LOVE IT!" Probably, Jeff thought, but was it really in their best interest to continue down this already beaten path? Still, he hadn't said a word and now here they were, one week later, meeting with a client who seemed to be nothing short of ecstatic over the agency's work. "This is great. No. Not great. TREMENDOUS! You guys really got it this time."

To his credit, Eric cautioned: "Remember that Flat Buns ad. That hadn't played too well."

"Exactly. But it was a DYNAMITE ad." The Carl's Jr. manager spoke exuberantly:

It was edgy. I loved it. It should *never* have run on the network. That was a mistake. Should have gone right on the Web. She's on YouTube, you know. And she gets a lot of hits every day, even today. A few teachers and feminists might have objected, but heck, they aren't in the target audience, are they? Boys absolutely loved it! They still do. And if somebody objects to this spot, if the babe doesn't play right, we'll put her on YouTube with the others. She'll be a big hit.

The client wound down enthusiastically.

Jeff sighed. The client certainly was right about the Flat Buns spot and the Paris Hilton spot before it. Both had received a lot of publicity. People thought they were sexist, hyper-sexualized, and retrograde; some even called them "pornographic." But the target market did like it, sales were up, and "the girls" (as the client insisted on calling the models) were still a big hit on YouTube. Ads that are "controversial" or "banned" are always a big hit on YouTube, though that's not exactly what Jeff would have called a sound media strategy. And then, there was the nagging question of social responsibility.

The situation facing Jeff is a common one. Relatively new on the job, he found himself alone in his belief/recognition that something was awry with the creative executions. He didn't speak up, so no one knew or considered his concerns. The creatives had thought they were "on strategy," and, in fact, they were. In that sense, Jeff's colleagues were doing their jobs. Wasn't it their professional responsibility to operate in the client's interest, to create ads that were effective in meeting the goals the client had set? But in this situation, by all appearances, the creative team was blind to any of the possible moral consequences. They were concerned only with whether or not the client would "buy into" the campaign, which the creatives themselves really thought was great. In all fairness, the team felt they had a particularly acute grasp of the consumers' taste and understanding of the client, and apparently they did. They knew they could "go a bit farther" to get their client's product noticed.

Some advertisers guard their corporate reputation with care and would never dream of being associated with any advertising that might be regarded as tasteless. Others, of course, are less discriminating. Clearly, there can be no reasonable argument against the contention that American culture has grown more tolerant of the sexually provocative. It's where we are as a culture at this moment. Sometimes it seemed you had to do "anything you can to get noticed; the ends justified the means." But did they?

This situation illustrates the complexities inherent in a profession in which we are bound to the service of our client; it becomes a matter of reflecting on what it is we think we are doing when we do advertising work, when we assume our role as advertising professionals. In that role, we are bound to the service of our client. But do we not also have some social responsibility to do the greatest good for the greatest number possible? A lack of awareness or concern for social consequences is not uncommon. Research has shown that those consequences farthest away, most abstract from the individual's own environment, are least likely to be recognized.

After conducting research on advertising practitioners' thoughts and actions with regard to ethics, Drumwright and Murphy suggested that "a paradigm shift seems to be needed regarding what it means to serve clients well."[63] "Many of [the informants interviewed] expressed a strong sense that as advertising practitioners, they are to do the client's bidding."[64] In all fairness, the client in this situation has had good return on his investment using images of questionable appropriateness and clearly recognizes the likelihood the ad will offend because he's planning ahead for when the executions either don't get accepted to air or create too much of a stir to keep airing. He has the YouTube escape hatch with which he clearly is enamored.

Then too, as noted earlier, the advertising profession is obligated to a number of constituencies. Those obligations cannot be met if all decisions are relegated to the client. Is the agency here in danger of "going native," of "overidentifying with the client's perspective to the point that they have lost the ability to be critical of clients and objective in assessing their behavior and advertising?"[65]

Certainly it was easier to leave the situation alone; clients aren't likely to want to be subjected to critical questioning, are they? Is it the agency's business to question the moral judgment of the client? But then, is the agency doing its job if it doesn't raise the question?

In adopting the client-is-always-right philosophy when making decisions, the agency sidesteps its professional responsibility to the client. After all, the agency's responsibility is to be the "objective outsider," advising the client, if necessary challenging long-held, tenaciously guarded perspectives and behaviors that may be operating to the client's detriment. The ability to be "neutral" is a professional responsibility. Although Jeff tangled with concerns about his social responsibility personally, he didn't confront the issue organizationally. Jeff failed to recognize that in keeping his silence, he was, in effect, abrogating his professional responsibility to the client.

In a fast-paced, competitive, creative industry, discussion of ethical concerns frequently takes a back seat to more urgent pragmatic issues. Finally, we too might ask, are the issues raised here merely a matter of taste differences rather than an ethical concern?

CASE 39. THE RISKY CLIENT: YES? NO?

By subjecting e-cigarettes to its regulatory regime, the FDA risks retarding the growth of what may prove to be a powerful new tool for harm reduction. But by failing to act, the agency risks undermining decades of progress in tobacco control. In either case, the public health impact is apt to be significant.[66]

Seth was the CEO of a mid-sized advertising agency in Fort Worth, Texas. The new business team at the agency had informed him that a new e-cigarette brand, N-lite-N, was considering hiring the agency for its product launch. E-cigarettes are metal tubes that heat liquids typically laced with nicotine and deliver vapor when inhaled. Did the agency want to be considered?

The new business folks had done the due diligence work. Yes, the client would pay, pay well, and pay on time. And, it would be a hefty bit of revenue for the agency. The industry is "smoking hot" (the trade journal's words, not his); sales are expected to reach $50 billion by 2025.[67] N-lite-N could end up being their biggest account in a year or two. Seth thought a lot can happen in a year or two. At this point, there were no federal regulations on the e-cigarette industry simply because the government didn't have enough data on health impact to provide a rational basis for regulations. That was bound to change because the product was a nicotine-delivery system. Yes, that would probably change very soon. Seth wondered what those regulations might be.[68] The government could choose to regulate e-cigarettes like tobacco. That would mean limiting the types of advertising and possibly imposing age restrictions. Choosing to regulate e-cigarettes like regulated smoking-cessation therapies would mean that only pharmacies could distribute them. That certainly would cut the visibility and the accessibility of the product, Seth thought. Of course, the FDA could create new regulations specific to e-cigarettes and who knows what those might be? They'd likely include restraints on the manufacture of the product as well as the marketing. No matter how he looked at it, Seth knew that any kind of regulation was bound to slow market growth and that would limit revenue-generating potential for the agency.

Seth also knew he should consider the possible risk to the agency's reputation. Sure, a number of well-known agencies were working for e-cigarette brands. The product category was seemingly in the "midst of a swagger" at the moment, that was true enough. But the product *was* controversial, and there were a number of agencies who didn't want anything to do with a "tobacco account." Tobacco was part of the problem too. While e-cigarettes claimed to be "safer" than traditional cigarettes, they *are* a nicotine-delivery system. That says "tobacco" to almost everyone—smokers, non-smokers, regulators—and tobacco "carries a lot of baggage." Still, Seth believed all legal products should have a right to advertise, and agencies had the right to represent them.

He'd thought through the financial risks involved, studied the research and he thought he was fairly comfortable that the potential revenue outweighed the financial risk. He was worried that he'd hire new employees to service the account and then, if things fell apart . . . well, he didn't like the idea of laying off employees.

Just then, Federica, supervisor of account services, stormed into Seth's office. She'd heard that the agency was thinking about pitching the account, and she wanted to talk about it. No, she wanted to protest! And protest she did. She laid out her case methodically. Did Seth realize the product might be harmful (*might* was the operative word in Seth's mind)? Sure, advocates saw e-cigarettes as a mechanism to help people quit smoking, but research on their usefulness in cessation was limited, and no major health or medical organization in the U.S. recommended e-cigarettes for that purpose. Others worried that e-cigarettes were a "bridge" to traditional tobacco use and addiction. The popularity of e-cigarettes was sky-rocketing; the Centers for Disease Control and Prevention reported that eighteen million middle- and high-school students were exposed to e-cigarette ads in 2014, and 2.4 million had smoked an e-cigarette in the last thirty days.[69] Though the e-cigarette industry claimed not to be targeting teens, the new flavors being added to the cigarettes—watermelon, bubble gum, sour apple—said something different. The companies appeared to be using the same tactics they'd once used to sell tobacco, Federica fumed. She'd even read an article in the *British Medical Journal* that called e-cigarettes "an on-going human experiment without ethics approval."[70]

Okay, she understood that "disruptive technologies" often faced controversy, perhaps unfairly, and that e-cigarettes were particularly polarizing because of the connection to tobacco and nicotine. She also understood that e-cigarettes might turn out to be a big boon to public health if they really did help people stop smoking or prevented them from starting. Yet, ending with her characteristic bluntness, Federica made her stance very clear. "At this point," she pointed out, "we don't know the possible health threats posed by e-cigarettes. The agency SHOULD NOT pitch the account."

Seth and Federica approach the challenge of a "risky" client from similar positions, but ultimately reach different conclusions. Seth views the risk involved primarily in terms of potential economic gains or losses, that is, in terms of anticipated consequences. As CEO of the agency, his loyalties clearly lie with its stewardship. The reputation, the quality of work, the welfare of the employees, and, of course, the financial stability of the agency are his primary concerns in assessing risk. His belief that any legal product has the right to advertise is a reflection of his inherent faith in the free-market system. This provides something of a short-cut (short-circuit?) through which he avoids consideration of the product's potential health risk. Though he acknowledges the reason for the government's delay in regulation of e-cigarette marketing—the lack of information on the health impact of the product—he seems to view the "risk" in e-cigarettes to be a function of the uncertainty surrounding the almost-certain regulation of the industry and the impact that would have on agency revenues. In a sense, he seems to have disconnected his view of risk from questions related to health impact that are at the heart of the present regulatory hiatus, and from any future questions of the future legal status of the product. Seth's decision apparently will be based on perceived impact of winning the client's business (he seems to be confident that a pitch would in fact lead to winning the account) on the agency's economic viability. Does the possibility of increased revenue generated by winning the account outweigh the risk arising out of the uncertainty of the imposition of regulations and the nature of those regulations?

Seth's faith in the functioning of the marketplace to provide greater good is based on a free-market perspective. Operating on the well-established principle that individuals should be allowed to make their own informed choices, advertisers are completely on moral ground advertising legal products truthfully. Seth's consideration seems to have little ethical depth beyond that; he doesn't engage with broader questions underlying this perspective, questions that are at the heart of the controversy surrounding e-cigarette marketing. As such, it might be useful to further consider the assumptions of a free-market perspective.

Acting in their own self-interest, advertisers present only a "partial truth" (that is, they are not likely to say "there are studies that counter our claims"), assuming many one-sided communications will collide in a marketplace of ideas, and rational individuals will make the wisest choice. If consumers understand that long-term impacts of smoking e-cigarettes are unknown, and choose to use the product anyway, the moral decision is theirs alone; they have every right to "self-abuse" as long as they aren't harming others. In striking a balance between placing personal responsibility on citizens and regulating what citizens are allowed to indulge in, adopting this perspective shifts the responsibility for determining whether it is ethical to market e-cigarettes to the government.

Do consumers have the information they need to make "an informed choice"? Are they relying on the seemingly reasonable expectation that sellers would not be selling the product if they had determined it was harmful? In the case of e-cigarettes, it seems plausible to ask if in fact *anyone* had enough information concerning long-term consequences of smoking e-cigarettes to suggest claims one way or the other.

Critics adopting an absolutist stance would argue that because e-cigarettes contain nicotine and nicotine is known to be detrimental to health, it is simply wrong to advertise them or any potentially dangerous product, regardless of the consequences.

Federica's position is not absolutist. Like Seth, she has an inherent faith in the free-market system; she believes legal products should be allowed to advertise. Yet in this case, the absence of scientific evidence firmly establishing the consequences (positive *or* negative) of smoking e-cigarettes, the acknowledgment that e-cigarettes *might* pose a health threat, overrode the edicts of the marketplace. E-cigarettes should not be advertised. Federica, it seems, is willing to take the responsibility for ethical decision-making out of government hands, and instead place it firmly in the hands of the agency.

The ethical positions taken in the e-cigarette controversy are wide-ranging. Looking from a utilitarian ethical perspective, determination of the ethicality varies depending upon how "greatest good" is defined. Those adopting an economic perspective might argue that the growth of the e-cigarette category alone indicates that consumer needs are being satisfied. Favorable consumer response is seen as a vote of confidence. A utilitarian position grounded in human welfare would view the situation quite differently. It would argue that it is unethical to advertise a product that cannot be shown to be harmless. The claim that e-cigarettes are "safer" is both untenable and unethical.

The ethicality of marketing e-cigarettes is a very complicated one, made even more complex by a lack of information upon which to base ethical decisions and the conflation of the ethicality of the product and the ethicality of *marketing* the product. Are e-cigarettes a booming industry or a health fiasco?[71] At the time of writing, the question remains unanswered.

NOTES

1. Talcott Parsons, "The Professions and Social Structure," *Social Forces* 17 (May 1939): 457–467.
2. Burton J. Bledstein, *The Culture of Professionalism: The Middle Class and the Development of Higher Education in America* (New York: W. W. Norton and Co., 1976), 90.
3. Vanderbilt Medical Center Patent Medicine Collection, www.mc.vanderbilt.edu/biolib/hc/nostrums/nostrums.html.
4. Peggy J. Kreshel, "The 'Culture' of J. Walter Thompson, 1915–1925," *Public Relations Review* 16:8, (Fall 1990): 88–89, fn. 3.
5. Local clubs included: Agate Club, 1894; Advertising Club of New York, 1906; and League of Advertising Women of New York, 1911. National organizations included: Association of Advertising Clubs of the World, 1905; Association of National Advertisers, 1910; and American Association of Advertising Agencies, 1912.
6. Printers' Ink (1888), Agricultural Advertising (1894), Mahin's Magazine (1902), Judicious Advertising (1903), and Advertising and Selling (1909).
7. Northwestern University and the University of Minnesota (1903). By 1915, twenty-six universities had advertising courses for their undergraduate students.
8. Emile Durkheim, *The Division of Labor in Society* (New York: Free Press, 1964), originally published 1893.
9. Mark S. Frankel, "Professional Codes: Why, How, and with What Impact?" *22*s, 8 (1989): 110.
10. Greg Nyilasy, Peggy J. Kreshel, and Leonard N. Reid, "Agency Practitioners, Pseudo-Professionalization Tactics, and Advertising Professionalism," *Journal of Current Issues in Research in Advertising* 33:2 (2012): 146–169.
11. *AAAA Standards of Practice*, first drafted in 1924.
12. Thomas H. Bivins, "The Future of Public Relations and Advertising Ethics," in John Michael Kittross, ed., *An Ethics Trajectory: Visions of Media Past, Present and Yet to Come* (Urbana: University of Illinois/The Institute of Communication Research, 2008). See also Thomas H. Bivins, *Mixed Media: Moral Distinctions in Advertising, Public Relations, and Journalism* (Mahwah, NJ: Lawrence Erlbaum Associates, Inc., 2004).
13. D. Kirk Davidson, *The Moral Dimension of Marketing: Essays on Business Ethics* (Chicago: American Marketing Association, 2002), 7.
14. See, for example, Frank Newport, "Annual Update: Americans Rate Business and Industry Sectors," Gallup Poll, September 6, 2007, www.gallup.com/poll/28615/annual-update-americans-rate-business-industry-sectors.aspx; and Giselle Abramovich, "Americans Have Skewed View of Ad Industry," *DMNews*, September 25, 2007, www.dmnews.com/news/americans-have-skewed-view-of-ad-industry/article/98559/.
15. Matthew Creamer, "An Ad-ethics Code from Shona Seifert? Surely not." *Advertising Age*, May 18, 2005, 1, http://adage.com/article?article_id=103976.
16. Rakesh Khurana and Nitin Nohria, "It's Time to Make Management a True Profession," *Harvard Business Review* 86 (October 2008): 72.
17. Quentin Schultze, "Advertising Science and Professionalism 1885–1917," dissertation, University of Illinois at Urbana–Champaign, 1978, pp. 175–176.
18. www.aaaa.org/EWEB/upload/inside/standards.pdf, October 14, 2007. The AAAA is a national trade organization representing advertising in the United States, founded in 1917.
19. Creamer, "An Ad-ethics Code from Shona Seifert?," 1.
20. Ibid.
21. Minette E. Drumwright and Patrick E. Murphy, "How Advertising Practitioners View Ethics," *Journal of Advertising* 33:2 (Summer 2004): 7–24.
22. Mark S. Frankel, "Professional Codes: Why, How, and with What Impact?" *Journal of Business Ethics* 8:2/3 (1989): 110.

23. Drumwright and Murphy, "How Advertising Practitioners View Ethics," 16–17.
24. Ibid., 17.
25. Anonymous respondent quoted in Drumwright and Murphy, "How Practitioners View Ethics," 12.
26. Peggy H. Cunningham, "Ethics of Advertising," in John Phillip Jones, ed., *The Advertising Business* (Thousand Oaks, CA: Sage Publications, 1999), 500.
27. Bruce Weinstein, "If it's Legal, it's Ethical . . . Right?" Bloomberg Business, October 15, 2007, www.bloomberg.com/bw/stories/2007-10-15/if-its-legal-its-ethical-right-businessweek-business-news-stock-market-and-financial-advice.
28. Ivan L. Preston, Interaction of Advertising Law and Ethics in Matters of Responsibility," presentation at annual conference of American Academy of Advertising, March 27, 2009.
29. Keith Reinhard, "The Taste Debate: Making a Case for Decency in Advertising," *Agency*, Fall 2001, 30–32.
30. Ibid., 31.
31. Bernard Debatin, "The Future of New Media Ethics," in Thomas W. Cooper, Clifford G. Christians, and Anantha S. Babbili, eds., *An Ethics Trajectory: Visions of Media Past, Present and Yet to Come* (Urbana: University of Illinois Institute of Communication Research, 2008), 257.
32. Jay Black, *Doing Ethics in the Media* (New York: Routledge, 2011), 41.
33. American Association of Advertising Agencies, *Standards of Practice*, most recent revision June 2011, http://www.aaaa.org/about/association/pages/standardsofpractice.aspx.
34. Black, *Doing Ethics in the Media*, 41.
35. Barry Silverstein, "Voss: High Water," Brandchannel.com, March 5, 2007, cited October 21, 2007 at https://vossworld.wordpress.com/2012/10/21/message-in-the-voss-bottle/.
36. Charles Fishman, "Message in a Bottle," *Fast Company*, July 2007.
37. Attributed to Rosser Reeves, former Chairman of the Board, Ted Bates Agency and Company.
38. David A. Aaker, *Managing Brand Equity: Capitalizing on the Value of a Brand Name* (New York: Free Press, 1991), 7–8.
39. www.adbusters.org/.
40. Dwight E. Brooks, "In Their Own Words: Advertisers' Construction of an African-American Consumer Market, the World War II Era," *Howard Journal of Communications* 6:1–2 (October 1995): 48.
41. Roberta J. Astroff, "Spanish Gold: Stereotypes, Ideology, and the Construction of a U.S. Latino Market," *Howard Journal of Communications* 1:4 (Winter 1988–1989): 155–173.
42. The whole of this story is detailed in an excellent book by Arlene Davila, *Latinos, Inc.: The Making and Marketing of a People* (Berkeley: University of California Press, 2001).
43. Astroff, "Spanish Gold," 155.
44. Davila, *Latinos, Inc.*, 8.
45. Ibid., 8.
46. Ibid., 2, 4, 235.
47. Typescript of speech delivered by Carl Kravetz to the Association of Hispanic Advertising Agencies on the AHAA Latino Identity Project, September 20, 2006.
48. The material in this discussion draws heavily on Fred Fejes, "Advertising and the Political Economy of Lesbian/Gay Identity," in Eileen R. Meehan and Ellen Riordan, eds., *Sex & Money: Feminism and Political Economy in the Media* (Minneapolis: University of Minnesota Press, 2001), 212–229.
49. Ibid., 214.
50. Ibid., 219.
51. Ibid., 218.
52. Edward Spence and Brett Van Heekeren, *Advertising Ethics* (Upper Saddle River, NJ: Pearson, 2014), 54.
53. Sarah Childress, interview with Mark Andrejevic, "Mark Andrejevic: We Are All 'Lab Rats' Online, *Frontline*, February 18, 2014, http://www.pbs.org/wgbh/frontline/article/mark-andrejevic-we-are-all-lab-rats-online/.

54. Davila, *Latinos, Inc.*, 4.

55. Ibid.

56. Brooks, "In Their Own Words," 34.

57. Fejes, "Advertising and the Political Economy of Lesbian/Gay Identity," 218.

58. "New Campaigns–The World," *Campaigns* (UK), August 10, 2007, p. 29.

59. Ibid.

60. www.ocregister.com/articles/carl-329777-new-agency.html.

61. Kate McArthur, "Cheeseburger in Paradise; Big Burger Sales Boom Despite Obesity Epidemic," *Advertising Age*, July 17, 2006, p. 4.

62. Ibid.

63. Drumwright and Murphy, "How Advertising Practitioners View Ethics," 20.

64. Ibid.

65. Ibid.

66. http://healthaffairs.org/blog/2015/02/20/in-regulating-e-cigarettes-no-easy-fix-for-the-fda/.

67. http://www.prnewswire.com/news-releases/global-e-cigarette--vaporizer-market-2015-2025---analysis--forecasts-for-the-50-billion-industry-300124050.html.

68. Joshua Peterson, "Electronic Cigarettes: the Ethics of Marketing a Safer Cigarette," Texas Woman's University, School of Management, http://ssrn.com/abstract =2500600.

69. www.cdc.gov/vitalsigns/ecigarette-ads/

70. www.bmj.com/content/351/bmj.h5063/rr-0.

71. www.forbes.com/sites/ilyapozin/2013/04/11/electronic-cigarettes-booming-industry-or-health-fiasco/#2bb33b728b03.

THE HEART OF
THE MATTER IN
ADVERTISING ETHICS

Promotional communication permeates and blends with our cultural environment, punctuating our television watching, saturating our magazines and newspapers, and popping up in our Internet surfing, movies, and video games.[1]

Advertising is a major player in the global economy, an indispensable tool of business, and, in the words of media scholar James W. Carey, "a part of the very logic by which commerce is carried on."[2] Advertising provides the commercial foundation supporting most media, and, therefore, makes up a considerable portion of media content.

Of all media professions, it is perhaps advertising whose integrity is most frequently called into question. Surveys of public opinion consistently find advertising near the bottom of professions in terms of honesty and trustworthiness. A recent academic study examining practitioner views on ethics found that ethics frequently "didn't appear on the radar screen" of those practitioners interviewed and when they were noticed, they were often not discussed.[3] These scholars also identified what they called "seeing, talking" practitioners who "typically recognized moral issues and talked about them inside the agency with their co-workers and outside the agency with their clients and potential clients."[4]

We by no means want to imply that advertising or those who practice advertising are inherently unethical. They are not. Nor is it unethical to persuade, even to persuade passionately in advertising/promotional communication. However, it seems that advertising has developed a professional culture in which ethical dimensions of the work might easily be overlooked. Among these characteristics are: the tendency to equate ethicality and legality; a reluctance to "tell their clients 'no' regarding ethics or anything else," based on the rationale that the "client-is-always-right";[5] a hectic pace that leads many practitioners to believe that they simply don't have time to think about the ethicality of a situation; and, finally, a sense that is it is "difficult to institute processes that encourage ethical behavior without restricting the freedom that creativity requires to flourish."[6] As a result, practitioners must exercise extra vigilance, and work to provide an environment in which ethical decision-making takes on a higher priority.

What, then, characterizes the heart of the matter for developing ethical advertising practice?

Advertising as a profession, as well as individual practitioners within the profession, should recognize that advertising is not only a business tool, but also a vehicle of social communication. In addition to its economic power, it is, perhaps not by intention, a cultural teacher through which we learn ways of being and ways of relating to others, values, attitudes, and beliefs. These social messages are what marketing scholar Rick Pollay called the unintended social consequences of advertising, the "social by-products of exhortations to 'buy products.'"[7] Recognizing this social role of advertising adds an additional focus beyond that of efficiency and effectiveness. It recognizes and places additional emphasis upon our obligation to the public, and particularly to our "audiences." In order to practice ethically, we must view those audiences not merely as means to an economic end, but as ends themselves worthy of being treated with dignity, honesty, and fairness. Advertising can entertain, inform, and, indeed, persuade, but must do so with respect for personal freedom and autonomy of the audiences, or it becomes not persuasion, but manipulation.

As an "advocacy profession," advertising is contractually obligated to be an advocate of the client, working to advance the client's ends. Yet to fulfill our role of professionals, we cannot become so singularly focused that we fail to fulfill our duties to other groups of stakeholders to which we are obligated: the public; our professional colleagues; our audiences; and the media that carry our messages. Then too, Drumwright and Murphy suggest that as a profession we need to rethink "what it means to serve a client well."[8] We can fulfill our obligations to our client and to our profession only if we refrain from adopting the norm that we are to do the client's bidding. Doing so makes it more difficult to interject ethical judgments even as it hinders our ability to offer sound business strategies. We essentially abdicate our professional responsibilities; our professional obligation is not to please the client or do whatever the client wants but to serve as a neutral advisor in the client's interest. To do anything less reduces our "profession" to that of subordinate or technician.

Finally, the heart of the matter in advertising ethics is the necessity to self-consciously adopt a pattern of ethical sensitivity. A commitment to ethical values, articulated in revised codes of ethics, should be clearly and repeatedly expressed, not merely assumed. Moral issues should be recognized, discussed internally, that is, inside the agency as well as externally, with clients and potential clients. In these kinds of settings, an Aristotelian "good community" can form.

A professional is called not simply to *do* something but to *be* something.[9]

NOTES

1. William Leiss, Stephen Kline, Sut Jhally, and Jacqueline Botterill, *Social Communication in Advertising: Consumption in the Mediated Marketplace*, 3rd ed. (New York: Routledge, 2005), 3.
2. James W. Carey, Advertising: An Institutional Approach," in C. H. Sandage and V. Fryburger, eds., *The Role of Advertising* (Homewood, IL: Richard D. Irwin, 1960), 14.
3. Minette E. Drumwright and Patrick E. Murphy, "How Advertising Practitioners View Ethics," *Journal of Advertising* 33:2 (Summer 2004): 10.
4. Ibid., 15.
5. Ibid., 14.
6. Minette E. Drumwright and Patrick E. Murphy, "The Current State of Advertising Ethics," *Journal of Advertising* 38:1 (Spring 2009): 98.
7. Richard W. Pollay, "The Distorted Mirror: Reflections on the Unintended Consequences of Advertising," *Journal of Advertising* 50 (April 1986): 19.
8. Drumwright and Murphy, "How Advertising Practitioners View Ethics," 20.
9. Karen Lebacqz, *Professional Ethics: Power and Paradox* (Nashville: Abington, 1985), as cited in Thomas Bivins, *Mixed Media: Moral Distinctions in Advertising, Public Relations, and Journalism,* (Mahwah, NJ: Lawrence Erlbaum, 2004), 69.

3

PERSUASION AND PUBLIC RELATIONS

The practice of public relations shapes much of what we know of contemporary business, industry, government, sports, and entertainment—even religion. The act of helping an organization and its public adapt to each other or to "win the cooperation of groups of people"[1] calls on practitioners to "establish and maintain mutual lines of communications"; to manage problems or issues; to help management respond to public opinion and to use change in a positive way; to "serve as an early warning system"; and to help management understand how best to "serve the public interest."[2] In other words, practitioners are asked to serve a variety of roles within the organization, including those of spokesperson, listener, planner, surveyor, and counselor. These communication and relationship roles become increasingly important in the digital world where rumors or misinformation can fly around the globe with the stroke of a computer key and where interconnectedness makes information about business and government in Greece as pertinent in Athens, Georgia, USA, as it is in Athens, Greece.

Such a daunting task list has prompted calls for increased emphasis on ethical practice.[3] The two largest professional organizations have adopted formal codes of ethical practice, each with something distinctive within the field of professional communication ethics: enforcement processes. The Public Relations Society of America (PRSA) and the International Association of Business Communicators (IABC) have gone beyond the mere adoption of codes; they also teach, talk about, and try to enforce ethical practices. Practitioners from different industries, from health care to education, have adopted similar codes seeking to define and characterize the ethical principles that underlie best practices in their fields. (See www.case.org and www.hcpra.org for examples.)

Despite these efforts, the public image of public relations practitioners remains clouded. Terms such as *spin doctor*, *flack*, and *special interests* are all too familiar; phrases such as "It's just a PR stunt" and "It's all image control" come to mind too readily for the field to become complacent about its image or its role. The criticism may just reflect the general cynicism with which most institutions such as the press, big business, and government are regarded. But at other times, the criticism stems from the discordant relationships between practitioners and other communicators. Organizational downsizing and resizing have meant that marketers, advertisers, and practitioners often operate within the same department—indeed, sometimes with duties divided among two or three employees. This may foster the assumption that practitioners use the same one-way flow of persuasive information that advertisers or marketers traditionally rely on in sales campaigns rather than a belief that practitioners desire to build and maintain reciprocal communication flow. The interdependence between journalists and practitioners also has been an uneasy relationship, with questions arising about how much interaction can occur between the media and other organizations before ethical standards are breached. As new media emerge, these relationships become increasingly uncertain and undefined.

Criticism sometimes arises from a "kill-the-messenger" syndrome when practitioners, like reporters, are held personally responsible for the actions about which they communicate. The boundary communication role between the organization and the public played by the practitioner can become a convenient point of complaint for those discontented with the actions of politicians, corporations, or activist groups. Sometimes the criticisms are well deserved, such as when practitioners choose to divert public attention from the truth or distort it, or when they deliberately clutter the communication channels with confusing rhetoric or events.[4] Ethical suspicions also result from what appears to be the ever-increasing spread of the application of public relations into fields such as health care, litigation, and government.

The four chapters in this part do not claim to be encyclopedic, but they seek to raise the types of questions encountered by today's practitioners and audience members. Are there fields of interest so vital to the public good that public relations should not play a persuasive role in them? Is the polishing and shaping of a public image inherently deceptive? How does one loyally serve the interests of a client or an employer and still serve the public interest? How much social responsibility should a corporation or business be required to demonstrate, and how does one best balance social responsibility with fiscal responsibility? Some of the cases that follow are drawn from actual situations; others are hypothetical cases based on a realistic understanding of these pressures. Each seeks to focus attention on the needs, pressures, contradictions, and promises of this influential profession.

LEARNING OUTCOMES

After completing Part 3 of the book, you should be able to:

▪ **identify and understand key ethical issues faced by public relations practitioners;**

■ understand the interdependency of public relations practitioners and journalists, and explore the challenges present in this relationship;

■ evaluate the nature of other conflicting relationships and possible conflicts of interest that arise in the practice of public relations;

■ explore the nuances of truthfulness by exploring how loyalties and values may influence the amount of truthful information disseminated and publicized;

■ understand the social responsibility of businesses and organizations operating within a democracy; and

■ understand how a public relations campaign can be conducted in a socially responsible manner.

NOTES

1. Philip Lesley, "Report and Recommendations: Task Force on Stature and Role of Public Relations," *Public Relations Journal* (March 1981): 32.
2. Rex F. Harlow, "Building a Public Relations Definition," *Public Relations Review* 2:4 (Winter 1976): 36.
3. For background, see the "Special Double Issue: Ethics & Professional Persuasion," *Journal of Mass Media Ethics* 16:2&3 (2001).
4. For more discussion of public relations ethics, see Sherry Baker, "The Ethics of Advocacy: Moral Reasoning in the Practice of Public Relations," in Lee Wilkins and Clifford G. Christians, eds., *The Handbook of Mass Media Ethics* (New York: Routledge, 2009), 115–129; Jay Black, "The Ethics of Propaganda and the Propaganda of Ethics," also in *The Handbook of Mass Media Ethics*, 130–148.

10

PUBLIC COMMUNICATION

Information provider; advocate; activist: public relations practitioners frequently play multiple roles as they work with or against other stakeholders with particular viewpoints, needs, or causes. By definition, the practitioner is partisan—representing a certain group, organization, or public—with biases and loyalties apparent as he or she seeks to build or enhance critical relationships. In many settings, this partisanship raises few or no ethical questions. However, in the complex sphere of public communication in an open society, where successful or unsuccessful public relations may impact political campaigns, international diplomacy, judicial proceedings, and voter confidence, the motivations, tactics, strategies, goals, and objectives of practitioners may be questioned.

The work of this important profession is clearly informational and decidedly persuasive. And why not insist on both at the same time? Truth is never neutral, so why should the telling of truth be any less than the professional mandate of someone paid to communicate a particular perspective? In one important sense, this is a more honest mode of media work because one's biases as a communicator in a public relations setting are usually transparent. Shedding pretenses is normally the first lesson in public relations training.

Regardless of how it is categorized, the need for advocacy and information extends from Parent–Teacher Association councils to councils of war. Dwight Eisenhower recalled in his memoirs of the D-Day invasion that soon after his arrival in London in the summer of 1942, he recognized that the Allied plan to break into Germany through France would impose immense hardship on British families and farms as American sailors and soldiers gathered in preparation. His solution was to establish early "an effective Public Relations Section of the headquarters."[1] The general went on to describe battle plans, so readers were left to wonder what role public relations played in the success of the Allied cause and in the continuation of pluralist democracy in the West. We suspect that this part of the untold story is complicated and considerable.

What we do know is that contemporary politicians and strategists rely on the information and persuasion of public relations to raise funds for campaigns, to influence decision-making about legislation and policies, and to attempt to motivate what has become an inactive electorate to care about public affairs. A politician's choice of a press secretary or a campaign manager may be as avidly watched and debated as is the selection of a running mate or major policy initiative. Trade and professional organizations, labor unions, and industry groups routinely employ full-time lobbyists and send representatives to meet with policy-makers and politicians in local, state, and federal offices in hopes of influencing decisions. Indeed, the U.S. government employs thousands of public affairs specialists, writers, photographers, and editors, even though certain provisions of federal law seemingly prohibit such appropriation of funding.[2] At times, it seems that the channels of public debate have become so overloaded with voices representing special-interest groups that there is little room left for anyone who cares to articulate the need for the general public interest.

Who should control or influence the voices in the political and public affairs marketplace of ideas? Is the practice of journalism inherently more ethical than that of public relations because it strives more for objectivity and information? Or is public relations more honest because its practitioners admit their allegiances openly? Is there such a need to enhance the communication capability of some voices in the public forum that public relations must be employed? How far can the practice of public relations expand before it interferes with the democratic process?

The four cases in this chapter explore these questions. "Publicity and Justice" probes the expanding field of litigation public relations. Is the cause of rendering justice advanced when high-profile defendants or prosecutors use public relations tactics to communicate their views before trial? The second case, "The Many Friends of the Candidate," explains how the use of social and digital media has changed political communication. The next case, "Corporate Speech and State Laws" probes the dynamics of corporate activism in state political issues. The final case, "'Better Make Room' for Government Campaigns," explores the role of government-funded persuasion campaigns in a democracy.

CASE 40. PUBLICITY AND JUSTICE

Illinois Gov. Rod Blagojevich was arrested in December 2008 on charges of fraud and conspiracy. The Democrat was indicted in April 2009 by a federal grand jury on felony charges including racketeering, conspiracy, wire fraud, and making false statements to investigators.[3] Allegations included accusations that he sought favors or payment in return for naming the replacement for the U.S. Senate seat vacated when Barack Obama became president. Allegations in court documents made public in April 2010 also asserted that public funds in unneeded fees and commissions were given to Blagojevich's wife and that state contracts and some state positions were targeted for campaign donors.[4] Others, including Blagojevich's brother, some aides, and advisors, were also indicted.

Figure 10.1
Former Illinois
Gov. Rod
Blagojevich
speaks to the
media at the
federal building
in Chicago, after
he was
convicted on
multiple
corruption
charges for
attempting to
sell a Senate
seat (June 27,
2011).

Source: Associated
Press photo/M.
Spencer Green.

Following the arrests, the Illinois House and Senate began preparation for impeachment proceedings. On January 9, 2009, the House voted 114-1 in favor of impeachment. On January 26, 2009, the Senate impeachment trial began. While his attorneys were preparing his defense, Blagojevich hired The Publicity Agency, a Florida public relations firm, to represent him "in his dealings with the news media."[5] Those dealings were plentiful. Instead of attending the trial in the Illinois Senate, the governor appeared on ABC's *Good Morning America* and *The View* and NBC's *Today*. During the appearances, the governor argued the rules for the impeachment proceedings were unfair and compared himself to a character in a Frank Capra film or a cowboy hung for horse stealing before a trial.[6] The *Chicago Tribune* reported that *The View* hostess Whoopi Goldberg told the governor: "This is turning into a bit of a media circus, and I wonder if you're not hurting yourself more than helping yourself by doing all this because it feels a little bit like people aren't taking you seriously."[7]

Blagojevich's lead attorney, Ed Genson, resigned from the criminal case, telling reporters the governor was not listening to his advice.[8] On January 29, 2009, Blagojevich did appear to testify at the proceedings, but the Senate voted 59-0 to impeach him.[9]

But the media blitz continued. In March 2009, Glen Selig, Blagojevich's public relations counselor from The Publicity Agency, announced that a book deal had been signed with Phoenix Books for a reported "six-figure" fee.[10] In the book that was published, *The Governor*, Blagojevich proclaimed his innocence and compared himself to others such as Martha Stewart and *It's a Wonderful Life* character George Bailey, and said he had been unfairly treated.[11]

In April, Blagojevich sought the court's permission to travel to Costa Rica to participate on the NBC reality program *I'm a Celebrity . . . Get Me Out of Here*, but when it was denied, his wife Patti appeared as a contestant.[12] During the program, she was briefly shown discussing the case. During an interview on CNN's *Larry King Live*, Blagojevich said the reality appearance was necessary for the couple to "earn a living and – and be able to afford our mortgage and keep our kids in the same school that they're going in. And it was a very generous offer by NBC."[13]

But the ex-governor's turn in a reality series would come. He appeared as a contestant on Donald Trump's *Celebrity Apprentice 3* in March 2010[14] where during the show he, according to federal prosecutors, "repeatedly proclaimed his innocence"[15] (and got fired as an apprentice) all before his June 2010 trial date.

The ex-governor described his public relations counsel to the *New York Observer* in March 2010, saying: "Just as I was marching into the abyss, Glen came into my life and helped me navigate."[16] Sharon Cohen, an Associated Press writer, said Selig had "transformed Blagojevich into a cottage industry."[17]

Blagojevich was convicted on eighteen of the charges he faced in June 2011 and began serving a fourteen-year sentence.[18] A federal appeals court overturned five of the eighteen counts in July 2015.[19]

Should a politician or a celebrity embroiled in a legal scandal court positive public opinion as a "cottage industry" before trial? The notoriety of cases involving politicians, actors, athletes, musicians, and other celebrities means that accusations against them will get high-profile coverage across news and entertainment media in ways that likely will not be true for private citizens involved in litigation. The O. J. Simpson trials established a precedent for widespread media coverage that far exceeded what had been traditional, and the Clinton impeachment proceedings pushed the limits on what topics would be included in such coverage. Certainly, there are those celebrities who assert that they are not role models for others and that what occurs in their lives off the playing field, stage, or film should be kept from the public, but such an argument seems impossible for an elected official such as a governor to make plausible.

So, how should the celebrities and politicians who face serious legal issues approach their public communication or activities? Their access to media is far greater than that afforded most private citizens and may have unavoidable consequences when potential jurors and presiding judges are bombarded with carefully chosen and contextualized messages or when plaintiffs or their families are confronted repeatedly with painful disclosures or countercharges. In such a circumstance, is the highest duty to one's self to launch the best defense possible? What about the duty to one's family? The numerous media appearances by Blagojevich and his wife may have been ethically defensible as a utilitarian way of attesting to his innocence, or they may have been an exploitive way of generating empathy from potential jurors or opinion leaders or of profiting financially from the attention garnered by the impeachment.

Aristotelian analysis may offer the most useful insight here. Certainly, it would be virtually impossible for an indicted governor to avoid media coverage, and it would be virtually impossible for any such celebrity to totally control media coverage. But a balance that magnifies dignity and justice should be sought. What were the ex-governor's options? He might have avoided the spotlight as much as possible, relying on his defense team or public relations spokespersons to offer his declaration of innocence to the public. Or, he might have pursued news interviews or news conferences as an appropriate setting in which to posit his defense. The pursuit of entertainment venues such as reality programs where payment was acknowledged as being an important motivator for participation and where protestations of innocence are not questioned may be seen as a strategic way to bypass traditional judicial proceedings in order to sustain a disarming public image "full of political bluster, not criminal intent," as Associated Press writer Sharon Cohen described.[20] In these settings, the interests of the others who were indicted with him are not addressed, and the impact of continuing to publicize the political scandal in Illinois is not considered. Among these choices, consideration of others' interests, as well as those of Blagojevich, must be weighed heavily as decisions are made regarding public communications.

The role of assertive public relations efforts in litigation—such as news conferences, talk-show appearances, and special events—is becoming almost routine, even for non-celebrities, and both defendants and prosecutors use public relations as a tool. Many leading public relations firms have experts available to serve as counselors for attorneys and their clients in this arena. A moral judgment by the practitioners regarding participating in crafting and executing these communication strategies should not be made without considering the legal and ethical underpinnings. Contemporary media coverage of crime and the justice system can be volatile and sometimes prejudicial, as the U.S. Supreme Court has ruled.[21] Yet public discussion and media coverage of a crime, arrest, and trial can only be abridged in certain narrow circumstances. Generally, then, arresting police officers and prosecuting and defense teams enjoy great media access. Unless barred by specific court order, from the time of the crime until completion of a case, they can address the public and media in press conferences, interviews, and speeches and thereby potentially impact public perception of a suspect and the incident.

The ethical dilemma lies in deciding when information delivery co-opts justice to become trial by entertainment. News conferences, interviews, news releases, books, special events, reality programs: all may be employed by those hoping to alter the tone of the public debate before the trial begins and a jury is selected. Yet, by attempting to affect or alter public opinion in these ways, litigants may be undermining the judicial process. If indeed all the communication deals with only the abstract issues, the tactics may be defensible. However, typically such media contacts are more likely to be interpreted as attempts to influence potential jurors or to soften a potential judge into a sympathetic review of pre-trial defense motions than as objective truthtelling. Few would argue that justice is served when judgment is rendered in televised talk-show deliberations or edited reality programs rather than in a courtroom jury box.

VIRTUE Justice

Courts may seem the logical place to find justice. However, the result of litigation or prosecution may sometimes appear to rest more on communication strategies and legal maneuvering than on just decision-making. How might a practitioner balance a commitment to justice and truthtelling with loyalty to a client in litigation publications?

CASE 41. THE MANY FRIENDS OF THE CANDIDATE

Barack Obama's 2008 presidential campaign, highlighted by its "Yes, We Can" promise of change, and his White House succeeded in changing the ways in which candidates and the U.S. president communicate with the public. During the election campaign and the first years in office, the Obama camp sought to provide and control access to information in innovative ways, utilizing traditional media advertising, social media outlets, the internet, and text messages to offer first-hand messages directly to their stakeholders.[22] During the 2008 primary and general campaigns, more than two million individuals registered on the MyBarackObama.com website,[23] and the campaign collected more than thirteen million email addresses from supporters.[24]

Lawrence Lessig, a Stanford law professor who advised the campaign on internet policy, told MIT's *Technology Review*: "The key networking advance in the Obama field operation was really deploying community-building tools in a smart way from the very beginning."[25] Messages were sent directly to supporters by text, post, and email. Social communities such as MySpace and Facebook and viral video sites like YouTube were used, as Smith and French reported, "for developing an interactive, viral marketing-driven relationship with the Obama brand."[26]

Clay Shirky described the direct announcing of Joseph Biden as the candidate's 2008 running mate through text to "friends" as a way of preventing traditional news outlets from immediately analyzing the selection. This direct communication allowed text receivers to become the opinion leaders who would share the announcements with their friends and followers, enhancing the selectivity of the manner in which the news was spread.[27]

After the elections, the administration continued to use the internet to deliver controlled messages during the transition and to support initiatives throughout the two terms. In 2008, the website www.change.gov was created to maintain information flow during the post-election transition period, and the website www.whitehouse.gov was redesigned and launched virtually simultaneously with Obama's first inaugural oath. It provides far more than just photos and standard information about the President and First Lady. It features a blog written by different members of the administration, updates on important legislation and initiatives, and provides interactive features from an opportunity to sign up for email alerts to options to post information from the site on various user-content sites.

The *New York Times Magazine* described the care taken by the administration in crafting Obama's video image.[28] Heffernan reported:

> Obama has been criticized by some, including Rush Limbaugh, for relying on tele-prompters and electronic cue cards when speaking in public. . . . Obama's team, in producing and distributing more video (by far) than any past administration, has not so much won over political journalists as led the pack to become the new media on the White House beat.[29]

By the 2012 election, the Obama campaign embedded its videos directly in its website, without having to rely on YouTube.[30]

The 2012 campaign offered more examples of the skillful use of communication technologies to shape and deliver messages in timely, personalized, and innovative ways as both the Obama and the Romney presidential teams used Facebook, Twitter, Instagram, YouTube, Tumblr, email, and blogs to launch and sustain their campaign appeals.[31] The Obama campaign was able to direct digital messages segmented by states so that additional localized information could be provided.[32] After the election, the White House continued to use these channels to control administrative messages to micro-targeted groups. Followers received frequent direct email throughout the second term, some represented as from the President or Mrs. Obama, Vice President Biden, or members of the Cabinet. Some of the messages asked recipients to email their senators or representatives to urge action on a presidential initiative; some previewed upcoming speeches to be delivered by the President. Some had embedded photographs or videos. Tweets might criticize Congressional inaction or feature photographs of the First Lady at some official function. The President's and Mrs. Obama's individual Instagram sites contained photo and video depictions of special events and speeches, but also had direct messages urging individual action such as registering for health insurance or supporting military families.

Traditional media coverage of the campaigns in 2008 and 2012 was substantive, beginning long before the first caucuses and primaries and continuing through the national elections in November. Clearly some voters, however, wanted more immediate information and involvement, and the campaigns of almost all national candidates provided digital information, online donation sites, and social media communities in ever-increasing ways. The Obama campaigns and administration's reliance on direct media communications provide an opportunity to explore the ethical implications of reliance on these communication channels in public affairs practice.

Direct-to-voter communication has been practiced since the first days of democracy. Public oratory, fiery rhetoric, and political debate have inspired support, opposition, and action. Ethicists have decried overwrought emotional appeals, negative advertising, and campaign sabotage efforts while bemoaning the growing lack of voter participation amid a rise in cynicism and apathy. Even in the midst of direct-to-voter communication efforts, members of the public have relied on non-affiliated gatekeepers such as journalists and political commentators for help in sorting through claims of political parties and candidates whose words, appearances, and strategies have been crafted by public relations advisors: where are the issues among the images? What is true and important? Why should I care? Is there a place in political activity for me?

Digital social networks and internet sites now provide some instantaneous and alternative answers to these questions—and have energized a variety of political constituents to political advocacy and concern. Tom Sheridan, president of the Sheridan group, told *PR Week*: "New media platforms have created a new group of validators."[33] Want to attend a political rally or hear a speech? Interested in knowing more of a candidate's stance on an issue, or weigh his or her opinions against those of opponents? Excited about adding your voice to the debate, or in putting your money where your interest is? Click a browser. Join a network. Post a photo or video. Share your thoughts. The digital environment provides the contemporary agora, and democracy can be revitalized.

Yet the digital environment may limit at the same time it unites. The press has long provided a check-and-balance role deemed important enough in a democracy to be granted specific First Amendment protection. Professional reportorial ethics seek to prevent partisanship from shaping all political information; it does not restrain it, but it may contextualize or hold it accountable. Similarly, such traditional news outlets make information available to anyone who is interested on an equal basis. In the world of social networks and digital streaming, however, sharing information to "followers" exclusively or first may inherently exclude others. In a nation where a digital divide still exists, traditional media outlets provide information inexpensively and broadly.

This poses few ethical issues during a campaign, but the issue broadens when the campaign is over and the candidates are governing. New questions about access to public information arise: is internet access a requirement for active citizenship? Who would determine if donors are given information that non-donors are not? Are the best interests of democracy served when the image of the president or other politicians is controlled in-house with fewer opportunities for outside press scrutiny?

It may be uncomfortable for the occupants of the White House or other public offices to have journalists' notebooks, cameras, and microphones documenting their activities and statements. However, such media also provide open access for public servants to complain, explain, or expound when they deem it important. Similarly, it may be uncomfortable for journalists as they recognize the rise of the citizen journalists active in the digital sphere and the accessibility of public relations practitioners have in communicating directly to their interest groups without gatekeeping mediation. Aristotelian principles would posit finding a golden mean between potential extremes. In the agora of contemporary politics, yes, we can find room for in-house public relations practitioners who shape political images, the professional journalists who act as watchdogs, and the enlivened communities that form through digital tools.

CASE 42. CORPORATE SPEECH AND STATE LAWS

The introduction of the Religious Freedom Restoration Act in some state legislatures in 2014 and 2015 prompted public debates and political activism that involved some unusual speakers—national and multinational corporations and sports organizations. The rationale offered for the state bills was that they were designed to prevent a government body from "substantially burdening a person's exercise of religion," unless there were a compelling government interest involved that was applied in the least restrictive means.[34]

Proponents of the bills often argued that the owners of for-profit businesses should not be compelled to compromise their religious beliefs in order to comply with a state or federal law. Opponents said the wording of the statute could allow businesses to discriminate on the basis of sexual orientation. While many corporations and nonprofits did not participate in the often-heated debates, the corporations and management that did engage often argued that passage of such state laws would create an atmosphere that would harm their businesses or their employees. For example, leaders from Delta Air Lines, UPS, Coca-Cola, and Home Depot actively opposed passage of the measure in the Georgia Legislature,[35] issuing statements such as this one from Delta:

> As a global values-based company, Delta Air Lines is proud of the diversity of its customers and employees, and is deeply concerned about proposed measures in several states, including Georgia and Arizona, that would allow businesses to refuse service to lesbian, gay, bisexual and transgender individuals. If passed into law, these proposals would cause significant harm to many people and will result in job losses. They would also violate Delta's core values of mutual respect and dignity shared by our 80,000 employees worldwide and the 165 million customers we serve every year. Delta strongly opposes these measures and we join the business community in urging state officials to reject these proposals.[36]

Walmart opposed passage of a similar bill in Arkansas,[37] and negative reaction from such businesses and organizations as the National Collegiate Athletic Association (NCAA),

Angie's List, and Apple led to a revision of the law that had been passed by the Indiana legislature in 2015.[38] The NCAA's president, Mark Emmertt, expressed the concern of many in the sports community who had opposed the legislation. "The NCAA national office and our members are deeply committed to providing an inclusive environment for all our events," the statement said. "We are especially concerned about how this legislation could affect our student-athletes and employees."[39]

The corporations were not reluctant to flex their economic impact within states or cities as part of their argumentation. After the Indiana law was approved, Angie's List said it would cancel plans to expand its campus in Indiana, and the CEO of Salesforce tweeted that he was canceling all employee travel to the state. Similarly, some mayors and governors imposed prohibitions on paying for official travel to Indiana.[40] Convention planners worried that corporations and groups might avoid planning meetings in areas with controversial laws. For example, for almost fifteen years, the NCAA refused to hold championships in South Carolina as long as the Confederate battle flag flew on the Statehouse grounds, changing its rule in July 2015 only after the flag was removed.[41]

Taking Apple's opposition to a national platform, Tim Cook used the op-ed page of the *Washington Post* to explain the business concerns that prompted Apple's corporate opposition to the proposed legislation. He wrote:

> America's business community recognized a long time ago that discrimination, in all its forms, is bad for business. At Apple, we are in business to empower and enrich our customers' lives. We strive to do business in a way that is just and fair. That's why, on behalf of Apple, I'm standing up to oppose this new wave of legislation – wherever it emerges.[42]

The heightened corporate activism was not always welcomed. The Georgia senator who introduced the 2015 legislation, Rep. Josh McKoon, at a county political gathering, criticized the executives, saying: "They think that their cultural norms, their liberal, far-left cultural norms, should be applied to our state."[43] Groups such as the Family Research Council opposed the corporate involvement through such efforts as launching a boycott called "Take Angie off Your List," urging their members to drop their membership of Angie's List.[44]

The ability of corporate entities to engage in speech about issues of public concern has been legally protected since the U.S. Supreme Court decision in *First National Bank of Boston v. Bellotti* (435 U.S. 765) in 1978, and the Court continues to expand the ways in which corporations may engage in public debate and political movements. There's little surprise when nonprofits and cause organizations actively seek to influence public opinion on issues, but when multinational corporations become involved in highly divisive debates, more questions—and criticisms—are raised.

What principles might lead a corporation to engage in controversies when many businesses might seek to avoid polarizing issues? Certainly, many of the major corporations doing business in Indiana and Georgia did not engage in the political battles. They may have been concerned about offending current or future customers, investors, or employees. Of those that did, some offered an economic rationale, expressing concern about recruiting new employees or customers under the legislations. The challenge of maintaining consistent corporate human relations policies across varying state regulations likely impacted these concerns as well. The corporations could have simply been acting on the axiom cited by Apple's Tim Cook: "discrimination is bad for business."

However, there may be other values prompting the involvement. The published statements issued by almost every corporation pointed to their organization's commitment to respecting and protecting diversity among their stakeholders. Coca-Cola said its efforts were driven by a commitment to respect for all: "As a business, it is appropriate for us to help foster diversity, unity and respect among all people."[45] Amid the heightened lobbying efforts on both sides of the debates, some of the corporations issuing statements may have been trying to avoid being criticized for not participating.

Participating in public affairs is a common task for public relations practitioners. Knowing when and how to do so requires the careful weighing of values and loyalties. Understanding how best to foster diversity and show respect across the wide spectrum of political beliefs in charged political debates may continue to challenge the practical wisdom of corporations and nonprofits. Consumer and employee reaction to public stances on charged issues should be anticipated. The businesses that choose to engage in increased political speech, regardless of their ideological positions, may find that the marketplace of ideas is as competitive—or more so—than the economic marketplace.

You Think?

- What are the ethical constraints officials in a democratic government should consider when planning persuasion campaigns?
- Should government-funded persuasion campaigns be targeted only at adults?

CASE 43. "BETTER MAKE ROOM" FOR GOVERNMENT CAMPAIGNS

Text messages that encourage high-school students to complete the Federal Application for Student Financial Aid. A College Signing Day where alumni wear school colors and logos to encourage high-school graduates to attend college. Web links to resources such as the College Navigator that provides information on U.S. colleges and universities, the Net

Price Calculator Center, and the College Scorecard. Videos encouraging students to #ReachHigher. These were all part of "Reach Higher," a publicly funded initiative promoted by U.S. First Lady Michelle Obama that sought "to inspire every student in America to take charge of their future by completing their education past high school," as explained on the official website at www.whitehouse.gov/reach-higher. The goal? To encourage enough students to attend college so that, by the year 2020, America would again lead the world in having the highest proportion of college graduates. "Reach Higher" used videos, Twitter messages, public-service announcements, speeches, and special events to communicate information about college opportunities, financial aid, academic planning, and summer learning with high-school counselors, students, and parents.

The initiative has several areas of emphasis. The "Better Make Room" campaign announced in October 2015[46] offered a website as a space to foster encouragement and peer support; it is "about creating a space for all the great things you'll do next. It's about staking a claim, forging a path and lighting the way for others just like you."[47] Created in partnership with the creative firm Huge and Civic Nation, a nonprofit policy organization, the website (https://bettermakeroom.org/our-story) allowed visitors to post personal goals and to sign up to receive text messages that would remind them of key actions in the college-application process. Multiple partners from the Lumina Foundation to Vine participated in the campaign.

The College Signing Day promotion invited any college graduate—public officials, celebrities, athletes, faculty—to "celebrate students" on May 1, the usual deadline for college admissions deposits. Photos and videos available on the government website depicted individuals across the country proudly wearing sweatshirts or T-shirts or holding logo-decorated signs for their alma maters. A toolkit with guidelines for organizing and participating in the celebration was available on the website.

Encouraging high-school students to attend college may be a message as comfortable to Americans as the reminder from Smokey the Bear that "only you can prevent forest fires." Indeed, many government-funded public information campaigns may be viewed as highly positive, from the intensely patriotic encouragement to buy war bonds during the world wars of the twentieth century or the ongoing admonition to buckle up before driving.

Such campaigns can also prompt criticism. Indeed, the "Let's Move!" initiative launched in 2010 by Mrs. Obama, which encouraged school children to be physically active and school cafeterias to offer healthy food choices, was, according to CNN, criticized by "Republicans, food companies, school lunch professionals, and—perhaps most visibly—schoolkids themselves."[48] Yet CNN concluded that the campaign *had* been influential in helping to counter childhood obesity in the United States.

Ethical concerns about public information campaigns largely rise above particular message frames. Weiss and Tschirhart[49] studied a variety of such campaigns from around the globe and concluded that these campaigns offered a "normative paradox"[50] because they could "pose significant threats to democratic values but simultaneously create opportunities to strengthen those same democratic values."[51] Government-funded and -created messages may stimulate important action but could also stifle opposition ideas. Similarly, they could be self-aggrandizing or promote greater democratic involvement.

Virtue ethics provides a helpful frame for the examination of public information campaigns, particularly those funded by tax dollars (and corporate partnerships). What are the motivating factors that spark the campaign? Is moderation found by advancing the interests of the targeted publics as far as possible while still offering a place for a governmental interest? In what ways are public voices encouraged and protected from being drowned by the powerful interlocked voices of governments and funders? Similarly, deontological ethicists would call for all such messages to be truthful—information, not propaganda—intended to offer citizens the best information in order for them to be able to make free, rational choices.

A text message reminding a high-school junior to register for a standardized college entrance exam or a senior to work with his or her parents to file a financial aid application likely meets those ethical tests, as do most health and public safety campaigns. But whenever a government launches a multimedia campaign designed to stir citizens to act, it is best for citizens to make room—and time—to examine the messages and the motives behind them.

NOTES

1. Dwight D. Eisenhower, *Crusade in Europe* (New York: Doubleday, 1948), 58.
2. See the 1913 Gillett Amendment (Chap. 32, §1,38 Stat. 212; Pub. L. No. 89–554, §3107, 80 Stat. 416 [1966], Pub. L. No. 93–50, §305 [1973]).
3. CNN, "Blagojevich Indicted on 16 Felony Charges," CNN.com, April 2, 2009, www.cnn.com/2009/POLITICS/04/02/illinois.blagojevich/index.html#cnnSTCText.
4. CNN, "Details of Prosecution Case against Blagojevich Revealed," CNN.com, April 14, 2010, http://edition.cnn.com/2010/POLITICS/04/14/illinois.blagojevich/.
5. Dave McKinney, Chris Fusco, and Natasha Jorecki, "Gov. Enlists Drew's PR Firm to Oversee Dealings with Media," *Chicago Sun Times*, January 25, 2009, A17.
6. Joseph Ryan and Rob Olmstead, "They Are 'Just Hanging Me' Blagojevich Attacks Impeachment Process, Loses His Lead Attorney," *Daily Herald* (Arlington Heights, IL), January 24, 2009, www.highbeam.com/doc/1G1-192536169.html.
7. Phil Rosenthal, "Gov. Rod Blagojevich Gave No Ground in His Gamble of a Public Relations Blitz," *Chicago Tribune*, January 27, 2009, http://articles.chicagotribune.com/2009-01-27/news/0901270112_1_rod-blagojevich-blitz-gamble.
8. Ibid.
9. Kevin Mcdermott, "Blagojevich, 5 Others Indicted: Scheme to Extract Illegal Profits was Hatched before Illinois Ex-governor Took Office, Federal Charges Allege," *St. Louis Post-Dispatch*, April 3, 2009, A1.
10. Monique Garcia, "Ousted Ill. Governor Signs Six-Figure Book Deal," *Chicago Tribune*, March 2, 2009, www.chicagotribune.com/news/chi-blagojevich_book_deal03mar03-story.html.
11. Sharon Cohen, "Ousted Governor Seeks Spotlight," *The Atlanta Journal-Constitution*, May 30, 2010, A6.
12. Rob Olmtead, "Blagojevich Pleads Innocent," *Daily Herald* (Arlington Heights, IL), April 15, 2009, www.highbeam.com/doc/1G1-197814082.html.

13. Larry King, "Father of 9-Year-Old Speaks out; Interview with Rod Blagojevich," CNN *Larry King Live*, June 3, 2009, http://transcripts.cnn.com/TRANSCRIPTS/0906/03/lkl.01.html.
14. J. R. O'Dwyer, "'Blago' Credits PR Pro for Comeback," Jack O'Dwyer's Newsletter, March 31, 2010.
15. Natasha Jorecki, "Prosecutors Rap Blago Bid to Keep Evidence Sealed," *Chicago Sun-Times*, April 14, 2010, A14.
16. O'Dwyer, "'Blago' Credits PR Pro for Comeback."
17. Cohen, "Ousted Governor Seeks Spotlight."
18. Associated Press, "Rod Blagojevich Prepares for 14-Year Prison Sentence after Corruption Conviction, *Washington Post*, December 8, 2011, www.washingtonpost.com/politics/rod-blagojevich-prepares-for-14-year-prison-sentence-after-corruption-conviction/2011/12/08/gIQAHyD1fO_story.html.
19. Jason Meisner and Bob Sector, "Some Rod Blagojevich Convictions Tossed; Wife Tells Him Disappointing News," *Chicago Tribune*, July 21, 2015, www.chicagotribune.com/news/local/politics/ct-rod-blagojevich-convictions-20150721-story.html.
20. Cohen, "Ousted Governor Seeks Spotlight."
21. *Irwin v. Dowd*, 366 U.S. 717 (1961); *Sheppard v. Maxwell*, 384 U.S. 333 (1966).
22. K. K. Cetina, "What Is a Pipe? Obama and the Sociological Imagination," *Theory, Culture & Society*, 26:5 (2009): 129–140.
23. M. Moore, "Volunteers for Obama Plan to Keep in Touch; Supporters Stay Active Both Online and in Meetings about What's Next," *USA Today* Final Edition, November 21, 2008, 6A.
24. E. Saslow, "Grass-roots Battle Tests the Obama Movement; His Supporters Play Catch-Up on Reform," *Washington Post* Met 2 edition, August 23, 2009, A1.
25. David Talbot, "How Obama Really Did It: The Social-Networking Strategy that Took an Obscure Senator to the Doors of the White House," *Technology Review*, September/October 2008, para. 4, www.technologyreview.com/s/410644/how-obama-really-did-it/.
26. G. Smith and Al French, "The Political Brand: A Consumer Perspective," *Marketing Theory* 9:2 (2009): 209–226.
27. C. Shirkey, "Sidestepping the Media with a Text," August 20, 2008, www.technologyreview.com/blog/guest/22117/?a=f.
28. V. Heffernan, "The YouTube Presidency: Why the Obama Administration Uploads So Much Video," *New York Times Magazine*, April 12, 2009, 15–17.
29. Ibid.
30. Pew Research Center's Journalism Project Staff, "How the Presidential Candidates Use the Web and Social Media," *Pew Research Journalism Project*, August 15, 2012, p. 28, www.journalism.org/201208/15/how-presidential-candidates-use-web-and-social-media.
31. Jenna Wortham, "The Presidential Campaign on Social Media," *New York Times*, October 8, 2012, www.nytimes.com/interactive/2012/10/08/technology/campaign-social-media.html?_r=2&.&.
32. Pew Research Center's Journalism Project Staff, "How the Presidential Candidates Use the Web and Social Media," p. 35.
33. Gideon Fidelzeid, "The Path to Victory in 2016," *PRWeek*, July 2015, p. 43.
34. Indiana Senate Bill 101, https://iga.in.gov/legislative/2015/bills/senate/101.
35. Kelly Yamanouchi, "State's Biggest Companies Stand Firm on 'Religious Liberty' Bill," *Atlanta Journal Constitution*, September 2, 2015, www.myajc.com/news/focal/states-biggest-companies-stand-firm-on-religious-l/nnXBQ/.
36. Delta Air Lines Release, "Delta Issues Statement on Proposed Legislation," February 25, 2014, http://news.delta.com/delta-issues-statement-proposed-legislation.
37. Katie Lobosco, "Arkansas Gov. Sends Back Religious Freedom Law after Walmart Pressure," *Money*, March 31, 2015, http://money.cnn.com/2015/03/31/news/companies/walmart-arkansas-anti-lgbt-bill/.
38. Tony Cook and Tom LoBianco, "Indiana Governor Signs Amended 'Religious Freedom' Law," *USA Today*, April 2, 2015, www.usatoday.com/story/news/nation/2015/04/02/indiana-religious-freedom-law-deal-gay-discrimination/70819106/.

39. NCAA, "Statement on Indiana Religious Freedom Bill," March 26, 2015, www.ncaa.org/about/resources/media-center/news/statement-indiana-religious-freedom-bill.

40. "Backlash against Indiana Religious Exceptions," *New York Times*, March 1, 2015, www.nytimes.com/interactive/2015/04/01/us/backlash-indiana-religious-freedom-bill.html.

41. David Cloninger, "NCAA Lifts Ban on Holding Championships in South Carolina," www.ncaa.com/news/ncaa/article/2015-07-10/ncaa-lifts-ban-holding-championships-south-carolina.

42. Tim Cook, "Pro-Discrimination 'Religious Freedom' Laws are Dangerous," *Washington Post*, March 29, 2015, www.washingtonpost.com/opinions/pro-discrimination-religious-freedom-laws-are-dangerous-to-america/2015/03/29/bdb4ce9e-d66d-11e4-ba28-f2a685dc7f89_story.html.

43. Yamanouchi, "State's Biggest Companies Stand Firm on 'Religious Liberty' Bill."

44. www.frc.org/alert/take-angie-off-your-list.

45. The Coca-Cola Company, "The Coca-Cola Company Statement on Diversity Legislation, April 2, 2015, www.coca-colacompany.com/press-center/company-statements/the-coca-cola-company-statement-on-diversity-legislation.

46. Becky Supiano, "What's the First Lady's New Public-Awareness Campaign All About? And Could It Work?" *Chronicle of Higher Education*, October 19, 2015, http://chronicle.com/article/What-s-the-First-Lady-s/233831?cid=rc_right.

47. https://bettermakeroom.org/our-story.

48. Kevin Liptak, "Michelle Obama's Let's Move Turns 5; Is It Working?" CNN.com, April 6, 2015, http://www.cnn.com/2015/04/06/politics/michelle-obamas-lets-move-turns-5-is-it-working/, para. 5.

49. J. A. Weiss and Mary Tschirhart, "Public Information Campaigns as Policy Instruments," *Journal of Policy Analysis and Management* 13:1: 82–119.

50. Ibid., 100.

51. Ibid., 84.

TELLING THE TRUTH IN ORGANIZATIONAL SETTINGS

The pursuit of truth is common to all who seek to practice ethical communication. Yet public relations practitioners may be caught in one of the hardest arenas for truthfulness because of the special challenges arising from their liaison role. Practitioners enjoy multiple opportunities to shape information communicated to internal and external audiences. Controlling the dissemination of information—from carefully staging the news conference to artfully nuanced statements—offers practitioners a chance to stage manage the truth. For example, consider the typical corporate website. Graphics, copy, audio, and video are carefully selected and placed. Some sites are animated to draw viewer attention; some open only after other items have been highlighted or selected. Tabs link to pages filled with targeted information about management, performance, history, values, employment, and news. Archival data may be present. All the information presents the corporation's point of view. It may be completely accurate and yet still be incomplete or one-sided. Just as those who receive information from news releases or press conferences have always found, visitors to websites must remember that the information gleaned there has certainly passed through a public relations "gate" before moving out to various audiences. Similarly, consider an organizational blog post or a brand's Facebook page. All the information provided may be completely accurate, but its truthfulness may be diminished or lost completely because of what is omitted or recontextualized, or because of the lack of full disclosure about its sponsorship or partisanship.

Is the polishing and shaping of an image in such a manner deceptive? Does it violate the truth? Perhaps not in most cases or at least no more than any gatekeeping action does. But how far can one go in polishing before one becomes guilty of overt deception? The issue is complicated by many factors. Sophisticated technologies make it increasingly simple and quick to change or shape the reality of what audiences see, hear, or experience. The rapidity of the transmission makes it difficult for time-consuming verification or investigative processes to take place adequately. Audience impatience at involved presentations prompts practitioners to push for the pseudodramatic rather than relying on the "boring" truth. Intra-organizational pressures to please or appease managers or other key constituents are rising in this era of downsizing and reengineering. As partisan group members, practitioners may find their own enthusiasm a trap. It may be much easier to tell positive news than it is to tell negative news. Enthusiasm about something may lead one to overstatement and hyperbole.

Last, the truth is almost always more than one person's story or one person's perspective. In an organizational setting, truth is often negotiated and contains components of several opinions. Practitioners operating within the multiple layers of organizations are often charged with communicating a message composed so that its original elements of truth are well hidden. The litigious era also has prompted many attorneys to advise organizational spokespeople to hide behind "no comment," a statement that is certainly true in and of itself but may not be truthful in its level of disclosure. The luxury of the unlimited news hole of the internet means that multiple sides of a story may be heard, some without any attempts at objectivity or even accuracy.

The cases in this chapter will explore the demands of truthtelling within various organizational settings, both formal and informal. The first case "Private Issues and Public Apologies," focuses on the recovery of golfer Tiger Woods' public image following a personal scandal. The second, "#AskSeaWorld Faces Tides of Protests," looks at the challenges of truthtelling during a crisis and in controlling information shared through social media outlets. The role of corporate sponsorships and partnerships in scientific research is probed in "A Healthy Drink?" The need for accurate disclosure by nonprofits is examined in "Reporting Recovery," and the last case, "Posting #Truth @Twitter," questions the importance of authorship disclosure in the digital information flow across social networks such as Twitter.

CASE 44. PRIVATE ISSUES AND PUBLIC APOLOGIES

He was perhaps the best-known golfer in the world, and on many lists appeared as the best golfer in the world. His name was itself a brand, and his image promoted products from automobiles to watches to sports drinks, earning him an estimated $100 million annually. An Omnicom Group unit that uses polling data to assess celebrity appeals to consumers had ranked him at number eleven.[1]

But things changed for Tiger Woods on November 27, 2010, when a car accident near his Florida home—that included a report of his wife breaking the rear window of his car with a golf club—sparked revelations of extramarital affairs that were covered internationally in an explosion of news reports. While the news reports raged, Woods did not appear in public.

The timeline for the incident as explained by Agence France-Presse was simple.[2] The day following the accident, the Florida Highway Patrol reported it had not spoken with Woods or his wife; on December 1, it issued Woods a traffic citation with a $164 fine.

On November 29, Woods posted a statement on his website at www.tigerwoods.com that read: "I'm human and not perfect. Many false and malicious rumors circulating about my family and me are irresponsible." Then, news about an extramarital affair broke, and great media attention followed. Woods decided he would not play in the Chevron World Challenge tournament, a tournament he was to have hosted.

On December 2, Woods posted another statement on this website.[3] In it, he offered an apology:

> I have let my family down and I regret those transgressions with all of my heart. I have not been true to my values and the behavior my family deserves. I am not without faults and I am far short of perfect. . . . For all of those who have supported me over the years, I offer my profound apology.

He then criticized the media coverage the story had received, arguing that he and his family should be left to deal with the issues:

> Although I am a well-known person and have made my career as a professional athlete, I have been dismayed to realize the full extent of what tabloid scrutiny really

Figure 11.1
A woman, left, gives a thumbs down as Tiger Woods walks from the fifteenth hole during the second round of the Quail Hollow Championship golf tournament at Quail Hollow Club in Charlotte, NC (April 30, 2010).

Source: Associated Press photo/Chuck Burton.

means. . . . But no matter how intense curiosity about public figures can be, there is an important and deep principle at stake which is the right to some simple, human measure of privacy. I realize there are some who don't share my view on that. . . . Personal sins should not require press releases and problems within a family shouldn't have to mean public confessions.

Within a few days, thousands of comments were posted on the site in response—some supportive, some critical.[4]

In the next week, reports of liaisons with other women emerged, and media coverage was intense. On December 11, Woods reported he would take an indefinite break from the pro tour. Two days later, Accenture announced it was dropping Woods as a spokesperson, and on December 31, AT&T also ended its deal with Woods. Other corporations had stopped airing or printing commercials or ads featuring the golfer.

In January 2011, it was reported that Woods had entered treatment or undertaken therapy, but he made no public statements until he called a press conference on February 19, held in the TPC Sawgrass clubhouse in Ponte Vedra Beach, Florida.[5] His mother was a part of the audience, but his wife was not. Fewer than forty family members, friends, PGA Tour executives, and business associates were present.[6] One television camera was allowed. Only three reporters representing the Associated Press, Bloomberg, and Reuters wire services were allowed in the conference, but they were not allowed to ask questions.[7] Three members of the Golf Writers Association of America had been invited to attend, but the association voted to boycott the conference. President Vartan Kupelian told CNN: "As long as we're not going to have the ability to ask questions, as long as we're just going to be standing there like props, there's no point of us being in the room."[8]

About a mile away, the Jacksonville *Florida Times-Union* reported that more than 100 reporters from Florida newspapers, the four major golf magazines, television, and websites gathered at a hotel to watch the apology, which was being broadcast live on television and streamed on the internet. The conference was held while the WBC-Accenture Match Play Championship was being played in Arizona.[9]

During the conference, Woods apologized for what he called "irresponsible and self-ish behavior I engaged in. . . . I have let you down."[10] He acknowledged the many groups adversely affected by his actions, including his family, friends, fans, employees, Foundation associates, and business partners. He talked of the good work done through his foundation and pledged it would continue. He defended his wife who he said had been unfairly criticized, and he said he had been participating in inpatient therapy since late December.

He criticized some media coverage, saying the media should not have followed his daughter to school or staked out his wife or mother. He also said:

Some have written things about my family. Despite the damage I have done, I still believe it is right to shield my family from the public spotlight. They did not do these things. I did. I have always tried to maintain a private space for my wife and children.

Woods said he planned to return to golf competition, which he did by entering the Masters tournament in April. Just as he was preparing to play in the tournament, Nike began broadcasting a black-and-white commercial that showed Woods somberly looking into the camera while the recorded voice of his late father, Earl Woods, spoke: "I want to find out what your thinking was; I want to find out what your feelings are. And did you learn anything?"[11] Important questions for ethical theorists to consider as well.

This case demands two levels of analysis: a micro-analysis of the ethical options available to Tiger Woods once his sexual history became public and endangered not only his status as a husband but also as a commercial spokesperson and sports hero; and a macro-analysis that questions why this story commanded such public attention and media coverage.

Woods' life had been played on a public course. His meteoric rise to superstardom as a golfer was matched by his success as a brand spokesperson; television viewing soared when he played in tournaments and suffered when he did not. He benefited greatly from this attention, earning millions not only from his numerous tournament wins but also from his work in commercials and endorsements. The relationships with his family, from his mentoring father to his beautiful wife and children, were part of his carefully constructed public persona—a persona he seemed to lose control of as he lost control of his automobile the evening of November 27.

What was Woods then to do? What are the ethical options available to a sports hero whose embarrassing private life has become so public? Aristotelian thought can inform the decision-making here. What is the golden mean in this situation? Can truthtelling become excess? Some of the news coverage appeared so, as graphic details of sexual encounters were published and some of the "other women" became celebrities. Woods could have chosen to reveal all—on his website, in a tabloid, or on a *60 Minutes* appearance—or to publicize what was happening within his family as they dealt with the affairs, or to seek publicity as he sought therapy or treatment.

Conversely, what happens when truth is too limited? The initial statement on the Woods website seemed designed to turn away inquiry and suspicion, rather than to admit truth. The second web statement seemed to move toward a more candid and sincere admission of truth. Yet both of these appeared on his own website, one controlled by him and not open to public questions or personal elaboration. Hosting comments from responders, both critical and positive, was one admirable way of allowing a type of socially mediated discourse, but it fell short of the direct exchange and explanation possible through a media interview.

What about the press conference with its televised apology? Does this become the golden mean of truthfulness in this situation? Perhaps, but the carefully guarded nature of the setting, with restricted access and no questions, appeared too controlled, as if there was still much left undisclosed. A press conference is typically free-flowing, with reporters able to ask questions as they choose and the source freely choosing to respond or not. When initiating such a setting, Woods should have known the expectations and been willing to meet them. A press conference was not required from a public relations or an ethical standpoint. Had he chosen instead to issue a public statement or even a news release, it would have afforded him an audience eager to hear his side of this story and would have garnered great publicity. Truthfulness is not just expression, but it is also shaped by context. Allowing more reporters to attend and being willing to respond to open questions from them would have created a more even flow of information and likely helped foster a more positive image for Woods, which seemed to be the intention of the communication event. But, in its staged context, Woods' conference was just not up to par.

However, we should also acknowledge the rapacious nature of the media and audiences in seeking information about this story that might have affected Woods' choice of a venue for a lengthy public apology. The combination of the salacious sexual details, the physical beauty of those involved, and the influence and power of Woods himself made what could—or should—have been a private family issue all too public. Seeking every detail of every encounter was excess, a voyeuristic exploration of a hero's life. However, at least some of this interest arose from the disappointment and lack of understanding of such a failed exemplar. Woods had been seen as a model of skill and talent and dignity; his public service and his public demeanor had won him accolades from many outside professional sports. When a hero falls, even those not normally drawn to tabloid storytelling may find themselves searching for explanations and context.

Peter Roy Clark of the Poynter Institute suggests this incident offered an opportunity for a type of ethical reporting he calls "collateral journalism" that would help address some of these larger issues.[12] Such writing, he says, "attempts to take a current story and frame it to view its higher social, political or cultural significance." In the Woods case, he suggests stories that would explore the gender differences present in coverage and reactions to the coverage, or the power and status issues involved in the legal aspects of the accident and its aftermath. Such reportage would move readers and reporters beyond titillation to explore the larger meanings of this and other such events.

You Think?

■   In a world of 24/7 public media and social media coverage, do celebrities and public figures have control of their image?

■   Do we have control of our own images on social media such as Facebook, Instagram, and YouTube? Should we?

CASE 45. #ASKSEAWORLD FACES TIDES OF PROTESTS

SeaWorld, the corporation that operates eleven U.S. theme parks, found itself in a sea of protest following the broadcast of the 2013 documentary "Blackfish,"[13] which detailed what it depicted as harsh treatment of a SeaWorld killer whale that had killed a 40-year-old trainer after she fell or slipped into its pool in 2010.[14] The documentary was shown on CNN in October 2013, with an estimated twenty-one million viewers in the audience.[15] Protests against the use of killer whales in performance shows followed at SeaWorld Orlando, at the Macy's Thanksgiving Day parade, and the Rose parade, and some celebrities canceled performances at the park.[16]

In an attempt to counter the criticism, SeaWorld bought full-page ads in newspapers with the message: "The truth about SeaWorld is right here in our parks and people."[17] The ads described the efforts taken by the parks to create safe habitats for their whales.

PETA created a website titled SeaWorldofHurt[18] that encouraged activists to speak out about the corporation by sharing links to the documentary and to post negative comments on social media using hashtags such as #EmptyTheTanks. And respond they did. Some who posted on SeaWorld social media sites said their posts were deleted without response, according to CommPRO.biz.[19] But PETA told *USA Today Network* that more than 1.1 million people had used the PETA website to protest against the parks.[20]

More negative publicity resulted after the *Orlando Business Journal* reported that an informal poll it offered readers on December 31, 2013, asking "Has CNN's 'Blackfish' documentary changed your perception of SeaWorld?" had 54 percent of its 328 responding votes cast from a single IP address—a computer at SeaWorld.com—which suggested that the 99 percent "no" response was not random. CNN.com reported the polling result with the headline, "Did SeaWorld stuff ballots for 'Blackfish' poll?"[21]

As the criticism of its treatment of its killer whales continued, SeaWorld launched a television, video, and print advertising campaign in March 2015 to counter claims that confined killer whales die sooner than whales in open waters.[22] For example, an advertisement with the headline, "FACT: WHALES LIVE as long at SeaWorld,"[23] on the op-ed page of the June 18, 2015 *New York Times*, contained a message from Dr. Chris Dodd, a veterinarian at SeaWorld, who directly addressed PETA's criticisms: "There's no other way to say it . . . PETA is not giving you the facts." The ad invited readers to "Learn more at SeaWorldCares.com," a website that contained information about the parks' treatment of its whales and other animals.

At the SeaWorldCares website, the headline promised: "You Ask. We Answer. Learn more at AskSeaWorld.com." Visitors to the site were encouraged to post questions for SeaWorld's employees to answer. Questions with answers posted on the site ranged from "Does SeaWorld keep its killer whales in complete darkness for extended periods of time?" to "How does Tilikum the killer whale spend his day?" The site also offered information the corporation titled "Truth about 'Blackfish'" that sought to counter claims made in the documentary.

But once again, the #AskSeaWorld campaign was met with negative social media posts that were tagged with the suggested hashtag. By April 20, 2015, the *Wall Street Journal* described the corporation's communication efforts as a "whale of a crisis–literally."[24]

SeaWorld San Diego announced in November 2015 that it was going to stop offering killer whale performances in 2016.[25] In a release, President and CEO Joel Manby said:

> We see a growing trend within our core guest demographic that a vacation can and should be more than just fantasy and entertainment. Guests want to know that they're making a difference for the world we share and our parks deliver on that promise.[26]

Encountering criticism is never easy, for an individual or for a corporation, but countering criticism may be essential for a business seeking not to lose customers or investors. What are the ethical boundaries when defending an organization from accusations of mistreatment of employees, resources, or animals as endearing as whales or dolphins? The cardinal virtue of courage is certainly called for in such a setting. Ignoring critical reports or viral rumors might be more reflective of cowardice (ignore them, and maybe they'll go away; delete negative posts without direct responses), while orchestrating corporate group responses to an informal opinion poll might reflect more of a sense of bravado than courage.

Where is the golden mean found in such ongoing waves of crisis communication? At one extreme, SeaWorld could have brought legal action against the makers of the documentary in an attempt to silence what they believed to be false information. At the other, the park could have ignored the criticisms and continued its normal communication and public relations practices. By taking the initiative to provide information from its expert marine veterinarians and caretakers in advertisements and websites and inviting questions from those who were concerned about its animal-care practices, the park was seeking the golden mean between the two extremes. But questions about responsiveness and truthfulness still remained. Using a corporate website to respond to the questions suggested a lack of transparency. Visitors to the corporate website were shown some questions and answers, but how many questions were posed and by whom is not clear. Was the disclosure of information or answering of questions selective?

Identifying a primary critic in its newspaper advertisement is justifiable from a virtue perspective; justice requires that the accused be allowed to "face" one's accusers. Yet not all of the reaction to the documentary came from the controversial activist group. Framing PETA as the source of criticism may have been intended to deflect attention away from questions being raised by others not aligned with the group, but it also offered the activist group a dominant voice in the churn caused by the broadcast of the documentary.

The viral nature of social media increases the pressure on such decisions, however. A negative video post or a sarcastic hashtag can spread across the internet in seconds; reposted comments or tweets multiply exposures in ways that make a concerted response even more difficult. The type of respectful dialogic communication vital in easing conflicts can easily be swamped by such a flood. The tagline #SeaWorldCares provides a useful principle of communication behavior in a crisis setting: careful, caring communication that seeks to offer truthful information in accessible ways can help calm controversial waters.

CASE 46. A HEALTHY DRINK?

"Why in this day and age would a public health organization create even the possibility for there to be influence that might affect their ability to champion and promote public health?" asked Dr. Yoni Freedhoff, an obesity expert at the University of Ottawa, in a *New York Times* blog.[27] Dr. Freedhoff was reacting to news of Coca-Cola's disclosure of how it spent almost $120 million over five years to fund academic research, medical organizations, and community-based fitness programs designed to counter obesity. The corporate disclosure came after a page one story in the *New York Times*[28] a month earlier reported that the soft-drink corporation had provided $1.5 million in funding for the Global Energy Balance Network (GEBN),[29] a new organization that espoused "the science of energy balance" as a remedy for weight gain. (The newspaper investigation began after reporters received a tip from Dr. Freedhoff, the first to notice the connection between the group and funding from the soft-drink company.[30]) The news story reported: "The beverage giant has teamed up with influential scientists who are advancing this message in medical journals, at conferences and through social media."

Reaction to the story was largely negative[31] and prompted some critics to ask why the Coca-Cola funding had not been immediately disclosed on GEBN's website, and if and how corporate funding might influence the conclusions of other research results.[32] The *New York Times* published letters to the editor from individuals and groups of nutritionists and medical researchers disputing the theories espoused by GEBN.[33]

The Coca-Cola corporation responded to the article with a statement from Dr. Ed Hays, chief technical officer. In the corporate release, Dr. Hays said Coke was proud to provide funding for GEBN

> because their type of research is critical to finding solutions to the global obesity crisis. At Coke, we believe that a balanced diet and regular exercise are two key ingredients for a healthy lifestyle and that is reflected in both our long-term and short-term business actions. [34]

However, the criticism continued. About a week later, the CEO of Coca-Cola, Muhtar Kent, responded in an op-ed in the *Wall Street Journal*.[35] Mr. Kent said he was "disappointed that some actions we have taken to fund scientific research and health and well-being programs have served only to create more confusion and mistrust."

The op-ed detailed the actions Coke would take to increase transparency. Mr. Kent said that Coca-Cola would publish a list of the partnerships and research activities funded for five years, a list that would be updated every six months. Coke would recruit an oversight committee of independent experts to advise the corporation about research investments. Kent noted that the company was committed to continuing to provide smaller-sized sodas as well as other products such as waters and zero-calorie drinks.

GEBN responded to the controversy by posting information on its now defunct website seeking to clarify its mission and its relationship with Coca-Cola. In part, the response said:

> We recognize that there are those who believe that companies like Coca-Cola should not be at the table to develop ways to reduce obesity. Our position is that we need everyone at the table who is serious about helping solve this problem.

In November 2015, the University of Colorado School of Medicine where GEBN is housed announced it was returning the donation to Coca-Cola. In a statement, the university explained: "While the network continues to advocate for good health through a balance of healthy eating habits and exercise, the funding source has distracted attention from its worthwhile goal."[36]

The *New York Times* story was not the first time the corporation had been criticized in the media for its partnerships with nutritionists. The Associated Press had reported in March 2015 that Coke had paid several nutritionists during American Heart Month to promote the smaller 7.5 ounce cans of Coca-Cola as a healthy choice for a snack on their nutrition blogs or in some sponsored articles.[37] A Coke spokesperson explained that the corporation had a "network of dietitians" it worked with as consultants.

Corporations have the freedom and responsibility to promote the use of their products, goods, and services. When a 30- or 60-second commercial features products with corporate logos, jingles, and taglines, or when an event is sponsored, promoted, and even renamed by an acknowledged corporate sponsor, it prompts little ethical questioning. For a food or drink manufacturer, disclosure might seem to be routine as federal regulations require them to publish ingredients in proportional order and related nutritional information on the packaging or on menus. Such transparency is a utilitarian way to allow those with food allergies or aversions—or those who need to gain or lose weight—to make decisions based on truthful information.

Corporations that have been granted speech rights likely also enjoy the right of free association, so there's little question about their legal right to interact with trade groups, researchers, or related professionals. But do consumers have a reasonable expectation of such transparency when it comes to disclosing sponsorships or alliances that create and disseminate messages that promote consumption of food, drink, or other products that might have positive or negative effects, or those that are generally related to human health?

The Potter Box is helpful in determining if or when corporations should be ethically compelled to disclose the type of relationships described in this case study. The definition of the situation reminds us that Coca-Cola had offered donations to a variety of individuals, groups, and organizations that promoted physical activity as one antidote to obesity for several years. A full understanding of the situation would also reveal that at the same time, the soft-drink industry was facing proposed legislation that would have limited the sale of its products in some quantities and locations.

Several corporate and public values are in conflict in this case. Corporations value profits while also valuing social responsibility. They value news coverage and privacy, and they celebrate freedom from public or governmental regulations that impede their growth but welcome those that protect their trademarks and competitiveness. Truthfulness is valued, as is shareholder equity and return.

The values reflect the multiple stakeholders to whom Coca-Cola and their partners owe loyalty. From shareholders to employees to consumers to regulators to the research community, multiple groups can benefit or be harmed if the corporation does not flourish. In this situation, Coca-Cola must reconcile its duty to promote the well-being of its shareholders with the well-being of its consumers—and those who have come to depend on corporate funding for research and public health initiatives.

For a corporation that promotes itself with the tagline "Buy Happiness," it seems appropriate to ask how the happiness of the many can be achieved. Utilitarian principles may help inform this decision, considering the vast number of consumers across the globe who buy soft-drink products. Providing consumers with full information about the sponsorships, partnerships, and alliances that may be fostering research or persuasion or sales so that they may make reasoned decisions about their purchases would promote this goal, while minimizing harm to the corporation by avoiding the types of cynicism and criticism that resulted from the lack of transparency. It is not unethical to promote sales of a product, even when its overuse may be harmful, if those who are making decisions are given the autonomy that comes from complete information—a Kantian principle that coincides with Mill in this case.

As Mr. Kent noted in the *Wall Street Journal* op-ed, practicing transparency in its investments and focus on well-being will reflect the integrity with which Coke and its research and public health partners seek to serve their customers and their communities.

VIRTUE: Beneficence

Corporations often donate funds to nonprofit agencies, educational institutions, or arts and cultural organizations—in fact, without these donors, many such groups would suffer. These acts of beneficence can be misunderstood, however, when the motives of the donor or the recipient are questioned, as they were in this situation. How best can a corporation demonstrate beneficence in its charitable and donor activities?

CASE 47. REPORTING RECOVERY

The news report was shocking: a reported $488 million in disaster-relief donations that resulted in the building of only six permanent homes.[38] In June 2015, ProPublica and NPR reported that the American Red Cross had "broken promises, squandered donations, and made dubious claims of success"[39] while seeking to address the needs of the residents of Haiti following a devastating 2010 earthquake in which more than 200,000 people were killed and about 1.5 million displaced.[40] The report described issues with staffing, partnerships, land acquisition, and lack of expertise that prevented the charity from achieving its announced goals.

In one case the Red Cross sought to provide rental subsidies so that displaced Haitians could move out of temporary camps into rental properties. The report said that only 60 cents of each $1 donated actually supported the project directly. The American Red Cross used 9 cents of every dollar for its overheads—as it had reported publically—but 24 cents went to a partner, the International Federation of the Red Cross, for program management, and another 7 cents for other groups' overheads.[41]

The American Red Cross responded quickly to the report, issuing a statement that said it was "disappointed, once again, by the lack of balance, context and accuracy" in the report.[42] Work in Haiti had "made a difference in the lives of millions of Haitians who desperately needed help and humanitarian assistance." The statement directed those with questions to a special website, www.redcross.org/haiti, where it provided information such as summary data about expenditures in various categories of work in Haiti and questions and answers written by David Meltzer, its chief international officer, in response to the news report. He affirmed that only six permanent houses were built as part of a pilot project, but pointed to other housing efforts, including the distribution of 860,000 tarps for use in temporary shelters and work with groups such as Habitat for Humanity to provide more than 6100 transitional homes.[43]

This wasn't the first time a ProPublica and NPR report had criticized the charity. An October 2014 story titled "The Red Cross' Secret Disaster" had reported that relief efforts following Hurricane Isaac and Hurricane Sandy had been inefficient, "leaving behind a trail of unmet needs and acrimony."[44] The news report cited an internal assessment by the American Red Cross that said the charity had been "diverting assets for public relations purposes."[45]

The 2015 ProPublica and NPR report led to Congressional requests for a Government Accountability Office inquiry,[46] which recommended that Congress should set up a means for "conducting regular, external, independent, and publicly disseminated evaluations of the Red Cross's disaster assistance services in domestic disasters in which the federal government provides leadership of support."[47]

Following criticism of its aid efforts in the aftermath of Hurricane Katrina, the role of the Red Cross as the lead agency addressing national disasters shifted. From then on, it would coordinate with the Federal Emergency Management Agency and Homeland Security, rather than bear such responsibility alone.[48] The charity should not have been surprised that its work on subsequent natural disasters would prompt media scrutiny.

Disasters provide *agape* moments when the need to provide care for others is urgent. Measuring an agency's efficiency and precision in such a time is an awkward—perhaps irrelevant—calculation, for individuals, news organizations, or federal agencies. In situations so dire, ethical decisions always must be other-centered, with care of the suffering afforded the highest priority. Empathy, effort, and sacrifice are involved when individuals or groups rush help to those in need, hoping that those who are involved will act virtuously. Yet nothing goes perfectly, and the hardships encountered during and after disasters may take physical, fiscal, and emotional tolls on those offering aid as well as those in need of it. The internal report assessing the service offered during Hurricanes Isaac and Sandy cited by the journalists offered frank accounts of issues and problems, an indication that truthtelling was seen as a necessary component for improvement.

Certainly, the response provided those who suffer in a local fire or accident involves fewer volunteers, fewer donors, greater access, and easier reporting than does the multi-agency, long-term response needed in more widespread disasters. The millions of dollars donated to the American Red Cross—year after year, disaster after disaster—and the ways in which those donations are then used raise the level of public, government, and news media scrutiny of its work, an understandable obligation. When the amount of dollars given mounts, the accessed needs escalate, and the timeframe lengthens, organizing for efficiency and for accountability becomes more challenging. Such disclosure is not always easy. Explaining the issues associated with relief efforts in highly challenging settings may be complicated and politically sensitive. How and when might such an organization admit its shortcomings without losing public trust—and how should it describe its achievements?

Indeed, it may be that the overwhelming generosity of those who respond to the major disasters raises additional ethical challenges to truthtelling. What happens when disaster donations overwhelm traditional giving for the more routine responsibilities of the Red Cross? Are the public relations efforts criticized internally—and by the news account—justifiable if they help serve a greater need to sustain all the services provided by the Red Cross? Yet when so many give so much, the Kantian principle of truthtelling as an essential duty becomes clear. Individual and group donors need to know how funds are being used so that they have a factual basis for decision-making about additional giving, and employees and volunteers need to know how their efforts are helping to meet needs. Such truthtelling will strengthen the trust groups such as the American Red Cross have enjoyed for decades, thereby helping ensure that they will be ready when the next disaster occurs.

CASE 48. POSTING #TRUTH @TWITTER

Who is behind the posts on Twitter—the celebrity who thousands are following or someone hired to write the 140 characters that recount details about events, emotions, and promotions? Is the account being followed the actual account or a pseudo-account established by someone impersonating a celebrity or organization out of admiration or mischief? Are the retweets, comments, and followers valid or the product of what the *Wall Street Journal* called a "Twitter robot"?[49]

The *New York Times* reported in March 2009 that singer Britney Spears had advertised for a writer for her Twitter and Facebook accounts and noted that other celebrities from rapper 50 Cent to candidate Ron Paul and corporation executives relied on others to create content for their pages or accounts.[50] Forbes.com cited other celebrities who rely on staff members to post updates on their accounts, noting that such practices seemed to contradict the personal nature of the microblogging site.[51] The *Independent* of London noted: "Many celebrities are employing agents, social media experts and others to filter their tweets (Twitter postings) to the point of pointlessness."[52]

What about when it is not the authorship in question, but the authenticity of a celebrity or organizational account? Creating and posting material to a faked account is not uncommon, according to press reports. Tony LaRusa, then manager of the St. Louis Cardinals, sued Twitter in 2009, arguing that the establishment and content of a faked account bearing his name created emotional distress; the case was settled out of court.[53] The Associated Press reported that fake accounts with false information posted had been established for other athletes, including DeMarcus Ware and Ben Roethlisberger.[54] The *Hartford Courant* reported in an October 2009 editorial that the state Republican Party had created such accounts for well-known state Democratic politicians and had posted, concluding: "The truth? Republicans get an A for innovation but a D for ethics."[55]

During the spring 2010 Gulf of Mexico oil spill, those seeking news from BP may have begun following posts from the faked public relations account @BPGlobal PR, instead of the actual site @BP_America; reportedly, more than four times the number of followers had opted for the pseudo account than the real one.[56] No disclaimer was posted on the pseudo site.

In spring 2010, Twitter experimented with an attempt to authenticate accounts by offering a "Verified Account" feature that could be posted on accounts it had checked, but the site said that it would be impossible to verify each account on the site.[57] Twitter suggested that users wondering about authenticity should check the official websites of personalities they are following to see if there were Twitter links posted that would verify the actual account. Twitter noted, however, that having its "Verified Account" feature on the site would not guarantee the identity of the actual writers of the posts. Twitter has worked with university researchers to identify and then to cancel fake accounts,[58] although estimates of the number of these varies.

When is it ethical to use a ghostwriter? Public relations practitioners have for years been employed as speechwriters, articulating the ideas of politicians, leaders, and celebrities. Others have crafted quotations for use in news releases or publications, quotes that usually are approved before publication by the named source. Scripts for advertising endorsements are written to highlight the sponsors' benefits and features before they are voiced by the charismatic spokesperson.

Are these public relations practices deceptive? When is it necessary to explain that someone other than the speaker or the bylined author has written some, or all, of public or promotional content in order for the information itself to be deemed truthful? Creating a pseudo Twitter account, Facebook page, blog, or website seems to be clearly unethical; even when intended as satire or parody, some sort of disclosure is required. But when a site is authentic, the disclosed authorship of specific content materials seems to have far less impact on its truthfulness than the actual accuracy of what is reported there. Readers do not expect to see every section of a corporate brochure carry a byline, nor do audiences expect to hear speechwriters acknowledged periodically during a CEO's address at a shareholders meeting. In fact, many news reports from wire services carry no individual bylines; it is the credibility of the organization that underlies the believability of the content.

Perhaps the immediacy of the content of social media creates an assumption in its readers, friends, or followers that there are no intermediary assistants at work helping to craft the language or the presentation of ideas. The shortness of a tweet or the timeliness of a blog post may seem to imply that no one has intervened between the reported source and the audience. However, the *New York Times* explained that on Spears's account, posts not written by the singer are bylined, which should clarify the actual source of the information on the account;[59] this approach may provide an example of one way to address this issue, while another would be for the account owner to explain in his or her profile who will be responsible for posts and updates.

From an organizational standpoint, Twitter and other microblogging and audience-generated sites may seek to assure users that sites are accurately identified. The rapidly expanding and constantly shifting digital environment, however, is one in which audiences—followers, friends, and readers—also have an obligation to understand that the identity of any digital poster or follower may be unverified. Trust in a site or a source's truthfulness may only be developed through experience and verification by other public or social media—#healthyskepticism may be the best ethical defense.

VIRTUE: Friendship

In the world of social media, what does it mean to be a "friend"? Does "liking" an organization, brand, or company, joining a "fan" page, or following someone on a social media site create a lasting relationship that has mutual ethical obligations?

NOTES

1. Suzanne Vranica, "As Tiger Woods Returns to Golf, Nike & Others Embrace Their Links," WSJ.Com, April 6, 2010, http://thefutureforward.blogspot.com/2010/04/tiger-woods-returns-to-golf-nike-others.html.
2. Agence France-Presse, "Timeline of Tiger Woods' Fall From Grace," March 16, 2010, www.ndtv.com/sports-news/timeline-of-tiger-woods-fall-from-grace-412896.
3. Tiger Woods, "Tiger Comments on Current Events," December 2, 2009, originally on his own website but can now be seen at http://i2.cdn.turner.com/cnn/2009/images/12/02/woods.statement.pdf.
4. Roy Peter Clark, "New Questions about Tiger Woods Coverage," Poynter Online, December 4, 2009, www.poynter.org/2009/new-questions-about-tiger-woods-coverage/99728/.
5. CNN.com, "Tiger Woods Says, 'I'm So Sorry' in Public Apology," February 20, 2010, www.cnn.com/2010/US/02/19/tiger.woods/index.html.
6. Gary Smits, "'For All That I Have Done, I Am So Sorry': Tiger Woods Gives Public Apology in Pointe Vedra," *Florida Times-Union*, February 26, 2010, A-1.
7. Ben Smith, "American Writers to Boycott Tiger Woods Apology," TimesOnline, February 19, 2010, www.thetimes.co.uk/tto/sport/golf/article2340876.ece.
8. CNN.com, "Tiger Woods Says, 'I'm So Sorry' in Public Apology," para. 31.
9. Smith, "American Writers to Boycott Tiger Woods Apology."
10. CNN.com, "Tiger Woods' apology: Full Transcript," February 19, 2010, www.cnn.com/2010/US/02/19/tiger.woods.transcript/index.html.
11. Vranica, "As Tiger Woods Returns to Golf, Nike & Others Embrace Their Links," para. 3.
12. Roy Peter Clark, "New Questions about Tiger Woods Coverage."
13. "Blackfish" website, www.blackfishmovie.com/about.
14. CNN.com, "SeaWorld Trainer Killed by Killer Whale," February 25, 2010, www.cnn.com/2010/US/02/24/killer.whale.trainer.death/index.html.
15. Vivian Kuo and Martin Savidge, "Months After 'Blackfish' Airs, Debate over Orcas Continues," CNN.com, February 9, 2014, www.cnn.com/2014/02/07/us/blackfish-wrap/index.html.
16. Michael Pearson, "SeaWorld Takes Out Ads to Defend Itself Against Whale Mistreatment Accusations," CNN, December 20, 2013, www.cnn.com/2013/12/20/us/seaworld-newspaper-ads/index.html.
17. Ibid.
18. www.seaworldofhurt.com/.
19. David E. Johnson, "SeaWorld Crisis Management: The Textbook Case of What Not To Do," December 30, 2014, www.commpro.biz/corporate-communications/crisis-communications-corporate-communications/seaworld-crisis-managment-textbook-case/.
20. Lori Grishman, "'Ask SeaWorld' Ad Campaign Draws Criticism," *USA TODAY Network*, March 25, 2015, www.usatoday.com/story/news/nation-now/2015/03/25/seaworld-killer-whales-ad-campaign/70422606/.
21. Doug Gross, "Did SeaWorld Stuff Ballots for 'Blackfish' Poll?" CNN.com, January 3, 2014, www.cnn.com/2014/01/03/tech/web/sea-world-blackfish-poll/.
22. Grishman, "'Ask SeaWorld' Ad Campaign Draws Criticism."
23. Advertisement. "Fact: Whales Live," *New York Times*, June 18, 2015, A25.
24. Ben DiPietro, "Crisis of the Week: SeaWorld Has a Whale of a Problem," *Wall Street Journal*, April 20, 2015, http://blogs.wsj.com/riskandcompliance/2015/04/20/crisis-of-the-week-seaworld-has-a-whale-of-a-problem/.
25. Daniel Victor, "SeaWorld Ends Show with Orcas in San Diego," *New York Times*, November 10, 2015, B3.
26. SeaWorld Entertainment, "SeaWorld Entertainment, Inc. Announces New Partnerships and Business Initiatives during Investor and Analyst Day Presentation," News Release, November 9, 2015, www.seaworldinvestors.com/news-releases/news-release-details/2015/SeaWorld-Entertainment-Inc-Announces-New-Partnerships-and-Business-Initiatives-During-Investor-and-Analyst-Day-Presentation/default.aspx.

27. Anahad O'Connor, "Coke Discloses Millions in Grants for Health Research and Community Programs," *New York Times*, September 22, 2015, http://well.blogs.nytimes.com/2015/09/22/coke-discloses-millions-in-grants-for-health-research-and-community-programs/?_r=0.

28. Anahad O'Connor, "Coca-Cola Funds Effort to Alter Obesity Battle," *New York Times*, August 10, 2015, A1.

29. As of December 2015, GEBN no longer exists.

30. Meg Bernhard, "A Clinician, a Blogger, and Now a Thorn in Coca-Cola's Side," *The Chronicle of Higher Education*, August 14, 2015, http://chronicle.com/article/A-Clinician-a-Blogger-and/232381/?cid=at&utm_source=at&u.

31. Tony Dokoupil, "Coca-Cola's Misleading Anti-obesity Campaign also Targets Kids," MSNBC.com, August 11, 2015, www.msnbc.com/msnbc/coca-colas-misleading-anti-obesity-campaign-also-targets-kids.

32. Leon Stafford, "Company Defends Obesity Research," Atlanta Journal-Constitution, August 12, 2015, A7.

33. Letters to the Editor, "Coke's Pitch: Drink Coke. Get Exercise," *New York Times*, August 13, 2015, A20.

34. Ed Hays, "Setting the Record Straight on Coca-Cola and Scientific Research," August 10, 2015, www.coca-colacompany.com/coca-cola-unbottled/setting-the-record-straight-on-coca-cola-and-scientific-research/.

35. Muhtar Kent, "Coca-Cola: We'll Do Better," *Wall Street Journal*, August 19, 2015, www.wsj.com/articles/coca-cola-well-do-better-1440024365?cb=logged0.5834545353427529.

36. University of Colorado School of Medicine, "Coca-Cola Funds Returned," November 6, 2015, www.ucdenver.edu/academics/colleges/medicalschool/administration/news/ResearchNews/Pages/Coca-Cola-Funds-Returned.aspx.

37. Candice Choi, "Coke as a Sensible Snack? Coca-Cola Works with Dietitians Who Suggest Cola as Snack," March 16, 2015, www.startribune.com/coke-a-good-snack-health-experts-working-with-coke-say-so/296404461/.

38. Justin Elliott and Laura Sullivan, "How the Red Cross Raised Half a Billion Dollars for Haiti and Built Six Homes," *ProPublica*, June 3, 2015, www.propublica.org/article/how-the-red-cross-raised-half-a-billion-dollars-for-haiti-and-built-6-homes.

39. Ibid., para. 4.

40. Michael Martinez, "Red Cross Responds to Report about Building Only Six Homes in Haiti after 2010 Quake," CNN.com, June 5, 2015, www.cnn.com/2015/06/04/americas/american-red-cross-haiti-controversy-propublica-npr/.

41. Elliott and Sullivan, "How the Red Cross Raised Half a Billion Dollars for Haiti and Built Six Homes," infographic.

42. American Red Cross, "American Red Cross Responds to Latest ProPublica and NPR Coverage," June 3, 2015, www.redcross.org/news/press-release/American-Red-Cross-Responds-to-Recent-Pro Publica-Report-on-Haiti.

43. David Meltzer, "The Real Story of the Six Homes in Haiti: Answering Your Questions," June 5, 2015, www.redcross.org/news/article/The-Real-Story-of-the-6-Homes-Answering-Questions-about-Haiti.

44. Justin Elliott, Jesse Eisinger, and Laura Sullivan, "The Red Cross' Secret Disaster," ProPublica, October 29, 2014, www.propublica.org/article/the-red-cross-secret-disaster, para. 3.

45. American Red Cross, "Mass Care Observations/Lessons Learned from Hurricane Isaac and Sandy," January 14, 2013, PowerPoint presentation, www.propublica.org/documents/item/1225674-sandy-and-isaac-lessons-learned.html#document/p12/a184370.

46. Justin Elliott, "Red Cross CEO Tried to Kill Government Investigation," ProPublica, August 17, 2015, www.propublica.org/article/red-cross-ceo-tried-to-kill-government-investigation.

47. U.S. Government Accountability Office, "American Red Cross Disaster Assistance Would Benefit From Oversight Through Regular Federal Evaluation," Report to the Ranking Member, Committee on

Homeland Security, House of Representatives, GAO-15-565, September 2015, www.gao.gov/assets/680/672600.pdf.

48. Ben Gose, "Ready or Not?" *The Chronicle of Philanthropy* 19:19 (26 July 2007): 25.

49. Jeff Elder, "Inside a Twitter Robot Factory Fake Activity, Often Bought for Publicity Purposes, Influences Trending Topics," *Wall Street Journal,* November 24, 2013, http://online.wsj.com/news/articles/SB10001424052702304607104579212122084821400?cb=logged0.3823551454115659.

50. Noam Cohen, "When Stars Twitter, a Ghost May Be Lurking," *New York Times*, March 27, 2009, A-1.

51. Dirk Smillie, "Ghost Tweeters," January 14, 2010, Forbes.com, www.forbes.com/2010/01/14/tweet-ghost-writer-business-media-ghost-twitter.html.

52. Mark Borkowski, "The Twits Who Ruin Twitter," *Independent* (London), April 13, 2009, www.independent.co.uk/news/media/online/twits-who-ruin-twitter-why-some-stars-and-prs-miss-the-point-of-tweeting-1667816.html.

53. Associated Press, "La Russa, Twitter Settle Lawsuit," ESPN.com, June 5, 2009, http://sports.espn.go.com/espn/print?id=4235409&type=story.

54. Ibid.

55. "GOP's Fake Twitter Accounts Cross Line," *Hartford Courant*, October 8, 2009, para. 7, www.courant.com/news/opinion/editorials/hc-fake-twitter-gop.art.artoct08,0,3870422.story.

56. Craig Kinalley, "BP Fake Twitter Account: The Most Ridiculous Tweets Yet," *Huffington Post*, May 25, 2010, www.huffingtonpost.com/2010/05/25/bp-fake-twitter-account-t_n_588675.html.

57. Twitter, "Verified Account Beta," http://twitter.com/help/verified.

58. Elder, "Inside a Twitter Robot Factory."

59. Cohen, "When Stars Twitter, a Ghost May Be Lurking."

12

CONFLICTING
LOYALTIES

Consider the following situations:

- A major corporation decides it must reduce its workforce by thousands, and its communication department is told it must release the news.
- A public relations agency decides to accept a controversial new client who may be offensive to previously held clients or some of its employees.
- A consulting firm is asked to represent a political candidate with extreme views certain to arouse strong reactions.
- Beleaguered public affairs officers at a nonprofit agency are asked to explain the decisions of its executive officers to throngs of investigative reporters.

In each situation, practitioners and managers are challenged to find an ethical way to balance what may be strong personal values and loyalties with the values and interests of their various organizations.

Journalism ethicists have frequently dealt with conflicts of interest from the perspectives of news editors and reporters, warning against the lure of freebies, relationships with sources, and involvement in community or activist organizations. While these issues may have some relevance for practitioners, their professional conflicts may present a different set of challenges. Practitioners are expected to be partisan in their loyalties yet equitable in their actions. They are expected to represent the leadership of an organization and at the same time to serve as a boundary between that organization and its varied internal and external publics, ideally seeking to promote harmonious, beneficial relationships among them. Certainly, this may create situations in which clashing interests occur.

In an early analysis of public relations ethics, Albert J. Sullivan identified this conflict of interest as one between "partisan values" that are "highly personal and serve as a measure of the relationship between the managers of an enterprise and the men [and women] who serve as public relations counsel" and "mutual values," a concern that each group's rights and obligations are "carefully defined" and honored, with management but one of the groups considered. Sullivan said, by applying a mutual value system, "public relations may be called . . . the conscience of the institution." Partisan values involve commitment, trust, loyalty, and obedience to management. When practitioners become overly partisan, Sullivan warns, it may lead to a "my country, right or wrong" mentality, a utilitarian ethic, and one-way communication flow. Mutual values, Sullivan says, ensure the honoring of each person's right to true information and a right to participate in the decisions that affect him or her.[1]

In such a complex professional environment, how does a practitioner emphasize values that lead to mutual benefit with key publics, rather than personal or one-sided partisan values within the daily workplace? How might one balance numerous conflicting loyalties? What principles offer guidance toward arriving at an ethical solution?

The case studies in this chapter provide hypothetical and actual examples of ways practitioners, clients, associations, and corporations have struggled to balance conflicting loyalties and values. The pull of loyalties experienced by a corporation facing an expensive recall is discussed in the first case, "Accelerating Recalls." The pressures faced by agencies and practitioners when they are hired to represent clients whose goals may be at odds are considered in the second case, "Representing Political Power." The sometimes pressured relationships between journalists and practitioners are probed in "Paying for Play?" The third case, *Thank You for Smoking*," examines the film of the same name as a case study that provides an ironic analysis of the long-term implications when individual profit is allowed to outweigh loyalties and obligations to consumers. The values and loyalties called on during times of human tragedy are recounted in the fourth case, "Tragedy at the Mine."

CASE 49. ACCELERATING RECALLS

How should a corporation faced with a series of negative events balance its loyalties to customers, employees, regulations, and shareholders as it responds, and what are its ethical options in communicating about the issues? International auto leader Toyota had to make such decisions as it responded to questions about the safety of its most popular models from 2007 through 2010 while it was experiencing record growth in international sales.

The *Wall Street Journal* detailed the timeline of the 2007–2010 acceleration-related recalls.[2] In March 2007, the National Highway Traffic Safety Administration (NHTSA) began investigating five complaints about the gas pedals in the 2007 Toyota Lexus ES350; the pedals seemed to suddenly accelerate. Following a fatal accident involving a 2007 Camry, the NHTSA notified Toyota that it should recall its all-weather floor mats as they apparently could interfere with proper gas-pedal control. Toyota announced a recall of its all-weather floor mats on September 26, 2007. However, two years later in September 2009, a horrific accident occurred in which a California Highway Patrol officer, his wife, daughter, and brother-in-law were killed when the Lexus ES350 they were in reportedly raced to more than 100 mph and crashed. On September 25, 2009, the NHTSA notified Toyota that it should do more to address the acceleration issue. On October 5, Toyota recalled almost four million cars because of possible pedal entrapment from the floor mats.

Yet, in January 2010, Toyota told the NHTSA that there may be a defect in the pedal itself, prompting it to call for quick action. On January 16, the carmaker recalled 2.3 million cars. The NHTSA then told Toyota to stop selling cars with the suspected defect, and Toyota complied. An additional 1.1 million cars were then recalled.[3] The NHTSA was later to assert that Toyota had known of the pedal issue since at least September 29 when it notified European distributors, but it had not instructed its American division to stop install-ing the pedals.[4] While U.S. customers had also complained about the problem, Toyota did not notify the NHTSA or its customers of the potential problem.[5] Following the review, the NHTSA fined Toyota $16.4 million, the largest fine possible, which Toyota paid in May. Numerous other lawsuits have been filed in the United States against the carmaker.[6]

However, problems with model safety continued. In April, Toyota recalled the 2010 Lexus GX460 because of stability problems reported in *Consumer Reports* magazine, and a month later, Toyota announced it would recall the 2010 Lexus LS sedans with variable gear ratio steering for repairs.[7]

There had apparently been some internal debate about Toyota's slowness in addressing the problems publicly. The Associated Press reported that Irv Miller, the group vice president for environment and public affairs, had told the executive coordinator for corporate communica-tions that it needed to make the issue public several days before the public recall announcement. According to an email message reported by the Associated Press, Miller wrote: "We are not protecting our customers by keeping this quiet. The time to hide on this one is over."[8]

The recalls generated tremendous publicity in traditional media and social media con-versations and posts—most of it negative. Akio Toyoda, the president of Toyota, finally appeared at a news conference in Nagoya, Japan, on February 6, 2010, and apologized for the concerns raised by the issue. He also apologized to shareholders for the drop in the value of the corporate stock.[9] On February 24, he testified before the U.S. House Committee on Oversight and Government Reform. In prepared remarks, Toyoda said:

> We pursued growth over the speed at which we were able to develop our people and our organization, and we should sincerely be mindful of that. I regret that this has resulted in the safety issues described in the recalls we face today, and I am deeply sorry for any accidents that Toyota drivers have experienced.[10]

When some criticized Toyota's diagnosis of the acceleration problems, Toyota responded quickly to those statements. In one incident, ABC News broadcast an investiga-tive report by Brian Ross on February 22 that Toyota said included inaccurate footage of a tachometer on a Toyota; the network later admitted that a higher reading on a tachometer taken from another demonstration conducted under different conditions had been edited into the segment. Toyota responded with a release arguing the broadcast was misleading.[11]

Toyota further sought to counter criticism from Sean Kane, a safety consultant, and David Gilbert, a Southern Illinois University automobile technology professor, who had testified before the House Energy and Commerce Committee in February. Kane had asked Gilbert to run an experiment to determine if the acceleration problem might be linked to an electronic issue in the autos, rather than to sticking pedals. Toyota reported to the Congressional committee that it had hired a testing firm, Exponent, to investigate the problems; Exponent issued a 56-page report defending the corporation, and Toyota streamed a video of Exponent information on its website. However, the *New York Times* reported that Exponent had originally been hired by a Toyota law firm to conduct research to protect the corporation in the lawsuits it was facing. Exponent had received $11 million in consulting fees from Toyota from 2000 to 2009.[12]

The corporation also consulted the public relations firm of Robinson, Lerer & Montgomery and commissioned a poll called the "Kane/Gilbert Debunking Message Test." The House subcommittee then asked for all documentation related to the poll, questioning whether the poll was intended to intimidate the two witnesses.[13]

Toyota also began to address newer consumer complaints. The *Los Angeles Times* reported that Toyota had put together SMART (Swift Market Analysis and Research Team) groups to investigate and dispute consumer complaints. After a driver complained of sudden acceleration in his Prius, the SMART group called media to Qualcomm Stadium in San Diego to contest the charges. It also countered another Prius complaint in New York. However, another SMART group investigation of a complaint about a Camry found that the consumer was correct; the recall-prompted repair supposedly completed on her car had not been complete.[14]

Toyota sought to re-engage its consumers after the recall forced the suspension of sales. It conducted a national print and broadcast campaign to explain what actions car owners should take to have their models repaired. The corporation placed national ads on January 31, 2010, announcing suspension of sales of the recalled models.[15] Full-page newspaper ads on February 5, 2010, then acknowledged the publicity that had ensued about the gas-pedal recall: "There's been a lot of talk about the recall. Here are the facts for our customers." The ads explained the four steps the corporation was taking in response to complaints about sticking accelerator pedals, including sending letters to the 4.5 million owners of the eight various Toyota models involved in the recall asking them to set up an appointment with a Toyota dealer; extending the hours at dealerships so repairs could be completed quickly; offering repair training to service personnel at the dealerships; and halting production of the models involved in the recall.[16]

Toyota also turned to digital and social media to communicate with consumers. On February 8, 2010, Toyota Motor Sales USA President Jim Lentz engaged in an online interview on the Digg Dialogg site where he responded to the ten questions selected by Digg users from some 1,400 questions that were submitted; the interview garnered more than one million hits in its first five days.[17]

Tweetmeme, a Twitter aggregation service, hosted "Toyota Conversations" that provided the official Toyota Twitter feed, other Twitter feeds about the issue, and links to news coverage.[18] Denise Morrissey, a member of Toyota's Motor Sales USA social media team, explained that the site was designed "as both a listening post and an opportunity for interested consumers to continue those conversations." Toyota also communicated through a Facebook page, Twitter posts, and its YouTube account, along with a special recall webpage linked from the corporation's landing page.[19]

In April 2010, the corporation announced the creation of a global quality-initiative committee that would be asked to help it improve its communication about safety.[20] Toyota offered zero percent financing on many vehicles and cut lease prices on others in March, and buyers responded favorably. Sales rose 70 percent from February, back to the normal level before the recalls started.[21]

After a lengthy investigation, the U.S. Justice Department announced in March 2014 that the corporation had agreed to pay a $1.2 billion fine, the "largest ever for a carmaker in the United States," according to the *New York Times*.[22]

Using the Potter Box method for analysis may help clarify the ethical options Toyota could have exercised in communicating in the United States about these issues. The situation itself was complicated. Aggressive growth had placed Toyota as the world's automotive leader. Its brand had long been regarded as a symbol of quality; yet complaints about safety issues appeared to be recurring with consistency. The U.S. regulatory agency NHTSA was engaged in cautioning Toyota about its obligations, and Toyota had apparently begun to make changes in its European operations.

The primary values operating in this case are tied to these situational factors. As the global economy slowed, the economic values of profitability and brand equity were increasingly important, although truthfulness and concern for others demanded consideration as well.

Clashing loyalties may have affected how these values were weighed. The national pride accorded the corporation from its Japanese employees and the need for profits felt by global shareholders had to be balanced against the trust placed in the manufacturer by numerous global consumers and the demands of U.S. consumer safety regulations. U.S. employees of Toyota were dependent on the manufacturer not only for wages but also for long-term security.

To whom are the highest duties owed when choices about disclosure might affect people's physical safety and others' economic security? The Kantian categorical imperative that prioritizes truthtelling and providing duty to others would prompt Toyota to disclose problems as promptly as they are known, regardless of the economic costs that may result. The actions finally taken by Toyota, such as halting sales of new cars until problems could be corrected would be applauded; moving quickly to recall new models as issues came to be identified after the initial huge recalls would also be endorsed. Conversely, waiting to communicate about problems until forced to do so by regulators would be discouraged; countering critics would be recommended only if it promoted the disclosure of truth.

Interestingly, utilitarian analysis might lead one to a similar recommended action. The principles of Mill suggest that the more quickly the corporation addresses the problem, the more quickly it can be solved and put behind the corporation, benefitting consumers, shareholders, employees, and management. Delaying disclosure adds to the magnitude of the potential harm to many. However, once the recalls were instituted, the actions taken by Toyota to communicate through a variety of media with consumers to encourage them to seek repairs would be seen as an ethical way to minimize harm.

Encouragingly, Toyota seemed to grow far more eager to be accountable to its consumers and its regulators as this situation unfolded. Its CEO may have been reluctant to become engaged in the discourse as the crisis began, but Mr. Toyoda did become more active in articulating the corporate viewpoints and was humble enough to apologize in different settings to different audiences for the issues caused by the accelerating cars. While changing the tenor of communication within a huge multinational corporation may be difficult, Toyota has demonstrated that such change is possible.

You Think?

■ Is timely disclosure a necessary component of truthtelling?
▦ Is a truth told late still the truth?

CASE 50. REPRESENTING POLITICAL POWER

"A Plea for Caution from Russia," the headline declared on the op-ed page of the September 11, 2013 *New York Times*. The byline gave credit to Vladimir V. Putin, president of Russia. The column called for the United States to change its policy toward Syria and criticized a speech by U.S. President Barack Obama for its explanation of American exceptionalism. Putin said the time had come for him to speak "directly to the American people and their personal leaders."[23]

As might have been expected, reaction to the piece was swift. CBS News reported that U.S. House Speaker John Boehner was "'insulted' by it," and the chair of the Senate Foreign Relations Committee, Senator Bob Menendez "said it made him want to throw up"[24] while Ronn Torossian, the CEO of the award-winning firm 5W Public Relations, called it a "[m]ajor victory for Brand Russia."[25]

Attention quickly turned to the mechanics of such a prominent placement. Jackie Burton, the senior vice president of external relations for Ketchum, confirmed that the agency had submitted the piece to the *New York Times* and that Mr. Putin had authored it.[26]

The agency received both criticism and support. Roger Bolton, president of the Arthur W. Page Society, defended the agency's actions in a statement to Reuters that began:

> Many governments seek public relations and public affairs representation to help explain their policies, programs and cultures to foreign stakeholders. This is a very appropriate activity, and one that helps advance peace and justice. Here's how: Engagement by any institution – governmental, private for profit, NGO or other – is a recognition that public opinion and the needs of external stakeholders matter.

AdWeek's PRNewser posted a series of tweets from public relations practitioners questioning the tactic.

The *New York Times* piece was not Ketchum's only public relations achievement for the Russian president, however. According to Reuters, Ketchum successfully promoted *Time* magazine's selection of Putin as its 2007 "Person of the Year" and a flattering profile of Putin in *Outdoor Life* magazine in 2011.

The agency, a subsidiary of the Omnicom Group, had earned more than $25 million since 2006 working for Russia and more than $26 million since 2007 to promote the Russian state-owned gas company, Reuters reported.[27] Ketchum had been engaged by Russia in 2006 to promote the G8 summit in St. Petersburg and then continued to represent the country with more than thirty employees working in six countries on the account.[28] According to Bloomberg, it maintained the ThinkRussa.com website that featured economic, technology, and cultural news even as the conflict between Russia and the Ukraine escalated.[29]

However, Russia was not Ketchum's only government client. Ketchum has also represented the U.S. government in a series of campaigns, including producing prepackaged news stories promoting Medicare changes and the No Child Left Behind Act for the Bush administration and providing public relations support of the Obama administration's campaign to promote the use of electronic medical records.[30]

Ketchum ended most of its work for Russia in March 2015. Relations between the United States and Russia had chilled even further. *PR Week* carried a statement from the firm that simply said: "Ketchum no longer represents the Russian Federation in the US or Europe with the exception of our office in Moscow."[31] The *Holmes Report* reported that Dmitry Peskov, an aide to Putin, had told the media:

> We decided not to renew the contract because of the anti-Russian hysteria, the information war that is going on. If you spend a lot of money on communication, you want it to be fruitful—and that is not possible in this hateful environment.[32]

Ketchum appears to have complied with all legal requirements associated with representing foreign governments and did end its relationship with the Russian Federation after the violence in the Ukraine worsened. But this case raises the nuance of when the boundaries of legal actions are wider than the boundary of ethical actions. In his 2013 statement to Reuters, Roger Bolton said:

> Most leading global public relations firms are very careful about the clients they accept and decline business when they feel that the client's purposes are not legitimate or that the client is disinterested in building meaningful stakeholder relationships based on mutual understanding and trust.[33]

In choosing which international clients to represent, some agencies might agree with classic libertarian theorists who argue that all viewpoints deserve a place in the public marketplace, and that the First Amendment protects the exchange of even unpleasant ideas. In times of political uncertainties, perhaps discourse should be doubly valued. As Michael Cherenson, of the Success Communications Group, argued: "What the world needs now, more than ever, are ideas, facts, and a healthy public debate. The world needs more public relations."[34]

However, should there be ethical limits to the political or governmental viewpoints one might choose to promote and represent? This case presents a challenging opportunity to explore how various philosophical principles might guide the practitioner in weighing values and loyalties. The Kantian categorical imperative raises the question of role modeling and influence—and the imperative of truthtelling. Utilitarian principles ask about maximizing goodness or happiness and minimizing harm. Judeo-Christian tenets would challenge the practitioner to think about how to advance the worthiness and dignity of each individual impacted by the communications and campaigns, and Rawls's "veil of ignorance" would almost certainly ask the practitioner similarly to think about how to advance the power of those who have been without power, rather than how to promote the use of power.

Virtue ethics might challenge practitioners to examine the motivations for their client work—do these motivations reach toward justice or toward selfishness?—and the ways in which their actions align with virtuous motivations. After Ketchum announced that it would no longer be representing Russia in 2015, Roger Bolton noted: "Public relations firms often are criticized for taking on foreign governments, but they often say they are motivated by the opportunity to encourage reform. The fact that it doesn't always work doesn't mean it shouldn't be tried."[35]

You Think?

■ How do practitioners ethically balance patriotism and loyalty to various international clients?

■ How should agencies respond to shifting international alliances?

CASE 51. PAYING FOR PLAY?

Consider this hypothetical scenario. "Getting media coverage has gotten to be so complicated," Brian thought. "It used to be so much simpler. Newspapers, radio, TV, the occasional magazine pitch: write a release, craft a pitch letter, make a phone call or two–then if a reporter or editor or director were interested, I'd work with them to get the story out. If it ran, I'd write a thank-you note or call them or, occasionally, take someone out to lunch.

"Oh, but it's so specialized now. We've showcased the brand on video news releases featuring that hot chef from California. We've distributed recipes that highlight our vinegar in dressings and sauces to food editors and writers; I've offered to fly producers from the networks to Italy so they can see how the vinegar is produced. We catered their last show launch for free–and they invited 500 people to the party! I've supplied case after case of the product for use by their celebrity chefs–all for free, of course.

"Now," he said to himself, "it's all about social media and blogs. My client wants 'likes' on Facebook, followers on Twitter and Instagram, pins on Pinterest. The artisan bloggers or the foodies need to be raving about the product on their sites. I have sent small bottles of each of the new flavor varieties of our vinegar each season to the ten top food bloggers, but now one of them has written me back and instead of saying thanks, has said that if I want him to drop the name of the brand into a post or some recipes, I better send a check with a case of the product. No pay, no play.

"What more am I supposed to do? Who would ever have thought that promoting a new vinegar would be so expensive? I wonder what would my old PR professor would think about all this?"

The practice of "pay for play" has been debated and panned by media ethicists for decades. The radio payola scandals in the 1950s drew negative attention when DJs were accused of accepting payment from entertainment promoters for playing their artists' music on air. "Junket journalism," where reporters were provided free or low-cost travel arrangements to cover political special events or tourism destinations, is usually decried,[36] and most professional codes of ethics or publication standards call for journalists to disclose the circumstances of their arrangements–or to insist on paying for all their expenses.

The PRSA issued a Professional Standards Advisory against the practice in October 2008, arguing that when publicists "pay for play" in order to gain positive coverage for an employer or client, they are in violation of at least four of the provisions of the Member Code of Ethics.[37] To clarify their stance, the association updated the Code to more specifically identify the practice as unethical in 2009.[38]

But the practice hasn't gone away. With the boom in social media and blogging in the past ten years and the increase in the demand for native content on hosted sites, practitioners may be working with independent writers who desire compensation of some type when they are promoting a product, good, or service and hear clients calling for the type of positive word-of-mouth publicity that can be generated through such media.

The FTC issued guidelines for such endorsements that required disclosure of any compensation—free samples, products, or payment—in blogs or for published reviews first in 2009[39] and then amended these in 2013.[40] The FTC puts the burden of disclosure on the blogger.

But practitioners are not without ethical obligations, even in a complicated media environment. Offering small samples of a product, good, or service for free likely won't violate standards of good performance. If direct payment or more valuable product gifting is absolutely necessary, then practical wisdom might call for the practitioner to ask the blogger to disclose the business relationship. For practitioners to request such a disclosure in writing would not only align them with the legal guideline, it would also support the type of transparency that Kant would argue is required so that individuals can make rational decisions freely.

Such behavior will allow Brian's client's potential customers to decide for themselves: is the good product review deserved, or the result of a good payment? Let the informed reader—and taster—decide.

VIRTUE: Humility

The practice of public relations offers few bylines. In a field where most work is completed anonymously, practitioners may forego the ego and career boost that comes from public recognition in order to promote the client or employer's brand. The portrait of a successful practitioner is seldom a selfie.

CASE 52. *THANK YOU FOR SMOKING*

A handsome public relations spokesperson counters the talk-show appearance of a teen dying from cancer by asking why the tobacco industry would want to kill its best customers—those who are young and could buy cigarettes for years to come. Representing the Academy of Tobacco Studies, a lobbying group supposedly devoted to researching ties between tobacco and health, Nick Naylor works to counter proposed national legislation that would have imposed a skull and crossbones symbol on all tobacco packaging.

To accomplish this, Naylor bribes the cancer-stricken cowboy whose image had become synonymous with tobacco use to drop his lawsuit with a suitcase of cash. He convinces a major Hollywood producer to promote smoking in films as a way of gaining popular support, particularly among young people. Along the way, Naylor is shown lunching weekly with representatives of the alcohol and gun industries—the "MOD [Merchants of Death]

Squad" as they call themselves. Following a television debate with the sponsor of the "skull and crossbones" packaging bill, Naylor is kidnapped and almost killed by having numerous nicotine patches placed on his body. He is saved only because he has developed enough tolerance of nicotine through his smoking habit to survive the poisoning. Any more exposure to nicotine, even by smoking one cigarette, however, will kill him.

Naylor's no-holds-barred tactics are revealed in a tell-all newspaper article written by a reporter with whom Naylor has been having an affair. In disgrace, he is then fired by the Academy of Tobacco Studies. But he is not done yet. Just as the kidnapping did not kill him physically, getting fired does not destroy his career. He turns the table on his ex-lover and destroys her reporting career by revealing their relationship. Summoned to testify at a Senate hearing about the proposed legislation, he turns in a stellar performance in which he appeals to libertarianism in his cry against the regulation. At the end of the film, he has recovered prominence and is shown at the helm of a prosperous public relations firm about to take on other causes.

This plot of the 2006 film, *Thank You for Smoking*, directed by Jason Reitman and produced by David O. Sacks, was drawn from the 1994 novel of the same name by Christopher Buckley.[41] The film was nominated for a Golden Globe award.

The film *Thank You for Smoking* provides a satirical—and darkly comical—look at the interplay of lobbying, public relations, health communication, and newspaper sourcing and what may occur when careerism and client loyalty come before public interest and when dangerous products are promoted without much thought about consequences. It also provides an opportunity for two levels of analysis of public relations and social responsibility.

Within the plot of the film, the Potter Box method may be used as a tool in analyzing the ethics of the public relations practices depicted. The definition of the situation is easily summarized. What loyalties are felt by the public relations practitioner? Loyalty to his employer and to his "MOD Squad" friends is demonstrated. His loyalty to his reporter/lover is shown to be ill-advised. What other loyalties are demonstrated through plot interaction? What about his values? He obviously values money and influence but asserts that he values personal freedom. What philosophical principles might guide his behavior? Is he relying on utilitarianism, asserting that the greater good is served by maintaining the freedom of market choice, or is this a subversion of utilitarianism because the consequences of increased tobacco use, particularly by the young, are strongly linked to ill health and high costs? Or is he applying a balancing analysis, accepting some regulation of his client's products as an effort to protect users by informing them of potential harms, but maintaining the opposition to any more extensive efforts at warning or increasing the regulation of the products?

The philosophy of care and the respect for human dignity is noticeable by its absence. Throughout the film, Naylor manipulates or is himself manipulated by those seeking to maintain economic power. Neither he nor his employer cares about the real medical and financial needs of the cowboy; they offer money only as a bribe, not as a gesture of compassion. The reporter uses her sexuality to gain his trust and a huge byline.

The film itself also may be analyzed for its impact as a public relations message. Its central theme—that people should be free to make bad choices if they want to—omits many of the other issues within the debate, including the pain and suffering of others who have not chosen to smoke but who have become ill or whose loved ones have been ill, the cost of providing health care borne by those who have and who have not smoked, and the differences between the critical choice-making abilities of minors and adults. The definitions and locations of vice and virtue on an Aristotelian analysis may shift emotionally as the audience grows to sympathize with the unscrupulous lead as the "good characters" of the crusading legislator and reporter are shown to have flaws. In *Thank You for Smoking*, no group emerges as worthy examples of public servants—not the politicians, the reporters, the industrialists, nor the public relations practitioners.

You Think?

Should a practitioner represent clients whose legal products or services may be considered unhealthy or dangerous?

CASE 53. TRAGEDY AT THE MINE

Figure 12.1 A candlelight memorial service for the twelve miners who died in a mine explosion at the Sago Mine in Tallmansville, WV, is held at the Sago Baptist Church (January 4, 2006).

Associated Press photo/Gene J. Puskar.

CASE 53 CONTINUED

It was likely lightning that ignited the January 2, 2006, explosion at the Sago Mine in Tallmansville, West Virginia, in which twelve miners were killed and one was critically injured, according to a report commissioned by West Virginia Governor Joe Manchin, although the United Mine Workers of America union contests that cause.[42] The disaster was exacerbated by the spread of incorrect information both locally and nationally that mistakenly reported that the twelve miners had survived.

The search and rescue mission began around 5 p.m., nearly eleven hours after the explosion in the mine. The first body was found by rescuers at 9:10 p.m. on January 3. It took several hours more for the rest of the men to be discovered; rescuers searching the mine discovered the men about two miles inside the mine, and eleven of the group were already dead. The information was transmitted by the team using a series of five underground relay stations because their radios could not transmit through the rock. In a tragic manner, the message apparently was misunderstood and relayed over a speaker phone to the control center as "Twelve alive!"

The crisis command center was not secured, so information was not kept confidential until it was confirmed. CNN went live with the announcement. Cell phones then spread the word to the family members and friends who had gathered in the nearby Sago Baptist Church. The report to the governor said that family members were given erroneous information, such as that when the miners were rescued, they would come to the church before seeing medical providers. Family members and friends of the missing miners stayed in the church, waiting for their arrival.

However, within the hour, rescuers informed the command center that there appeared to be only one survivor. Several hours passed before the news was relayed to family members.[43] The tragic news was delivered to the church around 3 a.m. by Ben Hatfield, president of the mining company, who was escorted by state troopers. Following the announcement, the miners' families and friends left the church, some angry and yelling at the mining company officials and media, others crying.[44] Hatfield told reporters the next day that he had known within twenty minutes of the rescuers discovering the miners that a mistake had been made but that he did not inform the family members at that time because he did not know the extent of the deaths.

CNN corrected its story around 2:45 a.m., apparently the first medium to provide the updated information.[45] Headlines in morning dailies across the country carried the erroneous information and had to correct the stories in later editions.

The governor's commissioned report stated that rescue leaders should have been more cautious in confirming information before it leaked out. According to the report, no officials from the Mine Safety and Health Administration and the state Office of Miners' Health, Safety, and Training briefed the families of the miners during the entire rescue mission. The report said: "In any rescue situation, the highest-ranking federal, state and company officials on site must be personally responsible to ensure that miners' families receive timely updates of accurate and confirmed information." Apparently, the mining company had no press officer, and its president, Ben Hatfield, was responsible for conducting the press conferences.[46]

Facing such a tragedy would pose a challenge for any organization. Delivering tragic news is difficult, even more so in this instance because of the original misunderstanding. However, the communication or lack of communication in this incident by the mining and government organizations almost certainly compounded the pain for those involved and therefore raises ethical questions.

The *agape* principle calls for each person involved in such a crisis to be treated with dignity and respect; the operational principle calls for each individual involved to treat others as they would want to be treated if they were in the same position. From this ethical perspective, the actions taken or not taken by the mining company and the state officials are questionable. The time lapse between receiving the accurate information and informing the families at the church is hard to justify. Loyalty to the employees and their families and friends should have compelled communication. Providing avenues for families to receive prompt updates throughout the search would have demonstrated compassion and truthfulness. Creating a secure site for reporters to receive information regularly not only would have helped ensure accurate news reporting but also might have helped to protect families and friends from the intrusion of reporters and cameras during their time of high stress and great grief.[47]

While the full extent of loss may not have been known early on, allowing jubilant but false news to circulate raises false hope and then increases suffering and anger. The call to minimize harm to others should raise questions about process and planning. Whose best interests were considered here? Why was there so little preparation for a disaster like this when mining, after all, is among the most dangerous work in the country? The ethics of caring demand an investment in planning and preparation, thereby enabling organizations and employers to respond to tragedy in a more dignified, accurate, and compassionate manner. Crisis-communication planning calls for organizations to make certain they pass along only confirmed and accurate reports. This frequently involves designating spokespersons, holding briefings, and organizing a communication center where information flow is controlled.[48] Reports of life or death never should turn out wrong for lack of the preparation required to handle crises competently, compassionately, and professionally. At Sago, a nation was praying, and families were trembling. Every piece of news carried immeasurable value—as did the lives of the miners and those who loved them. Accepting responsibility for sharing accurate information is a duty owed.

VIRTUE: Compassion

Maintaining professionalism amid a crisis can be challenging, even for a very seasoned practitioner. In situations where there are injuries, loss of life, and loss of property, practitioners may want to demonstrate compassion and caring, while legal advisors may warn against expressions of concern that could be interpreted as an assumption of cause or blame. Is demonstrating compassion worth the professional and personal risks?

NOTES

1. Albert J. Sullivan, "Values in Public Relations," in Otto Lerbinger and Albert Sullivan, eds., *Information, Influence and Communication: A Reader in Public Relations* (New York: Basic Books, 1965), 412–428. See also Kevin Stoker, "Loyalty in Public Relations: When Does it Cross the Line Between Virtue and Vice?" *Journal of Mass Media Ethics* 20 (2005): 269–287.

2. Kate Linebaugh, D. Searcey, and Norihiko Shirouzu, "Secretive Culture Led Toyota Astray," *Wall Street Journal*, February 8, 2010, www.wsj.com/articles/SB10001424052748704820904575055733096312238.

3. Ibid.

4. Nick Bunkley, "Regulators May Pursue More Fines Against Toyota," *New York Times,* April 4, 2010, www.nytimes.com/2010/04/10/business/10toyota.html

5. Peter Whoriskey and Kimberly Kindy, "Toyota Faces $16.4 Million U.S. Fine for Waiting to Warn of Defect," *The Washington Post*, April 6, 2010, www.washingtonpost.com/wp-dyn/content/article/2010/04/05/AR2010040503200.html.

6. Jerry Hirsch and Coco Masters, "Toyota President Issues Rare Apology as Pressure Mounts," *Los Angeles Times*, February 9, 2010, http://articles.latimes.com/2010/feb/06/business/la-fi-toyota-recall6-2010feb06.

7. Micheline Maynard, "Toyota Pays Its $16.4 million Fine over Pedals," *New York Times,* May 18, 2010, www.nytimes.com/2010/05/19/business/19toyota.html.

8. Larry Margasak and Ken Thomas, "Toyota Official: 'We Need to Come Clean,'" Mercury News.com, April 7, 2010, www.mercurynews.com/business/ci_14838323?source=rss.

9. Bunkley, "Regulators May Pursue More Fines Against Toyota."

10. Brian Montopoli, "Akio Toyoda Congressional Testimony: 'I Am Deeply Sorry'" (full text), CBS News, www.cbsnews.com/news/akio-toyoda-congressional-testimony-i-am-deeply-sorry-full-text/.

11. "Is Toyota Positioning Media as Its 'Villain'? Embattled Carmaker Attacks ABC News Reporting for Casting 'Unwarranted Doubt' on Safety; ABC Admits to Editing Video," *Daily Dog*, March 10, 2010, www.bulldogreporter.com/toyota-positioning-media-its-villain-embattled-carmaker-attacks-abc-news-reporting/.

12. Micheline Maynard, "Lawmakers Cast Doubt on Report that Toyota Called Independent," *New York Times*, May 20, 2010, www.nytimes.com/2010/05/21/business/21toyota.html.

13. Michael D. Shear and Peter Whoriskey, "Toyota Had Attack Plan Against Congressional Testimony, Documents Show," *Washington Post*, May 15, 2010, A10.

14. Ralph Vartabedian and Ken Bensinger, "Toyota Response to Complaints Takes on a Confrontational Tone," *Los Angeles Times*, April 8, 2010, http://articles.latimes.com/2010/apr/08/business/la-fi-toyota-pushback9-2010apr09.

15. Michael Connor, "Toyota Recall: Five Critical Lessons," *Business Ethics*, February 3, 2010, http://business-ethics.com/2010/01/31/2123-toyota-recall-five-critical-lessons/.

16. Toyota Advertisement, "There's Been a Lot of Talk . . ." *The Atlanta Journal-Constitution*, February 5, 2010, A12.

17. Noreen O'Leary, "How Toyota Helped Digg Itself out of Trouble," *AdWeek*, April 5, 2010, www.adweek.com/news/advertising-branding/how-toyota-helped-digg-itself-out-trouble-101993.

18. Catherine P. Taylor, "Toyota's Crisis: Prism Into How Social Media Has Radicalized Public Relations," *SocialMediaInsider*, March 3, 2010, www.mediapost.com/publications/article/123625/toyotas-crisis-prism-into-how-social-media-has-r.html.

19. Denise Morrisey, comment posted at *SocialMediaInsider*, March 3, 2010, www.mediapost.com/publications/article/123625/toyotas-crisis-prism-into-how-social-media-has-r.html.

20. Toyota News Release, "Leading Safety and Quality Experts Named To Toyota North American Quality Advisory Panel," April 29, 2010, http://corporatenews.pressroom.toyota.com/article_display.cfm?article_id=1968.

21. Chris Arnold, "Toyota Deals Get Customers Back to Showrooms," NPR, March 19, 2010, www.npr.org/2010/03/19/124832230/toyota-deals-get-customers-back-to-showrooms.

22. Bill Vlasic and Matt Apuzzomarch, "Toyota Is Fined $1.2 Billion for Concealing Safety Defects," *New York Times,* March 20, 2014, B1.

23. Vladimir V. Putin, "A Plea for Caution from Russia," *New York Times*, September 11, 2013. Reprinted on September 12, 2013, in the New York edition, A31, www.nytimes.com/2013/09/12/opinion/putin-plea-for-caution-from-russia-on-syria.html.

24. CBS Interactive, "Selling the Message: How PR Firm Helped Place Controversial Putin Op-ed," CBS News, September 13, 2013, www.cbsnews.com/news/selling-the-message-how-pr-firm-helped-place-controversial-putin-op-ed.

25. Ronn Torossian, "Ketchum's Putin Op-ed Placement: 5WPR CEO Torossian Saluted Ketchum for Brilliant Russian PR Work," *Bulldog Reporter*, September 13, 2013, www.bulldogreporter.com/ketchum-s-putin-op-ed-placement-5wpr-ceo-torossian-salutes-Ketchum.

26. Brett Logiurato, "Meet the PR Firm That Helped Vladimir Putin Troll the Entire Country," *Business Insider*, September 12, 2013, www.businessinsider.com/vladimir-putin-nyt-op-ed-ketchum-pr-2013-9.

27. Andy Sullivan, "U.S. Public-Relations Firm Helps Putin Make His Case to America," Reuters, September 12, 2013, www.reuters.com/article/us-syria-crisis-usa-ketchum-idUSBRE98C00S20130913.

28. Ravi Somaya, "P.R. Firm for Putin's Russia Now Walking a Fine Line," *New York Times*, September 1, 2014, B1.

29. Kristen Schweizer and Matthew Campbell, "Putin Spin Doctors Pitch Russian Pancakes, Ignore Ukraine," Bloomberg Business, May 15, 2014, www.bloomberg.com/news/articles/2014-05-15/putin-spin-doctors-pitch-russian-pancakes-ignore-ukraine.

30. Logiurato, "Meet the PR Firm That Helped Vladimir Putin Troll the Entire Country."

31. Frank Washkuch and Laura Nichols, "Ketchum Calls It Quits on Russia Work," *PR Week*, March 11, 2015, www.prweek.com/article/1337821/ketchum-calls-quits-russia-work.

32. Arun Sudhaman, "The Unravelling of Ketchum's Russia Relationship," *The Holmes Report*, March 13, 2015, www.holmesreport.com/latest/article/the-unravelling-of-ketchum's-russia-relationship.

33. Roger Bolton, "Ketchum and Russia," March 13, 2015, *Page Turner Blog*, www.awpagesociety.com/blog/ketchum-and-russia.

34. Michael Cherenson, "Should a Public Relations Firm Represent Russia?" September 13, 2013, blog, http://scgadv.com/public-relations-us-russia/.

35. Ibid.

36. Ann Friedman, "What You Gonna Do With All that Junket?" *Columbia Journalism Review*, April 4, 2013, www.cjr.org/realtalk/what_you_gonna_do_with_all_tha.php.

37. PRSA. "Professional Standards Advisory PS-9," October 2008, www.prsa.org/aboutprsa/ethics/resources/ethicalstandardsadvisories/documents/psa-09.pdf.

38. PRSA Media Room, "PRSA Speaks Out on 'Pay for Play,' Strengthens Code of Ethics' Transparency Provisions," *Public Relations Tactics*, July 1, 2009, www.prsa.org/SearchResults/view/8138/105/PRSA_speaks_out_on_Pay_for_Play_strengthens_Code_o#.VzSW5YQrKUl.

39. FTC, "The FTC Publishes Final Guides Governing Endorsements, Testimonials," October 5, 2009, www.ftc.gov/news-events/press-releases/2009/10/ftc-publishes-final-guides-governing-endorsements-testimonials.

40. FTC, ".com Disclosures," March 2013, www.ftc.gov/sites/default/files/attachments/press-releases/ftc-staff-revises-online-advertising-disclosure-guidelines/130312dotcomdisclosures.pdf.

41. Fox Searchlight Pictures, www.foxsearchlight.com/thankyouforsmoking/.

42. Ken Ward, Jr., "Sago Report Proposes Reforms: Everything That Could Go Wrong Did Go Wrong," *Charleston* (West Virginia) *Gazette*, July 20, 2006, p. 1; Josh Cable, "Report Blames Company, MSHA for Sago Blast," *Occupational Hazards* 69:4 (April 2007): 14.

43. Ken Ward, Jr., "Report Criticizes Gap in Sago Rescue Info," *Charleston* (West Virginia) *Gazette*, July 25, 2006, p. 1.

44. Frank Langfitt, "Covering the Sago Mine Disaster," *Nieman Reports* 60:2 (Summer 2006): 103ff.; Randi Kaye, "Mine Disaster a Story of Private Pain Made Public," CNN.com, January 6, 2006, http://edition.cnn.com/2006/US/01/06/btsc.kaye.miner/.

45. David Folkenflik, "Sago: The Anatomy of Reporting Gone Wrong," NPR, January 4, 2006, www.npr.org/templates/story/story.php?storyId=5126627.

46. Jeffrey A. Dvorkin, "Listeners Upset by Mine Disaster Coverage," NPR, January 10, 2006, www.npr.org/templates/story/story.php?storyId=5147900.

47. Gerald Baron, "The Sago Mine Tragedy: Making a Bad Story Much Worse," *Public Relations Tactics* 13:2 (February 2006): 14.

48. Ibid.

13

THE DEMANDS
OF SOCIAL
RESPONSIBILITY

Perhaps one of the overriding ethical quandaries for a public relations practitioner is defining what is meant by the term *public*. One may define *public* narrowly from the perspective of the organization's and client's most critical stakeholders—those networks of interdependency and mutual benefit that demand ongoing attention, focus, and resources. Yet the tug of the greater *social public* or society also must be acknowledged. From the professional codes of ethics to the expectations that professionals will act on behalf of a greater good, this obligation is usually articulated by codes and practitioners as a first-order priority and is frequently eloquently tied to the responsibilities of citizenship. Yet the boundaries between acting in the best interest of the more narrowly defined public and that of the larger public are not clearly marked, forcing practitioners to search for ways in which somehow to balance or meet obligations to all.

To balance these interests, practitioners and the public must weigh such issues as:

1. What are the ethical considerations when the public good can be served only at great expense to the company?
2. Are time or financial constraints ever an acceptable rationale for compromising ethics? In other words, how much should these constraints be considered when choosing what should be done?
3. In an increasingly pluralistic society, how does one conceptualize the general public and then decide what is best for it?

One could describe this ethical quandary as one in which the principles of Kant meet those of Mill. One must decide when and how categorical duty and utilitarianism intersect or overtake one another. When does a practitioner have to decide that "the greatest good for the greatest number" becomes a categorical imperative for ethical behavior, and how does the practitioner's decision impact that of the organization or client? The mere question implies that it is possible to predict the consequences of actions taken on behalf of or in conjunction with a certain stakeholder group in a timely manner so that they could be stopped or changed quickly enough to mitigate harm or to expand the benefit. One also might argue that understanding the socially responsible action requires a commitment to accepting the ethics of caring as a fundamental obligation for both corporate and individual practices. Actions that honor the dignity and worth of individuals almost certainly result in socially responsible outcomes.

The cases in this chapter prompt you to consider different aspects of social responsibility from different philosophical and ethical perspectives. "One for One® . . . You Are TOM" highlights how TOMS has used its charitable outreach as a major component in its consumer relations. The next case, "Ice Bucket Challenge Fundraising," details the success of a grassroots nonprofit campaign. The third case examines how the NFL has addressed the issue of domestic violence, and the last case recounts a campaign at Starbucks designed to spark discourse about race relations in America.

CASE 54. "ONE FOR ONE® . . .YOU ARE TOM"

"With every purchase, TOMS will help a person in need. One for One®."[1]

Buy one, give one. For each pair of shoes purchased from the company, a pair of shoes is donated to a needy child at an event called a "shoe drop," which allows volunteers, often celebrities and shoe customers, to participate onsite in the distribution. The corporate website for #IAMTOM explains: "If you shop consciously, volunteer with an organization that is changing lives, take part in creating a sustainable future or help raise awareness of issues affecting lives across the globe – you are TOM."[2]

By spring 2014, the company had given away more than 20 million pairs of shoes to children in more than sixty countries. TOMS (short for "Tomorrow's Shoes") sells espadrilles and cordones. The shoes are constructed in factories in regions around the globe, from Haiti to Argentina to countries in Asia and Africa. The shoes are sold through the corporate website and in department stores and boutiques.[3]

But One for One® now includes more than shoes. In 2011, TOMS Eyewear was launched, and, for every pair of sunglasses sold, donations are made to partners who then provide treatment for eye-related diseases such as cataracts or who provide eyeglasses for those with some vision impairment in thirteen countries from Guatemala to Cambodia to the United States.[4]

More recent initiatives include: the launch of TOMS Coffee, sales of which trigger a corporate donation for each bag of coffee purchased that will be used to help fund one week of clean water to residents in five countries through the work of Water For People, a nonprofit partner; and the creation of the TOMS Animal Initiative by the founder's wife, Heather Mycoskie. This initiative works with the Virunga National Park in Rwanda to try to save the endangered mountain gorillas. Funding is prompted by the sale of special TOMS that offer an embroidered figure of a gorilla on the side of the shoe. Ms. Mycoskie explains on the website: "It's amazing to watch how the One for One® model can be applied to serve other needs in the world, and I am very grateful that we have applied it to helping animals."[5] Information about the One for One® projects is provided in an annual Giving Report available on the website.[6]

TOMS was founded in 2006 by Blake Mycoskie, an entrepreneur who started his first business while a college student and had appeared as a contestant on the reality program *The Amazing Race*, and Argentinian business partner Alejo Nitti. Mycoskie says he was inspired to start the company and its foundation once he learned of the grave diseases caused by parasites that enter through bare feet and saw firsthand the numbers of children and adults in the world who had no shoes. He told the *South China Morning Post* in a 2009 interview: "I've seen numbers that say a billion people worldwide are at risk of getting this disease and a pair of shoes is the most effective and simple solution."[7]

In a 2009 interview, Mycoskie told CNN that, beyond the health benefits, owning a pair of shoes may allow children to attend school in areas where proper uniforms are required. Describing the reaction to a shoe drop, Mycoskie said: "[T]he most common response we get from the kids and from their parents is that this shoe represents a passport to a better life."[8]

The social entrepreneur has been recognized for his creativity and best practice. Mycoskie received the People's Design Award from the Smithsonian's Cooper-Hewitt National Design Museum in 2007, an award presented each year in recognition of sustainable design achievements.[9] TOMS received the Secretary of State's 2009 Award for Corporate Excellence (ACE). The State Department present the ACE awards each year to U.S.-owned businesses that exhibit good corporate citizenship, promote innovation, and advance democratic principles around the world.[10]

Others have been inspired by the TOMS example. To help raise awareness of the need for shoes, TOMS invites individuals and organizations to become involved in an annual observance of "One Day Without Shoes," a day in which walking in barefoot reminds participants of the challenges of life without shoes. College students are encouraged to form organizations to promote the foundation.[11]

Doing good by doing well has become a mantra of corporate social responsibility statements, but TOMS offers a noteworthy example of developing an entrepreneurial response to human need that is, as Mycoskie often explains, sustainable because it is based on a for-profit model. In uncertain economic settings, it might be easier for a corporation to draw back from committing so openly to philanthropy. The rewards for donating shoes in underdeveloped areas are indirect at best. However, TOMS has demonstrated that a viable link can be established between good corporate citizenship and economic benefits, and that committing to doing good may become a compelling consumer motivation.

Indeed, TOMS has shown that its model can compel private individuals and organizations as well as other corporations to engage in charitable activism. The *Standford Social Innovation Review*[12] noted at least sixteen companies that now engage in some type of buy-one-give-one practice, ranging from the company Baby Teresa, which donates a baby outfit for each one purchased, to Nouri Bar, which works with Stepping Stones International by donating a school meal whenever someone purchases one of their snack bars.[13] Organizations that choose to act for others rather than just for shareholders or employees may exemplify the best of citizenship behavior. Acting on the basis of stated corporate values in such a public manner demonstrates an ethical commitment to living truth as well as telling truth, that ideal of Aristotelian *phronesis*—both knowing what is virtuous and how to practice it. Recognizing the positive efforts of such corporations is also ethically worthy. In a culture cluttered with what can be overtly negative views of corporate profiteering, identifying corporations that are financially successful and socially responsible offers moral exemplars that support continued belief in the possibilities for socially responsible capitalism.

However, the buy-one-give-one model is not without critics. Some advocates assert that asking what residents would like or believe they need would be a better step—true partnering—rather than having a corporation or organization decide on their behalf what to give or do without any consultations.[14] Other critics say donating products to low-income residents does not target their real needs and may, in fact, adversely affect local manufacturing and merchandising.[15] Mycoskie has pledged that by the end of 2015, at least one-third of its shoes would be manufactured in the areas where the shoes are also distributed for free.[16]

You Think?

- What does your donated dollar mean?
- Should individuals rely on an ethical principle to guide their charitable giving and involvement?

CASE 55. ICE BUCKET CHALLENGE FUNDRAISING

The videos seemed to be everywhere on Facebook, Twitter, Instagram, and YouTube: an individual or a group looking into the camera and challenging friends or colleagues to take the challenge and donate to the cause of defeating amyotrophic lateral sclerosis (ALS), the fatal neurodegenerative disease. From President Obama to Matt Lauer, from Justin

Figure 13.1
Massachusetts
Gov. Charlie
Baker
participates in
the Ice Bucket
Challenge with
its inspiration
Pete Frates,
seated left, to
raise money for
ALS research at
the Statehouse
in Boston
(August 10,
2015).

Source: Associated
Press photo/
Charles Krupa.

Timberlake to Jimmy Fallon, from the Boston Police Department to the New England Patriots, more than 2.5 million people responded to the #IceBucketChallenge, which raised unprecedented donations and awareness for the ALS Association.[17]

The idea of the challenge came from two young men who had been diagnosed with ALS, Patrick Quinn from New York and Pete Frates from Boston. Frates, who had captained the Boston College baseball team, started his own challenge on July 29—and the challenge went viral, with unprecedented results.[18]

More than seventeen million #IceBucketChallenge videos were posted on Facebook in 2014, according to the ALS Association, with more than ten billion views. Globally, more than $220 million was raised, with the U.S. Association receiving $115 million,[19] including what it called "an astonishing" $4 million in donations between July 29 and August 12, compared to $1.12 million received during the same two weeks in 2013.[20]

"We have never seen anything like this in the history of the disease," Barbara Newhouse, president and CEO of the Association in the August 12 release. "We couldn't be more thrilled with the level of compassion, generosity and sense of humor that people are exhibiting as they take part in this impactful viral initiative."[21]

By October 2014, the Association had designated $21.7 million to six programs and research alliances selected by its trustees in collaboration with key stakeholders,[22] and the number of research grants received by the Association had tripled.[23] Overall, the Association planned to devote $77 million of the #IceBucketChallenge funds to support research efforts, $23 million for patient and community service, $10 million for public and professional education, and $5 million for fundraising and external processing fees for credit-card donations.[24]

The research showed promise—in August 2015, the journal *Science* published results of a study supported by the Association that identified the important function of a protein related to ALS.[25] Summaries of other funded published research projects are presented on the Association's website.

The challenge returned in summer 2015, with the Association using the hashtag #EveryAugustUntilACure to raise awareness, prompting a new round of social media videos and an estimated $500,000 in donations received during the several weeks of August.[26]

Viral campaigns present challenges for nonprofits—they can spread false rumors, they can raise false hope, but they can also spur action and raise millions of dollars. In this case, the unexpected—and unplanned—publicity and its fundraising result appears to have been well managed. *Money* magazine examined the impact of the Ice Bucket Challenge and the performance of the ALS Association in response to it and found strong results.[27] The millions of dollars donated were targeted for efforts approved by stakeholder groups, with detailed descriptions of the expenditures and plans offered by the Association in publications and its website. Respect for those impacted by the disease and those investigating its causes and effects was demonstrated. Charity Navigator offered the Association a four-star rating, with a 92.94 out of 100 score for financial and a 97 out of 100 score for transparency,[28] satisfying Kant's call for transparency and truthtelling and establishing an example that could meet the challenge of the categorical imperative.

Those who participated in the ice bucket challenge may not have seen their icy moments—or their donations—in the light of such an ethical obligation. Some acted out of deep compassion, perhaps others in a quick impulse to participate in a social media phenomenon. The challenge itself, however, required individuals to establish themselves as at least a temporary exemplar calling others to imitate their behavior for a worthy cause. Whether this will lead to an ongoing commitment to financially support the fight against this fatal disease is unknown, but the willingness of millions of individuals to take positive action testifies to the power of social media to engage, activate, and unite friends and followers in ways as breathtaking as a bucket of iced water poured over one's head.

VIRTUE: Generosity

The digital world with multiple funding sites and need-based requests offers numerous ways for generosity to be demonstrated. One can contribute to a social cause, an entrepreneurial startup, or an emergency fund with just one click. Should generous giving become a public ritual?

CASE 56. TACKLING DOMESTIC VIOLENCE

The top sports story of 2014, according to the Associated Press,[29] was the NFL and its struggles to cope with domestic violence issues among some players.

In September 2014, a video of Baltimore Ravens star Ray Rice hitting his fiancée in an elevator was published by TMZ,[30] resulting in widespread controversy and some calls for the league to take tougher action. In July, the league had suspended Rice for only two games, but after the video became public, NFL Commissioner Roger Goodell suspended Rice indefinitely.[31] (Rice then appealed the suspension, and it was overturned.[32]) Just a short time after the Rice video aired, charges of child abuse were brought against Minnesota Vikings running back Adrian Peterson for switching his son. Other cases involving Arizona Cardinals player Jonathan Dwyer and Carolina Panther Greg Hardy also emerged in September, prompting many from the public and news media to question how the league should respond.[33]

The Associated Press described it this way: "The $9 billion industry that U.S. fans devour on a weekly basis ran into a public-relations crisis, the likes of which nobody could have predicted and not even the league's supposedly well-oiled spin machine could repair."[34]

According to the *Wall Street Journal*, internal NFL reports indicate that between 2000 and 2015, 135 domestic violence allegations were made against players. The typical league punishment was a one-game suspension.[35] But the 2014 incidents—and the publicity surrounding the Rice video—moved domestic violence from an internal issue to one that was intensely public and one to which the NFL had to respond. The league did so by changing its discipline policy, donating to a service agency, and launching an external and internal communication and education program.

Commissioner Goodell and other league officials began working in fall 2014 to address the public crisis. At a news conference on September 19, Goodell apologized for his handling of the Rice case.[36] A domestic violence working group also was established, with a female vice president appointed as its head.[37] In September, the NFL hired Lisa Friel, a Manhattan sex crimes prosecutor, as a consultant to help develop a new personal-conduct policy,[38] which was then announced in December. (The policy, adopted unanimously by the owners, gives the NFL the authority to put on leave all NFL employees who are charged or who face an independent investigation.[39])

In late September, Goodell spent three hours at the headquarters of the National Domestic Violence Hotline to talk with the staff members and hear stories of the women with whom they worked.[40] The league made a commitment to donate $5 million to the Hotline each year for five years.[41] The Hotline reported that it had dealt with an 84 percent increase in calls since the video with Rice and his fiancée was published.[42]

The league became active in developing a more consistent message about the dangers of domestic violence. An education program was launched for current players.[43] By late October, in cooperation with the group NO MORE, the NFL began airing public-service announcements during its games. The spots featured current and former NFL stars looking into the camera while offering messages such as "No more 'She was asking for it'" and "No more 'He just has a temper.'"[44] The NO MORE organization[45] had been formed the year before, in March 2013, as a private–public partnership that sought to combat domestic violence by developing messages and resources that could be used by its partners across the country. The NFL had donated airtime during the February 2014 Super Bowl for one public-service announcement created by the group.

In November 2014, in cooperation with several groups, the NFL distributed a seventeen-minute video, "NFL Call to Coaches–Domestic Violence and Sexual Assault Awareness," to college and high-school coaches. The video included messages from well-known college, high-school, and NFL coaches, including Pete Carroll of the Seattle Seahawks and Mike Tomlin of the Pittsburgh Steelers.[46]

It is not just some NFL players who are involved in domestic violence situations; unfortunately, the problem ranges far beyond professional and amateur sports players. However, the prestige and stardom of players and coaches does give them a platform for public messages and public actions they can use effectively as moral exemplars—and perhaps a duty to use this platform for the greater good. The position of the NFL commissioner also carries a duty to care, not only to the owners and their economic well-being, but to the well-being of the players, coaches, and their families—and the well-being of others who may be influenced by the players and coaches. While the funds donated to the Hotline—which could be increased by the very wealthy league—may help activists address at least some of the individual abuse cases across the country, the public-service announcements, videos, and educational meetings created and endorsed by the NFL can seek to prevent new cases.

Are these actions sufficient to solve the public relations crisis and, much more importantly, are they enough to change the attitudes and behaviors that catalyzed the issue? Perhaps. Writing in the *Chronicle of Philanthropy*, Fine decried what she called the "limousine philanthropy" of the NFL leadership where critical issues from social service to breast cancer awareness were too quickly addressed by quick visits, public donations, or pink sweatbands, "painless and impersonal ways to do good."[47] *Agape* ethics requires such caring to be based on an understanding of the innate worthiness and dignity of each indi-vidual—an ethic that must be taught, practiced, and enforced if the league is to change its culture. This type of caring will only be authenticated and demonstrated convincingly through consistent, ongoing actions that lead to real changes in attitudes and behaviors.

VIRTUE: Leadership

Aristotle stressed the importance of moral exemplars in helping shape the virtuous charac-ters of young people. In today's media-saturated world, are professional athletes, politicians, and corporate CEOs willing to exercise leadership with integrity?

CASE 57. BREWING RACIAL DISCOURSE?

> Starbucks mission . . . to inspire and nurture the human spirit – one person, one cup, and one neighborhood at a time.[48])

The round green sign has become a familiar part of the streetscape in cities, towns, and campuses in sixty-seven countries since the chain first sold coffee in its inaugural store in the Pikes Place Market in Seattle, Washington.[49] Tall, grande, and venti cups of various coffees, teas, and other drinks are prepared and sold, along with other food items and merchandise from music to mugs.

Figure 13.2
A Starbucks iced drink with a "Race Together" sticker on it is shown ready for pickup at a Starbucks store in Seattle, Washington, the day Starbucks CEO Howard Schultz announced the program for customers in an effort to raise awareness and discussion of race relations (March 18, 2015).

Source: Associated Press photo/Ted S. Warren.

The chain has distinguished itself by offering more than just pumpkin spice lattes, however. It offers stock options and health care benefits to qualified full- and part-time employees[50] and the opportunity to participate in the Starbucks College Achievement Plan,[51] announced in June 2014, which offered eligible partners full-tuition coverage for four years of enrollment in Arizona State University's online bachelor's degree programs.

One of the central tenets of the corporation is a commitment to diversity in hiring and service. The website explains: "Embracing diversity only enhances our work culture, it also drives our business success. It is the inclusion of these diverse experiences and perspectives that create a culture of empowerment, one that fosters innovation, economic growth and new ideas."[52]

With such a commitment, perhaps it was not surprising when the corporation announced a "Race Together" initiative in March 2015 following months of racially charged incidents and subsequent protests. For three months, employees had participated in open forums in Chicago, Los Angeles, New York, Oakland, and St. Louis where these issues were discussed.[53] The initiative called for employees to write the term, "#RaceTogether," on cups as they served their customers or to add a similar sticker on other purchases, and they were encouraged to talk with customers about the issue.

The campaign was announced with full-page ads in the *New York Times* and *USA Today* and a special newspaper section in *USA Today*.[54] Baristas began writing the hashtags while they were serving. The public reaction was largely negative but huge—with Race Together garnering 2.5 billion impressions in two days, many of which were tweets filled with what CEO Howard Schultz described to *Fast Company* as "visceral hate and contempt for the company and for me personally."[55] Some questioned the motives behind the campaign, and others complained about the increased time it was taking to be served in the shops.[56]

On March 22, Schultz sent a memo to employees telling them that the practice of writing on or placing stickers on cups would end, but that the initiative would continue.[57] The corporation planned to hold more employee forums and foster dialogue with community leaders, to hire 10,000 more "opportunity" youth within three years, and to build more stores in urban neighborhoods. In the memo, Schultz concluded: "An issue as tough as racial and ethnic inequality requires risk-taking and tough-minded action. And let me reassure you that our conviction and commitment to the notion of equality and opportunity for all has never been stronger."

"What should the role be for a for-profit, public company in [this] world?" Schultz asked during a panel discussion at Spelman College in April 2015.[58] It's a worthy question. Do corporations have a higher obligation than to make money for their shareholders or owners?

While economists and politicians may debate the question, some CEOs like Schultz have answered affirmatively. Moving beyond the more traditional understanding of the "triple bottom line" of corporate accountability for fiscal, social, and environmental sustainability, some are becoming engaged in CEO activism, using their bully corporate pulpits for commentary and agitation on key social issues.

Chatterji and Toffel, writing in the *Harvard Business Review*,[59] note that many activist CEOs have faced criticism from both political vantage points. Yet Chatterji and Toffel say such activism provides customers and investors insights so they can make informed decisions about how and where they want to spend their money. Internally, such activism must be "transparent and delimited,"[60] they argue, so that employees do not feel coerced to conform with the political or social opinions of their bosses.

The social and political opinions of the leadership at Starbucks are apparent, not only on the corporate website, but also promoted in advertising, signage, speeches, and practice. Customers who choose to patronize the chain have the information needed to act—or to stop acting. Shop employees may not have had such easy options, however. While Schultz says the idea for the campaign grew out ideas offered through the employee forums, the initiative was not voluntary. It's likely that some of the 2.5 billion web impressions were shared in person at local shops for local employees to deal with, and—as Schultz noted—many were not positive. Allowing employees to opt into the campaign would have offered them informed choice as well.

Did the "Race Together" initiative alter the nation's racial climate? Perhaps not. But it certainly raised a vital topic to the public agenda—as the billions of web impressions, talk-show commentaries, and news articles demonstrate—while it sought to brew some dialogue, one cup at a time.

NOTES

1. www.toms.com/our-movement.
2. www.toms.com/stories/we-are-en/iamtom.
3. Deidre McQuillan, "Feet First," *The Irish Times*, March 29, 2008, Magazine 21.
4. www.toms.com/gift-of-sight.
5. www.toms.com/stories/?lang=en.
6. www.toms.com/static/www/pdf/TOMS_Giving_Report_2013.pdf.
7. Daniel Jeffreys, "Blake Mycoskie; The Philanthropist and Entrepreneur Talks to Daniel Jeffreys about Providing Life-Saving Footwear to the World's Poor," *South China Morning Post*, September 6, 2009, Magazine 10.
8. Shannon Cook, "These Shoes Help Others Get a Step Up," CNN.com, March 26, 2009, www.cnn.com/2009/LIVING/homestyle/03/26/blake.mycoskie.toms.shoes/.
9. www.cooperhewitt.org/national-design-awards/history-of-honorees-jurors/.
10. www.state.gov/r/pa/prs/ps/2009/dec/133351.htm.
11. Jenna Bush Hager, "TOMS Shoes Helping Children Overseas," *NBC Saturday Today*, April 10, 2010.
12. Christopher Marquis and Andrew Park, "Inside the Buy-One Give-One Model," *Stanford Social Innovation Review* (Winter 2014): 28–34.
13. Ibid., 32.
14. Joyce Hackel. "TOMS Shoes Rethinks Its 'Buy One, Give One' Model of Helping the Needy," Public

Radio International, October 8, 2013, www.pri.org/stories/2013-10-08/toms-shoes-rethinks-its-buy-one-give-one-model-helping-needy.

15. April Joyner, "Beyond Buy-One-Give-One Retail," *The New Yorker*, April 8, 2014, www.newyorker.com/online/blogs/currency/2014/04/beyond-the-buy-one-give-one-model.html.

16. Hackel, "TOMS Shoes Rethinks."

17. Meg Tirrell, "The Ice Bucket Challenge Is Back," *CNBC*, August 27, 2015, www.cnbc.com/2015/08/27/the-ice-bucket-challenge-is-back-.html.

18. Bella English. "Stricken with ALS, Pete Frates Shows the Will to Live," *Boston Globe*, August 15, 2014,www.bostonglobe.com/metro/2014/08/15/stricken-with-als-pete-frates-closely-linked-ice-bucket-challenge-shows-will-live/m2Abeu4SIGROfg0aBlCTCM/story.html.

19. ALS Association, "As 2015 ALS Ice Bucket Challenge Heats up, Donations Fuel Significant Research Discovery," August 13, 2015, www.alsa.org/news/media/press-releases/cryptic-exons-release.html.

20. ALS Association, "ALS Ice Bucket Challenge Takes U.S. by Storm," August 12, 2014, www.alsa.org/news/archive/als-ice-bucket-challenge.html.

21. Ibid.

22. Carrie Munk, "The ALS Association Announced Initial commitment of $21.7 million from Ice Bucket Challenge Donations to Expedite search for Treatments and a Cure for ALS," October 2, 2014, www.alsa.org/2015-dev/site-default/ibc-initial-commitment.html.

23. Tirrell, "The Ice Bucket Challenge Is Back."

24. ALS Association, website infographic. "Your Ice Bucket Dollars at Work," www.alsa.org/fight-als/ibc-infographic.html.

25. ALS Association, "As 2015 ALS Ice Bucket Challenge Heats up."

26. Tirrell, "The Ice Bucket Challenge Is Back."

27. Ethan Wolff-Mann, "Remember the Ice Bucket Challenge? Here's What Happened to the Money," *Money.com*, August 21, 2015, http://time.com/money/4000583/ice-bucket-challenge-money-donations/

28. www.charitynavigator.org/index.cfm?bay=search.summary&orgid=3296#.VhToyflViko.

29. Charlotte Alter, "AP Votes NFL Domestic Violence Saga as Top Sports Story of the Year," Time.com, December 23, 2014, http://time.com/3645392/nfl-domestic-violence-2/.

30. D'Arcy Maine, "A Timeline of the NFL's and Ravens' Reactions to the Ray Rice Incident," espnW.com, September 10, 2014, http://espn.go.com/espnw/news-commentary/article/11489146/a-timeline-nfl-ravens-reactions-ray-rice-incident./

31. Alan Schwarz, "Handling of Ray Rice Case Puts Roger Goodell under Heightened Level of Scrutiny," *New York Times*, September 15, 2014, D1.

32. Alter, "AP Votes NFL Domestic Violence Saga."

33. Monica Langley, "NFL's Roger Goodell Seeks to Right Past Wrongs," *Wall Street Journal*, December 9, 2014, www.wsj.com/articles/nfls-roger-goodell-seeks-to-right-past-wrongs-1418182760.

34. Eddie Pells (Associated Press), "Domestic Violence at Forefront of NFL in 2014," *Washington Times,* December 23, 2014, www.washingtontimes.com/news/2014/dec/23/domestic-violence-at-forefront-of-nfl-in-2014/?page=all.

35. Langley, "NFL's Roger Goodell Seeks to Right Past Wrongs."

36. Ibid.

37. Ibid.

38. Jane McManus, "Domestic Violence and the NFL: What Impact Has the League Made?" espnW.com, http://espn.go.com/espnw/news-commentary/article/12235694/impact-league-made/.

39. Langley, "NFL's Roger Goodell Seeks to Right Past Wrongs."

40. Associated Press, "NFL Commissioner Visits Domestic Violence Hotline," NFL.com, September 28, 2014,www.nfl.com/news/story/0ap3000000401492/article/roger-goodell-visits-national-domestic-violence-hotline.

41. Langley, "NFL's Roger Goodell Seeks to Right Past Wrongs."

42. Ibid.

43. Ibid.

44. John Koblin, "The Team Behind the NFL's 'No More' Campaign," *New York Times*, January 4, 2015, ST7, NY Edition.

45. http://nomore.org.

46. Associated Press, "NFL Sends Domestic Violence Video to Schools," ESPN.com, November 19, 2014, http://espn.go.com/nfl/story/_/id/11903937/nfl-sends-domestic-violence-video-schools.

47. Allison Fine, "Against the NFL's 'Limousine Philanthropy,'" *Chronicle of Philanthropy*, October 14, 2014, https://philanthropy.com/article/Against-the-NFL-s/152461, para. 3.

48. www.starbucks.com/about-us/company-information/starbucks-company-profile.

49. www.starbucks.com/about-us/company-information/starbucks-company-profile.

50. www.starbucks.com/careers/working-at-starbucks.

51. http://globalassets.starbucks.com/assets/D43B807D47E14DEFAEC48AC0120EBFA6.pdf.

52. www.starbucks.com/responsibility/community/diversity-and-inclusion.

53. Starbucks, "What 'Race Together' Means for Starbucks Partners and Customers," March 16, 2015, https://news.starbucks.com/news/what-race-together-means-for-starbucks-partners-and-customers.

54. Ibid.

55. Austin Carr, "The Inside Story of Starbuck's Race Together Campaign, No Foam," *Fast Company*, July/August 2015, www.fastcompany.com/3046890/the-inside-story-of-starbuckss-race-together-campaign-no-foam, para. 2.

56. Hayley Peterson, "Here's the Starbucks Internal Memo Showing the 'Race Together' Campaign Was Always Doomed," *Business Insider*, March 29, 2015, www.businessinsider.com/heres-the-starbucks-internal-memo-showing-the-race-together-campaign-was-always-doomed-2015-3.

57. Howard Schultz, "A Letter from Howard Schultz to Starbucks Partners Regarding Race Together," Starbucks Newsroom, March 22, 2015, https://news.starbucks.com/news/a-letter-from-howard-schultz-to-starbucks-partners-regarding-race-together.

58. Carr, "The Inside Story," para. 5.

59. Aaron Chatterji and Michael Toffel, "Starbucks' 'Race Together' Campaign and the Upside of CEO Activism," *Harvard Business Review*, March 24, 2015, https://hbr.org/2015/03/starbucks-race-together-campaign-and-the-upside-of-ceo-activism.

60. Ibid., para. 8.

THE HEART OF THE MATTER IN PUBLIC RELATIONS ETHICS

Relationships lie at the heart of the practice of public relations, and in many ways the same character traits and practices that support the creation and maintenance of healthy, supportive interpersonal relationships are required for ethical public relationships. Who wants a friend to lie to them, or to misrepresent themselves to others? Who wants a friend to betray their loyalty or trust? Who wants a friend who will work only toward his or her best interests, not toward mutual interests? No one—and while we likely don't usually consider a corporation, a nonprofit, a celebrity, or a politician as our personal friend, we do likely expect to be treated with equality, justice, dignity, and respect in our communications and interactions. Similarly, we may not consider our clients, employers, or shareholders as traditional friends, but once we step into the role of public relations practitioner working for them, we are accepting the moral responsibility of *caring for*, in which their needs, rights, and expectations become as important to us as our own.

Public relations is not marketing, although marketing is a valid and respected field of its own. But, unlike marketing, public relations does not consider its interactions to be solely commercial transactions with consumers of our products, goods, and services. By defining groups as publics, practitioners acknowledge that there is mutuality, not just exchange. Such mutuality will last only as long as both parties find benefit, whether that is manifested through profit, service, knowledge, recognition, or meaning. Such relationships are risky. Balancing various loyalties may be difficult. It is possible to become so focused on the needs of one client, for example, that we disregard our responsibility to care for others, or to become so focused on the needs of one client that we are unable to balance our duty to our profession, our nation—or even our best selves.

So, what characterizes the *heart of the matter* for this type of ethical public relations practice?

Practice truthfulness: Ethical practitioners should engage in communication that is accurate, honest, and contextualized. Seek to be honest *about* sources and honest *with* sources. Be unashamed of your partisanship and frank in disclosures. Seek to maximize transparency, and minimize subterfuge. Only exaggerate in a context where such hyperbole is understood for what it is—and one in which no one is harmed or misled. At the heart of the practice is the ability to know and share the truth in an engaging manner.

Practice in humility: You are the spokesperson or the representative, not the organization or the client. Don't be tempted to confuse the roles. Be willing to listen to others' suggestions and to respond to their criticism, whether the one offering input is a client, a supervisor, or a philosopher. Gaining attention for your messages in what is both a diverging and converging media world isn't easy, so don't oversell your abilities. Public relations is typically a professional without bylines. At the heart of the practice is the willingness to focus on the other, not on yourself.

Practice with respect: Understand the power of the communications and organizations you're involved with. Persuasion and influence are powerful forces. The work of politics and public affairs, nonprofit service, industry, and business matters, and the influence of public relations in them, has real consequences. Take your work and yourself seriously. Each member of your publics and, indeed, each of your stakeholder groups or segmented publics, deserves to be regarded and treated with dignity, and is deserving of full participation in the public forum, even as you prioritize them in your communication efforts. The events, activities, and campaigns you plan and execute may be creative and clever, but don't allow the punchlines to ridicule or belittle. At the heart of the practice of public relations is an understanding of the value of the work being done—and the higher value of those for whom and with whom it is undertaken.

4

ENTERTAINMENT

A recent column headlined "Scuzz World" laments the misbehavior of then nineteen-year-old phenom Justin Bieber and the lascivious dancing of once Miss-Nicey-Nice Miley Cyrus, suggesting that American (and world) audiences must adjust to a new level of vulgarity on a vast (television) scale, or make the impossible trek "back to Kansas" (a tweak on Judy Garland in "The Wizard of Oz," for all readers born after 1999). "Wretched excess seems to be everywhere," the columnist observes, "on TV screens, movie screens, phone screens, in songs . . . websites. . . . It's an odd coincidence that LCD, the liquid crystal displays that put all of it in your face, also stands for lowest common denominator."[1]

Was this a rant by someone older than nineteen? Or a prudent observation by a sophisticated culture-watcher concerned with media content and its impact on youth? Either way, the sentiment expressed is not new. Studies come and go, research trends suggest this and that impact, and educators occasionally lament observably shortened attention spans. Should media ethics even take up this debate: popular entertainment as cultural literacy, or simple escapism?

When the question came before the Hutchins Commission on Freedom of the Press regarding whether the film industry was part of "the press," the first reaction of several of the assembled scholars was "rubbish." In their eyes, movies were diversionary, escapist, and silly. What claim could one make to count movies as part of the modern media?

Fortunately, a more farsighted view prevailed. Motion pictures are part of the culture and need to be looked at carefully. The commission invited Will Hays, then chief of the Motion Picture Producers and Distributors of America (later the Motion Picture Association of America), to present the case for industrial self-regulation. Eventually, the Hollywood model of codes and intra-industry regulations was adopted by the commission as the best way of expressing social responsibility in a democratic society.

On the importance of entertainment media and their responsibility to the public, the commission displayed wisdom in its landmark 1947 report. News and consumer information are vital to democratic life, but, clearly, entertainment occupies most of the broadcast spectrum, cinema screen, and a healthy share of the printed page as well. From these media we receive symbolic clues concerning what we should believe and how we should act. Entertainment, for all its recreational value, does much to educate and socialize us.

Should entertainment programs be subject to ethical reasoning? Robert Redfield, distinguished anthropologist and one of the Hutchins commissioners, urged that the direction of all our social productivity be toward a "new integrity" of idea and institution, a creative order wherein symbols and practices make "coherent sense when we state them and when we comply with them," leading to a "model society that will command the confidence of other free peoples everywhere."[2] Redfield, no dreamy chauvinist, was arguing for the interdependency of social institutions (such as the media) and social beliefs (such as the sanctity of life). Yes, he would argue, the entertainment media must be put to the test of ethical reasoning.

Redfield's intuitions were a preface to ethical theorizing in the 1980s, when narrative discourse and narrative communities became important concepts in the work of Duke University ethicist Stanley Hauerwas. Hauerwas argued that culture is built around stories that distinguish good from evil, hero from villain, success from failure. Because of the importance of story, a community that wants to live responsibly among other communities is obliged to set its compass on truthful narratives, without which a social ethic becomes detached intellectualism.

We organize the study of ethics around key questions: the relation of personal and social ethics, the meaning and status of the individual in relation to the community, freedom versus equality, the interrelation of love and justice. These are crucial categories for the analysis of a community's social ethics. The form and substance of a community are narrative-dependent, and, therefore, what counts as "social ethics" is a correlate of the content of that narrative. Good and just societies require a narrative that helps them to know the truth about existence and fight the constant temptation to self-deception.[3]

Hauerwas begins his appeal for narrative ethics with a long analysis of the novel *Watership Down*, a rabbit story with a profound political message, a fictional narrative that helps us to develop our own. Constructing journalistic narratives, public relations messages, advertisements, and entertainment programs involves process, hierarchy, imagination, constraint, profits, and power. Our aim is to examine the moral dimension and press toward justified solutions.

George Gerbner underscored the importance of this examination in his lecture at the fortieth anniversary of one of the country's premier communications research institutions: "I think of communications as the great story-telling process that guides our relationships to each other and the world." Later, he warned that "children are born into a home in which a handful of distant corporations tell most of the stories to most of the people and their families most of the time."[4] His point was to urge a more careful study of the field, entertainment primarily, and its cultural and moral foundations.

The emphasis on narrative and authenticity gathered momentum in the 1990s as philosophers and essayists as different as Richard Rorty and Wendell Berry began to explore how communities form, how people connect with each other, and how suspicion and distrust replace generosity as a first impulse.

Between the undefined "public" and the private individual, Berry writes, is the community, formed by a mutuality of interests and ennobled by "virtues of trust, goodwill, forbearance, self-restraint, compassion, and forgiveness." But, he adds, electronic media by nature "blur and finally destroy all distinctions between public and community." Television, for example, "is the greatest disrespecter and exploiter of sexuality that the world has ever seen."[5] Our narratives have gone crazy, self-destructive, and antihuman.

And from the time of Redfield's concerns to the late "naughties," we can do no better than cite Stephen Carter's book, wherein he urges us all to do better at (1) discerning right from wrong, (2) acting on that discernment even at personal cost, and (3) saying openly that we are acting on moral principle. He titled his book *Integrity*.[6]

The terrorist attacks on September 11, 2001, provided the most gripping real-time news coverage ever to appear on television screens. Those images and the new global realities following that frightful day have had an impact on entertainment as well. Movies scheduled for release were postponed, reworked, and reconsidered. How much fright could the public endure? How much bitterness and hate could the world endure?

The following chapters raise only a few of the ethical questions and suggest some ways of approaching answers. Violence is a pressing concern; its threat to social order is immediate and dramatic. Nearly 500 people in the United States die every week from gunshot wounds, many self-inflicted or tragically accidental. Many of these deaths are the result of a momentary act of passion among friends and relatives. Media violence, some argue, is the same threat one step removed and a hundred times more potent. Television violence sets the stage for social maladjustment, argues Purdue University researcher Glenn Sparks, especially among children.[7] While researchers debate the audience impact, ethicists ask how much media violence is tolerable, even though only one person might be affected or none.

And what about problems generated by big media's huge financial stake? Fortunes and careers ride on fractions of rating points. So many in the entertainment industry doubt that ethical reasoning has any word to speak at all—money alone counts.[8]

Other problems in entertainment programs are less overt than violence or greed: the stereotyping and typecasting of racial groups, age groups, geographic groups, and communities of faith; the bias expressed by the omission of substantive narratives about our society's small cultures; the offense created by our no-punches-pulled video and internet explorations of sexual experience and crime; or the monotony of canned laughter and endless reruns.[9] It becomes clear, as we proceed, that every level of the entertainment industry—producer, actor, writer, and viewer—closely encounters decisions of an ethical kind that require a thoughtful response.

The lines of debate between those who would protect the public from exposure and advocates of unfettered media violence have shifted in recent years from "my First Amendment rights" to "our flourishing common life together." We are less likely to scream for unlimited speech rights since 9/11; we are more likely to ask what kind of culture we wish to share. Robert Fortner has observed:

> If the press fails to foster within the community the conversation necessary to sustain it . . . and thus undergirds the links between people who constitute it . . . then it has become a tool of repression, propaganda, and self-interest.[10]

In the past, the oppressor has been the moralistic gavel pounder, the one who knows what's best for everyone. Today, we recognize gavel pounders and discount their inflamed rhetoric. It's more difficult to recognize the subtle, culture-changing, attitude-altering shift that happens when violent depictions do not seem that awful anymore, that crazy, that insane.

Lindsay Lohan's attorney, after one of his client's courtroom appearances, insisted she would henceforth live "with dignity, pride and respect."[11] Those old virtues sounded reassuring, but more like a museum walk than a late-night TV routine. In the new normal of "Scuzz World," are virtues such as dignity still marketable?

LEARNING OBJECTIVES

After completing Part 4, you should be able to meet these objectives:

- **Understand and assess research evidence and moral standards regarding effects of media violence and sexually explicit programming.**

- **Place entertainment choices in a context of life priorities, relieving the need to see everything and play everything.**

- **Adjust personal standards on exposure to recreational media of all kinds.**

- **Integrate personal moral sensitivities with broader social mandates of fairness, justice, and compassion.**

- **Spend personal resources (money and time) more wisely.**

- **Take a more active role in mentoring youth, engaging public conversation about media uses and effects, and determining personal boundaries.**

- **Appreciate First Amendment freedoms, but, beyond that, the social bonds that constitutions can only support, never create.**

NOTES

1. Daniel Henninger, "Scuzz World," *Wall Street Journal*, February 5, 2014, A16.
2. Robert Redfield, "Race and Human Nature," *Half A Century – Onward* (New York: Foreign Missions Conference of North America, 1944), 186.
3. Stanley Hauerwas, *A Community of Character* (Notre Dame, IN: University of Notre Dame Press, 1981), 9–10.
4. George Gerbner, "Telling Stories: The State, Problems, and Tasks of the Art," Fortieth Anniversary Program Highlights, Institute of Communications Research, University of Illinois at Urbana-Champaign, 1987.
5. Wendell Berry, *Sex, Economy, Freedom and Community* (New York: Pantheon, 1993), 124.
6. Stephen L. Carter, *Integrity* (New York: Basic Books, 1996), 7.
7. Glenn G. Sparks, Cheri W. Sparks, and Erin A. Sparks, "Media Violence" in Jennings Bryant and Mary Beth Oliver, eds., *Media Effects: Advances in Theory and Research* (New York: Routledge, 2009), 269–286.
8. See Clifford Christians and Kim B. Rotzoll, "Ethical Issues in the Film Industry," in Bruce A. Austin, ed., *Current Research in Film: Audiences, Economics, and Law*, vol. 2 (Norwood, NJ: Ablex, 1986), 225–237.
9. For balanced accounts, see Richard Winter, *Still Bored in a Culture of Entertainment* (Downers Grove, IL: Intervarsity Press, 2003); and William D. Romanowski, *Eyes Wide Open*, rev. ed. (Grand Rapids, MI: Brazos, 2007).
10. Robert Fortner, "The Public," in Linda Steiner and Clifford G. Christians, eds., *Key Concepts in Critical Cultural Studies* (Urbana: University of Illinois Press, 2010), 193.
11. Henninger, "Scuzz World."

CHAPTER

14

VIOLENCE

Media reformers gather to television and filmic violence like sugar ants to jelly. It's their cause, their concern—and the rest of us may have quickly dismissed them. At least until the 1999 tragedy at Columbine High School in Colorado. That day was so bizarre and brutal; everyone asked: "Why would teenagers plan and plot to kill their classmates and then themselves?"

News coverage of that terrible scene seemed like a surreal drama, yet the images were all too real. Had we—the American people—developed this culture of violence? Had entertainment violence made real-life violence less spectacular, more commonplace?

Three months after Columbine, two teenagers in Los Angeles stabbed and killed one boy's mother. They claimed their attack was inspired by the film *Scream*. Again we asked: "Is this *us*? Are we so vulnerable, or naive, or hardened that a B horror film can snap our sense of humanity and turn homes into slaughterhouses?"

Violence is inevitable in any drama, even in comedy and melodrama, such as when Spiderman fights the treacherous, spunky Green Goblin. But the irrepressible increase in real violent crime, much of it perpetrated by juveniles, often has been linked to video games and the internet. What a juvenile sees, it is argued, too easily becomes what a juvenile does. Because society cannot endure the anarchy of criminal rule, it must move to eliminate the causes.

Confronting the censors of violence are combat-hardened libertarians who insist that all speech be protected. Violent programming may or may not breed violent behavior, they contend, but curtailment of speech surely heralds a retreat from democracy into feudalism, a return to the medieval monastery where utterances were controlled and political choices programmed. Such a fate, they claim, is worse than all others, and avoiding it is worth the risk of too much latitude.

Much of the current debate over violence in entertainment takes up the arguments of the last national inquiry, the controversial Meese Commission, and its outspoken opponents.

Organized in 1985 by Attorney General Edwin Meese, the commission was charged to "determine the nature, extent, and impact on society of pornography in the United States" and to recommend to the Attorney General how pornography "can be contained, consistent with constitutional guarantees."[1] The commission's research included content analysis, participant observation, case studies, interviews, and experimental studies. Its findings supported the cultivation hypothesis advanced by George Gerbner and others, and at points suggested an even more direct link between pornography and the acting out of sex crimes by certain persons. The commission's ninety-two recommendations were nearly all in support of tougher enforcement of existing obscenity laws, with even stricter measures against child pornography. The rationale for control and enforcement was a widely shared conclusion that viewing and reading sexually violent material tends to create an incentive for violent sex crimes and to develop a socially destructive linkage of sex and violence in the minds of persons who may, under some conditions, act out their new attitudes.

From the first commission hearing, opponents issued charges of *comstockery* (a pejorative term recalling Anthony Comstock's antiobscenity crusades of the 1880s). The American Civil Liberties Union published a summary and critique of the commission, entertainment professionals organized to protest the commission's implied call to curtail cinematic art, journalists trailed the commission and reported on the bizarre nature of some of its testimony, and columnists pointed to "dark lunacy" and "potential danger" underlying the commission's report. Much of the opposition can be summarized around five claims:

1. Artistic freedom and aesthetic integrity demand a laissez-faire approach. Government has no business policing writers and directors.
2. No direct effects can be documented or proved. Indirect effects are the consequence of living one's life in a world of mediated messages and cannot be made the basis of criminal prosecutions.
3. Violence is a social and historical problem, not the result of violent television shows or films. To think otherwise is to blame John Wayne for the Vietnam War.
4. Worry over media violence is really our fear of changing social institutions. To suppress television and film is to forcibly maintain traditional notions of family, friendship, and marriage in an era when these social arrangements are undergoing radical change.
5. Boundaries between news and entertainment programming are fluid. Television newsmagazine shows are so hungry for material that anything visual (even if it must be staged for replay) is turned into a major "investigation." All the free-marketplace arguments that traditional news has enjoyed must now be applied equally to entertainment programs. The public has a right to know.

These objections seem less important in the face of enduring questions concerning the causes and cures of real violence. One author has suggested that media violence be treated like obscenity, which would remove its First Amendment protection in some cases.[2]

Ethicist Sissela Bok compares the attraction of modern media violence to the Roman gladiatorial contests, wondering why civilized peoples permit uncivilizing entertainment.[3] The Clinton administration called for better industry self-control and clearer prosocial messages for the nurture of youth. Here and there, a producer and a network executive toned down the violence to show respect for the most recent shooting victims. The Michigan state senate passed a bill to require warnings on tickets and ads where a performer's music also carries such warnings. Small gestures, cautious solutions.

The cases in this chapter struggle constantly with the impulse to freedom and the moral boundaries of liberty. The first case, "Hear it, Feel it, Do it," raises the effects argument: hear violent lyrics, do violent deeds; show a violent program, commit a violent crime. No matter that the violence is sometimes directed toward the self and sometimes others.

But what would stories tell if all violence were expunged on moral claims? The second case, "Violence-Centered," insists that violence has its purposes. It cannot be read out of human experience, and it should not be so tempered in entertainment that we fail to deal with reality and history.

The third case, "Comics for Big Kids," looks at the persistence of violence in media entertainment. The final case, "Video Gaming Changes the Rules," considers violent games. It should take the most dedicated video gamer to a new level of moral on-alertness, always a good level for video competition at any level.

CASE 58. HEAR IT, FEEL IT, DO IT

Friday evening in October. John McCollum, nineteen years old, is alone in the house. An Ozzy Osbourne fan, he cranks up the family stereo—loud, intense, reverberating. The first song, "I Don't Know," celebrates in the manner of heavy metal the chaos and confusion of human life. The second song, "Crazy Train," points to insanity as the inevitable result of our inability to explain life's contradictions. The third, "Goodbye to Romance," advocates cutting ties to the past as the only way to personal freedom. The last song is "Suicide Solution." That tune's lyrics convey a nihilism—a giving up on life—that even drug-induced addictions cannot solve. What's the solution to such bleakness? Ozzy points explicitly to the last and only act of the will available to a depressed soul who has lost every reason to maintain life. Then, masked in a twenty-eight-second instrumental break, and heard at one and a half times the normal rate of speech, are lyrics which, prima facie, advocate immediate self-inflicted death via gunshot.

John McCollum turns off the family stereo, walks to his bedroom, and puts another Osbourne album, *Speak of the Devil*, on his personal stereo. Volume up, headphones on, he lies on the bed. Nearby, a handgun, .22 caliber. Music. The cool small muzzle against his right temple. Volume up. A muffled pop.

McCollum's body was discovered the next morning. He was still wearing headphones, and the stereo's needle was riding around and around the center of the album. He had had problems with alcohol abuse that complicated other serious emotional problems, but in their suit against Osbourne and CBS Records, the McCollum family claimed that these lyrics had a cumulative impact on a susceptible listener; that the impact was antisocial in its emphasis on despair, Satan worship, and suicide; and that the record company had sought to cultivate Osbourne's "madman" image in press releases and sales promotions and to profit from it. The music was a proximate cause in McCollum's death, the suit alleged, because CBS negligently disseminated Osbourne's albums to the public and thereby "aided, advised or encouraged McCollum to commit suicide." The beat and the words had created in John McCollum "an uncontrollable impulse" to kill himself, a consequence entirely foreseeable and therefore intentional, the suit contended. Death, his family insisted, was brought on by pressures and forces hidden in the grooves and ridges of a plastic disc, made and sold by an industry that does not care.[4]

Can media inspire violent crimes? A celebrated murder case in 1977 confronted the nation with a Florida teenager who shot his neighbor, an eighty-two-year-old woman, took $415 from her home, and went on a spree to Disney World with friends. Ronny Zamora's defense attorney proposed that his client was the victim of "involuntary television intoxication." A person who is drugged or becomes intoxicated without his knowledge is not legally responsible for actions while under the influence. Zamora had seen up to 50,000 television murders in his fifteen years, and he could not determine whether he was on a television program or committing a crime when he shot the victim, the attorney claimed. The jury decided otherwise, however, and Zamora was convicted. But similar cases keep coming to the courts.

Can violent media inspire self-destruction, and, if so, who is responsible? The argument that linked repeated listening to rock albums to John McCollum's suicide is similar to the argument in the celebrated *Born Innocent* case that occurred a decade earlier. In September 1974, NBC sent to its affiliates a program starring Linda Blair as a girl whose innocence is shattered through her experience in a girls' reformatory. Because the drama would include violent scenes possibly objectionable to some viewers, NBC ran a warning at the start of the program:

> *Born Innocent* deals in a realistic and forthright manner with the confinement of juvenile offenders and its effects on their lives and personalities. We suggest you consider whether the program should be viewed by young people or others in your family who might be disturbed by it.

As a portent of the show's later troubles, fifteen sponsors withdrew shortly before the broadcast.

Born Innocent did, in fact, raise objections from viewers. Hundreds of calls and letters were received by NBC affiliates across the nation—700 in New York alone. Only a few callers, notably social workers familiar with reformatories, applauded the network for its realistic portrayal of a pervasive problem. Particularly troublesome was one scene in which Blair was raped by four female inmates using a plumber's helper for penetration. The character was shown naked from the waist up.

The program and its forthright realism would have been largely academic but for a real-life rape three days later. On Baker Beach near San Francisco, nine-year-old Olivia Niemi was attacked by three girls and a boy, ages nine, twelve, thirteen, and fifteen, who raped her with a beer bottle in a fashion similar to the attack on television. Olivia's mother filed suit for $11 million against NBC and the owners of KRON-TV, charging that NBC was guilty of negligence in broadcasting the program during family viewing hours (8 p.m. on the West Coast). One of the assailants had in fact referred to the television show when she was arrested.

The link between dramatic and real violence might not be strictly causal, but the network had not taken adequate precaution against the program's potential effects on young viewers. The case was strengthened by the absence of any similar type of rape in the casebooks of juvenile authorities. If Niemi's attackers had perpetrated a first-of-its-kind rape, their teacher and proximate cause was the television network that had prestaged the event.

NBC declined to argue the facts. Instead, defense attorney Floyd Abrams contended that the First Amendment protected his client from damages from alleged effects of a media program. California Superior Court Judge John Ertola agreed. In September 1976, he ruled in favor of NBC without calling a jury, claiming: "The State of California is not about to begin using negligence as a vehicle to freeze the creative arts." But the California Court of Appeals overturned the ruling. Niemi had a right to a jury trial on questions of fact, the appellate panel contended.

Before the case was argued, NBC urged the U.S. Supreme Court to quash the trial. At stake, the network claimed, were basic constitutional rights. On behalf of NBC, the American Library Association filed an amicus brief suggesting that the Appeals Court ruling might lead to lawsuits against libraries by victims of crimes suggested in books. The Writers Guild of America wrote of the "chilling effect" on popular drama that a trial on the facts could have. For Niemi, the California Medical Association filed a friend-of-the-court brief. The Supreme Court declined to intervene.

Each side geared up for the coming battle in the California courts. NBC would argue that a warning had been given before the drama, that the four attackers had previous juvenile records, and that some testimony suggested that none of them had seen the televised rape. Causal explanations for the crime other than the television show rested on stronger psychological evidence. One of the attackers, for example, had been molested by her father. In theory, NBC insisted, the plaintiff's case would shift accountability for criminal acts away from the persons responsible and toward the producers of televised drama.[5]

Niemi's attorney would argue that the rape scene in *Born Innocent* ignored NBC's own production code and the National Association of Broadcasters' code that proscribed graphic depictions of violence at that time. The rape scene, in fact, had been abridged in telecasts after the first showing. No one should be absolved of civil liability because of the First Amendment, the plaintiff said.

Commercial television networks would be hard pressed to justify graphic violence based on Kant's imperative. No reasonable person could will that such portrayals become standard television fare because reasonable people do not, by definition, seek to promote gratuitous suffering. There should be little argument here. People who delight in causing or feeling pain are pathologically disturbed or criminally insane. Reasonable people may not choose to avoid all suffering (e.g., running into a fire to rescue a child), but suffering without purpose (e.g., merely running into a fire or pushing someone else in) is irrational by any common definition. Likewise, a constant media diet of violence and pain is irrational, assuming even a remote connection between what one views and how one behaves.[6]

Notice how close Kant (the doer of duty) and Jeremy Bentham (the calculator of pleasure) are on this issue. Bentham, the father of modern utilitarianism, wrote: "Nature has placed mankind under the governance of two sovereign masters, pain and pleasure. It is for them alone to point out what we ought to do, as well as to determine what we shall do."[7] Kant's appeal to rational duty would have little prescriptive value if people were unclear about whether to seek pleasure or pain. Let us assume that the history of human civilization is not remiss here: Avoiding gratuitous violence is the normal response of a rational person.

But "Suicide Solution" is only one song, and *Born Innocent* is only one program, and the rape scene is only one sequence in that one program. This is hardly a trend and certainly not an unrelieved diet of mayhem and bloodletting.

Yet, to describe the problem in this way is to miss the point of even the utilitarian response. Hans Jonas, a modern utilitarian, has argued that the consequences of a nuclear holocaust are so incalculable that we must set our goals specifically at eliminating even its possibility.[8] (Notice an underlying Kantian-style commitment to the reasonableness of human survival.) A similar argument warrants eliminating graphic violence on television. If the possibility of increased real violence or loss of sensitivity to violence exists, and the means to avoid the possibility are available and not onerous, then reasonable people will take those means—and ought to, violence being hurtful.

What means are available for avoiding graphic violence on television? On the one hand, viewers can choose not to watch, which is the preferred solution of the networks because it imposes no direct obligations on them. Let the buyer beware!

On the other hand, the state could impose limits on television violence in the same way it regulates cigarette and liquor commercials. (Is there any objection to banning the advertising of unsafe medicines?)

Or again, the television industry—in this case NBC—could set its own limits based on steady evidence that television violence at least creates a culture of suspicion and fear[9] and in fidelity to the belief that violence is never inherently justified. But this would require rebuilding Rome, according to syndicated columnist Suzanne Fields. She argues that media violence, unlike the violence in classical literature, occurs in an "ethical vacuum." What's the point of most television violence? There is none. Even Hansel and Gretel do better than that, Fields claims.[10]

In 1993, the nation's four broadcast networks (ABC, CBS, NBC, and Fox) agreed to provide television viewers with warnings preceding shows that contain violent material. This concession was announced one day before congressional hearings on new technologies to let parents block out violent shows. The agreement was a step toward industry self-regulation and responsibility. Peggy Charren of Action for Children's Television called it a "benign solution, inadequate to the problem."[11] That was the same reaction of Lois Salisbury, executive director of Children Now, when the television industry announced its new rating system, the first of its kind for television programming, in December 1996.[12]

Important distinctions separate the McCollum case and the *Born Innocent* incident. First, John McCollum did not take his handgun onto the street to apply the "solution" to any passersby. Grievous as its consequences were to his family, the harm done was self-inflicted. Second, the message blamed for inspiring McCollum's violence was offered in an easily repeatable format, unlike the 1974 television show. Whereas Olivia Niemi's attackers could have been influenced by a single viewing, John McCollum had occasion for a total environment of Osbourne's music, as loud and as often as he chose to listen. Third, the Ozzy Osbourne persona created by marketers and PR writers—with his cooperation—corresponded to his music's destructive themes. Neither Linda Blair nor NBC suffers under a reputation aligned with shower-room violence. Finally, NBC issued a warning as part of its message; CBS did not.

Is moral blame less heavy if no one other than the self is directly harmed in a violent act? In quantitative terms, yes. Given the choice of a terrorist blowing up an airliner in the sky or that same person blowing himself or herself up on the ground, we would reasonably opt for the latter. But the McCollum case involves the suicide of a young man who had a history of emotional and behavioral problems. For these individuals, we bear obligations to offer aid, not a prompt to self-destruct. Suicide is no solution to life's turmoils, and promoting it in music, film, or word is perpetrating a lie. Osbourne did not hand the gun to John McCollum, but his music is distributed in a format that carries no alternative point of view. No voice is heard after "Suicide Solution" arguing that self-destruction is morally wrong. McCollum heard only the most errant element of a many-sided ethical issue.

Is artistic integrity in jeopardy if we attach moral blame to a mere message? Roxanne Bradshaw of the National Education Association, commenting on violence in media, said: "We're not interested in censorship. We're interested in reeducating ourselves and our children about electronic media."[13] No moral theory would excuse media managers and artists from helping in the task Bradshaw describes. The more vulnerable the viewer or listener, the greater is the obligation to talk, to help interpret, and to channel responses toward beneficent ends.

California courts excused both CBS and NBC from liability in these two court proceedings; the First Amendment would not tolerate damages sought by these aggrieved plaintiffs. But our mutual human responsibility to seek each other's best interests and to help each other avoid meaningless hurt and harm—a responsibility expressed in both Judeo-Christian and Kantian ethics—knows no constitutional boundaries. NBC need not graphically show the tools and techniques of sexual abuse. CBS Records has no moral right to profit from the genius of an artist who would be foolish and wrong to practice what he preaches. Nonetheless, if the corporation chooses to exercise legal rights to such expression, fair warnings—if not outright disclaimers—would put music buyers on notice. People closest to troubled, vulnerable users of such media could then make more informed choices. In the present case, our objective is to prevent the lie of Osbourne's music from becoming John McCollum's final tune, or worse, that another confused teenager shoots schoolmates for the experience of just being bad.

The flip side of audience impact is actor impact, but here the lines of responsibility become very clear. The entertainment world was shocked when actor Heath Ledger died of an accidental drug overdose, and film watchers wondered: was his role in *The Dark Knight* too dark? Was the all-consuming prep work for the role of the Joker too close to imbibing a new paradigm for one's real life? Ledger described his intense work ethic as a month of being "locked away" trying to develop his character's voice. He wanted to get the laugh right, and found, as he said to an interviewer, the mindset of a psychopath.[14] The Academy Award for Best Supporting Actor, accepted by Ledger's family on his behalf, as well as numerous other posthumous awards including the Golden Globe Award for Best Supporting Actor, was no compensation for a talent lost too soon. Yet no direct link is possible between movie role and overdose; causal connections are speculation. At any rate, professionals know the emotional weight of the job. They can get help or walk away.

CASE 59. VIOLENCE-CENTERED

Oliver Stone surprised the movie world in 2006 with a film about two New York Port Authority police officers buried in the rubble of the World Trade Center on September 11, 2001. Sargent John McLoughlin, a twenty-three-year veteran, and first-year officer Will Jimeno survived the towers' collapse and ultimately were lifted back to safety—after being buried for twenty-two hours and thirteen hours, respectively—in one of the least likely but most heroic rescue efforts in modern times. Stone told their story in *World Trade Center* much as they told it to him, straight up and without an explicit political agenda. The result was a film about two returned-to-life police officers and the meaning of their rescue for the rest of us.

Violence happens throughout this film. After all, 2,769 people died that day. Extraordinary violence took those lives—the violence of terrorism, jet fuel burning, crushing concrete; the eerie violence of bafflement, incredulity, failure to communicate, reckless courage; and the violence that chips away at hope when the chance of rescue seems so remote. No story of that day could be told without violence; 9/11 and violence are related terms.

Director Stone had the good fortune of casting two leading actors—Nicolas Cage and Michael Peña—who successfully conveyed the human sensitivities of McLoughlin and Jimeno, both above ground and near death underground. *World Trade Center* was not a documentary but a narrative of resurrection on a day of pain and grief. Stone let the story tell itself, granted with the panache of camera angle, lighting, sound, and one dramatic dolly-up sequence that set the New York rescue in its global context. *Newsweek* noted the movie's celebration of the "ties that bind us, the bonds that keep us going, the goodness that stands as a rebuke to the horror of that day."[15] *Rolling Stone*, in an upbeat review, called the film a "salute to heroes who could have easily walked away"[16]—a reference to the rescue work of David Karnes and Jason Thomas, who saw the violence as a call to extraordinary action and whose unblinking approach to the violence, their climb into the rubble, saved McLoughlin and Jimeno from the pit of hell.

Our first thought is that violence is bad. Road rage is the bad side of freedom to travel on highways. Hurting someone is the bad side of relationship building. Assault with a deadly weapon is the bad side of an argument. To avoid these calamities—to find alternatives to violence—is the path we celebrate as morally good. But not all violence is bad. Some violence is necessary to prevent worse violence. Police use force to apprehend criminals. Sports teams use violence to entertain. Some violence is unavoidable or accidental. Nature kills skiers in an avalanche, but we do not hold nature guilty of a moral lapse. Humans make mistakes, and people are hurt. Sometimes we must simply say: "what a tragedy, but no one is to blame." Some violence is humorous, as kids' cartoons have demonstrated since Mickey Mouse. Even Hallmark TV tearjerkers depend on violence to create drama and dilemma. Without violence, where's the story?

Yet violence that causes hurt for its own sake is morally condemned, along with violence done with such little sense of empathy as to contribute to the "banality of evil" that Hannah Arendt observed at the trial of Adolf Eichmann, Hitler's architect of the Holocaust. Arendt was

> struck by a manifest shallowness . . . that made it impossible to trace the incontestable evil of his [Eichmann's] deeds to any deeper level of roots or motives. . . . There was no sign in him of firm ideological convictions or of specific evil motives. . . . Except for an extraordinary diligence in looking out for his personal advancement, he had no motives at all.[17]

Eichmann's violence is morally without excuse. No appeal to "following orders" or "I didn't know" mitigates the moral judgment.

The violence of *World Trade Center* is anything but banal, pointless, or overwrought. The movie portrays the violence of Islamic jihadists taking the lives of ordinary (noncombatant) Americans, along with many citizens from around the globe, and their own lives, in a cause they regarded as holy war. That violence is portrayed in *World Trade Center* in brief sequences of blood-soaked victims fleeing the building, a man down on the sidewalk, the gasping horror of the jumpers who chose gravity as their doom instead of fire, and the ominous street shadow of a low-flying airplane just before impact.

Most of *World Trade Center*'s violence focuses on the small team of Port Authority police officers who entered the Trade Center that morning. The most troubling portrayal is the death of Officer Dominick Pezzulo, who survived the first tower's fall only to die while trying to free Jimeno from the rubble. Was Pezzulo committing suicide in his last moments or firing his revolver into the darkness to attract the attention of rescuers? We do not know and cannot know. Pezzulo dies violently on screen, as it really happened.

Clearly, *World Trade Center* brackets the violence of the jihadists themselves, offering no comment and focusing no attention. The violence of *World Trade Center* is violence suffered, not perpetrated. McLoughlin's firefighters are victims. We watch their fight for breath and hope against all odds.

Virtue ethics from the ancient world assumed violence to be part of human experience and celebrated courage as the proper human response. Moreover, the golden mean established moral limits on violence: it must be used proportionate to its need and only when other means of achieving a just result have been exhausted. These limits and conditions were brought into a coherent theory of "just war" by Augustine in the third century. The Christian tradition from which he speaks has challenged "just war" with claims that only radical pacifism follows the example set by Jesus. Yet "just war theory" remains the most widely accepted set of moral boundaries on violence, in no small measure owing to Reinhold Niebuhr's insistence that "Christian realism" accounts for the obvious need to meet immoral violence (e.g., the Nazi war and extermination machine) with measured violence.

Utility does not forsake all violence, and the "veil of ignorance" could achieve a choice for violence if conditions warranted. The Kantian imperative never imposes defenselessness, and the Qur'an famously permits war under certain bounded conditions.

The violence of *World Trade Center* is defensive. Only an airliner's shadow points to unjustified violence, and that judgment is so nearly universal that Stone need not underline it. Even within Al-Qaeda, the attack on the towers is considered ill-advised, if not wrong per se.[18] The gripping violence of *World Trade Center* is captured in scenes of people caught in events where escape is the rational and self-reflexive response, but they choose against it for the sake of trapped victims needing rescue. This we call courage.

Some viewers claim that even this violence is presented too soon after the real disaster and dishonors the dead by making a film (and lots of profit) while survivors and families still grieve. A morally attuned filmmaker must listen to these concerns. Five years is not five months, but wounds heal at different speeds, and some never do. Certainly, the world is morally richer for careful films depicting the Nazi Holocaust (although survivors are still with us) and the more recent Rwandan genocide. Pearl Harbor and D-Day took the lives of thousands, but filmmakers have yet to exhaust public fascination with that terror. Stone could have waited another five years, yet with the support of many New Yorkers, he had sufficient moral allowance to move forward without blame.

Viewers of *World Trade Center* are not without choice as well. No one mandates movie patrons to see this film. Even the mysterious corescuer, the Marine identified only as Sergeant Thomas, when he finally emerged from obscurity, indicated that he had not seen the movie. "I'm not ready," Jason Thomas told the press. "I don't want to relive everything."[19] By all accounts, the courage this man displayed on 9/11 warrants a society's gratitude, no matter his reluctance to see himself portrayed. Thomas's choice to pass on the film is a choice open to everyone.

Most who see *World Trade Center* will be stunned, but not morally offended, by its violence. The cringing we do watching this movie reminds us that our rough, belligerent, morally flawed social universe sometimes requires heights of moral action when one's deep commitments to human care outweigh the danger for the sake of the other. Violence that leads to courage has purpose and benefit, although we would choose, if we could, to smother the violence before its sparks burst into flame.

CASE 60. COMICS FOR BIG KIDS

Nemesis (Icon Comics) is the brilliant story (if you buy the writer's own blurb) of a psycho killer who targets police, especially if the police operate in a law-and-order mode and really especially if the target is a "practicing Catholic and a family man." There's plenty of collateral damage in this shooting spree. Nemesis always makes an appointment, and he's never late.

Trading on the theme of religiosity as pretense, Marvel's *King Pin* pits a killer Mennonite (he only uses tools that his religion allows, e.g., sledge hammers) against the toughest gun-totin' gangsters in the village. This horse-and-buggy hitman can make quite a mess of himself and his targets. Watch out, he rids the streets of some rough hombres, and their kin are none too happy about him.

Flesh Gordon carries on its cover an M for "mature readers," whether as a marketing device or as a warning is hard to say. The story line begins on Planet Porno, where Flesh has destroyed a "sinister ray" aimed at Earth by Emperor Wang. Flesh saves Earth from slavery to Wang with the help of his companions, the beautiful Dale Ardor and the bearded Dr. Flexi Jerkoff. The reader of this simplistic tale should expect plenty of double entendres to compensate for the colorless pages.

Ernie Evil, on the other hand, is full of color. Lots of red, as in blood. Lots of pale green, as in slime, rot, and poison. Plenty of white and black, and always a beautiful woman about to have her brains blown away. As Mary, the gorgeous brunette, says in one frame: "Think I'm gonna be sick." That seems to be Ernie's big appeal—the sicker you feel reading his tale, the more successful is the book.

Heavy Metal is a series of panels featuring sex, technology, and death, with a few devils for motive power and a few drinks for the orgy's afterglow.

The graphic novel *Mark of the Devil* is a richly textured tale of all the above, plus danger, pain, extraordinarily proportioned breasts, fearsome creatures shorn of human sympathy, and lots of Ur-passion. It's a novel that could send your night dreams into neverland, wherever that is for you.

Comics these days seem more and more pitched to ages higher than seven. Certainly, no hint of childhood mars the dark and lascivious worlds of these books. Some are artless; some are well drawn and doubtless literary, as the comic world judges writing merit. All are escapist, elemental, and sinister.

Violence dominates the comics. Researcher John DiFazio analyzed the comic book treatment of fourteen American values and found that "peaceful resolution of conflict" was one of the values least often portrayed.[20] Our own quick review of a comic rack revealed plot resolutions involving a woman blowing herself up with a shotgun while trying to save an infant from a monster, the crashing of a boulder on the cranium of a muscle-bound cyclops, and the introduction of a new team of superheroes in the Justice League of America series, just to prove, it seems, that nationalism survives as the last moral stand. So vicious are modern comics that one can almost hear Frederick Wertham, author of the classic 1954 *Seduction of the Innocent*, uttering "I told you so" to the numerous critics who disparaged his work.[21]

Such unrestrained violence was not always the rule in children's literature. Note, for example, the ethic of restraint that characterized the popular Nancy Drew detective series, according to James Lones:

> There was an abundance of violence in the Nancy Drew series, but it was controlled violence. Clubbings, wrecks, assault and battery were common. Attacks fell indiscriminately on many types of characters with Nancy often the target. Despite this violence no one was murdered. Criminals who assaulted their victims did not go beyond beatings. In a decade [the 1930s] when sensational real-life kidnappings stirred the population, these fictionalized kidnappings ended happily and no victim of abduction was killed. Guns were used but were either fired as warnings, and not directly at persons, or used as clubs.[22]

Commentary on the comic book industry as it was in the 1980s reveals an industry as troubling as Wertham's case studies. Joe Queenan of the *New York Times Magazine* wrote:

> Over the last decade, comics have forsaken campy repartee and outlandishly byzantine plots for a steady diet of remorseless violence. "Green Arrow" depicts a woman whose eyes have been plucked out by vultures. In "Spider-Man," seven men are ripped to pieces by a wolf. The back pages of "Wolverine" show the hero puffing on a cigarette as blood drips from his lips. . . . "Black Orchid" begins with a woman being tied up and

set on fire, then moves on to child abuse, a mutant fed live rats, and a jailed hybrid—half woman, half plant—who avoids rape only because her jailers find her too repulsive.[23]

The comic industry grosses millions per year, with DC Comics and Marvel in the distant lead, followed by Archie Comic Publications and then about 200 minor-league hopefuls, many of them willing to go beyond the editorial boundaries (broad as they are) still observed by the market leaders. One distributor explained: "Our readers are teenage boys [with] lots of repressed anger. [They are] going through puberty [and they] like to see characters act out their aggressions."

As a shortcut to moral analysis, some might close the case by waving the banner of First Amendment freedom. But, even among legal theorists, First Amendment freedom weighs in primarily with political speech as a means to democratic process, not with comic book speech as a means to personal entertainment happiness.[24] The issues most salient to freedom of speech today are campaign financing and workplace safety, not graphic novels or comic strips. Justice of the Supreme Court Stephen Breyer calls the First Amendment a tool of "active liberty," not a cure for limitless expression.[25] First Amendment enthusiasts may ring the bell, but the heart of this controversy must be settled in moral, not legal, terms.

A reasonable argument can be made that older readers are capable of discerning reality from fantasy. The older a reader is, the more credibly he or she will process imaginative stories. On this basis, the two-dimensional static violence of comic books may qualify for broader license than the violence in the so much more emotionally engaging dynamic images of films. Give greater freedom to media of lesser evocative power, one might say.

The avid reader of adult comics, like the fan of almost any media challenging common values, must face the matter of loyalties. Do the imaginative dimensions stimulated or satisfied by violent or sexually oriented material help or hurt a reader's capacity to be a responsible member of primary social groups: friends, family, community? Perhaps the moral test is whether you can freely talk about the content of your entertainment reading. Can this part of your life be shared with people who depend on you?

Certainly we do not share every notion of conscience with everyone else. Such a surrender of privacy is often taken as a sign of mental or emotional need today. Yet this is also true: we ought to live a singular (not dual) life of moral accountability to self and others. You are free to show masks, but you cannot do so with integrity. Your presentation to others ought to be the same self you know yourself to be. Loyalties depend on such integrity, and in the Potter Box analysis, loyalties keep us linked to the moral lives of others as an anchor to our own.

Stay loyal by choosing comic book entertainment about which you can speak openly to those you admire and respect.

CASE 61. VIDEO GAMING CHANGES THE RULES

The *Grand Theft Auto* series epitomizes a popular perception of video games: they are popular, profitable, and controversial. *Grand Theft Auto V*, released September 2013, rapidly became the biggest single entertainment title in history, pulling in $1 billion dollars in three days (by comparison, James Cameron's film *Avatar* took a pokey sixteen days to reach the same number). And just like the other releases in the same series, critics decried *Grand Theft Auto V*'s extreme violence and misogynistic representations of women.

Video games can present players with significant ethical challenges. This is true even of the many nonviolent titles released every year. It's the violent games, however, that grab ethical headlines.

Take *Fallout: New Vegas*, set in alternate-reality Nevada long after a nuclear war. The game has an elaborate political backstory about the struggle for regional dominance between a bloody and tyrannical empire called Caesar's Legion, a corrupt democracy called the New California Republic, and a hyper-rational homegrown dictator called Mr. House. The player controls a character that must choose which faction to support.

It would be easy to leave the description of the game at that. Fighting for Caesar would mean the player supports totalitarian terror. Except, of course, that there is, in reality, no post-apocalypse Mojave Wasteland to terrorize. Mowing down a tribe of innocent civilians in *Fallout* kills precisely zero physical, breathing people.

Not all interaction in a video game is solely between a player and a pre-programmed world. Many of the most popular video games focus on player-to-player interaction, and this can lead to tricky ethical situations. *World of Warcraft* (usually called *WoW*) is a massively-multiplayer online game that allows hundreds or thousands of players to be interacting simultaneously in the same imaginary world. Many players join groups called "guilds" that generally work together on completing quests or fighting other guilds.

In 2006, a member of a guild passed away (in real life). To commemorate her passing, her *WoW* guild arranged a funeral gathering. The event, however, took place in a version of the game that allowed player characters to attack and kill each other. So a rival guild decided to take the opportunity to ambush their enemies and attacked during the funeral. The attackers recorded the event. The video was posted on YouTube and widely circulated.[26]

Video gamers have to consider how to be wise about playing: it's easy for a play session to swallow up productivity, sleep, and money. And many games explicitly challenge video gamers to make ethical choices: the popular *Fallout* series, for example, allows players to either be murderous psychopaths or noble heroes.

This textbook has described a series of ethical systems that help guide decision-making. Should the use of those ethical theories change when engaging interactive fiction? Is it possible to apply virtue ethics to imaginary characters in the adventure game *The Wolf*

Among Us? Is it reasonable to use Kant's categorical imperative when deciding whether to be a peaceful or a warlike empire-builder in *Sid Meier's Civilization V*? Can Bentham's utilitarianism provide guidance on whether to hurt innocent bystanders in *Grand Theft Auto V*?

You Think?

- Imagining that ethics in all situations are important, what does ethical action in a game mean? May games change the way people interact with each other, without real-life moral blame?
- Is it morally acceptable for players to experiment with ethics by performing virtual actions that would horrify most people in our physical world? Must moral choices in games carry the same ethical weight as real-life choices?

Back to *WoW* . . . Attacking a real funeral would, of course, violate a wide range of social taboos, and would be hard to justify using any ethical system. But video games provide a considerably different context for social interaction than real-life conditions. One of the core purposes of games is competition, and most players realize that actions in a game have a different reality than actions outside a game—otherwise, chess would be a competition of bloodthirsty tyrants.

The funeral raid in *WoW* started a vigorous online discussion. On one side, many argued that the attackers were deeply insensitive and violated the golden rule. Other gamers, however, pointed out that the ambushing guild violated no rules and was, in fact, staying true to the spirit of the game. Because there are versions of *WoW* that don't allow players to kill other players, if the grieving guild wanted to avoid combat, it should have set the event in a place where an ambush would not have been possible.[27]

Our questions remain: does the context of a video game change the moral obligations of players? Is it even possible to apply normal ethical guidelines to game-playing, which to gamers is a kind of alternate social space with different rules? If the traditional, time-tested moral systems of world civilizations also oversee all the alternate worlds in 100 million game rooms, why play?

NOTES

1. U.S. Department of Justice, *Attorney General's Commission on Pornography: Final Report* (1986), 1957.
2. Kevin Saunders, *Violence as Obscenity* (Durham, NC: Duke University Press, 1996).
3. Sissela Bok, *Mayhem: Violence as Public Entertainment* (Reading, MA: Addison-Wesley, 1998), 15ff.
4. *McCollum v. CBS*, 15 Med. L. Rptr. 2001.
5. Material on *Born Innocent* was drawn from "TV Wins a Crucial Case," *Time*, August 21, 1978, 85; T. Schwartz et al., "TV on Trial Again," *Newsweek*, August 14, 1978, 41–42; "NBC's First Amendment Rape Case," *Esquire*, May 23, 1978, 12–13; "Back to Court for 'Born Innocent,'" *Broadcasting*,

May 1, 1978, 37–38; "Judge Restricts 'Born Innocent' Case to First Amendment Issue," *Broadcasting*, August 7, 1978, 31–32; Karl E. Meyer, "Television's Trying Times," *Saturday Review*, September 16, 1978, 19–20; *New York Times*, September 18, 1978; *Wall Street Journal*, April 25, 1978.

6. If media-effects research finally eliminates any connection, and even the possibility of connection, between viewing habits and behavior, then real harm is eliminated as a factor, and arguments to curtail media programming for any reason fall away. But the weight of our society's beliefs leans heavily toward a connection, the contours of which are the substance of effects-researcher debates.

7. Jeremy Bentham, *An Introduction to the Principles of Morals and Legislation*, eds. J. H. Burns and H. L. A. Hart (London: Athlone Press, 1970), 11.

8. Hans Jonas, *The Imperative of Responsibility* (Chicago: University of Chicago Press, 1984).

9. The many writings of George Gerbner and Larry Gross are just the tip of the iceberg supporting this contention.

10. Suzanne Fields, "The Trouble Is that TV Violence Occurs in a Moral Vacuum," *Daily Herald*, July 6, 1993, sec. 1, 8.

11. *Daily Herald*, June 30, 1993, sec. 1, 14.

12. Quoted in "TV Industry's Rating Plan Faces a Tough Audience," *Chicago Tribune*, December 19, 1996, 1.

13. *Media and Values*, Fall 1985, 9.

14. "World Exclusive: The Joker Speaks: He's a Cold-Blooded Mass-Murdering Clown," Interview with Heath Ledger, *Empire Magazine*, November 28, 2007, www.empireonline.com/news/story.asp?NID=21560.

15. David Ansen, "Natural Born Heroes," *Newsweek*, August 7, 2006, 53.

16. Peter Travers, "Heart from a Stone," *Rolling Stone*, August 24, 2006, 107.

17. Hannah Arendt, *Eichmann in Jerusalem* (New York: Penguin, 1994), 235–236, quoted in *Moral Leadership*, ed. Deborah Rhode (San Francisco: Jossey-Bass, 2006), 27.

18. So reported in a CNN documentary, *In the Footsteps of Bin Laden*, August 23, 2006.

19. Wendy Koch, "Quick to Save Lives, but Not to Take Credit," *USA Today*, August 25, 2006, 3A.

20. DiFazio's study is cited in Alexis S. Tan and Kermit Joseph Scruggs, "Does Exposure to Comic Book Violence Lead to Aggression in Children?" *Journalism Quarterly* 57 (Winter 1980): 579–583.

21. Frederick Wertham, *Seduction of the Innocent* (New York: Rinehart, 1954).

22. James P. Lones, "Nancy Drew, WASP Super Girl of the 1930s," *Journal of Popular Culture* 6 (Spring 1973): 712.

23. Joe Queenan, "Drawing on the Dark Side," *New York Times Magazine*, April 30, 1989.

24. Cass Sunstein, *Radicals in Robes* (New York: Basic Books, 2005), 229.

25. Stephen Breyer, *Active Liberty* (New York: Knopf, 2005), 55.

26. "Serenity Now Bombs a World of Warcraft Funeral," www.youtube.com/watch?v=IHJVolaC8pw.

27. For more on this issue, see Kevin Schut, "Games and the Culture of Destruction: Violence and Ethics in Video Games," in *Of Games & God: A Christian Exploration of Video Games* (Grand Rapids, MI: Brazos Press, 2013), chapter 4.

15

PROFITS, WEALTH, AND PUBLIC TRUST

Entertainment media in America are 90 percent business and 10 percent public service. Or are these figures too weighted toward public service? Gerry Spence, the well-known trial attorney, insists that "ratings are what television is about, not freedom, not truth. If American television could sell lies and falsehoods more profitably, we would never hear another word of truth."[1] Only the most unrepentant idealist would argue that social responsibility is a major consideration in most entertainment media decisions. If social benefits show up in the product, all well and good, but woe to the producer, director, editor, or recording executive whose product shows a financial loss, whatever the social gain. The profit motive is the most compelling concern in entertainment industry decisions; some observers insist it is the only concern.

As earlier parts of this book have indicated, the bottom line of profit and loss affects media of all types, but entertainment media feel the impact most directly. A major survey of executives in the motion-picture industry confirmed that here was a media system operating on essentially amoral criteria. A vice president of a major production and distribution company commented:

> There are no ethical decisions in the movie business. In a word, the profit motive renders ethics irrelevant. The only counterbalance is that certain individuals—and precious few at that—live their personal and professional lives according to some reasonably high standard.[2,3]

The first case in this chapter, "Copyrights and Cultures," raises two concerns: the moral infringements of pirated material and the morality of copyright laws that effectively disenfranchise vast populations from mainstream culture. "Deep Trouble for Harry" looks at the cost to actress Linda Lovelace of profits she never saw, in the first and perhaps most famous of all "porn" movies. Linda's issues, from another era altogether in terms of mediated sexual content, are still remarkably relevant. The third case, "Super Strip," points to an example of fairness that carries a note of human care when legal contracts did not require it. How rare is that? The fourth and fifth cases, "Duct Tape for TV" and *The Lone Ranger and Tentpoles*," ask whether truly great story-telling can survive, in television drama and on the big screen, in what appears to be weakening markets for creativity and novelty. The final case, "Faux Doc, Twice Baked," written by media scholar and producer Sam Smartt, notes moral limits on creativity when the story being told has a real history.

CASE 62. COPYRIGHT AND CULTURES

That new DVD you want will cost $18 to $60, depending on its packaging. The CD on your want-list will cost a little less and a download, less still, if you have an internet connection. That's the price of enjoying someone else's creativity. It's a price clearly pegged to the salary of a typical $10-an-hour worker who twice a month will spend a half-day's wage on take-home entertainment. The marketing system provides enough incentive to fuel the dreams of every garage band, and for the very talented, well, they land the big prize—more money than one person can spend. Consumers are happy, too, with unlimited use and reuse of the plastic they own, constrained only by the contract embedded in the small print, usually for home-use only.

Yet, in every major city around the world, you can buy counterfeits (unauthorized look-alikes that violate copyright) of nearly everything from Colgate toothpaste to computer software to this week's Hollywood releases. Chinese counterfeits are especially threatening to U.S. markets. Nearly two-thirds of all pirated goods seized at U.S. borders come from China. Many shops in Beijing, and especially at the Silk Street market, sell DVDs for less than $2. When Chinese President Hu Jintao visited the United States in 2006, his country's counterfeits were a major talking point. Not only is international law at stake but also the profits to be realized from China's immense market. U.S. entertainment giants have no way to tap that huge Chinese market unless the cost of counterfeiting exceeds the cost of copyright compliance. New Chinese legal initiatives are beginning to make that correction.

The U.S. Constitution, Article 1, Section 8, grants Congress the power to "promote the Progress of Science and useful Arts" by laws that protect intellectual property through a process we call "copyright." Anyone can use this law to protect a creative, original expression, saving its value for his or her own discretionary exploitation. The copyright process is among the simplest our government has ever devised. *Enforcing* your copyright gets complicated, but many creators do it successfully.

The heart of this protection is the exclusive right of the creator to determine the distribution of his or her work. And the phenomenal success of this protection is the most vibrant film, TV, book, writing, singing, acting, drawing, sculpting, dancing, composing etc.

industries in the world—and, one can easily surmise, in the entire history of the world. This is the American dream: the opportunity to make something new and capitalize on it. Without copyright protection, the super-affluent stars of Hollywood, Vegas, and New York would be working day jobs wherever.

But the system suffers one gaping blind spot. No, it's not the cheap-shot easiness of breaking the law here and there, copying a friend's CD or photocopying a high-priced text-book. The system still works despite these violations. Copyright's blind spot is the immense difference in economies between the affluent West and Middle East—and everywhere else.

Copyright, including international copyright, legally forecloses vast populations from enjoying the culture products marketed for profit by Western standards. When you earn the equivalent of $1.50 a day, you're not going to hear Tchaikovsky's Concerto No. 1 on that $24 Van Cliburn CD or pay $75 to get a back-row seat to hear him play it.

Federico Mayor makes the case clearly in his turn-of-the-century review of the developing world:

> Creation and innovation are certainly favored by adequate rights protection. But too much protection works against the interests of rights-holders and users. Over-restrictive intellectual property rights lead to secure incomes [and] monopolies without benefiting public interest in any way.[4]

This kind of appeal does not cut the cake for Louis Vuitton and four other international designers who recently hired the law firm of Baker & McKenzie to prosecute Beijing's counterfeiters. They want pirating stopped, and China seems to be making new efforts. A six-person team of intellectual property rights investigators was added to the police arm of China's Ministry of Public Security. Bounty hunters can earn up to $37,000 for a tip-off that exposes an underground DVD operation. An exhibition at Beijing's Military Museum of the Chinese People's Revolution now features intellectual property protection—a symbolic nod, at least, to China's commitment to link hands with other nations promoting the "Useful Arts."[5]

Mayor, however, thinks that better policing is not the long-term answer. He insists that we "broaden the notion of public domain and bring down the norms and standards currently used so as to offer free competition, free circulation of ideas, and creativity in all cultures." He advocates the idea of "copyleft," where authors reduce their control to "moral rights," a British common-law term that denotes the right of an author to keep his or her work intact, its meaning and character as he or she created and intended it.[6] In Mayor's view, the world's poor still would be required to pay for material, but the cost of access to world creativity would be proportionate to their ability to pay.

The problem of a fair return on creative material and increased access for cultures with lower gross national products should not present moral theory with insurmountable problems. No moral theory coaches us to eliminate all private interests, and none legitimizes a purely free and viciously competitive marketplace. The founders of the United States recognized the limits to property protection when they put a clock on intellectual property protection. Unfortunately, that clock has been reset by corporate reluctance to give up control. The Bono Amendment to the U.S. Copyright Act of 1976 was inspired by Disney's horror at Mickey Mouse going into the public domain. Mayor, speaking for the developing world, would urge us to resist those efforts to hold property for yet another twenty years of profit and control. He urges a shorter period of protected use before a work is legally open to all.

You Think?

▦   People cheat and steal all the time. It's as common as whistling, and maybe as morally neutral. Do you agree?

▦   Some situations need a Robin Hood. Other situations need precise moral clarity and utter honesty. How do you discern what a situation needs?

Mayor advises that we readjust our mean between profit and public good, that creators enjoy distribution rights and find their market but not to the point where only criminals and the wealthy have access to literature and art. A golden mean of equitable copyright might include adjusting a creator's and distributor's profit to local economies or providing "public copies" for communal use through agencies designed to serve the needs of the economic underclass.

At the same time, there is no moral justification for the widespread illegal copying of protected material among collegiate Americans, whose pocket change exceeds the weekly wages of most of the world's workers by many times. Only greed inspires the easy use of technology to usurp the real claims of copyright.

CASE 63. DEEP TROUBLE FOR HARRY

By any definition, *Deep Throat* is a pornographic film. Released at the crest of the sexual revolution, the film tells the story of a frustrated young woman (played by Linda Lovelace) who cannot "hear bells" during orgasm, no matter who is the partner. She consults a psychiatrist (played by Harry Reems), who diagnoses her problem as freakish: she has a clitoris in her throat. The promiscuous doctor then joins a long line of other bell ringers who gratify themselves on, according to the *New York Times*, "virtuoso talent for fellatio."[7]

Neither Reems nor Lovelace had great acting talent, and neither found fortune in this film that grossed $600 million. Reems had done bit parts in the National Shakespeare Company and other theaters when director Jerry Gerard invited him to join the production crew of this new "white-coater," a porn genre specializing in portraying flaky doctors. Reems was paid $100 for two scenes, then waived all editing, marketing, and distribution rights to the movie. Two years later, Reems was indicted as part of an alleged nationwide conspiracy to profit from the interstate commerce of an obscene movie. He became the first performer to be prosecuted on federal charges for artistic work—a dubious honor. Reems was convicted in Memphis but, on appeal, the government declined to retry the case (following the U.S. Supreme Court's 1974 *Miller* decision).

Deep Throat made Lovelace a sex queen. Her starring role helped produce the most successful porn film ever made to that time. The same film typecast her and essentially ended her career, but not before silicone injections enlarged her breasts and tainted blood gave her hepatitis. Wrote Lovelace: "I was a robot who did what I had to do to survive." Her first husband earned $1250 for Linda's role in *Deep Throat*; she never saw a penny.

Lovelace quit her movie career, remarried, and moved to Long Island. There she began to build a new identity, helping at her children's elementary school and giving lectures on the social and personal effects of pornography.

A liver transplant necessitated, she insisted, by the silicon injections she took to entertain men, lengthened her life but not her happiness. She divorced again, moved to Denver, where she worked for minimum wage, and died in 2002 at the age of fifty-three from injuries sustained in an automobile accident. In the last year of her life, she finally saw the entire movie from start to finish. Still trying to shake her star status, she remarked about the film: "What's the big deal?"

Civil libertarians point out that twenty-three states banned *Deep Throat* at some point during the ten years after its release. In one important legal battle in Texas, a nuisance abatement strategy was turned back by the federal appeals court and the U.S. Supreme Court as a dangerous movement toward prior restraint.

Whether the film deserved suppression at all is both a legal and moral problem. In a customs case in Massachusetts concerning the confiscation of a film print, the court heard an expert witness say that *Deep Throat* "puts forth an idea of greater liberation with regard to human sexuality and to the expression of it" that would help "many women" overcome particular sexual fears. Yet, to argue that *Deep Throat*'s blatant appeal to lasciviousness has redeeming social benefits that warrant First Amendment protection is really to nullify common definitions of obscenity. Only a First Amendment absolutist can effectively maintain that this film should be freely allowed to find its audience. Only the true believer in laissez-faire popular culture would want marketeers of this film to be let loose on the populace at large.

In its much-maligned *Final Report*, the Attorney General's Commission on Pornography created five broad categories of material around which to organize its ninety-two recommendations. The first two categories—sexually violent material and nonviolent materials depicting degradation, domination, subordination, or humiliation—were deemed harmful by most of the commission. Class IV, nudity, was an innocuous category that included both classical art and toddlers bouncing around in naked innocence. Class V ("the special horror of child pornography") was so blatantly exploitative that commissioners urged the strongest measures to disrupt and prosecute this market. But the Class III category (nonviolent and nondegrading materials) was the most controversial.[8] It included portrayals of consensual and equal vaginal intercourse and oral–genital activity or "two couples simultaneously engaging in the same activity." The commission could not cite any film titles that fit this category, so perhaps *Deep Throat* was, in the minds of commission members, an example of Class II. Yet many people would claim that *Deep Throat* and other nonviolent pornographic films are mere entertainment that hurt no one (in a demonstrably causal fashion) and attract no one other than interested, paying customers. As long as unsupervised children are not permitted to rent the video, the market logic goes, let adults choose *Deep Throat* if they wish. And obviously many wish.

But the free-market argument would pass no muster with Linda Lovelace Marchiano. She was the Agent Orange victim of pornographic profiteering, her body devastated by the chemicals that made her appealing and the trauma that made her desperate.[9]

And the free-market argument also must face the fact that this movie was a financial boon for organized crime. On a $25,000 investment, the Colombo crime family made well over $50 million on *Deep Throat*, with some of the profits being directed to Caribbean drug-smuggling operations.[10]

A principled market cannot exploit (in this case, it was a form of slavery) and abuse its artisans, and it cannot tolerate siphoning wealth into criminal empire building. The porn-film business, with *Deep Throat* a shaded example, is too regularly guilty of each count to warrant waving a free-market flag in its defense. Freedom, Kant argued, is in the pursuit of right reason. Freedom, Reinhold Niebuhr and his compatriots would urge, is in overcoming greed and prurience through a movement of love guarded by justice. Exploring sexuality in film is inherently a good goal, but this porn film was a heist on humanity. No market potency can justify destroying a life.

A real white-coater who sat on the attorney general's commission, Park Elliott Dietz of the University of Virginia, stated, as the work concluded:

> As a government body, we studiously avoided making judgments on behalf of the government about the morality of particular sexual acts between consenting adults or their depiction in pornography. This avoidance, however, should not be mistaken for the absence of moral sentiment among the Commissioners. I, for one, have no hesitation in condemning nearly every specimen of pornography that we have examined in the course of our deliberations as tasteless, offensive, lewd, and indecent. . . . It has been nearly two centuries since Phillipe Pinel struck the chains from the mentally ill and more than a century since Abraham Lincoln struck the chains from America's black slaves. With this statement I ask you, America, to strike the chains from America's women and children, to free them from the bond of pornography, to free them from the bonds of sexual abuse, to free them from the bonds of inner torment that entrap the second-class citizen in an otherwise free nation.[11]

CASE 64. SUPER STRIP

Jerry Siegel and Joe Shuster were high-school students in Cleveland, Ohio, when they came upon the idea of a cartoon figure who, born in a distant galaxy, would escape to Earth as a baby, grow up in an orphanage, and as an adult, impervious to gravity and mightier than a locomotive, would aid the forces of justice in their battle against evil.

Siegel actually conceived the idea. His buddy Shuster liked to draw. So the two fledgling cartoonists set out to sell their story. Five years of pounding on doors finally won them a contract with Detective Comics, and the first "Superman" strip appeared in 1938. Siegel and Shuster were paid $10 a page for their work, about $15 a week per man.[12]

The contract favored the company. The more popular Superman became, the clearer was Siegel and Shuster's loss. Finally, they brought suit against Detective Comics and were awarded some money, but still they had no rights to their hero. When the legal dust settled, Detective fired Siegel and Shuster, and the two creators were left to watch others get rich and famous off their idea. More lawsuits proved futile. With legal routes exhausted, the men defied the advice of their attorneys and went public with their story.

Their tale was one of sadness and struggle. Neither man had received any money from Superman sales since 1948, though profits from the Man of Steel were in the multimillions. Shuster now was legally blind, living in Queens with a brother who supported him. Siegel was ill and lived with his wife in a tiny apartment in Los Angeles, where he worked as a government clerk typist for $7000 a year. The men appealed to Superman's current copyright owner "out of a sense of moral obligation," said Shuster. The National Cartoonists Society and Cartoonists Guild lent their full backing to Siegel and Shuster's moral claim.

The appeal brought results. Warner Communications, which owned movie rights to Superman, claimed "no legal obligation," but "there is a moral obligation on our part." Two days before Christmas, Siegel and Shuster signed a contract with Warner: They would each receive $20,000 yearly for life, and their heirs also would be helped. The creators' names would appear on all Superman productions. At the signing, a Warner executive commended the two cartoonists. The contract, he said, was "in recognition of their past services and out of concern for their present circumstances."

The money awarded Siegel and Shuster presented no threat to the profits of Warner Communications. The sum of $40,000 a year may be less than the company spends in processing receipts from Superman sales. But, as a gesture neither required by law nor essential to public relations, it represents an application of the Judeo-Christian ethic of other-mindedness.

Consider the dynamics of the award. Siegel and Shuster had sold their idea under the duress of the Depression and at a time in their youth when neither could be expected to negotiate a contract with business savvy. Events had changed dramatically since then. One had become disabled, the other ill; both were living on a bare-bones income. Exhausted by fruitless legal efforts, they nonetheless persisted in a moral claim for some relief.

Warner could have called their appeal a nuisance. Business is business, after all. Investors who cash in stock certificates, for example, never qualify for *ex post facto* profits. Farmers who sell a corn crop in November may not appeal for extra payment when the bushel price rises in January. Buyers and sellers each assume part of the risk, and each understands that one could emerge from the deal a clear winner. Because the terms are understood, the bargain is fair.

But contracts are not independent from the economic milieu in which they are made. Were they selling a cartoon character today instead of in 1938, Siegel and Shuster might negotiate for a compensation clause should their idea become a bonanza. Indeed, they could have insisted that direct successors to their character, should Superman ever die (inconceivable until he met his fate in 1992 saving the world from Doomsday), be part of their legacy also. The economic climate of the late 1930s was not ripe for such risk-reducing appendices.

So the recognition awarded Siegel and Shuster was for the cartoonists a humanitarian gesture of life-sustaining aid, whereas to Warner it represented no loss to shareholders and no risk to corporate solvency. Perhaps a thorough application of "others as ourselves" or Rawls's ethic of undifferentiated negotiators would have resulted in larger awards or royalties for Siegel and Shuster or a cost-of-living adjustment in their $20,000 annual amount or life-insurance policies to establish an estate for each man. Maybe so. It may be argued that Warner hemmed and hawed until it was expedient for it to make a gesture, quite apart from what was fair for the two poor cartoonists. But the award, such as it was, points to a residual sense of group solidarity and caring, a dissonant but hopeful interlude in the normally amoral entertainment business.

CASE 65. DUCT TAPE FOR TV

Television critics are still raving over the success of ABC's six seasons of *Lost*, the story of survivors of Oceanic flight 815, downed on a Pacific island that won't behave itself. The now famous band faced threats from polar bears in a bamboo forest to a pack of "Others" who seemed like Vikings in their sensibilities and Visigoths in their appetites. The plot of *Lost* is nearly impossible to summarize, with twists and turns, characters in and out, and time zones intermingled. If you were an avid viewer from day one or later on DVD, you know *Lost*'s intriguing complexity. This show was unique, if sometimes an overload of never-ending plot twists.

Lost's problem, however, was a record of diminishing returns for the Walt Disney Company, owner of ABC. In 1983, the finale of *M*A*S*H* drew 105 million viewers and *Cheers* drew 80 million in 1993. *Lost* drew only 13 million in 2010, despite weeks of advertising and marketing buildup. The finale's 142 ads (in 150 minutes of television) rang up as much as $90,000 per thirty seconds, whereas the finale of *Friends* in 2004 pulled in $2 million for the same half minute.[13] During the same week that *Lost* said goodbye, *NCIS*'s weekly episode drew three million more viewers. Producers Carlton Cuse and Damon Lindelof gave their fan base an extraordinary drama, but their financial base was rated as a so-so performance.

Not since the scripts of the writer Horton Foote has television seen such transcendence, mystery, and a longing for the big answers. *Lost* supplied all of that, along with feats of the imagination that caused viewers to revel, to examine, to dissect, and then, finally, to let go. Much of what begged for explanation in the finale was left hanging. Only the big question— "Why are we here?"— was confronted, and then, answers only raised a host of new questions. Most critics praised the six-season show, including the decision in the third season to end the show on time, despite popularity, before the story ran amuck.

Foote's dramas (*Tender Mercies*, *Trip to Bountiful*, *To Kill a Mockingbird*) were tough viewing but redemptive. Religious themes and images appeared not only as backdrop to a culture but also as important elements to people sorting out their woes and recovering their loves. When Robert Duvall played the sloshed country singer Mac Sledge opposite Tess Harper as Rosa Lee in *Tender Mercies*, Foote used a title directly from the Psalms and brought his plot to its dramatic peak with a baptism. *Lost* was neither tied to the Bible nor so clear-cut in its references that one faith, more than any other, could claim symbolic preference. Yet symbols abounded throughout the show, including the dramatic drink wherein the mysterious woman, then Jacob, and then Jack commissioned their disciples: "Now you're like me." The stained-glass window in the final scenes displayed a panoply of world faiths, while the dramatically lit Christ statue outside the church tied the island's mystery light to Christian Shepherd's whiteout as his son Jack and others embraced their true loves. Evil, brutality, greed, subterfuge, physics, time travel, fear, and finally sheer mortality gave *Lost* its confounded twists, its pretzeled plot. The leader of the Dharma Initiative, at first the embodiment of oppression, becomes at the end the MC of a concert, not great by musical standards but the right note as sound track for new life begun and lost loves found—Dharma comes through. Explain all that? No way, just experience it, and maybe hope for brief glimpses.

In the finale, tough guy Miles Straume (Ken Leung) is sent below to fix a break in the hydraulics of the aircraft that will take survivors off the quaking island. Miles is shown wrapping some gizmo at the aircraft's front strut, remarking: "I don't trust in much, but I do trust in duct tape." Were all television shows the quality and depth of *Lost*, viewers might beg for pablum, something simple with just enough plot to justify the time wasted sitting and glaring. But American commercial television should not forsake the expense, complexity, and probe into the human condition that *Lost* once offered. If only as duct tape in the world of TV, *Lost* resonated to a public interested enough in mind–soul entertainment that its producers were commissioned to produce, its actors to act, and its financiers to take what they got. Once in a while, we, the world's most over-entertained people, can handle it.

CASE 66. *THE LONE RANGER* AND TENTPOLES

"Justice is what I seek," said Montesquieu, or was it Jefferson or John Stuart Mill? Wait, bro, hold your horses, it was Tonto, faithful companion to the Lone Ranger in the script written by Justin Haythe and Ted Elliott for the 2013 Western drama produced by Jerry Bruckheimer, the one Disney hoped would bring the "Hi-Yo, Silver! Away!" guy back into public play. The masked man was, after all, a childhood hero to Baby Boomers—why not to Generation Y and those following?

The Tonto quote was only one of several in the quirky, mixed-message script that doomed this remake. Reviews were vicious. B. H. Martin of "At the Movies" wrote about "a train wreck of a Western, a deeply boring film . . . The Lone Ranger is a noisy, never-ending nonsensical mess, which easily tops the flops in a silly season of summer blockbusters."[14] Opinions such as that put the $225 million production under expected revenues, despite its railroad stunts and Johnny Depp-style humor. Critic Jason Best called *The Lone Ranger* "overlong, over indulgent and totally uneven" but allowed that the "critical and commercial flop" is still a "breathtaking visual spectacle."[15]

There were issues of political correctness as well. Liam Lacey in Toronto wondered why Disney and its filmmaking professionals would choose "a bit of mid-20th-century cowboy kitsch" for another box-office go-around. The story of a masked Ranger and his native sidekick (played by a white actor) was "neither in demand nor politically sensitive. When it comes to mining boy's adventure stories . . . pirates may be fair game . . . but . . . western justice and Native Americans? Not so much."[16]

In its relatively short run, *The Lone Ranger* reaped $89 million, roughly 40 percent of its production costs. Viewers ratings on Rotten Tomatoes were 4.9/10. Peter Travers's comment in *Rolling Stone* did not help ticket sales: "Your expectations of how bad The Lone Ranger is can't trump the reality."[17]

Spin ahead two years to the 2015 flop *Rock the Kasbah*— a Western set in Afghanistan— starring Bill Murray, called "atrocious, cheesy and cynical," and duly avoided by nearly everyone at its debut. Is Hollywood misjudging its audience? Well, maybe so, maybe not. Two weekends following Murray's empty-seater, Daniel Craig's (007) *Spectre*, though poorly reviewed, and *The Peanuts Movie* (which needs no introduction unless you're under twenty-two), made movie exhibitors and big-screen viewers happy again.[18] Box-office headlines exploded again late in 2015 with the all-time blockbuster *Star Wars: The Force Awakens*, compelling evidence that tentpoles can hold up, when oldies refurbish with élan and originality, drama and charisma, character development and scenery integrity. In the hands of the right team, perhaps the masked man of yesteryear will have his Hi-Yo again, down the big-screen road.

The Lone Ranger first appeared (in audio form) as a radio drama in 1933 on WXYZ Detroit. Its long history on the air included a successful TV series (1949–1957 starring Clayton

Moore and Jay Silverheels). The show made Rossini's "William Tell Overture" one of the most recognized pieces of music in America. Then followed seven motion pictures, beginning in 1938, and spin-offs aplenty: toys, novels, comic books and strips, and parodies and spoofs. *The Lone Ranger* is a story that has made a lot of people rich and a lot of youngsters a tad more conscious of "the fight for law and order in those thrilling days of yesteryear"–the show's introductory tag.

Lynda Obst, Hollywood producer, explains why films like *The Lone Ranger* constitute the "New Abnormal," her term for Hollywood's big change from original scripts to market-driven remakes. She writes: "In the last ten years or so, the studios have tried to patent a formula for surefire hits," called "tentpoles" in the industry. They are sequels, prequels, and reboots, designed by committee (and Ms. Obst does not mean the Creative Committee) "meant to work with or without a star and have a built-in audience in the United States and overseas."[19]

Marketing departments run the culture industries more aggressively now than ever. International box office accounts for 70 percent of revenue. "These huge tentpoles, $200-million-fueled missiles, are lined up on the studio distribution pads . . . like international thermonuclear devices toward foreign capitals."[20] George Lucas's *Star Wars* was the model. We all know titles in its wake: *Harry Potter*, *Transformers*, *Twilight*, *Pirates*, to name a few.

Is there room now in Hollywood for the original story? Not much room, claims Ms. Obst: "Movies are now an endangered species in the very place that make them."[21] Films such as *Field of Dreams* and *Forrest Gump* would never get made in the "New Abnormal," she says, where near-guaranteed international audiences have replaced DVD sales as backup to the so-so American box office. Stories produced today must be recognizable overseas, understandable in translation, and entertaining. Comedy is in trouble, since humor is most difficult to export; historicals and musicals too. Positive buzz yields production approvals, not the traditional pitch meetings where, Obst recalls, creative possibilities were the "superfood of the life of Hollywood."[22]

You Think?

■   If you must choose between producing sequels (low on creativity, high on revenue) or producing creative drama (and not necessarily getting rich), how do you make the decision?

■   Why do you still pay to see a film on a big screen? Is there virtue in supporting film as a big-screen art form?

Markets are vital to any industry. Too many films like *The Lone Ranger* in a row and deficits bury the future of any business. Movie attendance is voluntary, not government mandated, so appeal and art and other intangibles not available to statistical analysis must make audiences happy they attended.

An odd but discernible resonance brings people and artists to the entertainment venue. Responsibility rests on both sides: producers must entertain with language and visuals lifting people temporarily from the humdrum reality, sometimes even inspiring them, at the least contributing to their cultural literacy; audiences must pay for it, a slice (growing slice, we note) of their seemingly shrinking monthly income devoted to refreshment and sometimes enrichment.

The "New Abnormal" changes the terms. The studios, once "caretakers of an indigenous art form" are in the process of "relinquishing responsibility for that art form altogether. Sure, it was always show *business*, never show *art*. But now it is *business* business."[23]

Ms. Obst's plea for balance and creativity has yet to reverberate in the studios. After *The Lone Ranger*'s stunning losses (estimated at $160–$190 million) Disney chief executive Robert Iger said: "We still believe that a tentpole strategy is a good strategy–big story, big cast . . . big budget . . . and big marketing."[24] Hi-Yo, silver (the metallic currency kind) Away!

CASE 67. FAUX DOC, TWICE BAKED

In 2005 Robert Houston and Robert Hudson took home the Academy Award for Best Documentary Short with their inspirational portrayal of the 1963 "Children's Crusade" in Birmingham, Alabama. *Mighty Times: The Children's March* tells the compelling story of thousands of Birmingham children who abandoned their classrooms en masse and marched on Birmingham, despite Civil Rights leaders' misgivings about their exposure to police violence. Hundreds of children were arrested, many of them more than once, and their courage ultimately led to talks with Birmingham's mayor and the intervention of President John F. Kennedy. The film features a dramatic soundtrack and uses archival footage to bring powerful moments in history to life–but there's a catch.

Shortly after the Academy Awards, complaints began rolling in about the filmmakers' blended use of archival footage and scripted reenactment. As it turned out, the makers had filmed over 700 extras with trained dogs, period automobiles, firefighters, and police in Southern California. What's more, they shot on old film stock and digitally altered the footage to match the authentic archival footage as much as possible.[25]

The filmmakers did not shy away from these criticisms, but embraced them as a technique they called "faux doc." Director Robert Houston said:

> The way we make our films is like baking a biscotti. We make a classic documentary using the archival record. We then make another layer of film. We bake the cookie twice, like a biscotti. That second layer of film fills in the gaps, and what you end up with is a seamless telling and definitive telling of unknown chapters from civil rights history.[26]

Houston and Hudson's previous film, *The Legacy of Rosa Parks*, which was the first installment of the *Mighty Times* series, also employed "faux doc." But there was one significant difference: with *Rosa Parks*, the filmmakers employed a device when reenacted footage was being used—a "visual footnote"[27] of shadowy film sprockets running along the right side of the screen. Interestingly, *Rosa Parks* was nominated for the Academy Award but did not win. Two years later with *Children's March*, Hudson and Houston captured the Oscar . . . without the sprockets.[28]

Shortly after the Awards, documentary filmmaker Steve Kalafer wrote to the Academy calling Hudson and Houston's technique an "intentional deception." Kalafer had produced *Sister Rose's Passion*, one of the films *The Children's March* beat out for the Oscar that year. "In comparing the two films," Kalafer said, "it is clear that they chose to realize the full potential of their 'faux doc' technique, raising it to a new level as a well-crafted, cunningly deceitful art form – but not documentary filmmaking." [29]

Houston said the reason the sprockets were left out of *The Children's March* was that HBO preferred it to be broadcast without them—a claim that an HBO spokesperson later denied—and that *Rosa Parks* had been on HBO "for two years without film sprockets."[30] The final DVD release of the film—which was only available for educational use through the Southern Poverty Law Center—included both the sprockets and a disclaimer at the beginning of the film stating: "Portions of this film were reenacted using vintage cameras and film stocks."[31]

To complicate matters, Houston and Hudson also used authentic archival material from other events in the Civil Rights Movement, edited into the film to look as if they were in Birmingham. Jon Else, documentary filmmaker and series producer for *Eyes on the Prize: America's Civil Rights Years*, pointed out that *The Children's March* contains some footage from the Watts Riots in Los Angeles in 1965, as well as at least one shot from the Little Rock school desegregation crisis in 1957.[32] Though the treatment of reenactments is the focus of our discussion here, the questionable use of the actual archival record might be considered the icing on the biscotti.

Documentary filmmakers frequently make use of reenactment for testimony representation—the visualization of a story authentically told by someone who was there. These reenactments typically have some sort of stylistic marker that helps viewers differentiate them from the rest of the film. Errol Morris, a documentary filmmaker who frequently uses reenactments in his films, shared his philosophy on the subject in a 2008 *New York Times* article: "My re-enactments focus our attention on some specific detail or object that helps us look beyond the surface of images to something hidden, something deeper—something that better captures what really happened."[33]

Such scenes in Morris's films, on the one hand, call attention to themselves as reenactments. Even in documentaries such as *Nanook of the North*, however, in which the director took liberties in staging certain scenes that are almost entirely fictional, this approach usually indicates an overall looser commitment to historical accuracy, and is not mixed with authentic samples of the archival record in order to piggyback on their veracity.

Houston and Hudson, on the other hand, were criticized for editing their reenactments together with authentic archival footage in a way that would be difficult—if not impossible—for the audience to discern. As Jon Else puts it: "The audience doesn't know the difference between the real Bull Conner and the actor Bull Conner."[34] Morris stated it more strongly: "Surely, this is not a question about re-enactments. It's a question about fraud. . . . But to what end?" [35]

To what end, indeed? The filmmakers certainly seem to have nobler intentions than simply profiting from a successful film. The *Mighty Times* series was co-funded by HBO and the Southern Poverty Law Center, and was intended from the beginning for educational use. The DVD was never released commercially. Thousands of children have undoubtedly been made aware of an extremely important Civil Rights story that they otherwise might never have heard of. This certainly seems to be a compelling argument, but is it worth the cost? What is the sanctity of the historical record?

You Think?

■ Do filmmakers have an obligation to help their audience distinguish between archival footage and reenactment? What is the sanctity of the archival record? Does archival footage provide a healthy tether for our imagination when dramatizing history?

■ Are there other incentives besides financial gain that could motivate us to stretch the truth? When do aesthetic and even educational considerations outweigh the need to be faithful to the facts?

The Children's March also brings up troubling questions about media literacy. A similar debate over docudrama centers around whether viewers should be educated to take the facts presented in a historical fiction film with a grain of salt. In documentary, however, the bar for historical accuracy is higher. When the Academy of Motion Picture Arts and Sciences bestows its highest honor on a film employing the "faux doc" technique, we find ourselves in dangerous waters. It would only be natural for viewers to "let their guard down," so to speak, when watching an Oscar-winning documentary, unaware that the filmmakers had made a concerted effort to keep them from recognizing the difference between the actual archival footage and reenactments. Ultimately, this "intent to deceive" is the crucial problem with *The Children's March*. Somewhere before "faux doc," there's a line of truth and falsehood that should not be twice baked.

NOTES

1. Gerry Spence, *From Freedom to Slavery* (New York: St. Martin's Griffin, 1995), 177.
2. See Clifford Christians and Kim B. Rotzoll, "Ethical Issues in the Film Industry," in Bruce A. Austin, ed., *Current Research in Film: Audiences, Economics, and Law*, vol. 2 (Norwood, NJ: Ablex, 1986), 225–237.

3. "Whose Values Run Hollywood?" *USA Weekend*, October 23–25, 1992, 8.

4. Federico Mayor, *The World Ahead: Our Future in the Making* (New York: UNESCO, 2001), 300–301.

5. "China Grows More Aggressive in Thwarting Counterfeits," *USA Today*, April 21, 2006, 4B.

6. Ibid.

7. Quotation and background material from Edward de Grazia and Roger K. Newman, *Banned Films: Movies, Censors, and the First Amendment* (New York: R. R. Bowker, 1982).

8. United States Attorney General's Commission on Pornography (1986). The report is summarized in Michael J. McManus, *Final Report of the Attorney General's Commission on Pornography* (Nashville: Rutledge Hill Press, 1986), xix–xxi.

9. Linda Lovelace has written (with Mike McGrady) on her experience in prostitution and pornography, her victimization, terror, and exploitation in *Ordeal* (New York: Bell Publishing, 1980).

10. McManus, *Final Report*, 295.

11. Ibid., 491–492.

12. Material in this case is from the *New York Times*, November 22 and December 10 and 24, 1975.

13. Shira Ovide and Suzanne Vranica, "'Lost' Finale Finds a Base, but Not Too Many Others," *Wall Street Journal*, May 25, 2010, B8.

14. Brian Henry Martin, "Who Killed the Lone Ranger?" Originally from At the Movies, August 15, 2013, www.rottentomatoes.com/critic/brian-henry-martin/movies.

15. Jason Best, "Movie Talk: The Lone Ranger," August 10, 2013, www.whatsontv.co.uk/blog/movietalk/the-lone-ranger-johnny-depp-s-tonto-seizes-the-reins-in-sprawling-action-comedy-reboot.

16. Liam Lacey, "The Lone Ranger," *Toronto Globe and Mail*, July 3, 2013, www.theglobeandmail.com/arts/summer-entertainment/the-lone-ranger-cowboy-kitsch-meets-major-studio-spectacle/article12925938/.

17. Peter Travers, "The Lone Ranger," July 8, 2013, www.rollingstone.com/movies/reviews/the-lone-ranger-20130708.

18. Joe Queenan, "The Mystery of the Five Filmic Flops," *The Wall Street Journal*, November 1, 2015, C11, and Ben Fritz, "'Spectre' and 'The Peanuts Movie' Give Box Office a Welcome Boost," *Wall Street Journal*, November 9, 2015, www.wsj.com/articles/spectre-the-peanuts-movie-give-box-office-a-welcome-boost-1447023829.

19. Lynda Obst, *Sleepless in Hollywood* (New York: Simon and Shuster, 2013), 5.

20. Ibid., 7.

21. Ibid., 10.

22. Ibid., 23–24.

23. Ibid., 13.

24. Ben Fritz, "'Lone Ranger' Hurts Disney," *Wall Street Journal*, August 7, 2013, B1.

25. Irene Lacher, "Documentary Criticized for Re-enacted Scenes," *New York Times*, March 29, 2005, www.nytimes.com/2005/03/29/movies/documentary-criticized-for-reenacted-scenes.html?_r=0.

26. Joseph Lon Lanthier, "Do You Swear to Re-Enact the Truth? Dramatized Testimony in Documentary Film, International Documentary Association," Documentary.org, Spring 2011, www.documentary.org/magazine/do-you-swear-re-enact-truth-dramatized-testimony-documentary-film.

27. Ibid.

28. Lacher, "Documentary Criticized for Re-enacted Scenes."

29. Ibid.

30. Ibid.

31. *Mighty Times: The Children's March.* Dir. Robert Hudson, Tell the Truth Pictures, 2005. DVD.

32. Robert Siegel, "Documentary Film's Oscar Win Draws Complaints," *All Things Considered*, March 29, 2005, *NPR*, www.npr.org/templates/story/story.php?storyId=4566421.

33. Errol Morris, "Play It Again, Sam (Re-enactments, Part One)," Opinionator, *New York Times*, April 3, 2008, http://opinionator.blogs.nytimes.com/2008/04/03/play-it-again-sam-re-enactments-part-one/.

34. Siegel, "Documentary Film's Oscar Win Draws Complaints."

35. Morris, "Play It Again, Sam."

16

MEDIA SCOPE
AND DEPTH

For every medium there is a scale; we may call it an "aesthetic scale." On one end are the serious artists and producers, careful about the integrity of their craft and insistent that their labors give audiences a better insight into meaningful human life. On the other end are writers and producers who want to provide the most popular product possible. They care little if lofty artistic visions are part of their work; theirs is the task of attracting the largest possible share of the audience—because if they do not, competitors will. Success is measured by best-seller lists and Nielsen ratings.

The pull of the media's commercial base inevitably may lead to television programs, movies, and books that trivialize human dilemmas or escape entirely from them. Perhaps forces resisting such trends are too weak to activate much of a counterthrust. Yet only the cynic will claim that money is really all that matters in popular culture, and only a misty ideal-ist will assert that money does not matter at all.

Between the demands of art and the marketplace are a host of moral questions that media practitioners face every day: must art be compromised when it passes from one medium to another? Are stereotyped characters fair to real people? How far should com-mercial concerns dictate cultural products? What is a fair portrayal of a religious or ethnic character on television?

In the first case in this chapter, "Reel History," the story of the Nixon presidency is retold with glaring historical boldness. Against this background, we have to ask what is truth if it fails to make emotional sense? In the second case, "They Call it Paradise," we examine one of our most current vogues, reality television, with a particular look at *Paradise Hotel*, a program supposedly about love but more about anti-love, jealousy, fickleness, and young exhilaration gone sour. Did these contestants know what they were getting into? The third case, "Tragedy Lite," wonders if some human trauma goes too deep for fictionalized accounts of it. The fourth case, "Training in Virtue," written by media scholar John C. Carpenter, profiles an actor who approaches his part in the vast entertainment business with intentionality. He means something by it. Imagine!

Long before television, Louis Brandeis (a justice of the Supreme Court from 1916 to 1939) wrote: "Triviality destroys at once robustness of thought and delicacy of feeling. No enthusiasm can flourish, no generous impulse can survive under its blighting influence."[1] Ought we to wink at mass-mediated entertainment—its romance and simplicity—or is it our only way to survive the stress and strain of the twenty-first century?

CASE 68. REEL HISTORY

It was the most famous "nothing" in American history.

On June 17, 1972, five men broke into Democratic National Committee Headquarters at the Watergate office building in Washington, DC. What at first appeared to be a second-rate burglary turned into one of the most devastating political scandals of all time. Suspicion grew that President Richard Nixon knew of or even approved the break-in. When it was discovered that Nixon secretly taped conversations in his office, the special prosecutor in charge of the Watergate investigation demanded that the President hand over his tapes. After months of legal haggling, President Nixon relinquished some of the tapes, including one of a June 20, 1972 conversation between him and top aide Bob Haldeman. Right in the middle of the tape, prosecutors discovered eighteen and a half minutes of nothing—a blank space that interrupted the Nixon–Haldeman discussion about what to do concerning Watergate. Prosecutors quickly suspected that the tapes had been tampered with.

What was said during the missing eighteen and a half minutes has been a topic of speculation ever since. No one really knows what was said—until now. In his three-plus hour docudrama *Nixon*, writer and director Oliver Stone "revealed" that the tampered tapes contained a Nixon confession that he planned and supervised "Track II," a 1960 assassination plot against Cuban President Fidel Castro. Apparently, Nixon explained to Haldeman that the mission involved a cooperative effort between the CIA and the Mafia, but the election of John Kennedy thwarted the plan. The film hints at some connection between Nixon's work on Track II and the Kennedy assassination.

Critics of *Nixon* were livid, while fans cheered Stone's portraiture. Gene Siskel and Roger Ebert gave it an "epic thumbs up, way up,"[2] and other reviewers crowned it "brilliant," "intriguing," and "extraordinary."[3] Anthony Hopkins and Joan Allen (playing Richard and Pat Nixon, respectively) were rewarded with Best Actor and Best Actress nominations.

Others were less impressed, however. Howard Rosenberg blasted the film on ethical and aesthetic grounds,[4] whereas most critics launched their response against Stone's alleged cavalier handling of the historical record. Foremost among the complaints was the Castro assassination story line, but Track II was not the only bit of scriptwriting that had film critics and Nixon scholars scratching their heads. Among the other surprising "revelations":

■   Nixon secretly met with right-wing fanatics in the Texas desert. They promised to deliver the White House in 1964 if Nixon would run, and again in 1968, even if political victory meant the elimination of certain Kennedys along the way.

- These same extremists threatened to bring Nixon down in 1972 when they perceived he had become soft on the far-right agenda.
- Nixon was a heavy drinker, often inebriated in the presence of aides, albeit sober in public and with visiting dignitaries.
- Nixon lost the 1960 television debate to Kennedy because Kennedy divulged the Cuban invasion plans while Nixon, as vice president, could not discuss them.
- Nixon and wife Pat came close to divorce several times.

When Oliver Stone was publicly chided for such historical revisionism, he produced a screenplay annotated with hundreds of footnotes from more than 100 sources, an introduction containing twelve articles defending the accuracy of his film, and a 200-page bibliography of Watergate documents and tapes.[5]

What does it mean for a docudrama to "tell the truth"? Clearly, many historically questionable details and events were included in *Nixon* for the purpose of dramatic impact. Some events, such as a scene in which Nixon aide John Dean and burglar E. Howard Hunt meet on a bridge, definitely did not occur.[6] Other events, such as Nixon's involvement in the alleged Castro plot, or the meeting between Nixon and extremists in the Texas desert, are highly unlikely.[7] But, as Stone said, this type of loose commitment to historical accuracy has always been part of the genre.[8] One critic ruefully pointed out that an artistic retelling of history can be traced back at least as far as Shakespeare.[9] Stone is right when he reminds his critics that all observers of history, including filmmakers and professional historians, view the past through their own agendas and biographies.[10] What is important, Stone insists, is that storytellers get the "deeper truth" right.[11]

Los Angeles Times media critic David Shaw remarked that one of the worst examples of the dangers of docudrama was the CBS production of *The Atlanta Child Murders*, the story of convicted child-killer Wayne Williams (implicated in twenty-three homicides, convicted of two). The obvious slant of *The Atlanta Child Murders* portrayed Williams as the victim of circumstantial evidence. CBS did precede the two-part show with an advisory that the program "is not a documentary but a drama based on certain facts. . . . Some of the events and characters are fictionalized for dramatic purposes." Viewers were left to their own knowledge of the case to sort out the factual from the fictionalized scenes. Shaw called this kind of television product the "bastardization and confusion of fact and fiction."[12]

Professor Gregory Payne was a consultant to NBC during the making of *Kent State*, a docudrama of the May 4, 1970 National Guard shootings of four university students. Although he is a proponent of the docudrama genre, Payne has meticulously described the fictionalized interactions of the National Guard members and students in *Kent State*. For example, the burning of the ROTC (Reserve Officer Training Corps) building at Kent State on May 2 has never been definitively explained, and only last-minute insistence by consultants and actors kept those ambiguities intact. Payne observes that whatever were NBC's exaggerations (such as building much of the drama around the romance of Allison Krause, one of the four students), they were nothing compared with the distortions of James Michener's book *Kent State: What Happened and Why*.

At a conference in Boston, actor Rick Allen, who played guardsman Wesley in *Kent State*, noted that his portrayal of being overcome with tear gas and retreating from the line of march was pure fiction intended to humanize the "bad guys" and, in addition, to win a couple of seconds of additional on-camera time (valuable for a young actor). Allen was troubled that history was being written for thousands of viewers on the basis of a director's urging his people to ad-lib.

In 1988, the plight of surrogate mother Mary Beth Whitehead put a spotlight on the womb-for-hire business and its legality. Whose child was Baby M? Her natural mother's or William and Elizabeth Stern's, who held the contract? (William was the natural father through artificial insemination.) ABC would help the nation decide with a four-hour, $6 million docudrama. Since neither the Whiteheads nor the Sterns would cooperate, ABC used court transcripts, published accounts, and psychiatric evaluations made public with court records. Of course, the obligatory disclaimer preceding the telecast notes that "certain scenes and dialogue are interpretive of this material."[13]

In 1644, John Milton was confident that truth would emerge in a free marketplace of ideas. Though falsehood might grapple for a while, human rationality eventually would make the distinctions, because the universe could not end on a lie. In 1985, psychiatrist M. Scott Peck began to forge a new vocabulary based on clinical observations that in some people, deception becomes truth and leads to the grim realities that destroy their lives.[14] Perhaps human rationality is not as powerful as the great liberal democrats believed. And, if not, is truthtelling all the more a moral imperative, as fragile of understanding as we are?

Is the docudrama genre a powerful vehicle for reviving our culture's important stories or a cheap distortion based on television's insatiable need for new material?

In favor of docudrama: how many students would know or care about Kent State's Allison, Jeff, Sandy, and Bill were it not for the efforts of NBC, albeit profit-tinged, to give new life to that fateful spring weekend in northeast Ohio? Few, we suspect. How many dry eyes and stoic hearts walked out of theaters after *Mississippi Burning* (a film about three murdered civil rights workers that fictionalized the FBI investigation) unmoved by the suffering and careless about the future of racial justice? Journalist Bill Minor covered the Freedom Summer of 1964 and won the Elijah Lovejoy Award for "most courageous weekly editor in the nation" after his exposure of Klan activity in Mississippi. He defended *Mississippi Burning* as "a powerful portrayal." For viewers who depend on film for stories not experienced firsthand, the movie "got the spirit right."[15]

If a film re-creates the texture of an event such that participants can affirm the veracity of context and struggle, is that not sufficient? History is more than mere facts, and no story corresponds exactly to events. Perhaps the docudrama is our best vehicle for keeping at bay those who claim the Holocaust, for example, never occurred. Yet audiences can do amazing things with a story. One high-school audience admitted to believing, after seeing Stone's version of the 1960s, that Lyndon Johnson had conspired to murder John Kennedy. When confronted with that reaction, Oliver Stone replied: "I am not responsible for the interpretation that an audience takes away. Sometimes [the film] is misinterpreted."[16]

The crucial variable is the judgment of the subject. If a docudrama wins the approval of those closest to the real-life drama, viewers are ensured that a truthful perspective on events survives the dramatic process. If the subject cannot recognize his or her struggle for all the romantic clichés and garbled characterizations, we rightly worry that rampant revisionism threatens to obscure and distort the meaning of the past. Morally sensitive producers of docudrama will incorporate fictional elements without padding history or violating the pain of those whose stories they tell.

CASE 69. THEY CALL IT PARADISE

During summer off-season, television networks struggle for viewers. How to get the right ages, the right consumers, inside to watch television instead of outside under the sun or on the beach? Fox Television answers with a beach, a pool, and sun on the screen, populated by tanned young adults, bikinis, kissing contests, faded-gray shots of bedroom snuggling, and the "tension" of each contestant trying to ingratiate himself or herself to the others so as not to be forced to "leave paradise, *forever!*"

Paradise Hotel began its run in July. Each week a new player was added from among thousands of viewers applying to get on the show. Newcomers had to prove their sexuality to the group at the hotel, who coaxed libidinous data from each wannabe before voting admittance. And each week someone at the hotel had to leave, usually amid tears and bravado mixed to hide the shame of exclusion. Host Amanda Byram kept her sturdy demeanor throughout, as if she were den mother to these eleven young twenty-somethings assembled at a resort in Acapulco to do nothing but drink, play, and touch. Five couples shared rooms, but one person was always left out, cast into the black room, as it were. Cameras and microphones recorded the smooching, the primping, the push-ups, the sipping, and mostly the gossiping, as this "lords of the pool" group sorted out their all-important relationships and defended the one part of their person that this unscripted reality show sought to exploit—sexuality. Indeed, at the start of each episode, Byram admonished her troop—these ripped and supple post-teens were promised no money and given no incentive other than to prove their cool—you either hook up or pack up.

Reality television uses no scripts. The setup generates the story, but the ending is unpredictable. Stars are not so different from viewers, and in the genius of the creators of *Paradise*, viewers become stars each week. Of course, some sort of fuel must propel whatever happens, and that fuel is normally sex or wealth or both. For viewers, there's the mystique of a relationship built on the flimsiest basis: will it take? For contestants, there's a short moment of fame and, for some, the hope of a casting director's call.

Contestants on *Paradise*, however, were not promised money and were not likely to break into professional acting. The incentive then? Simply that eleven cuties get a free sandy-beach, big-king-bed vacation together. The setting called to mind the omnipresent cameras of *The Truman Show*, but, in this case, all eleven allowed their hormones to rage and their pettiness and sobbing to become entertainment for millions. Kant, frankly, could not approve. That might be a minuscule worry to producers of this show, as long as advertisers did approve. The persons on this show were means to an end, pure and simple. Though each player chose freely to come, the normal progression, visible any week, was elation ("What a cool place") to disillusionment. The sulky twenty-one-year-old waitress from St. Paul remarked: "They call it paradise, but it's not."

Reality television as a genre must face up to Kant's claim that each person should be valued; no one should be treated as fodder for another's exploitation. To violate this principle is more than "dissing" an eighteenth-century philosopher. It is, rather, to put human relationships in jeopardy. As the *Hartford Courant* editorialized: "America's ravenous appetite for 'unscripted' reality shows reflects a cultural emptiness in an era of over-stimulation." Jane Eisner, columnist for the *Philadelphia Inquirer*, added: "We chase after money, good health and educational status, thinking they bring happiness; we deride marriage and faith, not believing they bring happiness; we waste our time watching dumb entertainment." And producer Aaron Spelling cogently testified: "The reality trend makes me puke."[17]

Paradise Hotel is an opera of raging hormones played by emotionally vulnerable young adults led to believe that sun, surf, and sex represent the ultimate human environment. The ethic of duty and human care imagines that to prosper and mature, people must discover the resilience to endure trouble with hopefulness, to plot a course that contributes to others, and to satisfy the appetite for happiness indirectly—in vocation and service or in strong, long-term relationships. *Paradise Hotel* undermines our best wisdom about happiness with its visceral, short-lived, superficial unreality. Paradise it's not.

CASE 70. TRAGEDY LITE

When Roberto Benigni, the director, writer, and star of the 1998 film *Life Is Beautiful*, jumped up on his chair in his excitement to get his Oscars for Best Actor and Best Foreign Language Film, many people were thrilled with both his over-the-top acceptance speech and the film itself, a comic "fable" about the Holocaust. Others, however, including some concentration camp survivors, were far less pleased. Even at its initial screening, the film provoked widely differing reactions; some critics found it to be a uniquely uplifting triumph, whereas others were disgusted and greatly disturbed by it.

The first half of the film is the charming but conventional story of Guido, an Italian Jew, who falls in love and courts Dora, finally carrying her off, in true romantic style, on a white horse. In the second half of the film, however, the tone changes drastically when, in the midst of planning for a birthday party, Guido and his four-year-old son, Joshua, are taken away to a Nazi concentration camp. What makes the film unique, and also the cause of the controversy surrounding it, is that director Roberto Benigni presents even this second part of the film as a semicomic fable. We enter the world of one of the greatest horrors of the past century, but we find ourselves laughing and being uplifted. Benigni elicits these responses through a brilliant conceit: Guido must protect his son from the terrible reality around them by pretending that, as a surprise birthday present, they have come to the camp to participate in a game.

Guido begins by telling his son that they have joined an elaborate contest in which they compete with the other prisoners for the prize of a real tank. One of the best examples of the comic potential of this situation occurs when they first get to the camp. A German officer enters their barracks, and although Guido does not speak German, he offers to translate the camp instructions into Italian so that Joshua will only hear his invented rules for the "game." While the guard lists rules in German, Guido translates:

> You'll lose points for three things: One, if you cry. Two, if you want to see your mommy. Three, if you're hungry and you want a snack. . . . Don't ask for any lollipops. You won't get any. We eat them all.

Amazingly enough, Guido is able to pull off this major deception; this feat is partly possible because Benigni's camp has almost no violence or terror. Benigni does hint at those aspects of the concentration camps that he assumes his audience will recognize: the child's grandfather is sent to the showers, and the boy himself ignores the call for all the children to go take a shower and thus survives. Late in the film, however, there is one scene in which Guido is carrying the sleeping Joshua back to bed, and he stumbles upon a staggering mound of corpses in the mist. He backs away, and shortly after this, we see the chaos of the Germans leaving as the Allies enter the area to liberate it. Guido tells Joshua to hide for the last time, but he himself is caught by a guard and killed off-screen. Joshua has survived the Holocaust having never even realized he was experiencing anything but a game. A voiceover representing Joshua as an adult says: "This is the sacrifice my father made. This was the gift he gave to me." Even as the young Joshua is reunited with his mother, he gleefully shouts that they have won the game.

The controversy is seen in the extremes of the reactions of the reviewers. Some proclaimed it a masterpiece, but other critics wrote scathing opinions. The most notable of these have come from Jewish Holocaust survivors, who fear that such an easy-viewing version of the death camps may have too great an influence on younger viewers who likely never have seen more explicit narratives or documentaries. Some concentration camp survivors, however, greatly appreciated the film and felt that it showed respect for those who died in the camps.

Criticisms of the film generally focused around three separate but related issues. First, people condemned the complete lack of violence, terror, and the horrifying reality of the death camps. The film's camp was a sanitized version of the real thing. Children were not immediately taken from parents. Nazi officers did not shoot or even hit the deportees. Second, a number of critics argued that using the Holocaust for a comic fairy tale is always wrong because humor is completely out of place in such an event. And finally, others were offended that Benigni seemed to be presenting the message that love and imagination were all it took to overcome the horrors of concentration camps.

All three criticisms relate to the question of what ethical obligation a writer/director has in using an historical event that caused great pain to the survivors and the relatives of the millions of victims. Are all events fair game for comedy? Benigni, in response to the criticisms about his glossy presentation of a death camp, claimed that he never wanted to make a historically accurate Holocaust film and that he purposely referred only obliquely to some of the worst terrors. In a later interview with Graham Fuller, he said: "Historically the movie may have its inaccuracies. But it's a story about love, not a documentary. There's no explicit violence because it's not my style."[18]

The problem with the argument that life in concentration camps can only be portrayed with detailed historical accuracy is that films will always distort and fail to re-create what many have called "indescribable." If filmmakers are not allowed to even attempt their own versions of horrific events, with the awareness that their films have to be palatable to a general audience if they wish them to be seen, we will have few, if any, Holocaust films for viewing by the general public. Film representations do educate and provoke controversies that then allow for further education. If artists do not feel the freedom to use the Holocaust story, the memory of it will fade, particularly for those people who do not have the stories of survivors as part of their family inheritance. So a demand for strict historical accuracy or true-to-life details would seem counterproductive in the end. But what about changing a horrifically tragic event into a comic, life-affirming tale?

You Think?

■   Is it morally OK to laugh at our own struggles . . . at other people's struggles?
■   Could laughter be an antidote to despair? (And despair is never morally OK, don't you think?)

The problem in re-creating a painful, terrifying period of time in which survivors and relatives are still affected by the presentation is not only related to the filmmaker's historical accuracy or attention to detail but also to the message that accompanies the story. To present a fairly comic, sanitized death camp is to use our collective memories of what these camps were really like. This is problematic for both younger viewers who may not have many other visual memories of this period and for those for whom the actual memories contrast so greatly with this picture. If you combine this picture with a message that evil can be survived and transcended through love and imagination, you add to this feeling: you are using our sense of the "worst" moments a person can go through to give a message of hope or survival that seems at odds with the experiences of most of those who actually lived in these camps. The film may just be a fable, but it is a fable that is using our memories of a real event. One Holocaust survivor, Daniel Vogelmann, reports of his own father's return from Auschwitz without his child (Vogelmann sardonically notes his father was evidently not able to save his child with a clever story).[19] He contrasts Benigni's comic and triumphant view of life with his father's who was able to proclaim that life was beautiful, but only with pain in his voice. For Vogelmann and others, the problem seems to be not merely the combination of humor and a death camp but also a sense of a too easy and glib response to the evils that were experienced.

At the same time, Benigni was clearly aware of the risk he was taking in making a comedy about the Holocaust. One can certainly appreciate his ability to create a fable that in the end supports the values of courage, sacrifice, love, and compassion that were opposed by the Nazis. Individual moments in the film show great restraint and concern that his depiction of the camps does not show any disrespect to the victims of Nazi violence. Benigni made a Holocaust film that can be seen by children—and this feat is both a triumph and a terror.

In fact, life is beautiful, tragic, hopeful, and desperate. An artist's vision of life may be outrageous but morally justifiable if those closest to the event depicted can affirm that they recognize the reality described and if some, at least, affirm the interpretation presented. Benigni polarized his audience but did not sacrifice his moral warrant. His "take," not universally applauded, is nonetheless a defensible effort to redeem a complex tragedy, the memory of which we keep alive in order never to repeat.

CASE 71. TRAINING IN VIRTUE

Detective Alonzo Harris is the worst of the worst. A corrupt narcotics officer in the movie *Training Day*, he kills with impunity, steals the drug money he's supposed to be confiscating and directs a hit against his rookie partner after deciding he can't be trusted to keep a murder quiet. The role earned actor Denzel Washington an Oscar for Best Actor, demonstrating his ability to throw himself into roles that are nothing like the spiritually minded Washington's real life. *Training Day* is one of a rash of movies involving public corruption, including *The Departed*, *Killer Joe*, *L.A. Confidential*, and a string of others.

In *Training Day*, Harris is driven by a debt to Russian mobsters, and the only way to satisfy it is to kill his drug dealer friend and steal his money. To make sure this goes off as planned, Harris calls together his retinue of underlings, each of whom is as rotten as he is. The lone exception is Jake Hoyt, a rookie on his first day on the streets, played by Ethan

Hawke. After shooting the drug dealer, Alonzo concocts a story that places Hoyt as the shooter. Alonzo promises Hoyt he will receive commendations for taking out a dangerous criminal, but when the rookie shows a little too much resistance, Alonzo decides it's time to visit a group of gang bangers. He leaves Hoyt stranded in their kitchen, later sending a text message telling their leader to kill him. It looks like the ultimate triumph of evil over good until the lead gang-banger discovers Hoyt saved his 14-year-old cousin from being raped earlier in the day. He lets him go and Hoyt heads to Alonzo's apartment to exact justice.

In the end, that's exactly what Alonzo gets, becoming target practice for Russian mobsters after people in the community where he lives turn their backs on him in favor of the straight-shooting Hoyt.

The fictional Alonzo Harris met a violent end thanks particularly to the actor Denzel Washington. Washington insisted on changes to the script after reading it through in its early stages. In a radio interview about his role in the movie, Washington said:

> I couldn't satisfy his living in the worst way unless he died in the worst way. . . . There was a bit of a cop-out the way the script was, and it smelled like they were looking to do a part two or something.[20]

Washington, who speaks openly about the role his faith plays in his life, believes characters on screen send important messages to audiences. "You never know who you touch," Washington wrote in *A Hand to Guide Me*, a book of seventy-four inspirational essays by people who reached the tops of their respective games:

> You never know how or when you'll have an impact or how important your example can be to someone else. Even when you're acting in a manner that's meant merely to entertain, you strike a chord in someone and you end up enlightening.[21]

Washington stands out in Hollywood for his openness about the role religion plays in his life. The son of a Pentecostal minister, Washington attends church regularly and begins the day on his knees in prayer.[22] He takes life advice from the Bible, and when asked by Oprah Winfrey about the role spirituality plays in his life, Washington replied that it doesn't play a role, rather, it's everything. "If I get away from that idea, I get lost," he said. "This business is not who I am. Anyone with a spiritual base understands humility. When you start using the words 'I' and 'me' too often, you get in trouble."[23]

Washington said his religious beliefs allow him to feel positively about the state of the world. "It has all been foretold and written," he said. "I just stay focused on the question of how I will serve while I'm here. How can I lift people up?"[24]

We tread on tricky territory here: entertainment programming and religious/moral conviction. The Legion of Decency in the 1930s wrote scripts for Hollywood, so to speak, but that era is long past. Nearly past, too, in the popular culture production industries, is any sense of respect, not to mention reverence, for moral obligations linked to faith.

Ethicist Clifford Christians (co-author of this book) notes that in conversations on pop culture and faith, Friedrich Nietzsche is the "elephant in the room."[25] Nietzsche's influence on ethics was a "scorched-earth attack" on presumed rational and religious foundations of Western morality. "Defending an abstract good is no longer seen as beneficence, but rather as imperialism over . . . diverse communities. . . . In our day, morality has appeared to reach the end of the line."[26] Yet he notes, with theologian Paul Tillich, that neither knowledge nor moral choice can exist groundlessly or totally open to personal configuration: "Something irrevocable must be claimed for everything else to make sense—in this case, God as the ground of being."[27]

For Denzel Washington, the "ground of being" is the Christian God, and if Clifford Christians' application holds, Denzel qualifies as a "steward of an alternative conscious-ness," as were the prophets of ancient Israel, among others.[28]

In New Testament language, faith—hope—love are pre-eminent values, and life lived under their banner is wise and good, ultimately fulfilling, akin to accord with the Decalogue in Judaism or obedience to the Qur'an and Hadith in Islam.[29]

Translating morality based on monotheism into Aristotelian rationalism makes claims to the good more palatable to modernity but no less radical. To live by virtue (*arête*, moral excellence) is to find happiness in the fullest sense (*eudaemonia*). The "four cardinal vir-tues" of ancient Christian faith—temperance, prudence, courage, and justice—can be found in the cadences of Aristotle's *Nicomachean Ethics*, which Nietzsche critiques with as much passionate disapproval as he does the four Gospels.

Despite Nietzsche and post-modern secularism, a "remnant community"[30] exists (and Denzel Washington is part of it) that hears a different drumbeat. Media scholar Quentin Schultze claims that "we humans dwell east of Eden" where mediated realities serve up "one or another pack of lies about God, ourselves, others, and the creation." Nonetheless, aligning with Augustine's claim that "all truth is God's truth," Schultze insists that

> the Hebrew and Christian traditions offer a prophetic means for human beings to find their way amid the miasma of mediated mendacity. This way requires humans to do something outrageous, even foolish by many of today's standards: to be faithful.[31]

You Think?

- Does a media professional dare to mix work (or art) and personal conviction?
- Every industry recognizes a chain of command. How much time must a person "put in" before she/he may begin to exert moral influence?

If Schultze is right about how reality is put together, then living virtuously makes very good sense, all other considerations (money and fame for two well-known examples) rendered secondary. Whatever your career—film star or forest ranger—the good life is built on *arête*, *agape*, and communal treasures such as mutual regard, kindness, and a dash of humility. Denzel Washington speaks that language, in his own cadence.

Not all the characters Washington plays stink as badly as Alonzo Harris. He played an alcoholic pilot who finally accepts that he has a problem in *Flight*, a debate coach in the segregated South in *The Great Debaters*, and Malcolm X in a movie of the same name. He accepts bad-guy roles, too, saying he doesn't want to be "pigeonholed into doing what people think is ethical." Washington brings unusual complexity to the screen, and an integrity that suits his worldview. Alonzo Harris didn't deserve to get away.

NOTES

1. Louis Brandeis, with Samuel Warren, "The Right to Privacy," *Harvard Law Review* 4:15 (December 1890): 196.
2. Quoted in Howard Rosenberg, "Critics' View of 'Nixon': A Dirty Trick on History," *Los Angeles Times*, December 22, 1995, F41.
3. Walter Goodman, "With Fact in Service to Drama," *New York Times*, January 3, 1996, C9.
4. Rosenberg, "Critics' View of 'Nixon,'" C9.
5. Eric Hamburg, ed., *Nixon: An Oliver Stone Film* (New York: Hyperion, 1995).
6. Stephen J. Rivele and Christopher Wilkinson, "Critic's Ploy to Review 'Nixon' Is the Only Dirty Trick," *Los Angeles Times*, January 1, 1996, F3.
7. Stryker McGuire and David Ansen, "Stone Nixon," *Newsweek*, December 11, 1995, 68–70.
8. Hamburg, *Nixon*, xix.
9. Rosenberg, "Critics' View of 'Nixon,'" C9.
10. Hamburg, *Nixon*, xix.
11. Quoted in Charles W. Colson, "Demonizing Nixon Is the Least of Stone's Sins," *Houston Chronicle*, December 31, 1995, 4C.
12. *TV Guide*, April 20, 1985, 5.
13. Tom Shales reported on and reviewed "Baby M." His column appeared in the *DuPage Daily Journal*, May 20, 1988.
14. M. Scott Peck, *People of the Lie* (New York: Simon & Shuster, 1985).
15. *Quill*, March 1989, 24–26.
16. Quoted in Richard Reeves, "Nixon Revisited," *New York Times*, December 17, 1995, H41.
17. Quoted in *USA Today*, February 21, 2003, 15A and July 14, 2003, D1.
18. Graham Fuller, "The Brave Little Film That Could," *Interview*, November 1998.
19. Daniel Vogelmann, "Can One Write Fairy Tales About Auschwitz?" *Triangolo Rosso*, www.deportati.it/filmografia_documenti/benigni_vogelmann.html.
20. T. Gross (Interviewer) and D. Washington (Interviewee), *Denzel Washington Remembers 'Malcolm X' and 'The Wizard of Oz'* (Interview transcript, 2013), www.npr.org/2013/03/01/173228434/denzel-washington-remembers-malcom-x-and-the-wizard-of-oz.
21. D. Washington, *A Hand to Guide Me: Legends and Leaders Celebrate the People who Shaped Their Lives* (Des Moines, IA: Meredith Books, 2006).
22. M. Hainey, "The GQ&A: Denzel Washington," *GQ*, October 2012, www.gq.com/entertainment/celebrities/201210/denzel-washington-interview-gq-october-2012.

23. O. Winfrey, "Oprah Talks to Denzel Washington," *O. The Oprah Magazine*, January 2008, www.oprah.com/omagazine/Oprahs-Interview-with-Denzel-Washington.

24. Ibid.

25. Clifford Christians, "Preface," in R. H. Woods, Jr. and P. D. Patton, *Prophetically Incorrect* (Grand Rapids, MI: Brazos, 2010), xxi.

26. Ibid., xxiv.

27. Ibid., xxvi.

28. Ibid., xxv.

29. For further observations, see Mark Fackler, "Religious Ethics in the World," in Mitchell Land, ed., *Contemporary Media Ethics*, 2nd ed. (Spokane, WA: Marquette Books, 2014), 75–86.

30. The exiled Israelites were so called during their seventy years in Babylon.

31. Quentin Schultze cited in *Prophetically Incorrect*, xi.

CHAPTER

17

CENSORSHIP

Censorship, on the one hand, one of the ugly words of the English language, speaks of the repression that democratic beliefs officially condemn. It warns of the consequences of state tyranny, church tyranny, union tyranny, corporation tyranny—the strong hand of any institution silencing the dissenting voice. *Liberty*, on the other hand, provokes cherished feelings that resonate with our deepest human longings—an elusive goal perhaps, but worth the sacrifice required for each step in its advance.

So by our ideals we set the stage for the great paradox of democratic theory: liberty can never be absolute; censorship can never be absent. Liberty requires constraints at every level—speech, sex, movement, health care, business, religious practice—in order for people to create an ordered society. That which we prize most must be taken in measured portions.

Few of our essential constraints partake of the spirit of the abuse of the Star Chamber in seventeenth-century England. (The Star Chamber was originally established to ensure the fair enforcement of laws against socially and politically prominent people but later became a tool of repression by the monarchy.) The jailing and hanging of writers no longer occurs at the whim of a monarch, in England at least. Yet many contemporary restrictions are nonetheless called "censorship." One of our fundamental questions, then, is where to draw the lines. This is the question of ethics.

At the end of World War II, the Hutchins Commission on Freedom of the Press struggled over this question as it deliberated toward a theory of press freedom that would promote social responsibility as a new and important concept in media studies. All the commission members were ardent democrats; some might even be called dreamy-eyed in their praise of democratic virtues. True liberals in the historic sense, they held free inquiry to be paramount. Yet they wrestled with the question of censorship. The chief philosopher of the commission, William Ernest Hocking of Harvard, captured the dilemma poignantly in an essay written as plans for the commission were being laid:

Are . . . thoughts all equally worthy of protection? Are there no ideas unfit for expression, insane, obscene, destructive? Are all hypotheses on the same level, each one, however vile or silly, to be taken with the same mock reverence because some academic jackass brings it forth? Is non-censorship so great a virtue that it can denounce all censorship as lacking in human liberality?[1]

The first case in this chapter, "The Voice of America," points the moral compass at an entertainer who became one of the most popular figures in the world, tops in his field with fans, sales, and significance. Were his messages healthy, morally speaking, and can that question even be on the table (without sounding so 1970s)? The second case, "Frontal Assault," focuses on the most destructive impulses that we as humans feel. Mediated experience not only gives vent to those feelings but also may propagandize and convert too many of us for public safety.

You Think?

▪ Should people fear the impact of what they are watching or listening to? Can repeated exposure to media violence or horror change how people relate?

▪ The right to read or watch, right to one's own media preferences, right to a mind-diet governed by personal choice . . . aren't those fundamental human rights, to be respected everywhere?

The third case, "*South Park*'s 200th," is comedy, irreverent and potentially dangerous. The fourth case, "Rescue Us," is dangerous too, and grimacing if you don't know what's coming. Your opinion on the fifth case, "Lyrics Not So Cool," will depend on how you judge the role popular arts play in sorting out human affairs.

While you puzzle with us over these democratic conundrums, we may be encouraged in the knowledge that to do so—to read this book and think about these questions—is testimony that we are at least on the way to answers. In too many societies, the range of permissible media is tightly defined by a powerful elite. At least we can claim the advantage of a bias toward latitude: censorship must be justified. In these cases, we ask whether modern censors have demonstrated their case for building dikes against the flood.

CASE 72. THE VOICE OF AMERICA

The white rapper Eminem, the blue-eyed, backward-capped genius of rhyme, has sold millions of CDs, appeared in films, and runs a successful recording company. If "he didn't care," as the lyrics suggest, at least he works hard at it. *Rolling Stone* lauds his work ethic, calling him "the Voice of America," the "original gangsta," all "hip-hop swagger and hard-rock self-loathing."[2]

If Eminem is America's voice, we live in a country of angry young adults, disillusioned by whatever, delighted to "dis" any cultural zone once recognized as prima facie worthy of respect, from family relationships to the president. Religion is in the "post-dis" zone—not even on the screen. At the same time, Eminem cannot be cornered; he resists stereotypes. If he hates his mother, he loves his daughter. As he projects the image of the "entertainer you love to hate," he remains popular. Although antiestablishment, he is the center of a multimillion-dollar business.

American entertainment has always celebrated the performer on the fringe, from Elvis Presley's hips to George Carlin's "seven dirty words." Yet Eminem's robust popularity has created a new and different class of star: young, caustic, and platinum rich. Eminem sings youth's disconnect from social values, an inner anger that seeks a cause, but absent a cause, anger that protests anyhow.

Eminem's high-charged "own zone" may be redefining America and the West. When those schooled by his music come of age, what will they believe? How will they live? Toward what will they aim?

Rap is not so much a message as a snapshot of emotions. Rappers and fans play dress-up in the various emotions of the "music." The overloaded anger, brutality toward women, and rejection of tradition that typify rap are like a set of new clothes, a word game that carries little more than play-at-it ferocity, if you allow the argument of fans who listen to rap but still say please and thank you and finish their homework.

Prosocial rap is a contradiction in terms. Rap aims at a culture's hypocrisies; it releases the pent-up anger of minorities long repressed by the values of moral elites. Were rap to turn prosocial, it would oppose its own opposition. Make sense? Why not?

Every moral principle holds this in common: the prize of doing well. For Kant, that prize was coherence—a life lived as life ought to be, rational and ordered, contributing capably to the "kingdom of ends." For Rawls, the prize was social fairness, a level playing field for all participants. What, then, if coherence is the enemy, and the assumption that everyone wants to play (why else work so hard for fairness?) turns out not to matter: no one shows up when the whistle is blown.

The collective wisdom of humanity's moral imagination distinguishes between good and bad behavior, good and bad attitude, and good and bad intention. These distinctions play out differently by eras and cultures, but they always show up. Intrinsic to human nature is the embrace of good and the rejection of evil. What if that distinction is itself the target of reproach and reaction? Where does the human soul go when the very idea of an end point is sick, ugly, boring, old, and hateful?

Rap castigates and criticizes. Good entertainment, whether comedy or tragedy, must do so. But Eminem offers nothing to fill the vacuum. Rather, he admits repeatedly throughout his albums that his lyrics are not to be taken seriously. They are feelings from the angry/hopeless side of his persona, Slim Shady. If the minds of rap's listeners are indeed whacked and brainwashed, that itself is not a moral point, just an observation. The problem child in Eminem's messed-up world has nowhere to turn, not even inward. Apart from the loner's conduit to rap itself—the message through the headphones—there is nowhere to go with nothing positive to do. For America's great "problem child," problem-solving is a matter of volume up.

Nihilism disguised as rhyme and artistry finally makes nonsense even of its own sense. There is no problem child apart from an aberration from what should be. Eminem rejects every "should be" and has no right, therefore, to call anything a problem or to register anger at anyone. To do so anyway—without moral warrant—is sheer self-infatuation—the very heart of every Eminem protest. No human life can prosper as a self-absorbed pod, blinkered by headsets, streamed by contradictions, nurtured by incoherence, in love with anger and angry with love. To live in the emotional world the rapper describes is to expire as a human person, which even a rapper moving toward his next million in CD sales would not advise.

Entertainment media must offer something worth living for. Those who claim otherwise are conning the audience. And even the best con eventually burns out. Adrenaline alone cannot sustain us. Escapist entertainment is only as good as the return to reality.

"Confused" is the motto embroidered on Eminem's backward baseball cap. That's okay, for confusion can be the forerunner and catalyst to solution. It's time for America's richest rap voice to acknowledge even his own accountability to articulate an answer. And it's time for millions of fans to ask for one.

CASE 73. FRONTAL ASSAULT

Stormfront.org began as a private dial-in bulletin board in 1990 for members of the David Duke campaign to communicate. In 1995, Stormfront was the first extremist hate-speech site posted to the internet. It now reportedly attracts 15,000 visitors daily. Visitors are greeted by a Celtic cross surrounded by "White Pride World Wide" and "Stormfront.org" in a gothic font. Don Black, who created the site, calls Stormfront a white nationalist resource page for "those courageous men and women fighting to preserve their White Western culture, ideals and freedom of speech and association—a forum for planning strategies and forming political and social groups to ensure victory."[3]

Don Black's involvement as a white nationalist began in high school as he distributed white-power literature. At the age of seventeen, Black organized a chapter of the White Youth Alliance, an organization led by David Duke. Black also joined the Ku Klux Klan (KKK) and climbed the ranks, becoming the grand wizard (national leader). A year after becoming grand wizard, Black and nine other white supremacists were arrested as they prepared to invade the small Caribbean island of Dominica to establish a "white state." Black served two years in prison, where he learned computer skills. On his release from prison, he said: "I am here to build the greatest white racist regime this country has ever seen."[4] He resigned from the KKK, moved to West Palm Beach, Florida, and began using his computer knowledge to further his white nationalist agenda.

Black uses the internet to promote his ideas worldwide. According to Black: "We previously could only reach people with pamphlets and by sending tabloid papers to a limited number of people, or holding rallies with no more than a few hundred people—now we can reach potentially millions of people."[5] People from around the world access Stormfront, which offers German- and Spanish-language sections.

Don Black said on an *ABC News Nightline* interview:

> We have recruited people to our point of view, many people which we otherwise wouldn't have reached. Sites such as Stormfront which are interactive, provide those people who are attracted to our ideas with a forum to talk to each other and to form a virtual community.[6]

The virtual community can be reached through Stormfront's White Nationalist Community Forum (www.stormfront.org/forum). According to Black, the forum exists "to provide information not available in the controlled news media and to build a community of white activists working for the survival of our people." The forum has more than 17,000 members, and over 500,000 messages have been posted. Included in the message boards are sections for news and announcements and a general section covering a variety of topics, including white nationalism ideology and philosophy, culture and customs, poetry, science/technology/race, privacy, self-defense, health and fitness, and education and home-schooling. An activism section offers topics such as events and strategy, and opponents can argue against white nationalism in an opposing-view section. The international section displays discussion boards on issues of interest to white nationalists in the following geographic areas: Britain, Canada, Australia, New Zealand, France, Ireland, Italy, Spain, Portugal, Latin America, Netherlands, Serbia, Russia, South Africa, Sweden, Norway, Denmark, and Finland. Another aspect of the virtual community is the white singles section, where one can "meet other white nationalists for romance or friendship." Stormfront even maintains a calendar of members' birthdays.

In addition to the forum, the site exhibits essays covering a variety of issues about white nationalism, including affirmative action, immigration, racial differences, National Socialism, Zionism, and revisionist materials that deny the Holocaust occurred. In the essay "What Is Racism?" the author claims that whites are taught to be ashamed of their race, and "Who Rules America?" decries the control of the media over society and claims that Jews are masters of the media. The article calls for white nationalists to do whatever is necessary to break Jewish control. The site posted the "Color of Crime" study that "proves" blacks are more dangerous than whites. Stormfront offers a White Nationalism FAQs section, a well-articulated statement of their philosophy. In response to the first question, "What is White Nationalism?" the answer is: "The idea that Whites may need to create a separate nation as a means of defending themselves." Stormfront also reveals a collection of racist graphics and logos.

Stormfront has special versions of the webpage for women and children. The women's page (www.women.stormfront.org) is "not a feminist page, but rather a page to celebrate and honor Aryan women." Janice, web master of the women's page, first became curious about Stormfront after a Don Black TV interview. She visited Stormfront and felt that it was not hate speech but pride in the white race. "I get angry with this whole hate thing because it's simply not true at all," she says. She wonders why it is permissible for other cultures to celebrate their race, but when European-Americans have "white pride" it's considered hate. Janice wrote on Stormfront's women's page:

> We must remain separate to maintain our past, our roots, who we are and where we come from. I do not want to mix with other cultures. I do not want to adopt their dress, their music, or anything about them. I want to keep what is mine, what I was born with. I can learn about the others, I can eat all kinds of weird other foods, but when I wake up in the morning, I'll still be a European-American.[7]

The women's page includes a "public service announcement" urging women to boycott any foods with Jewish kosher symbols so as not to support Zionism. The site presents sample kosher symbols, Janice's correspondence to companies requesting they remove the labels, and links to other anti-Semitic sites, including Aryan Nation's. The women's version of Stormfront also displays essays of and for women in the white racialist movement.

Derek Black, Don's teenage son, is said to be the web master of Stormfront for Kids (www.stormfront.org/kids). Visitors to this site see two Celtic crosses and a banner announcing "White Pride World Wide." Derek greets fellow youth with a message: "I used to be in public school, it is a shame how many White minds are wasted in that system." Now home-schooled, he says that he is no longer attacked by gangs of nonwhites and spends most of the day learning rather than tutoring slower learners. He is finally learning to take pride in himself, his family, and his people, he says.

Stormfront for Kids provides activities that include games, a kaleidoscope painter, optical-illusion puzzles, and sound files of white-pride songs. Youth can learn about the history of the white race, view European flags, and follow a link to the "real" history about Martin Luther King, Jr. An animated U.S. flag constantly changes into a Confederate flag, and a child can follow an antikosher link to the women's page.

The enduring popularity of Stormfront, and its apparently growing worldwide appeal, points to a festering boil in many lives—a sense of victimization—and to the daffy extremes some will go to win a feeling of security amid self-imposed fears. A racist, above all, approaches the world with tightly conceived presuppositions about trust and community. Only those who fit a preferred model are welcome to the club.

None of the moral traditions discussed in the Introduction to this book can be marshaled to support Stormfront's race bias. Kant's universal duty speaks strongly against it. Rawls's justice game could never condone it. The idea that one could "love one's neighbors" by hating them is nonsensical. Only the most twisted pragmatic logic might render momentary support, until the facts are in and the logic of race exclusion is fully calculated. Morally, Stormfront and its kin are bankrupt. Should a liberal, morally sensitive people permit an organization devoted to Stormfront's aims to communicate its message and perhaps convert others to its position?

Suppression is one tactic a culture can use to rid itself of tainted philosophy. Driving up the social cost of membership will reduce the benefits of joining and eventually marginalize or eliminate the movement. But utilitarian constraints can only contain, never defeat, dangerous and faulty ideas. At the end of the day, the attraction of hate—its (albeit perverted) sense of justice, its (albeit phony) sense of security—must be surrendered to a greater idea, a more satisfying way to live and think. That transaction occurs not under compulsion but in the open air of free choice.

Stormfront offers a worldview, a frame of reference, a "moral universe" to subscribers and followers of race-based prejudice. Its commitment to racism goes deep. Its preposterous political intentions are a fool's dream. But racism will not turn to neighbor-care unless its adherents are offered a better way by word and deed. As long as Stormfront does not act on its philosophy, let its creators have their space to brandish a way of life so morally impoverished and globally isolated that other messages—justice and unconditional mutual regard—will overcome it. Kant and Rawls and Judeo-Christian *agape* will all give space for that.

CASE 74. *SOUTH PARK*'S 200TH

The 200th episode of *South Park* featured a bunch of characters previously satirized on the long-running animated show for adults: Jesus, Moses, Joseph Smith, Buddha, and Muhammed. All were depicted as persons except the latter, who was shown in a bear costume. Nonetheless, an Islamic website posted this message: "We have to warn Matt and Trey that what they are doing is stupid. They will probably end up like Theo Van Gogh for airing this show. This is not a threat, but a warning of the reality of what will likely happen to them."[8] Alongside the message were photos of Van Gogh, dead on an Amsterdam street. He had produced a documentary called *Submission* on the topic of violence against Muslim women, with script writer Ayaan Hirsi Ali, famous for her opposition to the faith she once lived by. The website, now defunct, provided links to studios and homes of Trey Parker and Matt Stone, creators of *South Park*.

The Comedy Central television network and parent company Viacom wanted no such trouble and bleeped significant portions of the second part of the episode a week later. Both companies refused to allow *South Park* to stream the episode on its website, the customary courtesy on the day after airing.

Anderson Cooper of CNN asked Ali about the seriousness of the website's intimidation. "It was clearly a threat," said Ali.[9] She then said that she is alive, and Van Gogh is not, precisely because she accepted protection and he did not. Her advice to Matt and Trey:

take care. But the fabulously successful cartoonists did not seem particularly worried when they spoke to Xeni Jardin of Boing Boing Video:

> We'd be super hypocritical going against our own thoughts, if we said, "Let's not make fun of them, because they might hurt us" . . . no, no . . . *South Park* matters to us, it's our whole world. . . . The *New York Times*, Comedy Central, Viacom . . . they're just pussing on it.[10]

Among the virtues that percolate through *South Park* production studios, reverence would come toward the end of the list, from all appearances. Reverence, the sense that sacredness lies behind our mundane daily affairs, that more is at stake than appears, that premier values such as human dignity and racial equality are built on more than United Nations documents and historic speeches—this kind of reverence is the fuel of *South Park*'s humor.

That's because so much of what passes for reverence is hokum and pretense, bloated egos and self-congratulating piety. *South Park* loves those human frailties. Indeed, the comedic world is built on reverence gone wild and scary—sand fortresses waiting for comedic brilliance to wash them away like the incoming tide.

South Park pulls no punches, reveres no messiahs, permits no reserve on the targets of its satire. There is no sanctuary from *South Park*, no hiding place. Reverence is the great unpardonable on that show.

South Park's popularity has proven that irreverence sells. A nice market segment enjoys opportunities to laugh at the holy symbols and personages that in most other contexts must be shown inordinate respect and deference. We are relieved, a bit, of the awesome otherness of God when we can laugh, even at God. A Middle Eastern woman named Sarah once laughed at God, too, and her laughter is known to history as the lead-in to becoming the mother of a nation—perhaps the most important nation in all of literature and history (Genesis 18). *South Park* was not the first to find humor in the mysteries of religious faith.

Yet the style of humor and level of bashing that *South Park* sells to its audience has little sensitivity to the ancient virtue. *South Park* grounds its "right to publish" on the contractarian liberal state, the absolute freedom to express a point of view that majorities would deem devilish, if only to show that when the devil gets its due, nothing much changes, good or ill. It's a rhetorical game, this reverence thing, and in the liberal state where inalienable rights trump social norms, reverence is duly pegged as blunderbuss.

In the life-world of the Muslim believer, the Enlightenment-born right of free speech is never understood properly without first invoking reverence. The ancient virtue defines the universe in which humankind is accountable to Allah for life itself. There is no space in all the world where reverence is excused, where sacredness is on holiday. The community of faith, as one might call it, is a community whose identity, prosperity, and future are wrapped tightly in seamless reverence. This community does not contemplate laughter directed at matters holy, or persons holy, or writings holy. To laugh at the holy would be to join the side of the unholy, and thus sever loyalty to the community or faith irrevocably. Christians and Jews share these sentiments. Do "thick description" on these communities (Clifford Geertz's term)[11] and reverence shows up near the top of the virtues. Precisely for that reason, it is a favorite target of *South Park*.

In a liberal, free society, *South Park* has every legal right to laugh at people's beliefs and at people's messiahs. In a liberal, open society, where public speech is believed to wash the docket clean of pretense and hold every high idea to a utilitarian accounting, *South Park* may have a duty to laugh at theologies and their holy objects. But in a communitarian society, where relationships between selves are a first-order concern, there remains, even if reverence declines, a respect for the other that constrains satire and bounds laughter. In a communitarian society, commonly, the believer laughs at the foibles of faith, the contradictions of holiness, and the failures of the self to make much progress toward the divine. Failure is often funny, and the self has first-rights on laughter at one's own wickedness.

Laughter at a neighbor's pretenses takes on additional moral obligations. The neighbor is sincere, let's say, and devout. Sometimes that devotion is inconvenient. Sometimes it seems ridiculous. Still, open laughter and satire are constrained by respect for the neighbor's dignity and beliefs, by the neighbor's sincere efforts to stay true to practices that in every way (to the nonbeliever) may appear pointless or cumbersome. Friendship understands those points of difference and respects them, even as an outsider.

In *South Park*'s world, the Enlightenment goes all the way. Communitarian concern for the other would make this cutting-edge show little more than *The Andy Griffith Show* revisited. But *South Park* may want to take a beginner's lesson in reverence, if no more than a neighbor's handshake over the hedges that acknowledges one world and many faiths. Enlightenment faith has sustained the show's popularity for almost two decades; communitarian sensibilities may not add market share, but they could give the show balance, humanity, and empathy. Admitting that *laughter-at* another is not the highest human achievement will not dethrone *South Park* as one of the world's leading comedies. Recognizing, even honoring, the deep structures of a believing community's worldview—its points of solemn reverence—might be Cartman and Kenny's next right step toward mature comedic edginess.

CASE 75. RESCUE US

Launched in 2004 as a vehicle for comedian Denis Leary, *Rescue Me* capitalized on America's post-September 11 deifying of New York firefighters, albeit with a twist. Billed as a "dramedy" by the FX Network, *Rescue Me* would act as a worthy New York City Fire Department complement to the already successful Los Angeles Police Department Emmy-winning juggernaut, *The Shield* (2002), a gritty drama exposing the dark underbelly of America's "heroes."

At Engine House 62 in the Naked City, desires trump logic, and conflicts are resolved with playground justice: may the bigger asshole win. Arguably, the biggest at Engine 62 is Tommy Gavin, played by Denis Leary, a character you hate to love: a psychotic megalomaniac whose unfettered duty to self is at once both repulsive and surprisingly refreshing, an alcoholic, forty-something Irish-American firefighter whose phantom conversations with both his dead cousin and Jesus Christ are the least of his problems.

High on "vitamin testosterone" and low on political correctness, *Rescue Me* is a virtual Plato's Retreat[12] for the male ego, Spike cable TV, big fires, big attitudes, and bigger breasts. In the June 20, 2006 episode titled "Sparks," there is an exhibition for the male rape-fantasy—the fantasy of women turned on by their attackers.

The plotline from the previous episode, "Torture," acts as a precursor to this culminating rape scene. Tommy Gavin's soon-to-be ex-wife, Janet, is sleeping with Tommy's brother, New York City police detective Johnny Gavin. Tommy sees it and avenges himself by beating his philandering brother. In the closing minutes of the Sparks episode, Tommy arrives at Janet's apartment to discuss the pending divorce proceedings, including the division of material goods. What transgresses next shocked both dedicated fans of the show and television pundits.

As the discussion between characters escalates to rage, Tommy pushes Janet onto a nearby couch, receiving several pleas of "no" in the process. Fighting through her resistance, Tommy forcibly has intercourse with her or, in the opinion of many viewers and critics, rapes her. In addition to this violent and forced sex, what shocked viewers most is the scene's resolution, as Janet succumbs to the pleasurable, albeit brutal, nature of the act and seems to enjoy it. As Tommy exits the apartment with vindication on his face, viewers are stunned. Was this shock TV at its worst? Did the FX Network just condone its antihero Tommy as a violent rapist? Is this appropriate and responsible TV drama?

The promotional material for *Rescue Me* includes a tagline that hints at undercurrents of firefighters needing saviors of their own with the slogan, "They save us. But who saves them?" Yet, in the aftermath of the Sparks episode, many viewers questioned: "Who saves us from them?"

In the opening reel of the 2005 Oscar-nominated film *Crash*, Hollywood actor Don Cheadle, comments on the alienation and disconnect of modern Los Angeles, resonating truths about humanity at large. "It's the sense of touch," he says, pausing, "we're always behind tin, metal, and glass. I think we miss that touch so much that we crash into each other, just so we can feel something." *Rescue Me* is about crashing into each other. It's about men crashing into men, men crashing into fires, but ultimately, the cluster bomb: men crashing into themselves and the reality of their personhood. The Sparks episode reflects crashes at several levels.

Initially, the Sparks debate centered on whether the sexual encounter constituted a rape or forced (and reluctant) sex between lovers, and whether there is a difference. Where is the line of consent? These are situational dilemmas and questions that psychologists and psychotherapists may ponder forever. However, what is definitive in the episode is Janet's initial physical refusal, followed by her seeming enjoyment, resulting in the ambiguity as to whether the act was "forced, then consensual" or "rape." For the sake of this examination, however, the act will be referred to as rape. And the question we address is not rape as an act but television drama that includes rape as part of a rocky, unpredictable, coarse, mutually intriguing relationship.

Is rape-TV appropriate for a cable audience? Consider the viewers. The FX Network is available on cable TV only, making its viewing a form of paid-for entertainment much like going to theaters, downloading a CD, or buying a book. Implied in the purchase of this entertainment is the consumer's consent to the product. In short, viewers of *Rescue Me* have not been forced to watch the episode. They do so willingly, out of pocket, and with the foreknowledge of the product's tone and script strategy. In addition, it should be noted that *Rescue Me* airs at 10 p.m. (Eastern Standard Time), a time slot acting as a precaution against viewing by inappropriate age groups.

The appropriateness of any art—in relation to the viewer—depends on the viewers' sensibilities. Viewers are the final watchdogs, filtering out the inappropriate through the choices they make every day. Viewers familiar with *Rescue Me*'s tones and themes should find that a rape scene, while shocking in any circumstance, remains honest to the drama, not simply exploitative or shock-fodder TV. This is not *Bum Fights* or *Girls Gone Wild*. The Sparks episode is a devastating, violent, complex extension of the story line. And if cowriter Peter Tolan were in fact the writer of an internet post bearing his name, he said the day after:

> The idea of any woman "enjoying" being raped is repellant and caused all of us (and the network) a great deal of concern. But again, these are seriously damaged people who are unable to express their emotions—and so expression through brutality has become expected.[13]

You Think?

■ Should media programmers ever give sexual exploitation of women a "green light"?
■ Should mediated stories be as real as life itself?

Other entertainments, such as *A History of Violence*, a 2005 film starring Viggo Mortensen, follow similar logic. In that highly acclaimed film, Mortensen's character initiates sex with his wife only to be violently fought off, a scene culminating in both respect and passion. In some instances, sexually violent episodes, while unsettling, act as appropriate progressions of the story line.

Some argue that violence and obscenity are of one cloth and that First Amendment protections cover both. Some argue the contrary: that First Amendment protections protect neither.[14] This debate, so polarized by Supreme Court obfuscations and so little used in courtrooms today, will not help here.

The distinction between art and life helps to free the viewer to hate the act but embrace the act's depiction. Art does not equate to advocacy. Showing violence is not preaching on its behalf. Excessive modesty flies in the face of reality. The audience and producers of *Rescue Me* have together created a misfit hero whose edgy art draws no easy answers. In a wonderful understatement, Tolan told the *New York Times*, "What Denis likes to write . . . is never the expected thing."[15] This is also, simply and really, what a lot of TV viewers like to see. As long as people can choose (the off-button still works) and the drama has integrity (shock with purpose, albeit controversial), the viewer and producer may engage in morally troublesome material with their own integrity intact.

CASE 76. LYRICS NOT SO COOL

Daryl Gates spent his life in dangerous public service in the Los Angeles Police Department, rising to the office of chief, but gained fame and popularity only when his name became associated with a rapper who wanted Daryl dead, artistically speaking.

Ice-T, born Tracy Lauren Marrow, joined the Army Rangers to escape from the streets. Then back in Los Angeles, he aimed to become a DJ and club promoter. His skills at performance, however, led to singles "Coldest Rap" and "Cold Wind Madness" in 1982 and two years later, his break-dance films *Breakin'* and *Breakin' 2*. In 1987, his first album, *Rhyme Pays*, became a leader in the gangsta-rap genre. He went platinum in 1988 and made his masterwork (by most fans' estimations) in 1991 with *O.G. (Original Gangster)*, which included the item that brought national attention to Chief Gates, the cut titled "Cop Killer."

The lyrics of "Cop Killer" are copyrighted and cannot be reproduced here, but they are widely known. Performed from the perspective of someone who "loses it," the rap advocates hunting down and dispatching police, in language that even if not copyrighted could not appear here. Ice-T called it a "protest record [by someone who is] fed up with police brutality."[16]

Events catapulted Ice-T's message. Months after "Cop Killer" was released, a jury in California acquitted white police officers who beat up African-American Los Angeles resident Rodney King. Riots broke out. Police associations lay partial blame on Ice-T's lyrics. Nationwide boycotts of Time-Warner products were urged. Police in Greensboro, NC, announced they would not respond to calls from stores selling the rap.

What did Ice-T think about all this? He wrote: "When you're coming out of the ghetto you learn the cops aren't your friends, and you quickly realize they are the enemy. . . . You learn that by experience." Ice-T was not alone in supporting the theme of his art. Thousands of African-American police, he claimed, "know I was saying the truth." His fans, he said, knew the song's protest was true to the feelings of many urban residents and "smile[d] and understood it." Warner Brothers Records supported their artist, but pressure grew. Finally, Ice-T himself removed the cut from the album, claiming concern for the safety of Warner employees.

How free is the dissenter to direct his anger at a class of persons easily recognizable, in this case most often in uniform? American history is graced with the words and lyrics of dissenters who defied communities in order to revive them. Cornel West, a dissenter of the academy, describes the "oppressive effect of the prevailing market moralities" which leads to a "form of sleepwalking from womb to tomb, with the majority of citizens content to focus on private careers and be distracted with stimulating amusements."[17]

Interpretation is everything. Should Ice-T's literal call for murder be interpreted as a cry of anguish and a plea for the country to face and overcome racism?

Prudential judgment matters. Ice-T may perform his lyrical call to violence if his two strategic audiences understand and affirm the imagery of his music and the connotative limits of his rhetoric. This will not be easy. Police candidates are normally not attracted to police work because it affords manifold opportunity for artistic imagery and meaningful forays into metaphorical expression. Precinct chatter will not likely focus on the aesthetics of Ice-T's penetrating vision of urban injustice. Nonetheless, this audience has a particular responsibility to listen to the people they serve and protect. Listening requires the capacity, even the humility, to acknowledge that the dissenter speaks something significant.

Nor is proper interpretation an easy task for the second important audience, urban African-Americans. As this second group has no *professional* cadre (police have their captains), talented mentors are strategic, and such mentors are there, if they speak, West among them, and others. Even Ice-T himself. A decade after "Cop Killer," Ice-T reflected:

> I had a part of my life where I was a criminal. As a criminal, they [the police] were the opponent, so I was trying to beat them. Now I'm not a criminal and I need them to protect my house. . . . If you believe I'm a cop killer, then you believe David Bowie is an astronaut.[18]

Cultural alertness for producers, wisdom for listeners and viewers, a pinch of empathy, and moment of caution against literalisms leading to rage, these give artists freedom to do it all for us, with peace the long-term mutual goal, grounded in common pursuits of core community values.

NOTES

1. William Ernest Hocking, "The Meaning of Liberalism: An Essay in Definition," in David E. Roberts and Henry P. Van Dusen, eds., *Liberal Theology: An Appraisal* (New York: Charles Scribner's Sons, 1942), 54–55.
2. Keleta Sanneh, "The Voice of America," *Rolling Stone*, July 24, 2003, 64ff.

3. Statement of the Anti-Defamation League on Hate on the Internet before the Senate Committee on Commerce, Science and Transportation, May 20, 1999.

4. www.stormfront.org/dblack/racist_021998.htm.

5. Kent Faulk, "White Supremacist Spreads Views on Net," *Birmingham News*, October 19, 1997, 1.

6. Ted Koppel, "Hate Websites and the Issue of Free Speech," *ABC News Nightline*, January 13, 1998.

7. www.stormfront.org/forum/t38769-8/.

8. www.nytimes.com/2010/04/23/arts/television/23park.html.

9. www.youtube.com/watch?v=FdNKvREnOwQ.

10. http://boingboing.net/2010/04/13/south-park-turns-200.html.

11. Clifford Geertz, *The Interpretation of Cultures* (New York: Basic Books, 1973).

12. Plato's Retreat was a famous 1980s New York nightclub.

13. http://tubetalk.blogspot.co.uk/2006/06/rescue-me-rape-scene-explained.html.

14. Kevin W. Saunders, *Violence as Obscenity* (Durham, NC: Duke University Press, 1996).

15. Jacques Steinberg, "He's Cornering the Market on Misfit TV Heroes," *New York Times*, June 12, 2007, B1.

16. This case is based in part on chapter 15, "Art, Rage, Violence, Protest" in *Ethics for Public Communication* (Oxford, 2012). This quotation and those following are found on p. 265.

17. Ibid., 273.

18. Ibid., 276.

THE HEART OF THE MATTER IN ENTERTAINMENT ETHICS

"The Heart of the Matter," which appears at the end of each part of this book, is also the title of a novel by British author Graham Greene. In the novel, police inspector Henry Scobie deals with smugglers, crooks, failed colleagues, and illicit loves. These troubles consume him. Scobie's life is professional failure and fractured pride. Nothing works as it should. Scobie asks himself at one point: "Would one have to feel pity even for the planets . . . if one reached what they called the heart of the matter?"

Entertainment is where we go for refreshment, advice, or escape. Our own failures and fears are forgotten in a good story, a challenging game, or exciting music. We can win at play while we struggle at life. Entertainment puts color on the canvas of life.

Try using these words as replacements for *entertain* or *entertainment*: delight, charm, please, feast, throw a party. All good times. Friends, fun, and laughter. Do we really have to think about the ethics of it? Can't we just enjoy what we enjoy?

Here's the *heart of the matter* in entertainment ethics:

- Entertainment has its impact, for good or ill, on a life's plan and purpose. Do you want to be a person of generosity and conviviality? Your entertainment choices will help or hurt that trajectory. Want to be a person who delights in vicious power grabs and cunning ill-will? (We don't advise it, but many people seem to like this plan.) You can find entertainment that supports and deepens those motives. You choose the person you will become.
- What at first appear to be quite personal choices carry applications for people around you. The entertainment you produce or select invariably promotes some moral declarations and despises others. These moral declarations are communicated intentionally

or by indirection and nuance. When Tom Cruise's character Daniel Kaffee shouts his famous appeal for moral clarity to the corrupted Marine colonel on the witness stand (*A Few Good Men*), the reply he gets is the equally famous, "You can't handle the truth," delivered with Jack Nicholson's unique sneer. Who's lying here, who's covering, who's working the dark side? You have to consider courtrooms, uniforms, military roles, facial expressions, and simple words revealing character depth. Moral clarity is tricky, its arena is social, and it is never a private matter. "*Personal* entertainment choices—nobody's business but mine" is a myth. Your choices make a difference to other people.

▪ The human conversation includes popular arts. Moral awareness was not invented today. We the people have pondered moral truth and error for a very long time. Why miss that conversation and some of its conclusions, mistakes, and mandates? In real-life ethics, we the world's people believe that endangering lives is wrong, that bilking consumers is reprehensible, and that dehumanizing a race is morally tragic. In entertainment ethics, all of the above are fair game, unless and until popular art (or the artless) turns a culture against itself. Why miss the obvious application of a long conversation on these themes?

Cultural literacy is the *telos* (plan and purpose) of entertainment. If your entertainment choices are deepening your understanding of your own life, and other lives near and far from you, that is gain for all of us. If your entertainment choices are wasting your gifts and skills, subverting your sense of human empathy, and weakening your trust in truthfulness, we all lose something precious. Be wise in entertainment. Choose what expands, enriches, deepens, and discerns. Avoid time-wasting drivel and soul-shriveling nonsense. Moral wisdom knows the difference.

INDEX